327
M818r

D1106860

PRESENTED BY
Dr. Minos D. Generales

THE MACMILLAN COMPANY
NEW YORK · BOSTON · CHICAGO · DALLAS
ATLANTA · SAN FRANCISCO

MACMILLAN AND CO., LIMITED
LONDON · BOMBAY · CALCUTTA · MADRAS
MELBOURNE

THE MACMILLAN COMPANY
OF CANADA, LIMITED
TORONTO

IMPERIALISM
AND
WORLD POLITICS

IMPERIALISM
AND
WORLD POLITICS

BY

PARKER THOMAS MOON, Ph.D.
ASSOCIATE PROFESSOR OF INTERNATIONAL RELATIONS
IN COLUMBIA UNIVERSITY

New York
THE MACMILLAN COMPANY
1947

Copyright, 1926,
By PARKER T. MOON.

All rights reserved—no part of this book may be reproduced in any form without permission in writing from the publisher, except by a reviewer who wishes to quote brief passages in connection with a review written for inclusion in magazine or newspaper.

Set up and electrotyped.
Published October, 1926.

Reprinted February, 1927; April, 1927; November, 1927; June, 1928; April, 1933; April, 1936; May, 1937; January, 1939; April, 1940; June, 1942; July, 1944. September, 1947.

: Printed in the United States of America :

TO E. C. M.

25580

PREFACE

Of Greek and Roman imperialism there are admirable histories, but to what convenient volume can one turn for a similar general account of the greater imperialism of our own times? What Rome required three centuries to achieve has been dwarfed by modern nations in barely fifty years. The imperialism of these last five decades will rank, in the writer's opinion, as one of the major phases of modern history and one of the two or three foremost problems in world politics and world economics.

Seeing the trees but not the wood is so natural a tendency that world events such as the industrial revolution, the rise of democracy, and contemporary imperialism are not easily envisaged in their full magnitude until we have had time to put their many specific incidents together in some intelligible synthesis. In the case of imperialism, making such a synthesis is as difficult as it is important, because it means fitting together into one narrative such apparently unrelated persons as Gladstone and Gandhi, Roosevelt and Cecil Rhodes, Menelik and Mussolini, Kaiser Wilhelm II and King Thebaw; because it means combining in one story the Entente Cordiale and the Chinese Consortium, Dollar Diplomacy and pound sterling politics, alliances and loans, foreign missions and raw materials; because it means viewing as parts of one political panorama the Near East and the Far East, Mexico and Morocco, the Philippines and Fiji, Turkestan and Transvaal, Congo and Cuba. Difficult as it may be to accomplish the task at all satisfactorily, such a synthesis seems well worth attempting. That is the primary purpose of this book.

The second purpose is to present a more realistic view of world politics than is offered by conventionalized, chronological narratives of European diplomacy. Nothing is more striking in the mass of "secret treaties" and confidential official documents published since the war than the overwhelming evidence that the old diplomacy of Europe was feverishly and more or less frankly devoted to gaining economic or strategic advantages and political prestige by appropriating the backward lands of Asia, Africa, the Balkans and the Pacific. Imperialism was the reality, diplomacy its superficial expression. If this is true, as it appears to be, then the story of international relations before 1914 cannot be interpreted simply as a matter of narrowly European vendettas and erratic personalities. More attention must be given to the mines and railway concessions, the colonial markets and naval bases, in which the diplomats themselves were so vitally interested. By emphasizing the fact that the Great Powers are not nations but nation-empires, and by devoting a series of chapters to the reasons for international rivalry in arenas of conflict such as North Africa, the Near East, the Middle East, the Far East, and the Pacific, the writer has endeavored to concentrate attention on the things for which diplomats have contended, rather than on the diplomats themselves.

An effort has been made, likewise, to study the economic and social forces behind diplomacy. To say that Germany threatened France with war about Morocco, or that France seized Tunis, is worse than meaningless. Probably a majority of Frenchmen would have refused to seize Tunis, had they been consulted. Certainly on the Moroccan question the Kaiser and his own ministers were at variance. Nations are rarely units in such matters. The habit of regarding them as units has unfortunately been strengthened of late by passionate controversies respecting the causes of the Great War. Attempting to indict one nation and vindicate another, to make "Germany" or "the Allies" guilty or innocent, has the unfortunate effect of obscuring the dynamic factors of which the German and other governments were—and are—instruments. Stressing these factors, the first few chapters of this book analyze the business interests, the social groups, the professional propaganda, the popular sentiments, the theories, and the economic conditions which seem to have dominated imperialist diplomacy. Throughout the book, it is to be hoped, the reader will see the exporter, the factory-owner, the concession-hunter, the missionary, the admiral, peering over the shoulder of the diplomat.

The narrative might be more conventional if it culminated in the Great War. Instead it continues into the present year.

Perhaps we are now far enough removed from 1914 to realize that it is historically and psychologically inaccurate to treat European diplomacy before that fatal year as if its sole trend had been toward Serajevo. The ideas and interests productive of war in 1914 had caused many previous wars, and in large measure they have continued to exist since 1914. The present volume, therefore, is written around ideas and interests, rather than around the War, and its concluding chapter is devoted, not to the indictment of any nation or any diplomatist, but to an evaluation of the past achievements and present problems of imperialism. For the problems the author candidly confesses that he can see no solutions except more enlightened public opinion and more effective international cooperation, but no panacea is offered, for the purpose of this book is analytical and historical rather than controversial.

For specialists there exists an appalling number of works on various regional and topical subdivisions of the subject. With these the present volume is not intended to compare or compete. It is designed for the general reader and for college classes as a survey of the causes and motives, the history and the effects of imperialist world politics during the nineteenth and twentieth centuries. It can make no claim to finality. Before the definitive history of imperialism can be composed, there are many monographs to be written by qualified specialists. To exhaust even the existing printed matter bearing on the subject would require a busy lifetime. The writer does not pretend to have utilized more than a modest portion of the innumerable books, pamphlets, articles, and archives available on almost every chapter. Nor has any consistent effort been made to cite all sources or to give extensive bibliographical references, since in a book covering so broad a field a morass of footnotes could easily swamp the reader without satisfying the scholar. Here and there, however, a few notes are given to indicate some of the more interesting documents published in the post-bellum flood of diplomatic revelations, and occasionally other important public papers and secondary works are mentioned. For readers who wish to venture farther afield, the footnotes may be supplemented by consulting the selected bibliographies in my *Syllabus on International Relations* and the quarterly lists of books and documents in *Foreign Affairs.*

For their generous courtesy in permitting the use of maps previously published in their own works, I am grateful to Professors Carlton J. H. Hayes (for the maps of Asia and Africa from his *Political and Social History of Modern Europe* and the map of the British Empire adapted from a map in his *Brief History of the Great War*), Arthur M. Schlesinger (for maps of the Far East and the Pacific from his *Political and Social History of the United States*), Edward M. Earle (for the map of Turkish Railways from his *Turkey, the Great Powers and the Bagdad Railway*), Leonard O. Packard and Charles P. Sinnott (for the map of the Lands of the Caribbean Sea from their *Nations as Neighbors*), and Mr. James A. Williamson (for the map of South Africa from his *Brief History of British Expansion*). These maps are reproduced with the gracious consent of Macmillan and Company, Ltd., the publishers of Mr. Williamson's book, and of The Macmillan Company, the publishers of the other books mentioned. Credit is due also to the skillful engravers who transformed eight rude manuscript sketches into intelligible maps.

Full acknowledgment of my debt to the scholars and statesmen whose works have been drawn upon, often without special mention, and to the librarians here and in Paris, Geneva and London, who aided and tolerated a troublesome reader, would be impossible in these few lines.

Nor can I, finally, find fit words to thank that tenth Muse whose constant encouragement made the completion of this task possible, and for whose sake I would this were a better book.

PARKER THOMAS MOON.

New York,
September 3, 1926.

CONTENTS

MAPS

IMPERIALISM AND WORLD POLITICS IN THE NINETEENTH AND TWENTIETH CENTURIES

CHAPTER I

SIGNIFICANCE OF IMPERIALISM

World Conquest and World Unrest

The American public is barely beginning to realize the significance of the present-day imperialism, which is now approaching its dénouement. Of ancient imperialism, of the empires of Alexander, of Cyrus, of Cæsar, we have heard much and of Napoleon's spectacular exploits every schoolboy has read. But the realms conquered by military emperors of past ages were baubles, trifles compared with the far-flung dominions which have been won, more often with the pen than by the sword, in our own supposedly prosaic generation. It is with this contemporary empire-building, and its effects on international relations, on our prosperity and our security, on industry and civilization, that this study is concerned.

Little as the general public may realize the fact, imperialism is the most impressive achievement and the most momentous world-problem of our age. Perhaps this statement should be thrust home. More than half of the world's land surface, and more than a billion human beings, are included in the colonies and "backward countries" dominated by a few imperialist nations. Every man, woman and child in Great Britain has ten colonial subjects, black, brown and yellow. For every acre in France there are twenty in the French colonies and protectorates. Italy is one-sixth as large as her colonies; Portugal, one twenty-third; Belgium, one-eightieth. The nations of western Europe are dwarfs beside their colonial possessions.

How prevalent imperialism was in Europe before the war

and still remains, it is difficult for Americans to appreciate, since the "average" American has been accustomed, at any rate before the disillusionment of 1919, to think that seizure of territory was somewhat akin to theft, that militarism and aggressive war were out of date among democratic nations, that conquest was contrary to the normal principles of international morality, albeit some slight deviation from such principles might be pardoned or ignored. If we desired Louisiana or Alaska, we purchased it; if we annexed the Philippines, we paid a price in gold.[1]

This, however, is not and has not been the attitude of the imperialist nations of Europe, or of Europeanized Japan. French statesmen have vehemently declared the conquest of colonies to be not merely permissible, but imperative for France, and the Third Republic has won almost five million square miles. Italian patriots have proclaimed it a sacred duty, and Italy, despite all discouragements, has gained almost a million square miles. Englishmen have regarded it, in Kipling's words, as "the white man's burden" which civilized peoples dare not shirk; and in the last half-century four million square miles have been added to the British Empire, besides many a veiled protectorate and sphere of influence, not formally annexed. Germany at first under Bismarck's cautious guidance abstained from African and Asiatic empire-building, but at length plunged into world-politics, rather late, to appropriate a million square miles in Africa and the East Indies, to dominate the rich Asiatic empire of the Ottoman sultans; and, finally, to stake all and lose all in the titanic conflict of 1914. Austria-Hungary, as lesser partner in the Central European coalition, strove to master the Balkans. Russian tsars, not content with their broad domain in Europe and Siberia, stretched acquisitive hands into Central Asia, Persia, Manchuria and Mongolia, and looked hungrily on Turkey, Tibet, and Afghanistan. Japan, aptly imitating Europe, took Formosa, Korea, part of Manchuria, Shantung, German islands in the Pacific, and, during the Great War, attempted at a single stroke to make all China virtually a Japanese protectorate. All the Great Powers save the United States boldly and frankly set themselves to the

[1] The payment, in this case, was not strictly speaking a purchase price, *cf. infra*, p. 396.

epic task, in the nineteenth century, of carving out stupendous colonial empires; and even the United States, feeling the same urge to action, reached into the Pacific and into the Caribbean for modest parcels of colonial territory.

Nor were the Great Powers more imperialist than several of the smaller nations. Belgium, with her vast property in Central Africa; Portugal, with colonies larger than the German Kaiser's; Spain, clinging tenaciously to a strip of Morocco together with pitiable fragments of her former colonial grandeur; and Holland, glorying in a magnificent East-Indian island empire, have vied with stronger states in seeking the rewards which all hoped to win in the stirring game of world politics.

"World politics"—it is a phrase to conjure with! Imperialism has given birth to world-wide empires, to world-wide diplomacy. Great Britain is not, in truth, a European nation, but the nucleus of a universal power. The tricolor of France flies in the Congo jungle, on Sahara's sands, above Indo-Chinese rice-fields. European diplomatists act the drama of international relations on a stage as broad as earth. Often a single diplomatic bargain, signed so easily in a European capital, affects the destinies of unwitting millions in all four quarters of the globe. The Anglo-French agreement of 1904, for example, dealt with Newfoundland in America, the New Hebrides in Oceania, Siam in Asia, Morocco and Egypt and other colonies in Africa. Such is the meaning of world politics. And imperialism is the root and *raison d'être* of world politics.

If from this commanding standpoint one reviews the recent history of international relations, the alliances, ententes, crises and wars reveal a new meaning. Almost without exception, they were but surface manifestations of the swift, deep current of imperialism. When France and England trembled on the verge of war in 1898, during the Fashoda Crisis, imperialist rivalry for a million or so square miles of the African Sudan was the cause. The German emperor's celebrated telegram to President Kruger, congratulating him on having repulsed a British invasion, was more than a breach of international etiquette; it was a revelation of tense imperialist competition in South Africa, and as such it both angered and alarmed British statesmen. The Moroccan "crises" of 1905 and 1911, which so nearly embroiled all Europe in war, were not unique results of some peculiarly German—or peculiarly French—aggressiveness; rather, they were two of the innumerable explosions which have been caused when the aims of imperialist nations happened to cross. The South African War of 1899 may have been inaugurated by truculent Boers, but it would never have been fought had English imperialism not been active in South Africa; nor would the Spanish-American War have occurred if there had been no American interests in Cuba. The greatest war the twentieth century had witnessed before 1914 was the purely imperialist Russo-Japanese struggle for Korea and Manchuria. And the greatest of all wars was caused more by imperialism than by any other single factor. Americans who prefer to believe that the catastrophe of 1914 was brought about by the personal vagaries of William Hohenzollern may cherish their belief if they will, but the facts are opposed to it. The very alignment of European powers was dictated by imperialism, not by race or democracy or kinship of culture. Germany, Austria-Hungary and Turkey were allied by Teutonic domination of the Near East. Republican France and monarchist England were bound together by the far-reaching imperialist bargain of 1904; liberal England and tsarist Russia, by an agreement of 1907 regarding imperialist interests in Persia, Afghanistan, Tibet.

It is easy to heap up the evidence, though no labored proof is intended here. When the German ambassador in 1914 offered to respect the integrity of Belgium and France, the significant question of Sir Edward Grey was whether Germany intended to take the French colonies. During the war, even when hardest pressed on the battlefields of France, the Allies spared troops to conquer the German colonies and occupy choice portions of Turkey. When the German government secretly formulated its war-aims for communication to President Wilson, a larger share of the world's colonies was the important point. The Allies, for their part, while professing publicly their interest in small nations and the sanctity of treaties, quietly arranged by a series of secret treaties the division to be made of Germany's colonies and of Turkey if victory should be theirs. And when victory was achieved, the Allies made it one of their first concerns at the Paris Peace Conference to wring from President Wilson's unwilling lips an assurance that, though the coveted colonial and Near Eastern territories might be nominally internationalized as "mandates," the mandates would be given to the Allies in accordance with the secret treaties.

Contrary to a quite general impression, imperialism is not a closed story now that the German colonies have been divided. The climax has not yet been reached; the dénouement is still uncertain. Never was imperialist rivalry so keen as after the Great War. We are now entering a period of intensified international economic competition, in which the problem of imperialism is becoming all the more acute because most of the backward areas available for colonies have already been appropriated. Competition is stimulated by scarcity. There are no longer vast unclaimed reaches of Africa to sate the appetites of rising powers. Moreover, tariff barriers are being erected in hitherto open colonies; governments are taking a more vital interest and sometimes officially participating in the international scramble for oil, railway and mining concessions; the tide of immigrant "surplus population" from Europe and Asia is being turned back upon itself by American restrictions, to seek new outlets; backward peoples are fast becoming educated to the point of providing a really important, and rapidly increasing, market for manufactures; raw materials are becoming more and more the stakes of diplomacy.

A few instances of the increasing economic importance of colonies will make these general statements more convincing. The exports of the United States to our own and other colonies amounted in 1900 to less than one-fifth of a billion dollars; in 1913, to two-thirds of a billion; in 1920, to more than a billion and a half. In twenty years our exports to colonies were multiplied by 8.8, other exports only by 5.4. These figures are mute witnesses to the all-important fact that the United States, like other industrial nations, is becoming increasingly dependent on non-European countries as markets for manufactured goods. Colonial markets are growing much more rapidly than European markets. To put it even more clearly, non-European countries absorbed only 23% of the exports of the United States before 1900 (average 1895-9), but their share rose to 40% in 1913, then 46% in 1920, and 49.8% in 1923. Almost sixty per cent of the new business which American exporters have gained since the 1890's has been found in Asia, Africa, and America. To generalize, in the decade from 1913 to 1923 the imports of colonies increased by 51% while the imports of other countries increased by less than 16%. Colonies in 1923 meant five billion dollars' worth of export business, of which two billions had been added in a decade.[1]

Conversely, as industrial countries import more raw materials and foodstuffs, colonial sources of supply are drawn upon more and more heavily. To take the United States as an example, again, the value of imports from colonies increased almost ten-fold in the two decades from 1900 to 1920. From colonies and quasi-colonial "backward countries" we get our crude rubber, much of our oil, fertilizers for farmlands, fruit and coffee for the breakfast table, chocolate and sugar for the confectioner, tobacco, tea, hemp for rope, and jute for all the millions of bags in which goods are packed for shipment, indispensable manganese for our steel-mills. Inconceivably more do the less richly endowed European nations rely upon colonial products. Colonial investments, too, are multiplying, mounting into billions of dollars for the United States and into tens of billions for the imperialist nations collectively; more will be said later about their importance. Colonies and backward countries, spoils of diplomacy before the war, are vital features of everyday business to-day. Whether they are closed or open, developed or retarded, monopolized or shared freely, will be a much more significant question to-morrow than it was yesterday.

Perhaps even more challenging as an omen of the approaching climax of imperialism is the uneasy stirring of non-European races which have been subjected to enough of European rule to become restive. During the last few years a spirit of rebellious self-determination has seized upon hitherto inert subject races: Nationalist Turkey has turned against European exploitation, Nationalist Egypt has won independence; Indian Nationalism has assumed monumental proportions; Nationalist Persia and Afghanistan have cast off British shackles; Filipinos have become more insistent in their pleas for independence.

Whether this movement of the non-European peoples for self-government will reach peaceful maturity is a grave question

[1] The foregoing statements are based on computations using statistics in the *Statistical Abstract of the United States* and the *Statesman's Year-Book.*

for the entire civilized world, but even more interesting is the prospect, of which one can catch only faint glimpses now, beyond the question of self-government. What will be the situation when India's factories, now springing up like mushrooms, are numbered by hundreds of thousands instead of by thousands; when China's industrious masses are harnessed, as more than a million Japanese now are, to modern industrial machinery; when Asiatic manufactures on a large scale compete with European and American industries? Steadily and surely, and far more rapidly than many casual observers believe, the so-called backward nations are borrowing not only superficial traits of European civilization, but European methods of industry, of war, of government, of education. The day is dawning when the deficiencies which made these peoples "backward" and impotent in the face of European imperialism will no longer exist, and, like Japan, such countries as China, India, Persia, Egypt, Turkey, Siam, perhaps even parts of Africa will use the machines and the weapons and respond to the nationalistic and democratic sentiments which have given Europe her seemingly impregnable world-mastery. India has 320 millions to Great Britain's 44 millions of inhabitants; China has possibly 400 millions to the 39 of France; Asia and Africa have over a billion to Europe's half-billion. The imperialist "Great Powers" of to-day are but pygmies prodding giants into activity. Which will be the Great Powers of to-morrow?

In the following chapters, imperialism will be viewed both as an achievement and as a world problem, the significance of which has been merely suggested in the foregoing rather sketchy introduction. The most natural starting-point for a systematic study will be found in the background, beginnings, and causes of the movement. After that, we may proceed chapter by chapter with a survey of its development, and, at the end, look back over the material to generalize and criticize.

CHAPTER II

TWO CHANGES OF MIND

MOST of us are inclined to believe that our convictions are true and will remain true. Few realize with what astounding rapidity the most fundamental political and economic dogmas may be revolutionized. If for no other reason than to illustrate this changeability of ideas, it is worth while to review the interesting process by which Europe was first enamoured of colonial empire, then disillusioned, then reconverted to the old faith in the modernized form of imperialism. If one would analyze international relations to-day, one should first digest the fact that only fifty years ago the foremost statesmen of Europe were just as firmly convinced of the futility and folly, as their predecessors had been and their successors were to be persuaded of the value and virtue of imperialism. Another purpose, however, will also be served by a preliminary survey of the historical and economic antecedents of modern empire-building. Like trees, great historical events spring from a soil enriched by the remains of earlier growths. The to-days of our lives, and the to-morrows, arise from the yesterdays. The infant present cannot deny the parent past.

The domination of the world by European powers which in modern times seems so natural as rarely to provoke the student's curiosity, is in reality one of the most astonishing paradoxes of history. During long millenniums while powerful empires and civilized cities were rising and falling in ancient Egypt, in Babylon, in Asia and China, most of Europe was a savage wilderness. In the case of the Phœnicians, at least, backward Europe received colonists from Asia and Spain was colonized by Carthage. Only toward the very close of ancient history did Greece and Rome, the southern fringe of the European continent, in contact with Asiatic and African civilization, begin to play any conspicuous rôle in the world. With the decline of Rome, Europe once more fell into weakness, and again became subject to colonization and conquest by Asiatic and African powers. Into Spain came the Moors from northern Africa; into southeastern Europe the Asiatic Turks fought their way. Surely Europe seemed destined to be the footstool of other continents, not the imperial mistress of the world!

The beginnings, however, of Europe's rise to world-power became evident about the time of the Crusades, when Christendom, turning at bay, sent its armies to invade the Afro-Asiatic Mohammedan world, and when Italian city-states such as Amalfi, Venice, Florence, Genoa and Pisa, reaching out for the commerce of the East, established their warehouses (*fondachi*) in the cities of Asia Minor. From the twelfth to the fifteenth century the Italian cities monopolized the trade routes linking the eastern Mediterranean with Asiatic countries whence came spices, gems, drugs, and many other luxuries desired by nobleman and burgher. This commercial expansion into the Near East was the prelude to, and the economic reason for, the epochal fifteenth-century European voyages of discovery.

Mercantilism, or the Creed of Princes

One may well inquire why the great explorers of the fifteenth and sixteenth centuries were sent out not by the Italian commercial city-states, nor by the opulent Hanseatic League of German commercial cities, but by commercially backward countries, predominantly agricultural countries, such as Portugal, Spain, England and France. An answer is suggested by even a cursory sketch of certain economic conditions at the time.

Gold and silver were relatively scarce in medieval Europe. As commerce expanded, the supply of precious metals became so inadequate as to occasion inconvenience, even anxiety, especially in countries which had no mines. Furthermore, the rising national kings needed gold or silver to maintain their courts, to increase their power, to hire soldiers, to pay for wars. Yet it was difficult to obtain the precious metals, except in one of two ways. The Italian city-states, which monopolized the Asiatic trade, obtained supplies from Asia, and from their lucrative business as middlemen between Europe and Asia. The Germans had mines as well as profitable trade. Other countries resorted to many and curious, but largely futile, expedients.

such as engaging alchemists to transmute baser metals into gold, or forbidding the export of bullion and coins, or debasing the coinage. It is not difficult to understand, then, why enterprising monarchs in Western Europe hungered for new mines of precious metals; why explorers searched so avidly for gold and silver. That would be one solution of the difficulty. Or, if a West-European nation could open up a new route to Asia and trade directly with the East, not only could it escape paying the extortionate prices of Italian and German middlemen, but it could hope to amass wealth in the rôle of retailer.

The latter solution was found by the little kingdom of Portugal, whose explorers bravely ventured down the unknown West-African coast until they rounded the Cape, reached India from the south, in 1498, and brought back cargoes of spices by the new all-water route. Naturally, under prevailing standards of international ethics, they claimed a monopoly of their new route and sought to exploit it to the ultimate degree; naturally the Portuguese king declined an offer from mercantile Venice to purchase wholesale all the spices imported via the Cape (1521). Portugal's aim was not colonization, but commercial profit. Trading posts were established along the African coasts, on the shores of the Indian Ocean, at the entrance to the Persian Gulf, and above all in the spice-producing East Indies. To Lisbon the Portuguese vessels, sailing in secrecy under naval convoy, brought their rich freight, and to the Casa da India at Lisbon, wholesale warehouse of Oriental spices and luxuries, came Dutch and French and English merchants to buy from Portugal. The king's coffers received, it was estimated, $750,000 a year net profit, and hundreds of Portuguese officials and traders enriched themselves.

Spain, on the other hand, failed to find a new route to the spice islands, but discovered instead the silver and gold mines of America. It has been estimated that from 1493 to 1640 Spain got in America about 875 tons of gold and 45,720 tons of silver, and on this treasure the king levied a royalty of twenty per cent, the "*quinto.*" Admitting that these figures may be far from scientific accuracy,[1] and that much of this bullion was captured en route by British or other adventurous mariners,

[1] A. Del Mar, *Money and Civilization*, pp. 62, 102; *cf.* A. F. Dodd, *History of Money*, etc., p. 39; Keller, *Colonization*, p. 111. Max Weber, in

and that through commerce much found its way into other countries, and even that the influx of gold and silver may have been injurious to Spain's economic development, the facts remain nevertheless that the Spanish court was brilliant and powerful in the sixteenth century, and that Spain's colonial conquests appeared to be so marvelously profitable as to excite the cupidity of less fortunate West-European monarchs.

For a time, to be sure, France and England were content to purchase spices from Lisbon, and send out a few explorers. The Dutch, at that time subject to Spain, became the chief carriers and distributors of Spanish and Portuguese trade. But toward the end of the sixteenth century the Dutch rebelled against Spain, and, as Spain and Portugal were united under Philip II's scepter, began to prey on Portugal's colonial-commercial empire. It is not necessary to retell the familiar story here, but merely to emphasize the economic aspect which has so potently affected modern nationalistic economic policies. The East India Company, chartered by the Netherlands in 1602, wrested from Portugal the route round the Cape, the trading posts in the East and the East Indies, and for generations monopolized the spice trade, despite persistent efforts of French and English to seize a share. Dutch commerce prospered; stately ships crowded Dutch ports; and the trident of Neptune seemed well in the grasp of Holland.

The sequence of events which have been so roughly sketched here led almost inevitably to a national policy which has continued to sway men's minds even to the present day—the policy of Mercantilism. Seventeenth-century rulers naturally ascribed Spain's greatness to the fabulous wealth of American colonial mines, Portugal's ephemeral brilliance to the East Indian trade, and Holland's rise to her colonies and commerce. Less favored nations, unable to find exclusive trade routes to the Orient or to tap nature's treasures of silver and gold, must find some other method of gaining wealth if they would not be impoverished. Richelieu, the great French statesman of the early seventeenth century, looked with envy on the Dutch, whose trade with the

his *Wirtschaftsgeschichte* (Munich, 1923), p. 219, accepts 2½ million kg. of gold and 90 to 100 million kg. of silver as the best figures for the production of Mexico and South America from 1493 to 1800. It should be remembered that the Brazilian gold production, which assumed large proportions in the seventeenth century, was Portuguese rather than Spanish.

East and West Indies was so lucrative. France, he claimed, should emulate Holland. Instead of paying so dearly for imports from other countries, France should make her own cloth, raise her own food and press her own wine, manufacture goods for export, and thus "draw money from other countries." And, be it remarked, he considered naval power and colonial empire indispensable features of this economic program.[1] Similarly John DeWitt, Grand Pensionary of the Netherlands, in his *Political Maxims* linked colonies with commerce and industry as the trinity responsible for Dutch power. How general this conviction became may be inferred from the fact that Prussia, Denmark, Sweden, England and France, in the seventeenth century, all made some effort to found colonies, as well as to foster shipping, industry, and export trade. The theories inspiring these ventures were oftentimes so crude that the veriest tyro in economic science can demonstrate their falsity. Nevertheless, in one form or another with many a variation, the policy of colonial commercialism was so universal in the seventeenth century and so remarkably manifested in the eighteenth century, that it cannot be lightly dismissed as a fallacy. It was the direct application of political national monarchy to the economic conditions of the age.

Prefigured in the writings of Monchrétien, Richelieu, DeWitt, Thomas Mun, Raleigh, Sir Joshua Child, and others, and practised perhaps most conspicuously by Louis XIV's celebrated minister, Colbert, this policy of encouraging industries, exports, colonies and shipping came to be known as Colbertism or, more generally, Mercantilism.

Economic policies, more or less well suited to the conditions under which they were originated, survive long after the conditions have changed. And the policy of Mercantilism, dignified in its hoary age, still survives to-day, though it has donned the garb of modern economic phraseology and adopted an alias, imperialism. It will not be unenlightening to recapitulate the conditions which gave birth to Mercantilism, if we would clear our minds of tradition before attempting to judge the validity of mercantilist policies under twentieth-century conditions. In the seventeenth and eighteenth centuries, Mercantilism took

[1] See F. C. Palm, "Mercantilism as a Factor in Richelieu's Economic Policy," *Pol. Sci. Quart.*, XXXIX, pp. 650 ff.

form in response to a set of political, economic and religious conditions which have since been swept away. It was an edifice built on foundations which have been washed away by the current of progress.

One of these foundations was royal autocracy:[1] ambitious and despotic kings of England, of France, of Denmark, of Spain, of Prussia, of Sweden needed gold for their growing expenditures and men (obtainable for gold) and ships for their incessant wars. Hence the emphasis on obtaining precious metals by commerce, on which kings levied duties, or by discovery of mines, from which kings exacted "royalties," and hence the emphasis on national merchant marines, easily convertible into naval auxiliaries.

Religion played a less important part. Missionary zeal, one needs hardly say, was a significant factor in the early explorations and in later colonization. But missionary zeal is not a reason for wholesale colonial conquests unless, as in early modern times, it be generally assumed that monarchs should dictate the religion of subjects, and that conquered natives should be converted without choice.

More significant in this analysis was the economic situation. The first naïve greed for trade routes and gold mines, notable in the fifteenth century, was modified by subsequent economic transformations. To begin with, the building of larger ships for ocean voyages, and, incidentally, the improvement of roads in Europe, made commerce in bulkier goods possible and profitable. Manufacturing industries in Europe, stimulated by this event as well as by other causes, grew amazingly in the seventeenth and eighteenth centuries, until home markets were glutted and foreign markets bitterly contested. Woolen cloth and alcoholic beverages, probably the two leading commodities manufactured for export, were goods that could be made in almost every country. Competition was necessarily keen, and the European market was not only limited but fenced about with mercantilist restrictions and tariffs, since each nation endeavored to cut its own imports to the minimum. Under these circumstances, what could be more natural than for each nation to acquire colonies, from which it could obtain raw materials and non-competitive

[1] Although Mercantilism was practised in Holland and England after autocracy had fallen.

colonial products, and to which it could sell manufactures without hindrance or competition?

Such were the foundations of Mercantilism and of the so-called "Old Colonial System." By the middle of the eighteenth century France and England had emerged as the leading mercantilist powers, France applying Colbert's principles rigidly to her vast domain in the St. Lawrence and Mississippi valleys, and in the French West Indies; England enforcing the system less consistently in her West-Indian and American colonies. Spain still drew millions of pesos from the mines of the huge Spanish Colonial empire in America, besides plantation products from the West Indies and Philippines. The Dutch had exploited the spice-producing East Indies so ruthlessly, and the monopolistic management of these colonies had become so corrupt and inefficient, that decay had already set in. Portugal had lost most of the East Indies and on the African coast retained only a few scant footholds, but still had the immense colony in Brazil, in which gold and diamond mining yielded royalties to the king and fertile plantations produced coffee and sugar. Prussia had sold its holdings on the Gold Coast of Africa to Holland for 7,200 ducats in 1725 and dropped out of the race.[1] Denmark and Sweden held minor colonies.

Laissez-faire, or the Creed of Merchant Princes

Imposing as was its façade, this old colonial edifice of the eighteenth century was founded on shifting sands. Its fall was not long delayed. Sixty years, from 1763 to 1823, witnessed the shattering of the four greatest colonial empires. The French colonial empire was destroyed, or rather annexed, by Great Britain in 1763, at the close of a long series of wars. The British in turn suffered; the Declaration of Independence by thirteen important American colonies in 1776 seemed to presage the collapse of the empire. The grim hand of destiny touched next the Spanish realm in South America, and in the generation from about 1810 to about 1825 Spain was excluded from the continent. Simultaneously Brazil separated from Portugal, in 1822.

[1] The Netherlands in turn sold its Gold Coast holdings to Great Britain in 1867, *cf.* Hertslet, *Map of Africa by Treaty*, II, pp. 674-8. The Danish posts on the Gold Coast were ceded to Great Britain in 1850.

He must have been an incorrigible believer whose faith in the old colonial system was not shaken by this series of cataclysms. Turgot's famous dictum, "Colonies are like fruits which cling to the tree only till they ripen,"[1] uttered in the middle of the eighteenth century, seemed now to have been irrefutably proved. As if more proof were needed, in 1837 rebellion raised its head in Canada, and Lord Durham, who was sent to investigate, reported that the Canadian colonists should be granted responsible self-government. One by one the British colonies of Canada, New South Wales, South Australia, Victoria and Tasmania, New Zealand, Cape Colony, and Queensland received self-government, during the two decades that followed Lord Durham's report, and many Englishmen assumed that self-government was a step toward emancipation. Disraeli wrote to the British foreign minister, in 1852, "These wretched colonies will all be independent too in a few years, and are a millstone around our necks."[2] Gladstone sonorously expressed his conviction, in April, 1870, that colonies grow "until they arrive at that stage of their progress in which separation from the mother-country inevitably takes place"; in the past they have done so by bloodshed, in the future the mother-country should gracefully and peaceably surrender her authority.[3]

Even more devastating was the change in economic facts and theories in the century from 1775 to 1875. Colonial rebellions might shatter the pillars, but these economic changes swept away the foundations, of the old mercantilist colonial system. The altered facts of the economic situation may be considered first. The invention of spinning machines, power-looms, steam engines, and new metallurgical processes brought about an Industrial Revolution in England during this epoch. As the secrets of the inventions were at first carefully guarded, and as establishment of steam-power factories was in any case difficult for economically backward peoples, England during the first three-quarters of the nineteenth century was almost unrivalled in the manufacture of machine-made textiles, chiefly cotton cloth, and of iron

[1] Seeley, *Expansion of England*, p. 15.

[2] Monypenny and Buckle, *Life of Disraeli*, III, p. 385.

[3] Numerous quotations in similar vein are given by C. A. Bodelsen, *Studies in Mid-Victorian Imperialism* (N. Y., 1925), and by Professor R. L. Schuyler in "The Rise of Anti-Imperialism in England," *Pol. Sci. Quart.*, XXXVII, pp. 440-71, and "The Climax of Anti-Imperialism in England," *ibid.*, XXXVI, pp. 537-60.

and hardware, which could be sold at less than hand-made goods. Governmental restriction of colonial markets for such goods was quite unnecessary as long as English industry could undersell its lagging foreign competitors. Moreover, to sparse colonial populations less of such goods could be sold than to populous European nations. What the facts of the economic situation demanded, from the English manufacturer's point of view, was free access to European markets and indifference to colonial aggrandizement. The facts demanded a new political economy, antithetical to the principles of mercantilism.

By one of the most fateful coincidences of history, a new political economy was at hand, ready for application. Turgot and the French *Économistes* or Physiocrats in the third quarter of the eighteenth century had already sketched in broad lines a political economy of individual freedom which was summed up in the phrase, "*laissez-faire.*" Adam Smith, father of the classical political economy in England, had expounded somewhat similar, but more convincingly elaborated doctrines in *The Wealth of Nations* (1776). Greater gain, he argued, was to be obtained by free trade, permitting natural specialization of industry, than by mercantilist regulation of commerce. Some interference with commercial liberty (the Navigation Act) might be justified on the grounds of national defense, but, and this is the important point, it was certainly unprofitable economically. Applying his principles specifically to colonies, Smith asserted that although natural colonial trade would be profitable to all countries, attempts to monopolize colonial trade cause "mere loss instead of profit" to the "body of the people." The overgrowth of British colonial trade had sucked capital away from other branches of business and caused decay in Britain's general foreign trade. Then, too, the colonies were a heavy burden on the national exchequer. From an economic point of view, he concluded, Great Britain would profit by abandoning her empire.[1]

The truth of this bold statement seemed to be demonstrated when, after the successful rebellion of the American colonies, Great Britain's exports to the United States rose to higher figures than had been attained before the revolution. Later British economists of the classical school, Malthus, Ricardo, James Mill, J. R. McCulloch and others, made the economic value

[1] Adam Smith, *Wealth of Nations*, Bk. IV, ch. vii.

of free trade and the economic absurdity of Mercantilism fundamental principles of orthodox political economy. Cobden and Bright popularized the principles of free trade in their great campaign against the Corn Laws. Manufacturers fell into line. It is perhaps significant that the free trade movement became known as "the Manchester school," or simply "Manchesterism," taking its name from the city which was truly the heart of the cotton industry. Protective duties were taken off 750 articles in 1842 by Peel. The Corn Laws, emblematic of the old system, fell in 1846, and with them vanished the duties on about 150 other articles of food, raw materials, and manufactures. The Navigation Laws, enforcing a mercantilist policy toward shipping, were repealed in 1849. Shortly afterwards, Gladstone's reforms of 1853 and 1860 and the removal of the import duty on timber in 1866 demolished the last ramparts of English mercantilism.

While the doctrine of free trade was undermining the economic foundations of colonial imperialism, philosophical and political radicalism attacked the system from another angle. The doctrines of individual liberty, democracy, and cosmopolitanism which gradually gained popularity among radical thinkers in the early nineteenth century, and among other classes subsequently, were decidedly anti-imperialistic in their original tendency. Jeremy Bentham, father of British Philosophical Radicalism, expressed his views in a letter entitled *Emancipate Your Colonies,* addressed to the French National Convention in 1793 and published in 1830. Colonies, he held, were not only unprofitable, but involved great military and naval expense, danger of foreign war, and political corruption in the mother country. James Mill contributed an article on "Colony" to the 1818 supplement to the *Encyclopædia Britannica,* stressing the expense and corruption and enmities arising from the old colonial system, and condemning particularly the prevalent practice of settling convicts in colonies.

Far from convincing the masses, in the first half of the nineteenth century, these anti-colonial doctrines were long shared only by a handful of progressive thinkers; nevertheless their influence widened by degrees. Remarkably effective in the work of propaganda was the firebrand Richard Cobden, the popular apostle of free trade and pacifism, the man who called the British government "a standing conspiracy to rob and bamboozle the people." This fearless iconoclast assailed British rule in India as utterly unprofitable and unnatural. "Ultimately, of course," he predicted, "Nature will assert the supremacy of her laws and the white skins will withdraw to their own latitudes; leaving the Hindoos to the enjoyment of the climate to which their complexion is suited"; but in the meantime possession of India would breed "all kinds of trouble, loss, and disgrace," it would cost blood and gold; it might demoralize the British government just as Greece and Rome were corrupted by the East.[1] Recognizing the strong hold, however, which colonialism still had upon popular sentiment, even in 1842, Cobden declared: "The colonial system, with all its dazzling appeal to the passions of the people, can never be got rid of except by the indirect process of free-trade, which will gradually and imperceptibly loose the bonds which unite our colonies to us by a mistaken attitude of self-interest."[2]

As years rolled by the movement gained momentum. Soon we find, in 1862-3, an Oxford professor of history, Goldwin Smith, proclaiming in a series of letters to the *Daily News* that although colonies were once profitable, in days of commercial monopoly, there was no longer any reason for retaining them, now that "trade is everywhere free, or becoming free"; England should adopt a policy of emancipating her colonies.[3] Such views were by no means allowed to pass unchallenged, but they were shared by more than one official. Henry Thring, Home Office Counsel, who drafted legislation for the Government, proposed in 1865 that any colony at maturity should be permitted, as a matter of course, to become independent. Herman Merivale, permanent under-secretary for colonies from 1848 to 1860, accepted the doctrine that colonies eventually secede. Moreover, "with the colonial trade thrown open and colonization at an end, it is obvious that the leading motives which induced our ancestors to found and maintain a colonial empire no longer exist."[4] His successor from 1860 to 1871, Sir Frederic Rogers

[1] *Cf.* Cobden's pamphlet, *How Wars are got up in India* (London, 1853), pp. 255-7.

[2] Morley, *Life of Cobden*, I, p. 230.

[3] For a less inadequate summary of Goldwin Smith's views and influence, see Bodelsen, *op. cit.*, 52-7.

[4] Cited in Bodelsen, *op. cit.*, p. 35.

(Lord Blachford) said he always believed—so strongly that he could "hardly realize the possibility of anyone seriously thinking the contrary—that the destiny of our colonies is independence." Another Colonial Office official, Sir Henry Taylor, in 1864 referred to the British possessions in America as "a sort of *damnosa hœreditas*."[1]

Anti-Imperialism in the Mid-Victorian Age

The increasing prevalence of anti-imperialistic views helps to explain what would otherwise seem like astonishing indifference to colonial expansion in Victorian England, prior to the 'seventies and 'eighties. After the Revolutionary and Napoleonic wars, which had brought Heligoland, Malta, Tobago, St. Lucia, Mauritius, Trinidad, Guiana, Cape Colony and Ceylon into the fold, British colonial expansion was singularly sluggish for more than half a century. To be sure, the Indian realm was consolidated and expanded; Aden (1839) and a few other strategic points on the route to India were appropriated; the Australian colonies grew inevitably, New Zealand was annexed (1840), the Fiji Islands (1874) likewise, and Singapore (1819), and Hongkong (1842); while in Africa Natal was annexed in 1843, Basutoland in 1871, and Griqualand in 1874. But this record of expansion from 1815 to 1875 is indeed meagre, compared with the vast gains of later years. And especially it must be emphasized that during this period in numerous instances the British government exhibited a positive distaste for colonial aggression.[2] A few specific instances will enforce this point. The first attempts of British settlers in Natal to obtain British protection met with discouraging rebuffs, and only after much hesitation did Lord Stanley, then secretary of state for the colonies, consent to annexation of Natal in 1843.[3] In the case of New Zealand likewise, Downing Street stubbornly opposed projects of colonization and annexation was delayed until 1840, when there was good reason to fear that France might steal a march on her inactive rival.[4] A little later, Great Britain amiably

[1] Quotations from Schuyler, *loc. cit.* His articles and Bodelsen, *op. cit.*, may be referred to for scholarly estimates of the anti-imperialist agitation.

[2] *Cf.* Sir Charles Bruce, *The Broad Stone of Empire* (1910), I, ch. 4.

[3] Egerton, *Short History of British Colonial Policy*, pp. 343-5.

[4] *State Papers*, XXIX, 1111-4. Rusden, *History of New Zealand*, I, p. 241.

recognized the independence of Transvaal (1852) and the Orange Free State (1854), two republics founded by Boer emigrants from British South Africa, despite the fact that the elected delegates of the Orange River colonists desired to remain under British sovereignty.[1] In 1856, when the French promoter de Lesseps proposed digging a canal across the isthmus of Suez, Lord Palmerston, British Foreign Secretary, instead of welcoming the project, expressed a fear that such a canal might lead to British occupation of Egypt; a later generation might have regarded the same contingency with imperialist hope.

Perhaps the most interesting illustration is to be found in the Fiji Islands. Here a native chieftain euphoniously named Thakombau, embarrassed by rivals and rebellions, and alarmed by an American claim for $45,000 as indemnity for injuries to a consul, had first turned to the God of the Christian missionaries for aid, and then, that failing, to Queen Victoria, of whom he had doubtless heard as the mightiest of earthly potentates. He actually offered her in 1859 sovereignty over his islands.[2] The queen's advisers, however, sent out one Colonel Smythe to look this gift horse in the mouth, and Smythe ungratefully recommended refusal of the proffered sovereignty. A second offer was likewise spurned. Only on the third offer did Great Britain accept, and that was in 1874, after imperialism had revived in England.[3] Parliament apparently sympathized with this negligent policy. Indeed, in 1865 a committee of the House of Commons recommended the abandonment of all British holdings on the West-African coast, saving Sierra Leone, and abstention from further annexations in this region.[4]

As Professor Schuyler has convincingly pointed out,[5] the "Climax of Anti-Imperialism in England" was reached in Gladstone's Cabinet of 1868. Gladstone himself, as has been

[1] See Egerton, *op. cit.*, 346-52.

[2] Mr. Pritchard, who acted as Thakombau's emissary to England in making the 1859 offer, believed that the looms of Lancashire were to be kept going with the cotton which would be grown in Fiji. See *Proceedings of the Royal Colonial Institute*, VI (1874-75), pp. 86-119. The principal speaker at this meeting of the Institute expressed the hope that some day the population of Fiji "would be able, probably, to read Shakespeare and understand him." That, however, is not wholly typical of imperialist aims.

[3] See charter, Jan. 2, 1875, in *State Papers*, 66, p. 953.

[4] Bruce, I, p. 140.

[5] R. L. Schuyler, "The Climax of Anti-Imperialism in England," *Pol. Sci. Quart.*, Dec. 1921, pp. 537 ff.

said, was a "Little Englander" at heart, who desired that the inevitable separation of colonies from the mother country should be voluntarily and peacefully permitted. John Bright, a member of the Cabinet, favored the emancipation of Canada and stigmatized British ownership of Gibraltar as "contrary to every law of morality and honor." Lord Granville, the Colonial Secretary, and Robert Lowe, Chancellor of the Exchequer, were at least willing to acquiesce in independence for Canada, if the latter desired it. In accordance with the spirit of a resolution which had been unanimously adopted by the Commons a few years earlier, favoring withdrawal of British military forces from self-governing colonies, the Gladstone cabinet adopted the policy of removing Imperial troops from New Zealand, notwithstanding indignant protests both from New Zealand and from imperial-minded Englishmen.[1] Disraeli later asserted that the Liberal Party had been striving to disrupt the British Empire; but Disraeli himself, as late as 1866, had written to Lord Derby that England ought to "leave the Canadians to defend themselves; recall the African Squadron; give up the settlements on the West Coast of Africa."[2] Between 1866 and 1874, however, Disraeli's views had changed, and it was as an outspoken imperialist that he triumphed in the elections of 1874. These elections, as Professor Schuyler has observed, marked the defeat of anti-imperialism in England. Yet anti-imperialism as a lost cause survived the defeat. Gladstone, writing in *The Nineteenth Century* magazine, in 1877, expressed his apprehension lest by intervening in Egypt England might find herself burdened with a "North African Empire,"[3] and in his famous Midlothian campaign of 1880 the veteran Liberal leader stoutly resisted the advance of imperialism. History, ironically enough, made Gladstone himself the tool of British aggression in Egypt, but that is another story.

If one turns to France or Germany, one reads the same story of anti-imperialism, rising to a climax in the sixties and seventies, then suddenly overwhelmed by imperialism triumphant. France, after having made vain attempts in the war of American independence and again in the Napoleonic period to regain her

[1] Schuyler, *loc. cit.*
[2] Monypenny and Buckle, III, p. 476.
[3] *The Nineteenth Century*, Aug., 1877, cited by Morley, III, p. 72.

lost colonial greatness, found herself in 1815 with a few trifling shreds of former possessions—a dubious sovereignty over Haiti, two tiny islands in the West Indies, fishing rights in Newfoundland and microscopic St. Pierre and Miquelon nearby, a corner of Guiana, a foothold here and there on the African coast, an undeveloped claim in Madagascar, the Île de Bourbon, and five unimportant trading posts in India—a total of but 38,000 sq. km., embracing four hundred thousand souls. For a time in the 1820's there seemed to be some chance of acquiring Spain's colonies, but the English foreign minister threatened that England "would not tolerate for an instant" such a move, and France had to pledge her honor to keep hands off Spanish America.[1] In 1830 Charles X sent a naval expedition to conquer Algiers, just across the Mediterranean; in 1842 a French protectorate was declared over Tahiti; in 1842 the Gabun River was added; and Louis Napoleon, in the Second Empire period, engaged in scattered colonial ventures, in New Caledonia, Cochin-China and Cambodia, Somaliland and Mexico, all of which save the last were successful.

But how few and how small these gains were, as compared with later exploits, may be seen most clearly in cold statistics. In the sixty-two years from 1815 to 1877, the total acquisitions amounted to 928,000 sq. km. and 5,500,000 inhabitants; whereas in the much shorter space of time since 1877 (which year may be taken as an approximate dividing point between the era of anti-imperialism and the age of imperialism), France has gained about 14,500,000 sq. km. and 53,000,000 non-European subjects. In forty-eight years since 1877 the gain in territory has been almost sixteen times as great as in the sixty-two years before 1877.

Moreover the government of the Second Empire was strongly predisposed in favor of free trade; it made the celebrated "Cobden Treaty" of 1860 with England,[2] opening a wide breach in the mercantilist tariff wall; further, on July 3, 1861, it freely opened to all nations the commerce of the French colonies.[3] This was the very negation of colonial mercantilism. And under

[1] *Cf. infra*, p. 410.

[2] *Archives diplomatiques*, 1861, tome III, 5-12, and especially report on the same subject, *ibid.*, 12-40.

[3] M. Dubois et A. Terrier, *Un Siècle d'expansion coloniale, 1800-1900* (Paris, 1902), pp. 328-330.

the Third Republic, in the seventies and early eighties, anti-mercantilist principles were so strong that only with great labor could partisans of imperialism carry their projects through the gantlet of parliamentary criticism. It is hardly too much to say that in the 'seventies the prevailing spirit in France was opposed to colonies, either on the economic ground that they were unprofitable, or on the political ground that they were a dangerous diversion of energy from European politics, or on the ground that in the modern age of "cosmopolitanism" colonial greed was an anachronism.[1]

In Germany the all-powerful Bismarck shared, until perhaps 1876, the anti-imperialist *Zeitgeist.* In 1868 he wrote to a colleague (von Roon), "All the advantages claimed for the mother country are for the most part illusions. England is abandoning her colonial policy; she finds it too costly."[2] He had already refused a protectorate over the sultan of Sulu (in the Pacific); he likewise refused Portugal's offer to sell Mozambique (in Africa).[3] When France offered Cochin-China and other colonies in lieu of Alsace-Lorraine after the French defeat at Sedan, Bismarck scornfully refused colonial compensation, even though certain Bremen and Hamburg merchants favored it.[4] He wanted no colonies, he bluntly declared; their only use was to provide sinecures for officials; they were too costly a luxury for Germany. "A colonial policy for us would be just like the silken sables of Polish noble families who have no shirts."[5] Many were the pleas, from a limited number of interested merchants and travelers in the 'seventies, for the annexation of this or that overseas land, but the stubborn chancellor rejected them all.[6] And so strong was the anti-mercantilist sentiment of the National Liberal party, on which Bismarck then depended, and of the majority of the Reichstag, that even after he was personally

[1] On French policy and achievements before 1870 see Dubois et Terrier, *op. cit.*, pp. 1-369; from a different point of view, Joannes Tramond et André Reussner, *Éléments d'Histoire Maritime et Coloniale Contemporaine (1815-1914)* (Paris, 1924), pp. 1-220; and René Valet, *L'Afrique du Nord devant le Parlement au XIXe Siècle* (Alger, 1924).

[2] Zimmerman, *Geschichte der deutschen Kolonialpolitik* (Berlin, 1904), p. 6.

[3] M. E. Townsend, *Origins of Modern German Colonialism* (N. Y., 1921), pp. 17-18.

[4] *Ibid.*, pp. 45-7, 18; *cf.* Maxmilian von Hagen's more elaborate work on *Bismarcks Kolonialpolitik* (Stuttgart, 1923), pp. 42-50.

[5] M. Busch, *Tagebuchblätter*, II, 157.

[6] *Cf.* Townsend, *op. cit.*, and von Hagen, *op. cit.*

convinced of the desirability of founding colonies, Bismarck had to humor public opinion most cautiously, and reiterate his disclaimer of imperialist intentions. Not until the 'eighties, when imperialism was everywhere resurgent, could he dare to come out openly in favor of colonial aggrandizement.

The turning of the tide came in the 'seventies and 'eighties. Its cause need be no mystery. It came because economic and political conditions, and with them, theories, had been profoundly altered, since the middle of the century.

CHAPTER III

WHY EUROPE SHOULDERED THE WHITE MAN'S BURDEN

The Logic of Economic Necessity

Europe was converted to imperialism not by logic alone, nor by economic "necessity" alone, but by a combination of argument and interest, arising from an almost revolutionary alteration of economic and political conditions. The old order, the good old mid-Victorian order, had passed away, and if not a new heaven, at least a new earth was seen by the keen eye of business and politics.

First consider the alteration of economic conditions. Four signal changes appear, and first of these is the waning of the comfortable supremacy which English cotton mills and iron works had achieved by the inventions of the Industrial Revolution. As long as other nations worked with their hands, while Englishmen worked with machines and steam, England was secure from serious competition. And other nations were slow to install machinery. For approximately three-quarters of the nineteenth century English industry was as mighty as Gulliver in Lilliput. Even as late as 1870 Great Britain was smelting half of the world's iron, and more than three times as much as any other nation; she was making almost half of the world's cotton goods; her foreign commerce was more than twice that of any rival. But during the last quarter of the century the industries of Germany, United States, France, and other powers, after a long period of infancy, suddenly waxed mighty. England's share of the iron industry diminished with startling rapidity until, before the close of the century, United States had won first place and Germany was about to forge ahead of England into second place.

The following table tells the story:

PRODUCTION OF PIG IRON (thousands of tons)

	1870	1896	1897	1903
United Kingdom	5,960	8,660	8,796	8,935
United States	1,670	8,623	9,653	18,009
Germany	1,390	6,260	6,760	9,860

Even more important—and this needs emphasis—than the absolute volume of production is the rate of increase, because a high rate means reinvestment of surplus profits in the industry, whereas a low rate means either that profits will be low and work slack, or else that profits must seek other opportunities,[1] for investment. From this point of view, the figures are startling. During the period 1870-1903—the period of the great outburst of imperialism—the British iron masters were able to expand their business by a meagre 50%, as compared with 966% for their aggressive American competitors and 609% for the Germans.

Though Great Britain's monopolistic grip on the cotton industry seemed more secure, American and German, not to speak of other foreign competition, began to make itself very uncomfortably felt in the 1870's, 1880's, and 1890's. The following table shows the percentage increase[2] in ten-year periods:

PERCENTAGE INCREASE IN COTTON INDUSTRY

	1870–80	1880–90	1890–1900
Great Britain	19	18	—3
United States	90	42	50
Continent of Europe..........	33	53	25

Export trade tells the same tale. In the three decades from 1870 to 1900, while American exports were almost quadrupled and German exports doubled, English exporters increased their business by only forty-five per cent. While American captains of industry were accumulating fabulous fortunes, in England the pace was on the whole much slower. This fact is particularly impressive for England's two major export industries, iron and cotton goods. In the former, the exports (of iron and steel) during the decade of the eighties were slightly *less* than in the seventies; for expansion, the British iron industry had to rely wholly on domestic consumption, and that increased only by

[1] *Cf. infra*, pp. 30-32, 535.
[2] Using consumption of raw cotton as an index.

forty-one per cent. Cotton exports in the nineties stood at almost the same figure as in the late seventies; here again Great Britain failed to secure her share in the growth of the world market, and, as the table on the preceding page shows, the domestic market did not afford compensation.

This situation meant cut-throat competition. Each of the great industrial nations was making more cloth, more iron and steel, or more of some other manufacture, than its own inhabitants could possibly consume. Each had a surplus which must be sold abroad. "Surplus manufactures" called for foreign markets. But none of the great industrial nations was willing to be a market for the other's surplus, at least in the major competitive fields. All except Great Britain built around themselves forbidding tariff walls. United States, solicitous for "infant industries," took the lead in establishing a protective tariff during and after the Civil War, and raised it still higher in 1890 and 1897. Russia built up her tariff by degrees from 1877 onward. Germany began the erection of her tariff wall in 1879; France in 1881; and other countries followed the lead.[1] Business men and statesmen were not slow to take alarm. A French prime minister, Jules Ferry,[2] described the situation in 1885 clearly enough:

> What our great industries lack . . ., what they lack more and more, is markets. Why? Because . . . Germany is covering herself with barriers; because, beyond the ocean, the United States of America have become protectionist, and protectionist to an extreme degree.

There appeared, however, one bright ray of hope, one solution—colonies. How earnestly the rulers of Europe in the eighties and nineties viewed this situation, and how hopefully they sought to acquire colonies whose markets could be monopolized by the mother-country's industries, cannot fail to impress any reader of the political debates and imperialistic literature of the period. I cannot forbear to add one more quotation, from *The Rise of Our East African Empire* (1893), by Sir Frederick Lugard, who was at the time an influential advocate of imperialism as well as an administrator most active in securing new domains for his country:—

[1] See Moon, *Syllabus on International Relations*, pp. 160 ff., and references there cited.

[2] Dubois et Terrier, *op. cit.*, p. 405.

> As long as our policy is one of free trade, we are compelled to seek new markets; for old ones are being closed to us by hostile tariffs, and our great dependencies, which formerly were consumers of our goods, are now becoming our commercial rivals. It is inherent in a great colonial and commercial empire like ours that we go forward or backward. . . . We are accountable to posterity that opportunities which now present themselves of extending the sphere of our industrial enterprise are not neglected, for the opportunities now offered will never recur again.[1]

"Surplus manufactures," then, provided the chief economic cause of the imperialistic expansion of Europe in the last quarter of the nineteenth century.[2]

And "surplus manufactures" still provide an incentive to imperialism, though other factors have surpassed this one in importance. Colonies to-day provide a market for one-fourth, perhaps more, of the manufactures exported by industrial nations; and colonial markets are growing more rapidly than all other markets. Nations owning colonies are striving to monopolize their trade by means of tariff barriers. Even Great Britain, strong as the British tradition of free trade may be, has in the last few years quietly introduced into a number of the British crown colonies tariffs giving British goods a preference over foreign goods; and the British self-governing colonies are likewise practising imperial preference. Rivalry for colonial markets is a consequence of surplus manufactures.

The second great change in the economic world, to be noted as an explanation of Europe's conversion to imperialism in the last quarter of the nineteenth century, was the revolution in means of communication. To make colonial produce profitable, on a large scale, steamships were needed. To make commercial and military penetration of the interior wilds of Africa and Asia possible, railways were required. To bind colonies close to mother-countries, the telegraph had to be invented. To be sure, steamship, locomotive, and telegraph were invented long before the age we are considering; but their effect was not felt, in the world at large, until the last two or three decades of the nineteenth century. The following table offers the reason:

[1] Lugard, *op. cit.*, II, p. 585.

[2] The tendency of some writers to ascribe imperialism wholly or chiefly to capital investment is unhistorical.

	1850	1873	1880	1890	1900
Railways (thousands of miles)	24	—	224	—	500
Steam shipping (as per cent of world's total shipping).....	—	25	—	59	77
Telegraphs (thousands of miles)	5	—	440	—	1,180

The victory of steam and electricity over space made possible the gigantic increase of colonial trade between 1870 and the present; it also made possible the extension of empires, by transporting the troops that conquered the tropics. Incidentally, as it will later appear more clearly, the building of railways, the laying of cables and telegraphs, the operation of shipping lines, were economic enterprises which themselves were and still are prizes of imperialism.

The third economic factor to be examined is the demand of industrial nations for tropical and subtropical products. Cotton factories in Lancashire, England, are one of the reasons for British troops in Egypt and India. The millions of bales of raw cotton devoured by busy British spindles and looms had to be produced in southern United States, or in colonies. When the American Civil War cut off supplies of American cotton, England and other countries looked about for other sources of supply, and since that time colonies have become increasingly important as cotton-producers. Egypt, for example, produced only 87 thousand bales in 1850, but by 1865 this quantity had been multiplied by five; by 1890 it had been multiplied by nine, and Egypt had become the chief producer of fine, long-staple cotton. British India likewise multiplied its production, and in many another colony plantations were laid out.

Rubber affords another instance, spectacular in its effects. When the civilized world began to wear rubbers and raincoats, to put tires on its wagons and bicycles and automobiles, Europeans had to invade tropical jungles and, by persuasion or by force, induce the natives to tap the wild rubber trees and vines which grew in the Congo and Amazon valleys. The Congo became a colony, where natives were compelled to labor, and its rubber output increased from about thirty thousand dollars in 1886 to eight million in 1900. The Amazon, protected by the Monroe Doctrine against European annexation, was subjected to economic imperialism, almost as if it were a colony. And as the demand for rubber grew still more insatiable, vast rubber plantations were established in British colonies in the Malay Peninsula and Ceylon, and in the Dutch East Indies. Rubber means imperialism.[1]

Coffee, cocoa, tea, and sugar have also founded empires. Coconuts and coconut oil provided motives for the conquest of sunny islands in the South Pacific. The use of phosphate for fertilization of the soil in France is one of the reasons why France prizes her North-African colonies. To obtain tin the French endeavored to dominate southernmost part of China. Gold mines caused the British conquest of Transvaal. The universal hunger of industrial states for coal, iron, and oil has been a *leitmotif* in world politics.

Perhaps, one speculates, these objects of desire might have been bought in the normal manner of trade, without imperialism or conquest. Perhaps. But in fact they were not. Sometimes the complaint was that African negroes failed to appreciate the dignity of labor and preferred their accustomed life of sloth; or that South Sea islanders were unwilling to toil; conquest and compulsory labor were demanded. Or sometimes when Europeans laid out plantations, or opened mines, or drilled oil wells, in a backward country, they found the native government little to their liking, and desired the protection of their own imperial flag. Or in another case, one European government believed that only annexation of coconut-bearing islands would secure the output to its own citizens. In short, the northern world's desire for tropical products has been one of the conditions causing imperialism.

One more economic factor, the fourth, must be added. It is "surplus capital." (Although, as a careful reading of imperialist utterances in the eighties and nineties clearly shows, "surplus manufactures" rather than "surplus capital" provided the chief incentive at the outset, the latter has become the dominant force in twentieth-century imperialism.)

That anyone can possess too much capital will perhaps be denied by impecunious readers, if this volume should have such. But by "surplus capital" is meant a superfluity too great for profitable reinvestment at home. That such surpluses must be created by the industrial expansion of the last century was an inevitable result of the economic laws governing capitalist pro-

[1] *Cf. infra*, p. 546.

duction. The large incomes from factories, mines, rentals, return a profit on the capital; owners of the capital receive larger profits than they care to spend; wealthy capitalists reinvest most of their income. Fortunes accumulated from rents and finance must also be invested. Now it is a commonplace business law that the capital investment in an industry cannot be indefinitely increased by reinvestment of earnings, and still obtain a profitable return, unless the industry can be indefinitely expanded. But unlimited expansion is usually impossible; the world's demand for cotton stockings or for steel girders cannot be arbitrarily increased. If capital accumulation is proceeding more rapidly than industrial and agricultural expansion, the excess of capital must either be invested in relatively unprofitable enterprises, such as the construction of new railways along comparatively undesirable routes, at a profit lower than in the past, or lent out at lower rates of interest to be used in relatively unprofitable enterprises, or invested in less advanced countries, where capital is scarcer and returns larger.

To make this abstract statement more convincing, we may turn to a French economist, Paul Leroy-Beaulieu, who in 1886 observed: "The same capital which will earn three or four per cent in agricultural improvements in France will bring ten, fifteen, twenty per cent in an agricultural enterprise in United States, Canada, La Plata, Australia, or New Zealand." Sums invested in building new railways in France would hardly earn two or three per cent, but in new countries they would earn ten to twenty per cent.[1] Here we see plainly enough the reason why the investment of French capital in foreign countries, rapidly increasing after the middle of the nineteenth century, reached a total of fifty billion francs by 1914; why British capitalists before 1914 invested two billion pounds sterling in British colonies or dependencies and almost two in other undeveloped countries; why Germans invested twenty-eight billion marks abroad before 1914. Only a very small percentage of these staggering sums was invested before 1875; the age of large-scale foreign investments, like the age of imperialism, began in the 1870's.

Those who like to speculate on the future may find food for thought in the fact that the investment of surplus capital in

[1] *De la Colonisation* (1886 ed.), pp. 628 ff.

colonies and backward countries is still on the increase, and that the accumulated profits of the Great War enabled the United States to become, very suddenly, the foremost investing nation in the world, sending out its capital at the average rate of a billion dollars a year.[1] Money-lending countries of Europe, in the past, have shown a marked tendency to annex their debtors in Africa and Asia. Need America do the same? Is investment in backward countries a certain cause of imperialism?

Why investments have so often led to annexations needs just a word of explanation. French bankers lend money, let us say, to Morocco; it is a speculative venture, but the rate of interest is attractive. Morocco, being inefficiently governed by its native rulers, fails to pay interest. The French bankers appeal to their own government. And presently Morocco is a French protectorate, a French colony, in which efficient French officials make sure that French investors receive their due.[2] Whether there is any other way, one may well ask; but the question of solutions must be left for consideration after we have mastered the facts.

The Logic of Nationalism

The economic stage is now set for imperialism, with surplus manufactures, steam transportation, raw materials, and surplus capital ready to play their rôles. The cast is not complete, however, until we add another actor—the new doctrine of politico-economic nationalism. Upon this all the plot hinges. For if most men still believed, as they did a half-century or so ago, that the state has no concern with economics, the economic factors mentioned above would have been impotent to spur national governments to imperialist deeds. But the mid-Victorian doctrine of liberalism, which brooked no governmental intervention in business affairs, was after all a mid-Victorian

[1] The Department of Commerce has estimated that the private investments of United States citizens have reached a total in 1925, of 9½ billions of dollars. Of this sum, 43% is invested in Latin America, 27% in Canada and Newfoundland, 7½% in Asia and Oceania, and 22% in Europe. It is significant that almost four-fifths of the total is placed in non-European, undeveloped, relatively weak countries, and that the greater portion is in industrial and railway enterprises, rather than in government bonds. These figures, of course, do not include the war debts owed to the United States government by European governments. . . . On this subject see R. W. Dunn, *American Foreign Investments* (N. Y., 1926).

[2] *Cf. infra*, pp. 197-218.

doctrine, and it soon yielded the center of the stage to the rival doctrine of economic nationalism or Neo-Mercantilism, a reincarnation of that early modern Mercantilism which we have been at pains to describe.

If ever there was a "spirit of the age," the spirit of the second half of the nineteenth century was political nationalism. Germany achieved national unity "by blood and iron"; by blood and iron was Italy welded into nationhood; the Civil War cemented the American union; the Balkan nations emerged from Near Eastern turmoils; the Poles valiantly but vainly fought, in 1863, to regain national independence; Russia began to practise the nationalist policy of "Russification"; Disraeli revived British patriotism; the same ferment was at work among the Czechoslovaks and Yugoslavs and Magyars of Austria-Hungary; and in France nationalism became a bitter passion after the loss of Alsace-Lorraine. The nationalist wars of the period from 1848 to 1878 were succeeded by imperialist conquests.[1]

Nationalism means that people considering themselves similar in language, "race," culture, or historical traditions, should constitute a separate sovereign state; imperialism, on the contrary, means domination of non-European native races by totally dissimilar European nations. Antithetical as these two principles may seem, the latter is derived from the former through economic-nationalism or neo-mercantilism. German economists in the middle of the nineteenth century were peculiarly prominent in developing this doctrine. If Adam Smith's *Wealth of Nations* laid the theoretic foundations for free-trade England, Friedrich List's *National System of Political Economy* (*Das Nationale System der Politischen Ökonomie,* 1841) offered a basis for the protectionist policies of Continental nations. List boldly blasphemed against the first article in the creed of the orthodox or "classical" British and French economists, namely, that by the working of natural law, the free pursuit of self-interest by each individual would produce the greatest welfare for society collectively. Instead, List offered the dogma that the nation is a continuous and supremely important entity, whose well-being must be promoted by wise regulation of business. Private interests must bow to national needs. Nations

[1] See C. J. H. Hayes, *Essays on Nationalism* (Macmillan, 1926).

with infant industries should adopt "educational tariffs," until industry, agriculture and commerce reached the mature development and harmonious balance. List is cited as one among a host of European theorists who led the movement of ideas in favor of economic nationalism. And such doctrines fitted in well with practical exigencies of politics. The votes of workingmen demanded labor legislation; industrialists demanded tariff protection; humanitarians pleaded for social reform; and each of these urgent political forces made for greater control over economic matters by the national state. In tariffs, in labor legislation, in social reforms, economic nationalism became the order of the day in the waning years of the century. Imperialism naturally ensued, once it was assumed that government should promote business. For then it follows that nations may legitimately reach out for colonial empire, in order to preempt markets for their surplus manufactures, protect investments of their surplus capital, obtain business and coaling stations for their shipping, and secure raw materials. Such is the logic which combined with economic facts makes imperialism a necessity.

More humanly interesting, doubtless, than the abstractions and statistics through which it has been necessary to make our way thus far, is the story of the actual conversion of England, France, Germany, and other nations to imperialism. Conversions are always interesting. And this one is a peculiarly intriguing display of man's ability to combine egotism and altruism in a plausible amalgam.

On the eve of conversion individual sinners often possess a dual personality: an unregenerate dominant ego, and a more devout but suppressed self struggling to gain the upper hand. Without carrying over the ethical implications of this metaphor, we may say that the conversion of a nation to imperialism meant not an instantaneous *volte-face* on the part of the entire people, but the triumph of a hitherto submerged imperialist agitation reinforced by general economic and political changes, over a gradually weakening anti-imperialist party.

England's "Absence of Mind"

That England acquired an empire in fits of absence of mind, is a remark which Englishmen have been curiously fond of quoting, perhaps because it parries any charge of self-seeking imperialism. Not absence of mind, but absence of Gladstone, the historian might almost say.

It was the brilliant mind of Benjamin Disraeli, unrestrained by the respectable humanitarian moralities of a Gladstone, that conceived the idea of brazenly reintroducing imperialism into British politics, scandalized though the Gladstonians might be. It required a Disraeli to divine that the British public, growing weary of high-minded but unexciting commercialism, was ready for an emotional debauch and would welcome the thrill of a patriotic outburst. He made the rearing of a great British empire in Asia seem a romantic feat of daring, not a sordid business enterprise. He appealed to the popular imagination. The British Empire was a magnificent structure to be consolidated and enlarged, not permitted to disintegrate. He announced his campaign on June 24, 1872, in his famous Crystal Palace speech, adopting imperialism as one of the three chief aims of the Conservative Party.[1]

To be sure, in addition to this adventurous palladin, imperialism had its lesser knights.[2] A clever youth, Sir Charles Dilke, returning from extensive travels, had published a fascinating two-volume description of *Greater Britain* in 1866-67, and the rather surprising demand of the public for new editions attested the influence of the book.[3] A small but influential group of enthusiasts with the historian Bury at their head had founded the Royal Colonial Institute (1868) to promote the ideal of a "United Empire" as opposed to the Gladstonian belief in inevitable disintegration.[4] Sir George Grey, a former explorer

[1] See Buckle, *Life of Benjamin Disraeli*, V, pp. 194 ff.

[2] Carlyle, to be sure, has been styled the "father of British Imperialism," but see Bodelsen, *op. cit.*, pp. 22 ff.

[3] Dilke anticipated latter-day imperialism by emphasizing the economic and military value of uncivilized (*i.e.* tropical exploitation) colonies, while disparaging the alleged worth of white colonies, such as Canada.

[4] *Proceedings of the Royal Colonial Institute*, vol. 1 (1869), London, 1870, giving the names of those most actively participating, and the speeches. Viscount Bury was president. The lists of fellows of the Institute, given in subsequent *Proceedings*, afford a fair index of the organization's rapid increase of influence. Its members desired not merely to consolidate the existing empire, but to expand it. For instance, Lt. Cameron is cheered when he declares "I hope the day is not far distant when we shall see the Union Jack flying permanently in the centre of Africa" (VII, p. 282, June 13, 1876); the same year, Coleman Phillips urges expansion in the Pacific (*ibid.*, 193); there are similar exhortations in almost every meeting during this period.

and colonial governor, returning to England in 1868, had made a valorous but vain attempt to enter politics as a champion of imperialism. Professor John Seeley was just beginning (1869) the brilliant lectures at Cambridge on modern history which subsequently won so many converts to imperialism.[1] Another and a very influential historian, J. A. Froude, entered the lists in 1869; and in 1870-71 his articles in *Fraser's Magazine* were trenchant attacks on the prevalent anti-imperialist or indifferentist attitude. Several prominent politicians, too, had been converted, before Disraeli.[2] A number of British cotton manufacturers had been quietly working, since the American Civil War, to develop colonial cotton-growing. And, one might add, the Rothschilds and other financiers with whom Disraeli was at times connected, were beginning to become interested in the profits to be made by investment in colonial and "backward" countries.

Thanks partly to the efforts of these lesser prophets to make straight the path, but more to the magnetic quality of Disraeli himself, the British parliamentary elections of 1874 swept Gladstone's "Little England" cabinet out of office, and returned Disraeli and the Conservatives to power. For six years Disraeli's ministry pursued a "forward policy" of aggressive imperialism and flamboyant patriotism. The Fiji Islands in the South Pacific, twice refused by earlier governments, were promptly annexed in October, 1874.[3] The next year (1875) came the celebrated episode of the Suez Canal shares. A chance to purchase control of the French company which had just dug the Suez Canal had been offered to the British Foreign Office in 1870, during Gladstone's administration, and had been declined. But when Disraeli's foreign minister (Lord Derby), learning through a London journalist that the Khedive of Egypt was offering his block of 176,602 shares in the company to French purchasers, brought this news to Disraeli, the impulsive premier seized the opportunity eagerly. Without waiting for a parliamentary appropriation which might have been difficult to obtain (Parliament was not sitting), Disraeli bewitched his hesitant foreign secretary and cabinet to give him a free hand,

[1] See Bodelsen, pp. 149-176.
[2] *Ibid.*, pp. 106-112, 176-205.
[3] Buckle, *Life of Benjamin Disraeli*, V, p. 457.

borrowed four million pounds sterling from the Rothschilds (who, by the way, made a hundred thousand pounds on the transaction), and hastily purchased the shares for Great Britain. Though Gladstone, of course, was opposed, and cautious spirits were a bit breathless, Disraeli's coup was popularly applauded.[1] Hard on the heels of this event came the dispatch of a financial investigator (Stephen Cave) to examine the state of Egypt's public treasury, with special reference to British loans to Egypt,[2] and thus began the English intervention in Egyptian finance which led later to British conquest. In the following spring, 1876, Disraeli again startled Parliament by introducing a Royal Titles Bill enabling Queen Victoria, that housewifely model of virtuous royalty, to assume the resounding title of Empress of India, the title that had been borne in Oriental splendor by Moslem despots.[3] Here again was a challenge to Gladstonian anti-imperialism, a trumpet blast announcing the new imperialism. Disraeli said: "You have a new world, new influences at work, new and unknown objects and dangers with which to cope. . . . The Queen of England has become the sovereign of the most powerful of Oriental States." And again Parliament followed its master. In the same year the declaration of a British protectorate over the Khanate of Baluchistan, an important country on the northwestern borders of British India, showed clearly enough that empire meant conquest. Another winter passed, and the returning spring smiled on the annexation of Transvaal, the Boer Republic in South Africa which an earlier generation of British statesmen had allowed to become independent. But the climax was yet to come. When Russia in 1877 launched her armies against Turkey, obviously bent on conquest, and Constantinople seemed within the Tsar's reach, Disraeli sent the Mediterranean squadron to guard the sultan's city, and war between Britain and Russia was hourly expected.[4] Popular excitement reached the fever-pitch. London re-echoed the music-hall ballad of the day:

[1] Buckle, *op. cit.*, V, pp. 413, 439 ff. As there were 400,000 shares in all, Great Britain acquired not a majority interest, but practically a controlling interest.

[2] *Cf. infra.*, p. 225.

[3] Buckle, *op. cit.*, V, pp. 462 ff.

[4] Ward and Gooch, ed., *Cambridge History of British Foreign Policy*, III, pp. 115 ff.

> We don't want to fight,
> But by Jingo if we do,
> We've got the ships, we've got the men,
> We've got the money too.

Jingoism, in a word, was the spirit in which the country supported Disraeli. Great Britain's threatening mien, the hostile attitude of Austria, and Bismarck's diplomacy, induced Russia to submit the whole question of carving up the Turkish Empire to a congress of the Great Powers at Berlin in 1878. To this Disraeli went in person, armed with a secret Anglo-Russian convention regarding the Balkans and Armenia, a secret convention with Austria, and a secret Anglo-Turkish treaty pledging England to defend Asiatic Turkey against Russia, and permitting England to occupy and administer the Turkish island of Cyprus, ostensibly to facilitate fulfilment of this pledge.[1] To mollify the indignation felt by the French when these bargains were disclosed, a hint was dropped to the French delegate at the Berlin Congress that Great Britain would not object should France take Tunis.[2] Here we have imperialist world-politics, in full swing. Disraeli returned home from Berlin boasting he had brought back "Peace with Honour"—meaning peace with Cyprus. And there were at least some in Parliament who would have had him bring more of this kind of honor.

Whether it was honor, however, and whether it was peace, could be questioned. Gladstone heaped the vials of his wrathful oratory on his rival for sanctioning the iniquitous provisions of the Berlin Treaty as regards the Macedonian Christians, for dishonorably annexing Transvaal, and for embarking on the aggressive policy of jingo imperialism. Dishonor rather than honor, he felt, had Disraeli brought upon England. And jingoism did not mean peace. The annexation of Transvaal, mentioned above, brought on a cruel war with the fierce tribe of Zulus in South Africa, while aggressive imperialism in India led to trouble with the Mohammedan mountaineers of Afghanistan, on the border of India. Learning that Russian intrigue was active at the Afghan court, the British government sent a mission, followed by an army, into the country, and imposed what amounted to a British protectorate; but in September,

[1] *State Papers*, 69, pp. 744-6.
[2] Ward and Gooch, *op. cit.* III, p. 136.

1879, the British resident and embassy in Afghanistan were butchered by Afghan mutineers, and a new invasion, new bloodshed, ensued. Aghast at the consequences of Disraeli's imperialism, many Englishmen turned to the pacific Gladstone, whose anti-imperialist Midlothian campaign produced a Liberal landslide in the 1880 elections.[1]

Gladstone's return to power, for the years 1880-1885, was not so definite a setback to imperialism as might have been supposed. To be sure, Gladstone endeavored to refrain from aggression. He even undid the work of his predecessor, in the case of Transvaal, by restoring independence to the Boer Republic.[2] But against this courageous fulfilment of a campaign pledge there was a storm of indignation in England, for unfortunately the Boers had won a minor victory over British troops shortly before, and the grant of independence could be interpreted as a cowardly surrender. Emancipation of Transvaal had the effect of stimulating, rather than discouraging, imperialism. Furthermore, Gladstone found himself involved in the financial control Disraeli had established, with France, over Egyptian finances, and presently the force of circumstances, coupled with pressure from British financiers and diplomatic officials, drove Gladstone into the military occupation of Egypt.[3] Let him promise as solemnly as he would to withdraw his troops, Gladstone had become helplessly enmeshed. He had done what he had denounced Disraeli for intending; he had conquered the Nile. Imperialism had gained the upper hand in England.

On every hand there were evidences, in the eighties, of the imperialist awakening. Professor Seeley's book on *The Expansion of England,* portraying imperial expansion as Britain's historic mission, was published in 1883, took the public by storm, sold 80,000 copies in two years, and won its author knighthood, on the recommendation of Lord Rosebery. Rosebery himself, then a prominent Liberal, destined to become prime minister in later years, had just returned from a trip around the world in 1883, when he read Seeley's pages; he became a convinced imperialist, and as foreign minister in Gladstone's cabinets of 1886 and 1892, and as premier in 1894-5, he was in a position to

[1] Morley, *Life of Gladstone,* II, pp. 587-96, 609-15.

[2] *State Papers,* 72, p. 900 and 75, p. 5; *cf.* Ward and Gooch, III, pp. 204 ff.

[3] *Cf. infra,* p. 173, note 2.

give influential support to his new faith. Rosebery's conversion was significant as an indication that imperialism, no longer confined to Disraeli's Conservative followers, had invaded the Liberal party too. It was another Liberal, Mr. William E. Forster, who founded the Imperial Federation League in 1884, to work for closer ties between self-governing colonies and mother-country. The Colonial Conferences, beginning in 1887, lent additional force to this movement. Kipling's Indian tales and ballads cast a romantic glamour of poetry over even the most sordid features of conquest.

There is no need to follow through all its details the story of the development of this imperialist agitation in England. Yet in passing it is not inappropriate to notice four men who may stand as types of the many who toiled to extend Britain's empire. There is Sir Harry Johnston, versatile combination of explorer, anthropologist, administrator, historian and, in his last years, novelist, whose autobiography tells a story of indomitable labors to extend the advantages of British rule to barbarous African tribes and of hardly less courageous efforts to arouse lethargic Downing-Street officials, careless of abuses in colonial administration and negligent of opportunities for expansion.[1] There is Cecil Rhodes,[2] business adventurer and magnificent egotist, amassing millions by ruthless monopoly of South African gold and diamonds, dreaming of continents as British provinces, and using all the power of his wealth and personality to advance, by fair means or foul, the imperialism of which he was so lusty a son. There is the stalwart figure of a Sir Edward Grey,[3] high-minded Liberal Foreign Secretary for many a year, earnestly desiring to promote fair-dealing and peace among nations, yet so permeated with what, by his time, had become an unquestioned faith in Britain's world mission, that he barters in secret with France and Russia and Germany for the division of spoils in Asia and Africa. Last, there is Joseph Chamberlain,[4] successfully aggressive manufacturer, en-

[1] Sir Harry H. Johnston. *The Story of My Life* (London, 1923).

[2] Sir Lewis Michell, *Life of Cecil Rhodes* (London, 1910); T. E. Fuller, *Cecil John Rhodes* (N. Y., 1910); Basil Williams, *Cecil Rhodes* (London, 1921); *cf. infra*, ch. ix.

[3] Viscount Grey of Falloden, *Twenty-five Years, 1892-1916* (N. Y., 1925).

[4] Joseph Chamberlain, *Speeches* (Boston, 1914); A. Mackintosh, *Joseph Chamberlain* (N. Y., 1914); J. Gazeau, *L'Impérialisme anglais, son évolution: Carlyle-Seeley-Chamberlain* (Paris, 1903).

tering British politics as a radical Liberal in Gladstone's time, but wrecking the old party and later joining hands with the Tories, fearlessly preaching a doctrine of stark commercial imperialism. "The Empire," he said, "is commerce." India, he candidly claimed, was "by far the greatest and most valuable of all the customers we have or ever shall have." His arithmetic may have gone astray in computing India's commerce, but his argument was plausible. British capital and British workingmen must have employment; they could get employment only if there were a market for their manufactures; the colonies would afford the market, now and for future generations. Annexing colonies, said Chamberlain (quoting a happy phrase of Lord Rosebery's)[1] is "pegging out claims for posterity." Chamberlain could not persuade England to adopt a preferential tariff in 1906, but he did help mightily to persuade British manufacturers that civilizing Africans and Asiatics was a profitable business.

French Logic *Ex Post Facto*

It has been a favorite axiom of English critics that Frenchmen pursue logic *à outrance,* regardless of practical expediency. As a matter of fact, French statesmen are adept in the fine art of making expediency appear logical. It was to justify conquests upon which they had already launched that the rulers of the Third Republic elaborated their remarkable theory of imperialism. The logic was *ex post facto.*

The Third French Republic inherited a colonial empire of less than 1,000,000 sq. km. and 5,000,000 inhabitants, an empire whose total commerce amounted to only 600 million francs, a third of which was with foreigners; an empire which cost the French treasury 30 million francs a year in administrative expense; an empire which was quite generally considered, by French economists, politicians, and business men, to be burdensome and unprofitable. Few voices were raised in its defense, in the first decade of the Republic. It is rarely necessary to argue in defense of possessions. It was the new acquisitions that required justification.

Tunis and Tonkin were the conquests that needed apology. The seizure of Tunis in 1881 would probably not have occurred,

[1] London *Times*, March 2, 1893.

had not the adjoining country of Algeria, on the north African coast, been a French possession since 1830, when a desperate king had endeavored to save his tottering throne by a brilliant foreign venture.[1] Tonkin, likewise, neighbored a French possession, Cochin China, which had been acquired by the ambitious Louis Napoleon. A merchant's ambition to found an establishment there led to a minor military expedition (only 180 men), but by almost miraculous fortune this handful of soldiers had won for the French Republic in 1874 a protectorate over the extensive empire of Annam; this protectorate in turn led to a controversy with the Chinese government, which claimed suzerainty over Annam, and to war against pirates who infested the border province of Tonkin. Hence, the famous Tonkin expedition of 1883, which resulted, later, in a further extension of French empire.[2]

The Tunis expedition of 1881 and the Tonkin expedition of 1883, costly affairs both, required parliamentary votes of credit and parliamentary justification. There was strong opposition in the Chamber. One speaker pointed out that French colonies furnished less than 200 million francs out of a total French commerce amounting to nine billions.[3] Another declared:

> Instead of throwing yourself into the pursuit of new colonies which are supposed to be attractive because of alleged veins of gold which you do not know, not having seen them, and of alleged coal mines of whose existence you are ignorant although you proclaim them and indicate them on your fanciful maps, in order that public opinion may accompany you in this distant adventure, France will tell you not to look so far away . . . it is in France that you should look, and it is the poverty in France that must be alleviated.[4]

Georges Clemenceau vehemently rebuked the imperialist cabinet: "The tempter has led you to a high mountain, has shown you the nations at your feet, inviting you to make your choice, and you have made it."[5]

It was to defend himself against such assaults that Jules

[1] *Cf. infra*, p. 191. The French consul, Roustan, the foreign minister, Barthélemy Saint-Hilaire, and particularly Baron de Courcel, director of political affairs in the French Foreign office, seem to have been primarily responsible in urging Ferry (and Gambetta) to seize Tunis. See General Mangin, *Regards sur la France d'Afrique* (Paris, 1924), pp. 81-91.

[2] *Cf. infra*, pp. 315-16.

[3] Jules Delafosse, *Chambre des députés*, 7 décembre, 1883.

[4] Paul de Cassagnac, *ibid.*, 10 juillet, 1883.

[5] M. Clemenceau, *ibid.*, 31 octobre, 1883.

Ferry[1] stepped to the tribune as master of imperialist logic. He had been responsible, as premier, for both Tunis and Tonkin. He has been called "the apostle of the contemporary colonial renaissance." An apostle's creed of imperialism might easily be compiled from his speeches delivered in the early eighties.[2]

There are three articles in the creed. First: an industrial nation needs colonial markets, since other nations, notably Germany and the United States, have erected protective tariffs. Second: "The superior races have a right as regards inferior races. They have a right because they have a duty. They have the duty of civilizing the inferior races." France must combat the slave trade, "that horrible traffic," in Africa; she must continue her work of promoting "justice, material and moral order, equity, social virtues," in Africa. "Is it possible to deny," he asked, "that it is good fortune for the unhappy populations of equatorial Africa to fall under the protectorate of the French nation, or of the English nation?" There have been Englishmen, since then, who have denied it; but in Ferry's day the effects of imperialistic exploitation were not yet apparent. It was easy for Frenchmen to believe in the "*mission civilisatrice*" as for Englishmen to shoulder the "white man's burden." Third: for a marine and naval power, coaling stations were vital; a warship could not carry coal for more than fourteen days' cruising, and for that reason "we needed Tunis, for that reason we needed Saigon and Cochin China, for that reason we need Madagascar, and are in Diego Suarez, which we will never leave." In conclusion, if France refrained from imperialism, she would "descend from the first rank to the third or fourth."

[1] Born in 1832, Ferry became a prominent journalist and politician. As minister of public instruction in the Waddington Cabinet of 1879 and the Freycinet Cabinet of 1879-80 he took particular interest in advocating anti-clerical school legislation, but after he became premier in Sept., 1880, he embarked on the Tunisian venture which hastened his downfall in Nov., 1881. He was again minister of public instruction in the Freycinet Cabinet of 1882 and premier from Feb., 1883, to March, 1885, during which period he took the portfolio of foreign affairs and followed an imperialist policy in Tonkin and Madagascar. He was shot by a fanatic and died in 1893. Consult A. Rambaud, *Jules Ferry* (Paris, 1903), and *Discours et Opinions de Jules Ferry*, edited by Paul Robiquet (Paris, 7 vols.), especially vols. 4 and 5.

[2] Notably his speeches in the Chamber of Oct. 11, 1883, Dec. 11, 1884, July 28, 1885.

In a preface to a book on "Tonkin and the Mother Country" (*Le Tonkin et la Mère-Patrie,* 1890) he put the commercial argument with telling force. "Colonial policy is the daughter of industrial policy. . . . The protectionist system is a steam-engine without safety valve if it does not have as correlative and auxiliary a healthy and serious colonial policy. . . . European powers of consumption are saturated. New masses of consumers must be made to arise in other parts of the globe, else we shall put modern society into bankruptcy and prepare for the dawn of the twentieth century a cataclysmic social liquidation of which one cannot calculate the consequences."

It was the economic argument, after all, that had most appeal to the upper classes. The shrewd "opportunist" Gambetta, speaking with regard to Tunis in 1881, was blunt enough about it: "Do you not feel that the nations are stifling on this old continent? Do you not seek to create distant markets, exchanges, and to favor everywhere a necessary expansion? And necessary for what, gentlemen? Necessary for the increase of our material prosperity."[1] Chautemps, minister of colonies in 1895, frankly said he was in reality "a second minister of commerce."[2] Investment of capital was more emphasized at a later period, but even in 1895 Delcassé, the man who was later to become the guiding genius of French imperialism, was stressing the need of governmental protection and aid for French investments in the colonies; still, his main point was that France enjoyed at least 200 million francs of trade with her possessions, more than enough to compensate for the deficits in colonial budgets, and easily enough to warrant the outlay of several hundred thousands to round out the empire by a few more conquests.[3]

Alfred Rambaud and Paul Leroy-Beaulieu may be taken as typical of the academic protagonists of imperialism, few at first, ever more numerous as the decades passed. Rambaud, historian of Russia and the East, and first professor of contemporary history at the Sorbonne, had been deeply impressed by Russian expansion, and also by Napoleonic conquests; his imagination was touched also by Seeley's *Expansion of England,* a translation of which he joined with J. B. Baille in publishing, in 1885.

[1] *Chambre des députés,* 1 décembre, 1881.
[2] Dubois et Terrier, *op. cit.,* p. 418.
[3] *Chambre des députés,* 2 mars, 1895.

Why should not France also have a great historic mission of expansion? Such was the question that suggested itself to him. In 1886 he edited a volume containing contributions from explorers and public men, under the title *La France Coloniale,* setting forth the arguments for French imperialism. Possibly the fact that he had served as *chef du cabinet* for Jules Ferry, 1879-81, may help to explain Rambaud's conversion to imperialism. Leroy-Beaulieu, on the other hand, was primarily an economist. As a novice he had won a prize, in 1870, for an essay on the then rather academic topic of colonization. After he became a professor of economics and finance, his mind continually reverted to this theme. In 1874 he published his treatise *De la Colonisation chez les peuples modernes.* At that time, as he said, "public opinion in France was still almost indifferent to colonization"; and his book was put forth as a scientific study rather than as a propagandist appeal. But when he put out a second edition, in 1882, Tunis had been taken and France was beginning to manifest "all the fervor of a new taste." The change in public opinion was reflected in his new preface; no longer dispassionately academic, but rather, ardently imperialist. "Every day that passes," he wrote, "convinces us more and more of the importance of colonization in general, and of its importance above all for France." He was seizing every opportunity to proclaim, by tongue or pen, that France "has been a great colonial power, that she can and should become one again." To be sure, France had an annual increase of population of only 100,000 souls, sufficient to provide only modest contingents of colonists, but even these would suffice; and after all, "the true sinews of colonization are capital funds, rather than emigrants," and of capital France had abundance. French foreign investments amounted already (1882) to twenty or twenty-five billion francs, and each year this figure was growing by at least a billion. If even a quarter of this surplus capital could be directed to the French colonies, France would succeed in creating "a great African empire and a smaller one in Asia." Colonization, he concluded, "is for France a question of life and death: either France will become a great African power, or in a century or two she will be no more than a secondary European power; she will count for about as much in the world as Greece and Roumania in Europe." The third edition, appearing late in 1885, found public opinion "a little weary and discouraged"; to revive confidence was the writer's patent intention. While frankly admitting the vices of French imperialism—administrative arbitrariness, over-centralization, governmental interference with individual concerns, lack of perseverance—he nevertheless held out bright hopes to his fellow-countrymen. The concluding pages of his book glorified imperialism in dithyrambic strains. "Colonization is the expansive force of a nation, its power of reproduction, its dilation and multiplication across space; it is the submission of the universe or of a vast part of it to the language, the manners, the ideas and laws, of the mother country." From every point of view, "whether one restricts his view to the consideration of prosperity and material power, of authority and political influence, or lifts his eyes to the contemplation of intellectual greatness," one incontestable truth appears, namely: "the nation that colonizes is the premier nation; if it is not to-day, it will be to-morrow."[1]

But enough of such panegyrics. French imperialism in the eighties was chiefly the work of Jules Ferry, twice premier, and his foreign minister, Jules Barthélemy St. Hilaire (a professor of ancient philosophy, turned politician, who had been invited to inspect the Suez Canal project in 1855 and thenceforth cherished a weakness for Africa); it was taken up by the eminent historian Gabriel Hanotaux, foreign minister from 1894 to 1898, who saw in it something of historical inevitability as well as commercial gain; it was pushed to extreme lengths by Delcassé, Poincaré, and Clemenceau in the early twentieth century.[2] During the Ferry decade of the eighties France acquired sixty thousand square miles in Asia and one million in Africa; in the Hanotaux decade, the nineties, thirty thousand in Asia and three hundred thousand in Africa; in the first two decades of the twentieth century, the period of Delcassé, Poincaré, and Clemenceau, about a million and a third in Africa. Such achievements might be censured by a Socialist minority, but they gave to imperialists a confidence well expressed by Victor Beauregard

[1] Paul Leroy-Beaulieu, *De la Colonisation chez les peuples modernes* (Paris, 1886, third ed.), pp. 748-9.

[2] It should not be implied that these men were alone in the work. Behind them were business men, officials, officers, supporting and often originating their policies. The influence of the Comité de l'Afrique française was especially noteworthy; see files of its *Bulletin* and also H. Alis, *Nos Africains*, p. 552.

in 1924: "The study of history reveals a conclusion which has the certainty of an axiom: *France, more than any other nation has a genius for colonization.*" And, he added, "The future of France is in her colonies."[1]

BISMARCK'S CAUTION

It has often been said that Germany was born too late into the family of European nations to acquire her "place in the sun," her fair share of imperial possessions. Reiteration has made the statement seem plausible. In truth, however, Germany became a united empire, the most powerful state on the Continent, in ample time to participate in the imperialist world-division of the eighties and nineties. It was Bismarck's stiff-necked and hard-headed opposition, and the strong free-trade, anti-imperialist convictions of the Reichstag majority, that imposed a handicap on German empire-building. In no other country was so wordy a debate, so convulsive an internal struggle, required in the process of conversion to imperialism. Theoretical writings had to be reinforced by missionary activity, commercial and financial interests, intensive propaganda, and political pressure, before Germany was won over.[2] For did not Bismarck stubbornly refuse the French colonies in 1870-1, rebuff proposal after proposal for the annexation of this or that choice morsel in the seventies, and repeatedly proclaim his opposition to imperialism, while hundreds of projects for the establishment of colonies were neatly bound in volumes, with true German orderliness, and placed on the shelf with their forerunners? A well-informed German writer claims that thirty volumes of such plans had accumulated by the year 1885.[3]

Theory alone was too weak to convince Bismarck. All through the nineteenth century there were theoretical exponents of imperialism. Friedrich List, the influential nationalist economist, wrote in 1841 that "Colonies are the best means of developing

[1] Victor Beauregard, *L'Empire Colonial de la France: Formation, Résultats, Destinées*, published under the patronage of the Minister of War, Paris, 1924.

[2] The controversy is best described in M. E. Townsend, *Origins of Modern German Colonialism;* Maximilian von Hagen, *Bismarcks Kolonialpolitik* (Stuttgart, 1924); and A. Zimmermann, *Geschichte der deutschen Kolonialpolitik* (Berlin, 1914).

[3] Poschinger, cited in Townsend, *op. cit.*, p. 51.

manufactures, export and import trade, and finally a respectable navy."[1] Roscher, in 1848, asserted that "Germany must expand on the sea and over the sea into foreign lands if it wants to make up for the sins of past generations. New areas for production and consumption must be secured for our national interest, be they gained by means of political or economic colonization."[2] An official in the Prussian foreign office, Lothar Bucher, in 1867, reminded his compatriots that List's colonial program should be fulfilled, and specified the Philippines, St. Thomas, and Timor as desirable colonies.[3] Among the great historians who did so much to stimulate German nationalism, Treitschke was conspicuous, but not at all unique, in urging imperialism. "Every virile nation," he roundly asserted, "has established colonial power."

Missionary societies reinforced the nationalist theorists. Consider, for instance, the Barmen Rhine Mission, which established ten or more mission stations in South West Africa, engaged extensively in trade, and, through its inspector requested the protection of the German government. German missions were active in the Pacific islands, too. And devout Germans at home were eager to have the Flag follow the Gospel.

But not until "the colonial movement became a business proposition"—as one historian[4] so well says—did it make a serious impression on the anti-imperialist government. German industry and trade, having sunk thick roots in German soil during the middle of the nineteenth century, began to branch out into all parts of the world. The O'Swald company developed trade with Zanzibar and the eastern coast of Africa, and even obtained an offer of a protectorate over Zanzibar in 1874, an offer rebuffed by Bismarck. Woermann sent German vessels to carry the trade of the West-African coast, and to supply the negroes with salt and gin.[5] By 1880, 335,080 marks' worth of German goods were annually shipped to West Africa, and

[1] F. List, *National System of Political Economy* (London, 1904), p. 216.

[2] Roscher, *Kolonien, Kolonialpolitik und Auswanderung* (Leipzig, 1856), cited by Townsend, *op. cit.*, p. 30.

[3] Zimmermann, *Geschichte der deutschen Kolonialpolitik* (Berlin, 1914), p. 5.

[4] Townsend, *op. cit.*, p. 44.

[5] Woermann had established factories (i.e. warehouses and stores) in Liberia (1852), Gabun (1862) and Kamerun (1868), M. von Hagen, *op. cit.*, p. 18.

6,735,090 marks of African goods entered the port of Hamburg. It was a Bremen merchant, Lüderitz, interested in African trade, who founded Germany's first colony in South West Africa, in 1883. It was a Hamburg merchant, Godeffroy, who prepared the foundations for a German empire in the Pacific by building up trade with Samoa and the other South Sea islands; he had a virtual monopoly of the trade in copra (dried coconut meat, from which oil was extracted); it was no exaggeration to call him "the South Sea King." By 1875 Germany had fifty ships trading with Samoa and the Tonga Islands.[1]

To commercial interests was added the power of finance. Not only were great merchants such as Woermann and Godeffroy identified with important banks, the former with the Diskonto, the latter with the Norddeutsche Bank. But puissant Jewish financiers (Bleichröder, von Hansemann, etc.) were friends and advisers of Bismarck, and played no insignificant rôle in swaying the chancellor.

Propaganda, arising in part from missionary and commercial interests, in part from disinterested patriotism, in part from the numerous German explorers of African wilds, became exceedingly active in the seventies and eighties. Scores of books and hundreds of articles and pamphlets were poured out by busy presses to urge imperialism on Germany. Typical and prominent among the propagandists was Friedrich Fabri, who by long service as inspector of the Barmen Rhine Mission in south-western Africa had become an impassioned devotee of imperialism. In a persuasive little book, entitled "Does Germany Need Colonies?" (*Bedarf Deutschland der Kolonien?*) written in 1879 obviously for popular consumption, Fabri argued that the great stream of emigration flowing from Germany to America was the ominous symptom of an economic crisis. Germany must have colonial markets, new fields of investment, outlets for surplus population, if she would live. German Kultur, moreover, must be spread among the backward races. Fabri generously marked out a colonial empire to be acquired—Samoa, New Guinea, Madagascar, North Borneo, Formosa, besides commercial penetration of Central Africa and the Near East. And he suggested a method, that of letting the flag follow the trader in these regions.

[1] Townsend, *op. cit.*, pp. 39-41; von Hagen, *op. cit.*, pp. 71 ff.

A second figure towering tall in the legion of propagandists was Wilhelm Hübbe-Schleiden, lawyer, business-man, publicist, and, for a time, explorer in tropical Africa. His voluminous writings, especially his books in *Ethiopien, Studien über West-afrika* (1879) and *Deutsche Kolonisation* (1881), and his personal influence were devoted to the conversion of the younger generation from self-satisfied nationalism and from equally insidious cosmopolitanism to the new gospel of *Weltpolitik,* of imperialism. Germany, he wrote, must break away from Anglo-Saxon free-trade and cosmopolitanism; these were devices which had enabled England to obtain seventy per cent of the world's trade, at the expense of competing nations. Germany's future greatness, her honor as a nation, her prosperity, depended upon learning to think imperially in terms of *Weltpolitik.* "Ethiopia" (west-central Africa) and South America were to be the fields of German colonization. Hübbe-Schleiden, it is interesting to note, was a prominent member of the Westdeutscher Verein für Kolonisation und Export founded by Fabri in 1880, and joined with other members in founding a Guinea Company (1882), supported by Hamburg merchant princes, for the establishment of colonies on the western coast of Africa. This venture failed, but others took its place.

A most powerful agency of propaganda was the Kolonialverein founded in 1882, by a merchant (Friedrich Colin), a traveler (Freiherr von Maltzan), a widely read and traveled prince (Hohenlohe-Langenburg), and an interesting group of journalists, explorers, shippers, merchants, and geographers. Our acquaintances Fabri and Hübbe-Schleiden were of course to be found in this array. By 1885 the Kolonialverein had more than ten thousand members, many of whom were influential in the business world, the press, the universities, and the government.

While the Kolonialverein devoted itself chiefly to general propaganda in favor of imperialism, the Gesellschaft für deutsche Kolonisation founded by Dr. Carl Peters in 1884 had the more practical aim of raising capital to establish colonies in East Africa. As an imaginative youth, Peters had caught the fever of imperialism while on a visit to England. Returning to Germany in 1883, and finding it impossible to carry the Kolonialverein with him in his enthusiastic projects, Peters in

1884 founded the Gesellschaft für deutsche Kolonisation, issued fifty-mark shares, and raised four million marks capital. With characteristic impetuosity, he then made his way, through the most romantic adventures, to eastern Africa, to buy up land from the natives. His exploit will be described more fully in its proper place,[1] but his name belongs here as one of the chief apostles who evangelized Germany for imperialism.

All these forces, of economic theory, of religion, of commerce and finance, of propaganda, conspired to alter Bismarck's anti-imperialist policy. In the years 1875-1883 occurred his conversion. As early as 1876 he told the merchant Lüderitz, who desired to make Transvaal a German colony, that he favored colonization in principle, but must wait for further development of national spirit before taking action. This may have been little more than ordinary political suavity, but we find Bismarck showing by his deeds an increased interest in Africa and the Pacific. He protests to Spain against interference with German trade in the Sulu Islands; he allows trade treaties to be made with swarthy potentates in unclaimed South Sea Islands. His change of heart was hastened by a political crisis. When, sensing the decline of Liberalism, and needing increased federal revenues, he decided to adopt a protective tariff (1879) and rely on the Conservatives and Center instead of the National Liberal Party, Bismarck needed the support which the rising imperialist faction could give his new protectionist policy. To have influential imperialist merchants actively supporting him in the free-trade cities of Hamburg and Bremen was no small consideration. And Bismarck was willing to pay for such support in the coinage of political favors.

Intent on purely European affairs, the shrewd chancellor kept his opinions to himself, pretty largely, until a favorable opportunity for action should arise. The opportunity came in 1879. The Godeffroy firm, ambitiously reaching out for trade among the islands of the South Pacific, had formed a merger in 1878, the Deutsche Handels und Plantagengesellschaft der Süd See Inseln (German trade and plantation company of the South Sea Islands). Getting into financial difficulties, Godeffroy had borrowed heavily from London bankers, Baring Bros., and pledged as security a large block of shares in the South Sea

[1] *Cf. infra*, p. 123.

merger. Godeffroy's bankruptcy in 1879 placed German ownership of this merger, therefore, in grave jeopardy. It was time for Bismarck to act. Godeffroy's was perhaps the most influential firm in Hamburg, and loyal to the administration. Bismarck's method was characteristically cautious. With his encouragement a new company, the Deutsche See Handelsgesellshaft, was formed in January 1880, with two prominent Jewish financiers (Bleichröder and Hansemann) as directors-in-chief, representing the chancellor. For his part, Bismarck rushed through the Bundesrat a bill to guarantee the company with an annual subsidy of four per cent, from the imperial treasury, for twenty years, or until its dividends should reach a satisfactory figure. In the Reichstag, however, the Samoan Subsidy Bill encountered furious opposition from the liberal parties, whose leaders refused to be deceived either by official attempts to disguise the bill as a purely commercial measure, or by contradictory official declarations that "It is not a question of party, of free trade or protection, but one of the honor and glory of Germany." The "waving of the national flag and the blaring of trumpets," as one Opposition speaker put it, was of no avail. The bill was rejected by 128 to 112.

Between the rejection of the Samoan Subsidy Bill, in April 1880, and the establishment of Germany's first protectorate, in 1884, Bismarck discreetly felt his way, favoring imperialism, but hesitating to arouse sleeping dogs in the Reichstag. It was during these years that the Kolonialverein and similar organizations let loose a flood of propaganda, while imperialist merchants planned ventures with more or less secret connivance from the government which could be presented to the Reichstag as *faits accomplis.* The propaganda had its effect, and the imperialist activities of England and France at this time gave an additional stimulus to German imperialism, with the result that by 1884 Germany was ready. In that year Bismarck proclaimed a protectorate over South West Africa. Rapidly other protectorates followed—Kamerun and Togoland on the western coast of Africa, part of East Africa also, and part of New Guinea and adjacent islands in the South Seas.

Bismarck, however, was too much preoccupied with his system of alliances in Europe ever to become a furious imperialist. He remained unwilling to make conquests and annexations, as the

French did, simply for the sake of rounding out a colonial empire; on the contrary, he insisted that the way must first be paved by German merchants. The flag might follow trade, but would not precede it. As a result, Bismarck carved out only a relatively modest colonial empire.

It was after the accession of William II and the dismissal of Bismarck (1890), that German imperialism reached its apogee. Inclined by temperament to the grandiose and flamboyant, and keenly interested in Germany's commercial expansion, the new Kaiser threw himself without reservation or reticence into the enterprise of enlarging Bismarck's empire. In the period 1890 to 1914 the protectorates in Africa were extended; the German flag was hoisted over hundreds of South Sea islands; a port was obtained on the Chinese coast; through the Bagdad Railway German imperialism penetrated and dominated Turkey; and even more than these additions would have been made, had there been less opposition from jealous competitors. German parties still opposing imperialism were converted or defeated; even in the Socialist party an influential faction willingly learned to mouth the arguments for empire.

Others Share the Burden

Italy, like Germany, achieved nationhood just before the dawn of the day of imperialist world politics. Unlike Germany, however, the new nation of Italy was industrially backward and politically weak. Although many Italian patriots, mindful of Rome's ancient grandeur, cherished imperial aspirations, the country was neither weak enough to be permitted by other Great Powers to acquire colonies which might be exploited by them, nor strong enough to risk the enmity of powerful neighbors. With self-abnegation born of impotence, Italians looked on, furious but helpless, while imperialist France appropriated the most natural field for Italian expansion, Tunis, on the African coast just south of Italy, the site of ancient Rome's vanquished rival, Carthage. Italy could do nothing, until she had allies sufficiently powerful to bolster her claims. Grasping this fact, the then premier, Agostino Depretis, sued for the favor of Germany, and, after difficult negotiations, obtained admission to a Triple Alliance with Germany and Austria-Hungary in 1882, the year after the French seizure of Tunis. He made also a beginning of empire, by taking possession of a port (Massowa), on the western coast of the Red Sea. But he could not do more. His successor, the astute Francesco Crispi,[1] obtained from Germany, when the Triple Alliance was renewed in 1887, a secret pledge of aid in case France should attempt to conquer Tripoli or Morocco.[2] Tripoli, at least, he hoped to gain for Italy. He also enlarged Italy's foothold on the Red Sea coast, obtained another foothold, farther south, in Somaliland, and intrigued to gain possession of the great state of Abyssinia, which lay between these two Italian colonies. But an evil fate pursued him. A disastrous battle with the natives shattered his hopes in Abyssinia. Nor could he create any favorable opportunity for the realization of his designs on Tripoli. Italian imperialism was checked. The imperial impulse, being balked rather than sated, did but grow stronger. As the individual conscious of actual inferiority seeks compensation in dreams of power, the ruling class of Italy waxed more ardently imperialist and dreamed more extravagant projects to restore Rome's ancient sway over the Mediterranean coastlands. In the twentieth century, Italy was ready to send her armies once more into Africa for conquest, and, during the Great War and after, to manifest an imperialist hunger too keen to be sated with the colonial crumbs that fell from the Allies' table.

Very different was the case of Russia. As an ever-expanding empire of peasants and horsemen, Russia had pushed eastward into Siberia, southward toward Constantinople and toward the Caucasus, and westward to the Baltic, long before the fever of modern imperialism infected western Europe. Russia's early expansion was the work of restless frontiersmen, seeking new homes in virgin lands, and of ambitious tsars, seeking warm-water "outlets," "windows to the west." It was not the imperialism of surplus manufactures, surplus capital, and national pride. But in the late nineteenth century, though Russia as a whole remained agricultural, giant industries developed in Russian cities, capitalists arose, and imperialist doctrines identical with those of western Europe gained currency among the ruling classes. Capitalist projects for railway construction in Man-

[1] See his *Memoirs* (London, 1912-14), especially II, ch. 2.
[2] Pribram, *Secret Treaties of Austria-Hungary*, I, p. 110.

churia, capitalist interests in Persia, intensified the historic aggressiveness of Russia. And French financiers, after about 1890, supplied for Russian imperialism surplus capital which Russia herself lacked; for instance, the Russian Asiatic Bank, the agent of Russian imperialism in the Far East, was financed with French capital.

Austria-Hungary, like Russia, developed imperialism as an intensification of historic expansionist policies, and sought to dominate neighboring countries rather than to acquire overseas colonies. The emancipation of Germany and Italy from Vienna's control, occurring on the eve of the imperialist era, turned the Hapsburg monarchy to seek compensation in the Balkan Peninsula. The desire for compensation was stimulated by the economic interests of bankers and exporters, as well as by the political motive of bolstering up a tottering throne by means of a strong foreign policy, and, after 1890, by the German "*Drang nach Osten.*" Austrian capitalists purchased Balkan railways, while Austrian diplomats conducted subtle intrigues looking toward annexation of Bosnia and domination of the Balkan states.

For most small nations, imperialism was out of the question. They lacked capital, and, above all, they lacked strength to vie successfully with Great Powers. The Netherlands, Portugal, Spain, and Denmark, however, possessed colonies which had been obtained in earlier times. In these cases pride of possession was enhanced by the outburst of imperialism among the Great Powers. Portugal and Spain even attempted to expand their holdings in Africa.

Belgium entered the race largely because of the initiative of an unusually ambitious and foresighted ruler, Leopold II, who perceived the first flush of the dawning day of imperialism early enough to carve out for himself a huge empire, the Congo Free State, in central Africa, before the Great Powers had parcelled that continent out among themselves. This venture, a personal enterprise of Leopold II rather than a national undertaking, ultimately gave Belgium possession of the Congo and an important place among imperialist nations. Belgian imperialism, like Russian imperialism, afforded an indirect outlet for French surplus capital.

Imperialism, in the form that has been so conspicuous since

1875, is a peculiarly European product, but it has been acclimated in non-European nations, in proportion as they progressed in the economic institutions and political ideas characteristic of western Europe. Japan, apt imitator of Europe, became strongly and aggressively imperialist toward the close of the nineteenth century, after textile and metallurgical industries, export commerce and finance, had developed on European lines, to the point of requiring foreign markets for surplus goods, foreign supplies of raw material, foreign investments for surplus capital, and after Japanese political sentiment, forsaking old ideals of exclusion and conservatism, had become poignantly eager to maintain national prestige by doing successfully what the European Great Powers were doing.

America has not yet been converted, certainly not wholly converted, to European imperialism. Traditional principles enshrined in the Declaration of Independence have militated against imperialism in theory, while an abundance of unoccupied land, a prodigal profusion of undeveloped resources, and a lack of surplus capital and surplus manufactures, until very recently, have obstructed it in practice. The westward expansion of the United States, accomplished prior to the age of imperialism, was dictated partly by slave-holding interests, eager to add new territory and new votes to the strength of the cotton-raising "slavocracy," and partly by the westward urge of pioneer and prospector, and partly by an exuberant confidence in America's "manifest destiny" to expand. But conquering overseas possessions was quite another matter, distasteful to the prevalent opinions. Not until the close of the nineteenth century had American nationalism and American business enterprise reached the stage attained a generation earlier in Europe. At the time of the Spanish War of 1898 there was a vigorous imperialist movement, but after the excitement of the war had subsided, imperialism too declined. Washington officials and New York business men have since then coöperated in more or less imperialistic enterprises in Mexico, Central America, and the Caribbean area, but America has not yet embarked on a policy of open, enthusiastic, aggressive imperialism, frankly eager for colonial possessions the world over. But of this, more must be said in a later chapter, when we have more of the facts before us.

Up to this point our inquiry has shown that an anti-imperialist, free-trade Europe was converted to imperialism, rather suddenly in the seventies and eighties, when England began to feel the competition of other industrial rivals, when manufacturing nations began to raise protective tariff walls around their own markets and to compete bitterly for foreign markets, when steamships and railways provided facilities for world commerce and conquest, when greedy factories and hungry factory towns called out for raw materials and foodstuffs, when surplus capital, rapidly accumulating, sought investments in backward countries, when the doctrine of economic nationalism triumphed over the old individualistic liberalism. The next step in our investigation is to discover the dynamics of imperialism. Borrowing, to some extent, the method of the sociologist, we must inquire more specifically what classes or groups of men, and what motives, have been responsible for imperialism.

CHAPTER IV

DYNAMICS OF IMPERIALISM

Men and Motives

Language often obscures truth. More than is ordinarily realized, our eyes are blinded to the facts of international relations by tricks of the tongue. When one uses the simple monosyllable "France" one thinks of France as a unit, an entity. When to avoid awkward repetition we use a personal pronoun in referring to a country—when for example we say "France sent *her* troops to conquer Tunis"—we impute not only unity but personality to the country. The very words conceal the facts and make international relations a glamorous drama in which personalized nations are the actors, and all too easily we forget the flesh-and-blood men and women who are the true actors. How different it would be if we had no such word as "France," and had to say instead—thirty-eight million men, women and children of very diversified interests and beliefs, inhabiting 218,000 square miles of territory! Then we should more accurately describe the Tunis expedition in some such way as this: "A few of these thirty-eight million persons sent thirty thousand others to conquer Tunis." This way of putting the fact immediately suggests a question, or rather a series of questions. Who were the "few"? Why did they send the thirty thousand to Tunis? And why did these obey?

Empire-building is done not by "nations" but by men. The problem before us is to discover the men, the active, interested minorities in each nation, who are directly interested in imperialism, and then to analyze the reasons why the majorities pay the expenses and fight the wars necessitated by imperialist expansion.

Business Interests

First and foremost among the active imperialist groups come certain business interests. Not the whole so-called "capitalist class," as many an earnest Socialist would have us believe, but only a minority of business interests are directly interested in imperialism. They are easily identified. To begin with, there are the exporters and manufacturers of certain goods used in colonies. The following figures of English exports to India tell the story.

English Exports to India (Average 1920-2)

Cotton goods and yarn	£53,577,000
Iron and steel, tools, machinery, and locomotives	37,423,000
Wagons, trucks, and automobiles	4,274,000
Paper	1,858,000
Brass goods	1,813,000
Woolens	1,600,000
Tobacco	1,023,000

No other item over £1,000,000.

Obviously the cotton industry and the iron industry are the important factors. The imports of most other colonies and backward countries tell almost exactly the same story of cotton and iron, with minor variations. Many colonies provide a spongelike market for cheap alcoholic beverages. Cigarettes have fifth place in China's imports.

In some cases coal is important. Kerosene has also played a significant rôle. But cotton and iron have been dominant. In more human terms, the makers of cotton and iron goods have been very vitally interested in imperialism. Their business interests demand the opening-up and development of colonial markets, and, in many cases, the exclusion of foreign competitors. Such aims require political control—imperialism. One specific instance may show how important imperialistic control over colonies is to these business groups. India, if free, would long ago have established a tariff to protect Indian spinners and weavers against British competition, but the cotton manufacturers of Lancashire, England, have used imperial England's authority to prevent any such blow to their business; when in 1896 a small import duty of 3½ per cent was established by the Indian government, the London government, pressed by British cotton barons, insisted that the effect of the duty be nullified by a countervailing excise duty of 3½ per cent on Indian cottons.[1]

[1] In 1917 the duty on imported cotton goods was raised to 7½%, without a corresponding increase of the 3½% excise on Indian cottons, so that a net protection of 4% was afforded. In 1925 the excise was abolished. *Cf. infra,* p. 310.

As one Indian remarked, "There are indeed sixty good reasons" for this British interference, "for there are sixty Lancashire members who have votes in the House of Commons."

Next in line come the import interests. The British merchants who import tea from India, the Belgians who import rubber and palm nuts from Congo, the Frenchmen who import wines from Algeria are vital factors in imperialism. The development of such business enterprises on a large scale requires at least a degree of orderly government sufficient to protect investments in plantations, warehouses and railways; often it demands expensive public works, such as dams, irrigation systems, roads, and railways, which a backward native government cannot or will not undertake; occasionally, also, governmental authority is considered necessary to compel natives to work. In short, imperial control by a progressive nation is demanded. And the importers, together with planters and other allied interests, usually desire that the imperial control shall be wielded by their own nation, because from it they may hope to receive privileged treatment. There is only one reason why 197 million francs' worth of rubber, palm nuts and palm oil, copal, and copper from Belgian Congo are exported to Belgium and handled by Belgian merchants, whereas only 13 millions go to England, 17 millions to all America, and only two-fifths of a million to France. The reason is that Belgium owns Congo. And the Belgian importers are aware of this fact, as are their competitors in other imperialist countries.

Of late years this group of import interests has been enormously strengthened by the demand of giant industries for colonial raw materials—rubber, petroleum, iron and coal, cotton, cocoa. The oil trusts of England and the United States have enlisted the aid of naval and diplomatic officials in their world-wide rivalry. The cotton industry of Germany hoped to obtain from Asiatic Turkey, under German imperialist control, raw cotton for German spindles; the cotton interests of England have been striving for a generation to develop plantations in British colonies; their French and Italian rivals have been hardly less interested in colonial potentialities. The European cotton industry, it may be remarked, as an export business and as an import business, is doubly imperialist.

Shipping magnates form a third powerful business group.

The annals of empire-building bristle with the names of shipowners. It is no accident that the greatest shipping nation has the greatest of empires. Shipowners demand coaling stations for their vessels, and naval bases for protection; they desire development of colonial trade and of emigration. It was William (later Sir William) Mackinnon,—"a leetle, dapper, upright man, with an acquiline nose, side whiskers, a pouting mouth, and a strutting manner of walking"—chief owner of the British India Steam Navigation Company, who first proposed that the British should take Zanzibar, and who later organized a group of British capitalists to develop East Africa.

To these interested groups may be added the makers of armament and of uniforms, the producers of telegraph and railway material, and other supplies used by the government in its colonies. These have been aptly styled the "parasites of imperialism." They do not directly cause imperialism, but thrive on it.

Finally, the most influential of all business groups, the bankers, may be said not only to have a direct interest in imperialism, through colonial investments, but to represent indirectly all the above-mentioned interests, for banks have financial fingers in every industrial pie. The many billions of francs, pounds, and dollars invested in colonies have been invested through banks, for the most part. Banks underwrite the loans of colonies and backward countries, the capital issues of railways and steamship lines; they extend credit to colonial plantation-owners, to importers and exporters, to manufacturers and distributors. The six largest Berlin banks, in pre-war days, were represented, through interlocking directorates, in more than three hundred industrial corporations. The Deutsche Bank was the mainspring of German imperialism in the Near East. The Rothschilds, it will be recalled, lent Disraeli the money to buy shares in the Suez Canal, and, more than that, utilized their political influence to bring about the conquest of Egypt. The French conquest of Tunis has been called a piece of high finance—*un coup de Bourse.* The National City Bank has played an important rôle in the Caribbean policy of the United States.[1] British bankers have established literally thousands of colonial branches.

[1] The lists of financial interests given in Dunn, *American Foreign Investments,* offer impressive confirmation of the general thesis advanced in this paragraph.

All these business interests taken together may be much less important than the interests which have no direct concern in imperialism, since nothing like half of the world's commerce,[1] shipping, production, and finance, is accounted for by colonies. But the imperialist business interests are powerful, well-organized, and active. Through lobbies and campaign funds they influence political parties. For example, Mr. Doheny, being interested in Mexican oil, gave generous contributions to both of the major parties in the United States, in order to make sure that his Mexican interests would be favorably regarded in any case. Cecil Rhodes, the diamond king of South Africa, contributed to the Liberal Party on condition that it would not "scuttle out of Egypt," for he needed Egypt as the northern terminus for his projected Cape-to-Cairo Railway and telegraph line. But campaign contributions represent only one of innumerable methods of influencing the government. A Bismarck, a William II, a Nicholas II, or a lesser official may be induced to invest in colonial enterprises. The son-in-law of a president may be paid a handsome retainer, to use his influence at the White House in favor of American oil interests in Mexico. A Cecil Rhodes may purchase newspapers to praise his projects. The methods are legion.

Their Allies

Moreover, the imperialist business interests have influential allies. Military and naval officers are often predisposed in favor of imperialism. Rear Admiral Rodgers, retired, recently declared that "if our successors remain a virile people as the world fills up they will remain armed to take what they want at the expense of others"; the United States, he believed, would have to engage in imperialist conquests when its population passed the 200,000,000 mark. Admiral Dewey urged annexation of the Philippines. Lord Fisher, rugged British sea-dog, joined forces with the oil interests to secure Britain's navy an adequate supply of oil. Similar illustrations could be multiplied endlessly

[1] In 1922-3 the total international commerce of the world was almost fifty billion dollars, of which the colonies and protectorates accounted for about ten billions, and other partially dependent countries (Cuba, Nicaragua, Panama, Dominican Republic, Haiti, Egypt and Liberia) which are nominally independent accounted for another billion.

for every imperialist nation. Military and naval leaders who have helped to conquer colonies usually believe ardently in the desirability of extending the white man's dominion over the "inferior races." To think otherwise would be unnatural for an officer who has won his spurs in colonial wars, for one of the strongest of our impulses is to find some justification for our own work. Furthermore, by mental processes more often subconscious than conscious, fighting men sometimes proceed from the premise that promotions are more rapid in expanding armies and navies, to the conclusion that in a world of greed and force each nation must "remain armed to take what they want at the expense of others." Rarely is the militarist's belief in armaments and expansion consciously based on class interest or personal advantage; but it would be difficult to find a clearer case of class psychology.

Quite similar is the interest of diplomatists, colonial officials and their families. Prestige and advancement are almost assured for the diplomatist who obtains something for his country. Colonial officials make careers and names for themselves not by prosaic administration, but by adding new provinces to old. As their profession is the governing of backward races, they feel certain of their country's mission to govern more, and ever more, of the colored peoples. An altruistic professional faith blends with personal ambition. One needs but mention the name of a Lord Milner, a Lord Curzon, a Lord Cromer, a Sir Harry Johnston, to support this statement; their deeds will appear in later pages. But the host of more obscure administrators should not be ignored in favor of a few celebrities. Thousands of families in England and France have provided recruits for the colonial administration, and take a kind of family pride in imperialism. Some of these families are very influential, particularly in England where so many a proud but impecunious nobleman finds in imperialism a solution of the problem of "younger sons"; for all except the eldest heir must be located in honorable professions such as Parliament, the Church, the Army, the Navy, or the Colonies.

To this motley company of business men, fighting men, and "younger sons" must be added another incongruous element—the missionary. The nineteenth century, following hard on the heels of an age of doubt, witnessed a remarkable religious revival in Europe, and one of the most notable manifestations of increased fervor was the sudden expansion of missionary effort. Going out to preach a kingdom not of this world, missionaries found themselves very often builders of very earthly empires. Sometimes they promoted imperialism quite unintentionally; being killed by savages, for example, was a very effective though not a deliberate, patriotic service, inasmuch as it might afford the home country a reason or a pretext for conquest. Thus the murder of two German missionaries in China gave Germany a pretext for seizing a Chinese port. But more important was the direct impetus intentionally given to imperialism by missionaries. Livingstone, the famous Scottish missionary to Africa, desired with all his heart that British rule might be extended in the Dark Continent, to wipe out slavery, to spread civilization and Christianity. Fabri, whom we have mentioned as one of the leading advocates of colonial expansion in Bismarck's time, was inspector of a German missionary society active in South West Africa; he probably converted more Germans to imperialism than Africans to Christianity. Time and again missionaries in some savage land have called upon their mother-country to raise its protecting flag above them. Time and again British missionaries have persuaded a converted chieftain to offer his fealty to the British crown. Protestant missionaries representing national churches have doubtless been particularly predisposed to regard themselves as representatives, pioneers, of their own nation; but Catholic missionaries of France, though their creed was international, were hardly less nationalistic in aiding the expansion of French power in Africa. Often, too, missionaries by teaching natives to wear clothes and use tools have paved the way for the merchant, who in turn has brought the warship. And while missionaries toiled in heathen lands, enthusiastic missionary societies at home, and the leaders of the churches, learned to take a direct interest in Asia, Africa, and the South Sea Islands, and to urge upon statesmen the need of extending civilized Christian government over benighted pagans. In all this there is a note of tragic irony. Where grasping merchant and murderous machine-gun followed the missionaries' trail, the message of Christianity was not always appreciated, nor were Christian morals advanced by the gin and the venereal disease brought by trader and soldier. But the fact remains that the missionary organizations were among the active groups which promoted imperialism.

Explorers and adventurers—if we may couple them with prejudice to neither—were conspicuous in the early days of imperialism. Henry Morton Stanley was something of both, and a journalist to boot. By birth he was a Welshman, of the name Rowlands. Born in Wales, of a poor family, he ran away from school, to find work in the city of Liverpool, first in a haberdasher's shop, then with a butcher. When this grew tedious, he worked his way across the sea to New Orleans. There he was adopted by a merchant by the name of Henry Morton Stanley, whose name he accepted and later made illustrious. Young Stanley had begun a prosaic existence as a country storekeeper in Arkansas when the Civil War called him to a more stirring career. Enlisting in the Confederate army, he was captured by the enemy; with ready versatility he then joined the Union army to fight against his former comrades-in-arms. Toward the close of the war he discovered a latent talent for journalism, which, when peace returned, led him to Salt Lake City, to describe the extraordinary customs of the Mormons, then to Asia Minor in search of thrilling adventure; then with General Hancock against the Indians, with the British against Abyssinia, and to Crete, and Spain. When David Livingstone, the famous missionary-explorer, was lost in the heart of Africa, Stanley was selected by James Gordon Bennett, owner of the *Herald*, to find him. And Stanley did. This exploit, in 1871, converted Stanley into an African explorer. In succeeding years he made repeated trips into the interior of Africa. We are not concerned here with the details of his explorations, however, but with his influence on imperialism. After making his historic journey, in the years 1874-1877, across the hitherto unexplored Congo basin in Central Africa, Stanley became an apostle of imperialism. With eloquent pen and tongue he portrayed the marvelous economic potentialities of the region he had discovered; but, far from being sordidly materialistic, he urged the sending of missionaries, the abolition of the slave traffic, and the civilization of the natives.

How this extraordinary adventurer-explorer-journalist, failing to arouse the interest of cautious English capitalists, lent his services to Leopold of Belgium and established a huge empire for that monarch, a later chapter will tell. But a speech he delivered before a gathering of the Manchester Chamber of Commerce—chiefly cotton merchants—may perhaps be quoted in part. Assuming that civilization and Christianity would teach the naked negroes of Congo to wear decent cotton clothes, at least on Sundays, he estimated that one Sunday dress for each native would mean "320,000,000 yards of Manchester cotton cloth" (Cheers from the audience); and in time, when the natives had learned the importance of covering their nakedness on weekdays as well as Sundays, the amount of cloth required would amount to twenty-six million pounds sterling per annum. In his peroration he fused the mercantile and missionary motives in masterly style:

> There are forty millions of people beyond the gateway of the Congo, and the cotton spinners of Manchester are waiting to clothe them. Birmingham foundries are glowing with the red metal that will presently be made into ironwork for them and the trinkets that shall adorn those dusky bosoms, and the ministers of Christ are zealous to bring them, the poor benighted heathen, into the Christian fold.[1]

Stanley may have been unique in his versatility and his logic, but as an imperialist explorer he was in some measure typical of scores. It was an explorer, Gustav Nachtigal, who declared the German protectorates in Kamerun and Togoland. Henry Hamilton Johnston (later Sir Harry), began his career as a scientific explorer, interested in architecture, and art, and languages, and biology, but became an empire-builder in Africa, annexing vast territories for England, and striving to complete the Cape-to-Cairo route of which he dreamed. There is no need to lengthen the list beyond the reader's patience.

Last, but by no means least, let us add a sprinkling of politicians to our already heterogeneous array of active empire-builders, with definite personal interests at stake. Some premiers and presidents have acted, more or less unwillingly, at the instigation of business and other interest-groups: Gladstone, for example, was compelled to seize Egypt though his heart may have been heavy; Bismarck yielded to the imperialist only after long resistance; Woodrow Wilson opposed imperialism with extraordinary courage, yet was driven to more than one imperialist enterprise. But others have deliberately promoted imperialism

[1] Pamphlet issued by the Manchester Chamber of Commerce. 1884

either because they believed in it, or because they felt that it would bring prestige and votes, or campaign contributions. Disraeli, apparently, believed in England's eastern empire, and at the same time was very much aware of the strength of the appeal he could make to voters on the issue of national pride. Roosevelt, with his "big stick" policy and his "Rough Rider" campaign parades, skillfully stimulated and utilized imperialist sentiment in America.

Interests and Ideas

But, a sceptical reader may object, imposing as the array of importers, exporters, shippers, financiers, admirals, generals, officials, diplomats, missionaries, explorers, and politicians may appear when reviewed in detail, still it remains true that these active imperialist interests are minority interests. The overwhelming majority of a nation has no direct business, or professional, or military interest in colonial empire. Not only is this true of the poorer classes, who of course have no colonial investments,[1] but it applies also to many, probably a majority, of capitalists and business men. Indeed, imperialism might appear to be directly contrary to the economic interests of many business men. For instance, American ownership of Hawaii injures the beet-sugar producers, by admitting Hawaiian cane sugar free of duty. French ownership of Algeria may injure French wine-producers by developing the production of Algerian wine, much of which is used to slake the thirst of Frenchmen, in substitution for domestic vintages. The issue is not between "capital" and "the masses"; capital is divided, one section against another, one industry against another. Why, then, does the majority so cheerfully follow the leadership of the imperialist minorities?

Not direct interests, but ideas, not property or profession, but principles, actuate the public at large. The theories spread broadcast by imperialist propaganda are the dynamic factors impelling nations to send out armies, defray expenditures, risk wars, for the conquest of distant colonies and protectorates. It requires ideas, attuned to instinctive emotions, to make modern nations fight. The ideas which have been particularly potent in

[1] Although admittedly a considerable percentage of the working class is employed directly in the production of goods for export to colonies, or in industries utilizing colonial raw materials.

imperialism are the idea of preventive self-defense, which awakens the primitive emotion of fear; the idea of surplus population, resting on the instinct of self-preservation; the ideas of economic nationalism, and national prestige, appealing to instincts of gregariousness and self-aggrandizement; and an aggressive sort of altruism, which gratifies our innate pride. These ideas require analysis.

Fear, so easily aroused in the human soul, and so powerful when once awakened, is a cardinal factor in imperialist world politics. The citizens of modern nations fear attack, defeat, conquest. To persuade them that such calamities may be prevented by preparedness for war, is a relatively easy task, as the universality of armies and navies all too convincingly testifies. But of what use is a navy without coaling stations and naval bases? Thus the argument proceeds. If hostile fleets are to be held off from a vulnerable coast, the nation must have outlying naval bases and defeat the enemy's squadrons before they approach. That Great Britain has secured naval bases in all the seven seas, every schoolboy knows. But Great Britain is not unique in this respect. The need of naval bases was one of the chief arguments used by Jules Ferry in the eighties to justify French annexations. It is one of the most popular justifications for American ownership of the Philippines, Hawaii, Samoa, Porto Rico, the Danish West Indies. It has given anxiety to the Japanese, the Germans, the Dutch, the Italians.

A kindred theory, springing from the same motive of self-protection, is that a nation must control raw material in time of war. It is all very well, imperialists argue, to purchase iron, and coal, and cotton, and rubber, and nitrate, and oil from neighbors in time of peace, but in war a nation must have its own supplies, else its cannon will lack shells, its arsenals will stand idle without coal, its warships, tanks, and airplanes will have no fuel, its laboratories will look in vain for ingredients of explosives. What argument could be more plausible, or more moving? The unimpassioned student may perhaps inquire whether ownership of oil wells in some distant colony will be of value, in war, to any except the supreme naval power, that is, England. But to the "man in the street" such doubt rarely occurs.

Even more influential has been the idea that the great civilized nations, being "overpopulated," need colonies as outlets for their "surplus population." To France, of course, no such argument could be applied, nor was it much used in England; but it has enjoyed an extraordinary vogue in Germany, Japan, and Italy, and it is not unfamiliar in the United States. In a densely populated country, where competition for employment is keen and the cost of living is rising, it is easy to believe that overcrowding is responsible for unemployment and poverty, and that additional breathing-room for the teeming millions is an absolute necessity. The case is all the more convincing, if thousands of emigrants are annually leaving their "overcrowded" mother-country, to find homes in more spacious lands.

Germany was in this situation, on the eve of the outburst of imperialism. In the decade from 1871 to 1880, no fewer than 625,968 Germans forsook the Fatherland, to become inhabitants of the United States, Brazil, and other foreign countries. And yet, the population in Germany increased, at the same time, from about forty-one to over forty-five millions. After 1880 the figures became even more startling. In the years 1881-1884, some 747,168 Germans emigrated—more in four years than in the previous decade. Such figures the imperialist propagandists in Germany used with telling effect. Germans became so profoundly convinced of their "surplus population," that the argument was still being mouthed long after the emigration figures had sunk—as they did in the 1890's and after—to an insignificant figure, and after the growth of population in Germany to fifty, then to sixty, then to sixty-five millions had demonstrated that the anxiety expressed in the eighties was quite unwarranted.[1]

The Italian public, likewise, was alarmed by emigration figures, which rose from 94,000 in 1881 to 118,000 in 1891, to 282,000 in

[1] The following table computed from the *Statistisches Handbuch für das Deutsche Reich* (Berlin, 1907), shows the situation more plainly.

	Emigration in 5 Yrs.	*Increase of Population in 5 Yrs.*	*Total Population at End of Period.*
1871-75	394,814	1,668,558	42,729,360
1876-80	231,154	2,506,701	45.236,061
1881-85	857,287	1,621,643	46,857,704
1886-90	485,136	2,570,766	49,428,470
1891-95	402,567	2,651,431	52,279,901
1896-1900	127,398	4,087.277	56,367,178

1901, and have continued to exceed two hundred thousand a year. Most of these emigrants, to be sure, have gone to European and American countries, and many have returned to Italy with their savings, but Italian imperialists have eloquently urged the necessity of African colonies as outlets for this tide, regardless of the fact that emigrants seem to prefer civilized countries where employment is easily found.

In Japan, an increase of population from thirty-three to fifty-six millions during the half-century after 1872, and the emigration of about 600,000 during the same period,[1] provided imperialists with plausible grounds for their thesis that Japan must be permitted to conquer colonies to relieve overcrowding. Curiously enough, this was one of the arguments popularly used to justify Japan's seizure of the Chinese province of Shantung, in 1915, although Shantung happens to be more densely populated than Japan.

A little reflection reveals the fallacy of using "surplus population" as an argument for imperialism. Development of industry and commerce enables supposedly overpopulated countries to support ever-increasing populations. For such development, a country needs increased investment of capital at home. Emigrants leave, not because there is no room for them, but because they believe they can earn more money, or enjoy greater freedom, elsewhere, and they seek prosperity, regardless of flag or nationality, in the country that seems to offer the most attractive opportunities. The colonies that were to be had, and were taken, during the imperialist age from 1875 to the present, have been unsuitable for European colonization, and have failed to attract immigrants. We shall return to this problem later on, but for the present the point to be made is, that the idea of surplus population, fallacious as it may be, has been and still is a vital factor in popularizing imperialism.[2]

The third popular belief, which we have called economic nationalism, has already been elucidated but needs practical application here. The teachings of economists and arguments of List and Fabri and Ferry and Chamberlain and their compeers

[1] The census of 1925 showed a population of 59,736,704, not including Chosen (Korea), Taiwan (Formosa), and Karafuto (Sakhalin). In June, 1922, the Japanese Foreign Office estimated the number of Japanese residing abroad as 590,000 including 134,000 in South Manchuria.

[2] *Cf. infra,* p. 540.

have sunk so deeply into popular consciousness, that Europeans, except Socialists, and many Americans take it for granted that there is such a thing as "national wealth," and that this thing is increased if a rich colony or a profitable concession is secured overseas. The diamond and gold mines of South Africa are regarded as an addition to Britain's store of wealth; the resources of North Africa are added to those of France; the profits to be made by an oil concession in the Near East or in Mexico are added to the income of the American nation. Germany, it has been generally assumed, was made poorer by the loss of her colonies in 1919.

There might be other ways of looking at such matters. Norman Angell and other persuasive pacifists have endeavored to prove that conquests do not profit a nation. A sceptic may ask whether "national wealth" is more than a phrase; certainly the profits of Cecil Rhodes were not shared by the denizens of the London slums, nor have the dividends from Mexican oil been distributed equally throughout the American nation. One might even go further, and inquire whether the Boer War, while profitable to mine-owners, did not prove an actual loss, in money, to the bulk of English taxpayers. But national sentiment stills all such doubts, and perhaps even a pauper may have some share in the glorious consciousness that "we" own rich mines here and fertile fields there; that "we" have billions invested in tropical lands. And certainly national sentiment responds with instant thrill when one's fellow-countrymen clash with foreigners in rivalry for a railway concession in some backward country, or for the commerce of a colony. So strong is this sentiment, that applause rather than surprise greets the action of the foreign minister or secretary of state who officially takes up diplomatic cudgels to defend against foreign competitors the business interests of certain citizens belonging to his nation, albeit he would not think of giving the same governmental support to a private business interest at home.

Quite as subtle, and as potent, is the complex of imperialist ideas clustering around the notion that a nation's honor and prestige must be zealously cherished. The fundamental impulse is primitive enough to be easily comprehended. Each of us naturally desires any group or organization with which he is identified to be better than rival groups. Our own egotism, or vanity, may perhaps be at the bottom of the desire, for we enjoy the prestige reflected upon us by our group. We enjoy this prestige, whether it is reflected by our family, our fraternity, our college, our club, our team, our city, our state, or our nation. Most of all our nation. We are willing to die for that, but not for club or college. The impulse may be simple, but the applications in imperialism are subtle. For example, the desire for prestige, for greatness, impels Italian taxpayers to pour out hundreds of millions of lire on a relatively barren African empire. Possessing unprofitable and rebellious but impressively extensive colonies, enables Italians to feel that they belong to a Great Power; that theirs is one of the imperial races. The hearts of true Britons beat faster at the thought of England's world empire and world mission, at the sight of world-maps showing Britain's vast possessions all colored in conspicuous red. Germans—before the great defeat—demanded their "place in the sun," meaning a large share of tropical Africa and Asia, as the rightful heritage of a great nation, and eagerly published maps showing Germany's ambitious claims. Frenchmen, learning the phrases of Ferry, repeated the prophecy that unless France built up a great African empire she would become a second or third-rate power. And what patriot desires his nation to be third-rate?

The same solicitude for prestige is responsible for the belief that a nation, a great nation, must punish atrocities or insults to the flag, and protect its citizens and their property in other countries. To refuse protection, most of us feel, is to sacrifice national honor. No proud nation can tolerate affronts. The blowing-up of the United States battleship *Maine* had to be avenged in blood. If German missionaries are murdered in China, Germany must maintain her honor by seizing a Chinese port, and by exacting reparation and apologies. If British fortune-hunters surge into the South African Republic, attracted by the gold mines, and are denied the vote, British statesmen indignantly protest that Englishmen are not to be treated as "helots," and British armies are sent to conquer the country. If an Italian girl is kidnapped by a Moslem, Italy is justified in seizing Tripoli. If Mexicans refuse a salute to the Stars and Stripes, American marines occupy Vera Cruz.[1] If Chinese officials arrest murderers on a ship flying the British flag, Britain has reason to make war

[1] They did not actually refuse. *Cf. infra*, p. 444.

on China, and to demand Chinese territory. National honor must be maintained.[1]

National honor is at stake also when two imperialist nations contend for the dubious privilege of conquering a backward nation. When, for example, Germany questions the right of France to subject the unruly and bankrupt African empire of Morocco, it would be humiliating for France to yield, and no less humiliating for Germany: national honor is involved. Even though a compromise may be affected, there will be widespread resentment in both countries, for national honor admits of no compromise.

Finally, some attention must be given to what may be called, for lack of a better name, aggressive altruism. Kipling styled it "The White Man's Burden." His celebrated poem, written in 1899, urges us to—

> Take up the White Man's Burden-
>   Send forth the best ye breed—
> Go bind your sons to exile
>   To serve your captives' need;
> To wait in heavy harness,
>   On fluttered folk and wild—
> Your new-caught, sullen peoples,
>   Half-devil and half-child.

The white man's burden, in plain prose, is to govern and civilize the Asiatics and Africans, the backward peoples who are half devil and half child, sullen and wild. Jules Ferry made it plainer; the "superior races" (including France, naturally) have "the duty of civilizing the inferior races." France has a *mission civilisatrice* in Africa. Germans devoutly believed in their call to give German Kultur to the hapless negroes of Africa, —or, more accurately, to impose it upon them by force. Americans, to a lesser degree, take pride in the sanitary, educational, and other reforms which they have achieved in conquered islands of the Caribbean and Pacific. President McKinley declared, as a reason for annexing the Philippine Islands, that "there was nothing left for us to do but to take them all, and to educate the Filipinos, and uplift and civilize and christianize them as our fellow-men for whom Christ also died." Wilson's Mexican policy was, as Ambassador Page told the British government,

[1] See the interesting collection of interpretations of this concept in L. Perla, *What Is National Honor?* (N. Y., 1918.)

"shooting men into self-government." The British foreign secretary found this phrase difficult to grasp, but he had no difficulty in appreciating England's beneficent task of keeping order in India and other disorderly countries.

This is altruism, and aggressive altruism, because it means using force, brutal force, to impose on unwilling native peoples the blessings of French, or German, or British, or American civilization. Indeed, this altruism goes to such lengths that the civilizing nations are willing not only to shoot Hindus, or Zulus, or Filipinos, or Mexicans, into culture, but even to undergo the hardships of war with equally zealous civilizing nations, and to call upon savages from Africa, as they did in 1914, to join in the battle in behalf of the superior variety of European civilization. An altruism so earnest as this is a very important factor in the popular support for imperialism.

Altruism, national honor, economic nationalism, surplus population, self-protection—such are the principles or ideas which nerve nations to valiant feats of empire-building. The initiative, to be sure, is taken by interests; but the support is given by ideas. When a colony or a protectorate is acquired, the first steps are taken, as a rule, by the business or naval or missionary interests described in the first part of this chapter; not infrequently the public, ignorant not only of what has been going on, but even of the geographical location of the region about to be annexed, is confronted with an accomplished deed, a *fait accompli,* which needs only to be officially solemnified, popularly applauded, and, perchance, defended. Then the ideas function. The public rallies to the support of importer, exporter, banker, or shipper, missionary, administrator, admiral, or explorer. Imperialism, nay, all history, is made by the dynamic alliance of interests and ideas.

CHAPTER V

CLOTHES, CULTURE, AND CAOUTCHOUC IN CONGO

To the romance and drama in the story of imperialist world-politics, no normal human being can be entirely insensible, nor should he be. But the romantic element is incidental, and should not obscure the chief goal of this study—a factual analysis of the twentieth century's gravest problem.

The aim of the following fourteen chapters is to present the world drama of imperialism, that the reader may judge for himself of the rôles which ideals and interests have played. The tale may be told more clearly and interestingly, and its significance will be more easily appreciated, if we discard the customary chronological method, and instead of flitting back and forth between Asia and Africa, between the West Indies and the East, take one region at a time. Africa may well come first; then by easy stages the journey may proceed to the Near East and Middle East, to Southern Asia and the Far East, thence to the Pacific and to Latin America, and finally back to Europe. Then, and then only, shall we be in a position for generalized conclusions.

THE FIVE AFRICAS

There are five Africas. The northern coastland, washed by the Mediterranean, is temperate, more like southern Europe than like Central Africa. It does not belong to the so-called "Dark Continent"; on the contrary, it is a white man's country, inhabited by Arabs and Berbers, and mixed races, fairly advanced in civilization, and linked with Europe by more than two millenniums of history. South of the coastland lies the desert belt—the Sahara, the Libyan Desert, and the Nubian Desert—a region of parched and shifting sands, with here and there a palmy oasis to which Arab caravans resort for refreshment. Here the dusky white of Arab and Berber blends and contends with the black of the Sudanese negro; it is a racial transition region.

Farther south is true black man's Africa. Stretching across the continent from Cape Verde in the west to the Nile on the east is the Sudan ("land of the blacks") a belt of grasslands, prairies, forests, and rivers, a land inhabited by fairly dense and capable negro populations, skillful in primitive tillage and handicrafts. Next comes Central Africa, an equatorial land of drenching rains, dense jungles, tropical fevers; this, too, is black man's country, inhabited by barbarous negro tribes, and only the cool uplands are fit for white colonization. Finally, the southern tip of the continent emerges into a temperate zone, and its highlands, its rolling plains and upland prairies, invite the white settler.

Before 1875 not one-tenth of this, the second-largest continent, had been appropriated by the civilized nations of Europe. France had conquered Algiers, on the northern coast, in 1830, and had annexed the surrounding region. Great Britain had taken Cape Colony from Holland in 1806, during the Napoleonic Wars, and had annexed in 1843 the smaller and younger colony of Natal. Portugal had inherited historic claims to the region called Mozambique, on the eastern coast, and Angola, on the western coast, but the claims were undefined, and Portuguese authority had not been actively asserted in the interior. In addition, along the western coast there were a number of footholds, barely more than trading posts, in the possession of the French (Senegal, Gabun, Ivory Coast), the British (Gambia, Sierra Leone, Gold Coast, Lagos, the Niger delta), the Portuguese (Portuguese Guinea, Angola, and the islands of Principe and Sao Thome), and the Spaniards (Rio de Oro and Spanish Guinea). Better than words, the accompanying sketch-map shows how little of Africa had been taken, before the mad scramble for colonies occurred in the last quarter of the nineteenth century.

Intrepid explorers opened up the continent for conquest. Exploration was one of the ways in which nineteenth-century Europe gave vent to its scientific enthusiasm and at the same time found relief from the prosaic propriety and industrialism which were robbing European life of romance in measure as they added to its comfort. The public was fascinated by the thrilling adventures and bizarre experiences of explorers, while to minute descriptions of strange beasts, of pygmy races, of

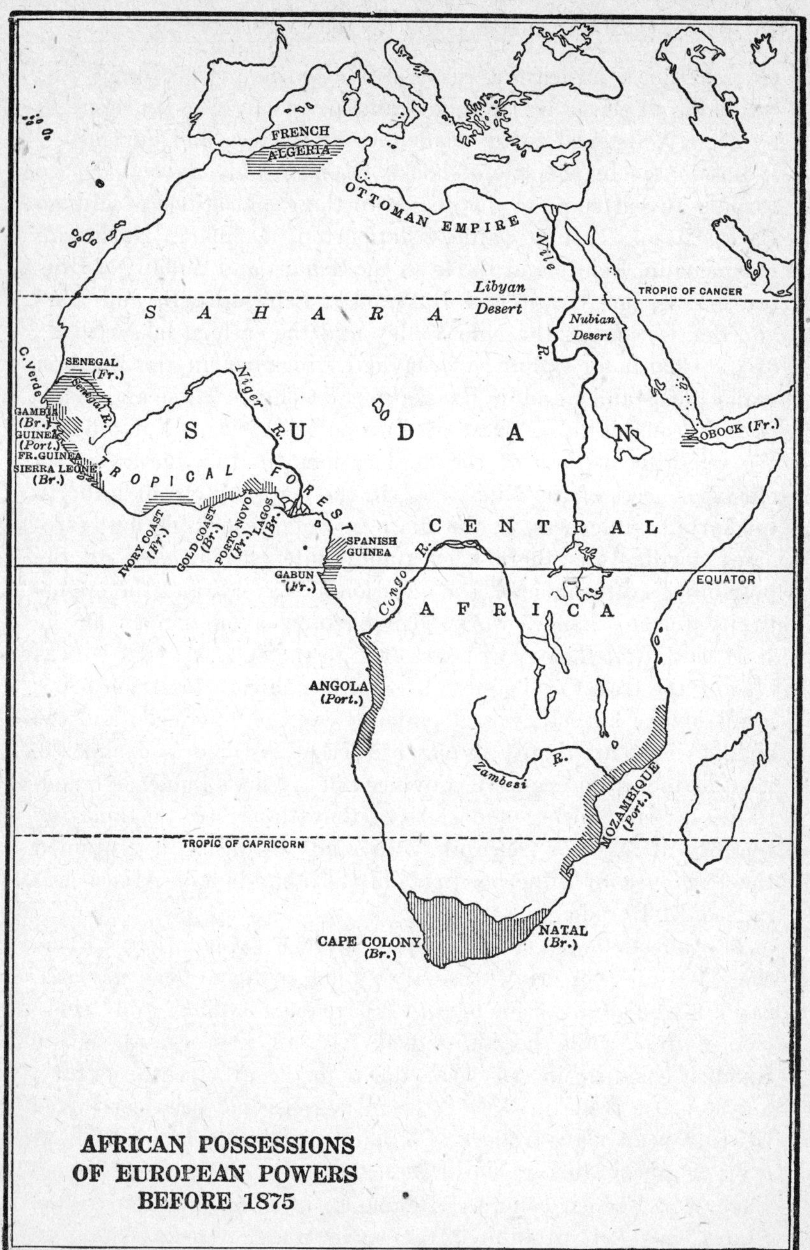

AFRICAN POSSESSIONS OF EUROPEAN POWERS BEFORE 1875

tropical flora, at least a respectful attention was given. The returning explorer was received and petted by royalty, lionized by society, listened to by academies of science, and enriched—if fortunate—by the sale of books describing his travels. Space forbids any attempt to do justice to the explorations of Mungo Park, Major Laing, Caillé, Clapperton, Denham, Nachtigal, Hornemann, Rohlfs and Barth in the Sahara and Sudan; of Burton and Speke, Grant and Baker, Dr. Schweinfurth and Karl von der Decken in the Nile Valley and the eastern lake region; of du Chaillu in Gabun; of David Livingstone in the Zambesi valley; of Stanley and de Brazza in the Congo. These and many others aroused the interest of Europe in Africa. Not only in the scientific aspects of the explorations, in the quest for the elusive sources of the Nile River, in the mapping out of hitherto uncharted wilderness, in the discovery of the manlike but ferocious gorilla, was there keen public interest, but also in the possibilities of commerce, the question of slavery, and the opportunity for missionary work. Livingstone, a missionary at the start, and a missionary at heart even to the end, felt that he was blazing the trail for the gospel. Stanley, though far from being a missionary himself, was at pains to point out the need and the opening for Christianity in pagan Africa. As regards commerce, most of the explorers were convinced of Africa's immense potentialities. In glowing superlatives they described the amazing fertility of Africa's rich soil; with ready intuition they divined the existence of minerals in fabulous abundance; Africa was indeed El Dorado.

The question of slavery merits further explanation. From the days of John Hawkins—that pious sixteenth-century sea-captain who enjoined his men to "Love one another" and "serve God daily" while he kidnapped African negroes, to sell to Spanish colonists in America—down to the nineteenth century, a systematic trade in West-African negroes had been conducted by European slave-traders. With awakening conscience, however, France, during the Revolution of 1789, had abolished slavery in French colonies; Denmark, in 1792, and the United States, in 1794, prohibited the slave trade; Great Britain in 1811 had forbidden British subjects to engage in the traffic; Sweden followed in 1813, Holland the next year; and the Congress of Vienna had proclaimed Europe's general, but ineffective, abhorrence of the commerce in men. But an illegal traffic still persisted. Moreover the Arab slave-traders who terrorized tropical Africa were under no compunction to obey European laws, and continued their business. Blood-curdling were the tales told by European explorers, in the nineteenth century, regarding the Arab slave trade. As I write I recall reading, as a boy, descriptions of Arab attacks on unsuspecting negro villages; the most likely negroes were seized, the others wantonly slaughtered; then the captives were linked in a long chain by a forked stick and cross-bar holding the neck of each; those that attempted to escape, or faltered on the long marches across-country, were killed, and their bones marked the trails. Here was an evil for Christian Europe to stamp out. Explorers and missionaries urged their governments to action. How much of the "crusade" against slavery was sincere, how much mere moral mask for imperialism, it is not easy to discover. Perhaps the fairest judgment is that a sincere desire to extirpate the slave traffic at first reinforced the economic and patriotic motives for conquest, and later was used to justify it.

Leopold's Altruism

The story of the Congo Basin reads like a romance, a romance with its touches of pathos and its lapses into bathos. It begins when Henry Morton Stanley, with a little band of Arab guides and negro porters, plunged into the African wilderness on the eastern coast, to push his way through prairie, jungle, and swamp, braving the poisoned darts of savages and the more perilous fever of the tropics, until he had reached the upper stretches of the Congo River, and followed that mighty stream down its long, winding course to the Atlantic. The three white men who started with him perished before the journey's end, and his four hundred porters had dwindled to a hundred and fifteen. But Stanley hastened back to Europe with manuscript for his publishers and, for the public, news of his discovery of the vast Congo basin.[1] The news traveled before him. When his steamer stopped at Marseilles in January 1878, he was met by Baron Greindl and General Sandford, who came in the name of King Leopold II of Belgium, offering to do "something sub-

[1] H. M. Stanley, *Through the Dark Continent* (London, 1878).

stantial'' for Africa, and begging Stanley to return to the Congo on a secret mission.[1]

The Belgian king who thus comes suddenly into the story was an interesting character, rakish in his incognito private life, an eloquent spokesman of mid-Victorian humanitarianism in his public utterances, a shrewd and ambitious monarch, much interested in industrial development, widely traveled, highly intelligent. Years before either his own fellow-countrymen or the Great Powers had been converted to the new imperialism, Leopold had the conviction that Belgium must gain a share in the ''new and vast market'' of the Far East, and had toyed with various colonial projects. Emile Banning, archivist in the Belgian foreign office, had helped to give point to such convictions by directing Leopold's attention to the opportunity for commerce and industry to profit by the opening up of central Africa.[2]

When Leopold in 1876 summoned at Brussels a ''geographic conference'' of geographers, explorers and prominent men of many countries, he did not speak of acquiring commercial outlets for Belgium. Rather, he said: ''To open to civilization the only part of our globe where it has not yet penetrated, to pierce the darkness which envelops whole populations, is a crusade, if I may say so, a crusade worthy of this century of progress.'' Then and there was founded an International Association for the Exploration and Civilization of Central Africa. The name itself is expressive of the disinterested and international spirit in which this new organization seemed to be conceived. And it was from this International Association that envoys were sent to meet the returning Stanley in January 1878.

Stanley, however, was too exhausted to return at once to Africa as the agent of the Association—or, let us say more simply, of Leopold II. Moreover, he wished an opportunity to interest England in the magnificent empire he had explored. Stanley, after all, was of British birth, and fighting on both sides in the American Civil War had failed to obliterate his native allegiance. England must have the first chance. Great was his disappointment when his eloquent descriptions of Congo's wealth

[1] H. M. Stanley, *The Congo and the Founding of Its Free State* (London, 1885), I, p. 20.

[2] See A. J. Wauters, *Histoire politique du Congo belge* (Bruxelles, 1911), ch. I.

failed to rouse any active interest in England. Says Stanley in his *Autobiography,* "All this (meaning the Congo basin) could have belonged to Great Britain, but was refused. Alas!" Discouraged, he crossed over to Brussels, saw Leopold, and consented to serve the latter's aims.

Leopold's plans now began to reveal a less disinterested nature. A prospectus[1] was circulated regarding the opportunity for railway construction in Africa. A group of Belgian business men and other prominent persons was organized by Banning, under Leopold's direction, with the rather noncommittal name of the "Committee for the Study of the Upper Congo" (*Comité d'études du Haut Congo*), and with a capital of a million francs with which to operate. This committee sent Stanley back to Africa, in 1879, under cover of absolute secrecy. He was going, now, to carve out an empire.[2]

To disarm suspicion, and to recruit porters, the explorer sailed first to Zanzibar, on the eastern coast, although he intended to ascend the Congo from the west. Then quietly he slipped back to the western coast, and with five small steamers sailed up the Congo River. Slowly the expedition progressed. Leaving the steamers behind at the rapids, Stanley's party had to cross marshes and ravines and forests, often literally chopping a road through the jungle. When at length in December, 1881, after two years of toil and peril, Stanley arrived in the neighborhood of Stanley Pool, above the cataracts, what was his chagrin to encounter the tricolor of France!

A French explorer, de Brazza, had stolen a march on Stanley by cutting across from the French trading station of Gabun (a little north of the Congo), to Stanley Pool on the Congo. De Brazza had arrived there fifteen months earlier, and had persuaded the local native king, Makoko, to sign treaties placing the northern bank (and part of the southern) under French protection. Vainly did Stanley sputter that the treaties were worthless scraps of paper. They were promptly ratified at Paris. The northern bank became "French Congo" and the town of Brazzaville, conspicuous on the map, still bears witness to De Brazza's foresight.

[1] One should read it in Wauters, *op. cit.*, pp. 24-6.

[2] On the keen interest of the Comité in the Congo's economic future, see Stanley, *The Congo*, I, p. 26.

Not to be disheartened, Stanley founded Leopoldville on the southern bank of the Pool, and pushed on more than four hundred miles up the river, before he returned to Europe, in October, 1882, to give his report. He had founded five "stations" (forts and trading posts) on the Congo. By constructing roads around the rapids and cataracts, making portages easy between the navigable stretches of the river, he had opened up an easy route for the future. Natives called him "the rock-breaker," for through many a rocky obstacle he had blasted his way. But this was not enough. He was immediately sent back, to open up and take possession of the upper valley. Seventeen more stations were founded. Four hundred treaties were made with native chieftains, conferring on the *Association Internationale du Congo* (the *Comité d'Études* under a new name, since 1882) a protectorate over their lands. Such treaties, easily obtained from illiterate natives, by presents, cajolery, or intimidation, were sufficient to establish before Europe a claim to sovereignty over the Congo. Stanley, however, had his own plans. Resigning his governorship of the Congo, he urged the English to take possession of the region. But to his urging the diplomats of Downing Street were deaf. They, too, had plans.

Gladstone was in power in England. And Gladstone had no desire to annex more colonies. Still, Lord Granville, his foreign minister, did not care to have Congo fall into the hands of King Leopold, behind whose humanitarian platitudes British statesmen were beginning to perceive a shrewd economic and political purpose. It were better that Portugal, for centuries a friendly satellite of England, should take possession, even though the Portuguese colonial administration was notoriously corrupt and oppressive. On Feb. 26, 1884, was signed an Anglo-Portuguese treaty[1] recognizing Portuguese sovereignty over the mouth of the Congo and providing for an Anglo-Portuguese commission to control navigation on the river; England, of course, was assured of free navigation and most-favored-nation treatment. The maneuver was clever. It would nip Leopold's project in the bud, for Portuguese possession of the outlet of the Congo could cut Leopold's projected empire off from commercial access to the sea.

Leopold therefore turned to France and Germany for help.

[1] Hertslet, *Map of Africa by Treaty*, II, 713.

With the former a bargain was struck in April, 1884.[1] Jules Ferry (his name continually recurs) promised to respect the International Association's territory; in return, the Association gave France an option on its possessions, in case the Association should wish to sell. Ferry accordingly protested against the Anglo-Portuguese Treaty. At this juncture the ever-watchful Bismarck intervened.[2] Here was an opportunity to promote better relations with France, by supporting the French policy, and by placing France under obligations now, to earn French diplomatic support in case England should oppose the colonial ventures Bismarck was about to launch—in Kamerun, Togoland, and South West Africa. And besides, German merchants feared exclusion if Portugal controlled the Congo. Bismarck supported the French protest, and adopted Ferry's suggestion of an international conference to deal with the problem. In the face of such opposition, Lord Granville announced that the Anglo-Portuguese Treaty would not be ratified.

Before the International Conference met at Berlin, the International Association's claims had been recognized by the United States (through the influence of General Sandford, who had served on Leopold's committee), and by Germany, and France was supporting it. It was therefore a foregone conclusion that the International Association's title to Congo would be generally recognized, as it soon was. The three months during which the conference deliberated were mainly devoted to other questions—trade, slavery, missionaries, tariffs.[3] At the end a General Act[4] was drawn up and signed by most of the European Powers and the United States (the latter, it may be remarked, took a prominent part in the proceedings, and employed Stanley as expert adviser).

International Altruism at the Berlin Conference

Remembering that missionaries, explorers, and statesmen had represented European activity in Africa as a humanitarian cru-

[1] Hertslet, *Map of Africa by Treaty*, I, 207.

[2] Documents nos. 684, 687, 688, 689 in *Die Grosse Politik*, III, throw interesting light on Bismarck's maneuver and on the way in which he and Ferry agreed in advance what the conference was to do.

[3] See the collection of documents in *Staatsarchiv*, vol. 45.

[4] Hertslet, *Map of Africa by Treaty*, I, p. 20. For its subsequent amendments, see United States Tariff Commission. *Colonial Tariff Policies*, pp. 87 ff.

sade to advance science, spread the Gospel, abolish slavery, and uplift the natives, we may profitably examine the provisions of the General Act. The signatories promised "to protect the natives in their moral and material well-being, to cooperate in the suppression of slavery and the slave-trade, to further the education and civilization of the natives; to protect missionaries, scientists, and explorers . . ." All this was excellent—as an expression of good intentions. When the discussion approached practical questions, such as forbidding the sale of liquor to the natives, humanitarianism proved weak. It was clear that the negroes were being debauched by the cheap gin and other civilized beverages to the use of which they were unaccustomed. But there was a profit in gin; and, as the American delegate wrote home, the Dutch and Germans claimed that "in portions of this region commerce is dependent on the exchange of such liquors for the native goods."[1] Of the blessings of European civilization, the natives had learned to appreciate only one—gin. Nor was the sale of fire-arms to the natives forbidden; that, too, was profitable.

More care was exercised as regards commercial opportunities. Detailed provisions were made for freedom of trade, for equal treatment of the commerce of all nations. This freedom was at first intended to apply only to the Congo, but, at the instance of Stanley and of the American delegates, the free trade zone was extended clear across to the Indian Ocean, between latitude 5° North and the Zambesi River, on the east coast. Ships of all nations were given freedom of navigation over the Congo and the Niger and all their tributaries. An American proposal that Central Africa should be neutralized and war forever banished from at least this much of the earth's surface, was unacceptable to France and Portugal, who possessed colonies partly within the proposed neutral zone; consequently the powers framed an optional neutrality clause which permitted Leopold's Congo state to declare itself "perpetually neutral."[2]

Such was the work of a conference which, meeting on the eve of the great scramble for African territory, might have safeguarded native rights against exploitation and devised means of international control to prevent greedy aggression and dan-

[1] G. L. Beer, *African Questions at the Peace Conference*, pp. 221-2.
[2] Beer, *op. cit.*, pp. 259 ff.

gerous conflict, had the diplomats at Berlin possessed either the foresight or the will. They were but human, and as patriots concerned themselves more with safeguarding the present interests of their own countries—even in the liquor and arms traffic—than with the future. One interesting provision they did make to prevent any one power from excessive land-grabbing. No power, it was agreed, should declare a new protectorate without first giving due notice to the others (this would enable the others either to protest or to make equivalent annexations). The territories claimed must be effectively occupied (this would prevent wholesale annexations, but it should not be taken too seriously, as "occupation" need not mean more than building a rude fort to "occupy" a vast province). Disputes were to be settled by arbitration—a good intention.

Altruism or Rubber—the Congo Free State

It is high time we returned to the broken thread of our story—the story of Leopold and the Congo. Having gained international recognition, Leopold's International Association—which had already undergone so many chameleon-like metamorphoses—transformed itself into the "Congo Free State" (*État indépendant du Congo*), with Leopold as its "sovereign" in July, 1885. The Free State was an independent sovereignty, ruled by the Belgian King, but not subject in any way to Belgium.[1] The next few years were employed in making agreements with France, Portugal, and Great Britain,[2] settling border disputes, and in building forts and trading stations. Establishing the Free State's authority in its vast dominion of 900,000 square miles was an expensive operation. Moreover, Leopold was determined to buy out the foreign interests in the organization. He therefore had to borrow heavily from the Belgian government, besides digging deeply into his own pocket. He is said to have advanced twenty-five million francs in the first five years. At one time, in 1895, the financial difficulties were so grave that Leopold was on the point of turning the whole enterprise over

[1] The Belgian Parliament, not yet won over to imperialism, stipulated that the union must be strictly personal.

[2] Texts in *State Papers*, 78, p. 112; Martens, *Nouveau Recueil général de traités*, 2d series, 20, p. 702; *State Papers*, 86, p. 19; 83, pp. 913, 915; Hertslet, *Map of Africa by Treaty*, II, p. 596.

to the Belgian government, but a sudden increase in the production of rubber and ivory occurred, and he continued to rule his enormous African empire for thirty-three years. It was a long enough period to show the truth or falsity of Stanley's prediction that "this unique humanitarian and political enterprise" would be "a fruitful blessing to a region that was until lately as dark as its own deep sunless forest shades."

One of the first humanitarian acts of the new Free State government, in 1885, was to declare all "vacant lands" the property of the State (*Domaine privé de l'état*). This, however, meant little, until there were issued in the years 1890 to 1895 a series of decrees and orders for the more effective introduction of European civilization. One decree conferred on the State a monopoly of rubber and ivory production in "vacant lands," and an accompanying order forbade the natives to sell these products except to the agents of the State. Rubber and ivory, it should be explained, were then looked upon as the chief resources of the region. The vast forests contained countless herds of elephants, whose tusks provided the ivory; the rubber came from the latex or sap of the rubber vines which grew wild in great abundance, likewise in the forests. And as the "vacant lands" included the forests and all land except the small patches actually cultivated by natives or occupied by their huts, it will be seen that the state was to have a real monopoly. But would the natives willingly go out into the jungle to collect rubber and tusks for the State?

Little appreciating the "dignity of labor," the Congo negroes evinced a marked distaste for the task which their humane sovereign expected them to perform. Accordingly, another civilized innovation was introduced—taxes. Each native village was assessed so many kilograms of rubber or ivory. And to enforce these decrees a native army was raised by conscription. This system was introduced gradually, in different parts of the *Domaine privé*. Leopold found it more expedient, for various reasons, to entrust the exploitation of parts of his domain to private companies, rather than to undertake the gigantic task directly. "Concessions" were granted to corporations to exploit large blocks—whole provinces—of the state's *Domaine*.[1] The

[1] The chief concessionnaire companies were: the Société Anversoise du Commerce au Congo (basin of the Mongala); the Abir (basins of the

concessionaire company was empowered to exact the tax in rubber and ivory from the natives; in some cases it received authority to raise troops and enforce its demands. Despite Leopold's patriotism, foreign capital was welcomed. The American Congo Company, for example, was given a large concession. But regardless of the nationality of the other shareholders, Leopold himself usually reserved a block of stock, usually half. To cap the climax, in 1896 he created by secret decree the *Domaine de la Couronne,* virtually a private estate for himself, comprising about 112,000 sq. miles of the choicest rubber forests, and formed a commercial organization or *Fondation* to exploit it in his interest.

The Leopoldian system produced gratifying results. From the *Domaine de la Couronne* alone were produced in ten years 11,354 tons of rubber, yielding a royal profit of about fifteen million dollars. The following table shows the results of the system:

Year	*Export of Ivory*	*Export of Rubber*
	In millions of francs	
1891	2.8	0.3
1892	3.7	0.6
1893	3.7	0.9
1894	5.0	1.5
1895	5.8	2.9
1896	3.8	6.6
1897	4.9	8.3
1898	4.3	15.9
1899	5.8	28.1
1900	5.3	39.9

Besides, Leopold enjoyed dividends from the concessionnaire companies. One of these corporations in six years made a net profit of over three million dollars on a paid-up capital of about forty-five thousand. The fortunate shareholders not only received annual dividends averaging more than ten times the original value of the stock, but also profited by the rise of the stock's market value to empyrean heights. Sir Harry Johnston, an eminent British authority, has estimated that Leopold's humanitarian enterprise netted him twenty million dollars. As an enlightened monarch he spent his revenue generously in construction of royal palaces, in realty purchases on the Riviera

Lopori and Maringa); the Isangi; the Comptoir Commercial Congolais (in the Kwango). The Société Anonyme Belge pour le Commerce du Haut-Congo (in the Busira district) and the Comité Special du Katanga (in the Katanga region) had proprietary rights.

(one of his favorite resorts), and in the laudable endeavor to make Ostend "a bathing city unique in the world."

All this, however, was a departure from the originally proclaimed intention of piercing the veil of darkness, and bringing Christian civilization to the benighted heathens of the Congo. Critics were not lacking, especially English critics, to point out the discrepancy between Leopold's professed aims and his practice. As early as 1893 an Aborigines Protection Society of Great Britain raised protests against the treatment of the natives. In following years foreign missionaries heaped accusation upon accusation. By 1903 the British Government was stirred to propose an international inquiry.[1] The next year was published the report of Sir Roger Casement, a British consul, who alleged that the natives were being treated with inconceivable brutality.[2] Other investigations followed. Although a few travelers found nothing but praise for the work of the Free State, the overwhelming burden of evidence was incriminating. It was charged that when a native village failed to produce its required quota of rubber, native soldiers were sent to punish the offenders, and often brought back the hands of the villagers as trophies to prove that the punishment had been effective. One writer alleged that officials in some districts employed cannibals as soldiers, and encouraged cannibalism at the expense of unproductive villages.[3]

Some of the accusations were undoubtedly exaggerated; others were based on occasional atrocities rather than on ordinary practices. But there can be little doubt that in some areas a practice was made of holding women as hostages for the delivery of the required rubber tribute by their husbands. Nor can it be denied that thousands of executions occurred; that native rebellions had to be put down in blood; that thousands of natives fled from the country to escape the Leopoldian variety of civilization. Perhaps the actual atrocities were the least injurious feature of the system. Wherever a district was in the charge of an exacting agent, so heavy were the levies of rubber that the natives had no time to cultivate their patches of grain; famine found its victims

[1] See correspondence in *Staatsarchiv*, vol. 71, pp. 233 ff., 239 ff., 259 ff., 328 ff., vol. 72, pp. 91 ff.

[2] One Belgian post-war writer, Pierre Daye, in his *L'Empire Colonial belge* (Bruxelles, 1923), p. 72, attempts to take the sting out of such reports by accusing Casement and Morel of being "*vendus à l'Allemagne*."

[3] See E. D. Morel, *Red Rubber* (1919), *The Black Man's Burden*, ch. ix, and documents there cited.

and infant mortality, always high, became appalling; many a prosperous village fell into decay; and some parts of the Crown Domain, travelers tell us, became deserted wilderness, where the silence of the forest was "broken only by the occasional trampling of the elephant and buffalo, the chatter of the white-maned monkeys, the scream of the grey parrot."

To disarm his critics, Leopold appointed a commission of inquiry, in 1904, to investigate the condition of the Congo. The evidence taken by the commission was suppressed; it would perhaps have made too racy reading; but the report and recommendations were published in 1905.[1] That the commission was not unduly captious in its criticisms may be inferred from the fact that it approved the concessions system, sanctioned compulsory labor as the only means of exploiting the Congo region, denied that white men had sanctioned mutilation of natives, and praised whatever it could find to praise in the Free State's administration. Yet even so well-disposed a commission was impelled to report that the freedom of trade guaranteed in the Berlin Act of 1885 was practically nullified; that no new concessions should be granted; that the concessionaire companies should be forbidden to employ force; that military expeditions needed regulation; that it was oppressive to require more than forty hours a month of compulsory labor from the natives; that the stationing of military "sentries" in native villages to exact the rubber tribute ought to be stopped; and that the land laws were too harshly applied. But these proposals failed to satisfy Leopold's critics. The British Government insisted on effective reforms.[2] The United States Senate offered to support President Roosevelt in efforts to better the natives' condition. The Belgian Parliament began to manifest a determination to take the Congo over from Leopold.

Whether for purely economic reasons, or to conciliate foreign opinion, Leopold in 1906 granted four sweeping concessions, one to the American Congo Company, for rubber; another for minerals in the Katanga district; a third for an ambitious railway project; a fourth for a combination of mining activity with deal-

[1] *Staatsarchiv*, 75, pp. 120-206.

[2] The English protests were continued even after 1908. See *Staatsarchiv*, vol. 79, p. 269; vol. 80, pp. 1 ff.; *cf.* Keith, *The Belgian Congo and the Berlin Act*, chs. 10-11, and Wauters, *Histoire politique du Congo belge*, ch. 63.

ings in forest products. As British, French, and American capitalists were largely interested in these new concessions, Belgian opinion became more than ever excited, and the Belgian Parliament determined to insist on the transfer of the Congo from Leopold to Belgium. Recognizing the inevitability of such a transfer, the monarch shrewdly endeavored to secure a guarantee of the profitable Crown Domain and of the concessions he had granted. Such a solution, the British foreign minister, Sir Edward Grey, declared, would be regarded by Great Britain as a violation of the Berlin Act. And Leopold was compelled to abandon the Crown Domain, in return for 50,000,000 francs (which he promised to spend in ways "beneficial to the Congo"), an additional 45,000,000 francs to be spent on his projected "works of embellishment" in Belgium, and a guarantee of annuities to the royal family. Moreover, the concessions of the American Congo Company and the Compagnie forestière et minière were to be respected. On such terms Belgium took possession Nov. 15, 1908, and the Congo Free State became Belgian Congo, a Belgian colony.[1]

Belgium's Future—in Congo

With admirable sincerity the Belgian government endeavored to substitute a better régime for the grasping autocracy which Leopold had practised. Belgian Congo was placed under a governor-general responsible to a colonial minister, who in turn must answer to the Belgian Parliament for his acts. The first colonial minister, Jules Renkin, visited the Congo, which Leopold had never seen. The natives were given the right to sell their labor freely; native chiefs were recognized and given local autonomy, many of the old monopolies were abolished, though not all the concessions could be cancelled. The difference between the new government and the old may be illustrated by one

[1] The report of the Belgian parliamentary commission, April 1, 1908, giving a lengthy survey of the Congo question, and the law of Oct. 18, 1908, are reprinted in *Staatsarchiv*, vol. 79, pp. 131 ff., 167 ff. The report gives the typical economic arguments for imperialism, and points out that of the 85 commercial companies operating in Congo, 57 with a capital of 143 million francs were Belgian, and 28 with a capital of 40 millions were foreign; Belgium supplied (in 1905) about two-thirds of the total imports (20 million francs) of Congo, and absorbed over nine-tenths of the exports (53 million francs). *"C'est un fait constant, et presque une formule économique, que la marchandise suit le pavillon."*

instance: in 1912 a Congo official was sentenced to ten years in jail for his cruelty in arbitrarily executing seven native men, four women, and a child; in the old days such executions would have passed without notice. Humanitarianism of the new type was less profitable, however, than Leopoldian methods. Throwing the colony open to international trade, abolishing forced labor, relinquishing the profitable Leopoldian monopolies, and assuming the debts of the Free State, left the Belgian government with a colony whose revenues were inadequate to defray current expenditures. The annual deficit has averaged 16 million francs in recent years (1920-4) and the colony's debt was 543 million francs in 1924.

Yet King Albert, on New Year's Day, 1924, declared that Belgium's chief hope for the future lay in the development of her Congo colony.

The Congo, says a Belgian publicist,[1] is "overflowing with riches of every sort"; it is "the vastest reservoir that a country can have at its disposal"; without it, Belgium would "stifle." This point of view is characteristic. Present burdens are to be shouldered cheerfully in anticipation of future profits. What prospect of profit does the future offer? Trade, certainly, is increasing with some rapidity, as the following figures show.

1895	$ 9,100,000
1908	31,770,000
1922	40,724,000
1924	44,500,000

In these figures rubber is a dwindling element. The rubber vines ruthlessly hacked to pieces under Leopold's régime now yield but a small fraction of the colony's exports; the rubber trees—twenty or thirty millions of them—planted by the natives under Leopold's supervision proved a disappointment. The Congo rubber industry to-day is a negligible factor in competition with the rubber plantations of the East. The Belgian Congo's rubber output has actually declined at a startling rate, as the figures show:

Year	*Value of Rubber Output*
1900	40 million francs
1905	44 " "
1908	31 " "
1924	3½ " "

[1] P. Daye, *L'Empire colonial belge*, preface.

More important now is the mining of copper (and to a less extent, of gold and diamonds) in the Katanga district of southern Congo. A chart exhibited in 1925 by the Union Minière du Haut Katanga shows how rapidly copper production has developed:

1912	3,490 tons
1914	14,042
1920	18,962
1921	30,464
1922	43,362
1923	57,886
1924	85,670

This Union Minière, by the way, was formed in 1906 as a stock company with ten million francs capital, half Belgian and half British, and obtained the right to exploit all copper mines in a zone about half as large as Belgium, until the year 1990, as well as to build railways and roads and to exploit certain coal, mica, iron, and gold mines. As the business of the Union expanded, Robert Williams, of the Tanganyika Concessions, Ltd., and the group of British capitalists he represented, was unable to take fifty per cent of new stock issues, and soon found itself a minority holder. The Union is now controlled by a Belgian engineer, Jules Cousin. It is now one of the greatest copper concerns in the world. Copper has become the chief export of Belgian Congo and has made Katanga the most prosperous and highly developed part of the colony. Indeed, the great mining plants there, and the neat white-washed, thatched-roofed huts of the black miners present a quite "civilized"—an almost European appearance.

As for diamonds, the so-called Forminière (Société Internationale Forestière et Minière du Congo), founded in 1906, with a capital of 3,500,000 francs, with a concession to prospect over nine-tenths of the colony, made important discoveries in 1912 and soon became an important producer. Its capital was increased by jumps, to eight million, then sixteen million francs. The output of diamonds in ten years from 1913 to 1922 was 1,390,500 carats; it will be more than twice that in the next decade, if the production remains at its present figure. The actual mining is done by seventeen thousand negroes working at a wage of from six to eight francs a month besides food and lodging—both very simple, to use a euphemism.

Another infant industry, almost entirely a post-Leopoldian development, is the production of coconuts, palm kernels and palm oil—used chiefly in making soap, candles, and margarine. This industry, by the way, is in the hands of British soapmakers, the Lever Brothers, who obtained concessions in 1911 giving them vast areas in which they have a monopoly of oil-palms. Although the Lever interests operate through a Belgian company, La Société des Huileries du Congo belge, Belgian publicists are prone to lament the predominantly British character of the enterprise, for imperialism tends to monopoly. However, these British soapmakers have built up a great industry in Congo; they have established plants, with hospitals, model native dwellings, and even football and tennis grounds, at Kinshasha and other places. And palm-nuts and palm-oil now occupy second place in the Congo's exports. The fertile, well-watered soil of the Congo can also bear cotton,[1] cocoa and rice, but these require the development of plantations, large-scale organization, railways[2] and waterways and industrious but cheap and plentiful labor. The railways Belgium is building; waterways exist; plantations can be created; but labor is the problem.

In the last analysis, the economic future of Congo depends upon the employment of native labor in copper mines and on plantations, and perhaps in exploitation of the immense timber resources. In Belgian Congo there are now about eight and one-half million Bantu negroes, thinly spread over an area eighty times as large as Belgium. Of whites there are only ten thousand, almost all officials, business agents, missionaries. Nor is it

[1] The Compagnie Cotonnière Congolaise (Cotonco.), with six million francs capital, has established a number of cotton farms and hopes some day to supply Belgium with raw cotton.

[2] There were 1,268 miles of railway open in 1924. The greatest interest has focussed in projects for a trunk line to provide an outlet for the Katanga mining region, which cannot conveniently use the Congo waterway. A line has been constructed which links Elisabethville and Bukama, in Katanga, with the Rhodesian and South African lines. But plans for a shorter line, reaching the sea at Benguela, in Portuguese Angolia, were backed by Belgian interests in agreement with Robert Williams, the British promoter so prominent in Katanga's development. Williams, however, ran short of capital, and appealed to the British Government for aid, which was refused at the instance of General Smuts, perhaps to prevent competition with the South African railways. Accordingly, in 1922 the Belgian government adopted a substitute plan, to construct and run a railroad entirely through Belgian territory from Katanga via Bukama, Ilebo, and Leopoldville, to the Matadi, near the mouth of the Congo. Small sections of the line are already in operation. *Cf.* article by G. Van der Kerken in *Congo*, Dec., 1924, p. 719.

probable that European immigrants will ever be numerous, even in the mountain areas, much less in the sweltering heat of fever-infested lowlands.[1]

I have before me an attractive illustrated booklet entitled "*Allez-y et Faites comme eux!*" which urges ambitious Belgians to colonize in the Congo, where they can "create very fine estates for themselves where they will lead a large life, free from the cares of Europe." The pictures are attractive, and so are the

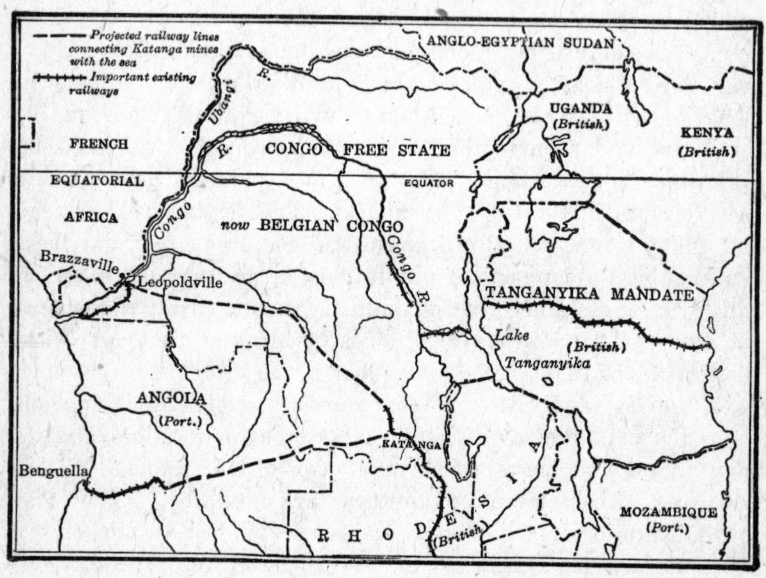

CENTRAL AFRICA.

biographies of successful colonists. The Goethals brothers, for example, have concessions covering 20,000 hectares, part cultivated, and boast possession of "*une auto Ford*"; they employ 170 negroes; and each acre cultivated becomes worth about 1000 francs. But there are not many Belgians willing to emigrate who have the 50,000 francs of capital considered necessary for the prospective colonist in Congo.

The negro population is the all-important element in the situa-

[1] The white population, according to the *Annuaire statistique de la Belgique et du Congo Belge*, vol. 48 (Brussels, 1924), has increased from 1958 in 1900 to 10,037 in 1923. The average annual increase since 1918 has been 910. Slightly over half the whites are Belgians. There are 365 Americans.

tion. And that negro population has declined; Stanley overestimated it at forty millions, other early estimates placed it at twenty, but to-day it is only eight and one-half. The negroes, moreover, have not forgotten the greed and cruelty with which Leopold introduced them to industrial civilization. Occasional revolts still reveal a bitter resentment. If the Belgian authorities rely on free labor, there is still a long process of education and civilization to be undergone before the negroes will give efficient voluntary labor in exchange for wages with which to purchase the goods of civilization; for the prodigal bounty of the tropical climate renders it easy for the native to live a carefree life little marred by toil.

The booklet which I have just mentioned informs us that negro labor in Katanga may be had for 25 to 31 francs a month (about five cents a day) without board, on a three-month contract. The Lever interests employ thousands of natives at fifteen to thirty francs a month, with rations provided by the company. Many of the natives work long enough to pay the government tax of fifteen francs and buy a little cloth, then return to their villages. On the other hand, skilled negro workers, machinists for example, earn as much as 800 francs (about $40) a month, wear European clothes, attend the "movies," dance the fox trot in their clubs, and order their wives' dresses from Paris department stores. In short, the need of work to pay taxes and in some cases a dawning taste for luxuries have spurred some natives to work, but the shortage of labor is generally admitted.[1]

There can be no doubt that the colony is valuable to some Belgian manufacturers, financiers and merchants. Before the war it provided a market for cotton cloth, machinery, liquor, arms, and other goods averaging about ten million dollars in annual value; after the war, the imports rose to about twenty-five millions. Of these Belgium provided almost half, and has usually supplied by far the largest quantity (except during the Great War, when the trade fell into British hands); and Belgians likewise handle the largest share of the Congo's export trade (43% in 1922)—chiefly the palm nuts, diamonds, gold, copal and ivory. But the copper goes to other countries.[2]

[1] *Cf. Congo*, Dec., 1924, p. 794.

[2] See illuminating itemized tables in *L'Annuaire statistique de la Belgique*, XLVIII, pp. 263-70, and 277.

How far we have wandered from the original theme of King Leopold! Civilization of the natives, not commerce, was the question in the seventies. If civilization means education, it may be said that, according to recent statistics (1924), the government was spending on education a little less than six million francs a year, less than one-twenty-eighth of its budget, less than New York City spends in pensions to superannuated teachers. The Belgian government, nevertheless, boasts that 200,000 negroes are receiving some sort of education. Many of the schools are conducted by the fourteen hundred missionaries who are inculcating Christian doctrines. The latter must seem, to the untutored native, a strange commentary on European rule in the Congo.[1]

Congo Diplomacy

A few words must be added about diplomacy concerning the Congo. France, it will be recalled, had obtained in 1884 an option on the Congo, then owned by the International Association. Subsequently France agreed that this option should not prevent the transfer of the Congo to Belgium; but even after Belgium had annexed the colony in 1908, France still held a first claim, in case Belgium should ever wish to dispose of the Congo. In 1911, however, as part of the settlement of the Morocco crisis, Germany demanded that France surrender her right of preemption. It was obvious that German imperialists hoped to incorporate the Belgian Congo, eventually, into a great German empire of Mittelafrika. France refused to yield her option to Germany. Instead, a compromise was adopted, providing that should the Congo ever be relinquished by Belgium, its fate would be decided by a conference of the powers which had signed the Berlin Act of 1885.[2] Later on, when England was endeavoring to settle her colonial difficulties with Germany, the English government secretly expressed its willingness to permit the Germans to regard the Belgian Congo as a German sphere of economic action, a region in which German capital would not be

[1] *Cf. Congo*, June, 1924, pp. 1-8.

[2] Art. 16 of the Franco-German Convention of Nov. 4, 1911. *Staatsarchiv*, 81, No. 14256. An interesting point in this connection is that Caillaux, French premier, thought of getting Belgium to lease to France a strip of territory along the Ubangi River, so that French Congo would not be cut off from the French Sudan: see Caillaux, *Agadir*, p. 226, and Daye, *L'Empire Colonial belge*, pp. 66 ff.

seriously opposed by British interests. This secret bargain, of course, was wiped out by the Great War. In March, 1914, the German foreign minister hinted to the French ambassador that Congo was too great a burden for Belgium.[1] At the outbreak of war, Belgium desired to maintain the neutrality of the Congo, in accordance with the Berlin Act of 1885, but France and England were determined to attack the German colonies in Africa, and presently Belgium, taking a German border raid as justification, used the Congo as a base for military attacks on German East Africa. Over ten thousand native troops were used in the campaign. At the close of the war, Belgium's native troops were in possession of the northwestern part of the German colony, and when peace was made this region—comprising most of the Ruanda and Urundi districts, about 19,000 square miles in all—was given to Belgium under a mandate from the League of Nations.[2]

Another important diplomatic change was the revision of the Berlin Act of 1885 [3] which had provided for free trade and the open door in the Congo Basin. In 1890, by the Brussels Declaration,[4] the powers allowed an import tax of ten per cent ad valorem, equal for goods of all nations. These open door provisions, however, were in effect nullified by the Leopoldian system of monopolies and concessions.[5]

Moreover, the declaration did not allow such freedom in adjusting the tariff as Belgians would have desired. At the close of the war, a new treaty was signed, allowing Belgium to fix tariff rates freely, subject only to the restriction that duties must be equal for goods of all members of the League of Nations and the signatories of the Berlin Act (all now members of the League except the United States and Russia).[6]

[1] *Deuxième Livre Gris Belge*, No. 2, Baron Beyens to M. Davignon, April 2, 1914.

[2] *Cf. infra*, p. 498.

[3] *Cf. supra*, p. 84.

[4] Hertslet, *Commercial Treaties*, 19, p. 304.

[5] See United States Tariff Commission, *Colonial Tariff Policies*, pp. 90-120.

[6] The treaty, signed at Saint-Germain-en-Laye on Sept. 10, 1919, by the U. S., Great Britain, France, Belgium, Italy, Japan and Portugal, applies to the "conventional basin" of the Congo, which includes parts of Cameroons, of French Equatorial Africa, of Portuguese Angola, British East Africa or Kenya, Uganda, Nyasaland, German East Africa or Tanganyika, and parts of Rhodesia and of Italian Somaliland. The text is reprinted in *Colonial Tariff Policies*, pp. 120-2.

CHAPTER VI

FIVE DECADES OF BUSINESS AND DIPLOMATIC BARGAINING IN WEST AFRICA

When King Leopold sent Stanley, in 1879, to obtain an empire in Congo, he unintentionally precipitated what may be described, with more accuracy than elegance, as an undignified scramble for possessions on the western coast of tropical Africa. Prior to this date, the malarial coastlands had appeared to be anything but prizes of diplomacy. To be sure, several nations had trading posts, scattered here and there, but since the abolition of the slave trade these had lost their chief reason for existence, and most of them were allowed to languish in neglect. One might, perhaps, make an exception in the case of Senegal, where a gallant French governor, General Faidherbe, had employed his restless energy in conquering native "kingdoms" until he ruled the coast from Cape Blanc to Gambia, a stretch of more than seven hundred kilometers, and the Senegal valley for two hundred kilometers or more inland.[1] But this, after all, was an exception.

Stanley's expedition of 1879 was taken as a challenge by Savorgnan de Brazza, then governor of the little French colony of Gabun; and as we have seen, de Brazza promptly took possession, in 1880, of the north bank of the Congo, thus giving France a claim to what later became "French Congo." The scramble began.

Earning Knighthood in Nigeria

Simultaneously keen rivalry appeared at other points of the coast, particularly at the delta of the Niger River. Like the Congo and the Nile, the Niger is one of the truly great rivers of Africa. Before railways were built, waterways were the arteries of commerce and of conquest in Africa. River-basins

[1] See Dubois et Terrier, *Un Siècle d'expansion coloniale*, pp. 330-48 and M. Petit (ed.). *Les Colonies françaises*, I, pp. 531-642.

were the stakes of diplomacy. And the Niger with its affluents was a magnificent highway through the coastal jungles into the far interior. Next to the Congo, the Niger seemed the choicest prize of western Africa. For its possession, empire-builders of three Great Powers contended. German merchants and explorers, and imperialist writers in Germany, made no secret of their desire to obtain the Niger for their Fatherland; but the cautious Bismarck delayed, and the real conflict was between French and English.

The conflict began as a skirmish between trading companies. In the very year that Stanley went to the Congo, an English ex-officer by the name of George Goldie Taubman established the United African Company, to trade in the Niger delta. More or less by chance of acquaintanceships, and of travels in Africa, Taubman had invested most of his small fortune in a Niger trading company, and, anxious regarding the value of his investment, had visited the area in person. In bold imagination he envisioned the future of the region. With persistence and tact, and business acumen, he built up, out of numerous companies doing business in the delta, the merger which he called the United African Company, with a capital of £125,000. He himself became a director, while for the presidency of the corporation he shrewdly selected Baron Aberdare, a former Liberal politician who had served in Gladstone's first cabinet, and subsequently a president of the Royal Geographical Society—an influential and dignified figure-head. Even with Aberdare's influence, however, Taubman long tried in vain to obtain from Gladstone a charter and official protection for the new company.

Meanwhile he had French competition to deal with. A French ex-officer, Count de Semellé, had persuaded several friends to form with him a French Company of Equatorial Africa (Compagnie française de l'Afrique équatoriale), with a modest capital of half a million francs. Untimely death had prevented the enterprising count from reaping his material reward, but his friends remained loyal to his project. They went to Gambetta, the great republican politician and premier, and from him received encouragement and authority to make treaties with native chiefs. Their agent then made numerous treaties with the dark rulers of the Niger valley, and established a score or more of trading posts. Between the French and the English company, the Niger was hotly contested, for both were seeking not merely present trade but also future dominion. The English company, however, had the greater capital resources—a million pounds sterling against a million and a half francs—and capital conquered. By cutting prices twenty-five per cent in all localities where there were French trading posts, Taubman's concern practically ruined the French. In desperation the French company asked the Paris government for aid. Gambetta, alas, was dead. And in 1884 the Compagnie française (along with another French concern) sold out to Taubman.[1]

Hopefully now Taubman attended the Berlin Conference of 1884-5, boasting that the British flag at last was unchallenged on the lower Niger. But a new menace appeared. A German merchant named Flegel had conceived the project of obtaining for Germany the great Fula (negro, mixed probably with white blood) kingdoms of Sokoto, Gando, and Bornu, which lay north of the British possessions. These were reputed to be fertile, rich, and populous. News of Flegel's plan reached England. Promptly a young Scot, Joseph Thomson, was sent to steal a march on Flegel. Thomson succeeded, made treaties with the "sultans" of Sokoto and Gando, and was returning down the Niger when he met Flegel, hopefully coming up river with blank treaties and bundles of gifts for the natives.

Britain had won, but with a narrow margin. Energetically Taubman drew up other treaties—more than four hundred of them—to be signed by native chieftains, accepting British protection. A protectorate over the coast was formally proclaimed in 1885. And, at last, in 1886, he obtained a charter, which converted his company into the Royal Niger Company, authorized by the Crown to acquire and administer territory as well as to conduct business. Incidentally, Mr. Taubman shortly afterwards became Sir George Taubman Goldie; the ruthless merchant, in other words, became an honored empire-builder. He had won the lower Niger for Britain.

There followed years of anxiety and restless activity. French "scientific expeditions" coming overland from French colonies, farther west, were making treaties with native kingdoms in the interior; they had already appropriated the upper and middle reaches of the Niger River, and were striving to hem the Royal

[1] *Cf.* J. Darcy, *Cent Années de rivalité coloniale* (Paris, 1904), pp. 235-40.

Niger Company in from the north and west. Meanwhile German "explorers" were encroaching, from the east, on what Goldie regarded as his preserves. Busily, therefore, the British pushed on up the river, and spread out in the interior, everywhere making treaties with native rulers, so that they might establish England's claim. We may well pause a moment over the narrative one of the British agents, Sir Harry Johnston, has given of a typical case of treaty-making; it possesses human interest, and it gives some idea of the realities which this brief narrative would else ignore.

In a long native canoe Johnston and his forty Kruboys (negro porters) and Callabars paddled up the Cross River, through lonely glades, startling an occasional chimpanzee or elephant herd, but seeing no human beings, until they neared a large negro village. Savages rushed out into the water, dragged Johnston from his canoe, and carried him off to a native hut. There, with a hundred human skulls grinning at him from the walls, he had to sit, while a crowd of savages stared at his strange complexion and clothes. At length his captors questioned him, through his native interpreter. He came, he said, on a friendly mission from "a great white Queen who was the ruler of the White People." He wished to "make a book" with the ruler of the village—that is, a treaty—to "take home to the Woman Chief" who had sent him out. The natives, fortunately, were agreeable. A burly individual carried him back to the canoe, and there Johnston took a treaty form (he had a stock ready for such contingencies) from his dispatch box, while three or four negroes, apparently persons of authority, crowded into the canoe to make crosses on the treaty. The natives, it seemed, had consumed enough palm-wine to be genial, even boisterous. Seeing their condition, Johnston "was longing to get away." Accordingly "after the crosses had been splodged on the treaty-form" and he had given them a present of beads and cloth, he made his adieux, but not before the villagers had generously compelled him to accept a hundred yams and two sheep—and "a necklace of human knuckle bones." Then, fearing that the natives might kill and eat his servants, Johnston made "a judicious retreat."

Such, in a general way, was the process of treaty-making by which the negro tribes accepted Great Britain's protectorate. A courageous but nervous explorer, bravely concealing his fears;

a half-explained treaty of "friendship"; presents of beads and cloth (and of liquor in the case of less high-minded explorers) —these were the typical elements in the situation.

Such exploits served to round out the domain of the Niger Company, until in 1900 the British government was ready to relieve the company of its political functions, in return for a payment of £865,000, and to proclaim protectorates over northern and southern Nigeria.

Bismarck Executes the Purposes of Providence

While Great Britain was appropriating the Niger and enlarging several minor colonies, Bismarck was planting German protectorates over other parts of West Africa. He had gradually been won over to imperialism, in the seventies, but hesitated to raise the German flag in Africa unless he could persuade his public that it was necessary to protect existing German commerce, and under favorable international circumstances. His hesitation was ended by the events of the early eighties—the activity of Stanley and de Brazza in Congo, of the British in Nigeria, and of the French in the Senegal region. Adolf Woermann, called by Bismarck the "royal merchant," was furiously indignant at the high duties now established by foreign powers, to the detriment of his trade in West Africa. Other German merchants were equally urgent, and Bismarck, ear to the ground, decided to act. To Lüderitz, a Bremen merchant, he gave a promise of support, on condition that a harbor unclaimed by other nations could be obtained. Lüderitz thereupon sent an agent, Heinrich Vogelsang, to discover an eligible port. Angra Pequena was selected, far down the coast, below the Tropic of Capricorn, for Lüderitz was determined to have a temperate colony. There Vogelsang landed, in April, 1883, and purchased from a local chief, for 2000 marks and 200 guns with ammunition, an area extending five miles in every direction. Later in the year, Lüderitz purchased a strip twenty miles deep, extending along the coast as far south as Orange River, the border of the British Cape Colony.[1]

It was a small venture—only three thousand square miles or

[1] See Townsend, *Origins of Modern German Colonialism*, pp. 165-9, and in more detail M. von Hagen, *Bismarcks Kolonialpolitik*, pp. 294 ff.

so—but important enough to arouse British opposition. A few years earlier (1878) the British had taken possession of Walfish Bay, the best harbor on the South West Coast, and British imperialists, particularly the British in Cape Colony, regarded this whole region as their preserve. And now the Germans were establishing themselves between Walfish Bay and Cape Colony. To Englishmen it was irritating.

Bismarck handled the affair with masterly subtlety. As early as Nov. 4, 1880, he had asked the London Government if it would protect certain German missionaries on this coast, and London had replied it would assume responsibility only for Walfish Bay. Again, on Feb. 4, 1883, he inquired whether Great Britain would give protection to a German merchant, who intended to set up a warehouse; and London replied that no definite answer could be given until the precise location was known. All this, before Lüderitz had made his purchase. Bismarck, on the face of the record, would appear to have been scrupulously correct. But the grizzled Realpolitiker took pains also to deceive London regarding his intentions. After the purchase was made, he inquired if England claimed sovereignty over Angra Pequena. Tardily shaking off its lethargy, the Gladstone cabinet replied that any claim by Germany between 18° S. (Portuguese Angola) and Cape Colony would infringe England's "legitimate rights." Bismarck tartly retorted by asking on what England based her alleged rights. To this pertinent question, answer was delayed while Lord Derby wired from London to Cape Colony, asking whether the Cape would annex the disputed area; and as a cabinet crisis intervened in the Cape, the decision to annex Angra Pequena was not taken by the Cape Parliament until July 23, 1884, almost six months later. Meanwhile Bismarck had sent a fateful telegram, on April 24, informing the German consul-general in South Africa of his decision to take Herr Lüderitz under Germany's protection. Here was a delicate situation.[1]

For a moment we may leave Bismarck and Britain contending for the honor of protecting Herr Lüderitz, while other events claim our attention. At this same time, in the year 1884, Bismarck had sent a celebrated explorer, one Dr. Gustav Nachtigal, in a German warship, to cruise down the western coast of Africa

[1] See correspondence in *State Papers*, 75, pp. 528-553.

on a mysterious mission. To the English he announced that Nachtigal was to secure information regarding German commerce;[1] to Nachtigal, he gave secret instructions, drafted by the "royal merchant," to hoist the German flag in Angra Pequena and other places.[2] Nachtigal arrived at Little Popo, on the Gulf of Guinea, July 2, 1884, and finding British intrigue busy, hastily made a treaty with the local native king, and hoisted the black-white-and-red flag of the Kaiser, July 5, for the first time in Africa. This act gave Germany what later became known as Togoland, a small but fertile colony. Then Nachtigal turned the bow of the *Möwe* toward the Cameroons river, farther along the coast. In the Cameroons region, German merchants had already made protectorate treaties with some of the native chiefs, anticipating Nachtigal's arrival. When English missionaries had warned the natives that German rule meant conscription, the Germans had replied that German rule meant freedom from taxes and customs duties. "And in fact," writes a German historian,[3] "this rashly made promise, *unfortunately given in writing,* was what above all held the chieftains to the German side," when a British warship suddenly made its appearance, a few days before Nachtigal was expected. The warship, however, could do nothing, except threaten the natives, since the British consul, Mr. Hewett, who had the treaty forms with him, had not yet arrived. When Nachtigal appeared on the scene on July 11, he hastily negotiated a treaty with "King" Bell, chief of a negro tribe at the mouth of the river, to whom he gave generous presents (about $5,000). He then hoisted the German flag, and sent word to the English, thanking them for their kindness in protecting German merchants in the past, but announcing that Germany would assume such duties in the future. A week later, a week too late, Consul Hewett arrived on the British gunboat *Flirt,* only to find Nachtigal in possession. "Too late consul," he was later called in England. However, Hewett made the best of the situation by establishing British protectorates over several places on the coast, which Nachtigal had neglected. If these protectorates were valid, the Germans were left, according to one British authority, with only about fifteen square miles—King Bell's realm.

[1] *State Papers,* 76, p. 755.
[2] Von Hagen, *op. cit.,* p. 347.
[3] Von Hagen, *op. cit.,* p. 386.

Nachtigal next sailed south to Angra Pequena, and there erected a black-white-and-red post, with the legend "*Kaiserlich deutsches Schutzgebiet.*" This, perhaps, was unnecessary; other German officials had already hoisted the flag at Angra Pequena on Aug. 7, 1884.

It was now Bismarck's task to obtain the consent of the other Great Powers for the accomplished facts. As regards France, this was easy. Bismarck had taken care to inform Jules Ferry in advance that even if Nachtigal should disobey instructions by poaching on French preserves, no claim opposed to French rights would be supported. In fact, Bismarck was at this time sedulously friendly toward France; he had virtually made a secret agreement with Ferry to cooperate against English pretensions in Africa.[1] This Franco-German cooperation made it more difficult for England to oppose German claims in South West Africa and elsewhere. The English cabinet found itself outwitted. Like a good loser, it recognized Germany's protectorate over South West Africa, from 18° S. to the Orange River (excluding the British harbor of Walfish Bay); it permitted the Germans to enlarge their Cameroons protectorate by pushing back into the interior and also by buying out the British Baptist mission station at Victoria, which Hewett had claimed; and Gladstone magnanimously welcomed Germany into the imperialistic arena with the words: "If Germany is to become a colonizing Power, all I can say is God speed her. She becomes our ally and partner in the execution of the great purposes of Providence for the advantage of mankind." [2]

Lord Granville told Herbert Bismarck in June, 1884, that "it cannot be otherwise than all right with us, if Germany pursues a colonial policy and opens barbarous lands to civilization and trade; we would certainly be glad of it. It is quite different with France, for wherever they colonize the French introduce high tariffs, up to 50%, and thereby injure us severely." But the elder Bismarck, reading these words, wrote an exclamation mark in the margin.[3]

[1] See documents nos. 680 ff. in *Die Grosse Politik*, III.

[2] See correspondence and "arrangement" in *State Papers*, 76, pp. 755 ff. and 772 ff. Interesting additional documents are published in *Die Grosse Politik*, IV, nos. 743-760.

[3] *Die Grosse Politik*, IV, No. 745.

France Rounds Out an Empire

France, meanwhile, had not been idle. Before the eighties, the only genuine French possessions on the western coast had been Senegal, in the extreme west, and the Gabun River, between the Congo and the Cameroons. During the early eighties, the French, as has been seen, added to their small Gabun River colony the extensive northern bank of the Congo. At other points, where French trading posts or uncertain French claims had formerly existed, they established bona fide colonies. Though ousted from Nigeria by British competition, they established themselves in Dahomey, just to the west of Nigeria. Here they had obtained a trading post by treaty with the negro king in 1878; over another locality, Porto Novo, they proclaimed a protectorate in 1883. When the Berlin Conference in 1885 agreed that all African territories claimed by a European power must be effectively occupied, France promptly sent garrisons to these posts on the coast of Dahomey. Was it too late? In the same year Portugal notified the powers that Dahomey had become a Portuguese protectorate, by virtue of a treaty with the king. Portugal, however, was a weak rival, easily pushed aside.[1] More troublesome was the native king, ruler of a fierce and primitive negro people. More than once his dusky highness compelled French representatives to approach his palace through a lane of freshly cut human heads. Patience ebbing, the French made war against him in 1889, and four years later, having defeated his armies, they sent him to Martinique, while they formally annexed the coast and set up puppet kings in the interior, under French protectorate.

A little farther west, France obtained the Ivory Coast, so named because it was once famed for its exports of elephant tusks. Here there had been French trading posts since 1842, neglected by Paris until 1883, when the French government suddenly took charge.

Still farther west, in the region now called French Guinea, French merchants had been active without official backing, until in 1884 a German officer proclaimed a German protectorate over part of the region. France immediately protested, and the next year Germany relinquished her claims here, in exchange for

[1] Hertslet, *Map of Africa by Treaty*, I, 253.

parts of Togoland to which the French laid counter-claims. Thus the colony of French Guinea was founded.

From these scattered footholds on the coast, France rapidly pushed into the "hinterland," the back country. First from Senegal the French fought their way into the interior, following the river up toward its source in the Sudan. From the Senegal Valley they crossed over, in the eighties, to the upper Niger, which is very close to the Senegal. Soon they had conquered the negro kingdoms in the upper and middle portions of the Niger Valley and were overrunning the great sweep of country enclosed by the great northward bend of the river. On the north they conquered Timbuctoo, on the edge of the Sahara. To the south, between 1895 and 1900, they connected their upper Niger territory with the coastal colonies of Dahomey, Ivory Coast, and French Guinea. What had been isolated coast colonies became windows on the sea—or, more realistically—commercial outlets, for the vast empire France created in the western Sudan and the Sahara during the eighties and nineties.

One remarkable feature of the story is that the work of conquest was achieved by a few thousands of Frenchmen. Take for example the justly celebrated Binger expedition of 1887. This intrepid young lieutenant, then thirty-one years old, started out with a dozen negro followers, to win for France the great stretch of unexplored forest and prairie country between the upper Niger and the Ivory Coast. It seemed a foolhardy venture. Yet, incredible as it might appear, Binger emerged from the wilderness, after a year and a half, carrying in his pocket treaties giving France protectorates over Kong and the other negro kingdoms which lay between the coast and the Niger.[1]

The mouth and lower course of the Niger were controlled by the British Royal Niger Company, but in the early nineties the French began to push down the Niger and soon clashed with their British rivals. Simultaneously French expeditions were pressing in toward the lower Niger from Dahomey in the west, while others were circling around to the north, cutting the British off from further penetration into the interior. How keen the rivalry was, may be seen in the case of Borgu. This negro

[1] Interesting accounts of these expeditions may be found in F. Rouget, *L'Expansion coloniale au Congo français* and M. Petit, *Les Colonies françaises.*

empire, situated on the western bank of the Niger, was coveted by France because it would give French trade access to the navigable lower Niger, below the rapids of Bussa. Though the British had a protectorate treaty with the King of Borgu, the French claimed that the King of Nikki was the real suzerain of the Borgu country. French and British expeditions were rushed to Nikki, but Capt. Lugard, forestalling his competitors by five days, obtained a treaty recognizing a British protectorate. He had hardly left when a French force arrived, too late. A few years later, France suddenly sent troops to occupy Nikki, Bussa, and other places in Borgu. The indignation of British officials may be imagined. British troops were moved toward the disputed borderlands; French troops likewise. War was in the air. Fortunately, however, calmer councils prevailed in London and Paris, and on June 14, 1898, a treaty was signed which divided Borgu, France obtaining Nikki and the western part, Great Britain retaining the banks of the Niger and, therefore, control of the waterway.[1]

Meanwhile the southernmost French colony, lying along the coast between the Gabun and Congo rivers, had been a starting point for ventures into the "hinterland." A plan to connect French Congo with French West and North Africa had been formulated by the Committee of French Africa and popularized in the nineties. Up the northern bank of the Congo went French explorers, while on the southern bank King Leopold's agents kept pace. Leopold's success in pushing the Congo Free State's borders north of the equator, north even of the middle Congo, to the Ubangi River (a branch flowing into the Congo on the north), stimulated the French in their penetration of the lands to the north. For a time it was hoped that the hinterland of French Congo could be extended around the rear of German Cameroons and connected with the French possessions in the western Sudan through the country around Lake Chad. The British, however, encouraged the Germans to extend Cameroons inland to Lake Chad, thinking by this means to cut the French off.[2] Instead, they provoked the French to bolder projects—the conquest of the central Sudan, east and north of Lake Chad, and the invasion of the eastern Sudan (which is the upper Nile

[1] *State Papers*, 91, pp. 38 ff.
[2] *Ibid.*, 85, p. 41.

Valley). But of these regions the story must be told in a later chapter.[1]

The Negro Republic of Liberia—and Mr. Firestone

It may be helpful to review the acquisitions of the powers in western Africa. The entire coast, with one exception, was appropriated by European powers. The exception is Liberia, a negro republic, about as big as the state of Ohio, with perhaps 30,000 civilized negroes settled along the coast, and between one and two millions of savages in the interior. The Republic was established in 1847 by negroes who had emigrated (beginning in 1822) from America, and has been regarded as a protégé if not a protectorate of the United States. To be sure, France and England have encroached upon its borders,[2] but its independence has been respected by Europe largely because of the benevolent interest with which the United States was believed to regard the little black republic. For instance, in 1879 the suggestion that France might establish a protectorate over the country was dropped because of the "peculiar interest" taken by the United States in Liberia.[3]

In 1908 Liberia sent a mission to the United States seeking financial and diplomatic assistance. After some delay, President Roosevelt in 1909 dispatched an American commission to investigate the situation, and as a result the United States began to take a more active hand in Liberian affairs. Previously, Liberia had borrowed money in London and allowed British supervision of her customs revenues. Now, in 1912, the outstanding bonds were retired and a new loan was floated (being taken up largely by the British) on the security of customs, rubber and other taxes; an American receiver general and financial adviser was installed; and United States army officers began to organize a police force. Liberia's independence was becoming quasi-independence.[4]

One result of this quasi-independence has been that Liberia

[1] See, however, F. Rouget, *L'Expansion coloniale au Congo français* (Paris, 1906).

[2] See particularly the boundary conventions of Dec. 8, 1892 (*State Papers*, 84, p. 626); Sept. 18, 1907 (*ibid.*, 100, p. 915); Jan. 21, 1911 (*ibid.*, 104, p. 181).

[3] See *Foreign Relations of the U. S.*, 1879, pp. 341-342.

[4] *Ibid.*, 1910, pp. 694 ff.; 1911, pp. 337 ff.; 1912, pp. 649 ff.

made less rapid economic progress than the neighboring French and British colonies. The comparison as regards commerce and railways is very striking:

	Republic of Liberia	*British Colony & Protectorate of Sierra Leone*	*French Colony of Ivory Coast*
Area (sq. mi.)..........	40,000	31,000	122,000
Population	1,500,000	1,500,000	1,500,000
Trade (1923)	$2,528,000	$17,786,000	$7,000,000
Railways	none	338 mi.	230 mi.

A great change was heralded in October, 1925, when Mr. Harvey Firestone, president of a great tire and rubber company, announced that the "Firestone Plantations Company" would invest a hundred million dollars in developing rubber plantations in Liberia. The company had a concession, it was reported, permitting it to select one million acres of suitable land. It was estimated that when the trees reach maturity in from six to eight years the crop will be 250,000 tons of rubber, more than half the world's present production. The Firestone concern, controlling this gigantic industry, and employing some three hundred thousand negro laborers, will be the dominant factor in the life of Liberia. That is to say, if the project is fully realized.[1]

Spain, as an old colonial power, still possesses the barren region of Rio de Oro, north of Senegal, and Spanish Guinea or Rio Muni, a small foothold near the equator, besides the Canary Islands and the island of Fernando Po, and a small share of Morocco. But these are mere shreds of an empire.

The Value of French West Africa

"French West Africa," as it is now called, includes the coast colonies of Senegal, French Guinea, Ivory Coast, and Dahomey,

[1] The foregoing inadequate account of Liberia may be supplemented by more elaborate historical and descriptive material in Sir H. H. Johnston, *Liberia* (London, 1906); R. C. F. Maugham, *The Republic of Liberia* (London, 1920); H. F. Reeve, *The Black Republic: Liberia* (London, 1923); British Foreign Office handbook, *Liberia*. The five-million dollar loan agreement of Oct. 28, 1921, reprinted in the N. Y. *Nation*, May 31, 1922, pp. 657-9, is interesting. See also *N. Y. Times*, Nov. 1, 1925, regarding the appointment of Mr. James L. Sibley as representative in Liberia of the Phelps-Stokes Fund, and the announcement of a comprehensive program of educational and social work. There is very illuminating material in T. J. Jones, *Education in Africa* (1922), ch. xii.

together with the hinterland (Mauretania, French Sudan, Upper Volta, Niger Territory) for which they serve as outlets. Its governor-general, seated at Dakar (on the coast, near Cape Verde), rules an empire of 1,400,000 square miles and more than twelve millions of negro Berber and Arab subjects (not including mandated territories). On the north, it is connected by the French Sahara with the French colonies on the Mediterranean coast; to the east, it is linked with the hinterland of French Congo. It is an imposing monument to the bravery of adventurous explorers and the methodical, persistent, unremitting aggressiveness of French colonial governors. From the commercial point of view, however, French West Africa is not as impressive as its extent would suggest.

Its trade to be sure has increased, from 79 million francs in 1895 to 155 millions in 1905 and 1418 millions in 1924. A popular manual telling "What every Frenchman should know about Our Colonies"[1] assures its readers that "Henceforth its future is assured, from now on the black Indies of France are in full prosperity." But the increase has been relatively slow; if one allows for depreciation of the franc since the war, the figure for 1924 means only about 380 million gold francs or less than 75 million dollars. This is but a third of the value of the trade of the Philippine Islands. This fact is the more surprising, inasmuch as during the years of conquest French statesmen made commerce the great reason for colonial aggrandizement, and in the western Sudan France was generally considered to have won an enviable prize.

Railways had to be built, before the products of the interior could be poured out in profusion, and although France has laid eighteen hundred miles of rails in West Africa, only a beginning has been made. French official maps show a projected railway network connecting the Sudan with ports on the Senegal, Guinea, Ivory, and Dahomey coasts, but only the line from Senegal has been carried any considerable distance into the interior. Automobiles on caterpillar treads have crossed the Sahara, and airplane routes have been planned, but for a large development of commerce, railways or waterways are still required.

Moreover, French West Africa has not yet developed staple

[1] Ch. Regismanset and others, *Ce que tout Français devrait savoir sur Nos Colonies* (Paris. 1924), p. 69.

products for export on a large scale. French imperialists like to think of West Africa as "a veritable empire whose resources are immense and whose inhabitants are profoundly attached to the mother-country."[1] No important mines have been opened up. Wild rubber, once highly valued, is losing out in competition

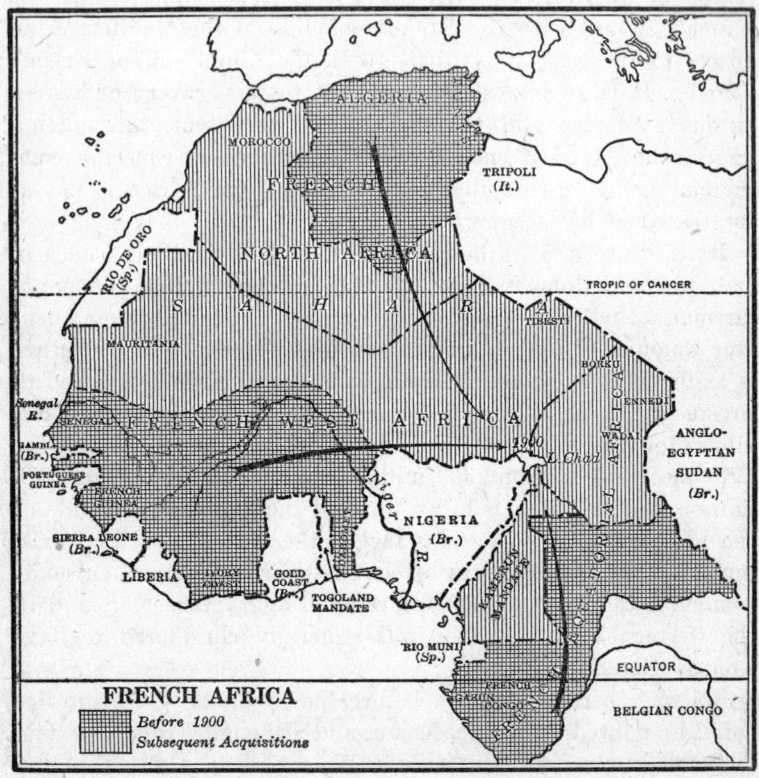

with East-Indian plantation rubber. Cotton plantations have been laid out, more or less experimentally, chiefly on the Upper Niger, but their output is still negligible in world markets, and irrigation is necessary. The capable negroes of Senegal have learned to use the curious combination of spade and hoe invented for them by an ingenious Frenchman, and some even use French plows; they, however, like the natives of the other colonies, tend to raise only the corn, rice, and manioc they need

[1] Camille Guy in *L'Afrique Française*, April, 1925, p. 173.

to eat, and find it difficult to understand why they should exert themselves to cultivate more groundnuts, from which imitation olive oil is squeezed. Nuts form the bulk of Senegal's products. Palm kernels and the oil pressed from them have accounted for a remarkable increase in the trade of Dahomey, and mahogany has begun to overshadow the other products of Ivory Coast. The future may make West Africa a rich land of cotton, coffee, and cocoa plantations, of grain fields and cattle ranches, of lumber mills, of palm orchards—for all these are possible in different regions—but billions of French capital and decades of constructive enterprise will be needed to make this imperial vision real.[1]

A Colonial Cinderella—French Congo

French Congo, together with the old colony of Gabun and the hinterland, is now known as French Equatorial Africa. Including the part of German Cameroons acquired by the Great War, this colony is almost a million square miles in area. The regions of Gabun and Moyen-Congo are covered with dense jungle; to the north lies a zone of broad savannahs, pasture lands, and semi-desert areas. It is so sparsely populated, however, and its production of wild rubber and palm oil so small in quantity, that the colony must be regarded as of insignificant present value, and uncertain future worth. Frenchmen call it "the Cinderella of our large colonial family"—Cinderella before the fairy godmother came.

Hoping to make it more profitable (or rather, less expensive), the government adopted King Leopold's system of concessions, forced labor, and monopolies, in 1899-1900.[2] To forty companies about half the total area of French Congo was parcelled out in

[1] See the interesting review of the assets and prospectus of development in A. Sarraut, *La Mise en valeur des colonies françaises* (Paris, 1923).

[2] See Rouget, *op. cit.*, p. 609, and E. Etienne, *Les Compagnies de colonisation* (Paris, 1893, brochure). The Freycinet Government had brought in a bill to authorize concessions in 1891, but it was killed in committee. Delcassé, later, as minister of colonies, granted three million hectares in the Ivory Coast to M. Verdier and eleven million hectares (an area equal to a fifth of France) in Congo to M. Daumas, but when the facts were made known, there were such protests that his successor, Chautemps, annulled the concessions. Nevertheless, a later minister, André Lebon, allowed Daumas to keep his land, and compensated Verdier. It was the apparent success of Leopold in Congo Free State that altered French opinion and

great concessions, each carrying monopolistic ownership of rubber and other forest products and industry and agriculture of the conceded area. Native tribes, suddenly prohibited from selling rubber, and compelled to deliver fixed quantities as a tax to the company authorities, rebelled. Punitive expeditions and atrocities followed. Reports of what was going on leaked into the press in 1905. Natives were being flogged to work, their wives were taken as hostages, idlers were being mutilated. One official wrote, in a letter, that natives had been used as targets for pistol practice. De Brazza, former governor and founder of French Congo, was sent to investigate. He died on his way home—of heartbroken disappointment, it is said. The commission he headed was forbidden to publish a report, and the evidence collected was suppressed, even though its publication was loudly demanded by some members of the French Chamber of Deputies.

In connection with the exploitation system, the following population figures are not uninteresting: the decline of population, it must be explained, is partly due to sleeping sickness, alcoholism, and abortions. Undernourishment has lessened resistance to disease; so it is claimed.

1900 (estimated)	8,000,000 to 10,000,000
1913 (estimated)	9,000,000
1921 (census)	2,845,936

The total commerce of French Congo before the concession system averaged about 10,900,000 francs (average 1897-9); during the transition period it was 18 million; from 1903 to 1905 it averaged 20,800,000; in 1922 it was 65,028,576 francs (but the franc had depreciated). In the first five years of the system, six of the companies made a profit of 2,645,045 francs, while twenty-six others lost 12,510,219 francs; the net loss of all the companies taken together averaged almost 200,000 francs a year.[1] In a word, it was speculative business, and on the whole unsuccessful. Partly because of this practical reason, partly because of criticism in France, and partly because of English

enabled Trouillot to grant concessions wholesale. *Cf.* L. Vignon, *L'Exploitation de notre empire colonial* (Paris, 1900); Henri Lorin, "La Crise du Congo Français" in *Questions diplomatiques et coloniales*, Dec. 1, 1900.

[1] From data given in Rouget, *op. cit.*

protests,[1] the concession system has gradually been weakened. By 1923 only eleven concessionaire companies remained in the field, and the total area of the concessions had been reduced from 730,190 sq. km. to 152,390 sq. km. Moreover, native rights to till farm plots, pasture animals, and hunt, were partly protected by the forest decree of December 31, 1919; and labor was declared free, though contract labor was allowed under certain safeguards, by the labor decree of May 4, 1922.[2]

Cocoa and Palm Oil in British West Africa

Less than a fourth as extensive, but fifty per cent more populous and at least twice as valuable commercially, are the colonies and protectorates which Great Britain took for herself in West Africa before 1914. Of these, Nigeria is by far the largest and most important; in itself it is an empire as big as France and Italy, with a population of 18,500,000 negroes—more than in all French West Africa. The other British colonies—Gold Coast, Gambia, and Sierra Leone, were cut off by the French from expansion into the interior, and remained small. In these British possessions, the districts along the coasts are "colonies," administered by British officials, while the less easily governed regions back from the coast are "protectorates," ruled by native "kings" and chieftains, subject to a varying degree of British supervision.

The system is characteristically British in its flexibility, and admirable in its success. Especially from a commercial point of view. British imperialism is epitomized in Sir Harry Johnston's statement: "Since we have begun to control the political affairs of parts of West Africa and the Niger basin, our annual trade with those countries, rendered secure, has risen from a few hundred thousand pounds a year to about £10,000,000. This is sufficient justification for our continued government of these regions and their occasional cost to us in men and money."[3] And since he wrote, the figure has increased to £25,000,000 (1924).

[1] The British government took up the cudgels in defense of Hatton and Cokson, John Holt, and other trading firms which had actually been fined by the French government for buying rubber and ivory. *Cf.* E. D. Morel, *The British Case in French Congo* (London, 1903).

[2] See H. Paulin, *Afrique équatoriale française* (Paris, 1924), pp. 86 ff.

[3] Sir H. H. Johnston, *The Colonization of Africa*, p. 446.

The relatively superior economic condition of the British as compared with the other colonies on the western coast, is due chiefly to the fact that instead of resorting, on a large scale, to forced labor and to monopolistic rubber concessions as means of exploitation, the British have allowed native industry to develop more naturally and freely. In Nigeria, for example, the production of palm kernels and palm oil has rapidly grown until it far surpasses that of other colonies, not entirely because of Nigeria's size or fertility, but because the natives, being free to sell their output, have gradually learned the advantage of earning money in this way. Similarly, in the Gold Coast, a few natives began to cultivate cocoa about fifty years ago; they were allowed to own small farms, and to sell their crops to traders; and in course of time the industry expanded. By the close of the century, about 715,000 pounds were annually exported; by 1913, the quantity was 113,000,000; by 1923 it was 443,000,000 worth about $33,000,000. Compare this last figure with the total exports, of all products, from the neighboring and larger French colony of Ivory Coast, namely, 35,000,000 francs (about $2,-125,000). The little colony of Gold Coast became with its two million negro inhabitants, through the voluntary efforts of the natives, the world's largest producer of cocoa. And Nigeria is rapidly becoming a competitor. Nothing could better demonstrate the folly of Leopold's Congolese system, or the capacity of the negro for advancement. Incidentally, natives working freely for what they can earn are able to buy more European manufactures than natives compelled to work for nominal wages or none. The imports of Gold Coast, where the natives are prosperous, were in 1920 almost ten times as great, per capita, as those of Belgian Congo or French West Africa.

To simple common sense these figures seem both astonishing and significant. Their demonstration of the economic and human fallacy implicit in the Leopoldian type of exploitation is so plain that it will not be obscured by adding a reservation or two. First, pessimistic but expert opinions have been quoted to the effect that in about a decade the climate will be too dry—because of deforestation—for the cocoa-tree and certain diseases will practically ruin the crop. Second, the Governor Sir. H. Clifford of the Gold Coast is quoted: "Cocoa is notoriously one of the least exacting forms of permanent cultivation known to mankind." The trees may be allowed to grow, without care, till they bear the cocoa-pods which the natives strip off. Yet it remains true that the natives, without forced labor, have produced immense quantities of cocoa, and also that they have purchased more manufactures than the natives of Congo. Sir Frederick Lugard,[1] a recognized authority on African problems, believes "there are few races which are naturally more industrious" than the African negro, and quotes with approval Captain Orr's assertion that "when the African native is given an incentive to work, he will work in a way that is sometimes almost astounding."

Germany's Share

The share of West Africa obtained by Germany between 1884 and 1914, but lost by the Great War, was larger, superficially, than that of Great Britain, though not more than a third as large as that of France. German South West Africa was larger by half than Germany; Cameroons (Kamerun, as the Germans styled it) was larger by half than France; Togoland, on the other hand, was only a small colony. But commercially the German share was less valuable than either the French or the British.

Cameroons, though it might appear on the map to be as important as British Nigeria, was a tropical wilderness, with only about two and two-thirds million negro inhabitants. Handicapped by its scarcity of labor and its lack of natural waterways, Cameroons exported only about seven million dollars' worth of goods, before the war, and these were chiefly forest products such as rubber, and palm kernels. Moreover, the attempts of the Germans to introduce cotton, cocoa and other staples, employing the plantation system, encountered two obstacles: native labor was difficult to obtain; and Germans with the capital and the wish to found plantations were even scarcer.

South West Africa, on the border of the south temperate zone, had a healthful climate suitable for white colonization, and was expected to become a prosperous land of German ranchers (water was too scarce for agriculture, except in certain regions).

[1] Rt. Hon. Sir F. D. Lugard, *The Dual Mandate in British Tropical Africa* (Edinburgh & London, 1922). This volume has become a classic on African administration.

But here again, it was discovered that few Germans were able or willing to establish cattle-ranches, and native labor was a problem. The natives, finding themselves expropriated from their tribal lands, and angered by the overbearing attitude of the German officials and ranch owners, gave continual difficulty, until the Hereros (one of the native races) desperately rebelled in 1904. The Herero and other rebellions were crushed with efficient ruthlessness, at the cost of five thousand German lives and six hundred million German marks. More than half of the Herero race was exterminated or driven into exile. The population, small enough before the war, was reduced to less than a hundred thousand. Had it not been for the accidental discovery of diamonds in 1909, South West Africa would have been little short of utterly unprofitable.

On the other hand, it should be recognized that the Germans were exceptionally earnest in the building of railways, roads, bridges and harbors; their government buildings were substantial and stately; their cities "were distinguished by order and cleanliness." In sanitation and medical work they were leaders. It was in their dealings with the natives, and hence in the development of prosperous industries, that the Germans proved relatively unsuccessful.[1]

The German government and German imperialists were far from satisfied with their share of West Africa. Repeatedly, after the main lines of partition had been roughly staked out, they endeavored to obtain more. Two possibilities presented themselves: the Portuguese colonies and Belgian Congo. Portugal had on the western coast a large colony of Angola, sterile enough near the shore, but with valuable interior plateaus and forests, and with four million negro inhabitants, thousands of whom were drafted as laborers for neighboring colonies. As England was the recognized ally and patron of Portugal, Eng-

[1] See Beer, *African Questions at the Paris Peace Conference*, part X; A. F. Calvert, *The German African Empire;* Paul Rohrbach, *Das deutsche Kolonialwesen;* Hans Meyer, *Das deutsche Kolonialreich*, vols. 1, pt. II, and 2, pts. I-II; *Comité de l'Afrique française, Les Colonies allemands d'Afrique d'après les rapports consulaires anglais;* German Colonial Office, *How Natives are Treated in German and in French Colonies* (a reply to charges in the *Journal Officiel* of Nov. 8, 1918, and Jan. 5, 1919), and *The Treatment of Native and Other Populations in the Colonial Possessions of Germany and England* (an answer to the British Blue Book of 1918). For an elaborate use of the *tu quoque* argument see Dr. Heinrich Schnee, *German Colonization Past and Future* (1926).

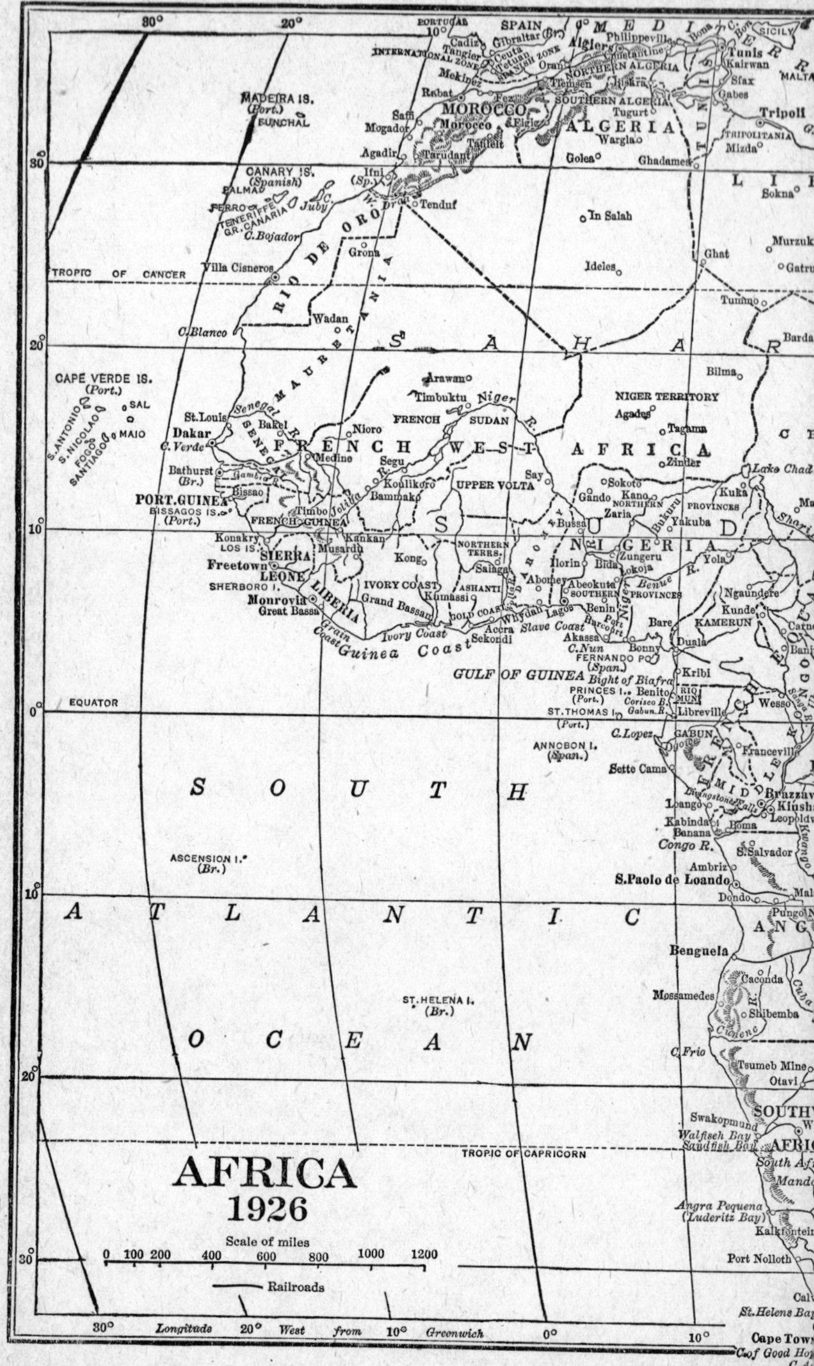
AFRICA
1926
Scale of miles
0 100 200 400 600 800 1000 1200
Railroads
Longitude 20° West from 10° Greenwich
PORTUGAL
SPAIN
Cadiz
Gibraltar (Br.)
Tangier
Ceuta
Tetuan
INTERNATIONAL ZONE
SPANISH ZONE
Algiers
Philippeville
Bona
Constantine
Oran
Tlemsen
Biskra
NORTHERN ALGERIA
SOUTHERN ALGERIA
SICILY
Tunis
Kairwan
Sfax
Gabes
MALTA
Tripoli
TRIPOLITANIA
Mizda
Mekinez
Fez
Rabat
MOROCCO
Safi
Mogador
Morocco
Figig
Tafilelt
Tarudant
Agadir
ALGERIA
Tugurt
Wargla
Golea
Ghadames
MADEIRA IS.
(Port.)
FUNCHAL
CANARY IS.
(Spanish)
PALMA
FERRO
TENERIFFE
GR. CANARIA
C. Juby
C. Bojador
Ifni
(Sp.)
Tenduf
Sokna
In Salah
Murzuk
Ghat
Ideles
RIO DE ORO
Grona
Villa Cisneros
TROPIC OF CANCER
Tummo
MAURETANIA
Wadan
C. Blanco
S A H A R A
Barda
Bilma
CAPE VERDE IS.
(Port.)
SAL
S. ANTONIO
S. NICOLAO
MAIO
FOGO
SANTIAGO
Arawan
Timbuktu
Niger
NIGER TERRITORY
Agades
St. Louis
Senegal R.
Bakel
SENEGAL
Nioro
FRENCH
SUDAN
Tagama
Dakar
C. Verde
FRENCH WEST AFRICA
Medine
Segu
Zinder
Bathurst
(Br.)
Gambia R.
Koulikoro
Say
UPPER VOLTA
Sokoto
Lake Chad
Bissao
Bammako
Gando
Kano
Kuka
PORT. GUINEA
BISSAGOS IS.
(Port.)
Timbo
FRENCH GUINEA
Joliba R.
NORTHERN
PROVINCES
Zaria
Bukuru
Yakuba
Bussa
Konakry
LOS IS.
Kankan
NORTHERN TERRS.
NIGERIA
SIERRA LEONE
Freetown
Musardu
Kong
Salaga
Ilorin
Bida
Zungeru
Lokoja
Benue R.
Yola
SHERBORO I.
IVORY COAST
ASHANTI
Abomey
Abeokuta
SOUTHERN PROVINCES
Monrovia
Great Bassa
LIBERIA
Grand Bassam
Kumassi
GOLD COAST
Whydah
Lagos
Benin
Ngaundere
Kunde
KAMERUN
Bare
Grain Coast
Ivory Coast
Accra
Sekondi
Slave Coast
Akassa
C. Nun
Bonny
Duala
Guinea Coast
FERNANDO PO
(Span.)
GULF OF GUINEA
Bight of Biafra
Kribi
PRINCES I.
(Port.)
Benito
Corisco B.
RIO MUNI
Wesso
EQUATOR
ST. THOMAS I.
(Port.)
Gabun R.
Libreville
C. Lopez
GABUN
ANNOBON I.
(Span.)
Franceville
Sette Cama
FRENCH MIDDLE CONGO
S O U T H
Loango
Livingstone Falls
Kabinda
Banana
Boma
Congo R.
S. Salvador
ASCENSION I.
(Br.)
Ambriz
S. Paolo de Loando
Dondo
A T L A N T I C
Pungo
Benguela
Caconda
Mossamedes
ST. HELENA I.
(Br.)
Shibemba
Cunene
O C E A N
C. Frio
Tsumeb Mine
Otavi
Swakopmund
Walfisch Bay
Sandfish Bay
TROPIC OF CAPRICORN
Angra Pequena
(Luderitz Bay)
Port Nolloth
St. Helens Bay
Cape Town

30°
40°
50°
60°
70°
Teheran
CYPRUS
Bagdad
PERSIA
ASIA
Alexandria
Damietta
Port Said
Cairo
Suez
Memphis
Ruins
Fayyûm
Siwa
Akaba
Farafra
Asyût
Qina
Thebes Ruins
Kharga
Dakhla
Kosseir
EGYPT
Esna
Aswan
Berenice
Syene
Ruins
Medina
Korosko
Wady Halfa
Mecca
RED SEA
Abu Hamed
Port Sudan
Suakin
NUBIA
Old Dongola
Berber
C. Kasr
Massaua
ANGLO EGYPTIAN
ERITREA
KAMARAN I. (Br.)
Omdurman
Khartum
Kassala
Atbara R.
SUDAN
Fasher
El Obeid
Sennar
Gondar
Adua
Assab
L. Tana
Aden (Br.)
PERIM I. (Br.)
Gulf of Aden
SOKOTRA (Br.)
Jibuti
Zeila
C. Guardafui
Shakka
Magdala
Beni Shangul
White Nile
Berbera
Ras Hafun
Ankober
BRITISH SOMALILAND
Kodok (Fashoda)
Addis Abeba
Harar
Sobat R.
ABYSSINIA
Bonga
Abaya
ITALIAN SOMALILAND
Obbia
Lado
Gondokoro
L. Stefanie
Webi
Juba R.
Welle R.
Logh
L. Rudolf
Albert Nyanza
Wadelai
UGANDA
Bardera
Mogdishu
Sanga
Kavalli
BRITISH
Barava
Mt. Ruwenzori
KENYA COLONY
PROTECT.
Kisumu
Mt. Kenya
Stanleyville
EQUATOR
Albert Edward Nyanza
EAST AFRICA
Kismayu
Victoria Nyanza
Nairobi
L. Rivu
Vitu
Lamu
CONGO
Taveta
Kindu
Kilimanjaro
Malindi
Nyangwe
Moshi
Mombasa
SEYCHELLES (Br.)
Kigoma
MAHE I.
Lake
Tabora
Pangani
Tanga
AMIRANTE IS. (Br.)
Kongolo
Ujiji
TANGANYIKA
PEMBA I.
Zanzibar
Kabalo
Mpapua
Bagamoyo
Albertville
TERRITORY
Dar es Salam
Kilemba
Tanganyika
MAFIA I.
British Mandate
Rufiji R.
L. Mweru
Kilwa
ALDABRA IS. (Br.)
Kalungwisi
Langenburg
Lindi
Karonga
Livingstonia
FARQUHAR I. (Br.)
Chilongo
C. Delgado
L. Bangweolo
Lake Nyasa
Rovuma
COMORO I.
COMORO IS. (Fr.)
C. Amber
IBO I.
NOSSI BE
Broken Hill
Kota-kota
Mayunga
RHODESIA
NYASALAND PROT.
L. Shirwa
Mozambique
Sitanda
Lialui
Zumbo
TROMELIN I.
NORTHERN
Tete
Blantyre
STE. MARIE
GARAYOS
Ayrshire
Mozambique Channel
Sena
Salisbury
Tamatave
Quilimane
Massi Kessi
Victoria Falls
Zambezi R.
SOUTHERN
Gwelo
Tananarive
DIEGO RODRIGUEZ (Br.)
Port Louis
Victoria
Beira
MASCARENE IS.
MAURITIUS (Br.)
Bulawayo
RHODESIA
Sofala
St. Denis
REUNION (Fr.)
Limpopo R.
PORTUGUESE EAST AFRICA
MADAGASCAR
Palachwe
Inhambane
TROPIC OF CAPRICORN
TRANSVAAL
C. Corrientes
Pretoria
INDIAN OCEAN
Johannesburg
Lourenco Marques
Delagoa Bay
C. Ste. Marie
SWAZI LD.
ORANGE FREE STATE
Ladysmith
NATAL
BASUTO LAND
Pietermaritzburg
Durban
Aliwal N.
East London
Grahamstown
Port Alfred
Algoa Bay
Port Elizabeth
Persian Gulf
G. of Oman
TROPIC OF CANCER
Williams Engraving Co., N.Y.
Longitude 40° East from 50° Greenwich 60° 70°

lish consent would be necessary for any German designs on Portuguese Angola. Such consent was obtained in 1898 by a secret Anglo-German treaty, which divided the Portuguese colonies in Africa into economic spheres of influence, Germany's share being the southern part of Angola, adjacent to German South West Africa (besides the northern part of Mozambique, on the eastern coast), the remainder being for England.[1] At that time it was anticipated that financial difficulties might compel Portugal to sell her colonies, in which case Germany would be able to purchase her sphere of interest. Portugal, however, suspecting the purpose of the agreement, became so alarmed that England signed a Treaty of Windsor (1899) reenforcing the Anglo-Portuguese alliance of 1661,[2] and years passed with no sign of willingness to sell, on Portugal's part.

Becoming impatient, the German government proposed a revision of the Anglo-German bargain. In 1913 Sir Edward Grey agreed, and a new secret treaty was drafted. As Germany's share, the new pact marked out most of Angola (except the part east of 20° E.), besides the rich cocoa-producing island of Sao Thome and its smaller neighbor, Prince's island (Principe), both lying off the western coast of central Africa, and also, on the eastern coast, the part of Mozambique north of the river Licango. This time it was agreed that it was unnecessary to wait upon Portugal's voluntary offer to sell; the Great Powers might step in ostensibly because of Portuguese misgovernment, and as soon as either Germany or England took its share, the other could occupy the rest.[3] Sir Edward Grey's willingness to conclude such a bargain disposing of the property of a small and allied nation behind the latter's back, may be explained partly on the

[1] The text of the convention, secret convention, and secret note, signed Aug. 30, 1898, and ratified Sept. 26, are given in *Die Grosse Politik*, vol. XIV-1, pp. 347 ff., and the German correspondence concerning them, pp. 257 ff. Portuguese Timor, in the East Indies, was also allotted to Germany's share. The public convention contemplated taking over the customs houses in the assigned spheres of interest, but the secret convention, article 3, contained the provision: "In case Portugal renounces her sovereign rights over Mozambique, Angola, and Portuguese Timor, *or loses these territories in any other manner*" (italics mine), each Contracting Party shall enjoy equal economic privileges in "such portions of the territories comprised in the present Convention *as may fall* to the other Contracting Party."

[2] See *International Conciliation*, No. 127, pp. 281, 289.

[3] Lichnowsky's memorandum, in *International Conciliation*, No. 127. Brandenburg, *Von Bismarck zum Weltkrieg*, pp. 399-400.

ground of his strong desire for a general agreement with Germany (he was at this same time settling Anglo-German differences in the Near East), and partly on the ground that English publicists had given Portuguese colonial administration a reputation for corrupt and cruel inefficiency, and for inhumane treatment of the natives.[1] The bargain, however, was never fulfilled, nor was it even ratified. Germany opposed its immediate publication, whereas Grey insisted on publication as a condition of ratification; as a result, the draft treaty, initialed by the negotiators, lay in a pigeon-hole awaiting signature until the outbreak of war in 1914 made signature impossible. Since then, the Portuguese colonies have increasingly become English spheres of influence, exploited by British capital.[2]

Another German project was the acquisition of Belgian Congo and French Congo, the possession of which, together with Angola and northern Mozambique, would connect German Cameroons, South West Africa and German East Africa in an unbroken empire of German *Mittelafrika,* sweeping from the Atlantic to the Indian Ocean, and from British South Africa to the Sudan. This was not, indeed, an openly avowed aim of the German government; it was the grandiose dream of imperialists, more or less shared by the government in secret, as an ultimate goal. An important step toward its achievement was taken in 1911, when Germany demanded "compensation" for permitting France to take Morocco. At first, Germany asked for French Congo and an option on Belgian Congo and on Spanish Guinea (wedged in between French Congo and German Cameroons). She obtained a hundred thousand square miles of French Congo, giving Cameroons a long arm reaching down to touch the Congo River, and another to touch the Ubangi. The option on Spanish Guinea was also granted.[3] But France refused to transfer her option on Belgian Congo, and a compromise was arranged

[1] H. W. Nevinson, *A Modern Slavery* (London, 1906); J. H. Harris, *Portuguese Slavery* (London, 1913); W. A. Cadbury, *Labour in Portuguese West Africa* (N. Y., 1920); *cf.* Foreign Office Handbooks on *Angola* and *Mozambique.*

[2] For example, northern Mozambique is exploited by a chartered company controlled by Libert Oury, an English financier of Belgian origin. For the significant Belgian economic penetration of Portuguese territory see Daye, *L'Empire colonial belge.* On conditions in Angola see *Afrique française, Renseignements coloniaux,* March, May, Nov., 1923; Aug, 1924; Oct., 1925.

[3] France had obtained this option in 1900.

whereby if Belgium should ever be willing to relinquish Congo, the colony's fate would be considered by a conference of the powers.[1] Taken all together, these German demands of 1911 show clearly the secret aim. In this connection, it is interesting to add that in 1913 Sir Edward Grey of England secretly offered to include Belgian Congo, along with most of the Portuguese colonies, in Germany's sphere of interest, so the German ambassador Lichnowsky claims, but Germany refused to incorporate this offer in a treaty intended for publication.[2] That her refusal was a matter of diplomatic tactics, not of self-denial, may be proved by the conversation which the German foreign minister, Herr von Jagow, held with the French ambassador in the spring of 1914. With the obvious purpose of sounding France regarding Belgian Congo, von Jagow declared that only Great Powers had the strength and resources needed for colonization; smaller competitors must disappear or gravitate into the orbits of the great.[3]

The Great War brought such German aims out into the limelight. Imperialists in Germany openly and enthusiastically demanded the creation of a German *Mittelafrika* extending from the Sahara in the north to the Zambesi in the south, and from the Atlantic to the Indian Ocean, and including all the Belgian, Portuguese, French and British possessions in this vast region. But the ordeal of arms decreed that instead of gaining, Germany should lose an empire. The former German colonies were to become "mandates" of the Allies, Togoland and Kamerun being divided between France and England, South West Africa assigned to British South Africa, and—we might as well add now—German East Africa being given to Great Britain, except a small corner in the northwest, which was handed over to Belgium, and a narrow strip on the south, to Portugal.[4]

[1] *Staatsarchiv*, 81, No. 14256.

[2] Lichnowsky's memorandum, in *International Conciliation*, No. 127, pp. 58-65.

[3] Beer, *op. cit.*, p. 49, citing Belgian *Correspondance Diplomatique.*

[4] *Cf. infra*, pp. 483, 498.

CHAPTER VII

THE CONQUEST AND EXPLOITATION OF EAST AFRICA

Anglo-German Rivalry

The partition of the western and eastern coasts of Africa was almost simultaneous, beginning in earnest about 1884, and reaching virtual completion within ten years. Before 1884, Portugal held a long but vaguely defined strip of malarial coast land, on both sides of the Zambesi River, which enters the sea just opposite the great island of Madagascar. All north of this Portuguese colony of Mozambique was eligible for conquest, since it belonged to no European power, but was claimed by a Mohammedan "sultan," who from his capital on the island of Zanzibar (a little below the equator) attempted rather unsuccessfully to assert authority over more than a thousand miles of the mainland coast. On one occasion (1877) the sultan had offered to let William McKinnon, a very God-fearing Scottish shipowner, collect all the customs duties in this empire, but the British Foreign Office had vetoed the project. Bismarck, likewise, had to discourage German schemes to acquire control of Zanzibar or East Africa—before 1884.

In 1884, however, a livelier tune was called by Dr. Carl Peters, an impetuous young German, who had absorbed the spirit of imperialism during a visit to England, and had founded in Germany a Company for German Colonization to provide capital for the acquisition of a colony. Not knowing just where to begin, Peters accepted the suggestion of Count Pfeil, another German who had lived in Africa and had profitably read Stanley's books. The expedition was planned in secrecy, for officialdom had frowned upon Peters' earlier proposals; moreover, Peters himself preferred stealth to publicity, melodrama to diplomacy. On October 1, 1884, Peters embarked at Triest, with Pfeil and two other associates. They were disguised as

English workingmen, and Peters took the alias, Mr. Bowman. Arriving at Zanzibar a month later, Peters found a telegram awaiting him, expressing Bismarck's disapproval of the enterprise. With characteristic verve, the young adventurer replied that he begged to have refusals delayed until he asked for something. With assistance from a German commercial house at Zanzibar, the little group of empire-builders obtained necessary supplies, and crossed over to the mainland. Ten days later, Peters was back in Zanzibar, with a dozen treaties, placing the native kingdoms of Useguha, Nguru, Usagara, and Ukami—about 60,000 square miles in all—under the protection of his company. How by presents, persuasion and cajolery he and his friends had induced the bewildered native chieftains to make their marks on the treaties, is a story that he himself has told.[1]

Hastening back to Berlin, he reorganized his company as the German East Africa Company, and demanded from Bismarck a *Schutzbrief*—a proclamation of governmental protection—for his acquisitions. When Bismarck seemed reluctant, Peters announced that he was going to Brussels, knowing Bismarck would suspect the purpose of the trip to be an offer of East Africa to the grasping King Leopold. Bismarck understood the move, and quickly published the *Schutzbrief*, March 3, 1885.[2] Whether his hand was forced by the importunate Peters, or the whole drama was but a puppet-show devised to mask the chancellor's own designs, has been a favorite theme for historical debate. A reasonable interpretation of the facts now available would be that Bismarck, ever an opportunist, cautious when uncertain as he was bold when assured of success, carefully assumed a diplomatically correct attitude of disapproval until the Peters expedition had succeeded, and then perceived an opportunity to gain a colony. His decision was made easier by the preoccupation of England with Anglo-Russian disputes in Asia.

[1] C. Peters, *Die Gründung von Deutsch-Ostafrika* (Berlin, 1906); *Lebenserinnerungen* (Hamburg, 1918). On this whole episode I am indebted also to Miss Townsend's *Origins of Modern German Colonialism* and M. von Hagen, *Bismarcks Kolonialpolitik*, pp. 510-552. *Cf.* Hertslet, *Map of Africa by Treaty*, I, pp. 303 ff.

[2] Hertslet, *op. cit.*, I, p. 303. This charter did not establish a protectorate in the ordinary sense of the word, that is, a tutelage by the German government over a native ruler; rather, it declared German "suzerainty" and "protection" over the territories and granted the company all rights of jurisdiction.

England, however, was not willing to permit the Germans to have things all their own way in East Africa. An English explorer, whose name—Sir Harry Johnston—must already be

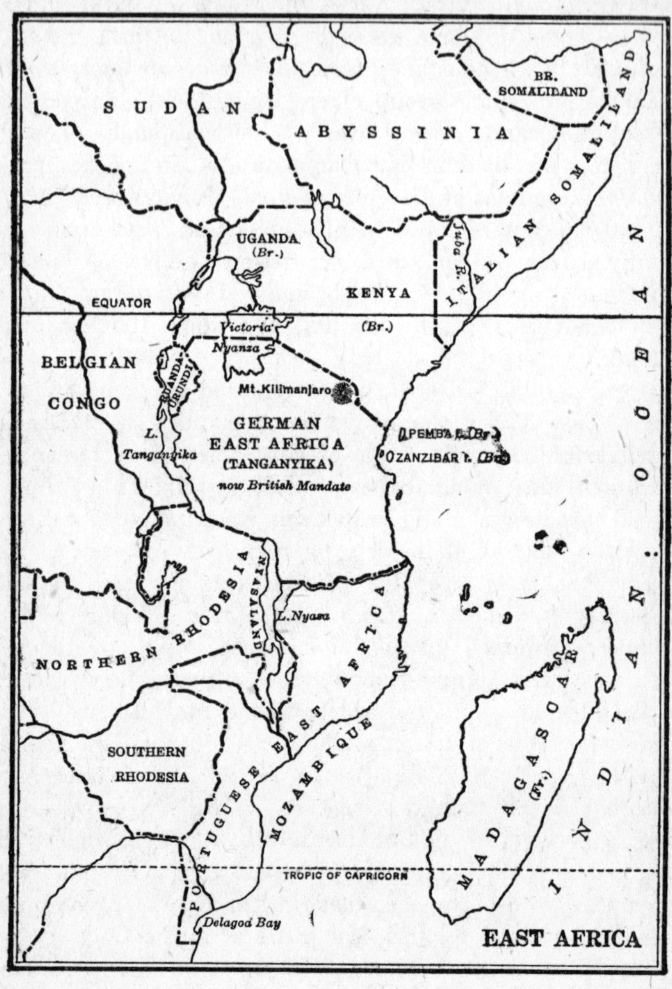

familiar to the persevering reader of these pages, had ventured into the locality of Mount Kilimanjaro, just north of Peters' domain, a few months earlier, to observe the flora and fauna, and, incidentally, to make treaties with native chieftains "if a French traveler seemed to be coming to the neighborhood" (he had no suspicion of the Germans). These were taken up, in 1885, by a group of Manchester merchants, and others, who formed the British East Africa Association, later reorganized as the Imperial British East Africa Company. As the French Government also claimed an interest in the East Coast, the three Great Powers—England, Germany and France—appointed a joint commission to settle their conflicting claims, and to determine whether East Africa was really the property of the sultan of Zanzibar. The decision, reached in 1886, allowed to the sultan only his islands of Zanzibar and Pemba, and a strip of the coast ten miles deep and about a thousand long. Of this the German company was to have the southern six hundred miles and the British the northern four hundred, as a sphere of interest. Back of the ten-mile limit, the hinterland was divided between Germany and England by a line drawn as far west as Lake Victoria. France, for her part, was left free to pursue interests in Madagascar.[1]

The next step was to obtain from the sultan the "littoral," the ten-mile coast strip. Each of the rival chartered companies —the German East African and the British East African— leased from Zanzibar its respective "sphere" of coast. But this arrangement could not last long. The Germans were eager to obtain outright possession of the coast, so that they might control the tariff. Moreover, the question of western extension raised problems. Were the Germans free to push their frontier back to meet the Congo Free State at Lake Tanganyika, leaving no corridor for the projected British Cape-to-Cairo Railway? Was the fertile inland kingdom of Uganda, described by explorers as the jewel of eastern Africa, to be British or German?

The future of Uganda became an urgent question in 1890. In earlier years French Roman Catholic missionaries, Cardinal Lavigerie's "White Fathers," had entered this negro kingdom and won many converts; British Protestants also sought to evangelize the kingdom. Islam, too, had found its devotees. Disliking the growth of these religious factions, the king, Mwanga, hit upon the interesting expedient of placing Christians and Mohammedans together on an island in Lake Victoria, and let-

[1] See Anglo-German agreement of Oct. 29-Nov. 1, 1886, in Hertslet, *Map of Africa by Treaty*, II, p. 615.

ting them starve. But his plan was discovered, and civil war resulted. Deposed by the Mohammedans, King Mwanga joined with the missionaries in asking aid from a British officer, Frederick Jackson, who had been sent to Lake Victoria by the British East Africa Company. Jackson offered to use his force of five hundred riflemen to help the king, if his expenses were paid and the British flag raised over Uganda. But he delayed, and once again, as they had so often done, the Germans profited by British procrastination. Carl Peters, founder of German East Africa, restlessly seeking new empires to conquer, was at this time leading a German expedition through Uganda to the Upper Nile Valley, to rescue a German (Emin Pasha) who was there beleaguered by fanatical Moslems. Peters happened to obtain some of Jackson's letters regarding Uganda, and was not a man to neglect opportunity. He quickly marched to the capital, and in February, 1890, concluded a treaty with the king, thanks to the help of the French missionaries, who preferred even German rule to English Protestantism.[1]

The Anglo-German Agreement

This time, however, Peters was not supported by Bismarckian diplomacy. Bismarck had previously been negotiating with Lord Salisbury for the cession of Heligoland in exchange for African territory. Though Bismarck fell from power early in 1890, his successor, Caprivi, continued the bargaining, and concluded on July 1, 1890, the famous Heligoland Treaty,[2] whereby Germany obtained Heligoland, and, in exchange, gave up all claim to Uganda (thus nullifying the exploit of Peters), Zanzibar and Pemba islands, Witu (a district on the British East African coast, hitherto claimed by Germans), Nyasaland (a region which Peters had coveted, as a southwestward extension of German East Africa), and some disputed territory in western Africa, on the border between Togoland (German) and Ashanti (British).

The treaty has been described as a one-sided bargain giving England a whole suit of clothes in exchange for a trouser-

[1] Sir Harry Johnston, *The Uganda Protectorate*, I, pp. 231 ff.

[2] Hertslet, *New Map of Africa*, II, pp. 642 ff. See the secret correspondence, now published in *Die Grosse Politik*, IV, ch. 29, and VIII, ch. 51.

button. But Heligoland was more than a button, it was a useful naval base for the protection of Hamburg and Bremen, and Germany got more than Heligoland. German South West Africa was given a long and narrow extension (often called "Caprivi's finger" or the Caprivizipfel), twenty miles wide, reaching eastward to the Zambesi River, on which an outlet was much desired. German Kamerun, in West Africa, was extended to Lake Chad. And, in the east, although Germany gave up all hope of penetrating through Uganda into the Sudan, nevertheless she did extend the boundary of German East Africa westward to the great lakes (Tanganyika and Nyasa) and Congo Free State, thus barring the road which British imperialists dreamed of stretching from Cape Colony to Cairo. In pursuance of this bargain of 1890, the Germans were able to purchase from Zanzibar for about a million dollars the coast they had hitherto leased.

There were minor boundary disputes still to be settled, but for all practical purposes, the German East Africa Company was in possession of a colony almost twice as large as Germany. The colony was taken over from the company by the German government in 1897. It was Germany's richest and greatest colony. In the highlands, German settlers could find healthful homes, although by 1914 only four thousand had done so.

The German aim was to transform East Africa into a land of productive plantations, conducted by German settlers with negro labor. Huge tracts of land were granted to capitalist companies, and smaller plots to individual planters. But labor was scarce, and rather than become landless serfs the natives rose in violent rebellion in 1905, a rebellion which is said to have caused the death, either in battle or by starvation, of 120,000 natives. After that, the natives were reduced to submission, and large numbers toiled as serfs on German plantations, growing sisal, hemp, cotton, rubber, and other tropical crops. The raw cotton exports increased from less than half a ton in 1902 to about 3000 tons in 1913-14, and about 32,000 acres of cotton fields were in the hands of white planters.[1]

Although the colony had not yet become self-supporting (deficit of 6.6 million marks in 1913) and though the trade was

[1] From British Parliamentary Paper, Cmd. 1428 (1921); *cf.* Lugard, *Dual Mandate* 391-2 on the British policy.

only 89 million marks in 1913, hope ran high that the plantations would some day supply many a German factory with raw cotton and other raw materials, and that the healthful uplands would become prosperous German cattle-ranches. But such hopes were cut short by the Great War of 1914.[1]

The Uganda Affair

In the meantime, England took advantage of the treaty of 1890 by declaring protectorates over Nyasaland, Zanzibar, Pemba and Uganda. Regarding the last, at least some suggestion should be given of a very interesting history.[2] In the winter of 1890, an able British adventurer-explorer (Capt. Lugard) was sent with three hundred armed natives to offer the king of Uganda the "protection and powerful assistance" of the British East Africa Company. Mwanga's lack of interest in this magnanimous offer was converted, by threats, into acquiescence, and a treaty was signed. But there was still such intense triangular conflict among "French" Christians, "English" Christians and Mohammedans, that Lugard sought to strengthen his position by bringing in several hundred Sudanese soldiers; with them he brought in unwittingly, it is said, the dread sleeping-sickness which killed off a quarter-million Uganda negroes in the next few years. Nevertheless, the "French" faction dared rebel, and only by force was order restored.

Alarmed by the cost of incessant fighting, the British company decided to withdraw its forces from Uganda, unless it could ob-

[1] For development of these points, see A. F. Calvert, *German East Africa.* (London, 1917); H. Fonck, *Deutsch-Ostafrika* (Berlin, 1909); F. S. Joelson, *The Tanganyika Territory* (London, 1920); British annual reports on the Tanganyika mandate; British Foreign Office, *Handbook of German East Africa;* H. Meyer, *Das deutsche Kolonialreich,* I, pt. 1; *Deutsches Kolonial-Lexikon* (Leipzig, 1920), *passim; Dreissig Jahre Deutsche Kolonialpolitik* (Berlin), *passim.* The chief products of the colony in 1913 were sisal (10.3 million marks), rubber (6.6), hides and skins (5.5), raw cotton (2.4), copra (2.3). But these were rapidly increasing. The sisal exports, for instance, grew from 15 tons in 1901 to 7,000 in 1910 and 20,834 in 1913. After the area became a British mandate, by the way, the sisal output dropped to 7,923 tons in 1921 but recovered to 18,428 in 1924. Under British rule, the natives have been encouraged to grow cotton on their own land, and the crop grown by natives has increased from 1,229,099 lbs. to 5,100,000 lbs. in two years, while the crop grown by European planters has remained about 1,700,000 lbs.

[2] See Johnston, *op. cit.,* I, pp. 232 ff.; F. D. Lugard, *Rise of our East African Empire* (1893), II, chs. 1 ff.

tain financial aid from the British government. Lugard went back to England to make a "buzz" against abandoning Uganda,[1] that is to say, to write letters to the press, to make speeches, to conduct a strenuous propaganda, in favor of a government grant to the company. The Church Missionary Society was persuaded to advance a few thousand pounds to postpone the evil day of evacuation, for to missionary organizations evacuation meant abandonment of Protestant converts to either native paganism or French Catholicism. The Church's contribution, a trifling sum, could doubtless have been raised by the East Africa Company's wealthy directors, but it was shrewd tactics to obtain the funds from the church, for it presented the issue as a matter of religion and altruism. The influential London *Times* likewise gave support, by editorials appealing to British patriotism, or representing Uganda (in very exaggerated terms) as a great market without which English labor would be unemployed, or as a field for British capital. Chambers of commerce joined in the plea.[2] Every motive, political, economic, humanitarian, was urged. Abolition of the slave-trade was put forward, along with other reasons.

What the Company actually wanted was almost half a million dollars a year from the Government, to defray the cost of retaining Uganda until that troublesome possession became orderly enough to be profitable.[3] The Government, however, had caution enough to investigate the enterprise it was asked to finance, and the commissioner sent to study the East Africa Company's administration presently returned to London with the report that "the history of British East Africa for the last five years, and its present condition, show us clearly that the experiment of combining administration and trade in the same hands has proved a failure, so far as this part of Africa is concerned; and that the sooner this system is discontinued the better it will be for native races, for British commerce, for

[1] F. D. Lugard, *op. cit.*, II, p. 514.

[2] *Cf.* Lugard, *op. cit.*, ch. 15. The London Chamber of Commerce in April, 1893, said in a report, apropos of Uganda: "The uniform experience of this country from 1568 down to the present reign is that colonies amply repay the first expenditure in blood and money, and that they pay both by extension of trade and shipping and in the growth of national power and status. . . . It should be sufficient for us to know that investments of this class are invariably good in the long run."

[3] *Ibid.*, II, p. 643.

Zanzibar, and, as I believe, for the Company itself."[1] This was plain enough. The Government decided to buy out the Company's rights and properties in East Africa and Uganda.

If the establishment of British protectorates in Uganda (1894) and British East Africa (1895) was "an answer to the Church's prayer," as the Church Missionary Society described it, Providence in this case worked through somewhat devious financial negotiations. An offer of £200,000 was refused by the Company as too small a valuation of its humane and patriotic achievements. By persistent haggling, the price was raised to £250,000. Even this sum, so it is asserted, left the Company, when its affairs were liquidated, with a deficit of about £194,000. Governing East Africa and Uganda was not a profitable business, as the British Treasury learned when it was called on to pay deficits ranging usually between one and two hundred thousand pounds a year, after taking over the Company's rights. East Africa has cost the British taxpayers over sixty million dollars (in budget deficits and payments for the Uganda Railway).

Black and White in Kenya

The British and German shares of East Africa were now well marked out. Germany had gained 384,000 sq. miles; Britain 353,000 (including British East Africa, Uganda, Zanzibar and Pemba). Neither was entirely satisfied. In 1898, as part of the secret bargain described in connection with West Africa, the two Great Powers agreed to divide the Portuguese colony of Mozambique between them, Britain taking the southern part, Germany the northern, in case Portugal should be willing to sell. And when Portugal evinced no such disposition, the two drafted an agreement, in 1913, for the division of Mozambique without Portugal's consent.[2] The outbreak of the Great War occurred in time to prevent final signature of this machiavellian compact. Instead of sharing with Germany, Great Britain was able, through victory, to take German East Africa as a mandate,[3] and to treat all Portuguese Mozambique as a British sphere of economic interest.

[1] As quoted by Leonard Woolf, *Empire and Commerce in Africa*, p. 300. I am indebted to his excellent chapter on Zanzibar and East Africa for this and several other facts in this section, particularly regarding the subsidy and purchase price questions.

[2] *Cf. supra*, p. 119.

[3] *Cf. infra*, p. 498.

A small but valuable part of German East Africa, namely the densely settled highlands of Urundi-Ruanda, was handed over to Belgium when the latter claimed compensation for the service rendered by troops from Belgian Congo in conquering the German colony—such is the lofty principle on which apportionment of the "white man's burden" is often based. And an insignificant wedge on the south, the "Kionga triangle," taken from Portugal by the Germans, was restored to the former. But most of the booty, as has been said, fell to Great Britain. The bulk of German East Africa became Tanganyika Territory, a British mandate, and, while inventing new names, the British Government renamed British East Africa Kenya Colony and Protectorate (1920). The map of Africa now shows these East African possessions as part of a solid block of British territory extending unbroken from Egypt to Cape Colony. The hopes of a Cecil Rhodes and a Harry Johnston, that through East Africa there might be built an all-British Cape-to-Cairo railway, are now in a fair way to be realized.[1]

British East Africa now includes Kenya (Colony and Protectorate) and Uganda (Protectorate) and perhaps we might add the Tanganyika Territory under British mandate—a solid block connecting the Anglo-Egyptian Sudan on the north with Nyasaland and Rhodesia on the south. In area British East Africa (688,000 sq. mi.) is two-fifths larger than British West Africa, and seven times as large as the mother country. But commerce measures the success of imperialism, and the total trade of British East Africa in 1923 was only 92 million dollars, as compared with 231 for British West Africa. This discrepancy is partly due to the fact that the eastern colonies are less densely populated (14 persons per square mile as compared with 48); but it is also true that per capita the trade of West Africa is a fourth larger than that of East Africa. And although a difference of natural resources undoubtedly exists, unfortunate methods of exploitation in East Africa are probably accountable in part both for the smallness of the population and for the relatively slower economic development.

There has been so much discussion, since the war, of conditions in Kenya (British East Africa), that the single word "Kenya"

[1] *Cf.* London *Times*, July 11, 1925; also *Afrique française*, Aug., 1925, p. 388.

conjures up a whole complex of controversies. One question is whether the British administration has been justified in granting about 10,000 square miles [1] to Europeans, while only 5,000 are set apart in native reserves for nearly two million Africans. More than half the arable area has been "alienated" to Europeans. About a fifth of Kenya is an elevated tableland, suitable for white settlement; the rest is desert or unhealthy coastland. Yet there are less than two thousand European farmers in the colony and protectorate and only a small part of the alienated land is actually cultivated. This situation arose because of a policy of introducing "an aristocracy of European landowners," in the words of Sir Charles Eliot, first governor of the colony. Eliot maintained very frankly that "the interior of the Protectorate is a white man's country, and it is mere hypocrisy not to admit that white interests must be paramount, and the main object of our policy and legislation should be to found a white colony." [2]

But the success of such a policy depends on the labor supply, for the white plantation-owners do not intend to cultivate their own huge estates. Lord Delamere, for instance, had 200,000 acres. He has been described, by the way, as "the leader of the European colony" and "mentor" of Eliot and succeeding governors.[3] Concessionaires like Lord Delamere, it appears, have strongly influenced the government to aid them in solving the labor problem. One method favored by the planters has been to limit the native reserves so drastically that the natives will be compelled to become "labour tenants on European farms." [4] Another expedient is the hut tax, first levied in 1901 at two rupees (about 60 cents) a hut, then increased gradually to sixteen shillings (four dollars), but later reduced to twelve shillings. This, in the opinion of Governor Sir Percy Girouard, "is the only method of compelling the native to leave his reserve for the purpose of seeking work. Only in this way can the cost of living be increased for the native." [5]

The average native has to work three or four months a year

[1] N. Leys, *Kenya*, pp. 79, 144. This figure includes 5,500 sq. mi. of leaseholds, 2,000 of freehold, and 2,500 promised but not registered. *Cf.* Lugard, *Dual Mandate*, pp. 324, 329; and Woolf, *op. cit.*, pp. 337-351.

[2] Eliot, *East African Protectorate*, pp. 105 and 310, cited by Lugard.

[3] Leys, *op. cit.*, p. 119.

[4] Lugard, *op. cit.*, pp. 324-6.

[5] Leys, *op. cit.*, pp. 186, 197.

to pay the hut and poll taxes for himself and dependents, for wages are as low as eight shillings a month for ordinary labor. Still only about 140,000 natives are employed, and this very inadequate number can hardly be much increased except by medical and economic measures which would increase the population, or by importing contract labor. The latter alternative suggests another of the burning questions in Kenya. Thousands of laborers were brought in from India to build and operate the Uganda railroad; they were followed by other thousands who engaged either in manual labor or in trade; and soon the Indians were demanding equality with the whites. The latter, however, were determined to keep the highlands for themselves, to restrict Asiatic immigration, and to control the government. The controversy on these points became so furious that it was brought before the Imperial Conference of the British Empire in 1921. Since then the affair has gone through a history too intricate to recount here; but the whites seem to have carried their points regarding the restriction of immigration, in practice, and the white monopoly of the highlands, while concessions were made to the political demands of the Indians. The 23,000 Indians in Kenya now have five representatives in the Legislative Council, but the latter is controlled by the elected and official white members.[1]

France in Madagascar

Up to this point we have left France out of the account, because France was interested not so much in the eastern coast as in the great island of Madagascar, about a thousand miles long and larger than France itself, which lies 240 miles off the East African coast. In the days of Richelieu and Colbert, the French East India Company of the seventeenth century had been interested in this island, then called Eastern France (*La France orientale*), but the French colonists had been massacred and French claims became a vague tradition, while English missionaries labored on the island converting the natives to

[1] *Cf.* Lugard, *Dual Mandate*, pp. 317-23; Leys, *Kenya*, 344-51; S. Rice, "The Indian Question in Kenya," *Foreign Affairs*, Dec., 1923, pp. 258-69; *Parl. Papers*, Cmd., 1922 (1923). On labor conditions in the mandate area see British reports on *Labour in the Tanganyika Territory*, Colonial No. 18 and No. 19, 1926.

Christianity, teaching them to read and write and to use the plow, and, in a word, forging a bond of union between Madagascar and England. The French, however, still cherished their historic claims. As one Frenchman remarked, "History, tradition, *and much imagination,* had created between Madagascar and us such bonds as no statesman could neglect."[1] The hope of profit has ever been a potent stimulus to imagination, and in this case a French explorer's exuberant description of the immense wealth of the island recalled to French statesmen the historic rights of France.

At this time, in the 1870's, Madagascar was a kingdom ruled with considerable intelligence and vigor by a queen belonging to the Hova tribe, the lightest in color and the most gifted of the Malagasy tribes who inhabited the island. The Malagasy, it should be explained, appear to be a mixed race derived chiefly not, as one would expect, from the African negro, but from the Pacific islands, with an admixture of Arab and negro strains. Barbarous in their social customs they may have been, and idolatrous in religion, disinclined to unnecessary toil and disregardful of human life; but their skill in terracing and irrigating their rice-fields, their artistic weaving and metal-work, and their readiness to adopt European innovations placed them far above the negro of the African jungle. In fact, their native queen seemed in a fair way to obtain general recognition for her government as a semi-civilized and sovereign state, when the French intervened.[2]

In the early 1880's France used a dispute with the Hova Queen as a pretext for sending a "punitive expedition" and reviving an old claim to a protectorate over the northwestern part of the island. The punitive expedition proved so successful that France was able to force upon the Queen a treaty recognizing her sovereignty but giving France control of her foreign relations, an indemnity of ten million francs, and the port of Diego Suarez (1885).[3] And now Madagascar enters the tangled web of African bargains. To obtain recognition for her "protectorate," in 1890, France recognized the English and German

[1] C. de Freycinet, *Souvenirs*, 1878-1893 (Paris, 1914), p. 268. *Cf.* M. Petit, *Les Colonies Françaises*, II, pp. 117-24.

[2] See Petit, *Les Colonies Françaises*, II, pp. 81-117.

[3] *Cf. Documents Diplomatiques: Affaires de Madagascar*, 1883, 1884, 1886. Also, Dubois et Terrier, *op. cit.*, pp. 707-753.

acquisitions in East Africa, and, to boot, made some concession to British aims in western Africa.[1]

As yet the task of France was hardly begun. The Hova Queen, too proud for mild submission, continually disregarded the protectorate, while her subjects, if French authorities may be trusted, showed their hostility to European domination by murders, thefts, and other outrages. Perhaps such charges should be taken *cum grano salis,* for European powers intent on conquest have rarely failed to find native atrocities to punish. At any rate, a new "punitive expedition" was sent from France, and after a hundred million francs had been spent and the lives of six thousand French soldiers (victims of fever) and 1140 French colonial soldiers sacrificed in breaking the will of the defiant Queen, the French protectorate was forced upon Madagascar.[2]

But for such sacrifices more than a sentimental compensation was required by French merchants. French trade, the *raison d'être* of French imperialism, must be given a monopoly. When France, however, announced the establishment of a tariff giving preference to French goods, there came a sharp protest from Lord Salisbury, British foreign minister, who stoutly maintained that by international law and by special treaty rights British traders were entitled to equal rights. The United States, too, had treaty rights to be considered.

With admirable ingenuity the learned historian Hanotaux, then directing French diplomacy, discovered that by annexing the island to France such treaty rights could be neatly evaded, and accordingly the native queen whom France had undertaken to protect was unceremoniously packed off to another island, Madagascar was annexed to France (1896), and French goods entering Madagascar were exempted from all import duties, while foreign goods were excluded by prohibitive duties.[3] Competent British historians assert that the French policy of monopoly was carried even so far as the issuance of orders to the natives to do business only with their new masters, disloyalty to whom might be punished with imprisonment in irons.[4] Such

[1] Hertslet, *New Map of Africa*, pp. 571 and 985.

[2] *Cf.* Dubois et Terrier, *op. cit.*, pp. 753 ff.

[3] *Ibid.*, pp. 767 ff.

[4] W. H. Dawson, in *Cambridge History of British Foreign Policy,* III, p. 221.

measures killed American trade with the island, and reduced British imports from £179,000 to £42,000 in a single year. France henceforth supplied the Malagasy with machinery and tools, "beverages" and cotton goods for the masculine loincloths and feminine aprons and inevitable lambas (toga-like wraps) affected by the natives. In return the French take the cattle and hides, the gold dust, the rice, produced on the island.

In passing, we may note that in Madagascar the "civilizing mission" of Europe is more genuine than in Central Africa. Not only have the natives progressed in industry, but compulsory education, practically unheard of across the Mozambique Channel, has been introduced, a hundred and forty thousand brown children are at this moment in public schools learning to read and write their native language, and one out of nine natives attends a Christian church. Oddly enough, however, the conversion of the natives has been the work more of the British missionaries, without governmental favor, than of the French masters of the island.[1]

Italy in Somaliland

A word more about Italian interests and we shall have done with the hot eastern coastlands of Africa. Just at the time when Great Britain, Germany and France were dividing East Africa among themselves, Premier Crispi of Italy was permitting himself to enjoy the seductive vision of an Italian empire stretching from barren Somali coasts on the Indian Ocean to the likewise barren coast of Eritrea on the Red Sea, with the mountain empire of Abyssinia included between them, as a jewel unworthily set in prongs of valueless brass. With Somaliland alone we are now concerned, as part of the East African littoral, for Abyssinia's history is linked with that of northern Africa and the Sudan. To the long Somali coast, stretching for twelve hundred miles northward from British East Africa to the easternmost tip of the continent at Cape Guardafui, Signor Crispi laid claim in the year 1889. So extensive and sudden a claim was made possible by the fortunate discovery of a certain Signor Filonardi, Italian consul at Zanzibar, that the chieftains

[1] On present conditions see *Afrique française*, Jan., 1925, supplement No. 1.

or "sultans" of the coast cherished an ardent desire for Italian protection. The annoying fact that at least part of this littoral belonged to Zanzibar was easily disposed of in 1892 by an arrangement with Great Britain, protector of Zanzibar; Italy leased the coast (the so-called Benadir Coast) for an annual rent of 160,000 rupees.[1]

As the reward of his enterprising patriotism, Signor Filonardi obtained, for a company which he organized and controlled, the privilege of governing and exploiting the newly acquired lands, while the Italian Government retained the privilege of paying the annual rent to Zanzibar and an annual subsidy to Filonardi's company. Despite subsidies, the company was so unsuccessful that a few years later the government entrusted to a new company, for fifty years, all rights over soil and minerals (if found), the power to collect taxes and conduct the administration, and an annual subsidy of about 200,000 lire in addition to the rent due Zanzibar. Could there be a more striking example of imperialism conducted for private profit at public loss?[2] Yet the Italian company was not at all unique; subsidized commercial companies were the almost invariable rule in African empire-building between 1880 and 1900. The Italian company further resembled its German, French and British compeers in proving inadequate to its task, and as the British and German East African companies had ultimately transferred their holdings to their governments, so also the Italian Benadir Company yielded to Rome, in 1905. Since then Italian taxpayers have more or less cheerfully, because unwittingly, paid several million lire a year to meet the deficits on a colony largely desert, while a private company headed by His Royal Highness the Duke of Abruzzi invested millions in the irrigation of a small area for agricultural colonization.

In later years the hope of raising cotton in Somaliland, especially in the Juba valley, stimulated new interest in the country. Moreover, in July 1924, Italy obtained from Great Britain—in fulfilment of article thirteen[3] of the London Pact of 1915—a strip of 33,000 square miles on the western bank of the Juba,

[1] Convention between Italy and Zanzibar, Aug. 12, 1892; *State Papers*, 84, p. 630.

[2] Woolf, *Empire and Commerce in Africa*, pp. 174-8.

[3] Whereby the Allies promised compensation to Italy in Africa if they should annex the German colonies.

formerly part of British East Africa.[1] Thus more potential cotton land was secured. In 1925 it was announced, also, that the Fascist governor of Somaliland had begun the military occupation of the sultanates of Obbia and Mijertins, in northern Somaliland, which had remained practically independent. It was about this region that an Italian foreign minister, Tittoni, said in 1904: "I do not anticipate any future for Italian Northern Somaliland, which consists in a great measure of unproductive sands."[2]

[1] Cmd. 2194 (1924).

[2] Tittoni, *Italy's Foreign and Colonial Policy*, p. 240. Compare P. d'Agostino Orsini di Camerota, *Espansionismo italiano odierno* (Salerno, 1923), on the resources and prospects of Somaliland.

CHAPTER VIII

A CLIMAX—IN THE SUDAN

The Setting for the Struggle

The melodramatic clash between the imperial projects of France, Britain and Italy in Abyssinia and the eastern Sudan is a natural sequel—one might say a climax—to the events which have unfolded themselves in the preceding chapters. Nowhere did visions of empire struggle for mastery with a greater intensity of conflict or a more colorful wealth of spectacular incident.

For France, the eastern Sudan and Abyssinia would provide the keystone of the edifice which bold-visioned architects of empire had been patiently constructing. In West Africa, as we have seen, isolated coast colonies had been made to serve as portals to a vast inland dominion, in the western Sudan, which in turn could be connected through the Sahara (at least in appearance on the map) with the French colonies of Algeria and Tunis on the Mediterranean coast. To complete the realization of their dream, French imperialists needed only a few million square miles in the Eastern Sudan, the Nile valley, and Abyssinia. These secured, the French empire would stretch from the Atlantic ocean to the Red Sea, from the Mediterranean to the Gulf of Guinea. All Africa north of the equator would be French, with the exception of foreign enclaves, here and there along the coasts. Such was the hope which in the early 1890's dazzled the eyes of French pioneers, of the Comité de l'Afrique française, and of statesmen.

There were obstacles, to be sure. A negligent and somewhat timid French cabinet had allowed England, in 1882, to occupy Egypt; but France had never accepted the British occupation as definitive, and French opinion found comfort in Mr. Gladstone's pledge that the British had not entered Egypt to stay. The upper Nile valley, known as the eastern or Egyptian Sudan, was held by fierce Arab tribesmen, and Abyssinia's hardy moun-

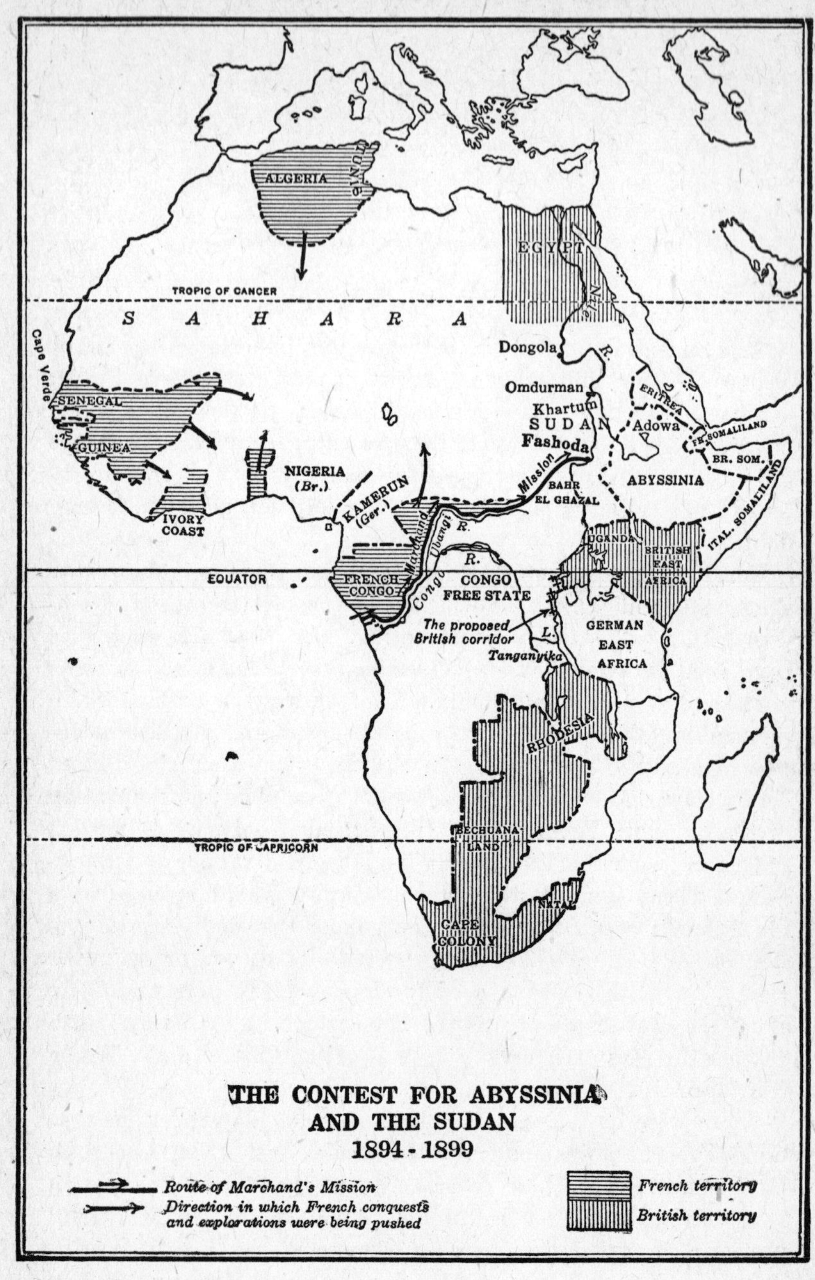

THE CONTEST FOR ABYSSINIA AND THE SUDAN 1894 - 1899

taineers would not be easily conquered, but, at any rate, no rival European power had possession. And France had at least a foothold in the east, on the Gulf of Aden, from which possibly French empire-builders might penetrate Abyssinia and join hands across the Nile with their co-workers from French West Africa.

This foothold, it may as well be explained now, was French Somaliland. Here a whole town (Obock) had been purchased for the surprisingly small sum of 50,000 francs, from a local sultan many years before (in 1862), and forgotten until 1883, when, the English having closed Aden to French ships during the Tonkin war,[1] the French decided to establish a naval base of their own here, and voted a subsidy of 450,000 francs a year for the development of the place. But the sandy roadstead of Obock was so ill-suited to the purposes of a harbor, that in 1888 the French took Jibuti, a nearby town with better prospects, and from Jibuti planned to build a railway across Abyssinia to the Nile. Need one add that railways are the steel girders of empire?[2]

Abyssinia, however, was coveted by Italian imperialists, whose modest aspiration was to carve off the eastern tip of Africa, including Abyssinia and its adjoining coastlands, as an Italian empire, small beside that of France or England, but satisfying to national pride. Beginning, naturally, on the coasts, the Italians hoped to push into the Abyssinian hinterland. As far back as 1870, an enterprising Italian shipowner, Rubattino by name, had paid about nine thousand dollars (provided by the government) to a local "sultan" for the town of Assab, on the Red Sea coast, intending there to establish a coaling station for his vessels. But fearing that the natives might oppose his taking possession of his purchase, Rubattino prudently refrained from occupying it, until, in 1880, an imperialist cabinet at Rome was ready to send a warship to help him. Encouraged by England for reasons that will presently appear, the Italian government now proceeded to install garrisons in neighboring towns, occupying several hundred miles of hot and sandy coast with a haste inspired partly by fear that France or Russia might take

[1] *Cf.* p. 315.

[2] Jean Darcy, *Cent Années de rivalité coloniale* (Paris, 1904), pp. 364-396; *cf.* G. Poydenot, *Obock* (Paris, 1889); Dubois et Terrier, *Un Siècle d'expansion coloniale* (Paris, 1902), pp. 677-87.

it, if given time. Soon the Italians came into conflict with the Abyssinians. An Italian garrison was slaughtered by Abyssinian soldiers. As the reader must be aware, nothing so stimulates imperialism as the killing of Europeans by natives. Furious for revenge, the Italian parliament voted five million dollars for a punitive expedition, and a strong army was prepared to fight Abyssinia.[1] But before proceeding with the drama, it will be well to set the stage more completely.

When African or Asiatic territory is being acquired, England is not often willing to be left out of account. In this case, British imperialists had a vital interest in thwarting French aspirations and encouraging Italy. On the bulk of Abyssinia, Britain had no designs; it could safely be left to Italy, more safely than to aggressive France. But in the fate of the eastern Sudan the British had a most compelling interest. Though a Gladstone might have promised to evacuate Egypt, imperialists from 1882 onward considered the Nile valley won, and ambitious empire-builders dreamed of connecting Cairo, in Egypt, with Cape Colony, in South Africa, by a railway system running through a solid band of British territory. In such a system, the upper valley of the Nile, that is, the eastern or Egyptian Sudan, would be an indispensable link.

The Sudan, it may be recalled, is the vast belt of African territory stretching from east to west, between the Sahara and the equatorial jungle region. The eastern part of the Sudan includes not only the swamp-bordered reaches of the Upper Nile and its tributaries, but great areas of fertile upland, dense forests, and, by contrast, the steppe countries of Kordofan and Darfur, and the Nubian and Libyan deserts—in all nearly a million square miles. Lying wholly within the tropics, where according to an Arab saying "the soil is like fire and the wind like a flame," the Sudan is obviously not a field for European colonization; its very name indicates its nature—"the country of the blacks" (Bildad-es-Sudan).

It was the "Nubia" or "Ethiopia" which ancient Egyptian emperors conquered, and from which they brought black Nubian captives and slaves. In more recent times, nomadic Arabs had pitched their tents in its steppes and desert oases, or plied their

[1] Woolf, *Empire and Commerce in Africa*, pp. 153 ff.; Darcy, *op cit.*, pp. 370-3; C. de la Jonquière, *Les Italiens en Erythrée*.

trades in its village bazaars, and more than one intruding race had mingled its blood with that of the negro masses. During the nineteenth century Egypt had once more sent troops up the Nile to conquer the "Egyptian" Sudan. Against this Egyptian aggression hot resentment was cherished by Arab slave-traders, whose profitable business was destroyed by the edicts of English and German adventurers employed as officials by Egypt. Taxes, too, were levied with a rigor that could not fail to provoke rebellion.

In such fertile soil the seeds of religious fanaticism were sowed by Mohammed Ahmed, who claimed to be the divinely inspired "Mahdi" (guide) appointed to revive Mohammedanism and expel European and Egyptian. With followers (called "dervishes") recruited from the natives, but chiefly from Arab tribesmen, the Mahdi in 1881 began his career of conquest. An Egyptian army sent against him was utterly annihilated. Soon the power of the Mahdi had waxed so great that Gladstone, who had sent British forces to occupy Egypt in 1882 and thereby had assumed a measure of responsibility for the Egyptian Sudan, decided to evacuate the latter and sent Gordon to arrange the withdrawal of Egyptians and Europeans. In vain efforts to placate the dervishes, Gordon recognized the Mahdi as sultan of a part of the Sudan, promised that the remainder should be given independence under the rule of a notorious slave-trader, and offered to permit the Arabs to resume their vicious traffic in negroes. Ominously the dervish forces closed in on Gordon and his handful of troops, at Khartum.

Frantic were the appeals Gordon sent to England for reinforcement. Help was sent to him by Gladstone's order, after painful vacillation. But it was too late. On January 25, 1885, Khartum was captured and Gordon killed by the dervishes.

Thenceforth the Egyptian Sudan was in the hands of the dervishes, and was ruled, after the Mahdi's death, by his successor the Khalifa (lieutenant) Abdulla. Worse than the slave trade were the evils endured by the Sudan under the misrule of this Arab despot; fire and sword, plague and starvation decimated the population. But England hesitated to intervene. Imperialism is rarely active against a formidable foe. Therefore the Sudan remained actually independent, albeit British diplomats might perhaps revive in British interests the defunct claims of Egypt to this lost dependency. The French, however, viewed the Sudan as a prize to be taken by him who could first lay hand upon it.[1]

France Thwarts British Plans

The drama now begins. The English, unwilling to undertake the conquest of the Sudan, yet fearful lest France might gain in Abyssinia a base of operations against the Sudan, decided to use Italy as a pawn in the complicated international chess-game. Italy was to be encouraged in a desire for Abyssinia, to forestall France.

It so happened that in the year 1889, Menelik, one of the local chieftains or "kings" in Abyssinia was scheming to usurp the imperial throne of the *negus negusti,* or king of kings of Abyssinia. To this aspirant for imperial greatness, the Italians furnished five thousand Remington rifles, and toward his designs they showed a benevolence not wholly disinterested, for Menelik was persuaded in recognition of their amiability to sign a treaty of friendship, the celebrated Treaty of Ucciali[2] (May 2, 1889), granting to Italy an extension of Eritrea back into the Abyssinian highlands, and stating, in article 17, that "His Majesty the King of Kings of Ethiopia (i.e. Abyssinia) *shall be at liberty to* avail himself of the government of His Majesty the King of Italy for the treatment of all questions concerning other Powers and Governments." This was an innocent enough sentence in the Ethiopian or Amharic text, but the Italian version instead of using the phrase meaning "shall be at liberty to," employed the word *consents* (*consente*). For a nation to consent to let another power conduct its foreign relations is, in common international usage, to accept a protectorate, and so it was interpreted by the Italian premier, Signor Crispi, who notified the European powers that their dealings with Abyssinia would henceforth be conducted in Rome.[3] As soon as Menelik discovered this neat Italian trick, he protested and denounced the treaty. Nor could the Italian diplomacy persuade "the lion of the Tribe of Judah" to acquiesce in such humiliation.

[1] *Cambridge History of British Foreign Policy,* III, pp. 176-84.

[2] *State Papers,* 81, p. 733; *Trattati e convenzione tra il regno d'Italia e gli stati esteri* (Turin), 12, p. 77.

[3] *Staatsarchiv,* 51, no. 10047.

Though Menelik might be opposed to an Italian protectorate, England was less unreasonable. In 1891 the British government signed two conventions with Italy, drawing a "line of demarcation in East Africa between the spheres of influence respectively reserved to Great Britain and Italy," and leaving to Italy all of Abyssinia as far west as the meridian 35° East of Greenwich. It is significant that this line safeguarded for England the Egyptian Sudan, including the valley of the White Nile and most of the Blue Nile, a generous territorial corridor leading from Egypt to Uganda and East Africa, a necessary link in the Cape-to-Cairo chain of possessions. In what way the diplomats of England and Italy, two of the six European Great Powers, were entitled to sit down at a table and mark out on the map vast areas as spheres of influence "reserved" for themselves, is a question which may be left for the subtle juristic mind. To the historian, the point of interest is that in Paris this Anglo-Italian arrangement was considered altogether high-handed and unjustifiable.[1]

Curiously enough, the conventions of 1891 were ignored in France, though they had been made public in England, until the spring of 1894, when the publication of a less important supplementary Anglo-Italian agreement brought them to the attention of French imperialists.[2] Two other events, occurring almost simultaneously, heightened French indignation. One of these events, the acquisition of Uganda by Great Britain, has been described.[3] The other event was the signature (May 12, 1894) of an agreement between England and King Leopold of Belgium, by which the latter, as sovereign of Congo Free State, received a lease of the Bahr-el-Ghazal district (in the southeastern part of the Egyptian Sudan) in return for a perpetual lease of a corridor of territory, 25 kilometers wide, running from Lake Albert Edward to Lake Tanganyika.[4] To grasp the significance of these arrangements, the reader should study the accompanying map, bearing in mind the British Cape-to-Cairo project and the French Cape Verde-to-Somaliland project. The British had by this time pushed their frontiers north from Cape Colony

[1] *State Papers*, 83, p. 19; 86, p. 55. *Cf.* also Dubois et Terrier, *op. cit.*, pp. 687-95; Darcy, *op. cit.*, pp. 376-9.

[2] Woolf, *op. cit.*, pp. 170-2, 221-7.

[3] *Supra*, p. 128.

[4] *State Papers*, 86, p. 19.

to Lake Tanganyika; the corridor leased to them by King Leopold would enable them to establish communications, running between Congo Free State and German East Africa, as far north as Uganda; Uganda in turn was now British; and by the Anglo-Italian conventions the Sudanese territory extending north from Uganda to Egypt was a British "sphere of influence." In short, the last gaps were being filled in, to complete the Cape-to-Cairo empire.

French imperialists, to their chagrin and amazement, could see the British plan working itself out before their eyes. And its success meant that the French dream of ocean-to-ocean empire was shattered. The disappointment was all the more maddening, because the Bahr-el-Ghazal, leased to King Leopold, had been regarded by the French as the next addition to their own dominions in equatorial Africa; they had just extended French Congo inland into the central Sudan, connecting it with French West Africa, and were now ready to push their undefined eastern frontier into the Nile valley.[1] In May, 1893, President Carnot had told Col. Monteil that Fashoda had been selected as the proper outlet on the Nile for French Upper Ubangi.[2]

To checkmate England, the French took two moves. First, they protested vehemently against the Anglo-Belgian treaty. "This treaty," said Gabriel Hanotaux, French foreign minister (speech of June 7, 1894), "puts the Congo Free State in a state of conflict, peaceful if you please, but nevertheless conflict, with the powers that signed at its cradle; it is in formal contradiction with the international law of Africa." And at the end of his speech, with the unanimous approval of the Chamber of Deputies, he announced that he would ask a vote of 1,800,000 francs to take necessary measures on the Upper Ubangi-that is, on the eastern frontier of French Congo. The Chamber approved, to a man.

M. Delcassé, who had been undersecretary for the colonies in 1892-3 when the unfulfilled plan of seizing Fashoda was formed, was now secretary, and the plan was revived. French forces were immediately concentrated in French Congo, and a cele-

[1] Darcy, *op. cit.*, pp. 380-6. Robert de Caix, *Fachoda* (1899), p. 106; Dubois et Terrier, *op. cit.*, pp. 633-6.

[2] Col. P. L. Monteil, *Souvenirs vécus, Quelques feuillets de l'histoire coloniale* (Paris, 1924), p. 67, *cf.* also pp. 65-72, 110-4.

brated empire-builder, Col. Monteil, was sent from France to take charge of them.[1] It was easy to perceive that the French government did not intend to permit the Bahr-el-Ghazal and Upper Nile to be divided by England and Leopold, when neither had accomplished the "effective occupation" prescribed by the Berlin Act of 1885.

The excitement regarding this English Congo treaty was not confined to France. Secret documents now published[2] show that the Berlin government was likewise disturbed, for article 3, giving England a corridor between Congo and German East Africa, might prevent that German colony from serving as a commercial outlet for eastern Congo. Germany joined with France in protesting to England and to Leopold.

A grave international crisis had arisen. Even Russia, Italy and Austria-Hungary were concerned. But on June 16 King Leopold agreed, and the next day England consented, to conciliate Germany by cancelling article 3. With this victory Berlin was content. France, finding herself deserted by Germany before the Bahr-el-Ghazal question was settled, continued her own diplomatic action, until on August 14, 1894,[3] King Leopold signed a treaty limiting the northern expansion of the Congo Free State to the M'Bomu River (about 5° North) and renouncing in favor of France the country north of 5° 30′ N. and west of 30° E.[4] That is to say, Leopold would occupy only a very small part (which became known as the Lado Enclave) of the large area he had leased; the larger part of the Bahr-el-Ghazal would be left to France.[5]

The imperial road to the Upper Nile was still open for France. Great was the jubilation in Paris. French orators flamboyantly boasted that the British dream of possessing the whole Nile was forever destroyed. The French missions which were to have

[1] Monteil, *Souvenirs vécus*, 110-114. Monteil's orders were modified in August, when France came to an agreement with Leopold, and the whole plan was again checked.

[2] *Die Grosse Politik*, 8, Nos. 2030-2072.

[3] *Ibid.*, Nos. 2061, 2066, 2069; *cf.* Bourgeois et Pagès, *Les Origines et les responsabilités de la grande guerre* (Paris, 1921), pp. 245-8.

[4] Martens, *Nouveau recueil général de traités*, 2d series, 20, p. 702.

[5] Subsequently the French renounced this region, in 1899, and Leopold reasserted his claims, but without avail. By an agreement with England, May 9, 1906, the lease of 1894 was cancelled, with the exception that the Lado Enclave would be retained by Leopold during his reign. It was transferred to the Anglo-Egyptian Sudan in 1910. See *State Papers*, 99, p. 173; 107, p. 34[illegible].

seized the disputed area in the Upper Nile were checked by new orders from Paris in August, 1894.

Curiously enough, by the way, rumors about the expeditions reached London the next year, and in reply to a question in Parliament, Sir Edward Grey, under-secretary for Foreign Affairs, made an impromptu speech (March 28, 1895) publicly and emphatically warning France that the whole Nile valley was a British sphere of influence, and that the advance of any French expedition, marching under secret orders, into this region would be "an unfriendly act." This, in the language of diplomacy, meant a threat of war. Then Grey went out to his cottage in Hampshire, to prune his roses.[1]

Italy's Defeat in Abyssinia

The second step taken by France was to cultivate the friendship of Menelik, the ambitious Abyssinian emperor. Menelik, it will be recalled, had at first been the friend of Italy, but had grown suspicious of Italy's good faith when the Treaty of Ucciali was interpreted by Crispi to mean an Italian protectorate over Abyssinia. Menelik denounced the treaty in 1893. French diplomats fanned his hot anger, encouraged him to resist Italian aggression, while French officers trained his army, and French arms and ammunition were supplied to his soldiers. Also, a French company secured a concession to build a railway from the French port of Jibuti, through Abyssinia, to the Nile (1894).

Meanwhile the Italians attempted to assert by force of arms their claim to suzerainty over that country.[2] In 1895 Italian

[1] *Cf.* Viscount Grey of Fallodon, *Twenty-five Years* (New York, 1925), I, p. 19. Mr. Woolf (*op. cit.* p. 188), following Darcy (*op. cit.*, p. 411), interprets the cancellation of Monteil's orders as the result of Grey's warning. But the result occurred in August, 1894, and the cause in March, 1895, as Monteil's *Souvenirs*, p. 114, clearly show. Mr. Dawson, in *Cambridge History of British Foreign Policy*, III, p. 251, represents France as giving Monteil and Marchand their orders "some time prior to the conclusion of the Convention of August 14th" (1894) "in spite of" Grey's warning (1895). In fact, Marchand did not receive his historic mission in 1894; rather, on February 24, 1896, Marchand, then in Paris, persuaded Premier Bourgeois to let him revive the project which had been confided to Monteil in 1894. (Monteil, *Souvenirs*, p. 121; Mangin, *Regards sur la France d'Afrique*, pp. 236-7; Rouget, *L'Expansion coloniale au Congo français*, p. 123.)

[2] On the somewhat tangled and very secret skein of diplomacy, reaching from Rome to Berlin and London, in connection with this Italian maneuver, one should consult the interesting documents in *Die Grosse Politik*, 8, espe-

armies invaded the Abyssinian province of Tigre adjoining Italian Eritrea. Menelik did not at first give battle; he preferred to wait until he had assembled an army of ninety thousand Abyssinians, many of whom had been trained by the French and equipped through French courtesy with modern rifles and artillery.[1] Then, in the famous battle of Adowa, March 1, 1896, Menelik routed two small Italian armies, each about five thousand strong. It was more than a defeat. Two Italian generals were captured, with more than two thousand of their troops, and more than six thousand were killed or wounded. It was a disaster. In Italy it caused such dismay that the Crispi cabinet was forced out of office, and the Abyssinian venture abandoned.

The new Italian premier, Marquis Rudini, told Prince von Bülow confidentially that he would like to withdraw from Africa entirely. Italy was "too weak and poor" to undertake colonial expansion. "As long as Italy has colonies, there will always be ambitious officers who will try to win new laurels there. Every engagement involves another and demands new sacrifices of men and money. The military expeditions to Africa were not only ruining Italian finances but disorganizing the Italian army."[2] In this frame of mind Italy made peace with Abyssinia. Italy paid Menelik an indemnity of about two million dollars, recognized his "absolute independence," and relinquished the province which Italian forces had occupied.[3]

Perhaps this disaster averted one even more serious. The German secret documents show that before the battle of Adowa there was some danger that France and Russia might take up arms to prevent Italy from conquering Abyssinia. Russia was keenly interested and prominent in the Abyssinian negotiations, partly because of traditional sympathy with the legended kingdom of Prester John, partly because of motives which the German chancellor keenly described in a dispatch to Bülow: "Abyssinia has been made popular in Russia as a legend, yet behind the legend hides a real aim. . . . The idea of extending Abys-

cially Nos. 2002, 2010, 2013; 11, p. 213. Germany was actively endeavoring to win favor in London for Italian plans in Abyssinia, which since 1894 had gone too far for the British. The latter were reluctant to permit Italy to use Zeila as a base, or to embroil them too seriously with France.

[1] *Die Grosse Politik*, 11, p. 213; Woolf, *op. cit.*, p. 187.

[2] *Ibid.*, 11, No. 2794.

[3] *State Papers*, 88, p. 481.

sinia to the coast under Russian protectorate, and making it a Russian base, such as England has in such number, on the sea route to Eastern Asia, has gained new significance especially since the piercing of the Isthmus of Suez."[1] Of course such Russian plans might not harmonize perfectly with French designs, but at least both France and Russia were in accord against Italy.

In fact, the peril was grave enough so that the German chancellor, von Hohenlohe, on February 13, 1896, warned the Italian ambassador that "A naval war of Italy against Russia and France on account of Abyssinia would not be a *casus foederis* for the Triple Alliance." He repeated: "A European war with the aim of enabling Italy to conquer Abyssinia would not be understood or receive assent in either Germany or Austria." A day or two later he had to reiterate, "The Triple Alliance is a conservative pact, not an acquisitive company." (*Der Dreibund ist ein pacte conservatoire, keine Erwerbsgesellschaft.*[2])

After Italy was defeated, the German Emperor pointed out to the British ambassador how mistaken England was not to have supported Italy, in view of the threat which Franco-Russian schemes in Abyssinia might offer to British route to India.[3] Although Lord Salisbury replied that he had always thought the Italian enterprise in Abyssinia a mistake,[4] the British Cabinet presently decided, "at the request of Egypt,"[5] to send a division of troops from Egypt up the Nile to Dongola, ostensibly to aid the Italians at Kassala (about 500 miles from Dongola!).[6]

A French Flag at Fashoda

The scene now shifts to the Upper Nile Valley, the Egyptian Sudan. This region, still under the despotic rule of the dervishes, was the goal of rival British and French desires. Italy being eliminated, the principals faced each other. Hardly had the news of Italy's defeat at Adowa been received, as we have seen, when orders were sent from London to Kitchener—the English officer who at that time was Sirdar or commander of

[1] *Die Grosse Politik*, 11, No. 2766.
[2] *Ibid.*, Nos. 2765, 2766.
[3] *Ibid.*, No. 2770.
[4] *Ibid.*, No. 2773.
[5] So it was announced. *Ibid.*, 2696. Egypt was under British control.
[6] *Cf.* W. S. Blunt, *My Diaries*, I, pp. 271-85; Hansard, 4th series, 32, cols. 1027-9.

the Egyptian army—instructing him to advance south from Egypt and occupy Dongola in the Egyptian Sudan. Kitchener proceeded, but the Sudan is a large place, and the methodical Sirdar's pace was slow, for he insisted on building a railway as he went, to ensure his communications with his base of supplies. Kitchener's caution was the opportunity of France.

In February, 1896, just before England ordered Kitchener into the Sudan, the empire builders at Paris decided to dispatch Captain Marchand, an intrepid French explorer, to lead an expedition from the French Congo, straight across the heart of Africa, into the Nile valley. Simultaneously two other French officers were ordered to start with an expedition from Abyssinia, to meet Marchand on the Nile. Menelik, in a helpful spirit of cooperation, supplied five thousand Abyssinians to join in the march on the Nile. The race was on, between the tortoise and the hare, or rather the hares; between Kitchener and his French rivals. And the prize was a million square miles.

There are few exploits in history more thrilling than that of the French explorer Marchand.[1] Boldly starting from French Congo, on the western coast of Africa, with a mere handful of men—nine officers, a dozen French subalterns, and not quite two hundred natives—he plunged into the unexplored wilderness. Through dense forests this little band had to thread its way, often using axes to clear the path; when they could, they packed their provisions on a steamboat (which was carried in parts on the backs of negro porters); then through dismal swamps they passed, braving fever and hunger. From the natives they purchased goodwill with cloth, beads, cotton wire, etc. Almost two years it took them to traverse the five thousand kilometers of their route. It was as long a journey as from New York to San Francisco, but through trackless tropical lands.

The journey's end came in July 10, 1898, when Marchand reached the village of Fashoda, on the Nile, and hoisted the tricolor over an old Egyptian fort. Happily he celebrated the national holiday, July 14. But as days passed, and his scouts could find no trace of the stronger French columns that were to have met him, his exultation gave way to alarm. The Franco-

[1] *Cf.* Mangin, *Regards sur la France d'Afrique*, 237 ff.; Monteil, *Souvenirs vécus*, 122 ff.; Rouget, *op. cit.*, p. 126 ff.; Castellani, *Marchand l'Africain.*

Abyssinian expeditions from the east had failed; one because it had no boats to cross the rivers and swamps, another because of fever. But Marchand held fast at Fashoda, and made a treaty with a local chief for a French protectorate over the left bank of the Nile.

Meanwhile Kitchener had been slowly pushing southward. It had taken him more than two years, and he was still in the northern part of the Sudan, fighting dervishes. Not until September, 1898, did he win the decisive victory of Omdurman, in which he slew twenty thousand dervishes. Entering Khartum, where Gordon had been killed, he avenged the events of 1886 by scattering the Mahdi's ashes.

When he learned that a French expedition had taken possession of the Nile, five hundred miles farther south, Kitchener took part of his army and made haste to Fashoda, to find Marchand and his tricolor. Marchand went aboard Kitchener's ship, and with polite irony welcomed him "in the name of France." Kitchener congratulated Marchand on his remarkable journey and announced that he would hoist the British and Egyptian flags in token of Anglo-Egyptian sovereignty, whereat Marchand pointed out that the tricolor was already floating over Fashoda. Kitchener courteously called attention to the numerical superiority of his own troops; Marchand retorted that he would be buried in the ruins of his fort rather than lower the tricolor without orders from Paris. Reluctant to precipitate a great European war by attacking Marchand, Kitchener decided not to force the issue. And so he complimented Marchand on his courage, agreed to refer the matter to London, presented Marchand with some wines, and received in return a gift of fresh vegetables. Courtesy was observed despite enmity.[1]

Théophile Delcassé, the able imperialist foreign minister of France, had forewarned the British ambassador that Kitchener might meet Captain Marchand at Fashoda, and that France had as much right there as England at Khartum. His intention seems to have been to use Marchand's exploit as a basis for bargaining, in hope of gaining at least the western bank of the Upper Nile, if he could not obtain more. But the British would

[1] One should read the account of this interview in Castellani, *Marchand l'Africain*, pp. 269 ff. Castellani, who was with Marchand, asserts that some of the native officers of Kitchener's army offered to betray their commander to the French, but Marchand refused to accept such treacherous aid.

not listen to any bargain; the whole Egyptian Sudan was theirs by right of conquest. Conciliatory as Lord Salisbury, then premier, was on most occasions, in this instance he was firm, and behind him was an enraged British public. Lord Rosebery, Liberal leader, declared in an interesting speech:

> In the face of a deliberate warning that a particular act would be considered as an unfriendly act, it has been deliberately committed. Behind the policy of the government is the united strength of the nation. No government that attempted to recede from or palter with that policy would last a week. The nation will make any sacrifice and go to any length to sustain them. On the other side of the Channel there is an element of great gravity, too; there is the question of the flag. I honor the flag. But the flag is a portable affair. It can be carried by irresponsible people, and I have some hope that the flag in this case is not necessarily the flag of France but the flag of an individual explorer. . . . I hope that this incident will be pacifically settled, but it must be understood that there can be no compromise of the rights of Egypt. Great Britain has been treated rather too much as a negligible quantity in recent years. . . .

As an expression of imperialist psychology this is a peerless gem. Particularly delightful is the reference to "the rights of Egypt," in view of the fact that England had seized Egypt by force, and was now using the rather tenuous Egyptian claims to lend some shadow of legality to the right of conquest, which Kitchener, with military bluntness, had openly asserted.

Urged on by the politicians and by the jingo press (notably the *Daily Mail*), the cabinet began to threaten France with war. The Chancellor of the Exchequer declared, "there are worse evils than war, and we shall not shrink from anything that may come." From September, 1898, to March, 1899, France and Great Britain were—in the words of an eminent Frenchman—"*à deux doigts des hostilités.*" Delcassé even called upon Russia, the ally of France, for a pledge of support; but received only the disappointing advice not to risk an actual break with England. Reluctantly Delcassé decided to yield. Early in November, 1899, he informed Salisbury that Marchand would be recalled. And Marchand came home, angry at his humiliation, and furiously indignant because Delcassé had endeavored to disclaim responsibility by styling him an "emissary of civilization." Marchand himself asserted that he had acted on official orders, as an emissary of France.[1]

[1] *Cambridge History of British Foreign Policy,* III, 253-5; Gooch, *History of Modern Europe,* 287-97; Debidour, *Histoire diplomatique, 1878-1904.*

As France had accepted the humiliation of unconditional retreat, Salisbury now consented to discuss the rival English and French claims in the Sudan. After rather delicate negotiations, an agreement was reached and signed in the form of an Anglo-French declaration, March 21, 1899, whereby France agreed to seek no territory east of a line drawn between the Nile and Congo basins, and England reciprocally engaged to acquire nothing west of the line. This left the Egyptian Sudan, including Bahr-el-Ghazal, to England, but France gained for her Congo colony free commercial access through this territory to the Nile, and, in addition, the kingdom of Wadai, in the central Sudan, was definitely assigned to France. It was further understood that France was free to consolidate her power in the central and western Sudan and the Sahara.[1] This France proceeded to accomplish. Military missions from (1) the French possession of Algeria in the north, (2) the French territory in the upper Niger valley or western Sudan, and (3) French Congo on the south, pursued converging paths toward the Lake Chad region. Their junction in February, 1900, southeast of Lake Chad, is memorable in the annals of French imperialism, for it meant not only the defeat of Rabah, a troublesome native chieftain, but also a definite occupation—according to imperialist conventions—of the territories in this region which France required to connect her Equatorial domain with French West and North Africa. In later years other expeditions rounded out French territory to the line laid down by the 1899 agreement, by conquering the Wadai and at least exploring Borku, Tibesti, and Ennedi.[2]

The Anglo-Egyptian Sudan

Free now to complete the conquest of the Sudan, the British quickly hunted down the remnants of the dervish forces and established their authority. Technically, the Sudan was a "con-

pp. 245-9; British correspondence in *Egypt No. 3*, 1898, Hanotaux, *Fachoda*. Castellani, *op. cit.*, pp. 338-9 alleges that the French government would not allow Marchand to publish a book giving his own story of the affair. Marchand later served as a general in the Great War and received the Grand Cross of the Legion of Honor.

[1] *State Papers*, 91, p. 55. One consequence of this agreement was the secret Franco-Italian accord of 1900 regarding Italian designs on Tripoli, *cf. infra*, p. 219.

[2] V. Beauregard, *L'Empire colonial de la France*, pp. 22 ff., gives graphic historical maps showing this process. *Cf. supra*, p. 112, map.

dominium," under the joint sovereignty of Egypt and Great Britain, and both flags were flown; in reality, the governor-general and his council of advisers, and most of the provincial governors, were British army officers, while Egypt's share in the government was chiefly the function of paying the annual deficits in the budget of the Sudan, amounting to a total of £2,750,000 in the period 1901-9, and of advancing even larger sums for railway construction and irrigation works. Sir Reginald Wingate, who succeeded Kitchener as governor-general in 1899 and held the office for seventeen years, was remarkably successful in overcoming native hostility and promoting economic development. By reducing taxes in the Sudan to a very low figure, by refraining from any attempt to impose European civilization on the natives, and by showing punctilious respect for the Mohammedan religion, the British authorities gradually won the sympathy of the Arab and negro inhabitants. As in all their colonies, the British labored chiefly to increase production and trade. The Sudan became the world's chief source of supply for gum arabic. Herds of cattle and sheep grazed on hitherto deserted prairies. In the fertile valley lands, watered by the Nile or by great irrigation works, Egyptian cotton of the finest grade was planted, and soon cotton surpassed all other products in its export value. Perhaps as succinct a way as any to describe the material results of British rule is to give the following little table:

	Trade of the Sudan	*Population of the Sudan (estimated)*
Before British rule.......	A few thousand l.	?
1905	£1,500,000	1,853,000
1910	£2,325,000	2,400,000
1924	£9,017,000	5,825,000

Said Sir Eldon Gorst, in a report (1909) on the condition of the Sudan, "I do not suppose that there is any part of the world in which the mass of the population have fewer unsatisfied wants." In like vein Kitchener declared, in 1912, "there is now hardly a poor man in the Sudan." Such self-satisfied British comments may perhaps be taken at a little less than face value; certainly in dry years there was some economic deprivation, but the importation of grain from India to relieve famine in the Sudan during a bad year must be put down on the credit side. In all fairness it must be recognized that in this country

British imperialism has been manifested at its best, as a constructive force, substituting order and economic progress for Arab oppression and general poverty.[1]

Perhaps it was in part due to the benefits of British rule that during the Great War of 1914-18 the greater part of the Sudan remained loyal. There was a revolt, to be sure, led by the Arab sultan Ali Dinar, in the province of Darfur, which had been allowed to remain as a semi-independent tribute-paying state, lying far out on the western border of the Sudan; and his revolt was only an outstanding incident in a general anti-British movement on the part of the Senussi—a fanatical Mohammedan organization of the desert Arabs. But Ali Dinar's army of dervishes and slaves was cut to pieces by Egyptian troops under British command, and the rebel leader himself was killed. After that, Darfur was definitely annexed to the Sudan, in 1916. Its western border, hitherto undefined, was fixed by an Anglo-French convention signed on Sept. 8, 1919.

Not long after the close of the Great War, Great Britain granted partial independence to Egypt, as we shall see in a later chapter, and thereupon the question arose, what should become of the Anglo-Egyptian condominium in the Sudan. The Egyptian Nationalist leaders insisted that the Sudan was Egypt's rightful heritage—so eager are newly emancipated folk to rule over others. Great Britain, as might be expected, found this claim little to her liking, for by this time Lord Rosebery's speech about protecting the "rights of Egypt" in the Sudan had long been forgotten, and the only rights that were remembered were British interests. In actual fact, British officials continued to rule the Sudan, as they had for a quarter-century.

Independent Abyssinia

But what about Abyssinia? A sequel to the story of Menelik and Italy may well be added here. As for Menelik, one might use the time-honored ending of novels—and he "lived happily ever after." At any rate, after defeating the Italians at Adowa he made good his claim to independence. Various foreign powers, including the United States, recognized his independence,

[1] P. F. Martin, *The Sudan in Evolution* (London, 1921); *Handbook of the Sudan* (London, annual); *Egypt and the Sudan*, Cmd. 2269 (1924).

made commercial treaties with him, and sent their envoys to his capital.[1]

French attempts to penetrate Abyssinia met with discouragement. A French concern, it will perhaps be recalled, had gained in 1894 a concession [2] to build a railway from the port of Jibuti (in French Somaliland) into Abyssinia, by way of the Abyssinian capital, Addis Ababa, to the Nile, and the laying of rails was begun in 1897. Financial difficulties led the company to part with some of its stock, but when it appeared that the purchaser was a British syndicate determined to obtain a controlling interest, the French directors appealed to Premier Waldeck-Rousseau, with such success that they obtained in 1902 a promise of 500,000 francs annually from the government, for fifty years, on condition that the company remain French, and that the French Government be given the right to ultimate reversion of the property. When this news was communicated to Menelik, French influence at his court vanished, for Menelik was by this time sufficiently sophisticated in the ways of European imperialism to distrust such plans.

As the French company encountered increasingly difficult obstacles, and again sought British capital, the British proposed the internationalization of the railroad. Italy supported the proposal. But Foreign Minister Delcassé of France refused.[3] In the end, a compromise was effected, by a tripartite agreement between France, Great Britain and Italy, signed July 6, 1906. The railway from Jibuti to Addis Ababa was to remain French,[4] but with British, Italian and Abyssinian representatives on the board of directors, and equality for the commerce of all powers; west of Addis Ababa, however, the line was to be continued by the British; and if any line should be built connecting the Italian colonies of Eritrea and Somaliland through Abyssinia, it should be entrusted to Italian enterprise. There would be a French director on the board of any British or Italian company, to ensure complete reciprocity.

This railway agreement paved the way for a political agree-

[1] Malloy, *Treaties*, 1, p. 466; *State Papers*, 98, p. 414, etc.

[2] Text of concession in Dubois et Terrier, *op. cit.*, pp. 697-8.

[3] Woolf, *op. cit.*, pp. 205-18, citing T. L. Gilmour, *Abyssinia: The Ethiopian Railway and the Powers* (London, 1905).

[4] This section, 495 miles in length, was completed in 1917 and is under French management, receiving a subsidy from the French government. Trains run twice a week!

ment, among the same three powers, in Decembr, 1906, by the terms of which all three agreed to maintain intact the integrity of Abyssinia, and to preserve the political and territorial status quo, if possible; should the status quo be disturbed, they were to act in concert to protect their special interests—that is, in plain English, they were to agree on the division of the spoils. Abyssinia, however, manifested so vigorous a spirit of independence, that this contingency never arose.[1]

The most dangerous crisis occurred during the Great War of 1914. The valiant and shrewd Emperor Menelik had left his throne, in 1913, to a young grandson, Lij Yasu, whose fondness for horses and women was greater than his statesmanship. Under the influence of Turkish and German propaganda, Yasu forsook Christianity, became a Mohammedan, married the daughters of leading Mohammedan chieftains, recognized the Turkish sultan as Caliph of Islam, and planned to intervene against the Allies, hoping to win for himself a great Mohammedan empire in Africa.

Yasu's action scandalized his Christian subjects, for, although more than half the population was Mohammedan, the ruling class had been Christian since the fourth century, when apostolic missionaries converted Abyssinia. The Christian princes met in council. One of them, the young Taffari Makonnen, boldly proposed that the apostate emperor should be deposed, his crown torn from his head and a Christian ruler set upon the throne. When asked to take the scepter himself, he modestly refused, and proposed that the Princess Zaodito (Judith), a daughter of Menelik, be made empress, with himself as regent and heir. His plan was adopted (in 1916) and forthwith he led the Christian princes with their retainers in battle array against Lij Yasu, with such success that the latter's Mohammedan army was defeated, and Lij Yasu himself captured. Had Yasu won, and attempted to carry out his Pro-Turkish policy, Abyssinia would doubtless have been partitioned, like Turkey, at the end of the war. But Empress Judith and Ras (King) Taffari found favor with the Allies, toward whose cause they maintained benevolent neutrality. The progressive and vigorous character of Taffari's administration, moreover, earned golden opinions. The combination of Allied favor and able government enabled Taffari

[1] *State Papers*, 99, p. 486.

in 1923 to obtain admission to the League of Nations, and thus to place his country's independence under international guarantee, while securing recognition for it as a civilized nation. Incidentally, it was necessary to promise that slavery, still existing in Abyssinia, should be abolished. As this book goes to press, Ras Taffari is reported to be protesting to the League against an Anglo-Italian agreement regarding a proposed British concession for a dam on the Blue Nile and an Italian railway project.

One is tempted to compare the development of this independent African state with the neighboring regions which have fallen under European power. In material progress, certainly, Abyssinia's record is not brilliant. The Anglo-Egyptian Sudan, for example, has more miles of railway, more irrigation works, a larger export trade. To be sure, the Sudan is three times as large in area, but Abyssinia has twice the number of people, and is well suited by nature to become a rich agricultural and pastoral country. Travelers have praised the sturdy physiques and active intelligence of the Abyssinians no less than the fertility and agreeable climate of their homeland. Education is legally compulsory but actually confined to a small minority; yet the Abyssinians are not for a moment to be classed with jungle savages. They have a written language, laws said to be based on the Justinian Code, and an established and ancient Christian Church. Economically and politically they are in a condition not very dissimilar to that of feudal Europe of the early middle ages.

A British traveler tells the story of an interview with the Abyssinian queen. He informed her of the many Asiatic and African countries through which he had journeyed, only to be surprised with her inquiry, "Are any of these countries independent?" "No," he replied. She remained thoughtful for a moment, then said, "Our father, the Emperor Menelik, reunited and held the empire against all enemies. We also will keep our country independent. We have no fear."

CHAPTER IX

THE LEGACY OF CECIL RHODES

For those who believe with Carlyle that great events are shaped by "heroes," the history of empire-building is replete with apparent proofs, and no better illustration of the theory can be found than the story of British imperialism in South Africa. So easily may the development of British South Africa be regarded as simply the expansion of the career of Cecil Rhodes, that for the purposes of our narrative his life may well be followed as the central thread of the tale. And yet, as it will be pointed out on occasion, the exploits of the "hero" were more closely related to geographical, political, and economic conditions, and therefore more essentially similar to the work of other empire-builders, than an uncritical admirer would suspect.

Diamonds and Gold

On September the first in the year of the Franco-Prussian War, a tall, lanky, rather pale young man, hardly more than a boy, stepped from the gang-plank of his steamer to the dock at Durban, on the coast of Natal, South Africa. Doubtless he wondered, as he looked about him in this unfamiliar town, what future this new land of opportunity held in store for him, for, like many another such immigrant, he was a "younger son" of a respectable but impecunious family. His father, a devout Anglican pastor, had sent four sons into the army, three to the colonies, to make careers for themselves, and had intended this youngest son for the Church or the Law. But the boy's health failed, and fearing he would fall victim to tuberculosis, his father felt that the bracing, dry climate of South Africa would benefit the lad. Years after, when the boy had become the great man of South Africa, he explained, "They will tell you that I came out on account of my health, or from a love of adventure, and to some extent that may be true; but the real fact is that I could no longer stand the eternal cold mutton."

The South Africa to which Cecil Rhodes came in 1870 was an interesting study in black and white. More than two centuries ago the first white settlers had arrived in Table Bay, to found a Dutch naval station at the place now known as Cape Town, in 1652. Slowly the naval station, intended at first merely to supply Dutch fleets en route to and from the distant Dutch East Indies, had grown into a Dutch colony of farmers or Boers (meaning farmers) employing negro slaves from West Africa to till their fields and watch their herds. French Huguenots fleeing the wrath of Louis XIV had found refuge in Cape Colony, in 1690, and mingled their blood with that of the Dutch. But during the Napoleonic Wars an English fleet had appeared in the Bay, to take possession of the colony (1806), and the British conquest, ratified by diplomacy in 1814, established the cornerstone of British rule in South Africa. At that time there were in Cape Colony about 26,000 "Boers," of Dutch and French extraction, with 29,000 negro slaves, 17,000 Hottentots, and a dwindling remnant of the race of Bushmen. The last-named were tawny-colored savages, diminutive in stature but untamable in disposition, who had been hunted by white settlers, and driven into the deserts north of the Colony. The Hottentots or "Tots," a copper-colored, woolly-haired race of herdsmen, described by one traveler as "without doubt both in body and in mind the laziest people under the sun," had proved less irreconcilable; many had become slaves and servants to the Boers while others retired to the inland deserts and prairies; many, too, had been swept off by smallpox and other diseases brought in by the whites; many of their women, serving the pleasure of Dutch settlers, had given birth to a race of half-breeds called Griquas or Bastards, who were led by a missionary, in 1803, to settle in the region now called Griqualand, on the eastern outskirts of Cape Colony.

East and north of the Colony were strong tribes of warlike negroes—the Basutos, the Zulus, the Kaffirs and the Bechuanas, all belonging to the Bantu division of the negro race. Their fierce opposition was a grave obstacle to the settlement of white pioneers in the healthful, upland prairies, the grass-covered veldt, northeast of the Colony, or along the eastern coast, where the rainfall was more abundant than in the west. For example, when five thousand British settlers were brought into South

Africa, in 1820-21, and attempted to colonize the eastern border of the Colony, they lived in terror of the Kaffirs, and a long succession of "Kaffir Wars" had to be fought before the pioneers could breathe freely. Nevertheless, hardy pioneers did push out into the back-country, particularly after the abolition of slavery (with inadequate compensation) by the English authorities caused several hundred Dutch farmers to "trek" out of the Colony in search of new homes, in 1836. These trekkers had established themselves on the grass-covered plateau or "high veldt" and in the eastern coastland. The coastland settlement became the colony of Natal and was annexed by Great Britain in 1843. But on the veldt arose the Boer Republics of Transvaal and Orange Free State, both recognized as independent in the 1850's.[1]

When Cecil Rhodes arrived on the scene, then, the coastlands of Cape Colony and Natal were British colonies, with about two hundred thousand white colonists, mostly Boers, with several times as many slaves and natives. The Orange River bounded British claims. To the northeast, on the high veldt, were the sparsely settled independent Boer republics. And to the north and northwest were vast expanses of dry plateau-lands, partly desert, partly covered with tufts of grass and stunted shrubs, thinly peopled by negroes, Bushmen and Hottentots, unclaimed by any European power.

Rhodes[2] arrived at an opportune moment, when British imperialism was beginning to revive, and when South Africa in particular was on the eve of marvelous expansion. He came just after a Dutch farmer had found his children playing marbles with a diamond worth twenty-five hundred dollars, just after glittering wealth was discovered at Kimberley and other places on the northern frontier, in the land of the Griquas. The rush of diamond-diggers to Griqualand had begun, and Griqualand was about to be annexed by Britain (in 1871). Among the prospectors was Cecil's brother, and him Cecil followed, in October, 1871. With cumbrous oxcart and provisions, the youth set out on his long and leisurely journey, equipped with a few volumes of classical literature to while away the time. It was

[1] On this earlier history of South Africa the standard work is G. M. Theal's *History of South Africa from 1795 to 1872* (5 vols., London, 1916).

[2] Biographies by Basil Williams, Sir Lewis Michell. Howard Hensman. Vindex. Gordon Le Sueur. Sir T. E. Fuller.

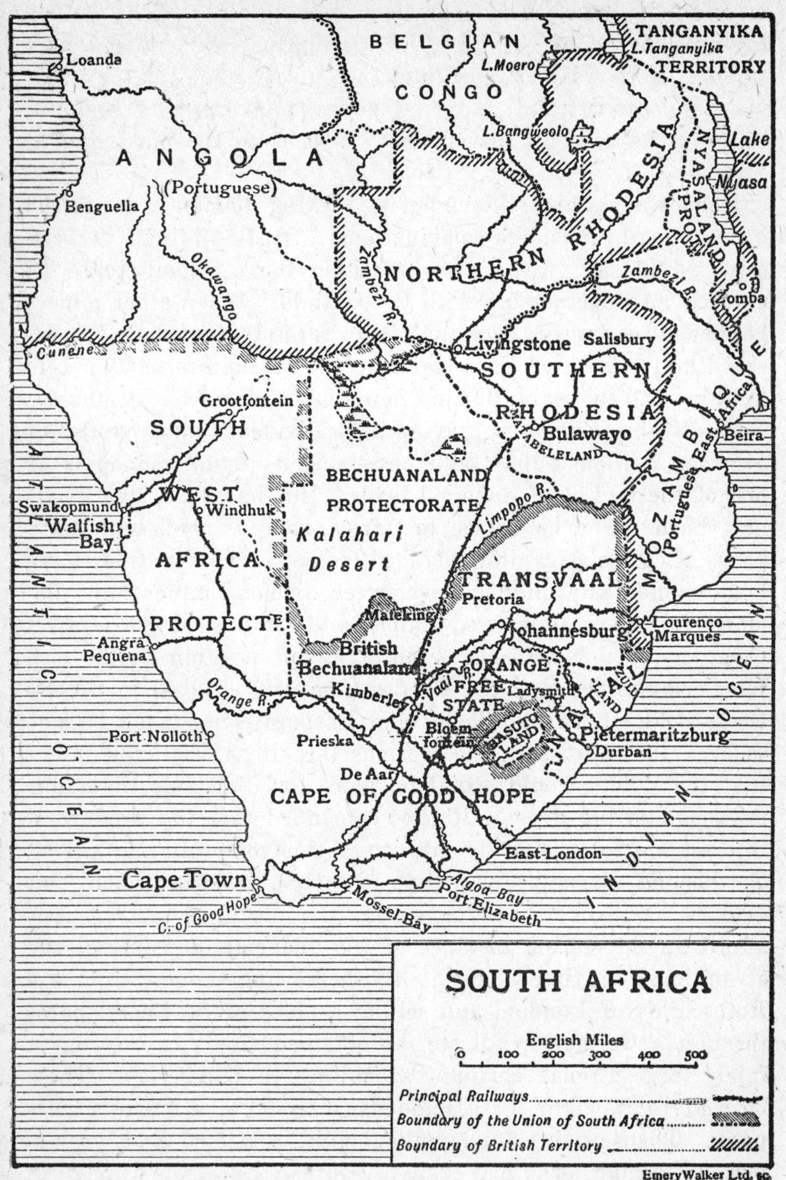
SOUTH AFRICA
English Miles
0 100 200 300 400 500
Principal Railways
Boundary of the Union of South Africa
Boundary of British Territory
BELGIAN CONGO
TANGANYIKA TERRITORY
L. Tanganyika
L. Moero
L. Bangweolo
Lake Nyasa
NYASALAND PROT.
Zomba
ANGOLA (Portuguese)
Loanda
Benguella
Okawango
Zambezi R.
NORTHERN RHODESIA
Livingstone
Salisbury
SOUTHERN RHODESIA
MATABELELAND
Bulawayo
Beira
MOZAMBIQUE (Portuguese East Africa)
Cunene
Grootfontein
SOUTH WEST AFRICA PROTECTe
Swakopmund
Walfish Bay
Windhuk
Angra Pequena
BECHUANALAND PROTECTORATE
Kalahari Desert
Limpopo R.
TRANSVAAL
Pretoria
Johannesburg
Lourenço Marques
Mafeking
British Bechuanaland
ORANGE FREE STATE
Vaal R.
Kimberley
Ladysmith
ZULULAND
NATAL
BASUTOLAND
Bloemfontein
Pietermaritzburg
Durban
Orange R.
Port Nolloth
Prieska
De Aar
CAPE OF GOOD HOPE
East London
Cape Town
C. of Good Hope
Mossel Bay
Algoa Bay
Port Elizabeth
ATLANTIC OCEAN
INDIAN OCEAN
Emery Walker Ltd. sc.

an inspiring experience. The clear, bracing air, and the endless grassy expanse of the high veldt awakened the young man's vision. Here was God's country, a country made for the white man, and for Britain. Later on, he was to attempt its conquest, but for the present, his energy was bent to the making of a fortune.

Rhodes made his millions not by picking diamonds out of the gravel, but by business combinations, "trust-building," Americans would say. Soon after reaching the diamond fields, he entered into partnership with C. D. Rudd. When other miners became discouraged, or found their capital exhausted, Rhodes and Rudd purchased their claims or took them into partnership. Within sixteen years Rhodes found himself master of the De Beers Mining Company, paying 25% dividends on a capital of over ten million dollars, and possessing a virtual monopoly of one of the two chief diamond fields. But he had a rival, Barnett Isaacs, who had come to Africa, so it is said, with sixty boxes of cigars as capital, changed his name to Barney Barnato, made money as a middleman between diamond miners and diamond exporters, purchased claims, and established the Central Company, which held the same dominant position in the rich Kimberley mines that the Rhodes Company enjoyed in the De Beers field. Between Rhodes and Barnato competition became so keen that both did some serious thinking. Figuring it out that the public would spend no more for diamonds than four millions sterling a year, Rhodes concluded that the producers' interest was to restrict the output and thus maintain high prices. To this end, Barnato was willing to enter a price-agreement, but Rhodes was bent on amalgamation. His dealings in this crisis afford an interesting instance of the financial internationalism of nationalistic imperialism. By borrowing money from the Rothschilds of London, and selling a block of de Beers shares through a German syndicate, he obtained funds to buy out a fairly large French company's holdings in Kimberley. These he sold to Barnato for a minority interest in Barnato's company. Then, raising funds with the aid of Alfred Beit, a prosperous German (who had come to South Africa from Hamburg, and later became a staunch British imperialist), Rhodes began to buy up other minority interests in Barnato's company, until Barnato admitted defeat and accepted amalgamation, in 1888.

Smaller independents were now easily swallowed up in the growing trust, and by 1890 De Beers Consolidated Mines, of which Rhodes, Barnato, Beit, and Stow were life-governors, had a monopoly of South African diamonds, ninety per cent of the world's supply.

Meanwhile Rhodes had begun a similar process of trust-building in the gold mines, which had been discovered in the Witwatersrand in Transvaal, in 1886. He had established a company, The Gold Fields of South Africa, Ltd., with a modest capital of £125,000, to buy up prospectors' claims. The company grew rapidly, changing its name to Consolidated Gold Fields of South Africa as it approached a monopoly position. Fifty per cent dividends were not unusual, nor was it exceptional for Rhodes to derive from one to two million dollars a year in profit from this concern. His combined diamond and gold interests, together with innumerable smaller enterprises, must have yielded him an income of about five million dollars a year in the 1890's, when he was at the height of his career.

Rhodes the Empire Builder

Not, however, as the ruthless business monopolist and manipulator, but as the patriotic imperialist, or as the founder of the Rhodes scholarships, is this South-African diamond and gold king usually remembered. He used his immense wealth to promote British imperialism, and imperialism, reciprocally, to promote his wealth.

His imperialism was undoubtedly sincere, and extraordinarily philosophical. One biographer[1] tells of the mental struggles through which Rhodes passed as a young man, in his search for an explanation of the universe and a view of life. There must be a God, he said to himself, and if there be a God, there must be a divine purpose in history. The purpose, it appeared, was the evolution of humanity toward a finer type. Now it is obvious, to any Englishman, that the breed of men best suited for survival in such an evolution is the so-called Anglo-Saxon race. The conclusion easily follows, that to serve the divine purpose, one should strive to promote the predominance of the

[1] Basil Williams, *Cecil Rhodes* (N. Y., 1921), ch. VI.

Anglo-Saxon race. And since the surface of the earth is limited, as Rhodes himself said, a vigorous effort should be made to obtain as much land as possible, while land is to be had, for the future expansion of this race. To be more specific, let us examine the terms of the will made by Rhodes in 1877, when he was still but a young man. He planned at that time to leave his property to endow a secret society, whose aim would be to extend British colonization and British rule throughout the world. All Africa was to be a British colony, and all South America—the Monroe Doctrine being surmounted by the simple device of reincorporating the United States into the British Empire—and in addition Oceania, the Malay Peninsula, the seaboard of China and India, Mesopotamia, Palestine, and various other smaller morsels. While others thought in provinces, said Rhodes, "I think in continents." Here was a grandiose vision, worthy of a Pan-German. But Rhodes did not intend despotic empire. The British colonies were to be self-governing, and the British flag was to mean defense, not domination. To bind the dominions together, there would be colonial representation in the imperial parliament, and colonial subsidies would be given to the imperial navy, but, above all, a system of preferential tariffs would be established, for "the future government of the world is a question of tariffs."

For all his altruistic philosophy of imperialism, the great imperialist was also a business man, not at all insensible to the importance of economic motives in politics. Perhaps no better summary of his attitude could be given than his own: "Pure philanthropy is very well in its way, but philanthropy plus five per cent is a good deal better." Fifty per cent, he might have said. And he used the "philanthropy plus" method, not only for himself, but in dealing with those who were necessary tools in the realization of his dream of empire. He gave business tips to obliging politicians and opportunities to political lieutenants. He contributed to the campaign funds of the British Liberals, on condition that they should not "scuttle out of Egypt."[1] He purchased newspapers to plead his cause. He knew the power of money.

[1] See Campbell-Bannerman's indignant denial, with a summary of the later proof of the contribution, in J. A. Spender, *Life of Campbell-Bannerman*, I, 202-7.

Just a thumb-nail sketch of "The Old Man"—as his protégés called him—may lend more reality, and perhaps more significance, to the political narrative that follows. A tall man he was, with piercing steel-blue eyes looking out from under a crop of curly gray hair. His careless dress and many eccentricities, such as taking a cow, some hens, and his own brands of champagne and kümmel with him on sea voyages, were amusing earmarks of a self-made man too arrogant for acceptance of ordinary restrictions. If he took champagne and stout mixed in the morning, champagne by the tumbler at dinner, and stronger potations through the evening, he was by no means an excessive, but merely a heavy and methodical drinker. That he enjoyed being told he resembled the Emperor Hadrian; that like Napoleon he tweaked the ears of subordinates, that toward opposition he showed the intolerance of a self-confessed "creative genius," indicated something of his magnificent egotism. But the fact that he succeeded so greatly must be ascribed to other and more admirable characteristics—indomitable grit, mastery of details, unflinching perseverance when weaker men would falter.

If he thought "in continents," Rhodes nevertheless had to deal, like other men, "in provinces," for only by fractions are continents won. The immediate task he set for himself was to extend British rule northward from Cape Colony, across the Boer Republics of the Orange River and Transvaal, and on to the lake region of east-central Africa. "All this to be painted red," he would say, as he passed his hand over this part of the map. And this South African empire of the future, he dreamed, would one day be connected with Egypt by a Cape-to-Cairo railway.

The first step was to acquire the wide expanse of arid deserts and grasslands known as Bechuanaland, directly north of Cape Colony. As this region lay like a corridor between the Boer Republics of Orange River and Transvaal, on the east, and German South West Africa on the west, it was aptly described by Rhodes as "the Suez Canal" of South Africa; it was the vital gateway to the north. Without it, British South Africa might be hemmed in on the north by a sea-to-sea band of Boer and German territory. It may be remarked, by the way, that German imperialists were eager to win the friendship of the Boers.

as distant linguistic kinsmen, and some even hoped that the Boers might accept German protection.[1]

To gain Bechuanaland Rhodes first exerted himself. Having entered politics in Cape Colony and made himself a power at Cape Town, Rhodes began a vigorous agitation for British acquisition of Bechuanaland. He himself made a visit to the region in 1884, but failed to achieve his aim, because of the opposition of the Transvaal Boers, who were at this time extending their influence into the region. However, the propaganda conducted by Rhodes, reinforcing the pressure of other imperialists, led the British government in 1885 to send an army into Bechuanaland, and on September 30 a British protectorate was proclaimed, extending as far west as the border of German South West Africa and as far north as the parallel of 22° S. The road to the north was now secure; it must now be used.

North of Bechuanaland and Transvaal was a great tableland, fertile and well-watered, within the tropics, to be sure, but high enough to be eminently suitable for white colonization. Its southern part was inhabited by negro tribes, the Matabeles and the Mashonas, under the rule of an able and warlike chieftain, King Lo Bengula. There was imminent danger that this desirable land would fall into other hands. Portuguese politicians were at this time exhibiting maps showing a broad band of Portuguese territory extending right across Mashonaland and Matabeleland, from Portuguese Mozambique to Portuguese Angola. The Transvaal Boers, too, having been foiled in Bechuanaland, were turning their attention toward Mashonaland. The British must act quickly. Yet the officials were hesitant.

It was Rhodes who acted. By offering to assume all the costs, he persuaded the British high commissioner for South Africa (Sir Hercules Robinson, whose name did not indicate his character), to permit a British missionary to have a talk with King Lo Bengula. That dusky sovereign was induced to sign a treaty, pledging himself to refrain from negotiations with other foreigners without the previous consent of the British high commissioner for South Africa. This was necessary to forestall rivals. Then, with the commissioner's consent, Rhodes sent three of his most trusted lieutenants to Lo Bengula's court. Theirs

[1] See M. von Hagen, *Bismarcks Kolonialpolitik*, pp. 414 ff., 477 ff. on the German attitude especially toward the Bechuanaland question.

was a dangerous mission, for the caprice of the negro king, or the intrigues of rival Europeans, might easily have brought about the murder of the small party. But at length Lo Bengula was induced to sign a most remarkable document, the celebrated "mineral concession" of Oct. 30, 1888, granting to Rudd, Maguire and Thompson (the delegates of Rhodes) "complete and exclusive charge over all metals and minerals situated and contained in my kingdom, principalities and dominions," together with the right "to exclude from my kingdoms, etc., all persons seeking land, metals, minerals, or mining rights therein." Perhaps when it is explained that the region was supposed to be rich in gold, the "plus" which usually accompanied Rhodes' altruistic imperialism will here be patent without specific mention. The mess of pottage for which Lo Bengula sold his birthright consisted of one thousand Martini rifles, a hundred thousand ball cartridges, and a hundred pounds sterling payable "on the first day of every lunar month." In addition, he had a strong desire for a steamboat, and to gratify it the negotiators threw into the bargain a second-hand steamer. How Lo Bengula himself understood this bargain may be learned from a plaintive message he later sent Queen Victoria:

> Some time ago a party of men came into my country, the principal one appearing to be a man called Rudd. They asked me for a place to dig gold and said they would give me certain things for the right to do so. I told them to bring what they would and I would show them what I would give. A document was written and presented to me for signature. I asked what it contained and was told that in it were my words and the words of those men. I put my hand to it. About three months afterwards I heard from other sources that I had given by that document the right to all the minerals of my country.

But Rhodes interpreted the concession as a permit to exploit and govern Lo Bengula's country, and, following the example of other empire builders such as Goldie of West African fame and Mackinnon of East African celebrity, he organized a company (the British South Africa Company) and applied for a charter from the British government. The British premier, Lord Salisbury, was at this time inclined to recognize Portugal's claims to the territory, but by much wire-pulling Rhodes won Salisbury over. By inviting the Duke of Fife to become vice-president, and the Duke of Abercorn to become president of the projected company, and by stating his intention that "the conditions of the natives inhabiting the said territories will be materially improved and their civilization advanced," Rhodes astutely enlisted both the prestige of British aristocracy and the zeal of British humanitarianism to serve the ends of his business enterprise.

The charter, signed by the Queen on Oct. 29, 1889, gave the South Africa Company for twenty-five years the right to make treaties and laws, maintain police, construct roads, railways and harbors, develop mines and industries, make grants of land, and, in short, govern a vast but purposely undefined area, north of British Bechuanaland and Transvaal, and west of Portuguese Mozambique, but with no northern boundary. The latter was left unmentioned, because Rhodes hoped to extend it far to the north.

The business aspect of the venture was interesting. The Chartered Company had a capital of a million one-pound shares. For themselves, the promoters took 90,000 shares and fifty per cent of any future profits. The De Beers company bought 200,000. The other shares were sold, in large part, to small investors, whose loyalty to Rhodes and his project was a useful political asset. There was not much difficulty marketing the stock, thanks to the helpful advertising which Rhodes obtained from the press. The *Times*, for example, described the land as being "fabulously rich" in metals; the soil was "only in need of scratching to smile with corn" and "cattle fatten in peace"; it was the storied "land of Ophir." The glowing optimism of the press regarding the natural riches and salubrious climate of about-to-be-acquired colonies is a phenomenon which recurs in almost any country, at almost every conquest, for some reason psychological or economic which conventional historical research has failed to expose.[1]

Getting a concession from a Matabele king who could not read, and actually occupying that king's territory to "scratch" the fertile soil and open the fabulous mines, were quite dissimilar propositions, of which the latter was the more difficult. Rhodes himself grew anxious, as he tried to make plans for the sending of settlers to make clearings in the forests and build their homes

[1] My account of the South Africa Company is based chiefly on biographies of Rhodes, J. H. Harris, *Chartered Millions* (London, 1920); P. F. Hone, *Southern Rhodesia* (London, 1909); Morel, *Black Man's Burden*, chs. IV-V.

in the wilderness, with a fickle and savage chieftain at their back. But a young daredevil offered to lead the way, and a slender band of a few hundred pioneers was brought together by a promise of fifteen gold claims and three thousand acres of farm-land for each man. They had to travel 460 miles on foot, making a road as they went and often cutting a way through forests, before they reached the Promised Land. There, as Rhodes later admitted, they "found that they could not pick up gold like gooseberries"; tropical rains fell upon their camp; enthusiasm gave way to dismal discouragement, and on the stock markets the shares of the company began to fall. Rhodes himself went out and restored confidence. Slowly the settlement grew, and its cattle began to fatten, not "in peace" as had been promised, but in constant danger of native raids, until at length the Chartered Company sent troops to conquer Lo Bengula, and take his cattle. Like the man who admitted the camel's foot into his tent, Lo Bengula found himself driven out (though his sons were magnanimously educated at the expense of Rhodes). What had been Lo Bengula's kingdom became "Rhodesia."

About the international difficulties that attended the marking out of the Chartered Company's domain of Rhodesia, we need not enter into detail. To the north, Rhodesia was extended to meet Congo Free State and touch Lake Tanganyika, as Rhodes had hoped, but it was cut off from further extension by the Anglo-German treaty of 1890,[1] which brought German East Africa and the Free State together, leaving no land passage between. To the northeast, there was some danger that Germany or Portugal might obtain a footing in the neighborhood of Lake Nyasa; a British company (the African Lakes Company), however, cooperated with the London Missionary Society in opening up this region for Britain, and in 1893 a protectorate was proclaimed over the western shores of the lake, then styled "British Central Africa," but later renamed Nyasaland.[2] On the east of Rhodesia there were boundary disputes with Portugal, and on the west with Portugal and Germany, but these

[1] *Cf. supra*, p. 126.

[2] *Cf.* Sir H. H. Johnston, *British Central Africa* (London, 1897); H. L. Duff, *Nyasaland Under the Foreign Office* (London, 1906); S. S. Murray, *Handbook of Nyasaland* (London, 1922) on a colony to which I give such scant notice here.

were cleared up by the Anglo-German agreements of 1890 and 1893, and the Anglo-Portuguese treaty of 1891.[1]

Though Rhodes never lived to see Rhodesia become—as it is to-day—a link in a completed Cape-to-Cairo empire, the region his company acquired for Great Britain was by no means contemptible—440,000 square miles of fertile land, suitable for white colonization and agricultural development. Only "Southern Rhodesia," a third of this great realm, has yet been colonized or developed to any considerable extent. Even here there were, when the 1921 census was taken, only 33,620 white settlers and 770,000 natives, less than a million all told, in a country three times as big as England. The best agricultural land was, of course, allotted to whites, while large but poorer areas were set aside, temporarily, as "reserves" for the natives. Natives living on the reserves paid a head tax of one pound per annum, while those living on white men's land paid an additional pound to the white owner. One of the purposes of these levies, it may be explained, was to provide the natives with an indirect incentive to work for the whites at wages that seem too incredibly small to mention. Intelligent and persistent efforts were made by the Chartered Company to promote farming and fruit-growing, in the hope of attracting English immigrants, but, as the abovementioned figures indicate, Southern Rhodesia has been less attractive than the United States to Englishmen seeking homes overseas, and desiring, not to break ground in an almost uninhabited wilderness, but to find well-paid employment in a civilized and prosperous country. Gold-mining, after all, has been the economic mainstay of the land. Though gold could not be picked up like gooseberries, it could be mined, and in the period from 1890 to 1921 the total amount of gold produced was no less than a quarter of a billion dollars. Northern Rhodesia, still larger and still more sparsely populated than the southern province, had in 1921 about a million negroes and 3,500 white men, scattered over high forested plateaus more extensive than England and France together. Here lead is mined, instead of gold, and in the clearings cattle graze.

For more than thirty years the Chartered Company governed Rhodesia pretty much as it pleased, though occasionally the

[1] *State Papers*, 82, pp. 27, 35; 85, pp. 41, 65; 92, p. 797; 104, p. 185; 105, p. 276.

London Government intervened to prevent too ruthless treatment of the natives. As the white settlers grew more numerous in Southern Rhodesia, however, and civilized towns sprang up here and there, the Company found it necessary to give the whites representation in a Legislative Council. The demand for complete colonial self-government became increasingly strong, for the settlers were by no means agreeable to the Chartered Company's privileges, both political and economic. At length, in 1922, a vote was taken, on the alternatives of joining the Union of South Africa or becoming a self-governing colony, and as the result favored self-government, Southern Rhodesia was created a colony with government responsible to an elected assembly, and the political rule of the Company in this part of its domain was ended.[1]

THE JAMESON RAID

From Rhodesia, the greatest achievement of Cecil Rhodes, we must turn our attention to the Boer communities of Transvaal and Orange River. These, as we have seen, had been recognized as self-governing republics,[2] and had been left to pursue their own interests, until with the discovery of gold in the northern republic, Transvaal, about the year 1886, a new factor entered into the situation. The thousands of prospectors, laborers, and tradesmen, who rushed into the Transvaal gold fields in the period after 1886, soon incurred the bitter hostility of the Boer farmers, who believed the land was theirs by right of conquest and settlement, and regarded the newcomers, with some cause, as a disorderly and dangerous element. The Boers, for their part,

[1] See *Parliamentary Papers*, Cmd. 1914 and Cmd. 1984 of 1923. For other aspects of Rhodesia, see Hone, *Southern Rhodesia;* E. T. Jollie, *The Real Rhodesia;* Harris, *Chartered Millions;* Ian Colvin, *Life of Jameson;* Annual Reports of the British South Africa Company.

[2] The independence of Transvaal (South African Republic) and Orange Free State was recognized in 1852 and 1854, respectively. Transvaal had been annexed in 1877 but by the Pretoria Convention of Aug. 3, 1881, it had been given self-government under British suzerainty. This action followed the famous battle of Majuba Hill. The London Convention of Feb. 27, 1884, went a step farther, omitting all mention of British suzerainty, but stipulating in article 4 that the republic "will conclude no treaty or engagement with any state or nation, other than the Orange Free State . . . until the same has been approved by her Majesty the Queen." See *State Papers*, 72, p. 900, and 75, p. 5; also, on the interpretation of this convention, 91, pp. 557-646.

angered the miners by excluding them from political rights, by levying heavy tariff duties on food and other supplies, by establishing dynamite[1] and railway monopolies which interfered with the miners' business. Furthermore, mine-owners like Rhodes and Rudd needed native labor, and believed that the natives should be forced to work by means of taxation or otherwise. As Rudd said, "If under the cry of civilization we in Egypt lately mowed down ten or twenty thousand dervishes with Maxims (he was referring to the battle of Omdurman), surely it cannot be considered a hardship to compel the natives in South Africa to give three months in the year to do a little honest work." But the Boer government interfered with the importation of native labor. John Hays Hammond, a well-known American engineer associated with Rhodes, estimated that "good government" would mean a saving of six shillings per ton on gold ore production costs, and that would mean an increase of about twelve million dollars a year in dividends. And to cap the climax, the Boer president, "Oom Paul" Kruger, showed altogether too friendly a disposition toward the German Emperor, who was known to have an indiscreet fondness for the Boers.

Under such circumstances some of the British gold producers and business men in Johannesburg conspired to overthrow the Boer government of Transvaal. Hearing of the plot, Cecil Rhodes with characteristic self-confidence decided that his was the genius to direct the revolt. He took charge of the scheme, provided funds, arranged for the smuggling of arms as company supplies, and planned to have his Rhodesian military police invade Transvaal in concert with the internal revolution. The capitalists backing the Johannesburg conspiracy, however, insisted that the aim must be to hoist the British flag, whereas the "reformers" in the so-called National Union, which was the backbone of the movement, desired an independent republican government. This dissension, and other circumstances, delayed

[1] This item alone, it was alleged, took $3,000,000 a year from the pockets of the mine-owners. For an interesting partisan discussion of this and other grievances, see the manifesto (Dec. 27, 1895) of Charles Leonard, President of the Transvaal National Union, in *State Papers*, 89, pp. 248 ff. *Cf.* J. A. Hobson, *The War in South Africa*. Leonard claimed: "We (the Uitlanders) are the vast majority in this State. We own more than half of the land, and, taken in the aggregate, we own at least nine-tenths of the property in this country; yet in all matters affecting our lives, our liberties, and our properties, we have absolutely no voice." Bryce's *Impressions of South Africa* (N. Y., 1897), ch. 25, is worth re-reading in this connection.

action until Dr. Leander Starr Jameson, an able Scottish physician whom Rhodes had made administrator of Rhodesia and who had been delegated to lead the Rhodesian police into Transvaal, grew impatient and resolved to wait no longer. Rhodes attempted to countermand the invasion, but the wires had been cut by Jameson's orders.

On Dec. 29, 1895, "Dr. Jim," as Jameson was called, set out with about five hundred men to invade the Transvaal republic. When Rhodes heard the news he exclaimed in consternation, "Jameson has upset my apple cart." He had. The invaders were captured on Jan. 2, 1896, after a little fighting. The Johannesburg conspiracy "fizzled out as a damp squib," in the words of Rhodes, and the leading conspirators, including John Hays Hammond, an American, were arrested.[1] The Jameson Raid[2] was a fiasco. Had it succeeded, perhaps it might have been sung by later bards as a glorious deed, but its ignominious failure allowed its true nature to appear clearly—it was an illegitimate armed attack on a peaceful neighbor. Rhodes himself had to resign office as a premier of Cape Colony and submit to a parliamentary inquiry which condemned the Raid and censured him.[3] For his accomplices Rhodes generously paid lawyers' fees and staggering fines.

More alarming was the effect of the Raid in releasing pent-up German animosity toward England. As soon as he heard of the Raid, the German foreign minister, Baron von Marschall, warned the British ambassador that Germany must insist on the "maintenance of the status quo" in South Africa, and that the London cabinet was perilously mistaken if it felt strong enough to pursue its aggressive policy without consulting the other

[1] They were tried and condemned to death, but later released on payment of large fines.

[2] On the Raid in general see Ian Colvin, *The Life of Jameson* (London, 1922), II, ch. 25; J. Hays Hammond, *The Truth About the Jameson Raid* (Boston, 1918); Lionel Phillips, *Reminiscences* (London, 1925), ch. 6. Compare Chamberlain's review of the affair in *State Papers*, 89, pp. 335-49, and correspondence in the same, pp. 247-335, and 91, pp. 474 ff.

[3] See *Second Report from the Select Committee on British South Africa* (1897). The minutes of evidence taken contain many racy items on the profits and methods of the mine-owners and on the fabulous careers of certain mining stocks. See also J. A. Spender, *Life of Campbell-Bannerman*, I, pp. 191-207, and A. G. Gardiner, *Life of Sir William Harcourt*, II, chs. 20, 22, for some of the inside story of the investigation and the views of the Liberal leaders regarding the Rhodesian variety of "stock-jobbing imperialism."

powers. Indeed, the Continental powers might combine against England. Secretly, the German ambassadors in other European capitals were instructed to sound the governments on this project of an anti-English coalition. As more news arrived, Marschall became more excited, and on January 2 he obtained the Kaiser's consent for a formal protest to England. This was delivered in a very sharp note, warning England that Germany was not minded to accept any alteration in the treaty status of Transvaal. This gruffly worded challenge, by good luck, was recalled the next day [1] when news of Dr. Jim's failure arrived. But the Kaiser himself, eager to show England that Germany could not safely be ignored in such matters, sent his famous telegram (January 3) to President Kruger of the Transvaal, congratulating him on his success in defending "the independence of the country against foreign attacks." [2] There has been much controversy as to the authorship of this amazing telegram, and the extent of William II's responsibility for its wording; [3] but the real point is that the telegram was not an isolated incident. The German foreign office, as we have seen, had previously issued harsh warnings to England; the foreign minister had suggested to Kruger an international conference on the status of the South African Republic; German public opinion was greatly excited. The telegram was merely a culminating incident, important because it was public and because it inflamed British opinion. War seemed not improbable. But Germany found the other European capitals lukewarm or cold toward the proposal of a Continental bloc against England, and the Germans themselves were astonished at the violence of British indignation. As gracefully as possible the Berlin government made its retreat. Incidentally, the Kaiser had hoped to obtain something for Germany—possibly a protectorate over Transvaal, or possession of the valuable port of Lourenço Marques in Portuguese East Africa, but his foreign office advised him that the former was impossible and that the latter would mean war against England and France, just as an English attempt to seize the port would mean a combination of France and Germany

[1] It had already been delivered at Downing Street, but not yet opened.

[2] Text in *Die Grosse Politik*, 11, No. 2610 with notes on its drafting.

[3] See especially *Die Grosse Politik*, 11, p. 32, footnote, and F. Thimme, "Die Krüger-Depesche," *Europäische Gespräche*, Mai-Juni, 1924, pp. 201-44.

against Britain. These suggestions are mentioned, only because they illustrate how statesmen must juggle with war and peace in the game of imperialist world politics.[1]

The Jameson Raid wrecked the hopes which Rhodes had long cherished for the eventual union of the Boer and British communities in South Africa. It was, indeed, contrary to his lifelong policy of cordial cooperation with the Cape Boers. After 1896 Rhodes retired from political life, more or less under a cloud, and in 1902 he died, leaving the bulk of his huge estate to endow 175 scholarships at Oxford for students from the British colonies, and also from the United States and from Germany. The inclusion of America and Germany is significant as an indication of Rhodes' belief in the mission of the English-speaking peoples and in the cultural solidarity of Anglo-Saxons and Germans. This use of his wealth is perhaps in part responsible for the fame he achieved, after death, as a disinterested altruist, his business practices being forgotten; certainly it helped Americans to look upon him as a far-seeing philanthropist rather than a far-reaching imperialist; and the name Rhodesia, writ large across the map of South Africa, is a reminder to the public of his patriotism, to the cynic of his bargain with Lo Bengula.

The Boer War

The inevitable effect of the Jameson Raid was to hasten the impending contest between Briton and Boer for supremacy in South Africa. Kruger, the Boer president of Transvaal, became increasingly anti-British in his policy, negotiated an alliance with the other Boer republic, the Orange Free State, and looked to the Anglophobe organization of the Boers in Cape Colony, namely the Afrikander Bond, and to Germany and Holland, for sympathy if not support. The British, on the other hand, were impelled toward conflict by three powerful forces. First and foremost, the British mining interests in Transvaal were dissatisfied with the Boer government because, representing the interests of the Boer farmers as opposed to British industrialists, it levied tariff duties on food, compelled British mining com-

[1] This paragraph is based on the recently published German documents in *Die Grosse Politik*, 11, ch. 63; the older documents are collected in *Staatsarchiv*, 58, nos. 10824-10913.

panies to buy dynamite and coal at exorbitant prices from monopolies, balked all attempts to establish convenient railway communications with the Cape, permitted the debauching of native laborers by saloons, and, in general, as Mr. Hays Hammond so admirably explained, reduced the profits of the mineowners by twelve millions a year. Secondly, certain British statesmen felt that British authority must be supreme in all South Africa or none; that sooner or later either the Boers or the British must gain the upper hand.[1] And finally, British public opinion was intensely concerned with the indignities suffered by the British citizens in Transvaal, who were treated as aliens or Uitlanders by the Boer government. By 1899 there were 180,000 Uitlanders (including many Germans, Americans, and others, as well as British), as opposed to 80,000 Boers in Transvaal. Though the Uitlanders owned two-thirds of the land and ninety per cent of the other wealth of the republic, and were heavily taxed, the Boer minority monopolized the government and insisted on a residence requirement of fourteen years for the franchise.

Though the economic grievance was fundamental, British statesmen with sure instinct stressed the franchise question in negotiations which brought on the war. The man chiefly responsible for the break was Sir Alfred Milner, a lawyer-journalist-politician-bureaucrat of mixed German and English blood, who had been appointed high commissioner for South Africa and governor of the Cape in 1897 by the arch-imperialist colonial secretary, Joseph Chamberlain. After learning the Boer tongue, and thoroughly familiarizing himself with the situation, Milner decided to bring matters to a head. On May 4, 1899, he cabled to Chamberlain: "The spectacle of thousands of British subjects kept permanently *in the position of helots,* constantly chafing under undoubted grievances, and calling vainly to Her Majesty's government for redress, does steadily undermine the influence and reputation of Great Britain. . . ."[2] The itali-

[1] The dispute as to whether by the Convention of 1884 England retained "suzerainty" over the South African Republic, although the word itself was omitted from that document, was important. See the elaborate controversy in *State Papers*, 91, especially pp. 557-646. *Cf. supra*, p. 173, footnote 2.

[2] The whole dispatch is worth reading, as it shows how Milner regarded the franchise question as a means of reasserting British determination, and as a cure for the many complaints regarding Transvaal legislation: see *State Papers*. 96. pp. 662-7.

cized phrase deserves study. As a matter of fact, the requirement of a few years' residence for the naturalization of alien immigrants was and is a familiar practice of civilized nations, and Milner himself recognized the right of Transvaal to require a five years' qualification; but any term longer than five years he considered tantamount to serfdom, helotage. This is a fascinating bit of logic, but still more intriguing is his statement "that the only effective way of protecting our subjects is to help them to cease to be our subjects," that is, to help them become citizens of Transvaal. Patriotism ordinarily dictates the opposite course, the retention of subjects, and the reader may perhaps wonder why a nation should be willing to fight in order to "protect" subjects so unpatriotic as to desire citizenship in another nation. But the paradox is easily explained if one remembers that underneath the superficial franchise question lay the fundamental economic reason why Englishmen desired power in Transvaal, and the imperialist desire for dominant power in all South Africa.

In a celebrated conference with Milner at Bloomfontein,[1] May 31-June 5, 1899, President Kruger offered to reduce the franchise qualification from fourteen years to seven, on condition that all future disputes be submitted to arbitration. "Such a demand," comments one historian, "no self-respecting nation could consider for a moment."[2] As a matter of fact, even the imperialist Chamberlain was willing to consider it,[3] but Milner was ready to fight for the difference of two years, or rather, he was ready to use the difference as a pretext for fighting, for when the Boers later offered to concede the two years, he found other grievances.[4] Milner persuaded his chief, and in September was begun the movement of British troops to South Africa from India, and the Mediterranean, while an expeditionary force was prepared in England. Kruger, for his part, was no less bellicose; there is little doubt that he considered war inevitable, that he was unduly contemptuous of British military strength and unwarrantably hopeful of German and other foreign sup-

[1] See Milner's reports to Chamberlain, *State Papers*, 91, pp. 697-728; *cf. Memoirs of Paul Kruger*, pp. 233 ff.

[2] N. D. Harris, *Intervention and Colonization in Africa*, p. 188.

[3] With modifications. See Chamberlain's long dispatch of July 27, 1899. *State Papers*, 91, pp. 763-771. *Cf. ibid.*, pp. 830-4 for the new franchise law promulgated on July 26, 1899.

[4] See their correspondence, *ibid.*, pp. 772 ff., especially 853-4, 867-74.

port, and that he prolonged negotiations from June to October waiting for the southern summer, which would bring grass on the dry veldt for his mounted forces. At length, on Oct. 9, 1899, he sent a forty-eight-hour ultimatum, demanding that all controversies be submitted to "the friendly course of arbitration," and that Britain should withdraw her troops from the borders of Transvaal and cancel her other military preparations.[1] The ultimatum was scorned, war was declared on Oct. 11, and the next day the Boers attacked a British armored train. The Orange Free State joined Transvaal. Most Englishmen rallied to their national cause. Only a few, such as David Lloyd George—then a young but promising Welsh firebrand—opposed what he called a war for forty-five per cent dividends.

The Boer War, thus begun, lasted from 1899 to 1902, and was the greatest foreign war in which Great Britain had yet been engaged, considering the number of British soldiers involved. The Boers never had more than about forty thousand men in the field, but their stubborn courage and the vast extent of the country made British victory difficult. After taking the offensive at the outset, the Boer armies were defeated and driven back by Lord Roberts and 250,000 men, the Boer capitals were captured, and Kruger fled to Europe, to be rebuffed by the German government but received as a hero in France and Holland. After Kruger's flight, however, the indomitable remnants of the Boer army continued to wage a bitter guerilla warfare against the invader, and in order to crush out resistance Lord Kitchener of Egyptian fame took command of the British forces and conducted systematic "drives," through one district after another, consolidating his conquests by chains of blockhouses, and sweeping the Boer women and children into concentration camps—in which, by the way, there was no little suffering. Only after forty thousand Boers had been captured, four thousand killed, and other thousands wounded,[2] did the Boer generals consent to sign the peace treaty of Vereenigung,[3] May 31, 1902, accepting King Edward VII's sovereignty, on condition that the Dutch language be permitted in schools and courts, that the conquered republics be given self-government as soon

[1] *Ibid.*, pp. 945-8.
[2] The war cost Great Britain 30,000 lives and £250,000,000.
[3] *State Papers*, 95, p. 160.

as possible, and that Great Britain pay £3,000,000 as compensation for destroyed farms.

In shaping Britain's foreign policy, and, therefore, in contributing to the international situation which led to the Great War in Europe, the Boer War played no small part. British statesmen, particularly imperialist statesmen, felt as never before the disadvantages of British isolation, when they found themselves in 1899 confronted by a disapproving world. Joseph Chamberlain, the mahdi of British imperialism, after holding conferences with the German Emperor and his foreign minister, Count von Bülow, publicly declared on Nov. 30, 1899—shortly after the outbreak of war in South Africa—that England could not remain isolated; the most natural alliance, he said, would be with "the great German Empire," and he even hoped for a "new triple alliance" of Germany, the United States, and Great Britain, to preserve the peace of the world. For two years secret negotiations for an Anglo-German alliance continued, but they were balked by the clumsiness of German diplomacy, the vehement Anglophobia of the German public, the difficulty of reconciling an Anglo-German bond with the Triple Alliance, and by German naval expansion.[1] During the war, it may be explained, British warships seized three German mail-steamers, thereby provoking such a storm of German indignation as could with difficulty be appeased by the release of the captured vessels; and this indignation was utilized by Tirpitz and the Kaiser as a convenient means of obtaining the Reichstag's assent to appropriations for the creation of "a fleet of such strength that war with the mightiest naval power would involve risks threatening that power's supremacy." There and then began that jealous naval rivalry which brought Germany and England into increasing antagonism, and which contributed with other factors to force England into the arms of France and Russia.

Briton, Boer, and Black in South Africa

Milner received the customary reward of successful British empire-builders—he was made a baron in 1901 and a viscount in 1902. He was offered a cabinet post as secretary for the colonies, but preferred during the reconstruction period to remain

[1] See *Die Grosse Politik*, 15, chs. 101-3; 17, chs. 109-111.

at his post in South Africa, acting also as governor of Transvaal and Orange River Colony, which had been annexed during the war. His every effort was bent to "restart the colonies on a higher plane of civilization." This apparently meant the speedy economic restoration of the country: Boers were repatriated, the gold mines reopened, tariffs and railway rates were brought into uniformity. At the instance of the mine-owners he permitted the importation of more than 50,000 Chinese coolies, bound by indentures for three years' work, to provide cheap labor in the mines. Less haste was made in fulfilling the treaty pledge of self-government for the conquered provinces. At last, in 1905, a constitution providing for representative institutions (but not full self-government) was granted to Transvaal, and Milner, with health exhausted, resigned. Later on, it may be added, he became one of the most prominent imperialist statesmen of England and a member of the war cabinet during the great struggle with Germany.

Milner's policy of importing Chinese coolies in South Africa accorded ill with his talk of "a higher plane of civilization," for the coolies were little better than slaves during their terms of indenture, working for insignificant wages and subject to flogging for even slight disobedience. This "Chinese slavery," as Liberals called it, was one of the reproaches flung at the Conservative Balfour Government by the Liberal Opposition.[1] When the Conservatives fell from power, the new British cabinet was headed by the anti-imperialist Campbell-Bannerman and included the radical Lloyd George, who had denounced the Boer War. The premier believed that the Boer War was a disaster; but it could not be undone, nor could its inevitable result, the annexations, be prevented; Great Britain could, however, at least fulfill the pledge of self-government.[2] This was done for Transvaal in 1906 and Orange River Colony in 1907, regardless of the danger that the Boer leaders would almost certainly control the two provinces, under any democratic white franchise. In fact, the first elections gave the Boers a majority in Transvaal and Orange River Colony, and shortly afterwards the Afrikander Bond—the Boer organization—won the elections in the Cape Colony.

[1] See J. A. Spender, *The Life of the Right Hon. Sir Henry Campbell-Bannerman* (London, 1923), II, 143-6. [2] *Ibid.*, II, 233-44.

The Boers now had the upper hand in three of the four colonies, and were soon to have still greater power. General Louis Botha,[1] the Boer premier of Transvaal, became a friend of Dr. Jameson—whose part in the Raid was now a matter of the past—and cooperated with him in promoting a movement for the union of the four South African colonies—the Cape, Natal, Transvaal and Orange River Colony. A convention summoned in 1908 drafted a federal constitution, which was approved as the South Africa Act (1909) by the British Parliament, and in 1910 the four colonies were federated in the Union of South Africa.[2] From the outset, the Boers dominated the Union government. Botha himself served as Union premier from 1910 until his death in 1919, and was followed by General Jan Smuts, who had been a comrade-in-arms in the campaigns against the British during the Boer War and right-hand man of Botha in politics since the war. Botha and Smuts alike believed, as practical statesmen, that in friendly cooperation with the British in South Africa and under the protecting aegis of the Empire the Boer people could best prosper. And why not? They were now masters of all British South Africa.

Botha and Smuts came increasingly under the spell of British imperialism. Botha conquered German South West Africa during the war and, as a delegate at the Peace Conference, insisted that it be given to South Africa (as a mandate). Smuts served as British commander in the campaign to conquer German East Africa, not for the Boers, but for the Empire; he was an influential member of Lloyd George's war cabinet and a trusted adviser of the London government in imperial affairs. At the Imperial Conference of 1923 Smuts stood forth as a most ardent advocate of imperial tariff preference and imperial economic solidarity. With the British owners of South African mines the Boer leaders had at first a quarrel; they opposed and ended the importation of Asiatic labor; but they permitted the importation of negro labor, on the contract system, from Portuguese Mozambique, and as time went on they found themselves in ever closer harmony with imperialist business interests. As a

[1] Earl Buxton's *General Botha* (London, 1924) throws much light on this interesting figure.

[2] See Professor D. P. Newton's valuable collection of *Select Documents Relating to the Unification of South Africa* (London, 1924, 2 vols.).

South African labor leader put it, they took "what may be termed the 'big finance' view of our various internal and domestic problems."

The alliance of Botha and Smuts with British imperialism encountered important elements of opposition. Against them General Hertzog, a talented Boer general, built up a "nationalist" party whose slogan was "South Africa first," and whose recruits were found chiefly among the Boer farmers of the "back veldt" and the Boer laborers in the mines (many of the white workers in the Rand mines were Dutch). The more extreme of Hertzog's followers would gladly have hauled down the Union Jack and hoisted a republican flag. Indeed, during the Great War, several prominent Boer officers attempted an armed revolution only to be crushed by Botha. Hertzog himself, however, refrained from definite treason to the Empire, and his party, surviving the rebellion, became strong enough in 1924 to coöperate with the Labor Party in overthrowing Smuts. With Hertzog as head of a Labor-Nationalist coalition cabinet in 1924, the Boer irreconcilables were fairly in the saddle, but they were pledged not to cut loose from the Empire. The very fact that such a coalition and such a pledge were possible suggests that the Nationalist movement had become less anti-British and more economic. Boer farmers and laborers were joining with British laborers against imperialist capitalists.

The trend of economic imperialism is suicidal. British imperialism in South Africa meant British investments in South Africa, which in turn meant the economic development of South Africa. So long as economic development was confined to producing more gold and diamonds, more wool, hides, ostrich feathers, copper, and other raw materials, and in return importing more British machinery, cloth, and other manufactures, colony and mother-country might be regarded as realizing the imperialist ideal. But inevitably manufacturing industries spring up to supply local needs. South Africa had 530 factories in 1890; 6,890, in 1920. These local factories in increasing measure are supplying the shoes, the clothes, the machinery, used by the colonists, while competing British and foreign manufactures are excluded by almost prohibitive customs duties. From an economic point of view, South Africa is still primarily colonial, in that it is chiefly a source of raw materials and a market for

British manufactures, but it is beginning the transition from the colonial to the competitive stage.[1]

In this transition South Africa is confronted by difficult labor and race problems. Not only is there the friction between the Boers, who number about eight hundred thousand, and the other (chiefly British) whites, who number about seven hundred thousand. There is also a growing antagonism between farmer and white labor on one hand and "big business" on the other, as in most civilized countries. But graver is the opposition between the white population, a million and a half in all, and the colored population of five and a half millions, mostly negroes. In the early days of Cape Colony, the Boers used the negroes as agricultural slaves, and it was the London Government that took the rôle of emancipator and champion of the black. Since then, the Boers have continued, on the whole, to insist, like the Southern planter, on the racial inferiority of the negro, and the London officials have leaned toward the humanitarian side, but not sufficiently to prevent the negroes from being divorced from the land. A recent issue of the *Official Year Book* of the Union of South Africa shows that the total amount of land owned by the whites is about 230 million acres, whereas the natives own 2 million, in addition to one million owned by missions and 23.5 millions set aside as "native reserves," a total of 27 millions. For a million and a half whites, 230 million acres; for five and a half million negroes, 27 million acres! Moreover, by General Botha's Land Act of 1913, natives were forbidden to buy from whites lands outside the native reservations. Only 123,000 natives lived on native-owned farms; more than two millions lived in the reserves, and the remainder either lived on European-owned soil or worked in the cities and mines. In the mines, some 281,000 were employed, at wages averaging about thirty pounds a year, as compared with the £478 received by the average white worker. Negro laborers for the mines were collected on the reservations by "recruiting agents" who took them on contract for a period of service; at the mines, the black laborers were herded together in "compounds" or barracks, under special supervision, much as though slavery had never been abolished. Such treatment accorded well enough with the attitude of the

[1] The facts in this and succeeding paragraphs are taken from various official reports.

Boers, and with the views of imperialists such as Rhodes, who considered the negroes lazy folk created by God to render compulsory labor in the mines. But the consequence of such policies was to aggravate the race problem. Instead of learning improved methods of agriculture, and becoming prosperous small farmers, as in Gold Coast, the South African negroes were divorced from the soil, and those employed in industry formed a dangerously discontented industrial proletariat. Moreover, the fact that negroes could vote in Cape Colony but not in the other three colonies, added a political grievance to economic unrest. Such inequalities were most acutely resented by "Cape Boys" (mulattoes) and negroes who obtained education in mission schools and entered into the skilled trades and professions. One has only to talk with educated South African negroes to realize that the ruthless exercise of white supremacy, under the aegis of British imperialism, has created a negro reaction of grave character, withal the bulk of the black population is still inert and impotent.[1]

By way of contrast, the other British possessions in South Africa, outside the Union, claim passing notice. Rhodesia has already been considered. There is also the vast semi-desert Bechuanaland Protectorate, with its scant population of 150,000 negro herdsmen; and the small protectorate of Swaziland, and Basutoland. The last-named has been called the Switzerland of South Africa; it is a beautiful mountain country, a third smaller than the Switzerland of Europe, and inhabited entirely by blacks. Here the land is owned entirely by the natives, under a communal system which they understand better than individual proprietorship, and neither mining nor industry has made inroads on rural simplicity. The native population, tilling its fields and tending its cattle in peace, has quadrupled since British annexation (1868) and prospered in a most remarkable degree, thanks to the exclusion of concession-hunters and white settlers. British imperialism has here been far more benevolent and beneficent than in the Union, partly for historical reasons, but chiefly because there was no great mineral wealth.

[1] See the semi-annual *Report of the Select Committee on Native Affairs* of the Union of South Africa (Cape Town, *Cape Times, Ltd.*, Government Printers) and, for comparison, *Native Life in South Africa* (London, King), by Sol. T. Plaatje, a Baralong (negro) journalist of Kimberley; and T. J. Jones, *Education in Africa*, ch. ix.

Taken all together, the Union, Rhodesia, and the former German South West Africa, and the other British colonies in South Africa, constitute a rich and extensive empire almost half as large as the continent of Europe, wonderfully suited, by climate, for white population, and richly endowed with minerals precious and utilitarian. Yet in all its history it has not attracted as many European immigrants as the United States received in the single year 1913, nor is it rapidly becoming a white man's country. The negroes still form four-fifths of the population. The dream of Cecil Rhodes, and of other British imperialists, that upon the healthful high veldt would some day live a sturdy British people, is not yet realized, or even near fulfilment. But the Transvaal alone had produced four billions of dollars' worth of gold since 1868, over a billion dollars' worth of diamonds have been exported, and the trade of South Africa, in which England has the largest share, is gradually rising toward the billion-dollar level which it exceeded in the boom year 1920. Here, if anywhere, is to be found the justification of the blood and treasure so freely poured out to make South Africa, in the words of Cecil Rhodes, "all red."

CHAPTER X

NORTH AFRICA AND THE GREAT POWERS

FROM the dark jungles of equatorial Africa, from the monotonous veldt of the South, the scene shifts to the smiling and temperate coastlands of the north. The most valuable parts of the Dark Continent for commerce, investment, and white colonization are the northern and southern extremities, and while Britain was appropriating the latter, France was endeavoring to make of the former a new and greater France.

Nowhere was the game of imperialist world politics played with greater abandon, or more vicious international consequences, than in the African lands north of the tropic of Cancer. Here France and England grimly played for Egyptian stakes; here Italy found reason to join, then later to desert, the Triple Alliance; here Germany and France desperately bid against each other for Morocco, until Europe was brought within a hair's breadth of war.

AVENGING AN INSULT—ALGERIA

White sails swelling full against blue water and bluer sky, a gallant French fleet coursed from Toulon through the Mediterranean, five hundred miles to the African shore, where among green palms gleamed the white mosques of Algiers. The Arab King or Dey of Algiers, so history relates, had recklessly struck a French envoy in the face with a fly-whisk or fan, and to clear the escutcheon of France there was but one conventional method. To be sure, three years had intervened since the Dey's indiscretion, and France during these years had diplomatically considered various projects of international intervention; but the lapse of years does not clear away an indignity to national honor. The French fleet, therefore, sailed in May, 1830, to punish Algiers. Furthermore, the French government announced its purpose to stop the attacks of piratical Algerian corsairs (then called "Barbary pirates") on European shipping in the Mediterranean. Still more important, though not publicly proclaimed, was the desire of Charles X and his ministers to achieve some brilliant feat of arms and diplomacy which would not only restore the lustre of French prestige, dimmed since Waterloo, but also revive the declining popularity of the tottering Bourbon monarchy. In vain British statesmen, fearful of anything which might destroy the quasi-sacred "status quo" or the still more sacrosanct "balance of power," argued and threatened and demanded a promise that the punitive expedition would withdraw from Algiers as soon as a brief lesson in good behavior had been administered to the Dey. The bulldog's bark was worse than his bite, in this case. With impunity the French expedition occupied Algiers and the neighboring coast district, and prepared to stay. The Dey was shipped to Naples. Though the exploit failed of its principal purpose, namely, saving the throne of Charles X, it established France permanently in Algiers.

To extend their power from the seaport of Algiers until it embraced the whole country of Algeria, larger than France itself, the French had to expend thousands of lives and millions of treasure, during three decades of almost incessant fighting after 1830. Little did they realize, at the outset, to how costly an enterprise the caprice of Charles X's cabinet had committed them. Particularly serious was the protracted warfare required to subdue Abd-el-Kader, a valiant Arab emir, who again and again roused the Mohammedan tribes to wage a "holy war" against the Christian invader. Not until 1847 was the emir taken prisoner and sent to France and not until 1871 was the last important rebellion in Algeria crushed.[1]

Conquered more or less by chance, before the age of deliberate imperialism had dawned, Algeria aroused relatively little enthusiasm in France until the latter part of the nineteenth century.[2] Then French imperialists found in Algeria not only a reason for new North-African conquests, but a colony valuable in itself. Much larger than the mother-country, Algeria was

[1] E. LeMarchand, *L'Europe et la Conquête d'Alger* (Paris, 1913); J. Darcy, *Cent Années de Rivalité Coloniale* (Paris, 1904); chs. 2-4; M. Dubois et A. Terrier, *Un Siècle d'Expansion Coloniale* (Paris, 1902), 154 ff., 203 ff., 262 ff.; C. Rousset, *La Conquête de l'Algérie.*

[2] See R. Vâlet, *L'Afrique du Nord devant le Parlement au XIX*[me] *Siècle* (Alger, 1924), part 1; P. Leroy-Beaulieu, *La Colonisation* (Paris, 1886); *livre deuxième,* ch. V.; Dubois et Terrier, *loc. cit.*

almost ideally suited for French colonization. Along its fertile coast plains the olive tree grew in abundance; on the mountains back of the coast were rich forests, and between the mountain ranges lay plains and valleys, fertile of soil and healthful of climate, where cattle and grain could be raised. The native population was small—even to-day there are but five million natives, and a generation or two ago there were less than four million. Unlike the negroes of equatorial jungles, the Algerians

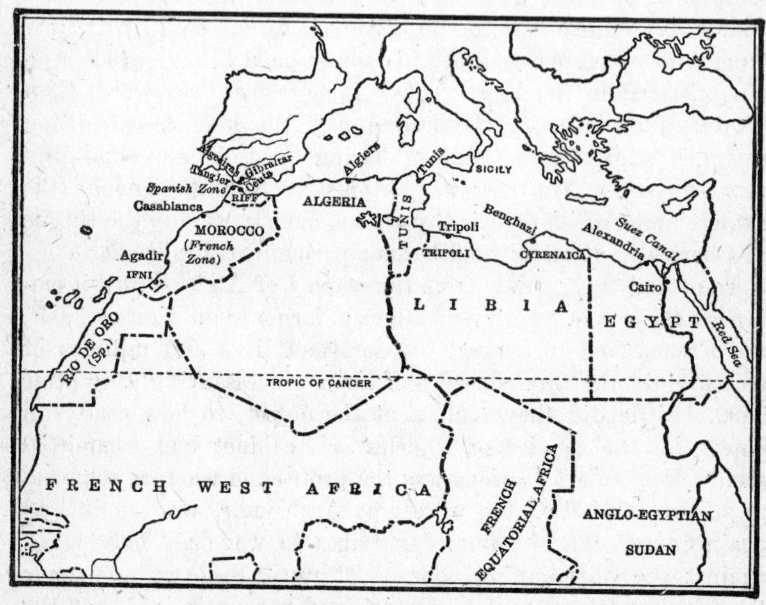

North Africa.

are industrious, accustomed to agriculture, handicrafts and trade. Some of the Arabs, who form the largest element in the population, were tent-dwellers and herdsmen wandering through the deserts and steppes of the back-country; but in the more fertile regions the Arabs had settled down, before French conquest, to live in villages of stone and to gain their livelihood by trade, tillage, or artistic handwork. Racially different, but culturally much influenced by the Arabs, were the Berbers, white but sun-tanned. Along the coast, where they lived in stone houses with red-tiled roofs, and tilled their fields with wooden plows, the Berbers are known as Kabyles; in the mountains they are the Shawiyas; in the desert, they are the Tuareg tribes. In addition, there are the "Moors" of mixed Berber, Arab and European blood, indolent but canny tradesmen of the towns, well able to compete with the traditional mercantile ability of the numerous Jews.

Though in Algeria there was room for colonists, Frenchmen are notoriously loath to quit *la belle patrie,* and after many decades of official attempts to attract French settlers, Algeria to-day has but half a million French inhabitants; of these no inconsiderable number are descended from immigrants who forsook Alsace when that province was conquered by the Germans.[1] French and other Europeans own the very fertile grainfields and vineyards and olive groves in the coast zone, and conduct the foreign trade and finance of the colony, leaving the natives to till the less fertile and more remote parts of the country, and to raise sheep and cattle for export.[2] And as General Mangin observed, *"Le coeur des Berbères reste à prendre."* [3]

Of all the French colonies, Algeria is now by far the most important from the viewpoint of economic imperialism. As a market for French goods it is three times as valuable as any other French possession; indeed, among all the customers of French industry Algeria ranks seventh (after Great Britain, Belgium, Germany, United States, Switzerland, and Italy).

It is not, however, very important as a source of raw materials, with the notable exception of phosphate; its chief exports to France are wine, grain and meat.

COUP DE FORTUNE OU DE BOURSE—TUNIS

From Algeria French imperialists naturally turned their eyes toward the neighboring land of Tunis, just to the east, much like Algeria in climate and race, but smaller. In ancient times, Tunis was the seat of the mighty Carthaginian empire, and later a prosperous Roman province of whose high civilization

[1] From 1871 to 1895 some 13,300 French families (54,000 persons) were colonized on 640,000 hectares of land in Algeria.

[2] *Exposé de la Situation Générale de l'Algérie en 1924*, présenté par M. Th. Steeg, gouverneur général de l'Algérie (Alger, 1925); V. Piquet, *La Colonisation française dans l'Afrique du Nord* (Paris, 1912), Chs. V-VIII; E. F. Gautier, *L'Algérie et la Métropole* (Paris, 1920).

[3] Mangin, *Regards sur la France d'Afrique*, p. 72.

mute testimony is offered to-day by marble ruins of Roman temples and amphitheaters, half submerged by the sands of the desert. These remains, by the way, seem to indicate that the regions in the south and interior of Tunis, now parched by winds from the Sahara, were once fertile and populous. But when Tunis began, in the second half of the nineteenth century, to attract the attention of European imperialists, it was a "backward" country, thinly populated, and ruled by a Mohammedan Bey, nominally subject to Turkish suzerainty but actually swayed only by his own despotic caprice.

In the 1860's European speculators, money-lenders, traders and concession-hunters began to swarm into Tunis. The Bey found it easy to borrow money, difficult to repay it. When his debts reached what for him was the stupendous figure of 28 million francs, at an average of 13% interest, he welcomed an apparently brilliant proposal that these miscellaneous obligations be repaid by floating a consolidated loan of 35 million francs on the Paris Bourse at a more reasonable rate of interest. To his chagrin he received less than six millions cash from the sale of his bonds, and found himself saddled with the interest charges on the new 35 plus the original 28 millions. When he levied heavier taxes to carry the interest charges, his subjects rebelled; the cost of suppressing insurrection necessitated new loans; the additional interest burden meant higher taxes; and so the vicious circle went on—loans—taxes—rebellions—loans. It is said that in desperation the Bey at length took to poisoning rich subjects and confiscating their property. His French creditors, growing anxious as they received no payments on their coupons, insisted on the establishment of a financial commission to supervise, or curtail, his free-handed expenditures. Italian financiers, and Italian patriots, remembering that Carthage was once subject to Rome, protested, with the result that Italy and England were admitted to the commission in 1869 and the Tunisian debt was "consolidated" at 125 millions.[1] Then ensued years of financial rivalry, French, English and Italian consuls at Tunis vying with each other in efforts to obtain influence at court and railway, telegraph or land concessions for their fellow-countrymen. It became increasingly apparent that, what with the disorderly condition of the country and the inse-

[1] The nominal amount before consolidation was 160 millions.

curity of its debt, and what with the awakening of European imperialism, one of the three powers would soon appropriate Tunis.

Though at the Bey's court the Italians enjoyed most favor, France was more fortunate in European chancelleries. The Disraeli-Salisbury government of England was glad, at the Berlin Congress of 1878, to inform the French diplomatist Waddington that England recognized the right of France, since she had occupied Algeria, to exercise decisive pressure on Tunis, and looked upon this result as inevitable. More plainly, Salisbury told Waddington France could take Tunis if she would offer no objection to the ambitions of Disraeli in Cyprus and the Near East.[1] Bismarck likewise dropped a hint that Germany would not object to French intervention in Tunis; his motive, doubtless, was to involve France in colonial ventures and to sow seeds of discord between France and Italy.[2] And France advised Italy that "Italy cannot cherish dreams of conquest in Tunis without clashing against the will of France and risking a conflict with her."[3]

Not long afterward, an English company offered to sell the railway property it possessed in Tunis. This apparently innocent business affair was viewed in Paris and Rome as a crucial event, for though the value of the railway was paltry (perhaps a million francs), imperialists are quick to interpret the acquisition of any concession by foreign rivals as a national defeat and humiliation. French interests offered a million francs. An Italian concern (the Rubattino Co., which had acquired the first Italian foothold in Eritrea, on the Red Sea) offered two and a half. Finally the Italians bought the property for 4,125,000 francs, four times the original French bid It is significant that

[1] Lady Gwendolyn Cecil, *Life of the Marquis of Salisbury*, II, pp. 332 f.; Mangin, *Regards sur la France d'Afrique*, pp. 78 ff.; G. Hanotaux, *Contemporary France*, III, pp. 576 ff.; (P. H. X.) d'Estournelles de Constant, *La Politique française en Tunisie.* (Paris, 1891); *Documents Diplomatiques, Affaires de Tunisie*, 1870-1881 and supplement, 1881.

[2] *Cf.* Bourgeois et Pagès, *Origines de la Grande Guerre*, p. 192; *Die Grosse Politik*, 3, nos. 655-7; London *Times*, April 4, 1881. On Bismarck's earlier suggestion to Italy, and on his later support of France, as well as on the whole complex of European diplomacy concerning Tunis, see the critical articles by W. L. Langer in *Amer. Hist. Rev.*, Oct. 1925 and Jan. 1926.

[3] A. Lebon, "Les Préliminaires du Traité de Bardo," in *Annales des Sciences Politiques*, 1893, p. 403, citing letter from M. Waddington to Marquis de Noailles, Oct. 13, 1878.

the Italian company made its extravagant offer only after receiving a promise of 600,000 lire a year from the Italian government.[1]

France, however, was not to be so easily balked. The sale of the railway occurred in July, 1880. In August, by one of the coincidences that abound in imperialist annals, Paris received most ominous reports of warlike unrest among the Tunisian tribes on the border of Algeria. Such reports accumulated rapidly, until in the spring of 1881 border raids provided the "incident" which is usually considered necessary to bring such matters to a head.[2] In April Jules Ferry obtained from the Chamber of Deputies authority and six million francs to send a punitive expedition, for the purpose of guaranteeing "in a serious and lasting fashion the security and the future of African France (Algeria)"; conquest, he explained, was far from his mind.[3] Thirty-five thousand French soldiers were then thrown across the Algerian border into Tunis, but instead of merely punishing the unruly border tribes, the French army compelled the Bey to sign the Treaty of Bardo, May 12, 1881, allowing the French to occupy any regions it considered necessary, promising not to act in international affairs without first consulting France, accepting a generous French promise to protect his person, dynasty and territories against attack, and, last but not least, authorizing France to make new financial arrangements in the interest of his creditors. French troops then overran the country and by the end of the month, in the words of a French historian, "pacification was complete." The conquest was complete.

Ferry, however, was furiously assailed in the French Parliament for what his opponent Clemenceau styled a "*coup de Bourse*"—a stroke of high finance. To such taunts Ferry retorted, it was a "*coup de Fortune.*" Could any "*bon Français*" he asked the Chamber (Nov. 5, 1881) bear the thought of letting

[1] *Discours et opinions de Jules Ferry*, IV, p. 538.

[2] In the meantime the French had warned Italy that the French cabinet could not look with indifferent eye while Italian interests secured the control of the cables and railways of Tunis; and the French consul, Roustan, had persuaded or browbeaten the Bey to give the French Bône-Guelma Company railway concessions to compensate for the one the Italians had purchased. That the border raids were not the reason for French aggression in Tunis, but merely provided a reason or pretext for armed action, appears pretty clearly from any detailed narrative.

[3] *Journal Officiel.* Chambre des députés, April 11, 1881.

some other power (Italy) have "a territory which is, in every sense, the key to our house"? Furthermore, he asserted, there had been in the last decade no fewer than 2365 violations of the Algerian frontier by Tunisian warriors: surely these were numerous enough to justify intervention! But particularly meaningful, in the light of the events we have described, was Ferry's guarded statement that the immediate cause of intervention was the hostility shown by the Bey toward "French influence." In the more candid words of the French foreign minister, Barthélemy Saint-Hilaire, the Bey had become hostile to "all French enterprises in Tunis." He had, it is true, favored Italian as opposed to French, concessions for telegraphs, railways and ports; and the Italians were gaining the upper hand. Not border raids, but economic rivalry, and strategic interests brought French troops into Tunis.[1]

Though Ferry and his foreign minister were forced out of office by the criticism of the Tunis venture, and though M. Roustan, the French consul, who had been so active in Tunisian concession-hunting, was openly charged in the press with having been implicated in not altogether honorable financial schemes in Tunis, France nevertheless retained the fruits of Ferry's *Coup de Bourse.* Two years later, on June 8, 1883, the new Bey of Tunis was presented with a treaty which he could hardly do otherwise than sign, and which openly established the French "*protectorat*" and provided for a loan of 125 million francs and the enactment of reforms desired by France.[2] Ferry, having returned to power, explained the advantages of a protectorate over annexation pure and simple. The protectorate was cheaper, since there would be fewer French officials to pay; it was easier, since the native administration would be responsible for details and petty difficulties; and it safeguarded "the dignity of the vanquished." The protectorate meant that the native Bey was retained (and his successors have been) as nominal ruler, with a staff of officials, but a French resident-general representing the French minister of foreign affairs presided over the Tunisian cabinet, conducted foreign relations, had veto power over the Bey's edicts and controlled the administration

[1] A strong statement to this effect is that in Woolf, *Empire and Commerce in Africa*, pp. 79 ff.

[2] *Archives diplomatiques*, 73, p. 12.

while French "civil controllers" or governors supervised the caïds and chiefs. At present eight of the eleven ministers of the Bey are Frenchmen.

Under French control Tunis was unquestionably more orderly and more prosperous than of old. A French army, supported by native regiments, preserved peace. Schools and colleges were opened, roads and railroads were built, a postal system established. Commerce figures rising from 27 million francs in 1881 to 100 in 1899 and 1,395 in 1921 afford an index of remarkable economic progress. After 1885 the mining of phosphate of lime, for fertilizer, became a big industry. The French government, of course, took care to safeguard French financial interests by suppressing the International Financial Commission, consolidating the Tunisian debt at four per cent interest (a profitable return, since the bonds had been purchased at much less than par). France could not at once exclude foreign commercial interests from Tunis, as Great Britain had obtained from the Bey in 1875 a treaty promise to limit the tariff to eight per cent ad valorem on imports,[1] and other powers had treaties providing for equal treatment. But in 1896-7 these powers gave up their rights[2] and permitted France to establish a high protective tariff in Tunis, from which French goods were in large part exempted. It is interesting to note that Great Britain consented to this step only on the explicit condition that British cotton goods should not be taxed more than 5% ad valorem, and as a result Great Britain continued to supply the Tunisian Arabs with most of their flowing cotton garments, while France practically monopolized the other branches of trade, after 1898.

Tunis like Algeria is temperate and suitable for white colonization, but, despite the earnest efforts of a "Committee of French Settlement" to promote French immigration, Tunis has attracted only 55,000 French settlers and business men. The French, by the way, occupy 2,530,000 acres, as compared with a total of seven million acres of tillage land available for the population of two millions. Strangely enough, there are almost fifty per cent more Italians than Frenchmen in Tunis.[3]

[1] *State Papers*, 66, p. 19.

[2] *Documents Diplomatiques, Révision des Traités Tunisiens*, 1881-1897.

[3] *Statistique générale annuelle de la Tunisie;* J. Saurin, *Le Peuplement français en Tunisie;* Piquet, *La Colonisation française dans l'Afrique du Nord*, chs. 10-13; L. Woolf, *Empire and Commerce in Africa*, pp. 325-30.

By the "punitive expedition" of 1881, then, France gained a fairly valuable colony. But she gained also an enemy. Tunis, remember, is the Carthage of ancient history, and, as such, was regarded by Italian patriots as the historic footstool of Rome. Great was Italian indignation when France occupied the country of Hannibal.[1] And in the very next year, Italy joined hands in the Triple Alliance with Germany and Austria-Hungary. The secret negotiations between Rome, Berlin and Vienna, published since the Great War, reveal the depth of Italian enmity toward France during the two decades that followed 1881.[2] When the Triple Alliance was renewed in 1887, Italy signed with Germany a secret treaty, article III of which provided:

> If it were to happen that France should make a move to extend her occupation, or even her protectorate or her sovereignty, under any form whatsoever, in the North African territories, whether of the Vilayet of Tripoli or of the Moroccan Empire, and that in consequence thereof Italy, in order to safeguard her position in the Mediterranean, should feel that she must herself undertake action in the said North African territories, or even have recourse to extreme measures in French territory in Europe, the state of war which would thereby ensue between Italy and France would constitute *ipso facto* . . . the *casus fœderis.*

In short, Germany and Italy together would fight to prevent any further extension of French imperialism in northern Africa. The reference to "extreme measures in French territory in Europe" was interpreted by Prince Bismarck to mean Nice and Corsica.[3]

Inevitable Necessity in Morocco

"Not insatiable land hunger, but inevitable necessity," says a French historian,[4] took France into Morocco. And he was not entirely wrong. It was inevitable in the psychology of imperialism: a French Bourbon having taken Algeria in a futile effort to save his tottering throne, imperialistic logic made Tunis, on the east, "the key to our house," and Morocco, on the west, became equally indispensable. As someone has said, a large empire is the best of all reasons for a larger empire.

[1] See Crispi's memoirs.

[2] Summarized by Pribram, *Secret Treaties of Austria-Hungary, passim; cf. Die Grosse Politik.*

[3] Pribram, I, 113; II, 80.

[4] Bernard.

Morocco is a country a little larger than France, situated at the western end of the north-African coast, south of Gibraltar. Thanks to the snow-crowned Atlas Mountains—the peaks on which by Greek legend the god Atlas dwelt, bearing the heavens on his shoulder—the northern and western parts of the country are sheltered from the hot Sahara winds; much of Morocco is not only fertile but marvellously pleasant and healthful in climate. Attractive as the country might be, however, and important in strategic situation, it was the last part of Africa to be appropriated by European imperialism. Until 1912 it remained an independent empire, ruled by a Mohammedan sultan or amir, "Prince of True Believers," directly descended from the son-in-law of the Prophet Mohammed, and entitled therefore to the Shereefian umbrella as insignia of exalted rank. Barbarous Berber tribes in the mountains, Arabs and "Moors," or Arab-Berber hybrids, in the plains and towns gave little obedience to the central government or Maghzen; in fact, only a certain number of tribes were directly subject to the sultan, the others being a law unto themselves. Perhaps their warlike spirit may account for the long preservation of their independence.

But a better reason is the fact that too many European powers were interested in preventing any one empire from swallowing up the sultan's realm. Spain, asserting historic claims, had sent General O'Donnel to Morocco with a strong army, in 1859-60, only to be checked by England, but still Spain retained a weak grip on Ceuta, just opposite Gibraltar, and several other places along the coast. England, for her part, not only had a strategic reason for keeping any strong European power out of the hills across the strait from Gibraltar, but also enjoyed, at the opening of the twentieth century, the largest share of Morocco's trade. Germany had had a representative at the sultan's court, since 1873, and by a treaty of 1890 obtained a guarantee of commercial rights equal to those of the "most-favored nation," although her share in Morocco's commerce was small. A number of other European powers, and also the United States, enjoyed the same right of "most-favored nation" treatment, under the Convention signed at Madrid in 1880 by fourteen nations.[1]

[1] See U. S. Tariff Commission. *Colonial Tariff Policies*, pp. 204-5.

Morocco, however, was on the border of Algeria, and Théophile Delcassé, foreign minister of France from 1898 to 1905, was determined to add it to the French African empire. Realizing that it would be necessary to gain the consent of other European powers, Delcassé resorted to secret diplomacy, before overt action. With Italy an agreement was quickly made. Fortunately for Delcassé's purposes, the Italian government inquired whether the Anglo-French agreement of 1899 (the agreement which settled the Fashoda crisis), marking out French and British spheres of interest in the Sudan, would infringe on the Turkish provinces of Tripoli and Cyrenaica, which Italians coveted for themselves. Promptly Delcassé instructed the French ambassador in Rome to reassure the Italian foreign minister, that France had no designs on Tripoli and Cyrenaica. In exchange, the foreign minister, in December, 1900, handed the French ambassador a note saying that Italy would not oppose France in "the exercise and the safeguarding of the rights which are the result for her of the proximity of her territory (Algeria) with that (Moroccan) Empire"—it being "understood that, if a modification of the political or territorial status of Morocco should result therefrom, Italy would reserve to herself, as a measure of reciprocity, the right eventually to develop her influence with regard to Tripolitania-Cyrenaica." Since, up to this date, the Italian government had been prepared to fight rather than permit France to take more of North Africa, the meaning of the rotund and dignified phrases just quoted is clear and simple. Italy would let France conquer the independent empire of Morocco, if France would let Italy seize the Turkish provinces of Tripoli and Cyrenaica. This secret agreement, we may add, so reconciled Rome and Paris that a little later, in 1902, further secret letters were exchanged, by which each nation pledged itself to neutrality in case the other should be attacked, or "should find herself compelled, in defence of her honor or of her security, to take the initiative of a declaration of war." Inconsistent in spirit though not in letter, with Italy's obligations to the Triple Alliance, this secret bargain made it practically certain that Italy would not join Germany in war against France. Thus in one more case, Africa shaped the destiny of Europe.[1]

[1] Pribram, *op. cit.*, II, pp. 226-56.

With Spain Delcassé next sought to bargain. Spain was to have the northern coast, including Tangier and Fez, and a part of the south, if France took the rest. But the Spanish Cabinet, probably fearful of British displeasure, refused to sign the pact, and Delcassé turned to England. The moment could not have been more favorable. The British government, afraid to remain longer in isolation, had been negotiating for an alliance with Germany, only to be irritated and angered by tactless German diplomatic bungling, by German press tirades against British conduct in South Africa, by German navy increases, and by the German Bagdad Railway scheme. From Germany, the English turned to Japan, with which power an alliance was made in 1902—and to France. We need not attempt here to evaluate the miscellaneous factors which brought France and England together in the Entente Cordiale of 1904. Only one point is relevant; that the agreements which sealed the Entente were nothing more nor less than imperialist bargains. One was a convention settling disputes in Newfoundland, West Africa, and Central Africa; another convention dealt with the New Hebrides, in the South Seas; there was a "declaration" concerning Siam, Madagascar, and the New Hebrides; but most important of all was the bargain regarding Egypt and Morocco. France to gain Morocco was willing that England should keep Egypt—such was the meat of the matter.

The details are not without interest as illustrations of imperialist diplomacy. Part of the agreement was published as an Anglo-French Declaration of April 8, 1904.[1] In this document France denied any intention of altering the political status of Morocco, that is to say, of annexing Morocco or establishing a protectorate; France was to make an agreement with Spain concerning Morocco; no fortifications were to be constructed opposite Gibraltar; and Great Britain recognized that "it appertains to France" to "preserve order" and to "provide assistance for the purpose of all administrative, economic, financial, and military reforms" in Morocco. In exchange, France gave Britain a free hand in Egypt, as will presently be explained more clearly.

Very different were the "secret articles" signed on the same day, and carefully concealed until they "leaked" out in a

[1] *France No. 1 (1904)*, Cd. 1952.

French newspaper seven years later.[1] The public declaration that France had no intention of altering Morocco's independent status was given the lie by the secret agreement that "whenever the Sultain ceases to exercise authority over it," the northern part of Morocco should "come within the sphere of influence of Spain," the bulk of the territory, of course, being left for France. If Spain should decline, the Anglo-French arrangement "would be none the less at once applicable," so little, after all, does the consent of a smaller power matter. Spain, however, did not decline, but rather joined France in making a public declaration that both powers were "firmly attached to the integrity of the Moorish Empire under the sovereignty of the Sultain," and in signing a secret convention which provided for the division of Morocco between France and Spain.[2]

With these secret treaties in his pocket, so to speak, Delcassé confidently appeared before the French Chamber of Deputies on Dec. 10, 1904, and announced that the time had come for France to convince Morocco that France in her own interest must serve the interests of Morocco: "for the sake of our tranquillity, to aid it (Morocco) in establishing internal security and order; for our prosperity, to furnish means (capital) to profit by the resources in which Morocco abounds; so that, continuing to live its own life, its customs, laws and chiefs being safeguarded, under a Sultan whose authority will be strengthened and extended, Morocco will know our power only through the benefits which will accompany it." Morocco, in plain Anglo-Saxon, was to be another Tunis.

The moment was favorable enough. The capture of an American citizen, Perdicaris, by the Moroccan bandit Raisuli, had called worldwide attention to the disorderliness of the country, and French diplomatic aid in obtaining the release of Perdicaris had made a good impression. Affairs in Morocco were approaching a crisis. The young sultan, Abd-el-Aziz, who had ascended the throne—or assumed the umbrella—in 1900 at the age of sixteen years, had been encouraged to spend money recklessly on

[1] The authenticity of the secret articles was admitted and they were officially published by the British Government in its *Treaty Series, 1911, No. 24* (Cd. 5969).

[2] *Archives diplomatiques*, 3d series, 96, p. 677; *Amer. Jour. Int. Law*, Supplement, 6, p. 30; secret agreement, *Parl. Papers*, 1912-13 (Cd. 6010) or Martens, *Nouveau Recueil Général*, 3d series, 5, p. 666.

fireworks, bicycles for himself and the ladies of his harem, player-pianos and other ingenious products of European civilization. To fill his empty treasury, he levied higher taxes, but they produced only revolts. He then turned to Parisian bankers, in 1904, for a loan of 62½ million francs, at five per cent, on the security of 60% of his customs revenues; he received in cash, by the way, only about three-quarters of the face value of the loan, as the investment was risky. Such was the situation when Delcassé sent M. Saint-René Tailliandier to Fez with a program of "reforms" for the Sultan's signature. A force of military police was to be organized under French officers; a state bank was to be established to bring financial order out of chaos; and various public works were to be undertaken with French capital.

A Crisis and a Conference

Just at this point occurred the proverbial slip twixt cup and lip. "By incredible blindness," writes a candid Frenchman, the French government "took precautions with everybody except the only one of its neighbors whom it had serious cause to fear."[1] Italy, Spain and England had been bought off; Russia was an ally; but Germany had been ignored. By the unwritten law of imperialist ethics, when one Great Power seizes an important colony, its rivals may justly feel aggrieved if they be ignored; they should be consulted in advance, and permitted to seize something for themselves by way of "compensation." The German government felt such a grievance, and was resolved to make its displeasure felt.[2]

Early in March, 1905, the Kaiser appealed to President Roosevelt,[3] urging him to join in promising to protect the Sultan against any nation seeking exclusive control; if Spain took Tangier and France the Moroccan hinterland, the Kaiser gloomily predicted, they would dominate the road of American commerce to the Near East and the Far East. As Roosevelt

[1] René Millet, *Notre Politique extérieure*, p. 224.

[2] *Die Grosse Politik*, vol. 20, pt. 1, shows voluminously how sorely Germany felt the grievance. In a memorandum of June 3, 1904, Holstein writes, "Deutschland hat nicht nur aus materiellen Gründen, sondern mehr noch zur Wahrung seines Prestiges gegen die beabsichtigte Aneignung Marokkos durch Frankreich Einspruch zu erheben"—*op. cit.*, p. 208.

[3] *Ibid.*, nos. 6558 ff., *cf.* Bishop, *Theodore Roosevelt*, chs. 36-37.

demurred, the Kaiser himself, acting somewhat reluctantly, at his Chancellor's suggestion,[1] landed from his imperial yacht at Tangier, and made two speeches, short but fateful. The Moroccan sultan, he said, was sovereign and independent; he should be cautious about adopting (the French program of) reforms; Morocco should remain open to the commerce of all nations on equal terms. These apparently banal reaffirmations of the existing legal situation were rightly interpreted in France, by reading between the lines, as a direct veto to Delcassé's plans, a deliberate challenge.[2]

This impression was confirmed when, after receiving advice from a German diplomatist, the sultan declined to ratify the French program of reforms, unless they were first discussed by an international conference of the numerous powers which had signed the Madrid Convention of 1880. Germany likewise demanded an international conference. Delcassé angrily opposed the idea; it would balk his scheme. War seemed very near indeed. When the French cabinet met, early in June, to decide between yielding and fighting—for there seemed to be no other choice—Delcassé pleaded with his colleagues to maintain the honor of France, and told them that Great Britain had promised to mobilize her fleet and land 100,000 men in Schleswig-Holstein, if necessary, to support France.[3] This British promise, by the way, is viewed by English historians [4] as a figment of Delcassé's imagination, and it is probably true that he wrongly interpreted British expressions of sympathy as promises of support; but it is also true that years afterward, in his speech of August 3, 1914, Sir Edward Grey declared England had come very close to war, in 1905, on account of Morocco.

Fortunately for peace, Delcassé's colleagues in the cabinet were against him. They dared not risk war, with Russia, sole ally of France, crippled by the Russo-Japanese War and torn by revolution. Delcassé therefore resigned, and the French

[1] On this point his memoirs are confirmed by *Die Grosse Politik*, esp. 20, pp. 262 ff.

[2] *Documents Diplomatiques, Affaires du Maroc*, 1901-5; Morel, *Morocco in Diplomacy;* The Kaiser's *Memoirs*, ch. 4; *Bourgeois et Pagès. Origines de la Grande Guerre*, p. 308; Debidour, *Hist. dipl. de l'Europe*, II, pp. 32-63, 96-102.

[3] Mévil, *De la Paix de Francfort à la Conference d'Algéciras*, Chs. 4 and 5, for this item and a justification of Delcassé. *Cf. Morocco No. 1 (1906)*.

[4] E.g., *Cambridge Hist. of British Foreign Policy*, III, pp. 342-3.

premier, Rouvier, agreed to a conference. That France yielded gracefully, averting war, was in part due to President Roosevelt's secret urging.[1] "It looked like war," Roosevelt reminiscently confessed, "so I took active hold of the matter . . . and got things temporarily straightened up." He persuaded France that war would be dangerous; and that if a conference were held he would exert his influence to safeguard legitimate French interests. "It was eminently wise," he told the French ambassador, "to avoid war if it could be done by adopting a course which would save the Emperor's self-esteem; that for such a purpose it was wise to help him save his face."

The Algeciras Conference

The Conference held at Algeciras,[2] from January 16 to April 7, 1906, included representatives of eleven European nations, and of the United States, and of Morocco. France had secret assurances of support from England and Russia, and could count also on Spain and Italy, while Germany was practically alone, save for Austria's half-hearted backing. The American delegates, Henry White and Samuel Gummere, took little part in the public proceedings, except to demand equal treatment for the numerous Jews in Morocco; but behind the scenes Roosevelt was working for France. The real contest was fought over the questions of police and finance; who would have military control, and who would exploit Morocco? That the sultan would remain nominally independent, with a nominally open door, was agreed in advance. But France wanted to officer the police and control the bank. Germany, of course, was opposed, and so stubbornly opposed that Roosevelt later wrote Whitelaw Reid: "The trouble is that with Russia out of the way as she now is, Germany believes that she can whip both France and England." Strenuously Roosevelt urged the Kaiser to accept a compromise, whereby France would accept "jointly with Spain a *mandate* from all the Powers, under responsibility to all of them for the

[1] Bishop, *Theodore Roosevelt*, I, chs. 26-7; *cf. Die Grosse Politik*, 20, chs. 147-148.

[2] The French yellow book, *Protocoles et Comptes Rendus de la Conférence d'Algéciras*, together with British *Parliamentary Papers* on Morocco, give the official diplomacy, but need to be supplemented by subsequent relevations, notably Bishop, *op. cit.*, and *Die Grosse Politik*, vols. 20-21.

maintenance of equal rights and opportunities." The word mandate, which I have italicized, and indeed the whole conception, anticipates in almost uncanny fashion the mandate system established fourteen years later.

Germany, however, refused the plan, and offered instead, through the Austrian representative, a project for French military "instructors" at Tangier, Safi, Rabat and Tetuan; Spanish at Mogador, Larache and Mazagan; Swiss, Dutch or Belgian at Casablanca; all supervised by the diplomatic corps representing all the powers, at Tangier. How Roosevelt interpreted such proposals, one may learn from his confidential letter to Reid: "We became convinced . . . that Germany was aiming in effect at the partition of Morocco, which was the very reverse of what she was claiming to desire. She first endeavored to secure a port for herself, and then a separate port, nominally for Holland or Switzerland, which we were convinced would, with the adjacent Hinterland, become German. The French said they would not yield on these points, and as you know it looked as if the conference would come to nothing and that there would then be the possibility of trouble between France and Germany."

Shrewdly taking advantage of the Kaiser's egotism, Roosevelt threatened to publish the whole secret correspondence, if Germany should persist in her refusal of compromise; but if Germany yielded, he would keep his own rôle secret and give all the credit for preserving peace to the Kaiser. The psychology was accurate. Germany yielded, and Roosevelt publicly declared, perhaps with a suppressed chuckle, "In no country is there a warmer admiration for Germany and for Germany's exalted ruler, Emperor William, than here in America." In private, Roosevelt admitted: "In this Algeciras matter, you will notice that while I was most suave and pleasant with the Emperor, yet when it became necessary at the end I stood him on his head with great decision." Or, to put it differently, "where I have taken part of the kernel from him, I have been anxious that he should have all the shell possible, and have that shell painted any way he wished."[1] After such decisive inter-

[1] Since this was written, volume 21 of *Die Grosse Politik* has appeared. The latter shows that Roosevelt did oppose the Austrian proposal and threaten to publish his correspondence with "certain Powers" (nos. 7113 and 7115) and that Germany promptly returned a conciliatory reply (no. 7121); but the German ambassador does not report Roosevelt's promise to

vention, by the President personally, the Senate rather incongruously ratified the agreement with a declaratory resolution which denied any purpose "to depart from the traditional American foreign policy which forbids participation by the United States in the settlement of political questions which are entirely European in their scope."[1]

The General Act of Algeciras,[2] signed on April 7, 1906, by the United States, eleven European powers and Morocco, was an elaborate affair, interesting both as a compromise between France and Germany, and as an experiment in international control of imperialism. Its preamble recognized the independence of Morocco. Government finances were to be entrusted to a State Bank at Tangier, managed by four censors appointed, respectively, by the Deutsche Bank, the Bank of England, the Banque de France, and the Bank of Spain; its capital was to be subscribed in equal parts by the signatory powers, excepting that France should have a larger share. Customs duties, likewise, were placed under international supervision. Concessions or contracts for public works such as railways, roads, telegraphs, harbors, etc., were to be granted upon impartial adjudication, which would accept the most favorable bids regardless of the nationality of the bidder. As for police, a force of 2,000 to 25,000 armed Moroccan police was to be organized, under 16 to 20 French and Spanish officers and 30 to 40 French and Spanish subalterns (*sous-officiers*). The officers would be Spanish at certain ports, French at others, mixed at others. This provision, favorable as it seems to French interests, was partly counteracted by the stipulation that the whole police administration should be supervised by a Swiss officer, as Inspector General.

Taken as a whole, the Algeciras Act would appear superficially to have been a German victory, because it definitely substituted international control for the French protectorate at which Delcassé had aimed. But in reality France was victor in the Algeciras duel. Precisely what privileges she obtained by the

give the Emperor the credit. On the other hand, Roosevelt in his conversation with the ambassador on March 21 (no. 7121) spoke very highly of the "masterly" conduct of German policy in the Morocco crisis, and the ambassador expressed the "firm conviction" that the President's words came straight from the heart ("*ganz und gar vom Herzen*").

[1] Malloy, *Treaties*, 2183.

[2] *State Papers*, 99, pp. 141 ff.; *Amer. Jour. Int. Law*, Supplement, 1, pp. 47 ff. *Cf.*, Walter Lippman, *Stakes of Diplomacy*, ch. 10.

Act mattered little. The reality was that France emerged from the Conference much stronger, because more certain of English support, of at least neutrality on the part of Italy, of America's friendliness. There had been some danger that the Entente with England might be broken by a clever German move; instead Germany's rather clumsy maneuvers had strengthened the Entente, as may be seen by the fact that in January 1906, Sir Edward Grey consented to "conversations" between the naval and military experts of France and England; such conversations were, of course, not binding pledges, but they were an indication that if war occurred, France and England would probably carry out jointly the plans their experts had drawn up against Germany.[1] About the same time, the British military attaché opened "conversations" with the Belgian military authorities,[2] with a view to preparing for resistance to German invasion of Belgium in case of war. Such being the attitude of England, France could soon venture—as soon as Russia had recovered her strength—to interpret the Algeciras Act in her own way, regardless of Germany.

That is precisely what happened. Sure of English and Russian support, France continued the policy called "peaceful penetration" (which means gradual conquest) as though nothing had happened at Algeciras. The weakness of the Algeciras Act was its failure to provide what should happen in case disorders and murders of Europeans should occur in Morocco: there would surely be a demand for armed intervention, but if France or any other state sent in troops the other powers would regard the deed as a violation of the treaty. Of disorder there was plenty. In the northern part of the country the celebrated bandit, Raisuli, captured Sir Harry Maclean and held him for £20,000 ransom. In the south, Mulay Hafid, elder brother of the sultan, and aspirant to the throne, rallied warlike tribesmen to his rebellion against European control and against the sultan who had accepted it. On the Atlantic coast, the Shawiya tribesmen, infuriated by a rumor that a Franco-Spanish syndicate was building a railway through a Moslem cemetery at Casablanca, invaded the town and killed five Frenchmen and three other

[1] Viscount Grey, *Twenty-Five Years*, I, p. 74; *cf.* his speech of Aug. 3, 1914 in the Commons; Loreburn, *How the War Came*, pp. 80-81.

[2] *Norddeutsche Allgemeine Zeitung*, Oct. 3, 1914; London *Times*, Aug. 26, 1915; Haldane, *Before the War*, pp. 181-2.

Europeans, whereupon France sent a warship to rain shells upon the town, killing guilty tribesmen and innocent townsmen alike (1907). Then, to "pacify" the Shawiya district, a French army of 3,000 men occupied Casablanca, the town of Rabat farther north, and the surrounding region, by dint of incessant fighting.

The effect was, naturally, to increase the hostility of the tribesmen, who flocked to the standard of Mulay Hafid, the Pretender. Strangely enough, the French gave no effective aid to the sultan, but permitted the Pretender to defeat him, in 1908, and seize the throne for himself. Still civil war continued, until Mulay Hafid had crushed opposition in the northern hill-country of the Riff, and captured a rival aspirant to the throne, whom he imprisoned in an iron cage. Even then, though the European powers recognized Hafid as sultan, peace was not secured; no sooner had the new sultan come to terms with the Europeans than his native supporters turned against him. No sultan could be popular in Morocco and Europe both.

One great difficulty was finance. To satisfy France, Mulay Hafid was obliged to accept, much against his will, a loan of a hundred million francs at five per cent, which was used to pay off the debts incurred by his predecessor and to indemnify France, to the extent of sixty million francs, for the cost of the French occupation of Casablanca and the damage done to French property by the French bombardment. As the customs taxes, his chief source of revenue, were entirely pledged to pay interest to European bondholders on this and previous loans, the sultan had to raise funds for his own expenditures by heavier direct taxes, which the tribesmen refused to pay. Within less than three years he found himself besieged in his capital by rebel forces, and appealed to France for military aid.

Obligingly France sent an army of 10,000 men to defeat the rebels and occupy the capital city of Fez. Though the French government claimed that such action was necessary to protect the European residents of Fez from violence, and that French troops would be withdrawn as soon as possible, the Spanish government suspected that France was aiming to conquer Morocco regardless of the Algeciras Act, and the German government had similar suspicions.

"Economic Equality" in Morocco

We must turn back, for a moment, to explain Germany's attitude toward French "peaceful penetration" of Morocco, from 1906 to 1911. At first, in 1906, Germany seemed unwilling to permit Franco-Spanish punitive expeditions, and the dispatch of German warships was considered as a protest, but vetoed by the Kaiser. Later, Germany remained passive, even when France occupied Casablanca in 1907. But the next year, an "incident" brought the two Great Powers to the verge of war. In September 1908 the German consul at Casablanca, cooperating with a private German organization to encourage desertions from the French Foreign Legion, attempted to smuggle six deserters out of the town, to a German steamship in the harbor. But the French authorities arrested the deserters, and two employees of the German consulate, attempting to prevent the arrest, were roughly handled. Trivial as it may seem, the Casablanca incident was regarded in Germany as an outrageous affront to the German flag. Germany promptly demanded an apology and liberation of three of the deserters, and compensation for the injured employees. War clouds gathered. But while France was firmly supported by Russia and England, Germany was urged by the Austrian emperor to be moderate—Austria had just become involved in the Bosnian crisis of 1908. Accordingly the Kaiser gave the word for peace, and the dispute was referred to the Hague Tribunal for arbitration. (The Tribunal, we may add, held the German consulate at fault for aiding deserters, and the French at fault for using needless violence.)

Shortly afterward, Germany, in February 1909, made an agreement with France, "to avoid all causes of future misunderstanding." Germany magnanimously promised not to thwart French political interests in "the consolidation of order and internal peace" in Morocco; Germany's interests were "merely economic." In return, France promised to preserve the independence and unity of Morocco, and to "safeguard economic equality." Germany, in short, was willing to let France control political and military affairs, on condition that German business interests were safeguarded.[1] Why Germany

[1] *State Papers*, 102, p. 435.

adopted so magnanimous an attitude was a mystery, at the time, to the French, and even to some of the German diplomats; the explanation, provided by German secret archives recently opened, was that the Kaiser himself insisted: "the wretched Morocco affair must be brought to a close, quickly and finally. Nothing can be done, Morocco will become French. So get out of the affair gracefully, in order that we may at last end the friction with France, now, when great questions are at stake."[1] The "great questions," it may be explained, were the Near Eastern negotiations arising out of the Bosnian crisis. Perhaps this Moroccan agreement is one reason why France left Russia in the lurch in the Bosnian question.[2]

The "economic equality" which Germany desired in Morocco, so it soon appeared, was in reality the formation of international syndicates, mainly Franco-German, for mining, railway construction, and other public works. A beginning in this direction had already been made on private initiative, in the Union of Mines, formed by the German armament firm of Krupp and the leading French armament firms, Schneider and Creusot, the French taking 50% of the stock, the Germans 20%, and the remainder being assigned in smaller blocks to English, Spanish, Italian and Portuguese syndicates. The same principle was applied in the big Moroccan loan of 1910: French bankers subscribed 40%, Germans 20%, British 15% and Spanish 15%. For railway and harbor construction, French and German capitalists formed a Moroccan Public Works Company. The idea seemed so attractive that plans were made for the cooperation of French and German business interests in west-central Africa. Had such economic cooperation been successful, it is possible that the Great War of 1914 would have been averted. But difficulties arose. The French refused to ratify the plans for a merger in central Africa; Great Britain objected to the proposed Franco-German monopoly of public works in Morocco; and a German firm, the Mannesmann brothers, having obtained extensive concessions for iron-mining in Morocco (they obtained the concessions by lending money to Mulay Hafid when he was fighting for the throne), refused to come to a reasonable agree-

[1] Kaiser's notation on Bülow's report of Oct. 5, 1908, cited from German archives by Brandenburg, *Von Bismarck zum Weltkriege*, p. 293.

[2] *Cf. infra*, p. 250.

ment with the Union of Mines.[1] Particularly discouraging was the controversy regarding railway construction. An agreement on this subject had been drafted, to be sure, but the French government had not yet approved it, when rumors began to reach Germany that France intended to send a French army to the Moroccan capital.[2]

Another Crisis—Agadir

The two threads of our story now come together, in the spring of 1911. Sultan Mulay Hafid, besieged at Fez by rebels, was appealing for French aid. European diplomats were beginning to discuss, secretly of course, the probable consequences of a probable French expedition to Fez. The French press clamored for the protection of the Europeans in Fez, and some of the jingo journals began to talk of the Tunisification of Morocco. In France an inexperienced foreign minister (Cruppi), who apparently knew little about the Algeciras Act or the Moroccan situation, was goaded into action by the French press and by Delcassé, father of the Moroccan venture, who was now once more a member of the cabinet. Despite German warnings that it was easier to occupy a city than to evacuate it, Cruppi announced in April 1911 that a French army would be sent to relieve the sultan and the endangered Europeans at Fez. Again the German chancellor warned Cambon: "If you go to Fez, you will stay there, and then the Morocco question will be raised in its entirety, which I wish at all costs to avoid." But the French persisted, and in May a French army occupied Fez. Spain, suspicious of French intentions, took the precaution of sending Spanish troops to occupy the part of Morocco which had been promised to Spain by the secret articles of 1904. Perhaps the French foreign minister, Cruppi, in his ignorance, believed that he was not violating the Algeciras Treaty; perhaps he intended sincerely that the Fez expedition should soon be withdrawn; so at any rate his intentions are pictured in a secret report, now published, of the Russian ambassador at

[1] See *Denkschrift und Aktenstücke über deutsche Bergwerksinteressen in Marokko*, an official white paper, Nr. 189, laid before the Reichstag in Jan. 1910.

[2] See Tardieu, *Le Mystère d'Agadir.*

Paris.[1] But the occupation of Fez afforded Germany a splendid opportunity to claim, and rightly claim, that the Act of Algeciras was being torn up by France.

Kiderlen-Waechter, the German foreign minister, decided to use the opportunity. He was willing enough to let France take Morocco, if he could get something in compensation. His plan, formulated early in May, was to ask the French how long they intended to stay in Fez; if they remained there, he would demand "compensation" for the violation of the Algeciras Act. To make his demand more forceful, he would send a warship to Agadir, the best port on the southwestern coast of Morocco, and hold Agadir as a *Faustpfand* until France offered part of her colonial possessions as satisfactory compensation. Incidentally, success in this move would have a good influence on the forthcoming elections in Germany, and silence the Pan-German critics who had censured the Government for excessive generosity to France.[2]

The plan was pursued faithfully. On July 1 the small German gunboat *Panther* dropped anchor at Agadir, and the Great Powers were notified that the ship had been sent to protect German lives and property. This, of course, was a transparently false diplomatic formula, which meant that Germany would hold Agadir until she obtained some other colonial compensation. Kiderlen seems to have expected that France would hastily offer such compensation, but to his chagrin, France delayed, and at length, to open the bargaining, he suggested that French Congo, from the Sanga River to the seacoast, would be satisfactory. Cambon, the French ambassador, replied that such a concession was impossible, even if, as Kiderlen suggested, Germany should throw her small colony of Togoland and part of Cameroons into the deal. Kiderlen retorted, "You have bought your liberty in Morocco from Spain, England, and even from Italy, and you have left us out."[3] This feeling, that Germany had been left out, was expressed even more vividly by Count Metternich, German ambassador in London, in a conversation with Sir Arthur Nicolson: "Between 1866 and 1870 Germany became a

[1] *Livre Noir*, I, pp. 56, 103-4. This seems to be confirmed by the instructions given to General Moinier—see General Mangin, *Regards sur la France d'Afrique*, p. 131.

[2] Brandenburg, *op. cit.*, p. 320.

[3] *Ibid.*, pp. 323 ff.; Gooch, *Modern Europe*, p. 475.

great State, victorious over all her enemies, but since then France, defeated though she was, and England, have divided the world between them, whilst Germany has only received a few crumbs; the time has now come for Germany to make just demands."[1]

Meanwhile Sir Edward Grey, British foreign minister, had become uneasy. Not that he was fundamentally opposed to German aggrandizement in Congo, for he was not; but as it was "obviously impossible" for France to cede French Congo, Germany might perhaps remain at Agadir and create a naval base there. Such was not the German chancellor's intent, it seems fairly clear now, but unfortunately the German ambassador had not been authorized to repudiate designs on Agadir. The ambassador at once wired Berlin for such authority, and received it, but before he could assure Grey that Germany had no intention of creating a naval base in southern Morocco, a speech was made that altered the whole situation. David Lloyd George, chancellor of the exchequer, who had been scheduled to speak at the Mansion House on July 21, introduced into his speech a violent tirade on the Moroccan crisis. If Great Britain were "to be treated, where her interests were vitally affected, as if she were of no account in the Cabinet of Nations, then I say emphatically that peace at that price would be a humiliation intolerable for a great country like ours to endure." Here was a threat of war which could not fail to imperil the peace of Europe. If Lloyd George had waited, the threat would never have been made. But the danger of war passed quickly, when Grey received Germany's explanation.[2]

The bargaining in Berlin between Germany and France proceeded slowly. Little by little Kiderlen retreated from his rash suggestion that France cede the whole Congo. Caillaux, the French premier, proposed that Germany and France should liquidate all their colonial disputes while they were at it—the Bagdad Railway, the Turkish debt, South Sea Islands, etc. But the Kaiser, fearful of war, was pressing for a quick conclusion, and the imperialists in Germany, especially the Pan-German League, were becoming more and more dangerous with their

[1] Siebert, *Entente Diplomacy*, p. 593.
[2] Brandenburg, pp. 325-328; *cf.* Grey's version, in *Twenty-Five Years*, I, pp. 215 ff.

unofficial demands for a German West Morocco. Though Kaiser and Chancellor alike desired peace, and, in fact, had gotten into the crisis without realizing its gravity, the jingo press, talking of national honor, made retreat difficult. By September the situation became so acute, and the danger of war so great, that there was a financial panic in Berlin. Perhaps the bankers averted war. At any rate, Kiderlen yielded to French views regarding Morocco, early in October, and on November 4 the whole bargain was completed and signed.[1] One treaty permitted France to intervene in Morocco, on condition that all nations should enjoy equality as regards customs tariffs, transportation charges, and mining. The exaggerated view which prevailed, at that time, regarding the iron resources of Morocco was reflected in the stipulation that no tax would be laid on the export of iron ore.[2] By way of compensation for Morocco, Germany received 100,000 sq. mi. of French Congo. It was a small reward for all Kiderlen's maneuvering, for the risk of war incurred by Germany. And it left German imperialists disappointed, German patriots bitter against France and England, while on the other hand, French and English public opinion had been rendered suspicious and resentful toward Germany. All Morocco would not have been worth such a price; much less was the stretch of thinly populated Congo jungle.

French Morocco and the Riffians

With German opposition removed, there was no longer need for France to pursue a hypocritical public policy of maintaining "the independence and integrity" of the Shereefian Empire, while secretly endeavoring to conquer it by degrees. The only obstacles to French imperialism now were Spain and the Moroccans. The former was overcome by a Franco-Spanish treaty,[3] November 27, 1912, whereby the northern coast, about two hundred miles long and sixty deep, was set apart as a "Spanish zone," to be administered by a Moroccan Khalifa or lieutenant

[1] German account based on secret archives in Brandenburg, ch. 14; *cf.* Caillaux, *Agadir;* Siebert, pp. 577-612; Debidour, II, pp. 125-163; *Diplomatische Schriftwechsel Iswolskis*, I, *passim*. Treaties in *State Papers*, 104, pp. 948 ff.

[2] Iron, by the way, is not even mentioned among the exports or mineral resources of Morocco in recent numbers of the official *Annuaire économique.*

[3] *State Papers*, 106, p. 1025.

of the Sultan, under the supervision of a Spanish High Commissioner; this zone would remain nominally part of Morocco, but would become to all intents and purposes a Spanish colony. Spain also received two pieces of territory in the south, making a total of about 18,000 square miles, a twelfth of the area and a tenth of the population of Morocco. Further, the strategically situated town of Tangier, with 140 square miles of surrounding territory, was to be internationalized. The remainder was the French zone, eleven-twelfths of Morocco.

But paper conquests, made by diplomats, have to be translated into reality by machine-guns and bayonets. Morocco had to be conquered by French troops. Profiting by past experience in Algeria, the French government realized that attempting to destroy the native government and treating Morocco as an annexed colony would so enrage the Mohammedan tribesmen as to make conquest exceedingly difficult, bloody, and costly; hence, instead of annexing the country, as they had Algeria, the French used the method employed in Tunis. The sultan was retained, with his lieutenants and chieftains, but compelled to accept a French protectorate, by a treaty signed March 30, 1912.[1] This meant, in reality, that a French Resident-General would supervise the government, with a staff of French officers and officials to supplement the native administration.

Yet even such tactful procedure was not wholly successful. Hardly had the protectorate been established, when Moroccan police mutinied, 80 Frenchmen were killed in Fez, and rebellion swept over the country. Mulay Hafid, who had unwillingly signed away his independence, prudently accepted a generous French pension and left the throne to his brother, Mulay Yusef. Yusef in turn would probably have been forced out, but France rushed troops into the country, under General Lyautey, and began the work of conquest in earnest. One district after another was subjugated.[2]

Lyautey's method was to conquer a district, establish a military post, a market, and an infirmary, and then move on to conquer another region, leaving the market and the infirmary

[1] *State Papers*, 106, p. 438. This and other treaties affecting the French protectorate are conveniently reprinted as an appendix to the *Annuaire économique.*

[2] The process is briefly summarized in the official *Annuaire économique* of Morocco; *cf.* Max Touron, *Notre Protectorat Morocain*, pp. 220-248.

to gain the goodwill of the natives. This, it may be remarked, was an advance on the strategy employed in Algeria and described by a patriotic French author in these words: "mobile columns which incessantly overran the country in all directions, firing grain crops, burning the villages, leaving nothing but ruins, until the natives asked for mercy."[1] Lyautey made conquest and conciliation go hand in hand. The most elaborate care was taken to avoid wounding native sentiment: Mohammedan colleges were established and Mohammedan institutions preserved. Above all, true to Cecil Rhodes' maxim that rails cost less than bullets and carry farther, the French exerted themselves to construct railways, and good roads. Native industries and agriculture were zealously fostered; artistic Arab pottery and weaving were encouraged; harbors were developed; Casablanca and several other towns began to take on the appearance of progressive European cities. In few cases has European imperialism been more intelligently and efficiently conducted. The reward to French commercial and financial interests need detain us but a moment. French investors who had purchased Moroccan bonds below par, as a risky speculation, were now assured of interest and repayment.[2] French capitalists found employment for many hundreds of millions of francs in the construction of Moroccan public works, in mines and trade. French merchants, who had enjoyed only 43% of Morocco's commerce when the protectorate was established, increased their share, under the protectorate, to 63% in 1920.[3] Yet so rapid was the growth of Moroccan commerce, that other nations, although enjoying smaller percentages of the total, found the absolute amount of their business with Morocco increased, not diminished, by the French protectorate.

During the Great War, German agents managed to convey funds to Moroccan rebels, thus increasing the difficulties of

[1] Touron, *op. cit.*, p. 240.

[2] *Annuaire économique et financier*, published annually by the French Protectorate, gives the details. Further loans of 242,000,000 francs in 1914-16 and 744,140,000 francs in 1920 were floated with a guarantee by the French Government.

[3] As shown by statistical tables in the Moroccan *Annuaire économique et financier*, Morocco imported sugar, iron goods, automobiles, spirits, coffee, silk, wood, cements, chiefly from France. England supplied the bulk of cotton goods, candles, and soap. United States provided gasoline. Morocco's exports of grain, skins, and eggs went chiefly to France; almonds to England.

pacification. But at the close of the war, France obtained from Germany, in the treaty of Versailles, a cancellation of all German treaty rights in Morocco. Shortly afterward German mining concessions in Morocco were annulled, and German trade with Morocco was placed under special tariff burdens. It is not idle prophecy to point out that the peace treaties marked a step toward the closing of the open door, for which Germany had contended. Morocco was on the road to Tunisification.

Spain was less successful in her twelfth of Morocco. The turbulent hill tribes of the Jebala district, shrewdly led by the ex-bandit Raisuli, refused to be pacified. Futile efforts to establish order in the Spanish zone cost Spain heavily in men and money. More than that, they destroyed constitutional government in Spain, for Spanish military leaders, impatient with the defeats which Spain had suffered, overthrew the Spanish cabinet in 1923, and established the military dictatorship of General Primo de Rivera. Spain's efforts to deprive the Moroccans of liberty cost her her own freedom. It may be added that General Primo de Rivera, although he withdrew Spanish troops from the Jebala hills, suffered shocking losses.

The defeat of the Spaniards was but the prelude to graver events in Morocco. While the Spaniards clung grimly to the coastlands of their zone, another Moroccan chieftain, Abd-el-Krim, who had made himself master of the Riff mountain tribes, and had won brilliant victories over both Spaniards and Raisuli, decided in 1925 to invade the French zone to the south. The French, it may be explained, had recently extended their military occupation to the upper Ouergha Valley (just south of the Riff), whence Krim's followers had hitherto obtained grain supplies. So effective was Krim's well-armed, veteran infantry, that France found it necessary to combine with Spain against him, to reinforce her army of occupation, and to send Marshal Pétain to organize the campaign against the Riffians. Lyautey resigned on September 28, 1925. Before the end of the year France had lost 11,419 men (mostly colonial troops), so the government announced. Krim was driven back into his mountains, but did not surrender until 1926.[1]

[1] See the interesting article in *Current History*, Nov., 1925, by Prof. M. M. Knight, who had recently visited Morocco, and the series of articles in *L'Afrique française*, 1925. Military operations in Morocco cost France (on the budget of the war department) no less than 4,268

A word about the international zone of Tangier. Exactly how Tangier should be internationalized, the Franco-Spanish agreement of 1912 did not specify. Plans were discussed, no agreement was reached before the War broke out in 1914; then, during the war, Spanish imperialists, lending an ear to German propaganda, cherished hopes of obtaining Tangier for themselves, and perhaps even of gaining Gibraltar from England, if Germany should win.[1] After the war, Spain was more reasonable. France, Spain, and England proceeded to draw up an agreement (1923) establishing a rather complicated system of international government for Tangier, giving France a preponderant influence.[2] It may be of interest to add that the United States, in July 1924, refused its consent to the plan, on the ground that it would curtail the rights guaranteed by the Algeciras Act of 1906. And in 1926 Spain again revived her claims to Tangier!

Italy's Vital Interest in Libia

The seizure of Morocco by France was in more than one way an indirect cause of the Great War. Not only did it exacerbate Franco-German and Anglo-German relations; it also precipitated the Turco-Italian War of 1911, which led to the Balkan War of 1912, which in turn led to the Serajevo Crisis and the catastrophe of 1914. It is with the Turco-Italian War that we now propose to deal.

That Italian imperialists should have looked hungrily upon the littoral of Africa, just across the Mediterranean from Italy, was almost inevitable, not only because of geographic proximity, but also because in these lands Italians outnumbered other Europeans, and above all because ancient Rome had once been mistress of North Africa. Soon after Italy had become a united nation in the nineteenth century, Italians turned their eyes toward Tunis, ancient Carthage, only to see France carry off this prize in 1881 with lordly disregard of Italian aspirations. Italy, as we have seen, promptly allied herself with the enemies

million francs from 1907 through 1924. For 1925 an expenditure of 344 million francs had been planned, but more was spent and in December it was necessary to vote 440 million francs in Moroccan credits.

[1] Touron, *op. cit.*, pp. 148-219.

[2] *Parl. Papers*, 1924 (Cmd. 2096).

of France, in the Triple Alliance of 1882, and looked elsewhere for colonies.[1]

Just east of Tunis, between that country and Egypt, lay two Turkish provinces, Tripolitania and Cyrenaica, much larger than Tunis if less valuable. These at any rate Italy would secure for herself. This time Italian statesmen took pains to secure promises of support from the other Great Powers. From Germany a pledge was obtained, in 1887, of armed assistance to prevent France from taking Tripoli.[2] Great Britain and Austria-Hungary also promised, in the "Mediterranean Agreement" of 1887,[3] to oppose any attempt of France to extend her domination on the northern coast of Africa. Spain, too, came to an agreement.[4] But these were negative pledges, not positive approvals of Italy's designs; nor did a favorable opportunity soon arise for Italian seizure of the coveted lands. Italy waited. Thirteen years later, Italy was able to strengthen her secret agreements, by obtaining, in December 1900, a promise from France to refrain from opposing Italian ambitions in Tripoli and Cyrenaica, if Italy would be equally considerate as regards French interests in Morocco.[5] England also was favorable; in fact Lord Salisbury in 1890 had suggested that to prevent the Mediterranean from becoming a French lake Italy should take Tripoli—but not just then.[6] To make assurance doubly sure, the Italian government, in renewing the Triple Alliance in 1902, obtained not only the pledge of German military support in case French aggression should move Italy to "undertake action" in Tripolitania and Cyrenaica, but also from Austria-Hungary a declaration that no opposition would be offered to Italian "measures" in these provinces.[7] Russia's consent was purchased by the secret pact of Racconigi (Oct. 24, 1909) in exchange for Italian benevolence regarding the Dardanelles.[8] Italy now had secret agreements with all the other Great Powers of Europe.

Pending a favorable opportunity for armed conquest, the Italians proceeded with what is known as "peaceful penetration" of Tripoli and Cyrenaica. Leading Italian banks, notably

[1] *Cf.* p. 197 and ch. viii.
[2] Pribram, *Secret Treaties of Austria-Hungary*, I, 110.
[3] *Ibid.*, p. 95.
[4] *Ibid.*, p. 117.
[5] *Ibid.*, p. 240.
[6] Gooch, *Modern Europe*, pp. 266 ff.
[7] Pribram, *op. cit.*, II, p. 232.
[8] Siebert, *Entente Diplomacy*, pp. 142 ff.

the Banca d'Italia and the Banca di Roma, invested money in olive oil and soap factories, olive groves and farms, sponge fisheries, steamboats, and other business enterprises in the promised land.[1] Italian newspapers grew amazingly optimistic regarding the potential grainfields, the potential cotton plantations, the potential phosphate and sulphur mines, the potential cattle ranches, which would be added to Italy's national wealth.[2] As the time for annexation drew near, atrocities such as the kidnapping of an Italian girl and insults to the Italian flag aroused the Italian public to the required pitch of warlike enthusiasm.[3] In July 1911, the Morocco crisis afforded the long-desired opportunity. In August Italy quietly informed the Great Powers that she intended to restore order in Tripoli. The Italian army was made ready.

Then, on September 28, 1911, Italy took the final step, by sending to Turkey one of the most amazing ultimatums in the annals of diplomacy. The Italian note of September 28 declared that "the state of disorder and neglect in which Tripoli and Cyrenaica are left by Turkey" must come to an end; this was for Italy "a vital interest of the very first order." It may have been "vital" for the Banca di Roma and the Banca d'Italia, but what difference the welfare of a half-million Arabs (mixed with Berber and negro) in the Tripolitan deserts made to Italy as a whole, must be left to the reader's imagination. The note continued in like exaggerated vein, to say that all Italian business enterprises "constantly encounter a systematic opposition of the most obstinate and unwarranted kind," and to complain of the "agitation prevailing against Italian subjects," and the "arrival at Tripoli of Ottoman military transports." And now comes the delightful dénouement: "The Italian government, therefore, finding itself forced to think of the guardianship of its dignity and its interests (note the combination, national prestige and business interests), has decided

[1] See interesting discussion of the financial interests in W. Lippmann's *Stakes of Diplomacy; cf. Come siamo andati in Libia* (Firenze, 1914), p. xxii.

[2] See the interesting critique of the propaganda by Salvemini and other prominent Italian writers in *Come siamo andati in Libia.* This volume exposes the over-optimistic propaganda by which the nationalists led the public to regard barren Libia as a promised land.

[3] Read San Guiliano's letter in Dr. Paolo de Vecchi's priceless pamphlet, *Italy's Civilizing Mission in Africa* (Brentano's, 1912).

to proceed to the military occupation of Tripoli and Cyrenaica." This in itself would be ironic, in view of the secret intrigues which the Italian government had been conducting for a generation, to prepare for the conquest, but the supreme touch of irony was added by a suave request that Turkey give orders so that the Italian invasion "may meet with no opposition."

Turkey replied, the next day, that anything short of territorial cession would be granted, if Italy would but specify what reforms were desired. But Italy declared war. Secretly, through Germany, Italy offered to be content with the occupation of Tripoli, on terms resembling the Austrian occupation of Bosnia, but before an agreement could be reached Italian troops had taken the town of Tripoli, and the Italian public was so aroused that nothing short of annexation (by decree of November 5) would suffice. It was not difficult to capture the ports on the Tripolitan coast, but to subdue the Arabs in the interior, or to bring Turkey to terms, proved unexpectedly difficult. The war dragged on into 1912; Italy occupied some of the Ægean islands and twice attacked the Dardanelles; but not until October, 1912, was peace concluded, and then only because Turkey was about to engage in war with the Balkan nations, to which the Turco-Italian War had offered an opportunity for attack on Turkey. Italy emerged from the war with Tripoli and Cyrenaica in her possession (though Turkey never formally recognized Italian annexation of these provinces until the Treaty of Lausanne, of 1923); in addition, Italian troops occupied the group of small islands known as the Dodekanesia.

Ever mindful of the imperial Roman tradition, Italy applied to Tripolitania and Cyrenaica the old Roman name of Libya (Libia Italiana). But Libia Italiana was not the prosperous province that Roman Libya had been. Since Roman days, much of the colony had become uninhabited desert. Moreover, the Arab and Berber tribes of the interior fiercely opposed Italian rule. "Pacification by extermination" may be a very unfair description of Italy's policy toward these tribes, but it suggests the difficulties of Italian conquest. During the Great War of 1914, Turkish and German officers encouraged and aided the tribesmen in an effort to drive the Italians into the sea, and at the close of the war Italy held only some of the coast districts. But in 1919 the Italian government adopted a new policy, of granting the natives equal citizenship with Italians, of governing so far as possible through the native chiefs, and of granting the natives representation in a colonial parliament (one for Tripolitania, one for Cyrenaica). By this means most of the chiefs were more or less successfully conciliated, but Italian rule was by no means solid or secure.[1]

The war by which Italy won Libia is said to have cost over $200,000,000. And after the war Italy continued to pay heavy military expenses. Each year Italy had to contribute a large sum (in 1922-23 it was 203,000,000 lire) to make good the difference between heavy expenditures and small revenues in Libia. Altogether, it was estimated that Libia had cost Italy three billion lire, about $600,000,000 up to 1924. Was it worth the price? The colony is large enough—580,000 sq. m. And if what Italian newspapers had said of Tripoli before the conquest were true, it would have been valuable enough. But after the conquest, Italy discovered that Libia was a relatively barren country.[2] A large part of the interior was actual desert, where shifting sands mocked the imperialist. Other parts were suitable only for grazing. There were, to be sure, some regions, particularly along the coast, where olive, palm and fruit trees were grown. But the value of their products was small. Unfortunately for Italy, the caravan trade from the Sahara and Sudan, formerly passing through Tripoli, was diverted to Egypt and Tunis; and even the extension of the Italian frontiers, after the war, at the expense of Tunis and Egypt, giving Italy control of important caravan routes, did not entirely remedy the situation. Moreover, the scanty population of 800,000, little more than one person to the square mile, was an additional handicap to economic development. The total exports, chiefly hides and wool, were worth only 4,774,147 lire in 1912, and actually declined after the conquest, to 4,493,638 lire in 1914; later they recovered and in 1923 reached the figure of 39,735,358 lire, but as the exchange value of the lira had fallen, this sum should be divided by about four. The imports, thanks to Italian investments and expenditures, increased after the conquest, and

[1] P. d'Agostino Orsini di Camerota, *Espansionismo italiano odierno;* vol. 1, pp. 41-53; *cf.* Article by Filippo Lo Bello in *Rivista Coloniale,* Jan.-Feb. 1925.

[2] On the resources and exploitation of Libia, see P. d'Agostino Orsini di Camerota, *op. cit.,* part II.

were many times larger than the exports. Even so, the total commerce was only 201,630,575 lire in 1921, less than the annual deficit, paid directly by Italy, in the colonial budget. But the Banca d'Italia and the Banca di Roma, through branches in the colony, may have made considerable profits. And, above all, Italian patriotism exulted in the possession of a colony so large, albeit so costly.[1] Mussolini, moreover, balanced the colonial budget.

The Entering Wedge in Egypt

Great Britain obtained what is generally though mistakenly considered the chief prize in North Africa, namely Egypt. Large as it appears on the map, one should remember the real Egypt is merely a narrow river-valley and delta, only 12,000 square miles in area, densely settled by 14 million people. The rest, the 370,000 square miles of desert, is unimportant save on the map.

When the age of imperialism dawned on Europe, Egypt was a province of the Ottoman empire, paying tribute to the Turkish sultan, ruled by the sultan's representative, a governor or pasha. France, rather than Britain, seemed the most interested European power. French interest was partly due to the Napoleonic tradition. Had not Napoleon declared, "Really to destroy England, we must make ourselves masters of Egypt," and had he not compelled the pyramids, for a fleeting moment at least, to bow to the glory of France? As every schoolboy knows, Napoleon had to flee from Egypt in defeat. But in after years French interest remained lively. It was to France that the ambitious Mehement Ali, pasha of Egypt from 1806 to 1849, turned for advisers to aid him in promoting technical education and irrigation. It was to the Frenchman, de Lesseps, that a later pasha granted a concession to dig a canal through the isthmus of Suez. England became interested after the canal was opened.

As in the case of Tunis, or of Morocco, the entering wedge for imperialism in Egypt was finance, and the wedge was driven in because of the reckless extravagance of the ruler. The ruler,

[1] An interesting example of opinions may be found in the proceedings of the Istituto Coloniale Italiano, *Atti de Convegno Nazionale Coloniale* of 1919 (Rome, 1920).

in this instance, was Ismail Pasha (1863-1879), a squat and rather stout, red-bearded gentleman, with a passion for power and for European culture. In twelve years he spent a half-billion dollars. Some of it was well expended, on schools, on canals and railways, and telegraphs, on harbors and on public buildings. He bought up-to-date ironclads for his navy. He poured out money to conquer the Sudan. Hoping to obtain European favor, he generously sent twelve hundred Nubian soldiers to help the French establish an empire for Maximilian in Mexico. When the Suez Canal—in which he invested eighty million dollars—was opened in 1869, he entertained the Emperor of Austria and the Empress Eugénie of France, and other European luminaries, in truly royal style; he even built a special road from Cairo out to the Pyramids and the Sphinx, for the convenience of his guests, and a special palace for a ball at the terminus of the canal, in the town called Ismaila in his honor. By increasing his annual tribute to the Turkish sultan, he obtained the more dignified title of Khedive, instead of pasha, and the right of succession by primogeniture for his heirs. Meanwhile he was buying land in Egypt, from private owners, until he had increased his personal estate to 916,000 acres.

All this cost money. Though he imposed crushing taxes on the peasantry, Ismail got into embarrassing financial straits, especially when the price of Egyptian cotton, which had soared high during the American Civil War, suddenly dropped after the war, causing terrible suffering in Egypt. But European bankers were accommodating. Year after year he added to the foreign debt, which had been only £3,292,800 at his accession, but reached a total of £68,497,160 after ten years of his extravagance. As his credit weakened, he had to sell his bonds for less cash; for example, he received less than twenty millions cash for 7% bonds whose face value was thirty-two millions, in 1873.[1] Short-term treasury bonds bearing twenty per cent interest could be sold, in 1875, for only a quarter of their face value. To stave off ruin, he offered to sell, to French interests, the 176,602 shares he held in the Suez Canal Company.[2] These, as we have previously explained, were bought up hastily by Disraeli, for £3,680,000 in 1875, for Disraeli believed that the Canal was "a

[1] From the Cave report, *Parl. Papers, Egypt No. 5* (*1876*).
[2] *Egypt No. 1* (*1876*).

highway to our Indian Empire." But even this sum was not enough.

In response to Ismail's appeal for further loans, the British cabinet sent Mr. Stephen Cave to investigate Egypt's finances, in 1875. Cave's report, asserting the economic wealth of Egypt but recommending sounder financial methods,[1] resulted in the establishment, the following year, of an international debt commission, the Caisse de la Dette Publique, comprising representatives of England, France, Italy, and Austria. All existing loans were to be consolidated into a general debt of £91,000,000 bearing seven per cent; revenues sufficient to bear the charges on this debt were to be received directly by the Caisse, and no new loans were to be issued without its consent.

Dissatisfied with this arrangement, the British and French bondholders induced the khedive to appoint an Englishman to take charge of the revenue, and a Frenchman to audit expenditures. A "bad Nile" and famine year, however, so reduced the revenues that interest payments could not be met, in 1878, and the Khedive proposed to reduce the rate of interest.

Such a proposal, naturally, was most unwelcome to the bondholders; they insisted on the appointment of a commission of six Europeans and one Egyptian to investigate the situation. The commission proposed wholesale reforms, a budget system, tax reform, cession of the Khedive's personal property to the state.[2] Helplessly, Ismail tried to placate his creditors by appointing a Christian premier (Nubar Pasha), with an Englishman (Wilson) as finance minister, and a Frenchman (de Blignières) as minister of public works. But dreading the proposed reforms, and knowing well that landowners would support him in resisting heavier taxation and army officers in opposing economy, Ismail in April, 1879, discharged his European ministers, appointed a new cabinet, and announced that he would resume his prerogatives and protect the privileges of the upper classes.

Loudly the foreign bondholders protested; vainly the French and British governments remonstrated.[3] And the two western powers did take joint action. First they asked Ismail to resign. When he refused, they persuaded the Turkish sultan to depose

[1] *Egypt No. 4* and *No. 5* (*1876*).
[2] France, *Documents Diplomatiques*, vol. 41, *Affaires d'Égypte, 1880*, pp. 28 ff., 204 ff.
[3] *Ibid.*, pp. 271 ff.

him; the sultan was willing enough to reassert his authority over an almost independent vassal. Ismail departed on his yacht, with the favorites of his harem and such jewels and funds as he could hastily gather together. The new Khedive, Tewfik Pasha, was compelled to revive the Anglo-French financial control, and was warned that "the establishment in Egypt of political influence on the part of any other Power, in competition with that of England and France, would not be tolerated."

The "Dual Control," by France and England, lasted from 1879 to 1883. A budget system was established, heavier taxes were laid on wealthy landowners and the crushing burdens on the peasants were lightened; and although the interest on the debt had to be lowered to four per cent, there seemed to be good reason for believing that if this could be paid regularly the foreign loans to Egypt would still prove profitable investments, since the price paid for the bonds had been very low.[1]

Trouble, however, arose soon. In 1881 Tewfik summoned an Assembly of Notables, a sort of aristocratic parliament, to meet, and the Notables promptly demanded the ordinary parliamentary right to control the expenditure of at least that part (about half) of the revenue which was not required for debt service. To this, France and England replied in a joint note,[2] Jan. 8, 1882, announcing their intention of supporting the Khedive's authority. Parliamentary rule, apparently, was not for Egypt. More than a note, however, seemed to be needed, in view of the fact that, to save money, the Anglo-French advisers had insisted on the dismissal of about 2500 Egyptian army officers on half-pay, besides other unpopular reforms, and had thus called into life a powerful nationalist anti-European agitation, led by Col. Ahmed Arabi. There was danger that Arabi's followers would become strong enough to insist on "Egypt for the Egyptians," and overthrow the Dual Control; there were even rumors that the foreign debt was to be repudiated.

The British and French governments now decided on a fateful step, whose consequences were quite unforeseen. In May, 1882, they sent an Anglo-French fleet to make a "naval demonstration," that is, to appear off the coast and by its mere presence terrify the Egyptians, and thus, in the British foreign minister's

[1] *Ibid.*, pp. 322 ff.

[2] *Egypt No. 2 (1882) : Affaires d'Égypte, 1881; idem, 1881-1882.*

words, "strengthen the authority of the Khedive." They also demanded the retirement of Arabi, who was now a member of the cabinet. This ultimatum, however, simply inflamed the Egyptian nationalists. In Alexandria a number of Europeans were killed by rioters. Arabi prepared an army to resist foreign attack, and began to fortify Alexandria. And in July, 1882, Admiral Seymour commanded the British ships to open fire on the city. Alexandria fell, British troops were landed, and in a few weeks Great Britain completed the conquest of Egypt.[1] France, it must be noted, took no part in bombardment or conquest; on the contrary, the French ships sailed away, and Freycinet, the French premier, fell from power when he asked the French parliament for funds to defend the canal, for public opinion in France, mindful of the recent Tunisian scandals, was hostile to imperialism and fearful of a quarrel with England.[2] England made some show of inviting Turkey and Italy to help, but both refused. How the British foreign minister, Lord Granville, felt about such refusals, may be inferred from his own words (in a confidential letter): "we have shown our readiness to admit others, and we have not the inconveniences of a partner. . . . If Arabi caves in, as appears probable, we shall be on velvet." [3]

Less enthusiastic, in all conscience, was the British prime minister, none other than William Ewart Gladstone, who had been an eloquent and impassioned opponent of imperialism in general and intervention in Egypt in particular. Against his own principles, Gladstone had been pushed into Egypt by the pressure of foreign office officials, financiers and shippers, and parliamentary opinion; he had taken one step after another, hardly realizing how far he would be carried.

Landing troops in foreign territory is not usually considered a conventional, legal procedure, but British statesmen, always eager to cover their actions with the dignified mantle of law, represented the seizure of Egypt as a matter of justice, of legal right, and of disinterested duty. Said Gladstone, "we seek the maintenance of all established rights" in Egypt, "whether they

[1] See reports of Admiral Seymour, *Accounts and Papers*, 1882, C. 3315 and C. 3305.

[2] See *Affaires d'Égypte 1882* and Freycinet's book, *La Question d'Égypte.*

[3] E. Fitzmaurice, *Life of Lord Granville*, p. 271; *cf.* the voluminous correspondence in *Parliamentary Papers* for 1882.

be those of the Sultan, those of the Khedive, those of the people of England, or those of the foreign bondholders."[1] The last was not least. Said Lord Granville, England sought the "maintenance of the sovereign rights of the Sultan, of the position of the Khedive, and of the liberties of the Egyptian people under the Firmans (decrees) of the Porte (Turkey), the prudent development of their institutions, and the fulfilment of all international engagements."[2] Dilke, the undersecretary for foreign affairs, held that intervention in Egypt would benefit the "British workingmen," through trade, but that "necessity," and "treaty right," and "duty" were the reasons for intervention.[3] But treaty rights, and the sultan's rights, and the khedive's rights, like the flowers that bloom in the spring, had little to do with the case.

The important factors were Ireland, bonds, and the Suez Canal. Ireland, because the violence of the Irish Nationalist movement at this time not only preoccupied Gladstone's mind but made it easier for him to yield to the clamor for action against Egyptian "Nationalists." Bonds, because about £30,000,000 of Egypt's debt was held in England, so Joseph Chamberlain said,[4] and the bondholders feared that the Egyptian Nationalists would repudiate the debts. Lord Cromer, of whom more will be said, bluntly declared, "The origin of the Egyptian Question in its present phase was financial."[5] Perhaps Gladstone and Chamberlain, however, were sincere in denying that the interest of the bondholders was the primary factor. The Canal was even more important to British public men. About eighty per cent of the shipping which passed through the Canal in 1882 flew the British flag, and a considerable portion (13% in 1881) of Britain's entire foreign trade went by way of Suez.[6] There is convincing evidence that the Canal was a factor of primary importance in Gladstone's mind,[7] and Granville's, but perhaps the clearest statement about it was made by Sir Charles Dilke, undersecretary in charge of the commercial division of the Foreign Office:

[1] Hansard, 3d Series, 270, p. 1150. [2] *Ibid.*, 269, p. 647.
[3] *Ibid.*, 272, pp. 1706 ff., 1720. [4] *Ibid.*, 272, p. 1850.
[5] Cromer, *Modern Egypt*, I, p. 11.
[6] *Accounts and Papers*, 1882, LXI, pp. 1914-6 and LXIV, p. 773.
[7] *Cf.* Hansard, 3d Series, 162, p. 1553, and Morley, *Gladstone*, pp. 591-2.

. . . The Canal is the principal highway to India, Ceylon, the Straits Settlements, and British Burmah, where 250,000,000 people live under our rule, and also to China where we have vast interests and 84% of the external trade of that still more enormous empire. It is also one of the roads to our Colonial Empire in Australia and New Zealand.[1]

To protect the Canal permanently, Dilke and others believed, it was necessary to control Egypt. "The dominance of a purely military faction at Cairo must place our communications with India and the East in permanent jeopardy." All things considered, it is not far from the truth to say conflict between foreign finance and native nationalism produced the crisis in 1882, inviting intervention, and that a desire to control the Suez Canal made British statesmen unwilling that any power other than England should occupy Egypt.[2]

As a Liberal who opposed imperialism on principle, Gladstone did not intend permanent conquest when he permitted British troops to occupy Egypt. On the contrary, so at least he declared, "of all the things in the world, that (permanent occupation) is the thing we are not going to do." [3] Great Britain formally and explicitly notified the other powers, on January 3, 1883, that the British army was to be withdrawn "as soon as the state of the country, and the organization of the proper means for the maintenance of the khedive's authority, will admit of it." [4] These pledges Gladstone regarded as peculiarly sacred: in his own words (Aug. 9, 1883) they were "specific and solemn pledges given to the world in the most solemn manner and under the most critical circumstances—pledges which have earned for us the confidence of Europe at large during the course of difficult and delicate operations, and which, if one pledge can be more sacred than another, special sacredness in this case binds us to fulfill." [5] But Gladstone, though he lived to an advanced age, never fulfilled his pledge. It is difficult to abandon conquests.

[1] Hansard, 3d Series, 272, p. 1719.

[2] W. S. Blunt's *Secret History of the English Occupation of Egypt* provides many colorful details and an intimate, sympathetic account of the Nationalist movement. It would be invaluable if it were at all trustworthy, but see my review in *Pol. Sci. Quart.*, and also *Egypt No. 27 (1884)*.

[3] Hansard, 3d Series, 273, pp. 1384 ff.

[4] *Egypt No. 2 (1883)*, p. 34.

[5] Hansard, 3d Series, 282, pp. 2196 ff.

British Reforms and the Independence of Egypt

The "organization of the proper means for the maintenance of the khedive's authority," which, according to the British pledge, would permit England to evacuate Egypt, proved to be a long process. The Anglo-French Dual Control gave place to British control.[1] A sort of constitution for Egypt was drawn up by Lord Dufferin in the winter of 1882-3, and promulgated as the Organic Law of 1883.[2] The khedive was to exercise his authority through a council of ministers, with the advice and criticism of a Legislative Council and a General Assembly, without whose consent new taxes could not be levied. The khedive with his ministers, council, and assembly, and native officials constituted the visible government. But the real government was a more or less invisible system of British "advisers," supervising and controlling every department of the administration, and taking their orders not from the khedive but from the British consul-general at Cairo. As British consul-general and high commissioner, Lord Cromer was the real monarch of Egypt for a quarter-century, from 1883 to 1907. At the time of his appointment Cromer had not yet earned his peerage; he was simply Major Evelyn Baring, a colonial official who had shown great ability in financial matters and who was related to the great London bankers of the same name. He won his earldom by his remarkable achievements in Egypt, of which he has left an ample record in his two-volume work on *Modern Egypt*.

His first great task was "the race against bankruptcy." For five years "the issue seemed doubtful," he writes, but soon the budget began to show a surplus, after paying interest on the debt and expenses of administration. The bondholders were saved.[3]

Another task of supreme importance was to regulate the water supply. Egypt, it must be remembered, is a practically rainless country, and the cultivated lands of the valley and delta depend absolutely on the water of the Nile. For thousands of years

[1] See *Egypt No. 20 (1882)*; *Egypt No. 2 (1883)*; *Affaires d'Égypte 1882-1883.*

[2] *Egypt No. 19 (1883).*

[3] Cromer, *Modern Egypt*, II, ch. 53; *cf. Egypt No. 28 (1884)*; on the London Financial Conference, *Egypt No. 29 (1884)*; and the gratifying budget statement for 1889, *Egypt No. 4 (1889)*.

Egyptian agriculturists were at the Nile's mercy; and the great river with fickle humor gave their fields too much in some years, too little in others, of the life-giving water. Moreover, for the increasingly important crops of sugar and cotton, a fairly regular supply of moisture, rather than an annual flood, was needed. British engineers solved the problem by constructing the great Assuan dam, more than a mile long and eighty-two feet thick, to check the floods and hold a reservoir of water, two hundred miles long, for gradual use in the dry season. By irrigation canals this water is distributed to the thirsty fields. It is the greatest achievement of the British in Egypt.[1]

Other reforms, also, the British accomplished. Three crying evils which Lord Cromer styles "The three C's—the Courbash, the Corvée, and Corruption," were attacked.[2] The Courbash was the strip of hippopotamus hide with which the peasants were almost universally flogged; it was the favorite means of forcing laborers to work, of prompting unwilling witnesses to give evidence in judicial processes, or suspected criminals to confess their faults, of persuading taxpayers to meet their due and tenants to pay their rent. Egypt was ruled with the courbash, until the British administration forbade its use. The Corvée was compulsory labor. Each year a vast amount of labor was required, during the period when the Nile was low, to remove the accumulation of mud from the bottoms of the irrigation canals. The poorer peasants were compelled to do this work; in one district they had to work, without wages, 180 days in the year. As long as the courbash sang over their backs, they did the work, but with its abolition a new system had to be found. And though it required an additional governmental expenditure of two million dollars a year, the British substituted free labor and wages for the corvée, to a large extent. The third "C," Corruption, could not be entirely abolished, but we have Cromer's word that it "was greatly diminished."

But these were only the most conspicuous of the many reforms, some economic and some humanitarian, that were carried out.[3]

[1] *Egypt No. 6 (1888)*; Cromer, *op. cit.*, II, ch. 54.
[2] Cromer, *op. cit.*, II, chs. 49-51.
[3] Cromer's annual reports (*Parliamentary Papers*) afford a comprehensive record of these reforms. I have not dealt with the thorny question of the capitulations, but see for example *Egypt No. 1 (1905)*; *Egypt No. 1, (1906)*; *Egypt No. 1 (1907)*; Cromer, *op. cit.*, ch. 52.

Railways were built, harbors developed, schools[1] established. And from such reforms there can be little doubt that the fellahin, the downtrodden peasantry, greatly profited. Saved from the whip and forced labor, protected by wise laws from grasping moneylenders, encouraged in a hundred ways by a watchful government, the peasants gained greater freedom and prosperity than had ever been theirs.

The welfare of the peasantry meant increased population (the population has doubled since 1882),[2] increased agricultural production, increased imports and exports and tax revenues. Cotton production was more than doubled, and the value of the crop rose from 9 million pounds (Egyptian) in 1881 to 52 in 1924. Most of the cotton was exported for manufacture, England taking the largest share.[3] Imports increased from seven millions sterling in 1881 to forty-three in 1922, and most of the imports were cotton manufactures, coal, and iron and steel goods from England.

Yet the Egyptian was not happy. Cromer says, "The want of gratitude displayed by a nation to its alien benefactors is almost as old as history itself."[4] But ingratitude is not the only reason why British rule was unpopular. There were instances of overbearing arrogance, and unfortunately in some cases, notably in the Denshawi incident, certain Englishmen felt it necessary to display ruthlessness in punishing native antagonism. But the chief and most obvious source of trouble was that the Egyptians, as they came more and more under European influence, learned to feel a crude sort of national consciousness and longed, like every other nation, for self-government whether it were good government or not. And in Egypt nationalism was intensified by Mohammedan hatred of the Christian.

Hoping to conciliate the natives, the British in 1913 modified the Organic Law, and merged the Legislative Council and General Assembly into a single Legislative Assembly with power

[1] But in 1921-1922 the schools accommodated only 17% of the boys and 5% of the girls of school age, and of the 511,671 attending school, 269,897 were in private Moslem schools, and only 48,894 in government schools. *Annuaire statistique de l'Egypte, 1923-1924*, pp. 74-82.

[2] From 6,831,131 in 1882 the population increased to 13,551,000 in 1922.

[3] But England's share is less than half the total. The United States, France, Italy, Germany, and other industrial countries secure more than half the Egyptian crop. See detailed figures in *Annuaire Statistique de l'Égypte 1923-4*, p. 385.

[4] *Op. cit.*, II, p. 571.

to propose, as well as to discuss, legislation.[1] But the new Assembly, in its first meeting, showed a strong nationalist hostility to British domination. Then occurred the Great War of 1914. When Turkey entered the war, against Great Britain, the latter took advantage of the situation to declare Egypt no longer a Turkish province, but a British protectorate, in December, 1914. The pro-Turkish khedive, Abbas Hilmi, was deposed, and Hussein Kamel was given the throne, with the new title "Sultan of Egypt." Thus England fulfilled the aim of safeguarding the rights of the Turkish sultan and the authority of the khedive.

During the Great War, England ruled Egypt with a strong hand, disregarding the puppet "sultan," refusing to convene the Legislative Assembly, censoring the press, and suppressing nationalist agitation. Such tactics only made more Egyptians nationalists. At the close of the war, the Egyptian leaders appointed a peace delegation to put Egypt's case before the Paris Conference, and to claim the right of self-determination which Wilson, and Lloyd George, and other Allied orators, had so eloquently proclaimed. The Egyptian delegates were quietly arrested by British police and shipped to Malta, and General Allenby, who had won splendid laurels during the war in the Near East, was sent as Special High Commissioner to prevent the ominous unrest of Egypt from developing into a full-fledged rebellion. But even Allenby could not silence the clamor for independence. Then a mission of inquiry, headed by the celebrated empire-builder Lord Milner of South African fame, was sent down to Egypt. Milner returned discouraged. In London the commission interviewed Saad Zaghlul, leader of the Egyptian "peace delegation." In its report, the commission admitted that "the spirit of Egyptian Nationalism cannot be extinguished," and recommended that England should abolish the protectorate and grant Egypt independence on certain conditions.[2]

"Independent" Egypt

Great Britain's recognition of Egypt as "an independent sovereign State" in February, 1922, was clear evidence that in London the Egyptian situation was considered extremely grave.

[1] Kitchener's report, *Egypt No. 1 (1914)*, Cd. 7358, pp. 2-8.
[2] See *Egypt No. 1 (1921)*, Cmd. 1131.

It is difficult, we repeat, to give up possessions. But England retained the rights which seemed most vital to imperial interests: (1) the right to defend the Suez Canal using Egyptian territory for military operations if necessary; (2) the right to defend Egypt against all foreign aggression or interference; (3) the right to protect foreign interests in Egypt; and (4) control of the "Anglo-Egyptian Sudan."[1]

While these matters, "absolutely reserved" by Great Britain pending future discussion, were left unsettled, the Egyptians were allowed to draw up a constitution (1923), providing for the government of Egypt as an independent constitutional monarchy, with King Fuad as sovereign, a cabinet responsible to parliament, and a parliament elected by the people. The formerly persecuted peace delegate, Saad Zaghlul, the nationalist who had been imprisoned in Malta, now became premier of Egypt, and nationalism had full sway.[2] So exuberant were the newly emancipated patriots, that they even ventured to insist, in firm tones, that the Sudan must be turned over to Egypt as her rightful heritage; one backward people, hardly freed from alien rule, demanded its right to rule another backward people—such is the circular path of human logic. England, however, retained the Sudan. And General Allenby, we may add, remained in Egypt with British soldiers, for all Egypt's "independence."

Egyptian agitation against British rule in the Sudan reached a climax with the assassination, by Egyptians, of General Sir Lee Stack, Governor General of the Sudan and Sirdar (Commander) of the Egyptian Army, on Nov. 19, 1924. The British Government seized this opportunity to insist upon the withdrawal of all Egyptian officers and troops from the Sudan, and the increase of the area to be irrigated at Gezira, in the Sudan, to an unlimited figure. If this meant that Great Britain would draw off from the Nile an unlimited amount of water for the irrigation of British cotton plantations in the Sudan, it would be a grave threat to Egypt, for Egypt lives by the waters of the Nile. The British foreign minister, however, soon silenced criticism on this

[1] *Egypt No. 1 (1922)*, Cmd. 1592, pp. 27-31.

[2] Zaghlul resigned in Nov. 1924 in consequence of the Stack murder affair (*infra*). His successor, Ziwar Pasha, was more tractable, as regards the British. Zaghlul's supporters claimed that Ziwar was kept in power by British influence and the presence of British garrisons in Egypt.

point by promising a joint inquiry as to the amount of water available for the Sudan after making full allowance for Egypt's needs.

This is the story of Britain in Egypt, but not the whole story. We have not mentioned the effect on American cotton planters of the increasing cotton-cultivation in Egypt. Nor have we mentioned the effect of England's aggression on European peace.

In January, 1882, just after the Anglo-French note was delivered to Egypt, Bismarck thought it "regrettable for the general European situation, to see the English cabinet gliding from one adventure into another"; and he predicted that England would have trouble with France. He had previously been inclined to favor France in the Egyptian question, but after England intervened, Herbert Bismarck told Lord Granville that Germany would not object even to annexation of Egypt by England. Granville of course was pleased, and Dilke (British undersecretary for foreign affairs) favored Herbert Bismarck with such frank expressions of his views as—"I am very much anti-French"; "They (the French) behave like children."[1]

England's intervention in Egypt, in 1882, not only antagonized France, but disturbed the status quo in the Near East. Fortunately Gladstone's promise to get out of Egypt soon reassured the other powers, and peace was preserved. But France continued to cherish her grievance, and during the next few years France cooperated with Germany, in opposition to England, as regards African matters. In another chapter we have seen how the Anglo-French rivalry reached its climax when Kitchener and Marchand met at Fashoda in 1898. It was in no small part for the purpose of ending French opposition to British rule in Egypt[2] that Great Britain formed the Entente Cordiale with France in 1904. The Anglo-French "Declaration"[3] signed on April 8, 1904, provided that France "will not obstruct the action of Great Britain in that country (Egypt) by asking that a limit of time be fixed for the British occupation or in any other matter"; France also agreed to give the British a free hand in rais-

[1] *Die Grosse Politik*, 3, No. 661; 4, nos. 724 ff. Bourgeois et Pagès, *Origines de la Grande Guerre*, pp. 205 ff. for French view.

[2] How important, from the Downing Street point of view, French obstruction in Egypt was, may be clearly seen in Viscount Grey's reminiscences, *Twenty-Five Years*.

[3] *France No. 1 (1904)* Cd. 1952.

ing new Egyptian loans without the consent of the Powers, and in disposing of the surplus revenue of Egypt, over and above the sum required for interest on the debt, which surplus had long been tied up by international agreements. In return, England agreed to equal rights in the Suez Canal for the ships of all nations. In the secret articles[1] signed the same day, France agreed in advance to the abolition of the treaty rights which had hitherto hindered Great Britain from effecting judicial reforms in Egypt. This agreement, as the reader doubtless recalls, was part of a comprehensive set of colonial agreements, but the essential element in the complex balance of gains and concessions was the simple bargain that France would not oppose British imperialism in Egypt if England would not oppose French imperialism in Morocco. Gladstone's stumbling into Egypt in 1882 was therefore one of the reasons, perhaps the chief, why twenty-two years later Great Britain should embrace her age-long enemy in an Entente Cordiale, why in 1905 and 1911 Great Britain should stand ready to join France in war against Germany for Morocco, why in the Great War of 1914 Great Britain fought side by side with France and Russia. It is a tangled web that imperialism weaves.

[1] *Treaty Series No. 24 (1911)*, Cd. 5959.

CHAPTER XI

NEAR EASTERN QUESTIONS OLD AND NEW

In the storied lands of the Near East, where successive empires in their rise and fall have left a history more fabulous than fiction, modern imperialism has built railways where once swaying camels marched in caravan, has sunk oil-wells where once proud Xerxes ruled, has won the walled cities for which Crusaders shed their blood. More subtle than in Africa, but not less intense, imperialism in the Near East has been and still remains not merely a dynamic factor transforming the life of the people, but also a peril to the peace of the world.

That among English writers the phrase, "the Near Eastern Question," or simply "the Eastern Question," and among French historians the same phrase, *"La Question d'Orient,"* has become a *cliché,* is clear enough proof that to Europeans the Near East has been a problem, possibly the most vexing problem of international politics. But the phrase is a misnomer. There have been a succession of Near Eastern Questions.

Two Near Eastern Questions

From the sixteenth century to the eighteenth, one question was, shall the great Moslem empire of the Ottoman Turks be allowed to carry the crescent of Islam, already triumphant in the Balkans, into the heart of European Christendom; and the answer was negative.

Throughout most of the nineteenth century, the principal question was whether Russia should be allowed to dismember "the sick man," the decaying Ottoman Empire, assigning fragments of his estate to Austria and England, and to this the answer was written in blood by the Crimean War of 1853-6, whereby France and England checked Russian aggression, and repeated less vigorously in diplomatic ink by the Berlin Congress of 1878 after the Russo-Turkish War of 1877-8. Disraeli's "Cyprus Convention" with the Porte, pledging England to defend the Ottoman Empire,[1] and the general Treaty of Berlin[2] checked Russian encroachment, but were tinctured by the spirit of compromise, for Russia was permitted to appropriate Bessarabia and the Armenian districts of Kars, Ardahan and Batum, while Austria-Hungary occupied the Turkish provinces of Bosnia-Herzegovina and the sanjak of Novi-Bazar, and Great Britain occupied Cyprus, and France was secretly encouraged by England and Germany to console herself in Tunis, then a tributary province of the sultans. Moreover, the Balkan nations of Rumania, Serbia, and Montenegro were given full independence, part of Bulgaria received autonomy, and Serbia, Montenegro, and Greece enlarged their frontiers at Turkey's expense. Yet, considered as a whole, the settlement of 1878 was an English veto on Russia's plan of partition: as the British foreign minister wrote, three months later, "The reluctance of England to enter on a full policy of partition . . . is now the solitary support on which the Sultan's Empire now rests."[3]

Perhaps in English eyes the importance of the English veto was exaggerated: one might add another obstacle to partition, namely, the unwillingness of Austria, backed by Bismarck, to permit the acquisition of a larger share in the spoils by Russia. Though he helped Austria to secure Bosnia, Bismarck considered the Near East unattractive, not worth the bones of one Pomeranian grenadier; his interest was to prevent Anglo-Russian or Austro-Russian rivalry from causing war. As he wrote to his son, "our chief interest is not in this or that state of affairs in the Turkish Empire, but in the attitude which the powers friendly to us may be brought to assume toward us and toward each other."[4]

[1] *State Papers*, 69, pp. 744, 746.

[2] *Ibid.*, 69, p. 749; *cf.* E. L. Woodward, *The Congress of Berlin; Cambridge History of British Foreign Policy*, III, pp. 115-144.

[3] Salisbury's dispatch of Oct. 17, 1878, quoted by Gooch, *History of Modern Europe*, p. 20. But Salisbury's attitude was not constant. For a time he favored the partition of Turkey into spheres of interest (Lady Gwendolyn Cecil, *Life of Robert, Marquis of Salisbury*, II, pp. 305-12), then took the opposite view, and still later, in 1895, proposed the partition of Turkey, *cf. infra.*

[4] *Die Grosse Politik* II, no. 246; this entire volume throws much light on the Near Eastern question in the seventies.

The Bagdad Railway Concession

A wholly novel Near Eastern Question arose after the accession of William II to the German throne. Whether Germany should, so to speak, swallow Turkey whole, now became the issue. And on this new question the Great Powers realigned themselves, Russia joining with her former enemies, France and England, to oppose German imperialism, abetted by Austria. On this new question the verdict was finally passed only by the method of ordeal by battle, in the Great War of 1914.

Unlike Bismarck, William II considered the Near East to be of immense importance. The ambitious young Kaiser, coming to the imperial throne in 1888, believed ardently in the imperialist creed, and was eager to gain what he could for Germany. The choice morsels in Africa were almost gone. But the Near East might prove to be a richer treasure-house. As early as 1889, William visited Constantinople, despite the grizzled chancellor's disapproval. The latter, concerned lest the young Emperor's visit might give offense to Russia, assured the Tsar that the visit was not dictated by any political interest, and that Germany could not consider adding Turkey to the Triple Alliance or assuming the duty of warring with Russia for the future of Bagdad.[1] And William's attempts, on his return, to inspire Bismarck with "more favorable opinions" toward Turkey, were "of little avail."[2] Still, a reading of the German foreign office documents in the early nineties reveals the absence of imperialistic designs in the Near East, on the part of Germany. When, in 1895, Lord Salisbury secretly proposed to Germany that Turkey ought to be divided up among the Great Powers, William II rejected the proposal, not with any thought of German imperialist interests in Turkey, but rather with concern as to the possibility of satisfying Italian and Austrian aims, and as to the effects which the partition might have on the general diplomatic situation.[3]

Quite different was the situation in October, 1898, when the

[1] *Die Grosse Politik*, VI, no. 1358.
[2] *The Kaiser's Memoirs*, p. 28.
[3] *Die Grosse Politik*, X, ch. 60, esp. nos. 2372, 2381, 2385; *cf.* Hammann, *Der Missverstandene Bismarck*, pp. 43-6; Eckardstein, *Lebenserinnerungen* I, pp. 210-4; Sir Valentine Chirol in London *Times*, Sept. 11, 1920; and R. J. Sontag, "The Cowes Interview," *Pol. Sci. Quart.*, XL, pp. 217 ff.

German Emperor made his second visit to Turkey, ostensibly to attend the consecration of the German evangelical Church of the Redeemer at Jerusalem, but incidentally to further political and economic interests. On this occasion he ostentatiously declared: "May his Majesty the Sultan and may the 300 million Mohammedans who, living scattered about the earth, venerate him as their caliph, be assured that at all times the German Emperor will be their friend."[1] Incongruous as this utterance may have been with the purpose of the visit, it was not less anomalous than Abdul Hamid's expression of admiration for the Kaiser's "true religious spirit and deep understanding of the meaning of religion"; the sagacious sultan felt that Wilhelm and he could agree on the value of religion in forming "the foundation of obedience and thereby of the welfare of the nations."[2]

The material results of the Kaiser's visit show how sudden and how great a change had occurred, within the last few years, as regards the nature of German interests in Turkey. According to a memorandum by Foreign Minister von Bülow, "As economic results achieved by the Kaiser's trip we may regard the allotment of a concession for the construction of a harbor in Haidar Pasha, the concession for a German cable between Constanza and Constantinople, the strengthening of the existing relations between the Turkish government and great German firms. Through the cable concession we arrive in possession of a direct telegraphic connection with Constantinople, which probably will serve as the beginning for a new world line. Here we should also note the plan for a continuation of the Anatolian railways to Bagdad, whereby, we may hope, the foundation will be laid for the further economic opening of Asia Minor. It is to be emphasized that all these concessions will benefit not only German trade and industry, but still more, the Turkish population."[3]

These were only a few of the new German interests in Turkey. Missionaries, shipowners, exporters and importers, bankers and investors, and military men—almost all the typical dynamic elements of Imperialism were becoming active in Turkey in the

[1] *Die Grosse Politik*, XII, pt. 2, p. 575; *cf.* Freiherr von Mirbach, *Die Reise des Kaisers und der Kaiserin nach Palästina;* Schulthess, *Europäischer Geschichtskalender*, 1898, p. 187 f.; Earle, *Turkey, the Great Powers, and the Bagdad Railway*, pp. 43-4, 134-5.

[2] *Die Grosse Politik*, XII, pt. 2, no. 3338.

[3] *Ibid.*, XII, pt. 2, No. 3347, note.

last two decades of the century.[1] But the salient factor was railroad enterprise.[2] The first German railway project in Turkey was launched, by coincidence, the very year of William II's coronation. In October, 1888, George von Siemens and Alfred Kaulla, representing a syndicate of German bankers, obtained from the Turkish minister of public works a concession to reconstruct and operate the 56-mile railway from Haidar Pasha (on the Asiatic coast, opposite Constantinople) to Ismid, and to extend it 300 miles further, to Angora, in the heart of Anatolia. This seemed an innocent business enterprise, but it led further.

Even before the able German railway engineer, Wilhelm von Pressel, had laid the rails to Angora, the question arose, whether and whither the line should be extended. Discussions began as early as 1890. The Sultan was eager to have it continued to Bagdad, and by the Germans.[3] But French, British and Russian competitors, with rival projects, intrigued against the Sultan's plan of confiding this project to the German Kaulla.[4] A provisional agreement was reached in 1899,[5] but immediately Russian complaints poured in upon Constantinople. By way of "moral compensation," Russia must have a monopoly of railway concessions in the Black Sea coastal region.[6] Moreover, Russia objected to the route (via Diarbekr, the Tigris, and Mosul) which the Turks and Germans agreed on in 1900. This route might have brought Turkish troops too near the Russian frontier, or might have strengthened the Turkish grip on lands coveted by Russian imperialists. So strong was Russia's influence that the Germans had to content themselves with a more southerly route, via Konia-Adana-Nesibin-Mosul-Bagdad-Basra-Koweit.[7] Finally the definitive contract was made, in the form of a convention or concession, dated March 5, 1903.[8] The Bagdad railway project was launched, on what stormy waters few men could then foresee.

The Concession of 1903 may well be analyzed as a type whose

[1] For details see Earle, *Turkey, the Great Powers, and the Bagdad Railway.*

[2] See the interesting correspondence in *Die Grosse Politik*, 14, ch. 94.

[3] *Ibid.*, no. 3961.

[4] See German ambassador's dispatch of Jan. 9, 1893, describing the situation as a "Nest von Intrigen," *ibid.*, no. 3970.

[5] *Ibid.*, no. 3992.

[6] *Ibid.*, XVII, nos. 5219, 5221.

[7] *Ibid.*, nos. 5214, 5219, 5226; *cf.* Marschall's long memorandum, no. 5247.

[8] *State Papers*, 102, p. 833; Young, *Corps de droit ottoman*, IV, pp. 163 ff., well analyzed in Earle, *op. cit.*, ch. 4.

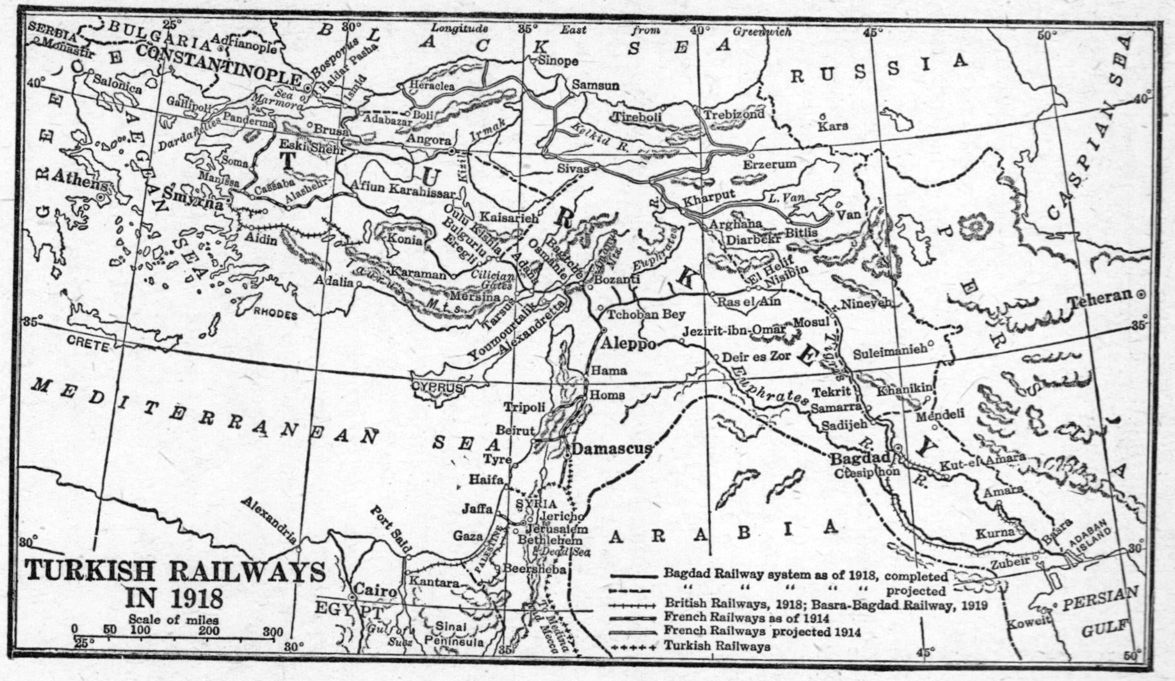

TURKISH RAILWAYS IN 1918
Scale of miles
0 50 100 200 300
Bagdad Railway system as of 1918, completed
" " " " " projected
British Railways, 1918; Basra-Bagdad Railway, 1919
French Railways as of 1914
French Railways projected 1914
Turkish Railways
Longitude East from Greenwich
BLACK SEA
CASPIAN SEA
AEGEAN SEA
MEDITERRANEAN SEA
PERSIAN GULF
RUSSIA
PERSIA
TURKEY
ARABIA
GREECE
BULGARIA
SERBIA
EGYPT
SYRIA
PALESTINE
CYPRUS
CRETE
RHODES
ADABAN ISLAND
CONSTANTINOPLE
Adrianople
Monastir
Salonica
Athens
Smyrna
Gallipoli
Dardanelles
Sea of Marmora
Bosporus
Haidar Pasha
Ismid
Panderma
Brusa
Eski Shehr
Adabazar
Boli
Heraclea
Angora
Kizil Irmak
Soma
Manissa
Cassaba
Alashehr
Afiun Karahissar
Aidin
Konia
Adalia
Karaman
Eregli
Bulgurlu
Oulu Kishla
Kaisarieh
Cilician Gates
Mersina
Tarsus
Adana
Osmanie
Baghche
Bozanti
Youmourtalik
Alexandretta
Sinope
Samsun
Tireboli
Trebizond
Kelkid R.
Sivas
Erzerum
Kars
Kharput
L. Van
Van
Arghana
Diarbekr
Bitlis
El Helif
Nisibin
Ras el Ain
Nineveh
Tchoban Bey
Jezirit-ibn-Omar
Mosul
Aleppo
Deir es Zor
Euphrates
Tigris R.
Teheran
Suleimanieh
Hama
Homs
Tripoli
Beirut
Damascus
Tyre
Haifa
Jaffa
Jericho
Jerusalem
Bethlehem
Dead Sea
Gaza
Beersheba
To Medina and Mecca
Tekrit
Samarra
Khanikin
Mendeli
Sadijeh
Bagdad
Ctesiphon
Kut-el-Amara
Amara
Kurna
Basra
Zubeir
Koweit
Alexandria
Port Said
Kantara
Cairo
Gulf of Suez
Sinai Peninsula

counterpart may be found in many an Asiatic or African or Latin-American country. The so-called "Bagdad Railway" was to be constructed from Konia (which was already connected with Constantinople by the rail and ferry), across the frowning Taurus mountains, skirting the Gulf of Alexandretta, but, for safety from British naval guns, not touching the coast, then stretching east across desert lands to Mosul on the Tigris, following that river down to Bagdad, thence down the Euphrates to Basra, and thence to the Persian Gulf. This would be the trunk line, from which branches would reach out, the most important being the proposed "feeder" to tap the trade of Persia at Khanikin. The total length would be 3,733 kilometers, or about 2400 miles.

The project was magnificent in its daring; it would mean spanning precipitous ravines, tunneling mountains, crossing great deserts; it would tap the almost untouched mineral resources of Asiatic Turkey; it would provide an artery through which European capital could pour into Anatolia and Mesopotamia, to transform wastelands by a magic touch into fields of snowy cotton or golden grain; it would open up an empire to European trade.[1] But it might not pay its promoters, at first. Like most railways meant to open up an undeveloped country, it would have to be built on faith, or with governmental aid. And as the builders of American transcontinental lines sought land-grants from Congress, or as railway pioneers in almost every other country asked public support, so in this case the promoters required financial help from the Turkish government. Similar assistance had been given to the railways previously built in Turkey; that it should be extended to this more vital yet more difficult project was a matter of course.

The financial arrangement was characteristic of concessions, and not so extraordinarily grasping as it has often been represented.[2] The German promoters were to form the Bagdad Railway Company, incorporated in Turkey. To this company the Turkish government would transfer bonds amounting to 275,000 francs per kilometer of railway to be built, and by selling the

[1] See especially Paul Rohrbach, *Die Bagdadbahn*, (1903) for a sample of German optimism regarding the economic results; *cf.* Earle, *op. cit.*, ch. 2, on economic resources of Turkey.

[2] *Cf.* MacMurray, *Treaties Concerning China*, I, pp. 74, 145, 367, 402, etc., and Earle, *op. cit.*, p. 79.

bonds to European investors the company would obtain the cash capital for its work. The bonds were not a gift, but a loan secured by mortgage on the railway. This, however, was not enough; the Company had to be guaranteed against operating the railway, after construction, at a loss. Accordingly, if the gross annual receipts should fall below 4500 francs per kilometer of railway in operation, the Turkish government was to contribute whatever sum was needed to bring the receipts up to this figure. *Per contra,* if the receipts should exceed the stated figure, the excess up to 10,000 francs would be paid to the government, and any excess over 10,000 francs would be divided between the government and the railway. That, in addition, the Company should be granted a free right-of-way through public lands, was in accordance with the normal practice. The provision for exemption of the Company's property from Turkish taxation was generous but not unprecedented.[1] The Company received the important right to exploit mineral resources found within a zone twenty kilometers on each side of the railway.[2]

Favorable to the German promoters, and burdensome to Turkey, as these terms may at first appear, they were in the main typical of railway charters in backward countries, let it be reiterated, and they were granted by the Turkish government not through fear or coercion, but in expectation of benefit. Abdul Hamid was, if anything, more eager than the Germans. The railway would undoubtedly increase the prosperity of Asiatic Turkey, and thereby swell the tax revenue; it would enable the Turkish government to send troops to maintain its authority in distant provinces, or to call up troops in case of war; and at the end of ninety-nine years the railway would become the property of the Turkish government.

[1] Even Professor Earle, who points out that the financial guarantees were far from unprecedented, seems to consider this exemption from taxation as an important and radical innovation. Yet for this, too, there were precedents in Chinese railway grants. For instance, the contract for the Chinese Eastern Railway in 1896 included tax-exemption (MacMurray, I, p. 76); so also did the Belgian concession for the Peking-Hankow line in 1898 (*ibid.*, pp. 138, 139, 141, 144) and other Chinese concessions.

[2] This likewise was not wholly novel. To cite but one instance, in the preliminary contract for the Peking-Newchwang Railway, in 1898, the syndicate was promised mining rights within five *li* of the railway (MacMurray, I, 180).

More Than a Railway

Considered as a business bargain, or as a beneficent economic enterprise, which would open up vast areas to civilization and progress, the Bagdad Railway could hardly be opposed by other nations. On the contrary, it won some praise, along with criticism, even in countries like England and France. The French ambassador at Constantinople, M. Constans, actually aided the German ambassador, Marschall, to secure the Sultan's approval of the project.[1] Moreover, French and British bankers seemed willing to join hands with the German promoters, who were eager to obtain foreign financial assistance in their gigantic undertaking. Von Gwinner and Siemens, representing the German syndicate, engaged in a series of negotiations with banking groups at London and Paris. It was proposed that French and German capital should each have a forty per cent interest, the remainder being assigned to minor groups. As the British, however, felt strongly that they should have an equal share, von Gwinner visited England in the spring of 1903 and an agreement was drafted [2] by which British, French and German syndicates would each take 25% of the stock, leaving 10% for the Anatolian Railway Company (which was predominantly but not exclusively German) and 15% for other groups. On the board of directors were to be eight German, eight French, eight British directors and six appointed by the Turkish Government and the Anatolian Railway Company. Though the British Government, after some hesitation, decided not to approve this proposal,[3] it is profoundly interesting, both as indication of German intentions and as a lost opportunity. So little was Von Gwinner actuated by German imperialism, that he would have given the French and English, combined, a controlling interest in the stock and a majority in the board of directors, to insure the financial success of the enterprise. And so short was the vision of British and French statesmen that they deliberately rejected an opportunity to obtain, by peaceful finance, control of a railroad which later had to be purchased in blood.

[1] *Die Grosse Politik,* XII, pt. 2, no. 3349. This refers to the preliminary agreement in 1899.

[2] Earle, *op. cit.*, ch. 8. *Die Grosse Politik,* XVII, throws light on the earlier negotiations.

[3] See Balfour's statements, April 8 and 23. 1903, *Parl. Deb.*, 4th Series, 120, pp. 1369-75; 121, p. 222

Why the Balfour Government, at first favorable, adopted an attitude of opposition toward the railway, will probably never be wholly clear, until its archives are opened to scholars. This much is clear, however, that the British owners of the Smyrna Railway, and the Lynch Brothers who handled the shipping on the lower Tigris, might suffer, and that British shipping interests might conceivably lose traffic to the railway. It is also true that in the press and in Parliament [1] a clamor was raised against the project, against German naval expansion, against German commercial rivalry; but to what extent this clamor was sincerely based on these ostensible reasons, and to what extent on the irritation which had arisen in recent unsuccessful overtures for an Anglo-German alliance,[2] and to what extent, if any, by hidden motives or financial influence, it is difficult even to guess. The German chancellor believed the anti-German agitation in the English press was solely responsible. The Kaiser suspected it was influenced by Russia, and Sir Clinton Dawkins, the London associate of Pierpont Morgan, in a very interesting letter to von Gwinner said his "impression is that the instigation proceeded from the Russian embassy in Paris." Dawkins felt certain that the failure of the Anglo-German agreement was due to the newspaper campaign, which coerced the Foreign Office.[3] On the other hand, Mr. H. F. B. Lynch, of the above-mentioned shipping firm, boasted that he had the Foreign Office and the press in his hand as regards Mesopotamia, and that if he chose he could guarantee the cooperation of the Foreign Office, as well as of such anti-German journals as the *Times,* the *Morning Post,* and the *National Review.*[4]

It may safely be hazarded that British imperial strategy weighed heavily in the hidden scales of judgment. The Bagdad Railway might be a menace both to the Suez Canal, if from the trunk line a branch running south through Palestine were constructed, and to India, if the trunk line reached to the Persian Gulf. To forestall the latter, the imperialist Lord Curzon, then

[1] April 8, 1903, *Parliamentary Debates,* 4th Series, 120, pp. 1358 ff.

[2] See brief accounts in *Cambridge History of British Foreign Policy,* III, 276 ff., Brandenburg, *Von Bismarck zum Weltkrieg,* ch. 7, and documents in *Die Grosse Politik.*

[3] *Die Grosse Politik,* XVII, esp. nos. 5261-2.

[4] He said this to von Gwinner in 1905, to support his proposal that the railway section in Mesopotamia should be surrendered to English financial control *Die Grosse Politik,* XXV, No. 8626.

viceroy of India, made an arrangement with the Arab Sheikh of Koweit, in whose small territory, at the head of the Persian Gulf, the German engineers planned to create their terminal. Accordingly, in 1900, the British amiably informed Germany that no concession of land could be obtained from the Sheikh of Koweit without British consent.[1] But after a lively diplomatic interchange, Lord Lansdowne, in October, 1901, said he would not oppose the construction of the railway to Koweit. In 1903 Lord Lansdowne, British foreign minister, declared in the House of Lords: "we should regard the establishment of a naval base or of a fortified port in the Persian Gulf by any other power as a very grave menace to British interests, and we should certainly resist it with all the means at our disposal."[2] To be sure, Lansdowne added, no proposals were on foot for such a naval base.

As for France, some French financiers did actually subscribe thirty per cent of the capital of the Bagdad Railway Company. Moreover, Delcassé, the foreign minister, is said at one time to have secretly favored the Bagdad Railway in the hope that by drawing Germany's imperialist energy to the Near East, it would leave Morocco undisputed in the hands of France.[3] Nevertheless the French Government, in October, 1903, adopted an attitude of hostility toward the project, and excluded Bagdad Railway bonds from the French Bourse. Perhaps this action was due to propaganda, perhaps to economic interests not clearly revealed, perhaps to fear that German penetration of Turkey would deprive France of the predominant influence which French missionaries, merchants, and railway builders had obtained in Syria. Perhaps also, pressure was brought to bear by Russia. The Germans suspected that the Russian ambassador persuaded Delcassé to oppose the project.[4]

Russia opposed the project from the beginning.[5] On economic

[1] *Cf. Die Grosse Politik,* XIV, no. 4000; XVII, nos. 5278-5331. The Russian consul at Bagdad also made an impressive visit to Koweit at this time, presumably to thwart German plans. The British denied having a "protectorate" over Koweit (no. 5293).

[2] *Parl. Deb.,* 4th Ser., 121, p. 134; *cf. Questions diplomatiques et coloniales,* 15, pp. 609 ff.; *Die Grosse Politik,* XVII, no. 5362.

[3] Earle, p. 169; *cf. Journal officiel, Débats, Chambre,* March 24, 1903, pp. 1468 ff.

[4] *Die Grosse Politik,* XVII, no. 5274; XXV, p. 186 footnote.

[5] *Ibid.,* esp. ch. 114, shows the tortuous course of Russian obstruction, which occasionally seemed to verge upon agreement with Germany, but persistently tended toward opposition, direct or indirect.

grounds influential Russian interests feared competition, but more important was the strategic problem. The German railway would revive the sick man, and strengthen his grip on Constantinople and on Armenia, both of which had long been coveted by Russian statesmen. Between Russian aims and the German railway, there was an absolute clash, just as there had been an irreconcilable collision between French and British designs in the Sudan. One or the other must give way.

Thus the business proposition of building a railway became a matter of imperialist diplomacy and international enmity. Nor were German imperialists loath to regard the railway as more than a railway. Many believed that the railway would open up Asiatic Turkey to German imperialism. This feeling, in all its joyous exaggeration of economic prospects, is perhaps best expressed in the words of Sprenger—"there are no virgin forests to clear away, no natural difficulties to overcome, but you have only to scratch the soil, sow, and reap. [This, of the exhausted soil in a worn-out country!] The Near East is the only region in the world not yet appropriated by a Great Power. Nevertheless it is the finest field for colonization. If Germany does not lose the opportunity, but seizes it before the Cossacks stretch out their hand in that direction, she will have acquired the best share in the partition of the world."[1] Others dilated on the as yet unprospected mineral wealth of Turkey, in copper, and coal and iron, and petroleum. Still others reminded the German public that Mesopotamia was once the Garden of Eden, that its agricultural wealth had been described by Herodotus, that it was the granary of ancient Rome, and that with irrigation it could regain its fertility. "Mesopotamia alone can provide all Germany with wheat and cotton," wrote Paul Rohrbach, in glorious disregard of realities.[2]

Rohrbach, by the way, was typical of the German publicists whose fervor excelled their common sense. What more foolhardy indiscretion can be imagined than to declare, in public print, that the railway could be used as a strategic menace to the Suez Canal and Egypt? Yet Rohrbach earnestly informed his fellow

[1] Quoted by Muratet, pp. 108-113.

[2] In all fairness it should be added that Sir William Willcocks, an eminent British irrigation engineer, believed an expenditure of about a hundred million dollars would reclaim about 2½ million acres of arable land in Mesopotamia.

countrymen—and England—that the only way for Germany to prevent her most dangerous foe, England, from oppressing or attacking her, was to menace England at the most vulnerable point, namely Egypt, loss of which would cut communications with India and the Far East and perhaps endanger other British possessions in Africa and India.[1] Rohrbach wrote as an irresponsible publicist, rather than as a spokesman for Von Gwinner and the bankers, or for the German Government, but indiscretions such as his could not fail to arouse suspicion in England. Nor could the glowing prophecies of German patriots concerning the roseate future of Turkey under German exploitation and political influence fail to strengthen the impression that the Bagdad Railway was more than a railway, that it was an imperial highway for the German *"Drang nach Osten."*

Foreign opposition did not prevent the successful, and profitable, completion of the first section of the railway, amounting to 200 kilometers, in October, 1904. But then difficulties arose. To build the next section, through the Taurus mountains, would be more difficult and more costly. Moreover, the German bankers had not been able to obtain the large financial assistance they had originally expected from France and England, and the Turkish Government, unable to issue additional bonds without increasing its own revenue from customs duties, had difficulty in obtaining the permission of the Great Powers for an increase of the tariff (which was fixed at 8% by treaties) to 11%. Not until June, 1908, were arrangements made for the issue of the 227 million francs of Ottoman bonds required for the building of the next 840 kilometers of railway.[2]

The Bosnian Crisis

Then German hopes were dashed to the ground by the Young Turk Revolution, in July, 1908. The Young Turks as fervent nationalists, educated for the most part in France or England, were suspicious of Germany and friendly to England and France. Germany had been too friendly with Abdul Hamid. Moreover, the Young Turk Revolution presented Austria-Hungary with an opportunity to annex the Turkish provinces of

[1] Rohrbach, *Die Bagdadbahn.*

[2] *State Papers*, 102, pp. 876 ff.; *cf. Die Grosse Politik*, XXII, nos. 7595-7668, XXV, nos. 8604-8680.

Bosnia and Herzegovina, which had been occupied since 1878, and the annexation of these provinces in October, 1908, by Austria-Hungary with the firm support of Germany, did not lessen the unfriendliness of the Young Turks toward the Central Powers.

The Bosnian crisis in the winter of 1908-9 was the sudden flare of diplomatic embers that had been kindled long before, and continued to burn long afterward. As we have seen, Bismarck had permitted Austria-Hungary to occupy Bosnia in 1878, partly in the hope of binding Austria close to Germany, and partly in the hope that Austria and Russia might agree to define for themselves separate spheres of influence in the Balkans. The former hope had been immediately realized in the Austro-German alliance of 1879; and the latter had seemed not impossible when the Three Emperors' League, of Russia, Austria and Germany was formed in the eighties, and Russia secretly agreed that in due time Bosnia should be annexed by Austria.[1] But Russia had subsequently, in the nineties, allied herself with France, in hostility to Austria and Germany, and the annexation had been postponed, until 1908. In September, 1908, however, the Russian foreign minister Isvolsky had agreed, more or less tentatively, with the Austro-Hungarian foreign minister Aehrenthal, that Austria might use the Young Turk Revolution as a pretext for annexing Bosnia, on condition that Russia be allowed to demand the opening of the Turkish Straits.[2] Austria had then gone ahead, rather high-handedly, to realize her part of the bargain, but Isvolsky suddenly turned about-face as though the annexation were an unexpected outrage. His *volte-face* was partly due to the fact that after sounding English sentiment, he concluded that the opening of the Straits might be a dangerous thing to attempt.[3] This was disappointing, for Russia had but recently formed an Entente with England, in 1907, and in June of 1908 King Edward and several influential British officials had held the celebrated "Reval interview" with the Russian Tsar and Russian statesmen; just what was done at Reval, has not yet been revealed, but it is certain that the Near Eastern question was discussed, and probable that the Russians were

[1] Pribram, *Secret Treaties of Austria-Hungary*, I, p. 43.

[2] Friedjung, *Zeitalter des Imperialismus*, II, pp. 222 ff.; Gooch, *Modern Europe*, pp. 410 ff.; Brandenburg, *op. cit.*, ch. 12; Siebert, *Entente Diplomacy*, pp. 229 ff.

[3] See Grey, *Twenty-five Years*, pp. 172-7.

encouraged to count on a conciliatory British attitude toward Russia's Near Eastern projects.[1]

What followed the annexation of Bosnia was even more disappointing to Isvolsky. When Serbia protested against Austria's action, and mobilized her little army, an Austro-Serbian war seemed imminent. Russian Pan-Slavists demanded that the greatest Slavic nation should support the smallest. Isvolsky rushed to Serbia's support, and gave every appearance of being willing to let Russian troops loose on Austria if the latter did not yield. So far, good. But German diplomacy intervened, to support Austria so strongly, and to exercise firm pressure in St. Petersburg. The Russian Government swallowed its wrath, persuaded Serbia to recognize the annexation, and thus accepted a great humiliation.[2]

In this crisis, Russia had looked in vain to France and England for support. England cared more for peace than for Russian prestige,[3] and France, in the midst of the crisis, signed a friendly agreement with Germany for joint economic exploitation of Morocco.[4] Russia, in short, had been left in the lurch. That the Russian Government resented the disloyalty of France and England, appears quite clearly from various secret documents which have been published.[5] For the moment, however, Russia was helpless. She could, and did, give secret encouragement to Serbia, holding out the hope that the time would come when revenge could be taken on Austria.[6] She could also make a secret military convention with Bulgaria, looking forward to a future struggle with the Central Powers.[7] With Italy, Isvolsky signed a secret pact providing for Italian neutrality if the Straits question should ever again be raised.[8]

Diplomatic Bargaining 1910-1914

But much more pertinent to our present theme was the bargain which Isvolsky, in his resentment, made with Germany regard-

[1] *Ibid.*, 202 ff., Siebert, *op. cit.*, pp. 478 ff.; *Die Grosse Politik*, XXV, ch. 159.

[2] Brandenburg, *op. cit.*, ch. 12.

[3] Siebert, *op. cit.*, pp. 229 ff.

[4] *Cf. supra*, p. 212.

[5] Particularly Siebert, *loc. cit.*

[6] Friedjung, *op. cit.* II, pp. 250 ff., *Deutschland Schuldig? Deutsches Weissbuch* (1919), p. 114.

[7] Stieve, *Iswolski und der Weltkrieg*, pp. 220 ff., text.

[8] *Livre Noir*, I, pp. 357-8.

ing the Bagdad Railway. If, as he had reason to believe, France was following the inclinations of French financiers toward reconciliation with Germany in Morocco and Turkey, and if, as he very well knew, England was already dickering with Germany on the compensation England was to receive for ceasing to oppose the Bagdad Railway, Russia might as well sell Russian consent to the Railway as quickly and dearly as possible.[1] For years Russian and German diplomats had been discussing this question, and haggling over the terms.[2] But now the bargain was concluded. At Potsdam, in 1910, the Russian Tsar and his foreign minister met the German Emperor and his ministers, and concluded the so-called "Potsdam Agreement," which was elaborated and confirmed by a formal convention in the following year.[3] Russia agreed to cease opposing the Bagdad Railway. In return, Germany practically recognized Russia's right to northern Persia as a sphere of influence.

Though accused of disloyalty by Russia, the English Government regarded the Potsdam agreement as a sign of Russian disloyalty, and Sir Edward Grey complained that Russia had weakened England's position in opposing the Bagdad Railway,[4] while French opinion resented the agreement and its confirmation (Aug. 19, 1911) at a time when France and Germany were at swords' points over Morocco.[5] It was an exceptionally dismal —or amusing, according to the point of view—illustration of the endless vicious circle of mutual suspicion among imperialist nations, even among imperialist allies.

After Russia, France and England also came to terms on the Bagdad Railway. England had enjoyed remarkable influence in Turkey immediately after the Young Turk Revolution; Englishmen had been appointed as advisers to the Turkish departments of finance, justice, and the interior; an English admiral had been asked to reorganize the Turkish navy; and an English banker had established a National Bank for Turkey. In November, 1909,

[1] Siebert, *op. cit.*, p. 507.

[2] *Die Grosse Politik*, XXV, ch. 185, gives documents showing how these discussions were proceeding simultaneously with the Anglo-Russian negotiations of 1907, and how closely the formula discussed in 1907 resembled the one adopted in 1910.

[3] *State Papers*, 105, p. 657.

[4] Siebert, *op. cit.*, p. 536.

[5] *Cf. supra*, p. 210; *Der Diplomatische Schriftwechsel Iswolskis*, I, nos. 4-9. See *Journal officiel* for debate on Jan. 12, 1911.

Anglo-German negotiations were renewed, looking toward some sort of compromise whereby Germany would give up the hope of extending the Bagdad Railway to the Persian Gulf.[1] To France, also, the Young Turks made overtures, promising railway concessions to French interests, but when Djavid Bey went to Paris in the summer of 1910 to borrow thirty million dollars for Turkey, he was shocked by Foreign Minister Pichon's demand that, as a condition of the loan, a French adviser should be appointed to control the Turkish budget.[2]

Indignantly, the Turks turned back to Germany, and the Germans made good use of the situation, by arranging the loan and tactfully winning the friendship of the Young Turks. It was in this same year, 1910, that the Potsdam agreement was made. Encouraged to hope for similar agreements with England and France, the Germans (and also the Turks) began negotiations with London and Paris. To conciliate England, the Bagdad Railway Company expressed its willingness, in March, 1911, to abandon the plans for the sections from Bagdad to Basra and from Basra to the Persian Gulf, and to permit the construction and operation of these sections by an international syndicate. The negotiations were not wholly interrupted by the Morocco Crisis of July, 1911, and the ensuing Turco-Italian and Balkan Wars.[3] And in 1913-14 a series of agreements were reached.

The secret bargains of 1913-14 are intensely interesting, because they show what England and France wanted in the Near East, and because they exemplify how far secret diplomacy could go toward the solution of this acute imperialist conflict, and because they make patent the close alliance between business interests and diplomacy. With France, or rather with French financiers backed by French diplomats, the German Bagdad Railway syndicate, represented by Dr. Von Gwinner and Dr. Karl Helfferich, backed by the German foreign office, came to terms which were sealed and signed in the form of a Franco-German Convention, dated Feb. 15, 1914.[4] France sold her con-

[1] Siebert, *op. cit.*, pp. 501 ff. On the earlier Windsor discussions, see Haldane, *Before the War*, pp. 48-52, and *Die Grosse Politik*, XXV, ch. 186, esp. nos. 8668-74. Grey proposed a discussion *à quatre*, that is, between Germany and the three entente powers, but this Germany refused.

[2] Earle, *op. cit.*, p. 224.

[3] Siebert, *op. cit.*, pp. 524-76.

[4] Earle, *op. cit.*, p. 248.

sent to the Bagdad Railway dearly. French capitalists were to receive concessions to build a system of railways in northern Anatolia along the Black Sea littoral, and to extend the French railways in Syria—about 2000 miles in all, almost as much as the mileage of the Bagdad Railway, and with kilometric guarantees and governmental aid similar to that received by the Bagdad Railway. The Deutsche Bank was to repurchase from the Imperial Ottoman Bank (French-controlled) the Bagdad Railway securities, amounting to 69,400,000 francs, which the latter owned, thus making the Bagdad Railway more definitely German, and liberating French capital for French enterprises. The French-controlled Imperial Ottoman Bank, it may be added, received the profitable task of underwriting the Turkish loan of $100,000,000 in 1914.[1] That France came off so handsomely was not due to any sentimental generosity on the part of the Germans. For the latter, it was highly important that France should cease to oppose the increase of the Turkish tariff and the allocation of Turkish revenues to fulfill the Turkish government's obligations toward the Bagdad Railway.

With England a series of Turkish agreements paved the way for the remarkable Anglo-German convention of June 15, 1914, the text of which was kept secret until Professor Earle, having obtained a copy from Dr. Von Gwinner, published it in 1923.[2] Though the British Smyrna-Aidin Railway Company obtained the privilege of extending its line by two hundred miles, and connecting it with the Bagdad system, the British government was primarily interested in other matters. One vital point was the German promise not to extend the Bagdad Railway farther than Basra, and not to establish a terminal or harbor on the Persian Gulf except by agreement with Great Britain: thus was to be safeguarded Britain's strategic interest in the Persian Gulf; thus was to be parried the potential thrust at India. Another important safeguard required by Great Britain was a pledge that there would be absolutely no discrimination against British goods and passengers on the Bagdad Railway, and that two British representatives should sit on the board of directors to see that justice was done. In addition, Great Britain had certain interests in lower Mesopotamia: any irrigation works

[1] *Parl. Papers*, 1920 (Cmd. 964).
[2] *Pol. Sci. Quart.*, 38, pp. 24-44.

here were to be British; a monopoly of river navigation in Mesopotamia was to be enjoyed by an Ottoman Navigation Company controlled by the affluent British shipping baron, Lord Inchcape; and British interests received a concession to exploit the oil resources of Mesopotamia, as far north as Mosul. To be more explicit on this last point, it was agreed that Turkey should grant exclusive oil rights in Mesopotamia to a Turkish Petroleum Company, half of whose stock would be held by the Anglo-Persian Oil Co. (British), one quarter by the Royal Dutch-Shell oil combine (British and Dutch), and one quarter by the Deutsche Bank.[1]

These Anglo-German agreements, one should remember, went hand in hand with secret agreements for the division of the Portuguese African colonies into British and German spheres of influence;[2] they were part of a general colonial entente, which never reached fruition, because, while Sir Edward Grey insisted that the agreements must be published, as a condition of British ratification, Herr von Jagow, German foreign minister, fearing that German imperialists would think him too generous toward England, desired to await "a suitable moment when the danger of hostile criticism would be less acute." In July, 1914, he decided to yield this point, but too late.[3] The outbreak of the war threw these secret conventions, initialed but never signed or ratified, into the scrap basket.

The secret agreements with France and Great Britain would have meant the partition of Asiatic Turkey into spheres of influence; Great Britain would have lower Mesopotamia and Smyrna; southern Syria and northern Anatolia would be French; Armenia, it was understood, would be reserved for Russian political and French economic interest; and the rest—central and southern Anatolia, northern Syria, and northern Mesopotamia, would be for German exploitation. The German official attitude toward the question of ultimate partition is shown clearly in a secret

[1] *Cf. infra*, p. 264. The total capital was £160,000. C. B. Gulbenkian was to enjoy a 5% beneficiary interest contributed by the Anglo-Persian and Royal Dutch-Shell.

[2] *Cf. supra*, p. 119.

[3] Brandenburg, *op. cit.*, pp. 400-1. On July 22, 1914, the day before Austria's ultimatum to Serbia, Bethman-Hollweg asked for authority to make the agreement definitive; it was given on July 27, and communicated to Lichnowsky, the ambassador in London, on July 30. *Cf.* Lichnowsky, *My London Mission.*

dispatch[1] of the German foreign minister (Jagow) to his ambassador in Constantinople (Wangenheim), July 28, 1913, stating that Turkey had no active strength, but must continue to exist "until we further consolidate ourselves in our zones of activity there and until we are ready for the annexation. That moment I would like to postpone as long as possible." For Germany was not ready.

It has been asserted that these diplomatic bargains would have been sufficient to settle the Bagdad Railway question, and perhaps to have prevented the Great War, had not the Central Powers precipitated the struggle in the summer of 1914. This is hardly true. English and French interests may have been satisfied, and German interests too; but no such bargains could permanently bridge the chasm between Russia and the Central Powers. The imperialistic faction at St. Petersburg might make temporary agreements for present advantage, but could not be sincerely satisfied without Constantinople. In February, 1914, a secret conclave or Crown Council of the Russian cabinet ministers and military and naval officials discussed this problem; the foreign minister considered Russian conquest of Constantinople as a well-settled aim of Russian policy; and plans were made to seize Constantinople when the next general war should break out.[2] Russia, it is plain, was not content.

A little later, in March, 1914, Russia made an interesting attempt to sound Germany on the Straits question. The Russian ambassador at Constantinople suggested to the German ambassador that Germany and Russia ought to cooperate in Turkey. Russia should be allowed to rule the Straits through a subservient Turkish Government, while Germany would exploit Asia Minor. The only real difficulty would be the question of Germany's support of Austria's Balkan policy. Such an entente, of course, might lead to difficulties with England and France, but Russia, said the ambassador, was quite indifferent to French hopes regarding Alsace. Germany, however, was unwilling to jeopardize her friendship with England, for an unreliable partnership with Russia, and so Berlin vouchsafed no reply to the Russian feeler.[3]

[1] Quoted in Brandenburg, *op. cit.*, p. 394.
[2] Stieve, *Iswolski und der Weltkrieg*, pp. 247-266.
[3] Brandenburg, *op. cit.*, pp. 397-8.

The Balkan Crisis 1912-1914

Moreover, the proposed settlement in Asiatic Turkey was closely related to the perilous Balkan situation, about which, fatuously enough, the diplomats had failed to make any agreement, so far as we know. For decades Russian and Austrian diplomats had been engaging in a sordid and subtle game of intrigue at the capitals of Serbia, Bulgaria, Greece and Rumania, the object being to secure the favor and friendship, or better still the puppet-like subservience, of the dynasty and faction in power in each of these Balkan countries, or, if that proved impossible, to aid another faction to seize power. Thus, for example, the Russians had gone to the length, on one occasion, of kidnapping an intractable ruler of Bulgaria.[1] In the case of Serbia, a pro-Austrian dynasty, allied to Austria by secret treaty, had been overthrown in 1903, or rather massacred, by a band of conspirators who placed the rival Karageorgevitch dynasty on the throne and pursued a pro-Russian policy. That Austrian statesmen should have considered, secretly, of course, plans for replacing this pro-Russian dynasty at Belgrade with a pro-Austrian sovereign, may be shocking, but can hardly be surprising.

In support of his Austrian ally, Bismarck had become involved in Balkan intrigues before 1890, but he felt that Germany had no direct interest in them. Once the Bagdad Railway was begun, however, in William II's reign, it became a very vital German interest to see that the Balkan nations were properly disposed toward Germany and Austria, because through the Balkans ran the railways, particularly the Orient Railway, which linked Constantinople and the Bagdad Railway with the rail systems of Central Europe. It is significant that these Balkan lines had been owned, since about 1888, by Austrian, German and Swiss-German banks, among which was numbered the Deutsche Bank, the financial fountainhead of the Bagdad enterprise.

With this background, we may examine a little more closely the imperialist interests involved in the Balkan situation from 1912 to 1914. In 1912 four of the Balkan nations—Bulgaria, Greece, Serbia and Montenegro—attacked Turkey. It was not

[1] Prince Alexander, in August 1886.

generally known at that time, but diplomats rightly suspected, that Russian diplomacy had secretly encouraged Bulgaria, Serbia and Greece to ally themselves and drive Turkey out of Macedonia.[1] Vienna was alarmed because Russian diplomacy had the upper hand; Berlin was anxious regarding Turkey, for German imperialists desired to preserve and strengthen Turkey as a Germanized vassal.[2] For Germany and Austria the overwhelming victory of the Balkan allies against Turkey was therefore a distinct setback; for Russia, proud parent of the Balkan alliance, a diplomatic triumph. Austria would have drawn the sword against Serbia in July, 1913, had Germany and Italy been willing to back her. Hoping to undo Russia's work, Viennese statesmen fostered disagreements between Bulgaria and her former allies, over the division of the spoils. This was all the more easily accomplished, since Austria and Italy by refusing to let Serbia take Albania made it almost inevitable that Serbia should seek consolation at the expense of Bulgarian aspirations in Macedonia. Between Bulgaria, on the one side, and Greece and Serbia, soon joined by Rumania and Turkey, on the opposing side, was waged an unequal contest in the summer of 1913.

This second Balkan War simply made matters worse for Germany and Austria, for in backing Bulgaria they had again picked the losing horse. Serbia emerged jubilant, enlarged and aggressive; by decreeing the nationalization of railways in her territory she served notice on the Central Powers that their railway imperialism was no longer to be tolerated. Rumania was, so to speak, flirting with Russia, although legally wedded to the Triple Alliance by a secret treaty. On the other hand, in Greece, Germany could count on King Constantine, a brother-in-law of William II; and of course there was Bulgaria, but Bulgaria was badly battered. Such was the situation on the eve of the Great War. The Austrian foreign minister was secretly planning to attempt the difficult diplomatic feat of forming a new Balkan alliance under Austrian patronage. Germany, for her part, was sufficiently conscious of her weakened position so that she was willing to make agreements, at considerable sacrifice, with France and England, in order to remove

[1] See Siebert, *op. cit.*, pp. 307-59; Stieve, *Iswolski und der Weltkrieg*, pp. 86 ff, 225 ff. *Diplomatische Schriftwechsel Iswolskis*, II, especially Nos. 243, 317, 401, and following documents.

[2] But see p. 256, *supra*.

opposition to the Bagdad Railway. At the same time, unfortunately, German military leaders felt it necessary to increase the German army, and to send a German general, Liman von Sanders, to reorganize the demoralized Turkish army. The former measure alarmed France and Russia; the latter provoked the Russians to hold the secret Crown Council of February, 1914, which has already been alluded to.

Only in the light of these clashing imperialist aims can one perceive the full significance of the crime that was committed in the dusty streets of Serajevo, in June 1914, and of the resulting Austrian attack on Serbia. It was more than a quarrel between Austria and her small neighbor; it was more than a question of suppressing pan-Serbian agitation for the dismemberment of the Hapsburg monarchy. It was also a crucial move in the Near Eastern chess game played by the financiers and diplomats of Europe. The Vienna Government probably intended to invade Serbia, assign some Serbian territory to Bulgaria and Albania, reduce Serbia to a properly servile condition, and found a pro-Austrian Balkan league. Berlin, though pretending disinterestedness for diplomatic reasons, was vitally concerned, not only to preserve Austria's strength and prestige, but also to insure Austro-German predominance in the Balkans. Behind Serbia loomed the Russian aim of dominating the Balkans and Constantinople; behind Austria towered German imperialism, determined to safeguard the "German road to the East."

War and Peace

During the war, the wildest dreams of German imperialists were realized, for a moment, in the Near East. Turkey, having secretly joined the Triple Alliance, was brought into the war on Germany's side, partly by the efforts of Young Turks like Enver Pasha, who felt that Russian victory would mean an end to Turkey, and partly by the presence of two German warships. Bulgaria, too, joined the Central Powers a little later, in October, 1915. Serbia, Montenegro, Albania and most of Rumania, were conquered by Germany and her allies. The Balkan peninsula was now a broad highway connecting Austro-German Central Europe with Germanized Turkey.

But Germany was defeated, as all the world knows, and it was left to the Allies to divide the spoils of Turkey. The Allies were not unprepared. Even in the darkest hours of the war, Allied statesmen were optimistically arranging the partition of Turkey. Russia was to annex Constantinople and the adjoining territory, so France and England agreed in March, 1915—just before the great Russian defeat in Poland. A year later, France agreed (Sazonov-Paléologue agreement of April 26, 1916) that Russia should also have about 60,000 square miles of northeastern Turkey, that is, of Turkish Armenia, while the region stretching southwestward from this region to the Mediterranean, including Syria, should be French. Next France and England defined their claims, by the Sykes-Picot agreement of May, 1916: France was to administer Syria and the hinterland reaching up to the Russian zone in Armenia, and a "zone of French influence" was to stretch eastward from Syria across the Euphrates and Tigris, as far as the Persian border. All south of this would be a British zone of influence, excepting Palestine, which would be under international control (the Palestinian ports of Akka and Haifa were to be British, however) and Mesopotamia, which would be under British administration. Italy, too, demanded a share. In the secret treaty of London (April 26, 1915) by which they purchased Italy's entry into the war, England, France and Russia promised Italy "a just share of the Mediterranean region adjacent to the province of Adalia." The demands of justice apparently were large, for when France and England came to settle details with Italy, in the St. Jean de Maurienne agreement of April 17, 1917, Italy would be contented with nothing less than the right to annex the southern third of Anatolia, stretching from Smyrna in the west almost to Adana in the southeast; and in addition a large area north of Smyrna was to be a zone of Italian influence. Of Turkey there would be left, after each of the Allies had taken its share, only the northern half, or less, of Anatolia.[1]

The promissory generosity of the Allies toward each other was never fully realized in fact. Russia by becoming Bolshevist for-

[1] F. S. Cocks, *The Secret Treaties and Understandings; Current History*, XI, pp. 339-41; Temperley, *History of the Peace Conference*, VI, pp. 1-22; R. S. Baker, *Woodrow Wilson and World Settlement*, I, ch. 4; Shane Leslie, *Mark Sykes*, pp. 250-8; Grannini, *I Documenti Diplomatici della Pace Orientale.*

feited her claims; it was convenient that she did so, for British statesmen were being besieged by the Mohammedans of India with petitions to leave Constantinople in the hands of the Mohammedan caliph, the Turkish sultan. Another change in the secret treaties was made, at Italy's expense, when, during the temporary withdrawal of Italian delegates from the Paris Peace Conference, Lloyd George, Clemenceau and Wilson authorized the Greeks to seize Smyrna; that province, one recalls, had been promised to Italy.

On the whole, however, the Peace Treaty of Sèvres [1] which the Allies compelled the Turkish Government to sign on Aug. 10, 1920, was a mosaic of the secret treaties, a document in which imperialism was writ large. The Ottoman Empire was to be shorn of its Arab possessions—Syria, Palestine, Mesopotamia, and the intervening deserts, and Hedjaz (now "independent" with a ruler salaried by England), and other Turkish provinces in the Arabian peninsula. These, it was planned, would be divided between France and England. The northeastern corner of Turkey was to become an independent Armenia, with borders later marked out by President Wilson. Smyrna was handed over, with unimportant reservations, to Greece, along with most of Eastern Thrace. Italy was to have a sphere of influence in southern Anatolia, instead of annexing it, as originally planned. And the Dodekanesia, the group of islands occupied by Italy since 1912, were (by a separate Greco-Italian treaty) to be transferred to Greece. What was left of Turkey—most of Anatolia, plus Constantinople—was to be saddled with such thoroughgoing Allied financial and administrative supervision that it could hardly be called independent.

The Treaty of Sèvres, however, was torn up by Kemal Pasha, a brilliant and daring Turkish officer, who gathered about him a patriotic army of Turkish "Nationalists," drove the Greeks out of Smyrna and practically expelled the French from Cilicia (north of Syria), regained Eastern Thrace, reconquered Turkish Armenia, deposed the Sultan, transferred the Turkish capital to Angora in the inaccessible heart of the Anatolian highlands, and declared Turkey a republic, an independent and pro-

[1] *The Treaties of Peace* (Carnegie Endowment), II, p. 789; to be read in conjunction with the agreement of 1920 between France, England, and Italy, *State Papers*, 113, p. 797.

gressive nation. This Nationalist revolution, accomplished in the years 1921-23, made the Treaty of Sèvres a dead letter, and necessitated a new peace conference between the Allies and Turkey. The conference met at Lausanne, in the years 1922-1923, and after many acrid interchanges of wit and sarcasm between the Turkish and Allied delegates, the Treaty of Lausanne was signed in the summer of 1923.[1] Recognizing the actual facts, the Allies had to allow Turkey to retain Smyrna, Eastern Thrace, Armenia, and Cilicia [2] as well as Constantinople and the unquestionably Turkish Anatolian plateau. Allied financial and judicial fetters on Turkey were struck off. The Straits were opened to ships of peace and war, with some restrictions. Turkish Nationalism, provoked by European imperialism, was apparently triumphant.

But European imperialism was by no means wholly thwarted. Syria, Mesopotamia, Palestine, Arabia, and the Dodekanesia were definitely severed from Turkey and appropriated by European powers. Moreover, all claims which the former Ottoman Empire might have had to Egypt, Cyprus, Tripoli and Cyrenaica, and Tunis were finally cancelled in favor of the imperialist powers occupying those former Ottoman provinces. But what needs special emphasis here is the fact that even in Nationalist Turkey the imperialism of the West was still entrenched. A protocol attached to the Lausanne Treaty confirmed the railway and other concessions which had been granted by Turkey, before she entered the Great War, to nationals of the Allied Powers.

What had happened, during all this turmoil, to the unfinished Bagdad Railway? The victorious Allies put into the peace treaties of Versailles (1919) and Sèvres (1920) clauses [3] which would mean practically confiscation of the German interests in the Bagdad and Anatolian Railways. The plan was to hand these railways over to a Franco-British-Italian company, at a price to be fixed by an arbitrator. Neutral and French citizens would of course receive their proper share of the price, but the

[1] *Parl. Papers*, 1923 (Cmd. 1929 and Cmd. 1814) give text of treaty and proceedings of conference.

[2] Cilicia had already been returned to Turkey by France under a separate Franco-Turkish treaty signed at Angora, Oct. 20, 1921—*Parl. Papers*, 1921 (Cmd. 1556).

[3] Notably article 260 of the former, and articles 293-295 of the latter.

portion due to Germans[1] would be "paid to the Reparation Commission." The Treaty of Sèvres, however, was thrown into the scrap heap by Mustapha Kemal's Nationalist Government, and the part of the Bagdad Railway which lay within the new Turkish frontiers was simply taken over and operated by the Turkish Government. The sections running through the French mandate of Syria were acquired by a French company, and the sections in Mesopotamia became the "Iraq railways," under British control.

Petroleum and Politics

In the international battle, after the Great War, for concessions in Turkey, American interests began to compete with European in ominous fashion. We refer particularly to the Chester concession granted in 1923. Years previously, in 1908, President Roosevelt had sent Admiral Chester to Turkey, and Chester had begun negotiations for rail and oil concessions in the Ottoman Empire.[2] Two causes, probably, contributed to his ultimate success. One was the fact that the Americans in 1923, like the Germans in 1903, appeared to be disinterested business men, devoid of imperialist ambitions for political domination of Turkey. The other was the possibility that by granting a valuable concession to Americans, the Turkish Nationalists might enlist American sympathy and diplomatic support in their diplomatic contest with the Allies at Lausanne.

At any rate, on April 30, 1923, the Turkish minister of public works signed the Chester concession,[3] granting to the Ottoman-American Development Company contracts even more ambitious than those which had been given, two decades earlier, to the Bagdad Railway Company. Chester's syndicate was to undertake the construction of a network of railways in eastern Anatolia and Armenia, connecting Angora, the new capital, with Samsun and Trebizond on the Black Sea, with the Gulf of

[1] It should be noted, however, that as the Deutsche Bank's interests were held by a subsidiary Swiss Bank, they could not easily be confiscated. It was reported in 1923 that British financiers had bought a controlling interest in this Swiss bank.

[2] Recently published diplomatic documents show that the danger that Chester might obtain these concessions was not without influence as a factor in predisposing the European rivals, before the war, to agree among themselves and exclude the Americans. There is an interesting popular summary by John Carter in *Current History*, Jan. 1926, pp. 492-7.

[3] *Current History*, XVIII, pp. 485-95; Earle, *op. cit.*, pp. 336-50.

Alexandretta on the Mediterranean, with Mosul and northern Mesopotamia on the southeast. The total length of these lines, 2714 miles, was considerably greater than that of the Bagdad Railway system; they were long enough almost to span the breadth of the American continent. The concessionaires were to have mining rights twenty kilometers on each side of the railway; the value of mineral resources thus assigned was estimated at ten billion dollars. In addition, the Chester syndicate was to erect a magnificent capital city at Angora, and to construct docks and port facilities at Samsun on the Black Sea and at Yomourtalik in the Gulf of Alexandretta.

Here was a truly stupendous business project. But, like its German forerunner, it could not be entirely divorced from international complications. To begin with, one of the railway routes now assigned to Chester had previously been promised to a French syndicate, in April 1914, in exchange for a loan of 800,000,000 francs, and though the Turks stoutly claimed that the promise had been cancelled by the failure of the French to pay more than 500,000,000 francs of the loan, the French felt convinced that they had been shabbily treated.

There was also a dispute with the British, over oil rights. One of the Chester lines was to traverse the Mosul district, supposedly very rich in petroleum, and the Chester interests would have oil rights twenty kilometers each side of the line. Now the exclusive right to prospect for oil in upper Mesopotamia, including Mosul, had been provisionally promised to the Turkish Petroleum Company, on June 28, 1914, as part of the Anglo-German-Turkish bargain of that year. And the Company resolutely insisted that this promise should be fulfilled, regardless of the conflicting Chester concession. The Turkish Petroleum, despite its name, was practically the British Government. Half its stock was owned by the Anglo-Persian Oil Company, and, in turn, a controlling interest in the Anglo-Persian was owned directly by the British Government. Another 25% was held by the Royal Dutch-Shell combine, an Anglo-Dutch syndicate (about two-fifths of whose capital was British). The remaining twenty-five per cent of the Turkish Petroleum stock formerly assigned to the Deutsche Bank was confiscated by the British Government in 1918, as enemy property; this quarter-share was promised to France by the San Remo Agreement of

April 25, 1920. It was against such a union of finance and diplomacy that the Chester concern entered the lists.[1]

Many Americans believed that the State Department at Washington should openly step forward to champion Chester, as an American, against British and French rivals. The Chester Concession, however, was not purely American; it was an international enterprise, in which British interests were strongly represented. The State Department announced that it did not view the Chester concession as a concern of the United States Government. But Secretary Hughes did protect the Chester interests indirectly. American diplomacy vetoed the attempt of the British at the Lausanne Conference to include the Turkish Petroleum concession among the concessions to be confirmed by Turkey.[2] With the United States refusing to recognize the British concession, and Great Britain discountenancing the Chester concession, the rivals were deadlocked.

Complicated though the story must appear, it may be well to add a little more, if for no other reason than to show how intricate such imperialist conflicts are, and how apparently disinterested political contentions may be built upon such things as oil. If Great Britain could obtain political sovereignty over Mosul, the Turkish Government would have no right to grant Chester oil rights in that region. In the original Franco-British secret agreement of 1916 for the partition of Turkey, Mosul had been assigned to France, on condition that France respect the Turkish Petroleum Company's concession there. Later, however, Lloyd George persuaded Clemenceau to draw a new line, leaving Mosul in the British sphere, in return for a share of Mosul's oil and certain other considerations. The San Remo Oil Agreement, by the way, was made in pursuance of this bargain.[3] Accordingly, Great Britain included Mosul in the British mandate of Mesopotamia.

The Turkish Nationalists, however, insisted that the inhabitants of Mosul were Kurds and by right of self-determination should belong with Turkey. Great Britain, on the other hand,

[1] See Earle, "The Turkish Petroleum Co.," *Pol. Sci. Quart.*, XXXIX, June 1924; Carter, "The Bitter Conflict over Turkish Oilfields," *Current History*, Jan. 1926; Davenport, and Cooke, *The Oil Trusts and Anglo-American Relations;* P. de l'Espagnol de la Tramerye, *The World-Struggle for Oil.*

[2] *Parl. Papers*, 1923 (Cmd. 1814).

[3] *Parl. Papers*, 1920 (Cmd. 675).

insisted that Mosul was part of the Mesopotamian mandate, and the vigorously expressed desire of the Mesopotamian Arabs to keep Mosul within their borders afforded a reason less sordid than oil for the British position. Behind all the talk of self-determination and native rights, however, lay the question whether London or Angora would dispose of the oil. So uncompromising were the contestants, that the fate of Mosul was left undetermined by the Treaty of Lausanne, and it was agreed simply that in case Great Britain and Turkey could not reach an accord, the dispute would be referred to the League of Nations.

When a boundary commission sent out by the League reported, after an investigation on the spot, that the best solution would be the award of Mosul to Iraq, on condition that Great Britain prolong her mandatory control of Iraq for twenty-five years, the Turks in the best nationalistic manner announced they would reject any decision, unfavorable to them, by the League. Even after the World Court had upheld the League Council's right (by the treaty of Lausanne) to decide the case, and after the League Council had awarded Mosul to Iraq, the Turks remained sullen. The British, of course, accepted the decision. Although there was some complaint on the part of taxpayers who considered the maintenance of British troops in Mesopotamia an extravagance, British imperialists might well be satisfied. Mosul would belong to Iraq, and Iraq would be controlled by Britain. Moreover, the British-controlled Turkish Petroleum Co., had obtained from the British-controlled government of Iraq a seventy-five-year concession to exploit the oil resources of the vilayets (provinces) of Mosul and Bagdad.

This was only one aspect of the "world-struggle for oil," in which Great Britain and the United States appeared, at the close of the Great War, as the foremost combatants. To enter into all the details of that struggle would be beside the point, here, but one or two points need to be touched on, in so far as they concern the Near East. When France and Great Britain by the San Remo agreement of 1920 proposed to divide between themselves the oil not only of Mosul but of the entire Near East, the United States promptly and strongly protested that it had a right to be consulted before the resources of the lands jointly conquered from the Central Powers were disposed of. This was only the beginning of a sharp diplomatic skirmish, the intricacies of which we need not pursue. But while the British Foreign Office composed masterly legal replies to American legal protests,[1] Sir John Cadman visited the United States and endeavored to come to a business agreement with American oil interests. It is asserted, perhaps without authority, that the Standard Oil was offered a quarter share in the Turkish Petroleum, a half-interest in northern Persia, and prospecting rights previously obtained but hitherto opposed in Palestine. But the Standard was not the only American oil company interested in Turkish oil. There were at least a half-dozen, and with these also the British had to negotiate. At length, in 1925, it was announced that a bargain had been made, permitting a group of American oil companies (including the Rockefeller, Doheny and Sinclair interests) to buy 25% of the Turkish Petroleum Company's stock. The remainder of this company's capital was to be held as follows: 25% by the Anglo-Persian Oil Co. (controlled by the British Government), 25% by the Royal Dutch-Shell (two fifths British), 25% by the Compagnie française des pétroles (representing 67 French companies).

Turkish Nationalism

If it would appear that much of the history of the Near East since 1918 has been written in oil, the reader should not too hastily conclude that oil alone will determine the fate of this much contested part of the earth's surface. Human beings count for something, and there are almost thirty millions of them to be considered in what was before 1914 the Ottoman Empire in Asia. They may be considered as falling into two main groups: approximately thirteen million, mainly Turks, in the Republic of Turkey, and approximately thirteen million Arabs and other racial elements mingled with the Arabs, in regions which have been detached from Turkey, namely, Syria, Palestine, Mesopotamia, Trans-Jordan, Hedjaz, Asir and Yemen.

The Turks form a pretty solid block of humanity, in their historic homeland, the rough plateau of Anatolia. To call them "Turks" is perhaps to beg the question of their identity, for, in the mass, they are doubtless a very mixed breed, in which a

[1] *International Conciliation*, No. 166; *Parl. Papers*, 1921 (Cmd. 1226).

relatively small element of Mongolian or Turkish blood has been mingled with many other strains, some of which probably go back to the prehistoric inhabitants of Asia Minor. But they speak the Turkish language, and seem to be learning to consider themselves members of a Turkish nation, as much entitled to nationhood as any other. This sentiment of nationality, be it noted, is a recent development, very different from the old Ottoman policy of considering any Moslem, regardless of tongue or blood, as Ottoman. The new nationalism is the product of Western civilization, transplanted by European imperialism into an Oriental soil. And this new nationalism, fiercely jealous of independence, resentful of encroachment, is an obstacle to European imperialism.

The full import of the opposition is just beginning to appear. Turkish nationalism will not be content with political independence; it will translate itself into economic life also. For many years the mass of the Turkish nation, the plodding peasants who till ungrateful soil, have allowed Armenians, Greeks, and, to a smaller extent, Jews, to keep the shops, market the rugs and crops, lend the money, in their country; and have permitted foreign capitalists to finance the railways, mines, and other large enterprises. Now there appear symptoms of Turkish revolt against economic vassalage: of Turkish determination first to supplant the Armenians and Greeks in local commerce and petty finance, second to make sure that foreign concessions in Turkey are not of such a nature as to place the country permanently in the grip of foreign capitalists. These aims are easier to express than to achieve, but in attempting their achievement Turkish Nationalists will inevitably find themselves at odds with the imperialist Occident, if the Occident remains imperialist.

One more word about the Turks. Contact with European imperialism has taught the upper classes something of Western social and political institutions. And the Turkish Nationalist leaders, many of whom have been educated in Europe, have shown remarkable energy and courage in attempting to reform Turkish institutions to suit European ideals. They have made Turkey a republic, with a constitution of a most radical democratic type, although probably the bulk of the people do not yet understand quite what a republic is, or what the exercise of the franchise means. The Nationalist leaders have destroyed the sultanate, and abolished the caliphate; that is to say, they have done away with the sovereign and his claim to be the spiritual head of the Mohammedan world.[1] They have taken other liberties with Mohammedan institutions. For example, the wife of Mustapha Kemal Pasha, the Nationalist leader, discarded the traditional face-veil, and advocated the emancipation of women from the harem system. Polygamy, practised only by the rich, but permitted by the Koran, was abolished. The fez gave place to the hat; European clothing was prescribed for officials; the Christian calendar was adopted; women's rights were recognized in a new civil code. Not to prolong the list, we may say in short that in certain vital respects Turkish Nationalism undertook the sudden Europeanization of Turkey. Whether this sudden transformation decreed by the leaders will provoke a temporary reaction by the masses, is of small moment, in the sweep of history. More important is the major fact that Europeanization has begun.

Arab Nationalism

A line drawn east from the Gulf of Alexandretta, at the northeastern corner of the Mediterranean Sea, to the Persian border would in a rough way separate Anatolia and its Turkish population on the north from the Arab countries on the south.[2] South of this line, in Syria, Palestine and Mesopotamia live six million Arabs, and still farther south, in the Arabian peninsula, are perhaps ten million more Arabs.[3] These figures are not much more than guesswork, because no census-taker visits the desert tents of Arabia. Long and lean of limb, brown of skin, strong and hardy, some of the Arab nomads are physically among the finest types of humanity; and mentally they have shown gifts of very high order. In past centuries the Arab has been a great warrior; receiving Mohammed's creed, he carried it by word and sword over the whole Near East, over northern Asia, into Persia, and for a space, in the Middle Ages, great was the renown of

[1] See article by W. L. Westermann, in *Asia*, vol. 24, pp. 349 ff.
[2] On the Kurds see Bowman, *The New World*, ch. 27.
[3] The term is used loosely, to include populations which speak Arabic and consider themselves Arabs, rather than to indicate any "race," for "races" are very much mingled in these regions.

Arab caliphs at Damascus or at Bagdad. North Africa, with its Arabicized population, still bears witness to the aggressive energy of this people, and Arab slave-dealers and traders have not yet been entirely swept out of central and east Africa. But the Arabs in modern times fell under foreign rule, except in the interior of the barren Arabian peninsula, into whose deserts alien conquerors were loath to venture. Perhaps it was lack of ability for political organization—more probably it was a traditional spirit of tribal independence, a spirit naturally bred of generations spent in wandering through desert and grassland, that rendered the Arab subject to conquest. At any rate, the Arabs of Syria, Palestine, and Mesopotamia became Turkish subjects, and Turkish rule was more or less fitfully maintained in Hedjaz, Asir and Yemen on the Red Sea coast of the Arabian peninsula.

The Great War released these regions from Ottoman rule, and transferred them to French and British imperialism. Syria became a mandate of France; Palestine and Mesopotamia, mandates of Great Britain; Hedjaz, an independent Arab kingdom more or less under British control. The other Arab states in the Arabian peninsula were considered to fall within the British sphere of influence, though it was hardly worth while for Great Britain to interfere with them, so small was their population, so certain their resistance, so insignificant their economic value. As regards the administration of the mandates, full discussion may best be postponed to the chapter in which the mandate system is considered.[1] But before leaving the Near East, we shall do well to take mental note that sixteen million Arabs, scattered over a region largely barren but almost half as large as the United States, represent an interesting problem for European imperialism. If the Arabic populations in north Africa are added, the problem becomes still larger in scope.[2]

As yet most of the Arabs are quite willing to be divided; racial or national consciousness has not translated itself, in the minds of the masses, into a desire for political unity. Nevertheless, a number of young Arabs, especially those who have been educated abroad, and officers who served in the Great

[1] *Infra*, p. 487.

[2] Temperley, *op. cit.*, VI, part III; Eugène Jung, *La Révolte Arabe*, esp. vol. II; Loder, *The Truth About Mesopotamia, Palestine and Syria*.

War against the Turks, have shown a fiery spirit of nationalism. Moreover, the fire is fanned by Arab colonies and Arab publications in Egypt, in New York, in Latin America. Whether this nationalism will communicate itself to the people at large, depends to some extent on British and French policy. And Great Britain and France have done much to promote Arab nationalism. During the war, to enlist Arab aid against the Turks, British and French authorities held out bright hopes of an independent Arab confederacy, then, by dashing these hopes to the ground, created a resentment that only intensified the national spirit. When Arab leaders in Syria and Palestine desired to make an Arab prince their king, a French general expelled the prince. Great Britain, nothing loath to discommode her ally, gave this same prince a crown and made him king of "Iraq" (the Arabic name for Mesopotamia).

More than that, the London cabinet adopted what seemed to be a brilliant general policy toward Arabia; it would conciliate the Arabs by putting the sons of Hussein the Arab king of Hedjaz on convenient thrones as kings or princes under British supervision. The new king of Iraq, Prince Feisal, was one of these sons; his brother was made emir (prince) of Kerak, or Transjordan, the land east of the Palestinian Dead Sea. Further, for a time the statesmen of London seemed inclined to favor the idea of making the King of Hedjaz caliph of all Islam, in place of the deposed Turkish sultan. The conception of this policy was unquestionably bold, and brilliant. If successful, it would make Britain ultimately the patron and protector of an Arab confederacy, and through the Arab caliph, Hussein, of the world of Islam. One difficulty, however, was that the very fact of British support made Hussein and his sons unpopular with other Arab chieftains, and perhaps with many of the tribesmen. Indeed, the warlike Ibn Saud, sultan of Nejd and leader of a puritanical Moslem sect (the Wahabis), invaded and conquered the Hedjaz. Hussein was overthrown, though his sons remained on their thrones in Iraq and Kerak. Admitting the failure of their former policy, the British, ever flexible, now made terms with the victorious Ibn Saud.

Quickly the moving finger writes. The Near East, penetrated by German imperialism through the Bagdad Railway, becomes an arena for Anglo-French imperialism, as Germany is eliminated; American capital enters the field as a politically disinterested third party, to seek oil, and business profit; Turkey, ceasing to be an empire, becomes a defiant nation; and the Arab tribesmen stir uneasily with the ferment of nationalism. The historic "question of the Near East" has passed through many transformations, until to-day it is but part of the world-wide question, what will be the issue of the conflict between Europe's imperialism and the new Oriental nationalism.

CHAPTER XII

ANGLO-RUSSIAN RIVALRY IN THE MIDDLE EAST

Between the Near East and the Far East, between Turkey on one side and China and India on the other, is an intermediate zone which may be called the Middle East,[1] in which the clash of Russian against British imperialism menaced the peace of Europe for a generation, prior to 1907, and in which, after 1907, the combination of Russian and British imperialism was one of the most potent factors in shaping the international situation which led to the Great War. The region is the more interesting to American students because since the war it has become one of the battlefields in which American oil interests have waged war against British rivals, and because American influence has here been arrayed against British imperialism.

Russian Aggression and British Precautions

One thinks of Persia as the home of ancient conquerors and emperors, or as the source of luxurious rugs; it would be nearer reality to visualize camel caravans crossing deserts infested by bandits, tribesmen dwelling in oases, a few cities where patient women weave rugs and loquacious tradesmen haggle in the bazaars. Persia is three times as large as France, but one-twelfth as densely populated, chiefly because most of the country consists of desert and semi-desert plateau; only in small and scattered irrigated spots are there more than thirty inhabitants per square mile. North of Persia is the desert, salt-encrusted basin of the shrinking Aral Sea, bordered by broad belts of steppe, of tablelands where just enough rain falls to cover the soil with grass for the cattle of wandering herdsmen. This is

[1] The designation is merely for convenience. Sometimes the "Near East" is made to include Persia, and the "Middle East" pushed farther east. There is nothing sacred about such terms.

Western Turkestan. But in the eastern part of this country and in Afghanistan the mountain slopes, rising toward the loftiest peaks of the earth's crust, are better watered and more thickly peopled. All things considered, this was not an attractive field of economic enterprise for imperialists of the last century.[1]

Yet there was a minor economic interest, financial and commercial. An English financier, Baron Julius de Reuter, founded the Imperial Bank of Persia in 1889 to lend money to the Shah, and to finance mines, if minerals should be discovered. A rival Bank of Loans (Banque des Prêts de Perse) was set up by the Russian ministry of finance, and between Reuter's concern and the Russians there developed a keen competition in the astonishing business of encouraging spendthrift shahs to spend and borrow more freely. A certain humor appears in the situation, when one remembers that Russia herself was borrowing from France, while lending to the Shah. Lending money to the Shah, however, was profitable, for like all such Moslem sovereigns, he had to pay exceedingly high rates of interest. Moreover, finance here as in Tunis was not wholly economic; there was always an ulterior motive, of obtaining political control through loans. And then, there was the possibility of obtaining valuable concessions; for example the Russians got concessions to build a railway from the Russian border to Teheran, the capital, and to prospect for oil and coal. Commercially, a few English merchants were interested in the Persian wares, and, even more, in the caravan traffic from western India, through Persia. Such economic interests in themselves were relatively small and insignificant, but as advance guards for other interests they formed a sort of skirmishing line, provocative of political rivalry.[2]

Much more powerful was the strategic interest. For British imperialists, the Middle East was tremendously important as a zone of defense protecting British India from European rivals, above all, from Russia.[3] For Russian imperialists, the same region was not only a natural field of expansion, south from the Caucasus and Siberia, and not only an approach to India

[1] Bowman, *The New World*, gives the setting in two vivid and authoritative chapters (29-30).

[2] See Maclean's report on trade prospects, *Parl. Papers*, 1904 (Cd. 2146).

[3] For example, see Curzon's dispatch of Sept. 21, 1899, *Parl. Papers*, 1908 (Cd. 3882), and his books on *Persia* (1892) and *Russia in Central Asia* (1889); compare Chirol, *The Middle Eastern Question* (1903).

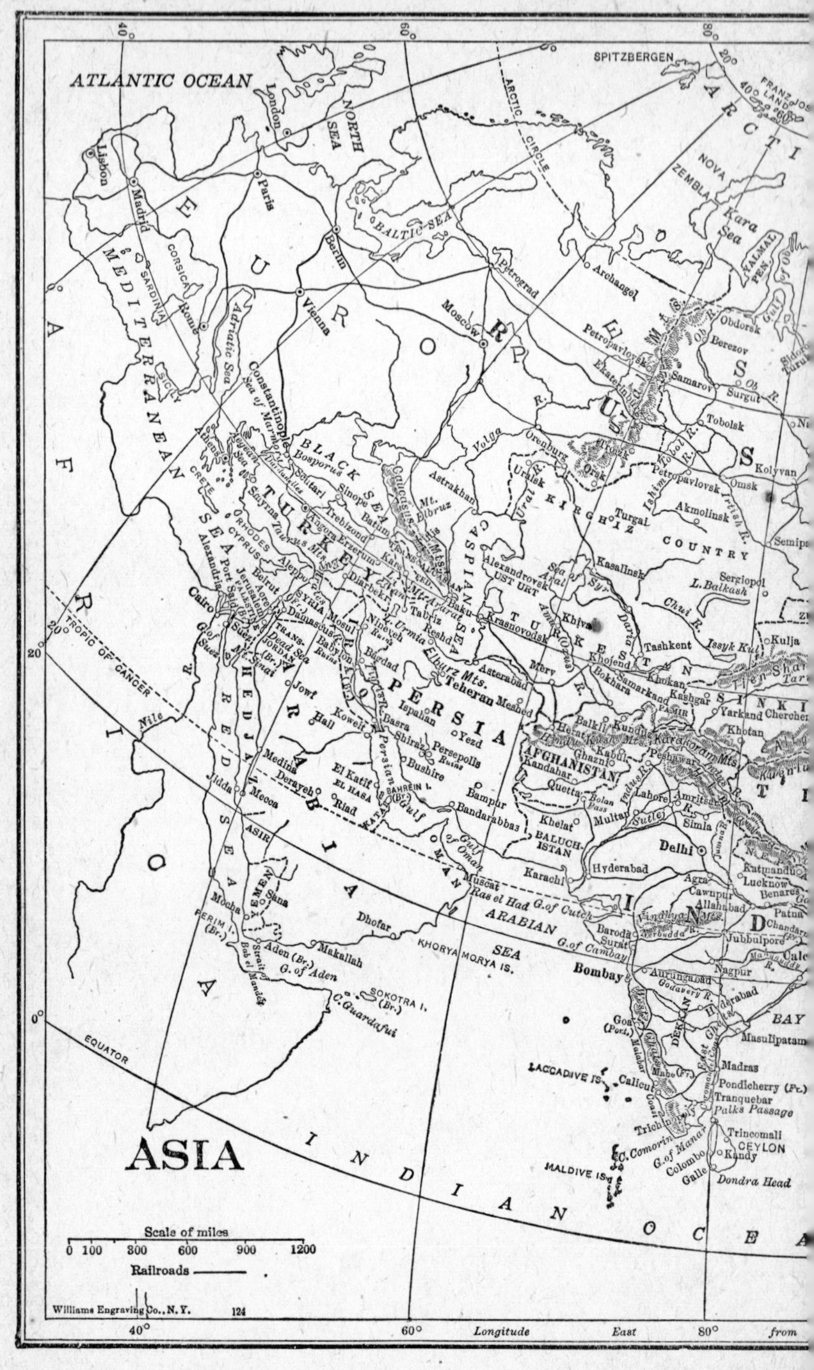

ASIA
ATLANTIC OCEAN
NORTH SEA
BALTIC SEA
SPITZBERGEN
FRANZ JOSEF LAND
NOVA ZEMBLA
Kara Sea
ARCTIC CIRCLE
TROPIC OF CANCER
EQUATOR
EUROPE
RUSSIA
AFRICA
MEDITERRANEAN SEA
BLACK SEA
CASPIAN SEA
RED SEA
ARABIAN SEA
INDIAN OCEAN
TURKEY
PERSIA
ARABIA
HEDJAZ
AFGHANISTAN
BALUCHISTAN
TURKESTAN
KIRGHIZ COUNTRY
SYRIA
IRAK
INDIA
CEYLON
London
Paris
Lisbon
Madrid
Rome
Berlin
Vienna
Petrograd
Moscow
Archangel
Constantinople
Athens
Smyrna
Angora
Trebizond
Batum
Erzerum
Aleppo
Beirut
Damascus
Jerusalem
Port Said
Alexandria
Cairo
Suez
Mt. Sinai
Dead Sea
Baghdad
Basra
Koweit
Medina
Mecca
Jidda
Riad
Sana
Mocha
Aden (Br.)
Makallah
Muscat
Teheran
Ispahan
Yezd
Shiraz
Bushire
Meshed
Herat
Kabul
Kandahar
Quetta
Peshawar
Lahore
Delhi
Karachi
Hyderabad
Agra
Lucknow
Bombay
Madras
Calicut
Colombo
Kandy
Trincomali
Galle
Tashkent
Samarkand
Bokhara
Khiva
Merv
Orenburg
Astrakhan
Baku
Tiflis
Tobolsk
Omsk
Obdorsk
Berezov
Ekaterinburg
Scale of miles
0 100 300 600 900 1200
Railroads
Williams Engraving Co., N.Y.
124
Longitude East from
40° 60° 80°

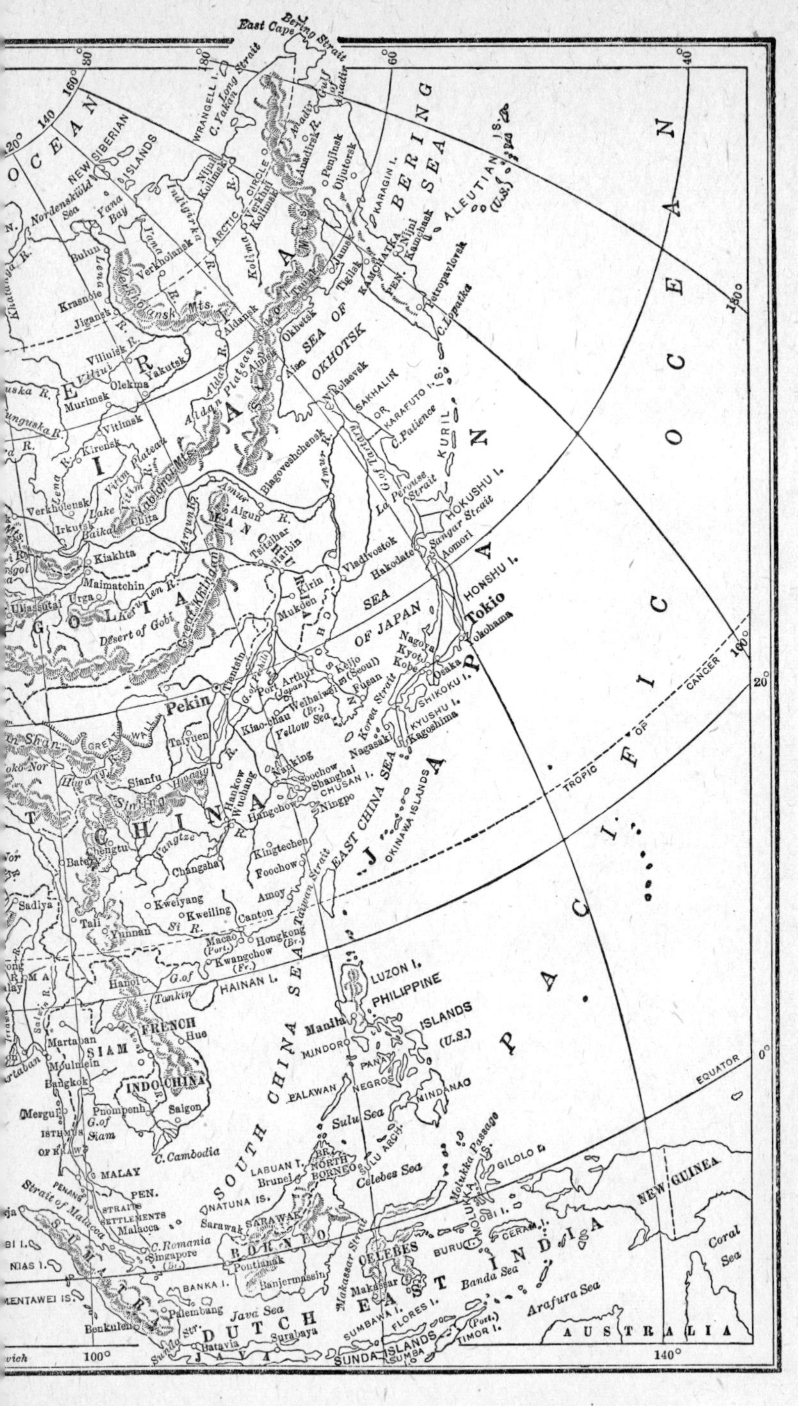

East Cape
Bering Strait
Gulf of Anadir
Anadir R.
Anadirsk
Penjinsk
Oljutorsk
KARAGIN I.
BERING SEA
ALEUTIAN IS. (U.S.)
Nijni Kamchatsk
KAMCHATKA PEN.
Petropavlovsk
C. Lopatka
WRANGELL I.
C. Yakan
Long Strait
NEW SIBERIAN ISLANDS
Nordenskiöld Sea
Yana Bay
Nijni Kolimsk
Verkhni Kolimsk
ARCTIC CIRCLE
Kolima R.
Indigirka R.
Yana R.
Bulun
Lena R.
Verkhoiansk
Verkhoiansk Mts.
Krasnoie
Jigansk
Viliuisk R.
Viliui R.
Yakutsk
Olekma
Aldansk
Aldan R.
Aldan Plateau
Stanovoi Mts.
Ayan
Okhotsk
SEA OF OKHOTSK
Nikolaevsk
SAKHALIN OR KARAFUTO I.
C. Patience
KURIL IS.
La Perouse Strait
G. of Tartary
HOKUSHU I.
Sangar Strait
Hakodate
Aomori
Vladivostok
SEA OF JAPAN
HONSHU I.
Tokio
Yokohama
Nagoya
Kyoto
Kobe
Osaka
SHIKOKU I.
KYUSHU I.
Kagoshima
Nagasaki
Korea Strait
Fusan
Keijo (Seoul)
Murimsk
Vitimsk
Kirensk
Vitim Plateau
Vitim R.
Yablonoi Mts.
Verkholensk
Irkutsk
Lake Baikal
Chita
Kiakhta
Maimatchin
Urga
Uliassutai
Kerulen R.
Desert of Gobi
Great Khingan Mts.
Argun R.
Amur R.
Aigun
Blagoveshchensk
Tsitsihar
Harbin
Kirin
Mukden
MANCHURIA
MONGOLIA
SIBERIA
Tientsin
G. of Pechili
Port Arthur (Japan)
Weihaiwei (Br.)
Kiao-chau
Yellow Sea
Pekin
GREAT WALL
Taiyuen
Sianfu
Hankow
Wuchang
Nanking
Soochow
Shanghai
CHUSAN I.
Hangchow
Ningpo
EAST CHINA SEA
OKINAWA ISLANDS
JAPAN
Kingtechen
Foochow
Amoy
Taiwan Strait
Changsha
Chengtu
Batang
Kweiyang
Kweiling
Canton
Si R.
Yunnan
Tali
Sadiya
Macao (Port.)
Hongkong (Br.)
Kwangchow (Fr.)
CHINA
TROPIC OF CANCER
HAINAN I.
G. of Tonkin
Hanoi
Hue
FRENCH INDO-CHINA
SIAM
Martaban
Moulmein
Bangkok
Mergui
Pnompenh
Saigon
G. of Siam
C. Cambodia
ISTHMUS OF KRAW
MALAY PEN.
PENANG
STRAITS SETTLEMENTS
Malacca
Strait of Malacca
Singapore (Br.)
C. Romania
SUMATRA
NIAS I.
MENTAWEI IS.
Benkulen
Palembang
BANKA I.
Sunda Str.
Batavia
JAVA
Surabaya
Java Sea
DUTCH EAST INDIA
NATUNA IS.
Sarawak
SARAWAK
BORNEO
Brunei
LABUAN I.
BR. NORTH BORNEO
Pontianak
Banjermasin
Makassar Strait
CELEBES
Makassar
Celebes Sea
SOUTH CHINA SEA
LUZON I.
PHILIPPINE ISLANDS (U.S.)
Manila
MINDORO
PANAY
NEGROS
PALAWAN
MINDANAO
Sulu Sea
SULU ARCH.
Molukka Passage
MOLUKKA IS.
GILOLO
OBI I.
BURU
CERAM I.
Banda Sea
SUMBAWA I.
FLORES I.
SUMBA
SUNDA ISLANDS
TIMOR I. (Port.)
Arafura Sea
NEW GUINEA
Coral Sea
AUSTRALIA
PACIFIC OCEAN
EQUATOR
100°
140°
160°
180°
20°
40°
60°

(which some Russians were bold enough to covet), but also a possible pathway to a warm-water outlet on the Persian Gulf. Russian strategy was purely aggressive; British, defensive, or rather, defensively aggressive.

With an open map before his eyes, the reader may see the situation at a glance. The story is a chess-game of the giants, with countries for squares. The game grew interesting in the latter part of the nineteenth century, after Russian armies, followed by colonists and railways, had moved across the Kirghiz steppes (north of the Aral Sea), southward into Western Turkestan. Slowly but surely they pressed on. In the sixties and seventies they conquered, one after another, the petty principalities or khanates of Turkestan. They began to encroach on the northern borders of Persia and Afghanistan, while British statesmen became increasingly nervous, especially about Afghanistan.

If once the Russians crossed the mountainous barrier of Afghanistan, no buffer would remain to shield India from their advance. To safeguard India, British armies were sent into Afghanistan, in 1878-81, and a puppet ameer (prince) was placed on the Afghan throne, in England's pay, and, as regards foreign policy, under England's control.[1] But still they were nervous. An acute crisis between England and Russia arose in the years 1884-85, when Russia moved into the town of Merv, and then marched south to Penjdeh, in northwestern Afghanistan. Queen Victoria appealed to the Tsar to restrain such dangerous aggression; and a British army was prepared to oppose the Russian advance. Gladstone, however, was unwilling to fight, and allowed the Russians to keep their gains. Again war threatened in 1895, when the Russians moved up into the high Pamir plateau, in the northeast of Afghanistan, where only a thin strip of Afghan territory separated them from India.[2]

With the dawn of the twentieth century the conflict grew keener. While England was occupied with the Boer War in South Africa, Russia stealthily resumed her progress in Central Asia,—in Persia, in Afghanistan, in Tibet. In Persia, the Russian bank made another loan to the Shah, and a Russian

[1] A good account of this episode is given in *Cambridge History of British Foreign Policy*, III, pp. 72-90.

[2] See *Parl. Papers*, 1895 (Cd. 7643).

warship attempted to establish a coaling depot on the Persian Gulf at Bandar Abbas. British statesmen were acutely alive to the situation. The British viceroy of India, Lord Curzon, had written home to London in 1899: [1]

> She (Persia) is one of those countries which must inevitably have attracted the attention of Europe, partly from increasing infirmity, but still more from the opportunities suggested by their latent though neglected sources of strength. Closely pressing upon Persia and Afghanistan is the ever-growing momentum of a Power whose interests in Asia are not always in accord with our own. The advance of Russia across the deserts that form the natural barrier between West and East Persia could not be regarded without uneasiness by the Government of India. . . .

After she had disposed of the Boers, Great Britain could take steps to counter Russia's moves. Lord Lansdowne could declare, in May 1903, that the establishment of a naval base in the Gulf by any other power would be resisted by England; [2] Lord Curzon could visit the Gulf, in November, 1903, with a formidable array of warships to impress the natives, and declare that British influence must remain supreme; and British officials could decide that the southeastern corner of Persia was essential to British security. Both Great Britain and Russia, watching each other's every move, waited; sooner or later Persia must fall to one or the other.

Simultaneously matters seemed to be coming to a head as regards Tibet. This vast table-land, lying east of Afghanistan, between India and China, was a tributary vassal state of the Chinese Empire; its ruler, the Dalai Lama, was supposedly a reincarnation of Buddha, and its governing hierarchy of Buddhist priests or lamas was so fanatically inhospitable to aliens that few Europeans had ever ventured into the bleak plateau, or to its forbidden sacred city of Lhasa. This seemed a secure enough buffer for the protection of India, but in 1901 the British heard, to their dismay, that a Russian who had been tutor to the Dalai Lama was in Petrograd as the Dalai Lama's envoy.[3] Was Russia about to establish a protectorate over Tibet?

Lord Curzon, the same imperious viceroy of India whom we encountered in the Persian Gulf, felt that Russia should be

[1] *Parl. Papers, Persia No. 1 (1908).*

[2] The statement was in answer to a question on German plans for a railway terminus at Koweit (*cf. supra*, p. 247), but it could cover Russian designs as well.

[3] *Parliamentary Papers*, 1904 (Cd. 1920).

forestalled. He himself attempted to communicate with the Dalai Lama, but his letters were returned unopened, and he exclaimed in exasperation: "It is the most extraordinary anachronism of the twentieth century that there should exist within less than three hundred miles of the borders of British India a State and a Government with whom political relations do not exist and with whom it is impossible even to exchange a written communication." He proposed a British expedition to Lhasa, to negotiate a treaty and install a British representative there. Russia, getting wind of the plan, protested; Lord Lansdowne retorted that Russia had concluded an agreement, so he had been informed, for a protectorate over Tibet.[1]

Perhaps Lansdowne's accusation was merely a diplomatic cover for what followed. Colonel Younghusband led a British "mission," well armed, into Tibet in 1904, fought his way to Lhasa, and dictated a treaty to the Lama's regent (the Lama had fled), providing for the opening of three trade marts and the opening of routes into Tibet. Tibet was to pay an indemnity covering the cost of the invasion. But most important was the ninth article of the treaty, to the effect that no other Power should be allowed to interfere with Tibetan affairs, send representatives to Tibet, or obtain concessions for railways, roads, telegraphs, or mining, or buy, lease, or occupy any Tibetan territory, without British consent.[2] This ought to safeguard Tibet against Russia. The Treaty, by the way, was confirmed by China in 1906, as suzerain of Tibet.[3]

While Tibet was being safeguarded, British imperialists again grew nervous about Afghanistan. The Afghan Ameer, Habibulla, who had come to the throne in 1901, declined to accept the British subsidy, and was inclined to treat the British with rather less than scant deference. Moreover, Russia was building new strategic railways in Asia.[4] Afghanistan still separated the Russian railways from India. Any attempt, said the British premier on May 11, 1905, to construct a railway in Afghanistan in connection with the Russian lines should be regarded as an

[1] *Ibid.*, especially pp. 113 ff.

[2] *Parl. Papers*, 1904 (Cd. 2054); 1905 (Cd. 2370); 1906 (Cd. 3088).

[3] *Ibid.*, 1906 (Cd. 3088).

[4] The Transcaspian Railway, built in 1880-8, connected the Caspian Sea with Merv and Samarkand, and sent a branch down to the border of Afghanistan. The Orenburg-Tashkent line (1905) further strengthened Russia's strategic position in the middle east.

act of aggression. It would be "the heaviest conceivable blow at our Indian Empire." Therefore, no railways must be built in Afghanistan except in time of war.

The Anglo-Russian Agreement

Toward the year 1906 the contest between Russia and England in Central Asia was approaching the stage where the rivals would have to become open enemies or friendly partners; there was no middle course. Where two nations meet as rivals only at one point, as France and Germany did in Morocco, compromise is difficult because one or the other must accept defeat and humiliation; where they are rivals in many regions, as France and England were in 1904, or as England and Russia were in 1907, it is easy to bargain. That Russia and England chose to bargain rather than to fight was due partly to this circumstance, and partly to other causes. For one thing, there was England's recently formed friendship with France, and France was Russia's ally. Perhaps England would have joined her ally Japan against Russia in the Russo-Japanese War had it not been for this Anglo-French entente. And then there was the growing British suspicion of Germany, which naturally impelled Great Britain into the arms of Germany's foes. Add to this the happy circumstance that since Russia was weakened by the Russo-Japanese War and seemingly liberalized by the establishment of a Duma, English Liberals no longer felt either the fear or the hatred for Russia that had been theirs in the past years. Moreover, it happened that in 1906, at the psychological moment, the direction of Russia's foreign policy fell into the hands of Alexander Isvolsky, who firmly believed Russia's destiny lay in alliance rather than conflict with England.

The record [1] of a secret meeting of the Russian council of ministers on Feb. 1, 1907, shows that Isvolsky urged acceptance of an English proposal for the division of Persia into spheres of influence. Until recently, he said, in Russian government circles, "the conviction even prevailed that Persia must come entirely under Russian influence, and that Russia must press

[1] Siebert, *Entente Diplomacy*, pp. 474-7; *cf. Parl. Papers*, 1909 (Cd. 4581).

onward to the Persian Gulf, which would necessitate the building of a trans-Persian railway and a fortified terminal station on the shores of the above-mentioned gulf." This "plan" he considered it impossible to realize. The idea of competing with the Bagdad Railway by building a Russian line, connecting the Russian railways with India by way of Afghanistan, must also be given up, as England would doubtless regard it as far more dangerous than the Bagdad Railway. Russia's best course, then, was to agree with England on Persia (and with Germany on the Bagdad Railway).[1]

On August 31, 1907, Isvolsky and the British Ambassador set their signatures to a convention embracing three agreements, one on Persia, the second on Afghanistan, the third on Tibet.[2] Let us consider them in reverse order. Tibet was to be a buffer state, in which neither power would seek railway, road, telegraph or mining concessions, or interfere with the government; neither should send representatives to Lhasa. They must conduct all negotiations with Tibet through China, the suzerain. Thus in Tibet there was a stalemate. As regards Afghanistan, Great Britain obtained the decision. Russia recognized Afghanistan as "outside the sphere of Russian influence" and promised to deal with its ruler only through the British government; Great Britain, on the other hand, would not annex or occupy Afghanistan as long as the Ameer fulfilled his treaty obligations—that is, remained in British pay, friendly toward Britain and obedient to her wishes in foreign policy.

There remains Persia. The preamble of the agreement on Persia, like most such preambles, was a dignified statement that Great Britain and Russia "sincerely desiring the preservation of order throughout that country and its peaceful development, as well as the permanent establishment of equal advantages for the trade and industry of all other nations," and intending, of course, "to respect the integrity and independence of Persia," had made an agreement. One should always read further than the preamble. The three articles show how Persia's "integrity" was to be preserved. Persia was divided into three zones. In the northern zone, containing about half the total area, Great Britain would neither seek concessions for herself,

[1] *Cf. supra*, p. 252.
[2] *State Papers*, 100, p. 555; *Parl. Papers*, 1908 (Cd. 3750 and 3753).

nor oppose concessions demanded by Russia: this was the Russian zone. In the British zone, comprising the southeastern fifth of the country, Britain was to have the concessions. Between the two zones was a neutral zone, open to both. Persia, of course, was not consulted in this partition. Persia's position was humorously shown by a sketch in *Punch,* representing the Persian cat torn between the voracious Russian bear and the British lion.

The agreement really meant an Anglo-Russian monopoly of concessions and control in Persia. In subsequent secret negotiations the British and Russian governments showed clearly enough that they took for granted their right to veto concessions and loans which were not to their interest. For example, when a gentleman named Cohen attempted to arrange a loan in Paris that would pay off Persia's debts to Russia and England, thus lessening Persia's subservience to these countries, Russia objected that this would be injurious to Russian interests, and the French government refused approval of the loan.[1] France, of course, would oblige her ally, and all the more willingly since the capital for Russian imperialism in Persia was furnished in part by Paris. But why should Germany and other powers permit Russia and Britain to appropriate Persia?

German financiers, as a matter of fact, hoped to tap the trade of Persia through the Bagdad-Khanikin branch of the Bagdad Railway, and the German Foreign Office was their champion—or tool. Nevertheless, the latter was not eager to offend the Tsar's government too deeply. Even before Russia and England came together in 1907, Germany and Russia had been bargaining. If Russia would cease opposing the Bagdad Railway, Germany might recognize Russian interests in Persia. After the Anglo-Russian bargain, Russia's attitude was for a time stiffened. Germany, accordingly, asked for equal commercial rights and a share in supplying materials for railways in Persia, although she was willing to recognize that Russia and England had a "privileged" position there. At length, however, a compromise between Russia and Germany was reached in the Potsdam Agreement, signed on August 19, 1911. Germany promised not to seek railway or other concessions in northern Persia; Russia agreed not to oppose the Bagdad Railway; and provision

[1] Siebert, *Entente Diplomacy*, esp. pp. 85-6.

was made to link the Bagdad line, via Khanikin, with a Russian line from Khanikin to Teheran.[1]

In one respect the Anglo-Russian agreement on Persia was successful: it prevented war between England and Russia. But if judged by its professed purpose, it was a dismal failure. It did not preserve order and commercial equality. Nor did it accomplish what Sir Cecil Spring-Rice, British minister to Persia, described as its aim: "Not only do they (the two Great Powers) not wish to have at hand any excuse for intervention, but their object in these friendly negotiations was not to allow one another to intervene on the pretext of safeguarding their interests." (Note the word "pretext.")

The Effect on Persia

A British historian complacently admits that this agreement "was cordially disliked by the educated Persians"; but, he adds, it "gave the unhappy and chaotic country seven years of peace and quiet."[2] Typical, this, of the way in which imperialist nations are self-deceived. We shall now see what kind of "peace and quiet" Persia enjoyed from 1907 to 1914 under the auspices of the Agreement.

On the eve of the Agreement, Persia had undergone an amazing transformation. A constitution had been granted by the autocratic Shah, in 1906, providing for the establishment of a National Council or Majliss, to be composed of representatives of the princes, nobles and chiefs, clergy, farmers, merchants, etc. The Majliss was to have control over finances, treaties, and concessions, among other things. Now it would be mere sentimentalizing to interpret this event as the establishment of a stable, democratic government. Persia was not ready for that. The tribesmen of desert and plain were a law unto themselves; the peasants were ignorant; the country had long been accustomed to a feeble but despotic autocracy limited only by the religious law of the Koran and the actual power of the leading tribes. But there was a small Nationalist Party, comprised of the more highly educated folk, ardently desirous of reforming

[1] *State Papers* 105, pp. 657-8; *Die Grosse Politik,* XXV, ch. 185; Siebert, *op. cit.*, pp. 61, 81-94, 501-76, 656-665.

[2] R. B. Mowatt, *History of European Diplomacy*, p. 273.

the government, adopting parliamentary rule, and preserving national independence. This party, dominating the first Majliss, was determined apparently to insist on financial reforms which would prevent Persia from falling into the clutches of European finance. In fact, the finance minister who was suspected of selling his country's liberty to Russia, was shot by a violent patriot, on the very day the Anglo-Russian Agreement was signed.[1]

Had Russia and England sincerely desired the peaceful progress and prosperity of Persia, one might have expected the Majliss to have received strong support from them. But such was not the case. The Shah was encouraged to surround himself with a "Cossack Brigade," officered by Russians, and this he employed against the Nationalists in Teheran. When the Majliss issued a manifesto to the powers of Europe, asking intervention to prevent the Shah from destroying the constitution, England and Russia, hastening to forestall any action of the other powers, counseled the Shah to promise respect for the constitution. But secretly the Russian consul-general supplied the Shah's supporters with arms, for use against the Nationalists, and civil war ensued, in which the "Cossacks" played a prominent rôle, against the Nationalists of course. Profiting by the disorder, Russia sent troops to occupy Tabriz, in northwestern Persia, until order was restored. Nevertheless the Nationalists gained the support of powerful Persian tribes, and were soon able to capture the capital and depose the Shah. That the Shah took refuge in the Russian legation, and was protected by Russian and British Indian troops in his exit from Persia, and found asylum in Russia may appear significant to those who look below the surface. It may appear still more significant if we anticipate our story enough to say that after the Nationalists had reestablished the Constitution and the Majliss, and were proceeding to reform Persia, the ex-Shah returned from Russia, with arms labeled "mineral waters," and with Russian encouragement began a new civil war in Persia.

The victorious Nationalists installed a new Shah, restored the Majliss in November 1909, and began their work of reform. Finding that they could not raise money, or obtain help, in Europe except with the consent of the Russian and British

[1] An interesting view of these events is given, through British official eyes, in *Parl. Papers*, 1909 (Cd. 4581 and 4733).

governments, the Persian Nationalists appealed to the United States, to send them a financier who would put the Persian treasury on its feet. At Washington the request caused some embarrassment, for it would be considered an intrusion on Anglo-Russian interests if the United States officially appointed a financial adviser for Persia. Tactfully, the Washington Government took no such action, but merely informed the Persians that Mr. Morgan Shuster might be a suitable man. Accordingly the Persian Government in 1911 appointed Shuster as Treasurer-General for a term of three years.

With splendid enthusiasm, with American energy and efficiency, Shuster plunged into the Persian tangle, hoping to put Persia on a sound business basis. But he soon encountered opposition, not from the Persians, who shared his enthusiasm, but from Great Britain and Russia. He had hardly announced his sweeping program of financial reform, when Russia sent the ex-Shah back into Persia, as we have said, to start a counter-revolution and make things interesting for Shuster. The ex-Shah was defeated and driven back into Russia. Shuster took this occasion to declare confiscate to the treasury the property of the ex-Shah's brother, who had taken part in the attempted counter-revolution; but the property was protected by Cossacks, acting under orders from the Russian consul-general. When Shuster, not to be balked, sent a larger force of Persian gendarmes to take the property, Russia proclaimed that his act was an insult to the Russian consul-general. It was sufficient pretext for a Russian ultimatum demanding the dismissal of Shuster, payment by Persia of the cost of sending Russian troops into Persia, and a promise to appoint no more foreign advisers without the previous consent of Russia and Great Britain.[1] Well might Persian patriots in the Majliss unanimously reject the ultimatum, and cry bravely, "Death or Independence." The Persian version of Patrick Henry's immortal phrase was unheeded. Russian troops marched on the capital. Great Britain urged Persia to yield. Some of the Persian leaders, in Russian pay, effected a coup d'état, dismissed Shuster, and dissolved the Majliss.[2]

[1] *Parl. Papers*, 1912-1913 (Cd. 6105), p. 81.

[2] On these events compare Shuster, *Strangling of Persia;* with *Parl. Papers*, 1910 (Cd. 5120); 1911 (Cd. 5656); 1912-1913 (Cd. 6103, 6104, 6105, 6264); and Sykes, *Persia*, II, p. 152.

From 1911 to 1914 Persia was misruled by a small clique of politicians willing to accept Anglo-Russian supremacy, to borrow money from the two protecting powers, and to allow Russian troops and Russian colonists to convert the northwestern part of the country into practically a Russian province; the people in that region did not even pay taxes to the Persian government. Despite Russian troops, and a Russian-officered Cossack brigade, and a Swedish gendarmerie in the British zone, banditry and disorder flourished. Disorder to Russia meant simply a pretext for extending Russian occupation in the North; and the British government, unwilling to oppose its partner in the Entente, had to permit Russian aggression. This was how the Agreement secured for Persia "seven years of peace and quiet."[1]

Persia was more unfortunate than countries which fell wholly under the imperialist domination of one power. In Egypt, or Tunis, imperialism meant at least orderly, efficient government, and the building of railways and rapid economic development of natural resources. Persia, on the other hand, was torn between two powers, neither of which would permit the other a free hand. Russia, for example, desired to build a railway straight across Persia, connecting with her own rail system, but Great Britain obstructed the scheme in one way or another, so that nothing came of it. A British firm, on the other hand, planned a system of railways in southern Persia, to be financed by issues of Persian bonds, but Persia was in no condition to undertake such financial obligations, and the surveyors sent out to lay out the routes encountered such native hostility that nothing was done. As a result, Persia to-day has 350 miles of railway, as compared with Egypt's 3,040, Algeria's 2,221, Tunis's 1,260. And Persia's commerce is likewise far less than it would have been, had there been but one dominating power.[2]

Nationalist Persia and International Petroleum

The Great War of 1914 profoundly altered the situation. We are not here concerned so much with the fact that, though

[1] *Parl. Papers*, 1913 (Cd. 6807), 1914 (Cd. 6807 and 7053).

[2] Persia's foreign trade in 1924 was $144,000,000, the largest part of the exports being petroleum, handled by the Anglo-Persian Oil Co.

neutral, Persia was used as a battleground by Turkish, Russian, and British troops, as with what happened to the Anglo-Russian protectorate. Early in the war, in 1915, as part of the secret bargain regarding Constantinople, England and Russia made a secret agreement that England should be permitted to add the middle or neutral zone to her own, and that Russia should be given a free hand in the northern zone.[1] Had Russia and England been able to carry out this bargain, it would have meant the partition of Persia in earnest. Russia, however, had her revolution in 1917, and the Bolshevists repudiated the Anglo-Russian agreements on Persia. The end of the war, therefore, found Persia occupied by British troops, and Britain relieved of Russia's partnership. In vain the Persians sought to avert the clearly impending British protectorate by appealing to the Paris Peace Conference. The Conference was deaf.

On August 9, 1919, the Persian cabinet accepted the inevitable by signing an Anglo-Persian Treaty[2] providing for British "advisers" for "the several departments of the Persian Administration," British officers and munitions for the Persian army, British capital for Persian railways, British experts to revise the Persian tariff, and a British loan of £2,000,000. If, in the preamble, the British government reiterated its pledge, "to respect absolutely the independence and integrity of Persia," the formula need not be taken too seriously. What Great Britain intended was a modern, subtle form of imperialist control no less effective, but much less candid, than what it used to be the fashion to designate by the euphemism, "protectorate."

The treaty, however, never went into effect. The Persian Majliss would not ratify it. Worse still for British plans, the Russian Bolshevists, renouncing all former Russian imperialist rights and interests, began a subtle campaign against British imperialism. Persian Cossacks seized control of the government and installed a premier who dared denounce the unratified Anglo-Persian Agreement. Over the shrewd military leader, Reza Khan, who became virtually dictator, the British could exercise no control, unless they used overwhelming military force. But the British taxpayers were unwilling to pay for a military conquest of Persia.

Once more the Persians turned toward the most distant, and

[1] *Cf. supra*, p. 260.

[2] *State Papers*, 112, p. 760.

therefore—they rightly inferred—the most disinterested, Great Power, for aid. Once more an American was installed as financial adviser, but this time there was no interference from Anglo-Russian interests.[1] When the word "disinterested" was used, it was meant to refer only to political aggrandizement, not to economic affairs. Certain Americans were very much interested in Persian oil. The Standard Oil Company purchased from the Persian government in 1921 an option on a concession to exploit the oil resources of the five northern provinces of Persia. But concessions covering these provinces had previously been granted to a Georgian adventurer named Khostaria, who has sold them at a high price to the North Persian Oil Company, which was owned by the Anglo-Persian Oil Company. The dispute between the Anglo-Persian and Standard was interesting, and intricate. In the end, the Anglo-Persian decided to offer a "50-50" compromise. But the Persian Majliss refused to sanction the bargain, and offered the concession to another American oil producer, Sinclair, in exchange for a loan of ten million dollars.

The Anglo-Persian company to which allusion has been made deserves a little more attention. Its founder was one of fortune's favorite sons, William Knox D'Arcy, who began his career as an impecunious lawyer in Australia; a client walked into his office one day, so it is said, with a chunk of gold quartz, and said he had a whole mountain of it on his sheep farm; whereupon D'Arcy helped him organize a mining company, and made himself a millionaire. Turning traveler, and looking about for new worlds to conquer, he decided to enter the oil business. Hearing that oil seeped from the soil in Persia, he sent a geologist to prospect, and, on the receipt of favorable reports, he persuaded the Shah of Persia to grant him, in 1901, an exclusive concession to exploit petroleum, natural gas, and asphalt deposits in all of Persia except the five northern provinces. Sinking wells and building pipe-lines was expensive work, and D'Arcy found his fortune disappearing so rapidly that he sought the aid of other British oil interests. An Anglo-Persian Oil Company was formed in 1909, owned by British capitalists, to develop D'Arcy's Persian concession. Gushers were struck in western Persia. Soon it became evident that the Persian field

[1] See A. C. Millspaugh, *The American Task in Persia* (1925).

was one of the richest in the world. And in 1914 the British government purchased a controlling interest in the Anglo-Persian Company, to make sure of controlling this supply of oil, in so far as control was necessary, for the British navy.

Barren Persia, it turned out, was a treasure-house of oil, the most eagerly sought for prize of post-bellum diplomacy. Persia was a nation, or rather a conglomeration, of eight or ten million persons, mostly Persian by tongue, and mostly poor, living over untold wealth of oil. The development of the oil industry may mean an end of Persian independence; but in these days of more subtle forms of imperialism, Persia is more likely to remain nominally independent, while her underground wealth is owned and exported by foreigners, from whose prosperity a few crumbs of economic benefit will fall to Persia's share, in the form of taxes, increased commerce, increased business.

Central Asia

A postscript must be added on the fortunes of the other Middle Eastern countries, notably Afghanistan, Tibet, and Turkestan, since the Anglo-Russian Agreement of 1907. The first of these, a mountainous country somewhat larger than France, inhabited by warlike Mohammedan mountaineers, was assigned to be a buffer state, more or less under British control, as the reader will recall. From 1907 to 1919 the arrangement worked well enough. The reigning Amir, Habibulla Khan, accepted a salary and advice from Great Britain; having visited India, he strove to institute in his own country the progressive policies he had there seen in operation; he had a few factories built, introduced telegraph and telephone, reorganized his army, established schools, and above all, built good roads. The curious fact that there are no railways in the country is explained partly by the reluctance of the British government to permit their construction, lest they prove a menace in time of war.

All went well until in 1919 Amir Habibulla was shot in his tent, and his son, Amanulla, proclaimed Amir in his stead. Amanulla promptly declared his independence and got in touch with the Russian Bolshevists, who were seeking to arouse Asiatic peoples against British imperialism. With fatuous courage, and Russian encouragement, he now proclaimed a holy war against the British, only to be summarily defeated. Peace was made a few months later, and confirmed by a treaty of Nov. 22, 1922, which recognized the complete independence of Afghanistan. Once a vassal, Afghanistan is now one of the few independent countries left in Asia or Africa.[1]

Tibet, that bleak plateau and mountain country sparsely peopled by inhospitable Buddhists, was to be a sort of "no man's land," as far as Russia and England were concerned, according to the Agreement of 1907. China was to be recognized as suzerain of Tibet, and no dealings were to be had with the Tibetan Dalai Lama except through China. When the Chinese Revolution occurred in 1911, and Chinese patriots planned to incorporate Tibet more definitely in China, the Tibetans rose in arms, expelled the Chinese officials and garrison, demanded independence, and thereby caused China to undertake the reconquest of the country. Just at this point, Great Britain interfered, imperiously demanding the withdrawal of the Chinese army. China was only "suzerain," not "sovereign" of Tibet, Great Britain firmly pointed out. The British proposed—quite openly in violation of the Anglo-Russian Agreement—that Tibet should be divided into two portions, one under Chinese control, the other "autonomous." Autonomous, in this case, would doubtless have meant under veiled British control. China refused, however, and there the matter rested, until Great Britain should find it to her interest to go further.

Finally, a word about Western Turkestan. This wide stretch of desert, steppe, and irrigated farmland had been appropriated by Russia in the 1860's and 1870's. Here there has been no great battle of international diplomacy, nor any significant conflict between imperialism and nationalism. The native peoples—akin to the Turks in race and language, and Mohammedan in religion, would doubtless have preferred independence, but they gave no sign of national rebellion. As a matter of fact, the native races were antagonistic toward each other: there were the pastoral Kirgiz herdsmen in the north, and the Turkoman herdsmen in the south, and the Uzbeg-Sarts, more civilized agriculturists, artisans, and merchants, between them. Under Rus-

[1] *Parl. Papers, Treaty Series No. 19 (1922)*, Cmd. 1786. See the interesting agreement of the German Afghan Company and the Afghan Government, in *Europäische Gespräche*, Nov. 1925, p. 576.

sian rule, the Turkomans ceased their favorite avocations of brigandage and slave-stealing and settled down, to some extent, as farmers and cattle-growers; the other races made even more marked progress. Russian railways afforded an outlet for cattle and dairy products, for millions of Astrakhan (Karakul) lambskins from Bokhara. But perhaps the most remarkable development was the introduction of cotton-growing on a large scale.

Since the Bolshevist revolution in Russia, a curious development has taken place in Russian Turkestan.[1] A small number of Russian colonists, aided by a minority of the native Mohammedans, followed the Russian example, set up Soviet republics, and remained bound to Russia. The significant aspect of this event was not that the Russians retained control even under a supposedly anti-imperialist Bolshevik government, but that Turkestan afforded a sort of corridor through which Russian Bolshevik propaganda could flow into Persia, Afghanistan, India, and China, stirring up Asia to throw off the galling yoke —so the Bolshevist phrase goes—of European imperialism. Russian propaganda was one factor, as we have seen, in expelling Britain from Afghanistan, and it has had marked influence elsewhere in Asia. Whether it succeeds or not in creating Asiatic rebellions, more or less serious, is probably of less moment than the certainty that it has already stimulated the growth of self-consciousness, of the spirit of self-determination, of resentment against European imperialism, among the peoples of Asia.

[1] See *Current History*, Jan. 1925, p. 534.

CHAPTER XIII

IMPERIALISM IN SOUTHERN ASIA

From Chartered Company to Empire

"In India," said Theodore Roosevelt, "we encounter the most colossal example history affords of the successful administration by men of European blood of a thickly populated region in another continent. It is a greater feat than was performed under the Roman Empire. The successful administration of the Indian Empire has been one of the most notable and the most admirable achievements of the white race during the past two centuries."[1] Set this statement over against the words of Mohandas Gandhi, the "holy one" who led India in passive resistance to British rule, in 1920-22:

> I came reluctantly to the conclusion that the British connection had made India more helpless than she ever was before, politically and economically. . . . The Government established by law in British India is carried on for this exploitation of the masses. No sophistry, no jugglery in figures can explain away the evidence the skeletons in many villages present to the naked eye. I have no doubt whatsoever that both England and the town-dwellers of India will have to answer, if there is a God above, for this crime against humanity which is perhaps unequalled in history.[2]

Colossal achievement, or unequalled crime, or perchance both achievement and crime, British rule in India is unquestionably the foremost example of modern imperialism.

When Indian patriots question the benevolence of British rule, or when British statesmen feelingly speak of England's benefits to India, there is danger of forgetting that the reason why the British first entered India, and the primary reason they have remained there, was not to benefit India, but to benefit Great Britain. It may indeed be true, as an eminent British scholar asserts,[3] that "the Emperor of India is the only sovereign known to history who does not draw one penny from the pockets

[1] *New York Times*, Jan. 19, 1909.
[2] Gandhi, *Speeches*, pp. 753-4.
[3] Ramsay Muir, *The Expansion of Europe*, p. 296.

of his subjects," but it is irrelevant. The plain historical fact is that British rule in India was established for purposes of commerce. The social and educational and political reforms which England has accomplished in India, the patriotic pride which Englishmen have learned to take in their great Asiatic Empire, important as they are, nevertheless are by-products of commercial imperialism. It was a commercial company, the East India Company, that first established British authority in a part of India. Commerce was the original purpose; unto it were added, later, sentimental and humanitarian motives.

How immense are the British business interests in India, and how rapidly they have grown in the last half-century, may well be emphasized at the very outset. Take first the capital invested. Though the precise amount cannot be stated, some rough estimates can be made. The public debt, that is, government bonds, of India, much of which is held by British investors, amounts to 3.5 billion dollars; the 634 foreign, chiefly British, companies doing business in India have a paid-up capital of two and one-half billion; of the 5,194 companies incorporated in India, with a total capital of one billion, a considerable portion are British owned; and in addition there are unincorporated investments.[1]

Add trade. Great Britain sells to India each year goods worth about half a billion dollars—a tenth of her total exports; and buys from India two-fifths of a billion dollars' worth, a ninth of her total imports. The importance of India, however, is even greater to certain powerful and well-organized industries than to British industry as a whole. No industries are more influential in British politics than cotton and iron, and both of these are supremely interested in India, for about one-fifth of their exports goes to India. India, in other words, means about $225,000,000 a year to the British cotton manufacturers. To the iron and steel industry, with the allied manufacturers of machinery, railway rolling stock, and automobiles, it means a hundred million dollars. Nor should we forget the interests of British importers. It may be a bit surprising to learn that tea is India's greatest export to Britain; that this item alone runs to 120 million dollars a year. Nor should one forget the mil-

[1] Sir George Paish estimated British pre-war investments in India at £379,000,000 or $1,895,000,000. This, however, does not include the important item of British companies doing business with India.

lions of pounds sterling represented by British imports of Indian jute, raw cotton, flax seeds, gums, wool and leather.

India has mineral wealth, too, which is just beginning to be exploited on any large scale. Some of the minerals found in India may appear insignificant, when one looks at tables of commerce, but, because they are rare, their industrial importance is great; such are chromite, tungsten, monazite. Of iron India has a modest supply, almost untouched. Of coal she produced only eight million tons in 1905, but twenty million in 1923. The increase is typical.

We have said that the British economic interest in India has grown with rapidity. The point is worth reiteration, because it helps to explain the intensification of British political interest. India's imports increased almost 500% in the period from 1875 to 1913; her exports, about 350%. British investments in India are almost entirely the product of the last half-century. To labor the point with statistics is probably unnecessary, besides being fatiguing; but to appreciate the fact, in interpreting the political events we are about to relate, is imperatively necessary.

Before the nineteenth century England had but a slight hold on India. Only a few provinces were actually administered by the East India Company; the greater part of the country was ruled by native princes, some of whom were puppets of the Company, in the sense that they knew they would be deposed by the Company's Indian soldiers, if they dared attack the Company or its commerce; but the native states had not yet felt the heavy hand of foreign interference in ordinary matters of government. Abuses and indiscretions in the Company's administration had led the British Parliament to extend a certain amount of control over the Company's affairs; a cabinet minister and board of control in London, and in India a governor-general appointed by the British cabinet, supervised the Company's governmental activity.

Such a situation could hardly be permanent. The Company, having conquered part of India, found itself impelled to conquer more. Did a native prince turn enemy, his land must be conquered and annexed; did a king on the border of British territory interfere with British ships, he must forfeit his kingdom. Consider, by way of specific illustration, the administration of Lord Dalhousie as governor-general of India from 1848-1856.

Hardly had he arrived at his post, when two Englishmen were murdered in the Sikh kingdom of Punjab, in western India, and the Sikhs arose in arms against the British. What could Dalhousie do but organize a strong army of Sepoys (hired native soldiers) under British officers, with a few British troops, and subjugate the kingdom, and annex it, and thereby earn for himself a step higher in the peerage, from earl to marquis? Or when the King of Burma, to the east of British India, insulted the British flag by stopping British merchant vessels, could Dalhousie do otherwise than punish such insolence, and annex part of Burma? [1] And when "a handful of scattered strangers"—to use Dalhousie's description of the British in India at that time—have to undertake such military expeditions, first to the west, then to the east, to countries fifteen hundred miles or more apart, it was the most natural thing in the world for an energetic, high-spirited governor like Dalhousie to conclude that the possessions of the Company ought to be consolidated by telegraph, road and railway [2] communications, and that the native states which separated the Company's territories ought to be brought under the Company's power. To this end Dalhousie practised what he called the policy of "lapse," namely, that whenever a Hindu ruler died without direct male heir, his kingdom should be annexed. During his short term of office, eight such cases occurred.

Such annexations could not fail to provoke fear and hatred among the Indian princes. And the steam locomotives, monsters in the eyes of the natives, and the telegraph, both introduced during Dalhousie's reign, as well as his attempts to establish an educational system under British auspices, angered the masses. Fear that the government intended to Christianize India was a part of the general reaction against Europeanization. Moreover, the Sepoys or native soldiers employed by the Company [3] had many reasons for discontent, including the fact

[1] The actual outbreak of the war occurred "more by accident than by design," in the words of Vincent A. Smith (*Oxford Hist. of India*, p. 702). Commodore Lambert, sent to ask redress for the British merchants, seized one of the Burmese King's ships, whereupon the Burmese opened fire, naturally, and the war began.

[2] He planned a system of railways. The first was opened for traffic in 1853.

[3] The Company had 200,000 native soldiers and 38,000 European officers and men.

that they had to bite off the ends of cartridges which they believed were greased with the fat of cows (sacred to Hindus) and pigs (forbidden to Moslems). The Sepoys mutinied in 1857, and from Bengal in the east rebellion spread like wildfire up the Ganges valley. The Sepoy Mutiny, as the rebellion is called, was crushed, at a terrible cost of life, the leaders were punished, some of them being blown to bits from the mouths of cannon, the native emperor was deposed and his sons and grandson shot.

This tragic event made it clear to British statesmen that the administration of India by the Company must end; Great Britain must assume direct control. India had outgrown the Company. As a matter of fact, the growth of the Company's territorial possessions in India had been paralleled by a gradual extension of the London Government's control over the Company. But now, on the morrow of the Mutiny, the Company's administration of India was taken over entirely by the British Government. By the Act for the Better Government of India (1858) the Company's powers were transferred to the Crown; India was to be governed by a viceroy appointed by the British cabinet, under the supervision of a member of the cabinet—the secretary of state for India—and an advisory council. The Company's army was merged with the British army. The British nation became sovereign of India.

Not of all India, as yet. "British India" then was less than half of what we call India to-day. There were still hundreds of native states, some large, some small; some subservient to British authority, some independent enough. Though after the Mutiny the doctrine of "lapse" was dropped, British India continued to expand at the expense of native India and border states, as the following figures show:

Area annexed from	1861 to 1871..........	4,000 sq. mi.
	1871 to 1881..........	15,000
	1881 to 1891..........	90,000
	1891 to 1901..........	133,000

Since 1901 the extension of British power has taken another direction—the gradual tightening of the reins by which the British governor-general controls the seven hundred states which still have native rulers. The maharajahs, rajahs, nizams, and other native sovereigns now rule not "by the grace of God," but by the grace of England. Indeed, the British have found them such convenient instruments of government, that their autocratic powers to-day may be said to rest on British support.

The transition from a chartered company's commercial enterprise to a nation's avowed imperialism was more and more definitely recognized, as British authority was extended, and—let us not forget—as British economic interests were magnified by the impetus which steamboats, steam locomotives, and steam engines gave to commerce and industry. In 1858 Britain had assumed direct control. In 1876 Disraeli, morning star of the dawning imperialist age, persuaded Parliament to confer on Queen Victoria the title Empress of India, as an advertisement of the fact that "The Queen of England has become the sovereign of the most powerful of Oriental States." [1] The sequel came in 1911, when King George and Queen Mary visited India, to be crowned with oriental pomp, as Emperor and Empress at Delhi, the ancient imperial capital, whither the headquarters of the British administration were moved from Calcutta. The dazzling magnificence of the coronation "durbar" (reception to the ruling princes of India) was intended to impress India with the fact that England assumed the sovereignty of the former Mogul emperors whose throne had been at Delhi. That Great Britain, traditional home of parliamentary government and political liberty, should revive in India the outward show of a defunct oriental despotism, probably seemed incongruous to few who witnessed that historic scene at Delhi in 1911.

If in India one finds modern imperialism displayed more openly, and dominant over a larger mass of humanity, and actuated by greater economic interests, than in any other part of the world, one finds in India also the reaction to imperialism in greater intensity than elsewhere. Nowhere can one find a more interesting experiment demonstrating the effects of the mastery of the West over the East.

Indian Nationalism and British Reforms

One of the effects is "Nationalism." An Englishman has said, "This is the first and most essential thing to learn about India—that there is not and never was an India, or even any country of India, possessing, according to European ideas, any

[1] *Cf. supra*, p. 37.

sort of unity, physical, political, social or religious; no Indian nation, no 'people of India' of which we hear so much."[1] He is profoundly right, and profoundly wrong. Right, in that it is true India has no unquestionable geographic unity (few nations have!); in that the Indian people are divided in race, language, religion, and loyalty. There are in central India wild and primitive tribes utterly different in race and language from the bulk of the Indian population. There are descendants of Arab and Afghan, and Mongol, and Persian invaders. There are the Dravidians in the south. And there are the "Aryan" Hindus, who, together with the great mass of mixed descent, constitute the Hindu majority of the population. No national language binds the diverse elements together. Hindi is spoken by almost a third of the population, Bengali by one sixth, and by lesser numbers dozens of other tongues are used. It is hard, very hard, to form a "nation" out of such discordant elements.

There is an even greater difficulty, created by religion. To be sure, the core of India is Hindu: the 217,000,000 Hindus form a majority in most of the provinces and two-thirds of the total population. But on the outskirts of India, there are eleven million Buddhists in Burma, three million Sikhs in Punjab; twenty-five million Moslems in eastern Bengal and eleven millions in Punjab. Worse, there are millions of Moslems scattered all through India, traditionally hostile to the Hindus, into whose midst they originally came as conquerors, to remain in some states as rulers, in others as oppressed minorities. In all, there are about seventy million Moslems. Still worse, the Hindus themselves are divided into "castes." Originally, perhaps, the higher castes were the conquerors and priests; the lower castes, the conquered and lowly. To-day the castes are social classes, within which each person is bound by religion to live and marry. At the bottom of the social scale are millions of "outcastes," to touch whom would contaminate a proud "Brahmin."

That such divergent elements should have been fused in an ardent Nationalism would be inconceivable, were it not for British imperialism. Britain has made India a nation, partly by giving political unity to the great peninsula which had been

[1] Strachey, *India, Its Administration and Progress*, p. 5. But compare Professor Radhakumud Mookerji's *The Fundamental Unity of India*, which adduces ancient Sanskrit and Vedic literature to prove India's unity.

a welter of warring principalities, partly by giving English education to Indians of the upper class, who thereby imbibed the European idea of nationalism; but most of all by giving India a universal sentiment which could serve as a bond of union. That sentiment is antagonism toward British rule. Perhaps no other could have brought Brahmin and pariah, Hindu and Moslem, Marathi and Bengali together. But they have been welded together in the heat of resentment against what they consider as wrongs done to them by England.

The Nationalist torrent which has raged in India of recent years is a flood swelled by innumerable rivulets of discontent, but its main current has been the desire for *Swaraj* (self-government). Indian youths, mostly of the higher castes and wealthier classes, having studied at English universities, returning to India found much to criticize in the British administration. Here and there local associations were formed to agitate for reform. At length, in 1885, was held the first meeting of the Indian National Congress—neither National, since it included only upper class Hindus, nor a Congress, since it was composed of delegates without authority and without mandate from the people. It was simply a gathering of those Hindus who felt the new impulse toward unity and self-government. It began by asking Great Britain to appoint a commission to investigate the administration of India; little by little it grew bolder in its criticism, and more representative in its composition, until it could claim to voice the aspirations of Hindu India, disregarding, of course, the lower classes. For years the chief figure in the National Congress was G. K. Gokhale, a Hindu who with temperate but determined spirit fought for the gradual emancipation of India.

Long after the Hindus had become aroused, the sixty million Mohammedans of India remained inert and inarticulate, for they seemed to be a minority which could hardly join forces with the Hindu Nationalists, nor claim separate nationality for themselves. But in due time the Mohammedans bestirred themselves, and in 1912 founded a Moslem League, which held annual meetings like those of the National Congress, and like the Congress criticized British despotism.

The two movements were brought into alliance in 1916, during the Great War, which indirectly gave a tremendous impetus to the demand for self-government in India, as in every other subject country. In 1916 the two organizations agreed to make a joint demand for representative government; in 1918, for complete self-government to be achieved by degrees within the next fifteen years.

What grievances against British rule could be strong enough to accomplish this miracle, of uniting Hindu and Moslem in a nationalist movement? Perhaps we had best let one of the Nationalist writers, Lajpat Rai, explain.[1] All Indians, he asserts, will agree:

(1) That the present constitution of the Government of India is viciously autocratic, bureaucratic, antiquated and unsatisfying.

(2) That India has, in the past, been governed more in the interests of, and by, the British merchant and the British aristocrat than in the interest of her own peoples.

(3) That the neglect of India's education and industries has been culpably tragic.

The indictment may be amplified.

The government of India was autocratic and bureaucratic. Bureaucratic, in that its routine was conducted by a staff of British officials strongly imbued with respect for custom and tradition and red tape, aloof from the natives, whom they regarded as inferior to the "white" man, serving in India and enduring the climate until their savings or pensions would permit honorable retirement in England. The bureaucracy was almost exclusively British, if we except the unimportant lower positions. Of 2501 administrative offices carrying salaries of 800 rupees ($266) a month, or more, only 242, less than ten per cent, were held by Indians, in 1913. The disappointment of brilliant young Hindus of good family, who secured educations hoping for government employment, only to find the higher offices closed to them, was a by no means insignificant cause of discontent.

The government was also autocratic. From 1858 to 1908 India was governed by a viceroy, with the aid of his official staff and provincial governors, and with the advice of a council of appointed, not elected, members, chosen because of their official experience or their prominence. Though he was to a certain extent subject to general direction by the secretary of state for India, in London, and by the British Parliament, London was

[1] Lajpat Rai, *The Political Future of India* (1919).

several thousand miles distant, and in India the viceroy's power was so great that he may well have been described as the most potent autocrat in the world. Autocratic the government remained until the agitation in India became serious. When the boast is made that Great Britain has given India generous but gradual reforms, and that England's purpose is to teach India the difficult Anglo-Saxon art of self-government as rapidly as India can learn, the cynic will suggest that the measures of self-government granted to India have been more in the nature of concessions, in response to Indian agitation, than of unwelcome lessons forced on a sluggish student.

The first great reform was adopted in 1909, and is popularly known as the Morley-Minto constitution, since it was adopted largely at the urging of Lord Morley, then secretary of state for India, and Lord Minto, then viceroy. It was adopted at a time when unrest was very prevalent in India. The Nationalist Congress had long been in existence. Native newspapers had sprung up all over the land, and were boldly criticizing the government. And there was a particular grievance. In 1905 the brilliant but high-handed Lord Curzon, then viceroy, had cut the huge province of Bengal into two provinces, largely for reasons of administrative efficiency, hardly realizing the dangers involved in the probability that the Bengalese, who might almost be said to possess a nationality of their own, would regard this act as an outrageous violation of their unity, or that the Hindus of eastern Bengal would resent being included in a new province with a Moslem majority, when they had previously enjoyed the position of a majority in the whole province. The division of Bengal aroused nothing short of fury.[1] Newspapers were loud in their complaints, until the Press Act of 1908 muzzled them. Bombs were mysteriously exploded, and officials murdered, not by ordinary criminals, but by determined young Bengalese of good education and family.[2] An Explosive Substances Act enabled the government to check the bomb-throwing to some extent, but the populace seethed with dangerous ferment, and even the arbitrary imprisonment of political agitators availed little. Repression failing, the British used concession. It passed the Mor-

[1] *Parl. Papers*, 1905 (Cd. 2658, and 2746).

[2] *Ibid.*, 1918 (Cd. 9190), *Report on Revolutionary Conspiracies in India*, chs. 2-5, and esp. p. 93.

ley-Minto constitution, and, two years later, announced that Bengal would be reunited.

Even after the reform, the government of India could hardly be called other than autocratic. The law of 1909 (India Councils Act) granted two important concessions.[1] First, it permitted native Indians to be eligible for high offices in the viceroy's executive council and the executive councils of the provincial governors. Second, it enlarged the existing "legislative councils," which had hitherto been little more than advisory bodies of officials. The provincial legislative councils were to include a number of British officials, but a majority of non-official members, some of whom were to be elected by an undemocratic system of class-representation. In the legislative council for the central administration, the officials still remained in the majority because control of this central council seemed more important to British interests. The councils could pass resolutions, subject to the British Parliament's overriding authority; they could discuss the budget and other measures; they could criticize and suggest. They could oppose and propose, but neither depose nor dispose. They could not overthrow the administration, or tighten the purse strings. They were, in short, experimental debating clubs. By Moderate Indian leaders such as Gokhale, the "generous and fair nature" of the reform was praised. By extreme Nationalists the reform was denounced as inadequate. And by all, it was considered unsatisfactory after a few years had passed. We may be permitted to comment, that giving a subject people the right to criticize, without the right to act, as England did in India and America did in the Philippines, cannot be anything but a half-way house. The right to criticize infallibly stimulates a demand for the right to act.

A next step toward self-government was taken in 1919. This time it was even more clear that Great Britain acted in response to Nationalist agitation. During the Great War India had remained loyal, or perhaps passive would better describe the condition. British imperialists like to point with pride to the fact that "India" contributed £150,000,000 and 800,000 soldiers, and 400,000 laborers for overseas service, to the winning of the war.

[1] See C. M. P. Cross's dissertation, *Development of Self-Government in India*, ch. 11, for a detailed study of the passage and effects of the reform.

The record is remarkable, but should not be taken quite at its face value, for the soldiers were recruited "from fighting classes and races which had little in common with the educated classes of the towns," and the financial contribution was made by a British-controlled administration. Certain native princes, true it is, contributed generously, but their reason is explained by A. J. Macdonald—"They realize that the maintenance of the principle of autocracy is wrapt up with the continuance of British domination."[1] For them the war was not to "make the world safe for democracy." A Mohammedan newspaper (*Hitaishi*) of Calcutta contributed another surprising reason why India should support England in the war: "The British Empire is known as a Moslem Empire. For under no other sovereign on earth is there such a large Moslem population."[2] But one of the chief reasons why there were relatively few attempts at revolution during the war, and why Nationalist leaders such as Mohandas Ghandi urged Indians to support Britain's cause, was that the Nationalists hoped that wartime loyalty would be rewarded with self-government. It was during the war that for the first time the Moslem League and the National Congress joined in the plea for home rule. Their action was followed by a lively agitation, led by Nationalists, for self-government. But at the close of the war they were to be disappointed. Early in the summer of 1918 was published a *Report on Indian Constitutional Reforms*,[3] setting forth the conclusions drawn by the Viceroy, Lord Chelmsford, and the Secretary, Mr. Montagu, after an inquiry into Indian conditions. The Montagu-Chelmsford Report admitted that the surprisingly rapid growth of home-rule agitation in India had rendered the Morley-Minto constitution obsolete, and that further reform was needed. It was needed to prevent revolution. But the Report pointed out that such reform must not be too radical.

The Montagu-Chelmsford proposals were adopted by Parliament in the form of a bill, the Government of India Act, 1919. By this new constitution was established a central legislature of two houses, the Council of State with sixty members, and the

[1] A. J. Macdonald, *Trade Politics and Christianity in Africa and the East*, p. 165.

[2] Quoted in *India and the War*, p. 61.

[3] *Parl. Papers*, 1918 (Cd. 9109) and supplementary report 1919 (Cmd. 123).

Legislative Assembly with 144. And in neither house was there to be any longer a majority of British officials. The provincial legislatures were also enlarged, by including more elected members. The new legislatures were more representative than the old; still they were far from democratic.

Only 909,603 persons, out of 247 millions in the British provinces, were eligible to vote for the 104 elective members of the central Legislative Assembly. The provincial legislatures were only a little less undemocratic: in Bengal one person out of 47 could vote; in Madras, one out of 34. A very interesting feature, though not novel, is the division of the electorate into classes. For example, the Bengal Legislative Council is composed as follows: [1]

Non-Mohammedan, urban	11
" rural	35
Mohammedan, urban	6
" rural	33
Landholders	5
University	1
European, General	5
" Commerce	11
Anglo-Indian	2
Indian Commerce	4
	113

Thus Mohammedans and Hindus and Europeans, though they live in the same block, must vote separately, as if in different electoral districts. The scheme has its merits in affording representation to minorities, especially minorities of wealth, education, or European blood. Note the eighteen seats given to Europeans and Anglo-Indians.

The same sort of community or class representation applies to the central assembly, to which Bengal—for instance—sends 6 Non-Mohammedans, 6 Mohammedans, 3 Europeans, 1 landholder, 1 representative of commerce. It is worth while to note this system, not only because it applies to a people of 320,000,000 souls,[2] but also because it is typical of the recent tendency in European treatment of similar subject peoples. Democracy of

[1] See electoral qualifications in *Parl. Papers*, 1920 (Cmd. 812), pp. 47 ff. Figures for the first election are given in *Parl. Papers*, 1921 (Cmd. 1261).

[2] Strictly speaking, it applies only to the 250 millions in the British provinces, as the native states are under their own princes; nevertheless all India is involved in the problem of home rule.

the Occidental type, where every man (and woman) counts as one voter, regardless of wealth, education, descent, or religion, seems virtually impossible at present where social and religious and racial differences are so deeply felt.

Perhaps the most interesting feature of the Montagu-Chelmsford reform was "dyarchy." To satisfy the demand for responsible government, and to make the assemblies more than debating societies, the provincial councils were given control over certain "transferred subjects," notably education, agriculture, public health and others, which are to be placed in the hands of "ministers" chosen from among the elected members of the councils. In these departments there would be self-government. But law, order, justice, police, are "reserved subjects," which remained in the hands of appointed officials, under the discretion of the governors, uncontrolled by legislatures. In defiance of Lincoln's principle regarding the fate of "a house divided against itself," the British Government made it a principle to divide the administration of India. India was to be "half free, half slave." Autocracy and self-government were to be twin columns supporting British imperialism. It is interesting to note the subjects which were reserved as of interest to Great Britain—the repression of disorder was a prime interest. Ingenious as it was, the scheme was by no means an unqualified success.

A Gentle Rebel—Gandhi

Yet the cry for *Swaraj*—self-government—was not appeased. It was after the announcement of what British statesmen considered so open-handed a grant of freedom, that the Nationalist agitation reached unprecedented heights. Not only were Indian extremists disappointed in the reforms, but there were other grievances. Bitter was the feeling against the Rowlatt Act, which gave the administration power to make arbitrary arrests and inflict summary punishment for the suppression of revolutionary violence.

More bitter was the indignation following the Amritsar "massacre." At Amritsar, in the Punjab, natives had committed several outrages—attacks on banks, and particularly an attack on an Englishwoman. General Dyer, the district military commander, endeavored to restore respect for British authority. When several thousand unarmed civilians essayed to hold a mass-meeting, against his general order, he mowed them down with machine-guns without warning or chance to disperse. His men stopped firing when their ammunition gave out, after killing four or five hundred and wounding about fifteen hundred, and then he marched his soldiers off, leaving the field covered with dead and dying. When he was later giving testimony regarding the affair, he said he could have dispersed them, probably without firing a shot, but "they would have all come back and laughed at me, and I should have made what I considered a fool out of myself."[1] Whether shooting down two thousand unarmed civilians saved General Dyer from folly or not, though it may be an interesting question, was not the main point. The significant thing was that Dyer believed, and many Englishmen believed, that such action as his was necessary to cow India. I was in England at the time Dyer's case was being discussed, and well remember how strong was the feeling in imperialist circles that Dyer had performed a courageous and necessary exploit. This point of view is interesting, when considered in connection with the affirmation which the same imperialists frequently make, that India is loyal to England, and that England's mission in India is one of peace and humanity. It is only fair to add, however, that the prevailing English sentiment was condemnation of Dyer's deed, as an unwarranted bit of "frightfulness." In India, of course, the Amritsar victims were martyrs, and Dyer's deed a bloody crime. The blood of martyrs is always a stimulant to Nationalism.

A third powerful factor was the Khilafat movement. When in 1920 the Great Powers imposed on Turkey a Carthaginian peace, dismembering the Ottoman Empire, great was the anger of Moslems in India, who had supported England in the war in the belief that Great Britain was the friend of Islam. There developed in India a fanatical Mohammedan agitation against the dismemberment of Turkey, because Turkey was Mohammedan, and the Turkish sultan was Caliph of Islam.

All these elements of unrest were fused under the leadership of that strange and saintly patriot, that gentle yet inflammatory

[1] Part of the testimony is reprinted in the N. Y. *Nation*, 110, pp. 121 ff.

revolutionist, Mohandas K. Gandhi. Gandhi was a Hindu, belonging to one of the higher castes, educated in India and in the University of London, with the intention of becoming a lawyer in India. Being called to Natal, South Africa, by Indian clients, he sprang into prominence there as leader of a movement of passive resistance to the laws discriminating against Indians. He became an ardent Nationalist, a believer in self-government for India, yet an opponent of violent revolution and an admirer of British institutions; at this stage in his career, all that he asked was the extension of British principles of parliamentary government and personal liberty to India. At the outbreak of the Great War he organized an Indian ambulance corps—then later aided recruiting in India, inspired by the hope of self-government as a reward for loyalty. But the events of 1918 to 1920, described above, were too much for his loyalty. He became the leader of the most amazing campaign for independence. Not by arms, but by the power of love and moral purity was India to gain freedom; not might but sheer right would triumph, he believed. By simply refusing to cooperate with the British Government, India could overthrow it.

Gradually the practical details of the Non-Cooperation plan were unfolded.[1] First all Indians must resign any offices or honors they held from the British Government; this was done, to some extent, but British rule did not collapse. Second, Indians were to boycott the British schools, and establish national schools of their own. That thousands of youths in the higher schools and universities followed this behest, risking their future careers, was a magnificent if tragic demonstration; but eloquent descriptions of national schools in which the Indian youth would learn to be self-reliant, proud of their nation, were difficult to translate into buildings and actual curricula.

The third item was more telling—the boycott. India must boycott foreign goods, above all, British cotton cloth. Gandhi's argument for this measure is worth summarizing.[2] Every person in India used on the average, he claimed, thirteen yards of cotton cloth per annum; this made a total of four billion yards, half of which was imported. Now if India supplied her own

[1] See *Speeches and Writings* of M. K. Gandhi, esp. p. 48.

[2] Gandhi, *The Wheel of Fortune*, published at Madras, 1922, in a binding of Indian homespun.

cloth, the chief reason—so he claimed—for British or any foreign imperialism in India would disappear. India would be freed. Let every Indian home have its *Charkha* (spinning wheel); let every patriot wear *Khadar,* the homespun, handwoven cotton cloth of India. Let even the school students spend four hours a day in spinning, during this national crisis, and two in study. Before the British came, said Gandhi, the spinning wheel and the hand-loom in each of millions of cottages enabled the agricultural masses to supplement the meager fruits of their toil on the land; India was happy and prosperous; but "the cottage industry . . . has been ruined by incredibly heartless and inhuman processes as described by English witnesses," and the living skeletons to be seen in Indian villages bear witness to the result. The spinning wheel is the remedy, and the sure cure for "an imperialism, which is built upon exploitation of the weaker races of the earth, and the acceptance of a giddy materialistic civilization protected by naval and air forces that have made peaceful living almost impossible." These words give some hint of the distaste which Gandhi and other Indian extremists felt toward European industrialism. Gandhi's Boycott was just one phase of an oriental reaction against the materialism and militarism, the competition and commercialism, of the West; an oriental reaction in favor of preserving the simplicity and calm of oriental life.[1] But to return to the Boycott—though huge bonfires were kindled of British-made clothes; though millions followed Gandhi's lead; though more than one English cotton mill had to close its doors for lack of business; nevertheless, British rule—the British *Raj* as Indians style it—survived.

Finally Gandhi was about to launch the final stage of Non-Cooperation, namely, "civil disobedience," or peaceful refusal to obey British laws and courts, pay British taxes, or cooperate with the British administration in any way. This might well have led to serious results, to violence and revolution, once the masses were embarked on it, although Gandhi himself regarded violence as a moral impurity to be avoided at all costs. Just at this point, however, the prophet was arrested and cast into prison. He told the British judge, "I am here, therefore, to invite and submit cheerfully to the highest penalty that can be

[1] Confirmed occidentals may perhaps agree with the writer in questioning the simplicity of oriental civilization.

inflicted upon me for what in law is deliberate crime and what appears to me to be the highest duty of a citizen.'' The judge condemned him, though admitting he was "a man of high ideals and of noble and even saintly life,'' and expressing the hope that the term of six years might be shortened. This was in March, 1922. Not quite two years later he was unconditionally released. The fact that British physicians saved his life during his jail term, and that he was released in accordance with medical advice, shows how unwilling the British Government was to make him a martyr. But it likewise afforded a telling commentary on the prophet's denunciations of Western civilization. After his release, Gandhi soon lost his commanding influence, as the Moderates gained power.

The power of "Mahatma'' (Holy One) Gandhi's personality had temporarily held together the divergent factions of Indian Nationalism. After his arrest, factional differences reappeared, among the Extreme Non-Cooperationists, the moderate Swaraj Party, the more moderate Liberals, and the Moslems. The Moslems were in part conciliated by Great Britain's action in giving asylum to the Turkish sultan and caliph, when that sovereign was deposed by the Turkish Nationalists. The Swarajists and Liberals took part in the election of the new legislatures, under the Montagu-Chelmsford reform act. The Extremists continued Non-Cooperation, scorning anything short of independence.

In the Legislative Assembly of India, the Moderate Swaraj (Home Rule) faction obtained a majority, and at first proceeded to demand the transfer of the government to the Indians. Of course the demand was refused. They defeated the budget. But the viceroy warned them the government would continue "as heretofore, save that the reformed constitution will be in abeyance.'' The new constitution was not working perfectly, it soon appeared. Yet the British Government was reluctant to modify it at once. It must first be given a fair trial. Progress in such matters must be cautious. On the other hand, there was an increasingly marked tendency on the part of the more moderate Indian deputies to cooperate with the Government and make the new legislatures at least partly successful.[1]

[1] For short but illuminating discussions see Sir Fred. Whyte, "Political Evolution in India," *Foreign Affairs*, Jan. 1926, and R. L. Schuyler, "India," *Pol. Sci. Quart.*. March 1926, pp. 91-6.

Indian Problems

Beside the problem of self-government, there are problems of education, economic welfare and social reform. Lajpat Rai stigmatizes the neglect of India's education as "culpably tragic." Many Englishmen believe, on the contrary, that England has been magnificently generous in educating India. It depends on the point of view. The British imperialist point of view is that any expenditure on education for India is magnanimous, and that in founding schools and colleges in India, Great Britain has conferred a great boon upon the natives. There were, in 1923, some 200 colleges giving instruction to 65,000 men, and 21 colleges with 1248 women students; there were about 9,000 secondary schools, 162,015 primary schools, and thousands of private institutions, technical and industrial, commercial and agricultural schools. All this is impressive. But from the Indian point of view it is not enough, nor is it rightly directed. It is not enough, because ninety-three per cent of the population of British India (1921 census) was illiterate; because only four per cent of the population was receiving primary instruction; because India needed six times as many primary schools for boys before she could attain the same level of literacy as England; because the expenditure for education in all India was less than half the expenditure in New York State. It is wrongly directed, so Indian Nationalists claim, because it is essentially Western. Since the time of Macaulay, who drew up a celebrated report on Indian educational plans, recommending instruction in English, the Government of India has generally held that Indian education should impart "a knowledge of English literature and science through the medium of the English language." But Indian patriots claim that such education teaches Indian students to ape the West, and to ignore the rich cultural heritage of India. Says Gandhi, "The strain of receiving instruction through a foreign medium is intolerable. . . . For this reason our graduates are mostly without stamina, weak, devoid of energy, diseased and mere imitators." Moreover, English education created a class of Anglicized Indians, of the upper social strata, out of touch with the masses who understood no word of English, no inkling of Western ideas. Against this system there has developed a powerful Indian reaction, and Indian presses are pouring out an endless stream of books and pamphlets written to restore respect for India's traditions, culture and institutions, as superior to those of the West and vital to India.[1] Strangely enough, many of these writings are in English. Lack of a single national language for India is one of the greatest obstacles to the nationalist agitation.

Then there is the economic problem. Englishmen justifiably boast that they have reduced taxes, built railways and roads, irrigated great areas, opened mines, developed commerce. They also boast that while giving India good government and naval protection, and diplomatic representation, they exact no tribute, but merely collect the taxes necessary for the administration's expenses. On the other hand, the taxes are more regularly collected, and perhaps more burdensome for that reason. The cost of railways and other public works has been paid by India, or saddled on India as a debt. Nationalists claim, moreover, that the salaries and pensions of British officials, and the large army maintained to fight in England's wars, are unjustified burdens on India.

There can be no doubt that the economic progress of India under British rule has been principally beneficial to British merchants and investors, and to Indian merchants and capitalists, whereas the great bulk of the population remains poor, terribly poor, hovering on the edge of starvation. British investigators and Indian patriots alike admit the appalling poverty of the agricultural masses, two-thirds of the population.[2] Great local famines may have been ended by the British-built railways, but semi-starvation remains, and has perhaps become more widespread than ever. There is probably some truth in Gandhi's assertion that the destruction of "cottage industry"[3] has caused inconceivable suffering. Indian peasants who eked out their earnings by using spindle and loom suffered the fate that overtook English hand-loom weavers in the Industrial Revolution. Machine-made cloth was cheaper. But in India's case, the machines were in a foreign country. Instead of a cloth-exporting

[1] I have a shelf of these before me as I write. They range from sober and scholarly books to inflammatory and mystical pamphlets.

[2] See W. D. Cole, *'Prosperous' British India, a Revelation from Official Records* (1901); Lajpat Rai, *England's Debt to India* (1917).

[3] Compare R. Mukerjee, *Foundations of Indian Economics*, especially Bks. II and IV, and also *Parl. Papers*, 1919 (Cmd. 51), the report of the Indian Industrial Commission, together with five volumes of evidence.

country, India became an importer of British cotton cloth. Great Britain took care that no protective tariff should be erected against British cloth. Imported cottons and Indian cottons were subjected to an excise tax at the same rate, 3½% ad valorem. This was the condition from 1896 until the Great War. Then, when India contributed £100,000,000 to the British Government's war chest, a concession was made; India was allowed to raise the duty on imported cottons to 7½% (1917) and later to 11% (1921); but even this measure was most vigorously attacked by the representatives of the Lancashire cotton industry, in the House of Commons.[1] If the 3½% excise tax was removed in 1925 it was only as a reluctant concession. The aim of British manufacturers was to keep India non-industrial, an exporter of raw materials, a buyer of manufactures. The right for India to establish a protective tariff is a most important boon craved by Indian Nationalists, and a danger feared by British industry.

A relatively new and very significant factor in the situation is the recent growth of factories, financed by British capital, in India. It is what one would expect. Indian labor is pitifully cheap; India has raw materials such as cotton, jute, coal, oil and leather. It is not surprising that in Indian cities factories are springing up like mushrooms. In 1923 there were six thousand factories and mills. In cities like Bombay the Industrial Revolution is at work. There are millionaire factory-owners, and there are squalid slums, where the infant mortality rate is one of the highest in the world. There are also trade unions. India has an industrial proletariat, a class of factory workers, now numbering about a million and a third, and rapidly increasing. As it grows, it will create a peculiarly grave labor problem, not only because in a country where human life is so cheap wages are likely to be pittances,[2] and hours long, and factory conditions atrocious, but also because the struggle between capital and labor will be in large part a struggle between India and England.

The Indian problem, it is clear, is far from simple. If emancipated to-day India might perhaps be worse off; there might, as the British claim, be a break-up of the empire, accompanied by

[1] See the long and candid debate between Chamberlain and Barton, Norman, and others in March 1917. *Parl. Deb.* 5th Ser., XCI, especially pp. 1148-1238, and *ibid.*, 186, p. 679 ff. on Japanese competition.

[2] In Bombay cotton mills in 1921 the average monthly wages of men were $17.50 and of women $8.50.

civil war and bloodshed—who can say? There would almost certainly be domination and exploitation of the masses by the classes—there is exploitation and domination now. Whether such a state of affairs would be worse or better than British domination and exploitation, one must judge according to his point of view. That British imperialism is step by step retreating before the advance of Indian Nationalism, appears obvious. Only judicious concessions can avert revolution. Perhaps if the problem were viewed without prejudice, it would be seen that India needs a gradually diminishing foreign political guidance, to make the transition to self-government safe and beneficial; that India needs foreign capital for her economic development and can learn much from Western civilization, especially from Western science; that, in a word, the proper kind of British administration could benefit India in the transitional period. On the other hand, it seems clear that passion and prejudice make such an easy solution difficult if not impossible; for on one hand Indian Nationalism can hardly avoid excesses of nationalist sentiment, and on the other hand, British imperialists of General Dyer's type are temperamentally unable to avoid provoking Indian Nationalists to rebellion, and British economic interests will not easily yield to India's welfare.

The problem has another aspect. India occupies a most important place in the British Empire, and in world politics. Protection of India has been a motive in British aggression in Persia, in Mesopotamia, in Afghanistan, in Tibet, in Burma, even in Egypt and the Mediterranean, because of the Suez Canal route. In the history of European diplomacy during the last century, India might well appear on every page, so far-reaching has been its influence.[1]

Moreover, India is the crucial internal problem of the British Empire in the present century. It is the greatest of British possessions and one of the least secure. Aside from the question of self-government, assuming that India were content with autonomy inside the Empire, there are two thorny problems concerning India's relations with the Empire. One is the question of India's voice in Imperial affairs. To conciliate Indian opinion, the British Government of late years has allowed representatives of India (carefully chosen by the British Government

[1] See Das, *India in World Politics*.

for their loyalty and dependability) to sit in with the representatives of the self-governing Dominions in Imperial Conferences. If India becomes self-governing, and sends Indian Nationalists to the Imperial Conference, the situation may become embarrassing, especially if the Indians demand for their views a weight proportionate to India's importance in population, for India contains three-fourths of the Empire's population. Only such a miracle as was worked in South Africa, the transformation of Nationalists into Imperialists, could easily solve this problem.

The other question is emigration from India. India's enormous population is ever increasing, and ever seeking outlets. Sanitation and peace only augment the problem. Why not fill up the empty spaces of Canada, Indians have asked, or Australia, or British Africa, with industrious and frugal Indian coolies? Many thousands have emigrated as contract-laborers, to work a term of years and return. But the white colonies do not welcome Asiatic immigration, to put it mildly. And the Dominion premiers were not even willing to permit Kenya Colony in British East Africa to be made an outlet for India's surplus population.[1] Indians resent such exclusion. They are infuriated by racial discrimination against them on the part of South Africa, Canada and Australia. Here indeed is a problem. If denied equal rights in the Empire, India will doubtless be resentful and disloyal toward the Empire; if given equal rights, India might overrun the wide areas which have been set apart for the future expansion of the European white man.

India, then, is not only the greatest example of imperialism, but one of the gravest problems of imperialism. It is a country in which imperialism has worked great good and wrought great evil; in which economic imperialism and humanitarian imperialism have been clearly enough revealed, often in conflict; in which imperialism has created what may prove to be—unless wisely dealt with—its own Nemesis, a native Nationalism.

French Admirals in Indo-China

French empire-builders of the eighteenth century had India almost within their grasp, only to lose it to England,[2] but French

[1] *Parl. Papers*, 1923 (Cmd. 1922); *cf. supra*, p. 133.

[2] France still retains five towns in India, with a total area of less than 200 square miles, as a relic of what was lost in 1763.

imperialists of the nineteenth century sought and found compensation—relatively small compensation—in the great peninsula which juts down east of India. The beginnings of French empire

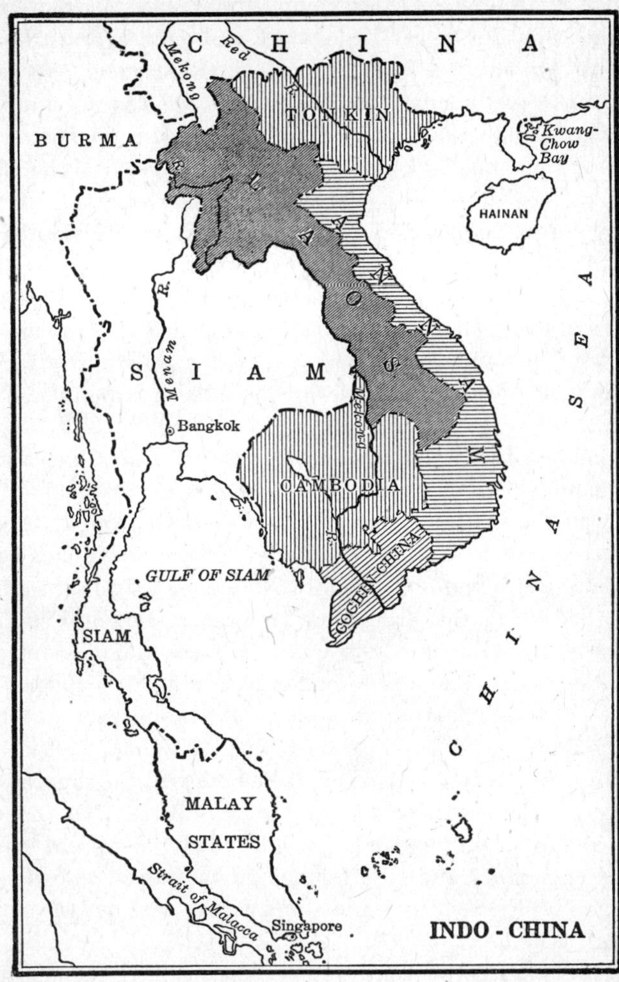

INDO-CHINA

in this region are traced back by French historians to the reign of Louis XIV, when a French missionary persuaded the emperor of Annam to seek the aid of France in his wars, with the result that in 1787 a treaty was signed giving France a bay and an island on the Indo-Chinese coast. The treaty was allowed, however, to become a dead letter. The new French empire in the east was founded by French admirals during the reign of Napoleon III.

To avenge the murder of a Spanish missionary bishop in 1857, a Franco-Spanish naval expedition was sent against the Emperor of Annam, Tu-Duc, who ruled the eastern part of the Indo-Chinese peninsula. So earnest was the French admiral in his indignation at the outrage upon the Spanish missionary, that the expedition ended with the signature of a treaty, June 4, 1862, ceding to France three provinces of Cochin-China, over which the Annamese emperor had been suzerain, and giving French merchants the right to ascend from Cochin-China up the great Mekong River. The treaty also permitted French and Spanish missionaries to endeavor to convert the natives in Annam. Here was a good beginning. A few years later the remaining three provinces of Cochin-China were conquered by another French admiral.

Just north of Cochin-China, astride the Mekong River, lay the kingdom of Cambodia, which was claimed as a vassal by both Annam on the east and Siam on the west. Here also Christians were being murdered. Accordingly a French admiral intervened, and the King of Cambodia was persuaded to sign a treaty (1863) accepting the protection of France, giving Frenchmen freedom to travel or reside in Cambodia and Cambodians a like freedom to travel and reside in France, admitting French merchandise free of duty, and allowing Catholic missionaries to preach and teach in Cambodia. France now had Cochin-China and Cambodia, a compact block of territory at the mouth of the Mekong, in the southern tip of the peninsula. To the north stretched the large kingdom of Siam and the empire of Annam, both independent; and still farther north was populous China, whose trade French merchants hoped to tap by way of the Mekong valley.

A shorter and better route into southern China was offered by the Red River, which runs through Tonkin, a northern tributary province of Annam. To this river a French naval lieutenant, François Garnier, was sent with 175 men and two gunboats, in 1873, under instructions to secure for Frenchmen the exploitation of the Yunnan mines in southern China, and also to settle a dispute between the Annamite officials who governed Tonkin and a French merchant who had contracted to supply a Chinese general with arms. Garnier settled the dispute by conquering the delta of the Red River, the most valuable part of Tonkin. France might then have held Tonkin, but Garnier was killed, and his successor, knowing that the cabinet at Paris would not approve a permanent occupation of Tonkin, contented himself with the signature of a most ingenious treaty (1874) between France and the somewhat awed emperor of Annam.[1] By this interesting document the President of the French Republic promised to protect the emperor of Annam and provide him with assistance in maintaining order, destroying piracy, and resisting attacks, and furthermore to give him five steamships, a hundred cannon and a thousand rifles as well as to furnish experts to reorganize the Annamese army and navy, financiers to take charge of Annamese finances, and professors to found an Annamese college. There were many other clauses, but perhaps it is sufficient to say that Annam became a French protectorate. And Annam included Tonkin.

An interesting and unfortunate episode followed. French merchants in Tonkin found themselves subjected to exactions, extortions, and attacks by the *Pavillons Noirs* or "Black Flags," who were generally considered as pirates, but certainly not of the familiar Captain Kidd variety. The French suspected, or at least alleged, that the Emperor of Annam and perhaps the officials of China were backing the Black Flags. But these quasi-piratical gentlemen had to be eradicated, if French commercial aims were to be satisfied. A naval officer was sent with a small force to restrain them, under strict instructions not to shoot, and not to attempt "a war of conquest." Like Garnier, however, he became a conqueror and met an untimely but glorious death, which had to be avenged by a new punitive expedition. And this led to war with China.

In view of the fact that Annam sent triennial tribute to Peking, the mandarins in that imperial capital considered Annam and its dependency Tonkin vassals of China. Peking therefore requested France to evacuate Tonkin. Chinese armies were thrown into the disputed land. The resulting war between France and China, from 1883 to 1885, convinced the Peking

[1] Text in Dubois et Terrier, *Un Siècle d'expansion coloniale*, pp. 833-839.

Government that obstructing European imperialism is rather dangerous. In a chastened mood China agreed to a series of treaties (1885, 1886, 1887) recognizing the French protectorate over Annam and French occupation of Tonkin, reducing the Chinese tariff by 20% and later by 30% on goods imported into China across the Tonkin border, and promising to seek the aid of French industry when railways were to be built.[1]

One of the quaint freaks of history is that the French politician who was most responsible for the conquest of Tonkin, Jules Ferry, was bitterly assailed at the time as *"le Tonkinois"* and was overthrown by a parliamentary vote of no confidence on March 30, 1885, after the victory over China had been won, but just before peace had been concluded.[2] Ferry's work is now regarded with pride in France, for Tonkin and Annam are cherished possessions.

Tonkin in the north and Cochin-China in the south, both great rice-growing regions, have been likened to two bags of rice hung at the ends of a rather flimsy stick, that is, the narrow coastal strip of Annam. France now had the bag and the stick. The next task was to enlarge the bags and thicken the stick. The French domain in Tonkin was rounded out by military operations in the process known as "pacification," which lasted from 1885 to 1887. The conquest of Laos, which lies between Annam and the Mekong River, thickened the stick. And in the south the French protectorate of Cambodia was rounded out at the expense of Siam.

All these territories—Cambodia, Cochin-China, Annam, Laos and Tonkin, and the leased port of Kwang Chow Wan on the coast of China[3]—are now grouped together under a French governor-general and constitute an imposing French Asiatic empire almost fifty per cent larger than the mother-country, inhabited by twenty million poor but industrious peasants and artisans. "No French colony," writes a French imperialist, "is more populous than the Indo-Chinese Empire, none has a richer soil, better suited to the most various production, or more abun-

[1] Treaties in *State Papers*, 76, p. 239; 85, pp. 735 and 744. The new Annam protectorate treaty of June 6, 1884, is in vol. 75, p. 1110. *Cf.* the French yellow books, *Affaires du Tonkin* for 1883 and 1884, and *Affaires de Chine et du Tonkin, 1884-1885.*

[2] The debates in the Chamber of Deputies through 1883-1885 will be of interest to the reader who cares to probe the psychology of imperialism.

[3] *Cf. infra*, p. 335.

dant or intelligent labor. The resources to exploit are immense."[1] In trade it is second only to Algeria. But unlike Algeria and the other North African colonies, it confers the advantage of its trade largely upon other Asiatic countries, leaving only a small percentage (about 28%) for France. That is because the chief export is rice and the chief import cheap cotton cloth. French imperialists hope, of course, that this situation will be changed. France must use more rice. Indo-China must produce large quantities of cotton and other raw materials for French industry. In the meantime, this empire for which French taxpayers have so generously poured out their francs, and French sailors their blood, is about fourteenth in the list of the customers of France.

Burma and Siam

It is time that we turned, as the French did, toward the kingdom of Siam, west of French Indo-China, and toward the kingdom of Burma, west of Siam. In the early 1880's King Thebaw of Burma was favorably inclined toward the French, and gave them the right to build a railway from Tonking to Mandalay, and establish a bank, and exploit ruby mines. Apparently he was endeavoring to play the French off against the British, who were (in India) closer and therefore more dangerous neighbors. With indignation the British learned of the progress of French peaceful penetration. The climax came when King Thebaw attempted to transfer to Frenchmen the rights of a British trading company. Protests to France had been vain. Not to be balked in this fashion, the British Government of India took the abrupt step of sending to King Thebaw a cool ultimatum, requiring him to welcome a British representative and to follow British advice in his foreign affairs. Ten thousand British (and Indian) soldiers followed the ultimatum, invaded Mandalay, captured King Thebaw, and sent him in safe custody to India. Then the viceroy of India announced, on Jan. 1, 1886, that Thebaw's kingdom of Burma was annexed by British India. So easy was it, in those days, to conquer an Asiatic kingdom larger than France.

With Britain in Burma and France in Indo-China, Siam

[1] *Ce que tout Français devrait savoir sur Nos Colonies*, by Regismanset, François and Rouget.

remained a buffer state. It was a kingdom centuries old, larger than France, and practically independent, although it had sent tributary embassies, as so many neighbors of China did, to the great emperor at Peking. Would it survive, caught between the upper and the nether millstone? France proposed that it should be preserved as a buffer to prevent Anglo-French conflicts, but when the British failed to act on this suggestion, the French began to push their claims westward, to the left bank of the Mekong River—another Left Bank problem arose. Curzon, whose acquaintance we have already made in India and the Persian Gulf, pointed out the danger to India, if France were allowed to appropriate Siam. Had not Britain long endeavored to prevent Russia, or any other Great Power, from coming into contact with India? Moreover, British commercial, mining, and railway interests in Siam would be endangered.[1] When France sent French gunboats to Bangkok, the capital of Siam, and presented an ultimatum to Siam demanding the whole left bank of the Mekong, British ships were posted at Bangkok too. France obtained, to be sure, the left bank of the Mekong (1893), but no more, at that time. The British then tried to create a neutral zone fifty miles wide, in the upper Mekong valley, where French and British borders were now too close for comfort. But in 1896 they gave up the effort, and the Mekong was recognized, up to the Chinese frontier, as the French boundary.

The next step was taken in 1904, when France and England formed their *Entente Cordiale.* One feature of the entente was an agreement[2] that all lands east of the Menam River basin (in which Bangkok lies) were under French influence, and all lands west of it under British influence. France thus gained a free hand to appropriate the Siamese province of Battambang, in 1907, and England to appropriate in 1909 four Malay states (Kedah, Kelantan, Trengganu and Perlis) situated on the smaller peninsula which runs south from Siam. England, we may as well note in this connection, had already secured the other Malay states and the island of Singapore at the tip of the peninsula, and thus gained command of one of the world's greatest waterways, the Straits of Malacca, through which passes the trade of the Far East and the East Indies.

[1] *Nineteenth Century,* July 1893, pp. 34-55.
[2] *State Papers,* 101, p. 629.

But to return to Siam. Though it had been sadly pared down, the "kingdom of the free" still retained a certain amount of independence, a territory almost as large as France, and a population of about nine millions. Like other oriental states it has had to accept foreign advisers and grant extraterritoriality to foreigners. Yet by employing an American diplomatic adviser, a British judicial adviser, a French legislative adviser, British and French police organizers, and many other foreign advisers, it has succeeded in avoiding too great subservience to any one Great Power.

As an independent oriental kingdom, Siam affords an interesting comparison with the neighboring lands which have fallen under European rule. Some time ago I made a rough computation of comparative school statistics. In Siam, 60 children per thousand of population were attending school; in French Cambodia, which adjoins Siam, the rate was 5 per thousand; in French Cochin-China, 23; in Annam, 7, and this despite *"la mission civilisatrice"!* On the other hand, in Bengal and Burma, under British rule, the ratios were 43 and 38, while in the Philippines the figure rose to 120. The comparison, superficial as it is, may at least enable the reader to draw his own conclusions.

On the material side, many readers might expect to find Siam far outdistanced by the neighboring lands which have been so zealously developed by European governments. The facts are rather surprising. Siam exports and imports more, much more, per capita, than either French Indo-China or British India. She has more railway per capita than either (but less per square mile than India). These, again, are crude measurements, but it is not easy to find accurate indices of progress. And it should never be forgotten that the masses in all three countries are incredibly poor tillers of the soil, who do not ride much on railways, who do not find themselves enriched as commerce grows, who do not send telegrams to their friends. They will share only very gradually in whatever progress is made. The point here, however, is that even according to the conventional measures of material and educational development, independent Siam with its foreign advisers and shrewd royal family, has a marked superiority over French Indo-China and, in some respects, over British India.

CHAPTER XIV

THE BATTLE OF CONCESSIONS IN THE FAR EAST

A CENTURY or so ago Napoleon Bonaparte, with one of his characteristic flashes of intuition, remarked of China, "There lies a sleeping giant. Let him sleep; for when he wakes he will move the world." The China of which he spoke was the dense mass of three hundred million human beings, patiently cultivating the valleys and rich alluvial plains of eastern Asia, reverently worshipping their ancestors and preserving their ancient culture, scorning all things foreign or novel, too much absorbed in the eternal realities of work and love and children and friends and family, too much accustomed to local and individual liberty, and too placidly certain of the unconquerable massiveness of their race and civilization, to be much agitated by the fears or the ambitions of smaller nations, or much concerned by the fact that their emperor and their bureaucracy were of the alien Manchu race. Invasions of the past had been mere pinpricks; invaders were slowly but surely assimilated. China was the eternal kingdom, the "Celestial Empire," around which other peoples gravitated like planets in subservient orbits.

China proper included, besides the thickly peopled lowlands, a back-country of hills and mountains, little cultivated, but stored well with unworked mineral treasures; all in all it was a country half as big as the United States is to-day. But around China proper lay dependent provinces—Sinkiang, Manchuria, Mongolia, Tibet—which in themselves made up an area as large as the United States; and, besides, the neighboring kingdoms of Korea, Annam and Tonkin, and Burma, and even the island empire of Japan, paid tribute and homage, or had occasionally done so, to the great empire from which all had obtained no small part of their culture. Surrounded by vassals and tributaries, China was truly a giant, a giant grown drowsy in centuries of unquestioned supremacy.

Europe woke the giant. The result may best be put in the words of a discerning American secretary of state, John Hay:

"The storm center of the world has shifted . . . to China." He added, "Whoever understands that mighty Empire . . . has a key to world politics for the next five centuries."

The first task of our inquiry, however, is not to understand China, but to discover what Europe did to China and the surrounding nations of the Far East, and for what purposes; because the Far East is to-day a melting pot in which Orient and Occident are being fused—in which the familiar saying, "East is East and West is West" is being hourly disproved. The Far East, to revert to Hay's metaphor, is the storm center of the world because the West has invaded the East.

Opening the Door for Merchants and Missionaries

Why Europe invaded the Far East may be simply stated. European industrial nations (and the United States) desired first of all an open door for their merchants, mariners, and missionaries, especially their merchants. This was the reason for the opening-up of China, Japan, and Korea, in the period from 1840 to about 1880. This was not true imperialism; on the contrary, the open door is almost the opposite of imperialism. But the opening of the Far East led inevitably to a desire for monopoly of markets, mines, and railway-building, hence for monopolistic "spheres of influence," and also for naval bases, and in some cases, territory. This was genuine imperialism, and it has been the dominant factor in the Far East since the 1880's. The early commercial motive, and the later imperialism, both required the use of force, but in their effects they were unlike; the former meant wars without conquests; the latter, conquests and bitter international rivalry.

The open door had to be forced open by violence or by threat, for Asia in the early nineteenth century did not welcome the trade and the creed of the West. A few European merchants, it is true, were permitted to buy silk and tea, or sell opium (from India) at Canton, in China, and similarly with Japan a few shiploads of goods were exchanged each year, but with these minor exceptions, the empires of eastern Asia were as effectively closed to the outside world as if they had been surrounded on every side by impenetrable walls. They were surrounded by walls, not of stone, but of prejudice, self-sufficiency, conservatism.

The first important breach in the wall of exclusiveness was made by the Anglo-Chinese War of 1839-42, often called the Opium War. A commissioner of the Chinese government, Lin Tse Hsi, determined to put an instant end to the opium trade, demanded that the British merchants at Canton surrender the stocks of opium which they had there for sale. When the British refused, he put the British community in Canton under quarantine, and brought it almost to starvation. This was one immediate cause of the war. Moreover, British sailors in quest of excitement had happened to kill a Chinese; Commissioner Lin had demanded the surrender of the murderer; the British had refused; Lin threatened to make the arrest by force; and the British naval squadron opened fire on the Chinese fleet, in November, 1839.[1] This was the immediate occasion of the war. The real issue was the commercial open door. Much to Commissioner Lin's surprise, the "barbarians" upon whom he looked with ineffable contempt proved amazingly powerful in war. British warships easily captured several cities on the Chinese coast, and the terms of peace were dictated by the British, in the Treaty of Nanking, 1842, and supplementary agreements.[2]

China paid an indemnity. Five Chinese cities—Canton, Shanghai, Amoy, Foochow and Ningpo—were to be "treaty ports," in which British and other foreign merchants could freely trade and reside and erect their warehouses. Near Canton, the small island of Hongkong was ceded to Great Britain, in order that British merchants might have a secure place for warehouses and residences. Moreover, British citizens residing in the "Treaty Ports" were to be subject to British rather than Chinese law, and were to be judged by British consuls. This exemption of foreigners from the laws of the country is called "extraterritoriality"; it is difficult to see how Europeans could have resided in China without some such arrangement, for Chinese law and Chinese punishments were incomprehensible and seemed barbarous to foreigners.[3] One other important pro-

[1] *State Papers*, XXIX, pp. 879-1069; XXX, pp. 4 ff., esp. pp. 20-1; compare Morse, *International Relations of the Chinese Empire*, I, chs. 9-10.

[2] *Ibid.*, XXX, pp. 389 ff.

[3] Chinese patriots are now eager to abolish extraterritoriality as a restriction on Chinese sovereignty and a reflection on Chinese courts and laws. An international conference met in January 1926 to discuss this problem. See discussion in *American Relations with China* (Johns Hopkins Press, 1925), pp. 49 ff.

vision of the peace settlement was that British goods imported into China would no longer be subject to arbitrary exactions, but to a fixed customs tariff, the rate of which was later settled at five per cent ad valorem. Thus China lost the right to regulate her own tariff.

The Nanking Treaty and its supplements were inspired, clearly, by a British desire for free access to the Chinese market, but not by latter-day imperialism. Great Britain could have taken a large slice of territory; she was content with the tiny island of Hongkong. She could have asked for exclusive privileges; she was willing that other nations enjoy the same rights. By separate treaties with China, the United States and France in 1844, and other Powers in later years, obtained the same rights that England enjoyed in the Treaty Ports.[1]

Three results of this first step toward opening China are worth noting. First, European trade with China increased marvelously, thereby intensifying the European interest in China.[2] Second, the treaty port privileges made it safer for European missionaries to work in China. Incidentally, there was in the fifties a great rebellion, the Taiping Rebellion, led by a pretender who had been converted to Christianity. The feelings of the Chinese emperor may easily be imagined. Third, the contact of European merchants and missionaries inevitably produced friction and conflict. In the Treaty Ports, the Europeans lived in peril, surrounded by a hostile Chinese population. Chinese officials were arrogant and overbearing. A French missionary was executed on the charge of stirring up rebellion. A ship flying the British flag was boarded by Chinese officials who sought to arrest one of the Chinese crew, a murderer. The latter incident led to a second Anglo-Chinese War in 1857, and France, too, made war on China.[3] Again China was defeated, and to save the capital from capture the Chinese government hastily made peace, by the Treaty of Tientsin (1858),[4] promising (1) to throw open additional treaty ports, (2) to permit trade on the Yangtse River and travel in the interior, (3) to permit a

[1] Malloy, *U. S. Treaties*, 1, p. 196; *State Papers*, 34, p. 1298. See list of treaties in *China Year Book*.

[2] The export of Chinese tea increased from about 42 million lbs. per annum before 1842 to over 100 millions in the 1850s.

[3] Morse, *op. cit.*, I, chs. 16, 20-22.

[4] *State Papers*, 48, p. 47.

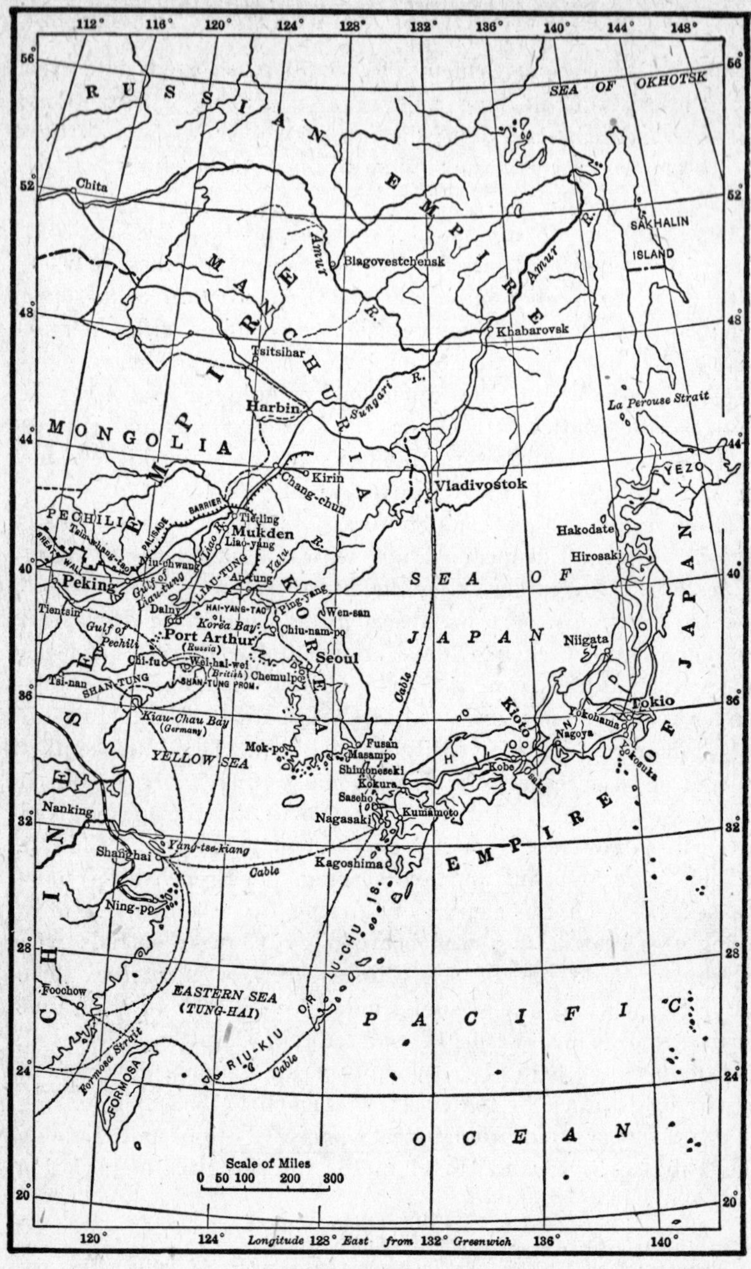

THE FAR EAST

British ambassador or minister to reside at Peking, (4) to revise the 1843 schedule of customs duties, which now amounted to more than five per cent since prices had dropped, and which the British wished to restore to an effective five per cent, and (5) to refrain from molesting Christian missionaries and converts. The last point was quaintly phrased: "The Christian religion, as professed by Protestants or Roman Catholics, inculcates the practice of virtue and teaches man to do as he would be done by. Persons teaching or professing it, therefore, shall alike be entitled to the protection of the Chinese authorities. . . ." France, United States and Russia promptly received similar rights by treaties made at Tientsin in 1858.[1]

When a British minister started up the Peiho River to Peking, to get the Treaty of Tientsin ratified by the emperor, he found a chain stretched across the river, and his ships were bombarded. This, of course, was from the European point of view an outrage. English and French forces were sent to punish the outrage; Peking was attacked; and the imperial summer palace was burned. Unable to resist such European methods of persuasion, the Chinese emperor now confirmed the Tientsin treaties, added an indemnity, and gave Great Britain a small area on the mainland near Hongkong, for the expanding British commercial community there.[2]

During the Chinese conflict with England and France, Russia had been represented to the Chinese as the protector and friend of China. As a reward, Russia received (by treaties of 1858 and 1860) all Chinese territory north of the Amur River and east of the Ussuri River—a vast region which became the Maritime Province of Russian Siberia.[3] The Russian aggression was inspired partly by the expansion of Russian colonization from Siberia into the Amur valley, and partly by the traditional Russian desire for an ice-free port. In the annexed territory Russia found an admirable harbor, which became the port and naval base of Vladivostok, free of ice during many months of the year. The other European powers, however, were less interested in territorial expansion, at this time; they wanted simply the open door, and they were willing that it should be equally open

[1] *Ibid.*, 48, p. 606; 51, p. 637; 53, p. 966.
[2] *Ibid.*, 50, p. 10.
[3] *Ibid.*, 50, pp. 964, 970.

for all. What they wanted, and what they had obtained between 1840 and 1860, may be summarized as (1) the right to trade at certain "treaty ports"; (2) a fixed, low tariff; (3) extraterritorial rights; (4) toleration for missionaries.

Compare the case of China with that of Japan. Japan likewise had been a hermit nation, with doors closed to Europe; Japan likewise was forced to admit foreigners and their trade; but the results were very different.

Not England, but the United States took the initiative with Japan. Like other nations, the United States had resented the refusal of Japan to permit trade or to receive diplomatic envoys, but the Americans had a special grievance. Occasionally American whaling vessels were shipwrecked on the Japanese coast, and the sailors were imprisoned, sometimes tortured. Hoping to stop this sort of thing, and at the same time to open up the island empire for American trade as China had been opened, President Fillmore in 1853 sent Commodore Perry with a letter addressed to the ruler of Japan, and many presents, typical of Western civilization—firearms, a toy railway, telegraph instruments, books, champagne, and "many barrels of whiskey."[1] When Perry's four warships steamed into Tokyo Bay, black smoke pouring from their funnels, the Japanese were terrified at the strange sight, and fled to their temples to pray for deliverance. But Perry landed, interviewed the officials, expressed his desire to conclude a treaty, and, on being refused, announced that after they had time to think it over he would return for an answer, with more warships. True to his word, he came back in 1854 with ten ships, and obtained a treaty allowing American ships to anchor in two Japanese ports and obtain provisions, and promising hospitable treatment of shipwrecked sailors. Immediately afterward, the United States sent as consul-general to Japan Townsend Harris, a man of such independence that he refused to crawl on his hands and knees—as had been the custom—before the Japanese ruler, and of such ability that he soon negotiated treaties granting Americans many new privileges and

[1] Foster, *American Diplomacy in the Orient*, ch. 5, for this and other interesting details; Perry, *The United States Japan Expedition; Sen. Exec. Doc.*, 34, 33d Congress, 2d Session; T. Dennett, *Americans in Eastern Asia*, ch. 14.

opening Nagasaki and Yokohama to American trade.[1] Other nations followed suit. In Japan, as in China, treaty ports were opened, the customs duties were fixed by treaty, and extraterritorial jurisdiction conferred on foreign consuls.

Korea, like Japan and China, was also compelled to open its ports. This mountainous kingdom, the "hermit kingdom" of the East, somewhat bigger than New England and twice as densely populated, had excluded foreign trade and put to death adventurous missionaries, despite French and American punitive expeditions. But when the Koreans fired on some Japanese sailors, Japan used the tactics which Commodore Perry had taught her, and forced upon Korea in 1876 a treaty opening a Korean port to Japanese traders.[2] Similar treaties with other nations completed the work, and soon Korea was in much the same position as China and Japan, as regards treaty ports and extraterritorial rights.[3]

In all three countries the first contacts with the merchants, missionaries, gunners and diplomatists who represented Western civilization produced profoundly disquieting effects. In China, a convert to Christianity became the leader of the "Taiping Rebellion," whose object was to overthrow the Manchu emperor, and only by employing a British adventurer, Major Charles Gordon, to lead the imperial troops, did the Chinese government suppress the insurrection, after more than a decade of civil war. After that, the Manchu officials in China generally regarded foreigners, especially missionaries, with suspicion and hatred; while, despite official hostility, many Chinese, especially in the southern treaty ports which had first been opened, came under the influence of European ideas. The smouldering enmity between South China and North, between Chinese and Manchu, was thus intensified.

In Korea Western ideas were accepted by a number of influential leaders, who became progressives, while other factions at the royal court cherished a bitter resentment toward the in-

[1] Foster, *op. cit.*, ch. 6; W. E. Griffis, *Life of Townsend Harris;* T. Dennett, *Americans in Eastern Asia*, ch. 19; Malloy, *op. cit.*, 1, pp. 996, 1000.

[2] H. Chung, *Korean Treaties*, p. 205.

[3] Treaty with U. S., 1882, *State Papers*, 73, p. 586; with Germany, 1883, Martens, *N.R.G.*, 2d Ser. 10, p. 473; with Italy, 1884, *State Papers*, 75, p. 308; with France, Martens, *op. cit.*, 15, p. 807, etc.

truders from abroad. The conservatives and exclusionists found sympathy and some support at the hands of the Chinese government, whereas the progressives looked to the Americans and to the Japanese, for Japan embraced European civilization with gusto.

Japan at first experienced the same internal conflict between progressives and exclusionists that occurred in China and Korea, but the progressives triumphed brilliantly. A little explanation is necessary. Before 1867 Japan was a feudal monarchy, whose nominal sovereign, the Mikado or Emperor, dwelt at his imperial city of Kyoto, and whose actual ruler, the Shogun or regent, greatest of the nobles, governed the nation from his capital Yedo. Feudalism was rampant; the country was divided into small provinces, each ruled by a noble chieftain; and each chieftain had his loyal band of swordsmen—samurai they were called—who like the knights of medieval Europe prided themselves on chivalric standards of honor, wore their arms as a badge of nobility, and scorned manual labor. The common people who tilled the soil were comparable to the serfs of the Middle Ages.

To the Japanese feudal system, the coming of Perry and the opening of Japan proved fatal. First the Shogun, who signed the treaty with Perry, and who admitted the foreigners, was denounced by leading nobles, especially those of the Satsuma and Choshu clans in southern Japan, who had long been jealous of the Shogun's power, and who now accused him of cowardice. But the chieftains themselves soon had a taste of Europe's power. It so happened that a procession of the Satsuma chieftain and his retainers was interrupted by three Englishmen, who discourteously tried to break through, and were promptly cut down by indignant Satsuma swordsmen; but soon the guns of a British squadron showed the Satsuma clan that European civilization was irresistible. The Prince of Choshu had a similar experience; by firing on foreign ships, his retainers provoked England, France, the United States and Holland to such a point that they sent warships to demolish his forts, punish his insolence, and exact an indemnity of three million dollars.[1] Choshu and Satsuma ceased to stand for exclusion; but they became the more determined to oust the Shogun who seemed so incapable of protecting the country. Other nobles, too, became convinced that

[1] Dennett, *op. cit.*, ch. 21.

the dual government and divided allegiance must be ended, and the emperor restored to power, if Japan were to survive. Finally, in 1867, the Shogun was overthrown by the nobles, and the young Mikado, Mutsu Hito, then only fifteen years old, was restored to full power.

This revolution, or "Restoration," was the turning-point for Japan. The boy-emperor allowed the government, henceforth, to be conducted by a little group of patriotic nobles and knights, chiefly of the Satsuma and Choshu clans, who were determined to resist European aggression by adopting European civilization. Most of them were ambitious young men, under thirty years of age. With a courage and a sagacity that would be hard to excel, these young men transformed Japan. Henceforth Europeans were welcomed, treated courteously by the imperial court, and studiously imitated. Englishmen were employed to direct the construction of railways, telegraph lines, lighthouses. French legal experts supervised the reform of the legal and judicial system, so that Japan could regain the right to try foreigners in her own courts. Americans helped organize a postal system and improve agricultural methods. Germans were drafted for the preparation of commercial laws, the reorganization of local government, and the teaching of medicine. After he had visited Europe to study Western methods of government, Prince Ito drafted a constitution (1889) establishing an aristocratic House of Peers and a not too democratic House of Representatives, with carefully restricted powers.[1] Factories began to spring up. Ships were built for foreign trade. The feudal lords were persuaded to make voluntary surrender of their fiefs, so that feudalism could be replaced by more efficient modern government. The samurai laid aside their swords, with magnificent self-sacrifice, and in their place a new fighting force, a modern army of conscripted commoners, was organized by French (later German) officers, equipped with European rifles and cannon, and drilled in European methods. The new army, distrusted at first, proved its value by defeating thirty thousand rebellious samurai of Satsuma in a bloody civil war. There was also a navy—Japan had hitherto possessed none. Warships were purchased from

[1] Hornbeck, *Contemporary Politics in the Far East,* one of the best general surveys of the Far East, gives a good discussion of the constitution in ch. 7; *cf.* Nichi Iwasaki, *The Working Forces in Japanese Politics.*

England and a fleet was organized under British guidance, until Japan could build arsenals and navy-yards of her own. Unquestionably Japan's sudden transformation was in some respects as insincere as the adoption of European clothes; Japanese officials might wear European costumes in the daytime, and might have mansions furnished in Mid-Victorian style, but in the privacy of family life they wore the graceful garments of their ancestors, and remained loyal to Japanese customs. It was chiefly the military and economic institutions of the West that were copied. As an indication of the imperviousness of Japan to Western spiritual ideals, the very small success of Christian missions among the Japanese is significant.

The Sino-Japanese War

Such were the first-fruits of the opening of the Far East. Later came imperialism. Toward the close of the nineteenth century, European powers began to seek something more than commercial opportunity in Asia. France began to encroach on Chinese territory from the south by conquering Annam and Tonkin in the eighties, despite Chinese claims of suzerainty over those regions. Great Britain annexed Burma.[1] Russia built a railway through Siberia, and began to covet China's northern, Manchurian provinces. And Japan, taking a leaf from Europe's book, marked Korea for her spoil.

Japan's intervention in Korea in 1894 was at once the natural result of the events, and the prelude to a fierce outburst of international imperialist rivalry. In Korea the incoming of European ideas had created two factions, as we have seen: a progressive faction fostered by the Japanese, and an anti-European faction favored by the Chinese government. Court intrigues, conspiracies, and acts of violence, growing out of the rivalry between the factions, were bound to involve China and Japan. In Korea the Japanese principle of assimilating Europeanism was opposed to Chinese conservatism. A crisis was reached in 1894, when at the appeal of the Korean royal family China dispatched a regiment or two to Korea, and Japan, not to be outdone, sent twelve thousand men to occupy the capital and treaty ports. It was unlikely that China would accept

[1] *Cf. supra*, pp. 293, 315, 317.

Japan's polite proposal that both powers should undertake to guide Korea into the path of progress. On the contrary, China revived her claims to suzerainty over Korea. Japanese forces entered the Korean royal palace, installed the King's father as regent. The regent promptly declared war on China, in July, 1894. Though the Chinese had some Krupp guns, and modern rifles, and ironclad warships, they were overconfident, ill organized, inefficient. In less than a year, the Japanese had overrun Korea and southern Manchuria, and were threatening Peking. It was a striking lesson in the value of Europeanization.[1]

By the peace treaty of Shimonoseki,[2] April 17, 1895, China recognized the absolute independence of Korea (this allowed the Japanese in the rôle of advisers to dominate the Korean government), and promised an indemnity of 200,000,000 taels or about $150,000,000 (more than enough to reimburse Japan for the total monetary cost of the war), and ceded to Japan the great island of Formosa and the smaller Pescadores Islands. But most important of all was the provision for the cession to Japan of the Liaotung Peninsula, the southern tip of Manchuria, commanding the entry to the Gulf of Chih-li and Peking. Was the island empire of Japan to gain a foothold on the Chinese mainland?

Hardly had the treaty been ratified, when Russia, Germany and France presented a joint note at Tokyo, offering their friendly advice that Japan refrain from annexing any part of the Chinese mainland. Rather than risk an unequal war, Japan took the advice, and returned Liaotung, and received 30,000,000 taels as additional indemnity. Superficially, it appeared that three chivalrous western powers had courteously protected China; yet in drab reality these three intervening powers were anything but chivalrous in their motives. Russian imperialists felt that Korea and the Liaotung Peninsula were of vital importance to Russia; if Japan dominated Korea, Japan would control both sides of the southern outlet of the Japan Sea, on which was situated the Russian port of Vladivostok, the intended terminus of the Trans-Siberian Railway. If Japan annexed

[1] Morse, *op. cit.*, III, ch. 1; Dennett, *op. cit.*, chs. 23-26.

[2] MacMurray, *Treaties and Agreements with and concerning China*, I, p. 18. Japan was also allowed to occupy Wei-hai-wei temporarily; China was to open up four new ports; and Japanese subjects were given the important right to import machinery and engage in manufacture in Chinese treaty ports and open cities.

Liaotung there would be no possibility of Russia's obtaining an ice-free port farther south, say Port Arthur. Japan, therefore, must be ousted from these regions. France joined with Russia, as a loyal ally in world politics. It was less natural that Germany should have participated in the triple intervention, but the publication of the so-called "Willy-Nicky" correspondence, between William II and Nicholas II, has shown that the German emperor was egging the Russian Tsar on against the "Yellow Peril"; Christendom, said the Kaiser, must stand firmly against the pagan Orient. From the pen of a ruler who a few years later proclaimed himself the friend of the Mohammedans, such sentiments smack of insincerity. But there can be little doubt that what the Kaiser really desired was to promote cordial relations with Russia, and by showing himself more zealous than France as a friend of Russian imperialism, to weaken the Franco-Russian alliance and rob it of its anti-German sting. Moreover, the memoirs of the Kaiser and of Von Tirpitz admit, and German documents prove, that at this time the German government eagerly coveted a Far Eastern naval base.[1]

The three Great Powers that had befriended China in the spring of 1895 were not unwilling to accept compensation for their aid. Indeed, China's friends were more grasping than the enemy from whom they had saved her. France, for her part, by a convention signed June 20, 1895, obtained an option on all mines in the three southern provinces, adjoining French Indo-China; and the right to extend French railways from Annam up into China; and confirmation of a reduction of the tariff by 30 to 40% on trade across the French Indo-Chinese border.[2] To the Chinese statesman Li Hung Chang, these privileges may not have seemed dangerous; to the student of imperialism, they appear as the familiar methods of economic penetration, the prelude to territorial annexation.

Russian diplomats reminded Li Hung Chang that chiefly to Russia was China's preservation due. After a visit to Russia, Li Hung Chang was persuaded to authorize, in 1896, a "Russo-

[1] Tirpitz, *Memoirs*, ch. 8; *The Kaiser's Memoirs*, pp. 64-7; *Die Grosse Politik*, 9, nos. 2219, 2227, 2238, 2252, and 14, ch. XC.

[2] By treaties of April 25, 1886, and June 26, 1887, France had already obtained a reduction of 30% on goods imported into China, and of 40% (of Chinese export duties) on Chinese goods exported through Tonkin. MacMurray, I, p. 28.

Chinese Bank," with largely French capital, to aid the Chinese government in arranging the payments on the Japanese indemnity, and to acquire concessions for the construction of railways and telegraphs.[1] In September of the same year, the Russo-Chinese Bank obtained an extremely important railway concession.[2] A "Chinese Eastern Railway" was to be built straight across the Manchurian provinces of China, connecting with the Russian Trans-Siberian. As a glance at the map will show, this meant that instead of constructing the eastern section of the Trans-Siberian by a circuitous route through Russian territory, Russia would build it by a shorter, direct route, through Chinese territory, to the Vladivostok terminus. China was to give the right of way through public lands free, and exempt the railway property and receipts from taxation, as Turkey did in the case of the Bagdad line; but China issued no bonds to finance the railway. In this case a Railway Company was to be formed, by Russian and Chinese (by way of courtesy) capital, the company's bonds being guaranteed by the Russian Government.

The last-mentioned provision points to the political nature of the enterprise; nominally a private industrial project, it was really an imperialist move on the part of the Russian Government. The railway was first and foremost a strategic railway, to advance Russian imperialist interests in the Far East. It would facilitate the movement of Russian troops in case of war; and even in time of peace Russian military guards could be stationed along the line to preserve order. Russia would dominate Manchuria from the military point of view. From the economic standpoint, also, Manchuria would be Russified. Of course the railway would give Russia the commerce of central and northern Manchuria; in addition the company was to have mining rights along the route.[3] Moreover, goods imported or

[1] The bank was organized as a Russian corporation, with a capital of 6,000,000 rubles, later increased to 11,250,000. It was merged with the Banque du Nord in 1910 and re-named the Russo-Asiatic Bank. A majority of the shares are said to have been purchased by French financiers and investors. See Witte, *Memoirs*, pp. 82 ff.

[2] MacMurray, pp. 74 ff., *cf.* pp. 35, 40. For the alleged Cassini Convention of 1896, *ibid.*, pp. 78-81, and Cordier, *Histoire des Relations de la Chine*, II, p. 343. See also Witte's *Memoirs*, pp. 82 ff. The Company was to pay China 5,000,000 taels and after eighty years of operation the Chinese Government would receive the railway gratis. China had the right to purchase the line after thirty-six years.

[3] Statutes of the Company, art. 1, MacMurray, p. 84.

exported over this railway would enjoy a reduction of a third of the established tariff rate. Russia's next step would be to get a concession for a southern extension of the line and a warm-water port, for Vladivostok was ice-bound several months in the year.

The Leased Ports

Germany meanwhile had been inactive. But German experts had been considering which port on the Chinese coast would be most desirable as a Far Eastern naval base and had selected Tsingtao, on Kiaochow Bay, on the southern coast of Shantung Peninsula.[1] Though the Russians had earmarked Tsingtao for themselves, in 1897 the German emperor in his most casual and friendly manner obtained the Russian Tsar's approval of the German plan: Tsingtao for Germany and Port Arthur for Russia.[2] By a coincidence that well suited German ambitions, two German missionaries happened to be murdered in November 1897 by Chinese, in Shantung, the very province which had been selected as the stage for German imperialism. Promptly the Kaiser sent Prince Henry of Prussia with a German squadron to display the German "mailed fist" in such manner as to inspire respect for Germans in China.[3] That the Kaiser, a Protestant, should have been so energetic in avenging the murder of Roman Catholic missionaries was a little surprising; but when Prince Henry proceeded to anchor in Kiaochow Bay and land troops on its shores, and when Germany demanded a lease of that Bay, the German Government's motives became clear. Germany intended to get her "place in the sun," her share of the spoils in China. The German method was ingenious. Instead of annexing Kiaochow, Germany asked merely for a "lease" of the shores of the Bay—about two hundred square miles—for ninety-nine years, during which period Germany could fortify and administer the leased territory as if it were hers. At Tsingtao, on the Bay, Germany constructed a first-class fortified naval base and commercial port. All the advan-

[1] Tirpitz, *My Memoirs*, ch. 8; *The Kaiser's Memoirs*, pp. 64-7; *Die Grosse Politik*, 14, nos. 3645-3685.

[2] *The Kaiser's Memoirs*, p. 67; *Die Grosse Politik*, 14, no. 3679, *cf.* nos. 3743-6.

[3] See William II's vehement telegram to the foreign office, *Die Grosse Politik*, 14, no. 3686.

tages of annexation were obtained without the appearance of territorial greed. But Kiaochow Bay was not only to be a naval base; it was to serve as an opening for German economic interests. German capitalists were to build two railways in the province of Shantung, and exploit the mines found near the railways (within 30 *li* from each side); and for public works in Shantung China would give preference to German capital and materials. In short, Shantung province was to be an economic sphere of influence for Germany.[1]

The leased port method was eagerly borrowed from Germany by other powers. Russia lost no time in obtaining a lease of 538 square miles, for twenty-five years, on the tip of the Liaotung Peninsula.[2] In this area, the harbor of Dalny was improved for commercial use, and Port Arthur was converted into a supposedly impregnable fortress and naval base. Furthermore, Russia was allowed to build a branch railway through southern Manchuria, connecting Port Arthur and Dalny with the Chinese Eastern, that is to say, with the Trans-Siberian. Thus Russia obtained an ice-free terminus for the Trans-Siberian; more than that, Port Arthur commanded the entrance to the Gulf of Chih-li, and was within striking distance of the Chinese capital, Peking. Russia's leasehold, it may be remarked, included part of the very region which Russia had prevented Japan from annexing in 1895.

Germany's lease of Kiaochow was signed on March 6, 1898; Russia's lease of Port Arthur, on March 27; France came next. On the day after the signature of the Kiaochow lease, France put in her successful demand for a lease of about 190 square miles, for ninety-nine years, on the shores of Kwangchow Bay, in southern China, near the border of French Indo-China.[3] Nor was Great Britain to be ignored. Great Britain presently obtained a lease of 400 square miles near Hongkong and a lease of Wei-hai-wei, on the northern coast of the Shantung Peninsula. The English purpose was to have a naval station conveniently near Port Arthur as a check on Russian aggression in the Far East, as the terms of the lease show, for England was to hold

[1] MacMurray, pp. 112, 240, 248, 252. See Bülow's comprehensive discussion of German policy in China, *Die Grosse Politik*, 14, no. 3778.

[2] MacMurray, 119 and 157; see British protests in *Parl. Papers*, 1898 (C 8814), *China No. 1*, esp. no. 133.

[3] Convention of May 27, 1898, MacMurray, p. 128.

Wei-hai-wei as long as Russia remained in Port Arthur.[1] Italy demanded a naval base, too, but was refused.

The year 1898, to sum up, was a year of leases in the Far East. Four European Great Powers had obtained leased ports —Germany in Kiaochow Bay, Russia in Port Arthur, France in Kwangchow Bay, and England in Wei-hai-wei. As each leased port was intended to serve as a naval base, it is clear that the strategic situation in the Far East was becoming tense. But strategic naval bases were not so much objects in themselves as trappings of economic imperialism. The Great Powers were intrenching themselves for the contest over the trade and resources of China.[2]

THE "BATTLE OF CONCESSIONS"

The economic aspect of the Far Eastern situation was taking on a new aspect. No longer were European powers seeking merely admission to the commerce of the Far East. That commerce had grown so rapidly that it was now of immense value, and European capitalism was beginning to reach out after the commerce of the interior of China, which could be reached and developed only by rivers and canals or railways. The first railway was built in 1876—and torn up! But others were constructed. Building a railway into the interior involves a capital investment that must be protected against disorder and banditry; it naturally tends to give the constructing power a monopoly of the commerce of the region; and as railway companies often received mining rights, a railway concession meant much more than the laying of tracks.[3] Furthermore, if capital-

[1] MacMurray, pp. 130, 152; *Parl. Papers*, 1898 (C. 8814), nos. 90, 95, 129, 144.

[2] *Cf.* P. Reinsch, *World Politics* (1900).

[3] Read Lord Salisbury's telegram—"It does not seem that the battle of Concessions is going well for us, and that the mass of Chinese railways. if they are ever built, will be in foreign hands is a possibility that we must face. One evil of it is that no orders for materials will come to this country. That we cannot help. The other evil is, that by differential rates and privileges the Managers of the railways may strangle our trade. This we ought to be able to prevent, by pressing that proper provisions for equal treatment be inserted in every Concession."—*China No. 1 (1899)*, no. 232. On the Chinese railways see P. H. Kent, *Railway Enterprise in China (1907)*; Overlach, *Foreign Financial Control in China; China Year Book;* Willoughby, *Foreign Rights and Interests in China;* J. V. A. MacMurray, "Problems of Foreign Capital in China," *Foreign Affairs*, Apr. 1925, p. 411.

ists of one country build a railway to open up a certain region, they do not wish capitalists of another country to construct a competing line into the same region. For instance, when in 1898 Great Britain obtained the lease of Wei-hai-wei, she informed Germany that there was no intention of competing with German railway construction in the province of Shantung.[1]

Railway-building thus led naturally to the marking out of "spheres of interest." France, as we have seen, laid claim to the three southern provinces of China, south of the Yangtse valley, as her sphere for railway construction and mines, as early as 1895; Germany in 1898 obtained railway and mining rights in Shantung which made that province a German sphere. In fact, by an Anglo-German agreement of September 1-2, 1898, British financial interests formally recognized the German right to a monopoly of railway-construction in Shantung and the Hoangho valley, in exchange for German recognition of a British monopoly in the Yangtse valley and the province of Shansi (north of the Yangtse, and just west of Shantung), which was needed to connect the Yangtse valley with Peking and north China.[2]

Similarly Great Britain and Russia agreed not to compete, but only after a lively contest which is worth summarizing here. In 1897 a Belgian syndicate obtained a concession [3] to connect Peking, in north China, with Hankow, on the Yangtse, by rail, and it was reported later that Belgian interests were to build railways across central China, from east to west. The meaning of this concession becomes clear when it is explained that the Belgian syndicate was acting in conjunction with French and Russian interests; operating through this "Belgian" syndicate, Franco-Russian finance [4] would construct a great system of railways dominating Central China and connecting the Russian railways in the north with the French in the south of China. It would also cut across the British sphere in the Yangtse valley. With extraordinary heat the British foreign minister, Lord Salisbury, instructed the British minister at Peking to protest

[1] *China No. 1 (1899)*, nos. 2, 31.

[2] MacMurray, p. 266; *Die Grosse Politik,* 16, ch. CV.

[3] MacMurray, pp. 145, 148, 135, 462.

[4] The prospectus showed that three-fifths of the loan for the Peking-Hankow line came from France—*China No. 1 (1899)*, nos. 135, 139, 175, 196, 239, 278, 286; *Documents Diplomatiques, Chine, juin-octobre 1900*. p. 23.

that "a concession of this nature is no longer a commercial or industrial enterprise and becomes a political movement against the British interests in the region of the Yangtse. You should inform the Tsungli-Yamen (Chinese Government) that Her Majesty's Government cannot possibly continue to cooperate in a friendly manner in matters of interest to China, if, while preferential advantages are conceded to Russia in Manchuria and to Germany in Shantung . . . these or other Powers should also be offered special openings or privileges in the region of the Yangtse."[1] When China, not daring to offend France and Russia, sanctioned the "Belgian" concession for the Peking-Hankow line, the British fleet was menacingly concentrated, and Mr. Balfour instructed the British minister at Peking to demand reparation in the form of concessions for British capital, and to threaten that if such concessions were refused, "we shall regard their (China's) breach of faith concerning the Peking-Hankow Railway as an *act of deliberate hostility against this country*, and shall act accordingly."[2]

This was indeed a strange method of obtaining Chinese consent to business propositions supposedly designed to benefit China. It was a threat of war. It put the British fleet at the service of British financiers in China. And in what Lord Salisbury called the "battle of concessions," Great Britain's method proved successful. China agreed to concessions for about 2,800 miles of railway (longer than the German Bagdad Railway in Turkey, or the Russian line in Manchuria) to be constructed by British capital.[3] The lines projected by the British would cross ten of China's twenty-one provinces, including Shansi and Honan, which were then considered to be very rich in minerals.

As one of the lines in which British capital was interested would run from Peking to Newchang, in Manchuria, penetrating the Russian sphere, the Russians became alarmed, and warm protests were exchanged between Petrograd and London.[4]

[1] *China No. 1 (1899)*, no. 175.

[2] *Ibid.*, nos. 286, 314.

[3] Comparative figures given in a letter from the British minister, MacDonald, show how well Great Britain succeeded. The British had secured nine railway concessions representing 2800 miles; the Russians, three, for 1530 miles; the Germans, two, for 720 miles; the French, three, for 420 miles; Americans, one, for 300 miles. The Belgians, it may be added, had the Peking-Hankow concession. Americans were interested in the Hankow-Canton line. See *China No. 1 (1899)*, no. 459; MacMurray, p. 149.

[4] *China No. 2 (1899)*, especially nos. 9, 23.

Finally, in April 1899, England and Russia came to an agreement which may be quoted as a sample of its kind:

1. Great Britain engages not to seek for her own account, or on behalf of British subjects or of others, any railway concessions to the north of the Great Wall of China, and not to obstruct, directly or indirectly, applications for railway concessions in that region supported by the Russian Government.

2. Russia, on her part, engages not to seek for her own account, or on behalf of Russian subjects or of others, any railway concessions in the basin of the Yangtse, and not to obstruct, directly or indirectly, applications for railway concessions in that region supported by the British Government.[1]

It was a strange mixture of business and politics—all this negotiation about railway construction. In most cases, the primary factor was the desire of a group of capitalists to obtain the diplomatic backing of its own government in order to secure profitable contracts, and to ward off foreign competitors.[2] Thus in 1898 the manager of the Hongkong and Shanghai Banking Corporation, a British concern, wrote a letter to the British Foreign Office, announcing that a syndicate of British capitalists was to be formed, and asking that the British minister at Peking should be instructed to give them "such support as they may require" in obtaining railway concessions from the Chinese government.

It is significant that before making this plea, the bank had hitherto worked with the German syndicate for the construction of railways in China, but, in order to enlist the aid of the British Foreign Office it severed its German connection, and represented itself as the champion of British, rather than of international financial interests.[3] Thus finance became nationalized, at least to a degree sufficient for the purpose of gaining national support. As a matter of fact, it was impossible to avoid some entanglement; railways built by British capital and those built by Ger-

[1] *Ibid.*, nos. 84-138; MacMurray, p. 204.

[2] In the case of Great Britain, interests such as the Hongkong and Shanghai Bank and Jardine Matheson Company were supported by powerful financial syndicates in Great Britain, and by such organizations as the China Association and the London and Liverpool Chambers of Commerce. *Cf. China No. 1 (1899)*, nos. 380, 25, 214, 456.

[3] This bank was organized in 1865 and had become a very important concern, with paid-up capital of ten million dollars and a reserve of eight million. *China No. 1 (1899)*, no. 5; *Banker's Magazine*, Feb. 1899 and Apr. 1902.

man capital had to cooperate, to some extent; and in one of the biggest British railway ventures in China Italian capitalists enjoyed an interest.[1]

Indeed, from an economic point of view, it was a sad mistake to regard Chinese railways as separate British, German, French, or Russian ventures; it would have been to the economic benefit of all concerned had the railways of China been planned as mutually dependent links in a unified system, laid out so as to develop the country in the most efficient way. But the banking concerns competing for Chinese railway contracts were less interested in the economic welfare of the whole country, and ultimate profitability of the railway system, than in the immediate advantage of obtaining for themselves big concessions, by enlisting diplomatic aid. And the diplomats readily joined hands with the bankers, and made the gaining of a concession, as Lord Salisbury said, not a purely industrial proposition, but a "political" matter.

The diplomats went further. Not content with marking out a sphere of interest in which its own capitalists would have a monopoly of railways and mines, each Government looked beyond, to the day when economic partition would be followed by territorial partition of China. For example, France in 1898 obtained from China a promise never to cede or lease any part of the three southern provinces and the Island of Hainan to any power other than France. England obtained a similar pledge regarding the provinces in the Yangtse basin.[2] In other words, each regarded its sphere of interest as the part of China which would fall to its lot when and if China should be dismembered. Russia would have Manchuria and all the territory north of the Great Wall; Germany, Shantung; France, the three southern provinces; and Great Britain, as usual, would carry off the richest share, the great Yangtse basin, with perhaps the mineral regions of Honan and Shansi.

This was imperialism, and short-sighted imperialism. It made the Far East in all earnest a "storm-center" of world politics. It was an extremely important and irritating factor in the relations between England and Germany at the opening of the

[1] Also MacMurray, pp. 537, 747, on the Anglo-French-Belgian combination of 1905 back of the Chinese Central Railway Company.

[2] *Ibid.*, pp. 98, 104, 123, 126.

twentieth century. It brought Anglo-Russian rivalry to such a pitch that more than once war was threatened, and England joined with Japan in an alliance (1902) originally directed against Russian aggression,[1] but subsequently utilized for Japan's own aggrandizement in a most provocative manner. The reaction in China against European imperialism was nothing less than a calamity, as will be explained presently.

As far as the United States was concerned, the events of these years, from 1895 to 1900, gave rise to grave concern. American commerce with China and Japan had grown to large proportions, and not without anxiety could the merchant princes engaged in this trade witness the monopolistic tactics of Europe in China. As a faithful solicitor for American business interests, Secretary Hay in 1899 addressed a circular note to the Great Powers, asking them to respect what is now generally known as the "Open Door" principle. Specifically, Hay's celebrated note asked that each power claiming a "sphere of interest" should pledge itself: (1) not to interfere with any treaty port or "any vested interest" in its sphere; (2) to permit the application of the Chinese treaty tariff to ports within its sphere without discrimination against other nations; (3) to maintain equal harbor duties and railway rates for all nationalities. This set of principles shows clearly enough that Hay was interested in American commerce, rather than in American investments, in the Far East; he was defending commercial equality, and ignoring the vital factor, the building of railways, which carried with it the opening of mines and the virtual monopolization of trade in the region traversed by the railways. To Hay's note Germany, Great Britain, France, and Japan, agreed, on condition that the other Powers do likewise; Italy (not having any sphere of interest) agreed readily enough; but Russia ignored point three. Hay, however, considered the replies satisfactory, and announced that the pledge would be regarded as "final and definitive."[2] It was anything but final. During the next two decades the Washington Government was to give much attention to what Hay had overlooked, namely, the fact that when American

[1] *Ibid.*, p. 324.

[2] *Ibid.*, pp. 221-235. Compare Hay's broader circular of July 3, 1900, p. 308; Anglo-German open door agreement of Oct. 16, 1900, p. 263; Thayer, *Life of John Hay*, ch. 26; Dennett, *op. cit.*, ch. 22; M. J. Bau, *The Open Door Doctrine in Relation to China.*

capitalists attempted to build railways in China and share in the profits of developing that country, they came up short against a stone wall of monopoly, for the European "sphere of interest" doctrine meant monopoly of railway and mineral development.

The Boxers

As regards China, the effects of the leasing of ports and demarcation of spheres of interest were unfortunate in the extreme. On the eve of the scramble for leased ports, the young and impressionable Chinese Emperor, Kwangsu, had issued a series of reform edicts, in 1898, in the hope that China would modernize herself no less successfully than Japan. Peking University was to be reorganized on modern lines; schools and academies were to be opened in the larger cities for instruction in modern European civilization; the civil service examinations, hitherto based on the Chinese classics, were to be revised; railway and mining development was to be encouraged; the budget was to be balanced and the host of officials reduced in the interest of efficiency and economy. Rash and over-enthusiastic the young Kwangsu may have been; but Japan was regenerated by young men, and few great transformations have been achieved without the enthusiasm which scorns tradition and overleaps practical obstacles. However, in addition to the discontent naturally engendered by such reforms, Kwangsu suffered in popularity because of the leasing of ports to foreigners, and these elements of opposition were skilfully utilized by an elderly but decidedly vigorous lady, Tsze-Hsi, Dowager Empress, who had been living in retirement on the Mount of Ten Thousand Ages.

One day in September, 1898, this lady firmly seated herself in her sedan chair and ordered her eunuchs to carry her down to the imperial palace. There, with the aid of a treacherous general, Yuan Shih-kai by name, she seized the Emperor, made him acknowledge her as regent, executed his liberal advisers, cancelled his reform edicts, and set her face against all innovation and all European influence. In particular, an Imperial decree of Dec. 18, 1898, announced that no more railway projects would be entertained, for the present, by the Chinese Government.[1] The reform movement was nipped in the bud. Worse

[1] *China No. 1 (1899)*, no. 428.

still, a virulent type of reactionary and anti-European agitation was encouraged more or less secretly by the Dowager Empress, and in 1899 there began a series of popular attacks on missionaries and other foreigners. By 1900 the local riots had become an anti-European rebellion, and the European legation quarters in Peking, filled to overflowing with frightened foreigners, were being besieged by fanatical Chinese. This was the Boxer Rebellion, or Boxer War, so called because the leadership was taken by a Chinese organization whose name was rather inaccurately translated as the society of Boxers. The Boxers were not professional pugilists, but patriots, who believed in using force to expel the foreigners. That the Boxers believed themselves invulnerable to European bullets and considered their campaign as a religious war to prevent the desecration of Chinese soil by foreigners and their railways will perhaps indicate the nature of the movement. The law of physics that the reaction is equal to the action, was here exemplified in politics; the anti-foreign reaction was as unrestrained as had been the imperialist provocation.

The Great Powers rushed troops to rescue the legations at Peking, and to punish the Boxers. Great Britain, Russia, Germany, and the United States all contributed small forces, and, significantly, Japan was recognized as sufficiently Europeanized to participate in chastising her refractory neighbor. This joint intervention by five powers is interesting because it was an example of international cooperation; it had to be that, for no one power would have been permitted by the others to intervene alone. It was also more effective than most punitive expeditions undertaken by a single power. Chinese resistance was speedily crushed, Peking was taken, and the Boxer movement stamped out. The one shameful blot on the record was the looting of Peking by European soldiers—a wholly undesirable object-lesson in European ethics. And the punishment of China was unduly severe. It was well enough to execute guilty officials, and to exclude the rebellious districts from civil service examinations for five years, and to station legation guards at Peking, but the indemnity of $325,000,000 was unwarrantably heavy. The United States at least had the grace to remit part of her share of the indemnity, thus enabling China to use the relinquished funds for the education of Chinese students in America.

The Russo-Japanese War

While a few of the Great Powers, notably Great Britain, Germany, and the United States, declared that the Boxer War should not be made a pretext for dismembering China,[1] Russia endeavored so to use it. Russian troops, sent into Manchuria during the war, remained there. When Japan protested, Russia promised to withdraw them, but they still remained. Some Japanese statesmen felt that Japan would have to fight Russia; others, more timid, preferred to agree and cooperate with Russia. As so often happens in imperialist world politics, rivalry leads either to alliance or to war. While still uncertain which to choose, the Japanese carried on negotiations in Petrograd and London, and when London showed itself more hospitable to the idea of an alliance with Japan, the project of a Russo-Japanese alliance was thrown overboard. By allying herself with England, in 1902, with the declared object of preserving (against Russia) the integrity of China and the independence of Korea, Japan chose war with Russia. In 1903, more confident now, Japan demanded that Russian troops be withdrawn from Manchuria, and suggested that she might recognize Russia's interest in most of Manchuria, if Russia would recognize Japan's right to intervene in Korea (Korea being "independent" but dominated by Japan), and to build a railway from Korea into Manchuria connecting with the Chinese Eastern (railway imperialism again!). Russia dilly-dallied, refusing to give a definite answer, until Japan lost patience, withdrew her ambassador from Petrograd, and, on February 8, opened the war by attacking Russian warships at Port Arthur. The formal declaration of war came the next day. Japan was the aggressor, on the face of the record; yet Russia was at least as much responsible. The Tsar's cabinet ministers were determined to seize Manchuria without making any bargain with Japan. They were even endeavoring to gain concessions and political influence in Korea, which since 1895 Japan had considered as hers to exploit, reform, and protect. For Japan's imperialism in Korea little excuse can be offered, but for Japan's determination to prevent the insatiable Russian empire from seizing Korea—so close to Japan—

[1] MacMurray, p. 308; Thayer, *loc. cit.;* Dennett, *op. cit.*, ch. 23.

there was good reason. And if Japan began the war, it was in part because Japanese statesmen rightly believed that Russia was simply stalling for time, until her strategic railways were completed and her Far East fleet was unimpeded by winter's ice.[1]

It was a modern combat between David and Goliath. For Japan, a small and relatively poor nation, to attack the huge bulk of Russia seemed little short of suicidal, but Russia was handicapped by the impossibility of bringing her full strength to bear; her armies had to be transported thousands of miles over the Trans-Siberian's single track, and her European squadrons were unfit for battle after cruising half-way round the world. Furthermore, the Russian army of illiterate peasants, scandalously mismanaged by corrupt and incompetent generals, was opposed to an army carefully drilled, well equipped, and tremendously in earnest. With fierce determination the Japanese army besieged and captured the supposedly invincible fortress of Port Arthur; and, a little later, defeated a great Russian army at Mukden, in Manchuria, while on the high seas Russia's fleet of thirty-six ships, sent from European waters, was annihilated.

Japan was exhausted by the cost of the war; Russia had still great resources and might have sent new armies and fleets to the Far East. But both the German Emperor and President Roosevelt urged peace,[2] and at Roosevelt's invitation a peace conference was held at Portsmouth, New Hampshire, in April, 1905. The treaty of Portsmouth, Sept. 5, 1905, signed only after long haggling, transferred to Japan Russia's lease of the Liaotung peninsula, including Port Arthur and Dalny (renamed Dairen by the Japanese), along with the Russian railway extending north from Port Arthur to Changchun, and Russian coal-mining rights in Southern Manchuria. Southern Manchuria thus became a Japanese sphere of influence. Japan was recognized as having a preponderant interest in Korean affairs, and the right to protect and control the Korean government. In addition, Japan obtained half of the island of Sakhalin, just north of Japan, then considered relatively small in value though

[1] Hershey, *International Law and Diplomacy of the Russo-Japanese War;* Asakawa, *The Russo-Japanese Conflict;* Witte, *Memoirs.*

[2] *Die Grosse Politik*, 19, no. 6193; Dennett, *Roosevelt and the Russo-Japanese War.*

large in area, but recently discovered to possess oil and minerals of great value.[1]

This purely imperialist war had far-reaching effects. It gave rise to anti-Japanese feeling in America, where popular sympathy with the small power as opposed to an enormous and undemocratic empire soon gave way to suspicion and even fear of the "Yellow Peril."

In Russia, the war so damaged the autocracy's prestige that a revolution occurred, and a Duma was created. On European international relations the effects were many and significant. As Russia was the ally of France, and Japan the ally of England, there was danger that France and England might come to blows; realizing the danger, French and English statesmen decided to avert it by becoming friends if not allies, and the Entente Cordiale was concluded shortly after the first shots were fired in the Far East. This victory for French diplomacy spurred Germany to attempt first to wean the Russian Tsar away from the French alliance,[2] and, that failing, next to test the strength of the new French friendship with England by challenging France in Morocco, in 1905.[3] Instead of breaking up the French coalition, German opposition consolidated it; England drew closer to France and supported her throughout the crisis; and—as we have seen—England and Russia were brought together in 1907.

Japan, by victory in war, had achieved a recognized place among the Great Powers. Moreover, her alliance with England was renewed and strengthened, in August 1905. By the new treaty, each ally was pledged to aid the other in case of attack by any Power (hitherto any two Powers) on their interests in Eastern Asia and India. Instead of preserving the independence of China and Korea, the new pact accorded to Japan the right of guidance, control and protection as regards Korea. In other words, Japan could do what she liked with Korea. This bond was followed in 1907 by other agreements, with France and Russia, by means of which Japan was reconciled with Russia, and became practically a fourth member of the Triple Entente. Russia was to give Japan a free hand in Korea and southern

[1] MacMurray, p. 522.
[2] *Die Grosse Politik*, 19, ch. 138.
[3] *Cf. supra*, p. 202.

Manchuria; Japan would allow Russia to treat northern Manchuria as a Russian sphere of interest.[1]

It appears that President Roosevelt also gave his consent to Japanese plans. A secret memorandum, published in 1924, records the assurances given to Japan on July 29, 1905, by a representative of Roosevelt, that the United States would not oppose a Japanese veto on Korean treaties, and that the United States could be counted on to act in harmony with Japan to maintain the peace of the Far East. In return, the Japanese premier denied harboring any secret designs on the Philippines.[2] Roosevelt's policy of entente with Japan was reaffirmed in November 1908 by the Root-Takahira agreement, in which both powers agreed to respect each other's possessions, maintain the *status quo* "in the region of the Pacific Ocean," preserve the independence and integrity of China, and uphold the principle of "equal opportunity for commerce and industry of all nations in China."[3]

No serious obstacle remained to impede Japan's imperialist aims in Korea. The country was occupied by Japanese troops, and Japanese officials managed its government, though the Korean Emperor (he had assumed that title in 1897) still remained theoretically sovereign and independent. Year by year Japan tightened her grasp, and finally in 1910 the annexation of Korea was announced.

Revolution in China

On China the lesson of imperialism had been more and more strongly impressed. If the Boxer war had shown the futility of attempting to shut out the Western World, the Russo-Japanese War had quite as emphatically demonstrated the advantage of borrowing from the West the governmental, economic, and military methods which had enabled Japan within a few decades to become more than a match for Russia. The lesson was the more deeply impressed, because the Russo-Japanese War was fought largely on Chinese soil, and for the Chinese provinces

[1] MacMurray, pp. 516, 640, 657, and, for 1910 agreement on *status quo* in Manchuria, 803. *Cf.* Russo-Japanese treaty of 1916, *ibid.*, p. 1327. A. L. P. Dennis, *The Anglo-Japanese Alliances.*

[2] Tyler Dennett in *Current History*, Oct. 1924, p. 15.

[3] MacMurray, p. 769.

of Manchuria, while China's Government looked on helpless and aghast. Even the aged Empress-Dowager could see the handwriting on the wall. With the same vigor she had once shown in opposing Westernism, she now embraced it. In 1905 she began the reorganization of her army on European lines—a significant point of departure. She decided to encourage the building of railways, under Chinese control. Education in European science and modern languages was to be promoted. And the government itself was to be remodeled, as Japan's had been. A Commission sent abroad in 1905 to investigate constitutional methods of government, reported in 1906 that the Chinese government should be liberalized gradually. The Empress promised a constitution and the gradual introduction of representative assemblies. But when the Empress Dowager died in 1908, and a weak man was installed as regent for the infant emperor, the reform movement got out of hand. Just as Louis XVI of France provoked revolution by his vacillation in the face of the Estates General, so the new regent proved incapable of handling the provincial assemblies and the National Assembly which was convened in 1910.

The Chinese Revolution of 1911 may be traced to several causes, the most fundamental of which was the effect of European imperialism on Asiatic monarchy. Another general cause was the enmity of Chinese toward the Manchu dynasty. A more specific difficulty was the unwillingness of the provincial authorities to bear the burden of national railway loans, for the construction of a Chinese-owned railway system as planned by the central Government. But the immediate occasion of the revolution was an attempt of the Government to arrest a conspiracy which had been revealed by a bomb explosion. Various radical secret societies, it should be explained, had sprung up, especially in South China, where the European influence was strongest and oldest. These societies, exhilarated with the new wine of European ideas, aimed at the establishment of democracy and republicanism, rather than a cautious transition from despotism to constitutional monarchy. And in October 1911, when it seemed likely that a group of these radicals would be arrested and executed, they decided to strike. Revolution broke out in the Yangtse Valley and spread through the southern provinces. An exiled radical. Sun Yat Sen, was brought back to be President of the revolutionary Government. Against the revolutionists, the imperial Government sent an army under the ablest of its generals, Yuan Shih-kai, the man who had betrayed Kwangsu in 1898. And Yuan, instead of giving battle, came to a friendly agreement with the revolutionists, whereby the Emperor was to be dethroned, a republic established, and himself elected as President. In February 1912 the oldest of empires became the youngest of republics.

Great was the enthusiasm with which the Chinese Constituent Assembly met in April 1913, to draft the constitution for a republic of more than three hundred million souls; and great was to be their disappointment. For their disappointment there were several reasons, not all good, but all effective. One was the attitude of the foreign powers. Russia seized Mongolia. To be more exact, when the Chinese Emperor was dethroned, his vassal, the Hutuktu (the "living Buddha") of Mongolia refused allegiance to the Republic, or rather, the tribesmen of Mongolia, stirred up by Russian agents, took this action in the Hutuktu's name, and made an agreement with Russia whereby Mongolia was thrown open to Russian imperialism. The Chinese Republic of course protested, and would have endeavored to repress this insurrection, but Russia stepped forward as Mongolia's champion, and compelled China to recognize most of Mongolia (Outer Mongolia) as an autonomous province, over which China would retain a fictitious "suzerainty" while Russia would have a protectorate in all but name. The Eastern or Inner fraction of Mongolia was left under Chinese rule; it was left because Japan had eyes on it.[1]

Simultaneously, as if by preconcerted arrangement, England took similar action as regards Tibet; Tibet revolted against the Chinese republic; England forbade China to suppress the revolt, and proposed the division of Tibet just as Russia divided Mongolia. China in this case refused, but her refusal meant nothing, as she could not thereby regain actual authority in Tibet. Thus most of Mongolia and most of Tibet, the two great outlying dependencies of China, became, respectively, Russian and British spheres of interest, practically detached from China, though shown on the map as parts of the Chinese Republic.

Such foreign entanglements as these served to arouse resent-

[1] MacMurray, pp. 992, 1066, 1178, 1239.

ment in China not merely against Great Britain and Russia, but also against the Chinese President who permitted China to be despoiled, and who aspired to make himself dictator with the help of foreign gold. Yuan Shih-kai, praised in the European and American press as "the strong man of China" (there was a popular fancy for "strong" men at that period), had no sooner become Provisional President than he began to replace revolutionary officials by old-time bureaucrats, and to turn his hand against the radical majority, the Kwo Ming Tang or People's Party, in the Assembly. From the Great Powers of Europe—and Japan—he obtained a loan [1] without the sanction of the Chinese Parliament, and the money thus gained he used to run his administration and pay an army, while he crushed a republican insurrection in the South, expelled the People's Party from the Assembly, then dissolved the Assembly, and finally dared announce that he intended to restore the monarchy, with himself as Emperor. Yuan died without consummating his purpose, but the mischief had been done; he left China in the throes of civil war.

After Yuan's death the Republic survived, but without strength, or unity, or peace. More and more clearly there appeared other reasons why a stable and progressive republican government could not be easily established. Between the people of the North and the people of the South there were physical, linguistic, and cultural differences which made union difficult; for although China has one official written language, the oral expressions of that language in different sections are sufficiently diverse to be regarded as different tongues. Moreover, radical ideas of democracy and republicanism had gained a stronger footing in the South than in the North. One might add that many Southerners had never forgotten that centuries ago the capital had been in the South, before the alien conqueror, the Manchu, established Peking, "the northern capital," as the seat of the Emperor.

Another difficulty was the fact that for centuries Chinese officialdom had been accustomed to easy-going ways, with little central government and much provincial autonomy, and a great deal of what Americans call graft. These traditions remained strong and pernicious. Provincial military governors, "tuch-

[1] MacMurray, pp. 1007 ff; *China No. 1 (1912)*, Cd. 6446.

uns" they were called, had little regard for the weak central authority of the republic; they plundered their provinces, maintained separate armies, made war on one another or on the central Government, and occasionally a strong tuchun was able to overthrow the Government, and put puppets in the cabinet to do his will. And unfortunately it was usually possible for such trouble-makers to purchase arms from abroad, and in some cases financial aid was forthcoming from Japan.

It is impossible here to trace the rise and fall of the rival tuchuns and their political puppets. After Yuan's death General Li Yuan-hung as President and General Tuan Chi-jui as premier, with a clique of tuchuns of the northern provinces, dominated the Peking Government for a time, while Dr. Sun Yat Sen and the liberal leaders set up a separate Government in the South. Tuan and his clique were opposed by Chang Tso-lin, super-tuchun of the Manchurian provinces, Tsao Kun, another powerful general, and General Wu Pei-fu, who controlled the Yangtse provinces. These rivals, in shifting combinations, alternated as masters of the central Government. They made politics a synonym for civil war.[1]

Japan's Opportunity

While China's republic was going through its ordeal of blood and fire, the Great European War of 1914 began. The War afforded a splendid opportunity for Japanese imperialism. As the ally of England, Japan on August 15, 1914, gave "advice" to Germany to withdraw all German warships from the Far East and to deliver the Kiaochow Bay leased territory to Japan "with a view to the eventual restoration of the same to China." Receiving no reply, Japan declared war on Germany, August 23, and proceeded to capture the German territory. Although at the outset the Japanese premier solemnly declared "that Japan has no ulterior motive, no desire to secure more territory, no thought of depriving China or other peoples of anything *which they now have*," after the conquest had been made Japan remained in Kiaochow Bay, and soon revealed "ulterior motives" of a most ambitious kind.

[1] On the factors in the Chinese political situation see M. J. Bau, *Modern Democracy in China* (1923); E. J. Williams, *China Yesterday and Today* (1923), a most valuable study of Chinese conditions.

On January 18, 1915, the Japanese minister handed the President of China a most remarkable document, containing twenty-one demands, arranged in five groups.[1] Group One required China's consent in advance to whatever Japan might agree with Germany regarding German rights in Kiaochow Bay and Shantung. Group Two gave the Japanese the right to open mines in South Manchuria and Eastern Inner Mongolia, the right to purchase land, and an option on all railway construction and loans, and ninety-nine-year leases of Port Arthur and Dalny, and the Antung-Mukden, South Manchurian and Kirin-Changchun railways, in South Manchuria and Eastern Mongolia; in short, these provinces were to become a sphere of Japanese economic monopoly and colonization. But Japan was not content with clinching her hold on Shantung, South Manchuria and Eastern Mongolia. Group Three would convert the Hanyehping company, a great Chinese iron and steel concern, into a "joint concern of the two nations," and give the company a veto on the working of "all mines in the neighborhood" of its own. As the Hanyehping Company's mines and mills were situated at Hankow, on the Yangtse, this demand meant encroachment on the British sphere of influence; moreover, one of the demands in Group Five was for concessions to build several important railways, some of which had already been promised to British concerns, likewise in the British sphere of influence. Ironical in connection with the other demands was Group Four, which required that, "with the object of effectively preserving the territorial integrity of China," China should promise "not to cede or lease to a *third* power (note that this does not include Japan) any harbor, bay or island along the coast of China." The most extreme demands, however, were included in Group Five and characterized by the Japanese minister as "wishes." These would have put all China under Japanese tutelage, as a veiled protectorate. Japanese "advisers" were to supervise "political, financial and military affairs"; in the "important places in China" there was to be a joint Sino-Japanese police force; China was to buy at least half of her munitions from Japan, or from a joint arsenal using Japanese material and employing Japanese experts. China would be a Japanese Egypt. Further,

[1] MacMurray, p. 1231; Reinsch, *An American Diplomat in China*, chs. 11-12.

Fukien province, opposite the Japanese island of Formosa, was to become a Japanese sphere of interest. And Japanese were to have the right of religious propaganda in China, hitherto accorded only to Christians.

So stubborn was China's resistance to the Twenty-One Demands, that after almost four months of wrangling Japan presented an ultimatum demanding immediate consent to all but five of the demands. These five, relating to advisers, schools and hospitals, the railways in the Yangtse valley, arsenals, and Buddhist propaganda, were to be postponed. To the threat of war, China yielded, and sixteen of the Twenty-One Demands were incorporated in a series of treaties and notes signed May 25, 1915.[1] Shantung, Fukien, Eastern Mongolia, as well as Southern Manchuria, were now Japanese spheres of influence, and the biggest iron concern in the Yangtse was to borrow money only from Japan.

In normal times, the European powers would not have tolerated such aggression, unless they received compensatory gains. But Europe was deadlocked in the trenches of Flanders and Champagne and Poland. Japan had a free hand. Even when the Allies desired, in November 1915, that China should enter the war on their side, Japan was able to veto the plan; it was not well that China should organize an efficient army. China did enter the war, later, in August 1917, but by that time China had been so weakened by internal civil strife that Japan was fairly confident of being able to control the situation.[2] Moreover, Japan had succeeded in extracting from the Allies secret promises to support her claims at the Peace Conference.[3]

The United States Government, too, was disinclined, after entering the war, to oppose Japan, for Japan was one of the "Allies." Secretary Lansing went so far as to exchange notes with Viscount Ishii, on Nov. 2, 1917, recognizing that "territorial propinquity" gave Japan "special interests" in China. Probably Mr. Lansing did not fully realize the import of this acknowledgment; in the customary language of imperialist diplomacy it would permit much Japanese aggression in China, even though time-honored and ineffectual formulas such as "the

[1] MacMurray, p. 1216.

[2] See interesting reminiscences of Paul S. Reinsch, *An American Diplomat in China*, chs. 21, 24.

[3] Temperley, *History of the Peace Conference*, VI, p. 634, texts.

territorial sovereignty of China'' and ''the principle of the so-called 'open door' or equal opportunity for commerce and industry in China'' were reaffirmed in the Lansing-Ishii notes.[1] Japanese statesmen interpreted the agreement as a permission to pursue their imperialist policy. China being in turmoil, and venial politicians at Peking being willing to promise anything to obtain loans, Japan found it an easy matter in 1918 to obtain additional railway concessions in China, and to make a secret military agreement with a pro-Japanese Chinese cabinet, allowing Japanese troops to operate on Chinese soil in Manchuria.[2]

Not only in China was Japanese imperialism intrenched during the war, but also in Russia. With Russia Japan had made a secret treaty,[3] practically an alliance, in July 1916, providing for joint action against any attempt of another power to dominate China; but when Russia became Bolshevist, in 1917, the secret alliance was, of course, discarded, and Japan could despoil her former ally. In ''cooperation'' with China, Japanese troops now occupied the Russian sphere of influence in northern Manchuria. But there was an even greater prize within reach. Eastern Siberia, vast and thinly populated, rich in minerals, lay to the north, inviting seizure. President Wilson, however, would not permit Japan to intervene, single-handed, in Siberia. Not until August 1917 did he consent to intervention, and then only on condition that it should be joint intervention, no one of the Allies being permitted to send more than 7500 men. Nevertheless, Japan soon had seventy thousand soldiers in eastern Siberia, and was flooding the country with Japanese merchandise.[4]

The end of the Great War, in 1918, found Japanese imperialism triumphant in eastern Asia. Japan had added Shantung, Eastern Mongolia, Northern Manchuria, and Fukien to her spheres of influence in China; her troops were in Eastern Siberia, apparently to stay; and, in addition, by arrangement with England, the islands formerly possessed by Germany in the Pacific Ocean north of the equator had been occupied by Japanese forces. Japan dominated the Far East.

[1] *Ibid.*, p. 637. This agreement was cancelled as a result of the Washington Conference, *cf.* p. 356.

[2] MacMurray, pp. 1407-1415; 1448, 1450.

[3] *Ibid.*, p. 1328.

[4] See interesting details in Buell's *The Washington Conference;* Kawakami, *Japan's Pacific Policy*, chs. 33-38.

At the Peace Conference of 1919, however, the Japanese demand for the simple transfer to Japan of the German lease of Kiaochow Bay and the German railway, mining and other rights in Shantung, met with strong opposition from the American delegation, for the Americans felt that Kiaochow should be returned to China, as a matter of general principle. Only by threatening to withdraw from the conference, and by giving an oral promise to return Kiaochow to China, retaining only economic rights in Shantung, did Japan obtain President Wilson's consent to the clause in the peace treaty transferring the German rights to Japan.[1] These clauses were regarded in the United States as a flagrant and cynical violation of China's national unity.[2]

Few Americans realized that what Japan demanded in Shantung was no more than what she had obtained in Manchuria; that leased ports and spheres of influence were nothing new in China; and that Russia, Germany and France had in past years shown as little regard as Japan did now for Chinese rights. The really significant point in the whole matter was that by 1919 the seizure of Chinese territory seemed less permissible than in 1898 or 1905. It seemed less permissible because in the United States and to a lesser extent in Europe and even to some extent in Japan, the doctrine of self-determination had made headway, and because in China the younger generation, especially the college students, had become ardent national patriots, and bitterly resented any further encroachment on their country. Contact with Europe and with Europeanized Japan was making China, or at least young China, a nation.

The Washington Conference

The reaction against Japanese imperialism became more pronounced after the Peace Conference. Chinese merchants caught the spirit of the new Chinese nationalism, and boycotted Japanese goods. The United States Government protested against the continued Japanese occupation of eastern Siberia; and in the Senate at Washington, as well as in the press, Japan's retention of Shantung was denounced; and anti-Japanese senti-

[1] Baker, *Woodrow Wilson and World Settlement*, II, ch. 36.

[2] In the Senate reservations and in the American peace treaty with Germany the Shantung clauses were specifically repudiated.

ment in the United States reached a dangerous pitch. In Canada and Australia, moreover, there was strong opposition to the renewal of the Anglo-Japanese alliance, partly because it might offend the United States. Japanese imperialism had gone too far and too fast. Even in Japan there were liberals bold enough to oppose the aggressive policy of their government. But most serious of all was the fact that the United States was building superdreadnaughts more rapidly than Japan, with her small financial resources, could hope to do.

Out of this situation grew the Washington Conference of 1921-1922.[1] At that conference, the United States and Great Britain worked together with such effect that Japan found it expedient to purchase naval security by sacrificing, in part, her imperialism. Japan agreed to evacuate Siberia. She also agreed, by a separate treaty with China, to give up the leased territory of Kiaochow Bay, to sell the German railway in Shantung to China, and to allow the exploitation of the Shantung coal mines by joint Sino-Japanese companies. To make this surrender easier, Great Britain offered to give up the leased port of Wei-hai-wei, and the French delegate promised to relinquish Kwangchow Bay. Thus three of the leased ports were to be returned to China; but Great Britain did not offer to restore Hongkong, nor did Japan loosen her grip on Port Arthur. Nor had Wei-hai-wei and Kwangchow been surrendered when this was written.

At the Washington Conference Japan also consented to an Open Door Treaty signed by nine powers and embodying anti-imperialist principles advocated by the Chinese and by the United States. As defined by this treaty, the Open Door in China was to mean more than a nominal respect for China's independence and territorial unity, and more than equal treatment as regards tariff duties, railway charges, and harbor duties. It was to mean that the powers would not seek monopolistic economic rights in any part of China, or agreements "designed to create Spheres of Influence." This was a blow at the vitals of imperialism. The conference also resolved that in the future there must be no secret agreements with or concerning China; this struck at the chief method of the old imperialist diplomacy. Moreover, the conference formally voiced its hope that China

[1] Buell, *op. cit.; cf.* Willoughby, *China at the Conference;* Kawakami, *Japan's Pacific Policy.*

would unify the various Chinese railways into a national railway system, under Chinese control, employing such foreign financial and technical assistance as might be needed; this was a definite repudiation of the railway imperialism that had prevailed since the 1890's, the building of railways in China as separate enterprises under British, or French, or German, or Russian, or Belgian, or Japanese control.[1]

Were the principles enunciated by the Washington Conference to be fully carried out, China would be emancipated from the most undesirable features of European and Japanese imperialism, and the imperialist policies that had prevailed since about 1895 would be suddenly reversed. Unfortunately these were declarations of principles, not tangible and specific alterations of fact, and in world politics declarations of principles have not always been strictly observed in practice. How effective the principles would be in this case, was a matter of dispute. Some critics believed that despite the principles, Japanese imperialism would in reality be unrestrained, because at the Washington Conference the United States and Great Britain promised not to fortify their island possessions in the Pacific (not including Hawaii), and without fortified naval bases it would be difficult for either to undertake naval action against Japan. "There is only one force which can now be brought to bear upon Japanese imperialism," writes Professor Buell in his book on the Washington Conference, and that force "is world opinion." World opinion is the only force that can check Japanese imperialism without substituting for it some other imperialism.

The Stakes of Imperialism

It is time to take stock of imperialism in the Far East. The stakes for which imperialists have contended in eastern Asia are so enormous as to beggar description. China, let it be remembered, is with her dependencies a third larger than the United States in area, and three times as populous. Add Great Britain (without her colonies), and France, and Germany, and Italy, and Japan together, and you would have a nation a fifth as large as China, and only three-quarters as strong in man-

[1] These principles should be studied in connection with the Consortium, *cf. infra*, p. 370.

power. Then remember that in China there are beds of coal and ores of iron, besides tin and other minerals, and an unknown quantity of oil, that will provide the vital raw materials for an incalculable industrial development. As a nation, and as an industrial power, China may one day be so gigantic that one will wonder how the so-called "Great" Powers of the early twentieth century could ever have laid the shackles of their imperialism upon her. And besides China, there is Eastern Siberia, vast in extent, an undeveloped country.

European and Japanese imperialists, however, have looked primarily to immediate profits, rather than to ultimate results. Their concern has been with their own generation. The stakes in which they have been interested are the Chinese railways, and mines, and commerce, and loans, and, naturally, the strategic and territorial accompaniments of such economic affairs. In the half-century since 1876, about eight thousand miles of railway have been built in China; this in itself meant the investment of hundreds of millions of dollars of foreign capital. The mines of coal, iron, copper, tin and antimony have been developing rapidly; they represent a more or less speculative interest which is bound to increase in importance. Chinese commerce has developed from almost *nil* eighty years ago, to 1800 million dollars a year (average 1919-24). Japan obtained 24%, United States 17%, Great Britain 9% and the Anglo-Chinese port of Hongkong 25% of this trade. Chinese trade [1] means over two hundred million dollars a year to British merchants, chiefly British importers of tea and exporters of cottons; it means as much to Japanese importers of beans and beancake, silk and raw cotton, and Japanese exporters of cotton and metal goods; it means many millions to American cigarette manufacturers, to the Standard Oil, to silk dealers. Incidentally, the Chinese trade gives employment to thousands of British, Japanese, American and other ships. Finally, foreign bankers have lent China a billion dollars, usually at a relatively high rate of return, as the investment is somewhat risky; and in addition to these public loans, there must have been hundreds of millions invested in private commercial and industrial ventures, and in banking institutions in China. The stakes are large.

[1] Including Hongkong, although the British do not handle all the trade of this British port.

Among European powers, Great Britain obtained the largest share of these economic stakes of diplomacy, obtained them not so much through superior diplomacy as through more highly developed finance and trade. British capital built a sixth of China's railways; for years British merchants almost monopolized the China trade, and although they have suffered from Japanese and American competition, still Great Britain and Hongkong have about a third of it. French capitalists obtained the copper and tin mines of Yunnan, and, through Russian and Belgian syndicates, a considerable share of railway profits, but little commerce. Germany's modest share, in Shantung, was lost by war. Italy had almost nothing.

Bolshevist Russia at first seemed disposed to surrender what Tsarist Russia had won in the Far East. The Russian Communists denounced and renounced imperialism. Moreover, for a time, Allied troops occupied Manchuria and Eastern Siberia, and the Japanese occupied northern Sakhalin. But when the Allies evacuated Manchuria and Siberia, the Bolshevists engaged in a most interesting Far Eastern policy. To begin with, they reclaimed the former Russian territories, by reintegrating Eastern Siberia with Soviet Russia, and by persuading Japan—at the price of oil concessions—to relinquish northern Sakhalin.[1] They also made a treaty with China, May 31, 1924, whereby they renounced special rights and privileges, notably extraterritoriality, in China, and their share of the Boxer Indemnity, yet they asserted ownership of the Chinese Eastern Railway.[2] Generously, they agreed to permit China to purchase it—if China could raise the funds. But in the meantime a Russian was to be manager. Communism claimed to be heir to imperialistic capitalism. The claim was disputed, however, by the Russo-Asiatic Bank, which had financed the railway company and was now controlled by French financiers and non-Communist Russians. France and the United States also entered protests. Difficulties arose, too, with the Chinese war lord of Manchuria, Chang Tso-lin, who desired to use the railway for troop movements, without necessarily paying fares for his soldiers very promptly. In another quarter, Soviet Russia was even more aggressive than the Tsars had been. The old Russian Govern-

[1] Russo-Japanese treaty of Jan. 20, 1925, *Current History*, May, 1925, p. 240.

[2] *Current History*, Sept., 1924, p. 960 (text).

ment had made Mongolia a sphere of interest. Soviet Russia made it a soviet state, dominated by Russia. Despite these variations, the main trend of Russian Soviet policy in the Far East was propaganda against Anglo-American imperialism and capitalism. If such propaganda won converts in China, and if some Chinese politicians found Russian support useful, it was not surprising, nor necessarily ominous. Its chief immediate effect was to add additional complications to Chinese internal politics, while accentuating the Chinese reaction against foreign financial control.[1]

Japanese Imperialism

That Japanese business men and statesmen wished to share in the spoils was not at all surprising. That they should have gained so large a share was due to the accident of geographic proximity, and to the intense zeal with which Japanese militarists and millionaires plunged into the mêlée. By appropriating the Russian and German spheres of interest, and by utilizing the opportunity afforded by the Great War, Japan obtained first place in the Far East, from a political point of view; while in the economic exploitation of China, Japan is rapidly overtaking Great Britain and will doubtless soon surpass her. As I write these words, however, I realize that they misrepresent the situation. Political influence in China is a shifting, evanescent thing. And to view the Japanese commerce with China and Japanese investment in China, as "Japan's share" obtained by imperialism, is misleading; for without imperialism Japanese merchants would still trade with China, and Japanese capitalists would invest in China.

Specifically, Japanese imperialism has meant the annexation of Formosa and Korea and the virtual annexation (by a ninety-nine year lease) of a few hundred square miles around Port Arthur and Dalny in southern Manchuria, and the establishment of "spheres of interest" in Manchuria, Eastern Mongolia, Shantung and Fukien.

Formosa (Taiwan), an island about twice as large as the state of New Jersey, has proved a burden rather than a benefit to Japan since it was annexed in 1895. Japan has built many good

[1] H. K. Norton, "The Trouble behind the Trouble in China," *Asia*, Jan., 1926, pp. 26 ff.; Dennis, *Foreign Policies of Soviet Russia*, chs. 11-12.

roads, constructed 369 miles of railway, established telegraph, telephone and postal services, opened Japanese schools, encouraged mining and fishing and agriculture, all at a cost, and with small return. The taxes raised in Formosa have been insufficient to pay the cost of administration; even in recent years Japan has regularly paid a deficit of from five to nine million yen. Formosa produces most of the world's camphor, under a Japanese Government monopoly, and exports a few million dollars' worth of tea, sugar and coal to Japan, but the game is hardly worth the candle. Nor has the island proved an outlet for Japanese "surplus" population. After thirty years of Japanese rule there are only 167,000 Japanese on the island. Most of the population consists of Chinese, who frequently rebel and bitterly resent Japanese rule. In the mountains are about a hundred thousand aborigines, most of whom have been subdued, and compelled to become more or less civilized, even though many a Japanese soldier gave his life in the process.

Korea (Chosen) was a more promising colony. After the Japanese annexation, Korea's exports (chiefly rice, beans and cattle products) multiplied tenfold in ten years; the imports (chiefly cotton, machinery, coal, from Japan, and kerosene from United States) were multiplied by seven; and Japan enjoyed the bulk of the growing trade. The development of Korea's abundant coal and iron resources, restricted to Japanese corporations after 1916, was retarded by lack of transportation facilities, yet the yield of minerals rose from six million to twenty-five million yen in ten years. Moreover, the abundance of cheap Korean labor enabled Japanese capitalists to establish numerous and profitable factories. Materially, Korea was benefited. Handsome government buildings, neat railway stations, up-to-date school buildings, 1500 busy factories, gave the country a progressive appearance, and impressed foreign visitors with the efficiency of Japanese administration. The Japanese official reports on the administration of Korea tell of reforms and progress. Koreans, on the other hand, complained that Korea became "a paradise for Japanese loan sharks and speculators"; that intellectual liberty was strangled; that Korean farmers were systematically driven off their land, to take refuge in Manchuria. A report made to the Presbyterian Board of Foreign Missions stated that nearly half a million Koreans had fled across the border.[1] If this is true, the exodus of Koreans was greater than the influx of Japanese immigrants; for only 337,000 Japanese were counted in 1924. The Japanese, it may be added, preferred to live in the towns, as tradesmen, rather than to engage in farming. It is easy to see why the Koreans should feel that they were being reduced to the position of "hewers of wood and drawers of water." And it was almost inevitable that sentiments of nationalism and therefore of rebelliousness should spread among a population of eighteen million Koreans, governed by alien officials. The Korean nationalist agitation flared up at the close of the Great War, when nations everywhere were demanding self-determination. But by ruthless repression of the insurgents and imprisonment of suspects, Japan suppressed the movement, for the time being. Korea was a rich colony, but would Japan be able to hold it permanently, in the face of Korean nationalism?

As I write I have before me a beautifully illustrated little book entitled *Manchuria, Land of Opportunities.* It shows handsome hotels and banks in the port of Dairen (Dalny); it pictures "the famous South Manchuria Railway Express, the only train in the Orient with all-American equipment"; there is a photograph of the great coke ovens of the Anshan Steel Works in South Manchuria, and a snapshot of an American steamshovel at work in the Fushun collieries; and another picture shows an endless vista of bags of soya beans, piled high in the railway yard at Changchun, awaiting shipment to Japan. That, perhaps, is the best summary of what Japan has done in Manchuria. The book is distributed free of charge by the South Manchuria Railway Company, a concern partly owned by the Japanese Government. With property, valued at $700,000,000, and share capital of $220,000,000, this company has made net profits rising from one million dollars in 1907-8 to thirty-one in 1921-22. Its dividends have risen to ten per cent. The Japanese sphere of interest in Manchuria is a matter of ten per cent dividends. It is not a matter of colonization; Manchuria is inhabited by about fifteen or twenty million Chinese, mostly hard-working farmers —the exact number is uncertain.

[1] Henry Chung, *The Case of Korea*, pp. 115-117. This is a typical presentation of the case against Japan, to be balanced against the reports of the Government-General.

Japanese imperialism rests its case, as popularly presented, on four arguments. *First,* that Japan has a "surplus population" for which outlets must be found. Japan's population is relatively dense, it is true, and appallingly poor, on the whole; but as must now be clear the territories Japan has annexed have not been outlets for population. Japanese prefer to remain in Japan, if they cannot gain admission to countries like the United States, Canada and Australia, where wages are high and profits easy. "Surplus population" is not a tenable argument for Japanese imperialism. *Second,* that Japan needs raw materials and food, especially rice and iron and coal. This, indeed, is true; it is true in one form or another of every industrial nation. The chief question is whether a nation should buy its raw materials or annex them. *Third,* that Japan has a civilizing mission in Asia; that Japanese imperialism means the economic development of Korea, or Manchuria, or Formosa, and efficient administration, and sanitation, and fine public buildings, and railways. This also is true, though the whole truth would include a statement that the mines and railways and fine buildings are owned by Japanese capital and the economic progress inspired by motives of profit for Japanese capital. *Fourth,* that Japan has the right, in self-protection, to declare a Monroe Doctrine for Asia, like the American Monroe Doctrine for the Western Hemisphere. This was one of the points for which Viscount Ishii tried in vain to obtain Secretary Lansing's approval in 1917; it is one of the most popular of Japanese imperialist arguments. It is true enough in a way. But it seems to ignore the fact that whereas the United States contains more than half of the population of the Western Hemisphere, Japan contains about six or seven per cent of the population of Asia.

The real causes for Japanese imperialism are chiefly the profit motive on the part of certain Japanese capitalists; the aggressiveness of the militarist class; and the supporting patriotism of the common people. Since the Revolution of 1867, a small group of military leaders, drawn largely from the old noble clans of Satsuma and Choshu, have enjoyed such influence in the Japanese government that, where military or naval interests have been concerned, the constitution and the parliament have been a sham. The militarists, like militarists the world over, have been intent on conquest, and have looked upon the Far Eastern situation almost exclusively from the point of view of warlike strategy. Opposed to them, there has developed a strong liberal movement among the bourgeoisie, and a demand for democracy on the part of the masses. In course of time, there can be little doubt, the liberals will triumph, the Japanese Government will be made genuinely responsible to the people, and the militarists will be forced into the background.[1] Such a change would not necessarily mean a total abandonment of imperialism—England and France reconcile imperialism with democracy easily enough. But it would probably mean the substitution of the more peaceful and subtle methods of economic imperialism, of investment and trade for the aggressive military imperialism of the old régime.

China's Risorgimento

Otherwise a clash must come with China, perhaps with the United States, perhaps also with the British empire. China, as we have repeatedly suggested, will not permanently remain an inert Gulliver, to be bound by Lilliputians. The present impotence of the nation which Napoleon described as a "sleeping giant," is not due, as one often hears, to an inherent inability to fight—there are more soldiers under arms in China to-day than in Japan, and they are continually fighting. Nor is it due to lack of capacity for organization—the strength of Chinese commercial "tongs" and boycotts is a marvel of organization. It is due, in the first place, to the weakness of the Chinese central government, and that is due primarily to the vastness of the country; and secondarily to historical traditions; and thirdly, to the diversity of vernacular languages. The factor of area, however, is very rapidly being overcome by railway and telegraph and postal service; these are unifying China. The lack of able leaders and of popular interest in the national government is being overcome by the rising generation of enthusiastic Chinese students, educated either in Chinese colleges or abroad, and ardently interested in methods of government as well as in

[1] In 1925 the franchise for the Japanese House of Representatives was extended to the common people, and the House of Peers was reformed. The crucial questions now are cabinet responsibility and the ordinance-making power of the Emperor.

the welfare of their country. The present generation of self-seeking "tuchuns," apparently devoid of patriotism, is likely to be followed by a generation of only too zealous patriots. And public schools are beginning to make some slight progress in the matter of linguistic unity.

China's impotence is also due to an economic backwardness that cannot long continue. Because China needed foreign capital to build railways, open mines and create factories, and above all, because the Chinese tax system was antiquated, China was a borrowing nation, at the mercy of creditors. The Chinese government could not raise adequate revenues from customs duties, because from 1842 on, the tariff was held down to a nominal five per cent (actually much less) by treaties which European powers had forced on Peking. In 1922 at the Washington Conference, China was given conditional permission to raise the tariff to an actual rate of five per cent, with provision for a further increase to ten per cent when the antiquated Chinese tax known as the "likin" should be abolished. In accordance with the Washington agreement, the five-per-cent rate was made effective at once, and in 1925 a Tariff Conference was held to discuss the proposed increase of the percentage. The Chinese demanded "tariff autonomy" and desired to impose different rates on raw materials, manufactures and luxuries, as so many modern nations do. The foreign Powers agreed to grant China tariff autonomy in 1929, but insisted on a low maximum rate—much lower than their own tariff rates—in the interim.[1] The internal taxes are obsolete; they are dishonestly collected; and some of them are pledged to foreign bankers. The revenue of the Chinese government is less than that of Japan, though China has six or seven times as many taxpayers, a considerably larger foreign trade, and infinitely greater economic resources. China's foreign debt of about two-thirds of a billion dollars, exclusive of railway loans which are taken care of by railway receipts, is less than Japan's foreign debt, and her internal debt is a mere trifle compared with that of Japan, or the United States, or any other Great Power; yet China staggers under the burden. However, the rapid development of railways, mines, factories and agriculture warrants the prediction that such a debt will be

[1] The rate had not been determined when this was written.

easily borne in the future. Since the importation of machinery was first permitted in China, in 1895, there have sprung up 19,000 factories employing power-driven machinery (1923), and the value of Chinese factory products exported annually has increased to about a hundred million dollars (in 1922). Hand in hand with this industrial development goes the development of capitalism, the increase of private wealth, the expansion of Chinese banks.[1] All this means clearly that China is becoming a great industrial power, which in turn means that China will be a Great Power. And against such a Great Power a comparatively small nation like Japan cannot safely continue the imperialist game.

Dollar Diplomacy

There is also the United States. President Wilson said in 1913 that the American interests in the Far East "are those of the Open Door—a door of friendship and mutual advantage." On the whole this is true, if we exclude the Philippines for the moment. It is to the interest of American exporters and importers, manufacturers and producers, to have the right of trading on equal terms with foreign competitors in the Far East. American exports to China were $24,628,000 in 1913-14, and $124,436,000 ten years later. It is to the interest of a considerable number of American capitalists to participate in lending money to China, or in financing Chinese railways.[2] There is also a strong missionary interest in China,[3] and a powerful popular sympathy with China's struggle for freedom.[4]

In pursuance of such interests, the United States Government, until the Great War, pursued with remarkable continuity its policy of advocating the Open Door, of protesting against, but not seriously attempting to prevent, the leasing of ports and demarcation of spheres of interest. This American policy conflicted, before the Great War, with British, Russian, French, as well as with Japanese imperialism. But the conflict with

[1] See *American Relations with China*, pp. 70 ff.

[2] See Dunn, *American Foreign Investments*, pp. 159-162; Pan, *Trade of the United States with China;* Nearing and Freeman, *Dollar Diplomacy*, pp. 35-66.

[3] See *The China Mission Year Book* and on Catholic missions Rev. B. Wolfertson, S.J., *The Catholic Church in China.*

[4] *American Relations with China* for a symposium of American opinions.

Japanese interests was becoming more acute before the war, and since the war has assumed first-rate importance.[1]

The crux of the matter has been the question of American participation in Chinese railway concessions and loans. In the first Battle of Concessions, in 1898, a valuable prize in the form of a concession for a railway from Hankow on the Yangtse to Canton in South China had been won by the China Development Company, a New Jersey corporation representing Standard Oil, the American Sugar Refining Company, and other interests.[2] The China Development Company also made an agreement in 1899 with British interests regarding their railway projects.[3] Americans, however, did not push the enterprise and consequently in 1905 the concession was cancelled and the company compensated by payment of $6,750,000.[4] American interests were given a new direction by Edward H. Harriman, the American railway magnate, who dreamed of establishing a round-the-world railway, and who hoped to obtain the South Manchurian Railway as one link in the globe-circling system. As Japan had just conquered this line from Russia, by the war of 1904-5, Harriman made a tentative agreement, in September 1905, with Prince Ito and Marquis Katsura for joint American-Japanese ownership and control.[5]

The Japanese Government, however, under the influence of business and military interests, dropped this plan, and likewise refused its consent to Harriman's scheme of purchasing from the Russians the Chinese Eastern Railway. Not to be defeated so easily as this, Harriman next considered the possibility of building a parallel line that would connect Chinchow (on the Gulf of Liao-tung and connected with Peking by rail) with Aigun on the north-Manchurian frontier, and thus with the Trans-Siberian. Willard Straight, at first as consul-general and later as representative of Harriman and his financial associates, negotiated an agreement, Oct. 2, 1909, according to which this line was to be constructed by a British engineering firm, financed by a group of American banks (J. P. Morgan

[1] See *International Conciliation*, No. 211; *Diplomatic Relations between the United States and Japan*, 1908-1924.

[2] Rockhill, *China Treaties*, p. 252; Reinsch, *World Politics*, pp. 128-9.

[3] Rockhill, p. 245 and *Parl. Papers, China No. 1 (1899)*, p. 322.

[4] MacMurray, p. 519; U. S. *Foreign Relations*, 1905, pp. 124 ff.

[5] Bland, *Recent Events in China*, ch. xi; Croly, *Willard Straight* p. 239; Straight, *Politics of Chinese Finance*, p. 4.

and Co., Kuhn Loeb and Co., First National Bank, and the National City Bank), and operated by an Anglo-American-Chinese company.[1]

Secretary Knox seized upon this opportunity to suggest to Great Britain his famous "neutralization" plan. In a memorandum, November 6, 1909, he wrote: "Perhaps the most effective way to preserve the undisturbed enjoyment by China of all political rights in Manchuria and to promote the development of those Provinces under a practical application of the policy of the open door and equal commercial opportunity would be to bring the Manchurian highways and the railroad under an economic and scientific and impartial administration by some plan vesting in China the ownership of the railroads through funds furnished for that purpose by the interested Powers willing to participate." He suggested that Japan and Russia might welcome this opportunity to shift part of their responsibilities and expenses in Manchuria. Of course the project should be made attractive to bankers by liberal terms, and the lending powers should supervise the railroad system for a period of time, and enjoy "the usual preferences for their nationals and materials." [2]

Knox's expressed hope that Russia and Japan would welcome the plan to share with England and America and Germany their spheres of influence in Manchuria, perhaps more inspired by suavity than by naïveté, was rebuffed without either. Russia pointed out that the Chinese Eastern Railway, the bonds of which were guaranteed by the Russian government, represented Russian economic and strategic interests in Manchuria which might be gravely injured by the projected Chinchow-Aigun line. Moreover, by a secret agreement of June 1, 1899, China had promised Russia an option on any railways built in the future from Peking to the north or northeast toward the Russian border, unless built with Chinese capital.[3] Japan simultaneously, on January 21, 1910, expressed her objections to the project, and reminded the American Government that "in the regions affected by the Japanese railways in Manchuria, there have grown numerous Japanese industrial and commercial un-

[1] MacMurray, p. 800.
[2] U. S. *Foreign Relations*, 1909, p. 211; 1910, p. 234.
[3] *Ibid.*, 1910, pp. 261 ff.

dertakings which owed their inception, as they owe their continual existence, to the fact that the Imperial Government, possessing the railways in question, are able to extend to those enterprises and to the persons engaged in them due protection and defense against attack and pillage by lawless bands that still infest the country."[1] Great Britain supported her ally, Japan, in this stand, as France supported her ally Russia.[2] Furthermore, in order to offer united resistance to American encroachment on their interests, Japan and Russia signed a convention, July 4, 1910, pledging themselves to cooperate in developing their respective railway lines in Manchuria, abstaining from competition with those lines, maintaining the *status quo* in Manchuria, and opposing interference with the *status quo*.[3] That *status quo*, of course, was a Japanese monopoly or sphere of interest in South Manchuria and a Russian monopoly in North Manchuria.

Defeated in Manchuria, the American bankers' syndicate was successful in the battle simultaneously waged for a share in the Hukuang Railway Loan, which was to cover the completion of the old Hankow-Canton railway project, besides the construction of important branch lines. Learning that the Chinese Government intended to award this big contract to a syndicate of German, French and British bankers, the American syndicate demanded the right to participate. Secretary Knox acted as their official champion, and when Knox appeared ineffective, President Taft himself, disregarding diplomatic practice, sent a personal telegram on July 15, 1909, to Prince Chun, Prince Regent of China, in which he said: "I have an intense personal interest in making the use of American capital in the development of China an instrument for the promotion of the welfare of China, and an increase in her material prosperity without entanglements or creating embarrassments affecting the growth of her independent political power and the preservation of her territorial integrity."[4] The weight of Taft's intervention helped to tip the scales in favor of the American group. The Deutsch-Asiatische Bank, the Hongkong and Shanghai Banking Corporation, and the Banque de l'Indo-chine took

[1] *Ibid.*, p. 251.
[2] *Ibid.*, p. 269. Sir Edward Grey's statement.
[3] MacMurray, p. 803.
[4] U. S. *Foreign Relations*, 1909, pp. 178, 144-215.

into partnership the Morgan-Kuhn-Loeb-First National-National City syndicate, and signed an agreement on May 20, 1911, to lend China thirty million dollars for the Hukuang railway system.[1]

The same four-power group of banking syndicates also drew up an agreement with China, April 15, 1911, to lend the latter fifty million dollars to be used in standardizing the Chinese currency and in promoting industrial enterprises in Manchuria, the bonds being secured by a surtax on salt and by certain taxes in Manchuria.[2] The Knox policy at last appeared to be on the way to success. The four-power group had invaded Manchuria.

The Consortium

This policy of internationalized financial imperialism was strengthened after the Chinese Revolution of 1911, when Yuan Shih-Kai sought a Reorganization Loan of $125,000,000. Russia (the Russo-Asiatic Bank) and Japan (the Yokohama Specie Bank) were now admitted to the combination. An agreement signed on June 12, 1912,[3] by the British, French, German, American, Russian and Japanese bankers, representing syndicates of powerful financial houses in their respective countries, established what has been known as the Six-Power Consortium of 1912. The six national groups were henceforth to share equally in the Reorganization Loan and in future loans. Just when the Consortium seemed well established, President Wilson was inaugurated, and on March 18, 1913, he announced that he did not approve American participation, because the conditions of the Reorganization Loan seemed to "touch very nearly the administrative independence of China itself." Wilson felt that the international financial monopoly might lead to objectionable and perhaps forcible interference with Chinese independence. Thus the Americans dropped out.[4] Then came the war, which ruled out Germany, and the Bolshevist revolution, which eliminated Russia.

During the war period, there was a return to the older methods of financial rivalry in China. Japan, as we have seen, presented her Twenty-One Demands, made several new loans

[1] MacMurray, p. 866
[2] *Ibid.*, p. 841.
[3] *Ibid.*, p. 1021.
[4] U. S. *Foreign Relations*, 1913, pp. 143 ff.

independently, and sought to strengthen her hold on South Manchuria, Eastern Mongolia, Shantung, Fukien. Americans, however, were not wholly idle. In 1916 the American International Corporation secured the contract for a loan of three million dollars to improve the Grand Canal.[1] At the same time Siems and Carey, a Chicago firm, got a concession to build 1500 miles of railroads in various parts of China.[2]

In June 1918, however, the State Department at Washington held a conference of representatives of the thirty-six American banks interested in Chinese finance, to discuss a revival of the Consortium policy. President Wilson apparently saw the problem from a new angle. International financial cooperation now appeared the best way to prevent China from becoming, through Japanese loans, a Japanese protectorate. A new Consortium was to be formed of American, British, French and Japanese banks, to share alike. The Japanese expressed their willingness, if Manchuria and Mongolia, Japanese spheres of influence, were excluded from the Consortium's operations. Obviously Japan preferred to play a lone hand there. The United States Government objected to any such exclusion. For several weeks the controversy continued, until the United States agreed that the Consortium would not attempt to internationalize Japanese vested interests, such as the South Manchuria Railway, and Japan came into the Consortium. The new Four Power Consortium agreement was signed in 1920.[3] Through all these tortuous financial maneuvers there ran the conflict between the imperialist doctrine of spheres of influence, of which Japan had become the chief protagonist, as regards Chinese affairs, and the American doctrine of equal opportunity. The Open Door Treaty of the Washington Conference of 1922 was a victory in principle for the American position, though in practice Japan was allowed to retain her vested interests. More and more clearly it appeared that the American tendency was to erase the partition lines which imperialists had drawn in China, and demand for ambitious American bankers their share in Chinese finance. Against American finance Japan had little prospect of waging a successful struggle. The attempt of the

[1] MacMurray, p. 1287.

[2] *Ibid.*, p. 1913. The terms are interesting. Compare Reinsch, *An American Diplomat in China*, ch. 18.

[3] Carnegie Endowment, pamphlet series, No. 40, *The Consortium.*

Japanese to float in the New York market securities of the South Manchuria Railway and of the Oriental Development Company was a significant indication that Japanese captains of finance saw a way out of the difficulty—cooperation.

CHAPTER XV

FORTUNES OF WAR AND PROFITS OF PEACE IN PACIFIC ISLANDS

The Setting

It has been said that just as the center of the civilized world was once the Mediterranean and shifted to the Atlantic in early modern times, so in the coming age it will move farther westward to the greatest of all oceans, the Pacific. The Pacific is almost as large as the other four oceans put together; it occupies more than a third of the world's surface; it is ten thousand miles across at the equator, and almost ten thousand from north to south. Its magnificent distances are an obstacle to present means of transportation, but the tendency of civilization has been to overcome distance. Certainly the last century has witnessed an amazingly sudden development of trans-Pacific commerce, and in our own day the mighty ocean has become the most important theatre of imperialist world-politics. If the population and resources of the lands which look out upon this broad expanse of water are any guide to its future importance, the Pacific will be prominent in the history of coming centuries, for on its western borders lie Japan and China, and the rich but undeveloped realm of Siberia, and Indo-China, the East Indies, and Australasia, all together comprising a population of about half a billion, with immense resources and potentialities; while on the east lie the most rapidly developing countries in the world, United States and Canada, and ten Latin-American republics.

These considerations lend enhanced significance to the several thousands of islands which lie scattered across the Pacific. Even small islets may be of large importance as naval and coaling depots, or cable landings, or radio stations. The tiny island of Yap, as a cable and radio station, is not so small that it could not excite serious controversy between two great Powers and figure in the headlines of newspapers in cities ten thousand miles to the east.

But some of the islands are important for their own sake. On the ordinary mercator's map, which compresses areas in the tropics and expands the arctic zones, these islands appear much smaller than they really are. Borneo, for example, is bigger than Germany; New Guinea, larger than France and Italy; Sumatra as large as Great Britain; Java, larger than Portugal; Celebes, equal to Austria and Hungary; the Philippines as large as Rumania; New Zealand, larger than Yugoslavia; and Australia would account for most of the remaining countries of Europe. The islands lying on the southwestern border of the Pacific are another Europe. In population, it is true, they are less considerable, but not so insignificant as is generally supposed. The Philippines, for instance, contain a larger population than Canada; the Dutch East Indies are more important, both in area and in population, than France, or Italy, or the British Isles.

The natives of the islands are of many races, which for our purposes may be considered as falling into three principal groups. First, in the islands of Polynesia (the "many islands") scattered in the mid-Pacific from Hawaii in the north to Samoa and Easter Island in the south, live the Polynesians, tall, well-built, copper-colored, intelligent, capable of assimilating Western civilization easily, but averse to labor; these are the attractive "South Sea Islanders," whose surf-boards, and dances, and idleness, and picturesque customs have kindled the imagination of urbanized Americans. The second and most important group consists of the Malays, also copper-colored or brown of complexion, with straight black hair and the slanting eyes and short nose of the Chinese, intelligent and artistic, some of them civilized to the point of having a written language and of building beautiful temples. The Malays predominate in Java, Sumatra, Borneo, Celebes, the Philippines—in short, in the Malay Archipelago—as well as on the Malay Peninsula, which is more a part of the archipelago than of Asia. The third group consists of various black or chocolate-colored peoples, for the most part primitive savages. Among them are the aborigines of Australia; the Papuans of New Guinea (Papua), the Solomon Islands, and Fiji; and the Negritos or small negroes,

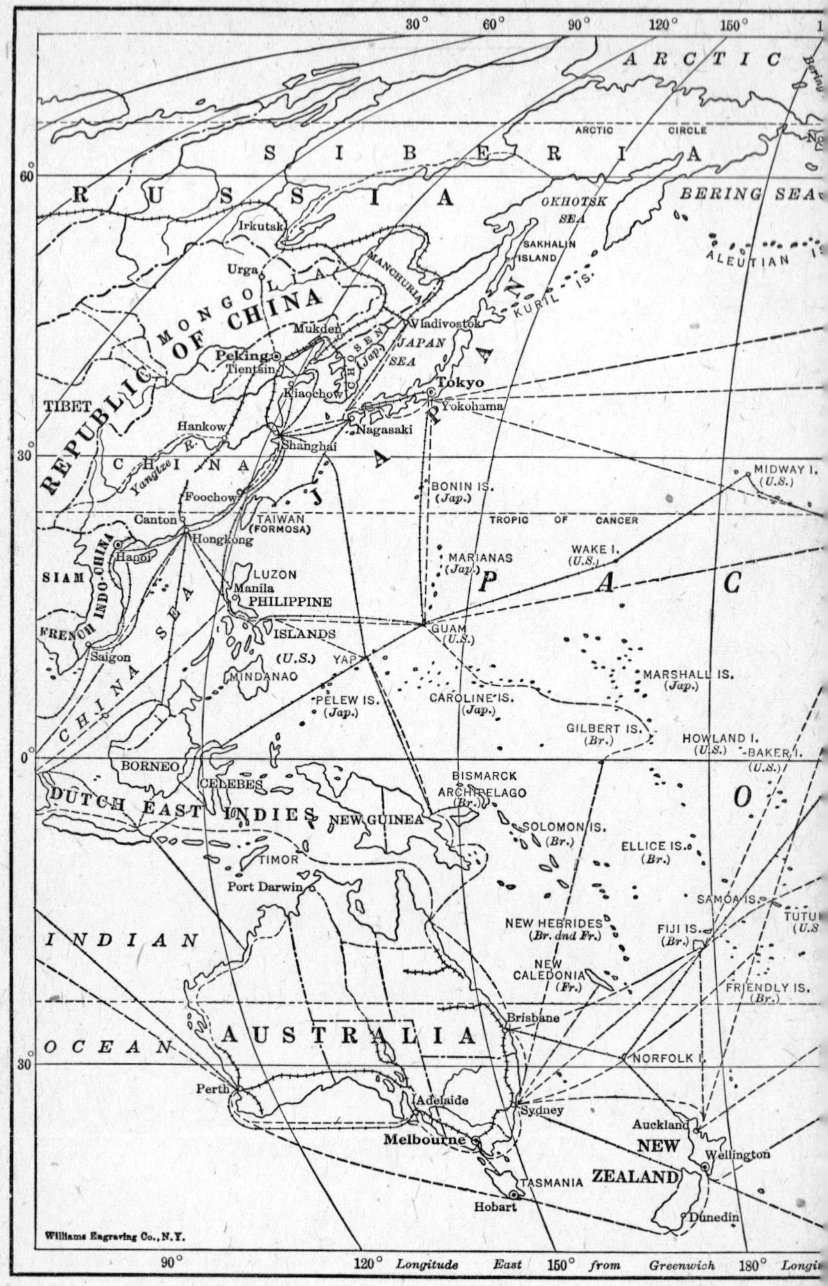

30°
60°
90°
120°
150°
ARCTIC
ARCTIC CIRCLE
SIBERIA
RUSSIA
BERING SEA
OKHOTSK SEA
Irkutsk
SAKHALIN ISLAND
ALEUTIAN
Urga
MANCHURIA
MONGOLIA
REPUBLIC OF CHINA
KURIL IS.
Mukden
Vladivostok
Peking
Tientsin
CHOSEN (Jap.)
JAPAN SEA
Tokyo
Yokohama
Kiaochow
TIBET
Hankow
Nagasaki
JAPAN
Shanghai
CHINA
Yangtze R.
MIDWAY I. (U.S.)
BONIN IS. (Jap.)
Foochow
TAIWAN (FORMOSA)
TROPIC OF CANCER
Canton
Hongkong
WAKE I. (U.S.)
Hanoi
FRENCH INDO-CHINA
MARIANAS (Jap.)
SIAM
LUZON
Manila
PHILIPPINE ISLANDS (U.S.)
PACIFIC
GUAM (U.S.)
Saigon
YAP
MARSHALL IS. (Jap.)
MINDANAO
PELEW IS. (Jap.)
CAROLINE IS. (Jap.)
CHINA SEA
GILBERT IS. (Br.)
HOWLAND I. (U.S.)
BAKER I. (U.S.)
BORNEO
BISMARCK ARCHIPELAGO (Br.)
CELEBES
DUTCH EAST INDIES
NEW GUINEA
SOLOMON IS. (Br.)
ELLICE IS. (Br.)
TIMOR
Port Darwin
SAMOA IS.
TUTUILA (U.S.)
NEW HEBRIDES (Br. and Fr.)
FIJI IS. (Br.)
INDIAN OCEAN
NEW CALEDONIA (Fr.)
FRIENDLY IS. (Br.)
Brisbane
AUSTRALIA
NORFOLK I.
Perth
Adelaide
Sydney
Auckland
Melbourne
NEW ZEALAND
Wellington
TASMANIA
Hobart
Dunedin
Williams Engraving Co., N.Y.
90°
120° Longitude East 150° from Greenwich 180°

TH

scattered through the Philippines and other Malaysian islands. This sketch will perhaps forestall any tendency to classify all "South Sea Islanders" as fierce headhunters, or, on the other hand, to regard them all as handsome and intelligent folk, devoted to strumming the ukelele.

Before the age of nineteenth-century imperialism, the Pacific islands, especially the East Indies, had been repeatedly subjected to conquest and invasion. The East Indies had once been overrun by Buddhists from India, as the remains of splendid Buddhist temples in the mountains of Java mutely attest. Later had come Arabs, who converted the Malays in the western islands to Mohammedanism. Then followed the Europeans, first Portuguese explorers in quest of spices, in the early sixteenth century; then the Dutch and English East India companies, contending for the spice trade; while Spain established missionaries and governors in the Philippine group. But in the nineteenth century European merchants and missionaries and men-of-war swarmed among the islands, and other Great Powers entered on the scene—France and Germany and the United States. And in the twentieth century, Japan. It will be simplest to consider each separately.

The Culture System in the Dutch East Indies

The Dutch empire in the East Indies is a heritage from the days when Dutch seapower was in its glory; when Dutch fleets were bold enough to beard the British lion in the Thames, or to prey on the colonies of Portugal and the heavy-laden galleon of Spain. In the seventeenth century the Dutch East Ind Company had ousted Portugal from the spice islands, and gun its long career of ruthless exploitation, exacting fixed q tities of spices from native Malay chieftains, forcing th tives to work, overcharging Europe for East Indian spice enriching fortunate Dutch stockholders. The Company h lapsed in 1798, however, and its island possessions wer over by the Dutch government, only to be lost to Engl ing the Napoleonic Wars and ruled for several yea celebrated Sir Thomas Stamford Raffles, before the turned to Holland in 1818.

It was no mean empire that Holland thus inhe

cluded the great islands of Java, Sumatra, Borneo, Celebes, and the Moluccas. To-day, though part of Borneo has been taken by the British, the Dutch East Indies total 734,000 square miles, fifty-eight times the area of Holland, and their population of forty-nine millions is seven times that of the mother-country. Says a Dutch historian:

> In the possession of her splendid Indian Empire, she (Holland) feels on a level with more powerful States; without it she would understand the bitterness of that saying of Leopold II of Belgium: "It is such an infirmity for a country to be small!" This is why the Low Countries . . . would shed the blood of their last soldier rather than abandon the Indies.[1]

Modern Dutch imperialism in the East Indies—or Netherlands India as the Dutch call their empire—has been largely a question of how best to govern and exploit the natives. In olden days, officials of the East India Company had been content to exact tribute in spices from the native chieftains, without establishing any elaborate administrative organization, or caring much about the labor problem, or concerning themselves with native education. But as the spice trade declined in relative importance, and other products, such as sugar, coffee, tobacco, tea, cinchona and cacao began to be cultivated, it became necessary to lay out plantations, and build roads, and, above all, to make the natives work. One Dutch governor, for instance, decreed that every village in a certain district must cultivate a thousand coffee trees per family, giving two-fifths of the crop to the government as a tax, and selling the other three-fifths to the government. The same governor, Daendels, built many roads by means of compulsory labor; he would make each village along the proposed route responsible for building a section of the road, and hang the village chief if the allotted section was not built.

More celebrated was the "Culture System" introduced in Java by Count Van den Bosch, in the 1830's. One-fifth of the natives' land was set aside to be cultivated for the government. The government decided what crop was to be cultivated on this land. And of course the cultivation was done by the natives, who were compelled to work one-fifth of their time without pay.

[1] A. Cabaton, *Java, Sumatra and the Other Islands of the Dutch East Indies* (1914), p. 371.

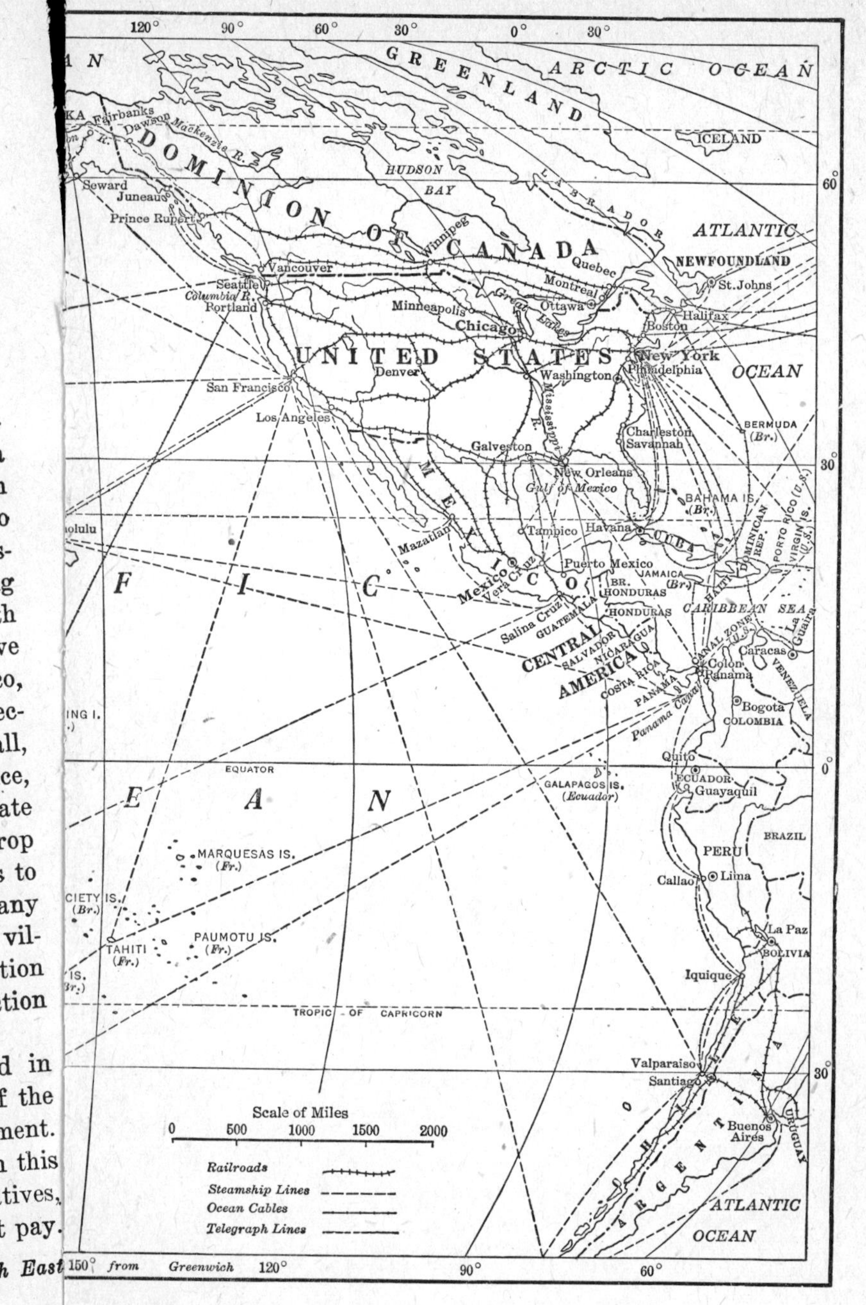

The Culture System enabled the government to extend the cultivation of sugar, coffee, tea, tobacco, indigo, pepper and cinnamon, especially sugar and coffee; in this respect it was perhaps beneficial. Moreover, the Dutch colonial budget—it was almost if not quite unique in this—showed a regular net profit from 1840 to 1874, chiefly from coffee and sugar; this profit, however, is explained by Professor Day in his penetrating study of Dutch colonial administration,[1] as the result of European price conditions rather than of the system. On the other hand, the natives performed the work unwillingly, and inefficiently; only coffee and sugar cultures were really profitable. Moreover, in some districts the natives were not allowed sufficient land or time to raise the rice they needed for food, and famines were frequent. The oppression and cruelty in the administration of the system were exposed in a book by Edouard Dekker, in 1860, a book which, like *Uncle Tom's Cabin,* stirred popular sentiment to the depths.[2] The liberals in Holland demanded reform. Between 1860 and 1865 the tea, tobacco, indigo, pepper and cinnamon cultures were abandoned, and after 1878 the sugar cultures were gradually reduced.

In place of the Culture System, "free labor" prevailed. The government compensated itself by levying a poll tax, in order to pay which the natives would have to work. Private proprietors were allowed to exact dues in labor and in kind from native tenants, and to appoint and pay village head-men or chieftains, who served as instruments in obtaining practically compulsory labor, in some cases. In other cases, Dutch planters employed the ingenious system of advancing two or three years' wages to a native, and then making him work to pay off his debt. It may be explained that although most of the soil had been claimed as government property, Europeans were allowed by a law of 1870 to appropriate waste lands for the term of seventy-five years; by 1920 a million and a quarter acres in Java were held, under this law, by 929 companies and Europeans.

[1] Clive Day, *The Policy and Administration of the Dutch in Java* (1904). On this subject see also Cabaton, *op. cit.;* A. G. Keller, *Colonization* (1908), pp. 463-95; Van Coenen Torchiana, *Tropical Holland* (1921); A. Ireland, *Far Eastern Tropics*, ch. 9; F. G. Carpenter, *Java and the East Indies* (1923).

[2] E. D. Dekker (pseud. Multatuli), *Max Havelaar, of de Koffiveilingen der Nederlandsche Handelsmaatschappy* (1860).

Instead of ruining the prosperity of the Dutch East Indies, the gradual substitution of private enterprise for government plantations, and of "free" or hired labor for the Culture System, produced effects which may be seen most clearly in figures. The total annual crop of coffee, in the old days (average from 1869 to 1878) was 6036 tons; in 1921 it was over 45,000. The sugar crop averaged 170,831 tons when the Culture System was in its glory (1869-73); it was 1,577,528 tons in 1920. The population of Java increased amazingly: from twenty million in 1880 to twenty-nine in 1900, to thirty-five in 1920. And the commerce expanded in volume until it reached the value, in 1920, of almost one and one-half billions of dollars (more than five times the trade of the Philippines, and almost three-quarters of the trade of Japan for that year).

Education goes naturally hand in hand with free labor. If natives are to learn to work without compulsion, they must be educated, for without education they are pretty generally disposed to follow nature's promptings. In the old days, Dutch administrators did not trouble themselves about educating the natives. But in recent decades they have rapidly established a system of native schools. In 1924 about 598,601 native children were attending *desa* or village schools, for a three-year elementary course, and a somewhat smaller number were attending other public schools with more thorough courses of instruction. The interesting thing about the Dutch school system is that it is not Dutch. Whereas Americans in their colonies try to duplicate "the little red schoolhouse," teaching Filipinos the same subjects that would be taught in America and in the same language, the Dutch, unlike most other imperialist nations, seem to feel little impulse toward making good Dutchmen out of the Malays. Instead, their schools use the native tongue, emphasize native literature, customs, music, and dancing, and omit such subjects as civics and European history. It has been called "an ostrich policy." It seeks to avoid the danger of breeding in the natives too great a familiarity with the ideas which have acted like social dynamite in Europe and in Europeanized countries. It is the only kind of education really suitable for imperialism, that is, for the permanent domination of one race by another.

Yet carefully as the Dutch have avoided "Europeanizing" the

Indies, they have not prevented the development of a native demand for representative government. Up to the last half-century, as we have said, the Dutch were content to govern largely through native chieftains; and this system still survives in great part. In Java and Madura, the most important and populous of the islands, there are seventeen provinces each governed by a native regent under the supervision of a Dutch resident, and with the aid of a hierarchy of subordinate local officials, natives, likewise with Dutch supervision. Outside of Java, there are several hundred native rulers, who govern with the aid of Dutch advisors or *controleurs,* and a number of native chieftains, in practically unconquered mountain regions, who do not even have this assistance from the Dutch.

In 1903, however, the government authorized the creation of municipal, district, and provincial councils, and in 1917 the capstone was put on the new system, by the creation of a Volksraad, or Assembly to advise the Governor-General, especially on the budget. This was a radical step for Holland, and it was taken because of the increasing demand for self-government, stimulated by the introduction of partial self-government in the Philippines and in India, and by the establishment of the republic in China. Yet the Dutch legislators did not throw caution to the winds; they would not have been Dutch had they done so. The Volksraad was given no power except to discuss and advise, and it was far from democratic. Half its members were appointed by the Governor-General, half elected by the local councils—and the local councils were limited to those who paid fairly heavy taxes and could speak and read Dutch. Only the richer natives had any voice at all, and the very small minority of Dutchmen, Eurasians, Chinese, and Arabs, being more wealthy and better educated than the natives, held half the seats in the Volksraad, in which "stalwart white-clad Dutchmen, marked by the air of mastery which distinguishes that race in the tropics, slim Javanese, Sudanese, Macassars, or other Natives, often wearing Bond Street coats and haberdashery in combination with Batik sarongs and Oriental footgear, and Arab Hadji in his fez, and impassive Chinese, all mingle together in the usual legislative fraternity."[1]

[1] Hayden, "Political Progress in the Netherlands Indies," *Atlantic Monthly,* Sept., 1924.

A motley assembly this, but an assembly which marks the beginnings of self-government in what had been regarded as a "colony of officials," governed by and for the Dutch.

The "impassive Chinese" mentioned above is worth notice. The census of 1920 revealed the presence of 878,986 Orientals, including a few Arabs and Japanese, but mostly Chinese. The Chinese outnumber the Europeans in the larger cities—more than three to one in Batavia, the capital city. As tradesmen and artisans they are more successful than native or European, and are rapidly becoming a very influential, though still a numerically small element in the population. If any alien nation is "colonizing" the Dutch East Indies it is not the Dutch, but the Chinese. There were only 169,355 European residents.

The comparatively recent development, on a considerable scale, of rubber plantations and petroleum wells has given the Dutch East Indies a sudden increase of importance in the eyes of great industrial powers seeking supplies of vital raw materials. For instance, in 1921, the Washington Government felt it worth while to conduct a heated correspondence with The Hague, because the Dutch Government had granted to the Royal Dutch-Shell syndicate an exclusive concession for the Djambi oil fields in Sumatra. In this matter, the Dutch worked hand in glove with British interests. In fact, the Royal Dutch Petroleum Company, the chief concern in the field, was allied with the Shell Transport, a British concern, by means of a holding company; and the head of the Royal Dutch-Shell syndicate, Henri Deterding, became a British citizen during the Great War.

The rubber plantations were not established until the twentieth century, but their output rapidly increased, especially after the British adopted the Stevenson scheme of restricting production. The plantations are by no means all Dutch in ownership: some are British, some American. And the crop goes largely to American tire manufacturers.[1]

Partly because of rubber and oil, partly perhaps because of Japan's aggressiveness in other quarters, and partly because Great Britain had begun to convert Singapore into a great naval base uncomfortably near the Dutch islands, there was in the years following the Great War a good deal of discussion

[1] On the rubber plantations see below, pp. 547-554.

of the future of the Dutch East Indies. Would Japan one day seize them? Did the Singapore fortifications portend a British menace? Such speculations agitated the public mind in Holland as well as elsewhere, and produced a violent agitation in the Dutch States-General over the question of increasing the Dutch navy, so that it might better defend the colonies. Dutch politicians, apparently, did not appreciate the humor of this. A few small Dutch warships would not protect the East Indies. Small nations hold colonial empires not by their own strength, but by their weakness. Their security depends on the unwillingness of world opinion to sanction spoliation, or on the unwillingness of some of the Great Powers to permit any one of their rivals to swoop down on a weakly defended morsel. And in the coming age, it will be more important for Holland to improve her colonial administration so that it will be beyond reproach, than to build battleships, if she is to retain the empire which Dutch patriots regard as Holland's salvation from insignificance.

The British Islands

The chief island empire in the Pacific area, that of Great Britain, is largely the product of nineteenth- and twentieth-century expansion. In earlier times, Great Britain neglected the Pacific, although, to be sure, the British East India Company did compete with the Dutch company in the seventeenth century for the spice-bearing islands. Crowded out of the East Indies by the Dutch, the British company concentrated its energy on building up an empire in India, during the eighteenth century. Great Britain, however, was not wholly inactive in the islands. British explorers during the second half of the eighteenth century cruised about among the smaller islands of the Pacific, usually tacking up lead plates or cutting inscriptions on trees, to claim for Great Britain the islands they discovered. Thus Wallis discovered Tahiti, and Carteret claimed the Solomon Islands, and the celebrated Captain Cook rediscovered and claimed New Zealand and Australia (previously known to the Dutch as "New Holland" and rechristened by Cook "New South Wales"). But most of these discovery-claims were ignored, for the islands, even Australia and New Zealand, were considered to be of little value. Australia, now so important a British possession, was then regarded as fit only for a penal station. The sending of a shipload of British convicts, in 1787, to Port Jackson (now Sydney) on the coast of New South Wales, seemed of little moment at the time. Who could foresee that it was the beginning of British Australasia? And when British forces seized the Dutch East Indies during the Napoleonic Wars, the British Government, instead of clinging to this possession, returned it to Holland in 1818.

Slowly British interest in the Pacific grew keener, as the nineteenth century progressed. Australia, though regarded as only a penal colony until 1840, began to attract free settlers, especially after the introduction of sheep-raising by McArthur in 1805, and still more after the discovery of gold in 1850. Colonists spread out from New South Wales, on the southeastern coast, into other parts of the island-continent, to found what became the separate colonies of West Australia (1829), South Australia (1836), Victoria (1851) and Queensland (1859), while the neighboring island of Tasmania, settled as a dependency of New South Wales in 1803, became a separate colony in 1825. The growth of these Australian colonies, due not to any imperialist policy, but to free immigration, lent new importance to the neighboring islands, and became in time the chief factor in British imperialism in the Pacific. With the spirit of pioneers and frontiersmen, the Australian colonists have been much more eager than London officials for the annexation of other islands.

Thirteen or fourteen hundred miles east of Australia lie two large islands and many smaller ones, all together as large as the state of Colorado, which were inhabited by Polynesian tribes, the Maoris, of cannibalistic proclivities but nevertheless hospitable to the traders and missionaries who frequented their shores in the early nineteenth century. The missionaries, indeed, were able to induce the native chieftains to ask for British protection. But the indifferent London Government was willing neither to grant this request nor to sanction the scheme of Gibbon Wakefield and his New Zealand Association, which desired to buy land in New Zealand and settle British emigrants there. Wakefield went ahead, without official permission, and the first shipload of English colonists arrived in January 1840. This act, in conjunction with a report that a

French company was intending to colonize the islands, forced the Government's hand, and reluctantly the cabinet sent a governor to make New Zealand a British colony. The governor arrived in January 1840, and in the following month, with the aid of missionaries, negotiated a treaty with the Maori chiefs, recognizing British sovereignty, but guaranteeing the natives the right of possessing their lands as long as they desired. When a French man-of-war arrived in May, with French settlers, the British were safely in possession. From the beginning, New Zealand, unlike Australia, was a free colony rather than a penal settlement. Wakefield's company, chartered in 1841, bought from the natives about a third of the land with guns and presents, and systematically imported British settlers. Earnestly as the colonial governor, backed by the missionaries, might strive to prevent the natives from losing their land, and from obtaining liquor and arms, trouble with the natives was bound to arise as land speculators and white settlers swarmed into the islands, and a "Ten Years' War" (1860-70) had to be fought with the Maoris. After that, white supremacy was unchallenged, white settlers soon greatly outnumbered the Maoris, and most of the land passed into the hands of white colonists. The Maoris, however, were not exterminated, as the Tasmanian aborigines had been, nor were they driven into the interior as the Australian "blackfellows" were; they retained several million acres of land, and rapidly adopted European civilization. At the present time there are 50,000 Maoris (as compared with a million and a quarter whites), and about six thousand Maori children are attending school; the Maoris are allowed to vote, and have four members in the House of Representatives and three in the Legislative Council.

Very different is the story of the other British possessions in the Pacific. Australia and New Zealand were acquired before the age of aggressive contemporary imperialism, and developed into populous self-governing white colonies, self-governing Dominions; whereas the islands acquired in the last half-century have been neither settled by white men nor granted self-government, but are strictly imperialist possessions. The aggressively imperialist period began in the seventies. It was ushered in by missionaries, who often persuaded native chiefs to ask for British rule, or, by being killed, provoked the British government to intervention; by traders and "beachcombers," who built up a traffic in pearls, tortoise-shell, trepang, coconuts, and copra (the dried coconut kernel, from which oil is extracted for margarine and other uses), and bird-of-paradise feathers; by "blackbirders" who kidnapped islanders for work on Australian and South American plantations; and by a sudden outburst of international rivalry for coaling stations and naval bases.

In 1871 a British missionary, Bishop Patteson, was murdered by natives in the Santa Cruz islands. The murder called the attention of the British government to what was going on in the Pacific islands, and especially to the effect of "blackbirding" which was provoking the natives to acts of violence against missionaries and traders. The Gladstone government decided that the inhumane practices of the blackbirders must be checked by governmental regulation. This step led easily to the next, the annexation of the Fiji Islands in 1874, by Disraeli.[1] There were about two hundred islands in the Fiji group, with a total area about equal to that of the state of New Jersey. The natives, a type intermediate between the brown-skinned Polynesian and the darker Melanesian or negroid race, were fierce savages, inordinately fond of "long pig," as they called human flesh, but they had been converted by dauntless Wesleyan missionaries in the early nineteenth century, and their king, embarrassed by debts to the United States (for injuries to a consul) and to a neighboring king (for help in quelling a rebellion), had requested British protection as early as 1858, on condition that Great Britain pay his debts for him. Not until 1874, however, when imperialism was beginning to stir the minds of European statesmen, did Great Britain annex Fiji. Since that time, the native population has been decimated by European diseases, especially measles, whooping cough, and tuberculosis. The unwillingness of the Fijians to work on British sugar plantations was a problem which the British solved by importing coolies from India, after 1879, as contract laborers, and as many of the coolies remained in Fiji after their term of service had expired, the Indian population is now (census of 1921) sixty thousand, as compared with the native population of eighty-four thousand. This suggests the possibility of utilizing the larger Pacific islands as outlets for the population of India or of

[1] *Cf. supra.* pp. 19, 36.

China; it has the advantage of supplying laborers who are more willing and better able to stand the work on the plantations; but if generally adopted it would mean that the Pacific islands would become Asiatic or Chinese, and the native Polynesian and Melanesian races would be doomed to the fate of insignificant minorities in their ancestral islands.

A few years after annexing Fiji, Great Britain invaded two of the very large islands north of Australia, namely Borneo and Papua (New Guinea), both of which had long been claimed, but not seriously occupied, by the Dutch. The northern part of Borneo was ruled by independent native chieftains, and its coasts were infested by pirates. A British North Borneo Company was organized in 1881 by merchants interested in developing trade, and British men-of-war cleaned out the pirates, and it soon became obvious that northern Borneo was destined to become a British colony. Holland protested, on the ground of her historic claims, as did also Spain, on the ground that northern Borneo was tributary to the Sultan of Sulu, in the Philippines; but it was not to be expected that such protests would deter a Great Power from appropriating an unoccupied territory. The northern tip of the island, about a tenth of the whole, was made a British protectorate in 1888. In the same year, Great Britain declared a protectorate over Sarawak, a district about as large as Cuba, in the northwestern part of the island. Sarawak's romantic story can only be suggested here.[1] A British ex-official, Mr. James Brooke, while on a voyage in this region, had happened to notice the natural beauty of the place; he had aided a native chieftain in putting down a rebellion, and as a reward he had accepted from that chieftain the kingdom of Sarawak, over which he ruled as "rajah" or king; his grand nephew still holds the throne.

New Guinea or Papua, the largest island, excluding Australia, in the world, almost as extensive as France and Italy combined, was also practically unappropriated when the age of full-blown imperialism arrived, although the Dutch had some claim to the western part. Time and again the British colonists in Australia urged the mother-country to annex at least the southern portion of Papua, which is separated from Australia only

[1] See Sir John St. John, *Rajah Brooke*; S. Baring Gould and C. A. Bampfylde, *History of Sarawak*.

by the Torres Strait. No foreign power, declared the Australians, could be tolerated in such close proximity to Australia. But London was indifferent, unwilling to incur the expense of installing British officials in a wilderness of savages. When the Australian colony of Queensland in 1883, excited by rumors of German designs on the island, declared the annexation of Papua, Lord Derby in London vetoed the annexation, declaring, that the "natives have given no sign of a desire that their land should be occupied by white men." The next year, however, when Bismarck informed London that Germany would take measures to protect her trade in the South Pacific, and hinted at New Guinea, the British cabinet was at last spurred to action, and in November 1884 a British protectorate over southern Papua was proclaimed, just in time to forestall the Germans, who hoisted their flag on the northeastern coast in December. Indignantly the British protested against Germany's action, but in 1886 an agreement was made, whereby the northeastern quarter of New Guinea was allotted to Germany, the southeastern quarter to England, and the western half was left to Holland. The partition of New Guinea was, as a matter of fact, a paper partition, for none of the three powers seriously endeavored to establish effective occupation in the mountains and jungles of the interior. They were content to establish commercial footholds and a few plantations along the coasts, leaving the conquest and exploitation of the hinterland to the future. It may be added here that British New Guinea was made a dependency of Australia. Thus Australia became an empire within an empire.

East of New Guinea there is a chain of fairly large volcanic islands, the Solomon group, whose canibalistic inhabitants had disposed of more than one missionary before they were brought under British rule. The attempts of "blackbirders" to kidnap Solomon islanders for plantation labor led to such unhappy incidents that Great Britain intervened in 1893, and established a protectorate over the southern part of the archipelago, to see justice done between white man and black. At least such was the ostensible reason. Incidentally, British statesmen desired to forestall Germany. As it was, Germany obtained the northern islands in the group. Under British rule, the headhunters were set to gathering coconuts for the copra export trade, and to cultivating pineapple, bananas, cacao, and coffee.

As the century drew toward its close, and international rivalry for coaling stations grew keener, even the smaller archipelagos were appropriated. Thus the Gilbert and Ellice Islands, on the equator just west of the date line, became a protectorate in 1892, and the Tonga or Friendly Islands, not far from the Fijis, were added in 1900. But it would be useless to enumerate them all. Nor is there space to dwell on the curious twists and turns which British imperialism has taken in some of these islands—the leasing of Christmas Island entire to the Pacific Coconut Plantations Ltd., for 87 years; the settling of Pitcairn Island by nine mutinous sailors, castaways who married native women and left behind them a mixed breed of swarthy Seventh-Day Adventists to be annexed by Great Britain.

The Great War added most of the German possessions to the already numerous British holdings. The German quarter of New Guinea and the adjoining Bismarck Archipelago and German Solomons, were given to Australia under a mandate. German Samoa became a mandate of New Zealand. And the small German island of Nauru, practically an island of phosphate, was taken on a mandate by the British Empire, because of the value of phosphate.[1]

The Copra King and Germany's Lost Islands

About these German colonies it will not be amiss to give a little information. The Germans became interested in the Pacific through trade. In the middle of the nineteenth century a Hamburg merchant named Godeffroy established a trading station on one of the Samoan islands, far out in the Pacific, and began to build up a monopoly of the traffic in coconut kernels or copra, which he brought back to Germany to be pressed in German machines; the oil was used in substitutes for butter and in various other forms, while the residue could be used for cattle fodder. As the Godeffroys and other firms developed their commercial and shipping interests in the Pacific, Bismarck was in time won over to the policy of giving them diplomatic support. First this took the form of making commercial treaties

[1] On these mandates see pp. 502-503, *infra.*

with various native chieftains, kings, and sultans. Soon Bismarck was ready to ask the Reichstag's consent for a bill guaranteeing to a new German Company, the Deutsche See Handels Gesellschaft, a fixed rate of dividend on its capital of eight million marks. The Reichstag's refusal did not long check the plans of the imperialists, however. In 1884 a German New Guinea Company and various other companies were formed for business in the Pacific, and in the same year a celebrated German traveler, Dr. Finsch, was sent out, ostensibly for scientific purposes, really to claim for Germany good harbors. And in December Dr. Finsch raised the German flag in northern New Guinea. An epidemic of German flag-raisers occurred in other islands. The situation was much like that in Africa at this time. "Explorers" and merchants were eagerly claiming what they could, in hope that the Government would declare protectorates over their holdings, before other powers seized the desired territories. Not all of the German flags were raised to stay. But in May 1886 Bismarck did issue a *Schutzbrief*, or proclamation of protectorate, for the holdings of the German New Guinea Company, and by agreement with England these holdings were so defined as to leave to the Germans a quarter of New Guinea, some of the Solomon Islands, and a host of small islands north of New Guinea. With characteristic patriotism and enthusiasm, the Germans promptly renamed their part of new Guinea Kaiser Wilhelmsland, and the archipelago to the northeast became the Bismarck Archipelago, its individual islands being Germanized in name with a thoroughness that was no less amusing than patriotic—New Britain became Neu Pommern, New Ireland became Neu Mecklenburg, and so forth. With these possessions Bismarck seemed to rest content.[1] These, we may remind the reader, were the islands received by Australia, at the close of the Great War, under mandate from the League of Nations.

William II, however, deeply interested as he was in naval power, injected new energy into German imperialism in the Pacific. In 1898, as we have seen, he acquired in Kiaochow, on the coast of China, a naval base for the northern Pacific.[2] He

[1] On these acquisitions see Townsend, *Origins of Modern German Colonialism*, pp. 39-42, 57-74, 113-135, 161-2; M. von Hagen, *Bismarcks Kolonialpolitik*, pp. 70-96, 435-451, 552-570. (This last is interesting on the Caroline Islands question.)

[2] *Cf. supra*, p. 334.

also had his eye on the South Pacific. There is some evidence to indicate that he contemplated purchasing the Spanish possessions—the Philippines and the multitudinous but microscopic islands east of the Philippines. Perhaps that is one reason why when Admiral Dewey, during the Spanish-American War, attacked the Philippines, a German squadron in Manila Bay looked on with unconcealed disapproval.[1] But after the United States had taken the choicest of Spain's insular possessions, Germany was able to purchase the remnants for $4,200,000 in 1899.[2] The purchase included the Caroline, Pelew, and Marianne groups of islands (excepting Guam), literally hundreds of infinitesimal coral islets and lagoon islands, many of them uninhabited. From some of them, small quantities of copra could be obtained, and some had valuable phosphate deposits, but on the whole they were practically valueless except as coaling stations or cable landings. For the latter purposes they were strategically situated, athwart the routes from Hawaii to the Philippines, from China and Japan to Australasia.

One of the Caroline group, Yap by name, became an important cable station, where the trans-Pacific cable from San Francisco to the Far East met cables from Japan, from Shanghai, from the Philippines, and from the Dutch East Indies. It was the commercial and naval importance of these cables, and the possible use of other islands as coaling stations, wireless stations, or minor naval bases, that made American naval strategists unwilling to permit these archipelagoes, and especially Yap, to fall unconditionally into the hands of Japan at the close of the Great War. When the Caroline, Pelew, Marshall, and Marianne islands were assigned to Japan under a mandate from the League of Nations, the United States Government raised a protest, and demanded that Yap be internationalized. For a time, Yap was in the headlines and figured as an important bone of contention between the two Great Powers. At the Washington Conference, however, the difficulty was solved in 1922, by a special treaty, which permitted Japan to have her mandate, but guaranteed to the United States full equality in the use of the cables, and the right to establish a radio station if necessary.

Samoa, famed as the home and burial place of Robert Louis

[1] *Cf. infra*, p. 393.

[2] *Die Grosse Politik*, XIV, nos. 3801 and 3806 n., and XV, nos. 4167-4200.

Stevenson, was also the center of early German commercial activity in the Pacific, and would doubtless have been annexed by Germany in the 1880's had it not been for English and American rivalry. An enterprising American naval officer made a treaty with the native king, in 1878, whereby American goods were to be admitted free of tariff duties, and the splendid harbor of Pago-Pago (pronounced Pango-Pango) was to be put at the disposal of American ships, and in dealing with foreign powers the king was to use the "good offices" of the Washington government. According to European usage, such a treaty would have laid the foundation for an American protectorate. But Germany protested that she had interests also, and seized two Samoan ports, and compelled the king to grant her a naval station, exemption from tariff duties, and any privileges granted to any other power. The British, not to be outdone, obtained similar privileges. The native king, seeing the Great Powers swooping down upon his little realm in such eager greed, decided to choose what he considered the least of three evils, and to ask for a British protectorate. Getting wind of this plan, the Germans forced a new treaty on the king, creating a German-Samoan council, and in 1885 the German consul hoisted his flag, as if to proclaim Samoa a German possession. There followed years of protests, negotiations, and intrigue, among the three interested powers, and civil war in Samoa between the pro-English King Malietoa and the pretender Tamasese set up by the Germans. By 1889 the crisis was reached; Bismarck was about to have German troops landed from German warships; President Cleveland was determined to oppose such action; and English, German, and American warships were hovering off the Samoan coast ready to fight either the Samoans or each other, when a merciful hurricane swept the islands, leaving the warships stranded helplessly on the beach, and the international tension much relieved. The three powers now came to a peaceful agreement at Berlin, in 1889, recognizing Samoa as independent and neutral, under King Malietoa, with a sort of triple supervision.[1] Malietoa, however, had the bad taste to become bankrupt, and the worse taste to die, leaving rival claimants to dispute his throne. Then the three powers decided that joint supervision was unsuccessful, and in 1899 a new

[1] U. S. *Foreign Relations*, 1889, p. 353.

treaty was drawn up, whereby Great Britain withdrew from Samoa entirely (being compensated by the cession of part of the German Solomon Islands), leaving Germany and the United States to divide the Samoan Islands.[1] As there are three main islands, division was not difficult. Germany took the two larger islands, and the United States annexed the easternmost island, Tutuila, which though small in area, was far more desirable than the western islands, because it contained the harbor of Pago-Pago. Germany held her share of Samoa for nearly fourteen years, before the Great War broke out, and British warships took possession. At the close of the war New Zealand obtained a mandate for Western Samoa.

The Minor Rôle of France

French imperialism, to which we may now turn, has been an almost negligible factor in the Pacific,[2] except in so far as the fear of French rivalry spurred British imperialists to annex islands which the British Government would not otherwise have desired. In more than one case, and most notably in the case of New Zealand, Frenchmen arrived just too late, after the British. The share obtained by France in the islands of the Pacific was small, because French missionaries were less active than English in this part of the world, and because France did not have such aggressive and important commercial or naval interests in the Pacific as either the British or the Germans, or the United States for that matter.

French missionaries paved the way for a French claim to New Caledonia, in 1843, and the murder of a French survey party afforded the pretext for French occupation and annexation in 1853. Though New Caledonia is a fairly large island (as large as Massachusetts) with a good harbor, fertile soil for plantation agriculture, and mines of nickel and chrome, the French used it until 1896 simply as a penal station, to which convicts could be sent from France. To this island were sent four thousand of the political rebels who participated in the Commune of 1871, and thousands of ordinary criminals. Not inappropriately the capital was known as Criminopolis. Since 1896 the

[1] *Ibid.*, 1899, p. 665.

[2] Excluding French Indo-China (*cf. supra*, pp. 312-17). On Kwang Chowwan, see p. 335.

island has been slowly recovering from such treatment, plantations have been laid out, and the mines have supplied a large part of the chromite employed by European and American steel mills in the manufacture of chrome steel.

French missionaries also went to the New Hebrides islands, just north of New Caledonia, and a French trading company began to buy up land, and French military posts were established to protect the traders and missionaries. French annexation seemed imminent, when the Australians stirred up the British Government to take a hand. As a result, a joint Anglo-French government or "condominium" was established (by a convention of 1887 modified in 1906 and 1922), but it has never been brilliantly successful.

The most interesting of the French possessions was Tahiti, in the middle of the South Pacific. Here British missionaries early in the nineteenth century converted the natives, reformed the native laws, made the Sabbath a holy day, and got the native Queen Pomare to ask for British protection. Canning's refusal gave the French their opportunity. French missionaries, Roman Catholics, voyaged to Tahiti. When they were turned away, French warships appeared, collected an indemnity (the money was raised by English Protestant missionaries), presented Queen Pomare with a barrel organ, obtained her permission for Frenchmen to visit her island, and sailed away. This was the beginning. By 1842 the French had declared a protectorate; and in 1880, after the death of Queen Pomare, came formal annexation. In addition to Tahiti, the French annexed the numerous Society Islands, of which it is the chief, and several far-flung archipelagoes (Tubuai Island, Marquesas Islands, and the Tuamotu Archipelago), in this part of the Pacific, and grouped them all together as one "colony."[1]

An Unintentional Conquest

We come at length to American imperialism in the Pacific. Like England, France, and Germany, the United States had her missionaries brave enough to preach the Gospel to South Sea cannibals, and merchants enterprising enough to build up

[1] See Dubois et Terrier, *Un Siècle d'expansion coloniale*, pp. 231-250, 365-9, 1025-1028.

trade with palm-covered islands, and mariners bold enough to navigate uncharted seas, and naval officers imaginative enough to see the value of distant naval bases; but until the very end of the nineteenth century the predominant spirit at Washington was opposed to "imperialism" and little inclined to the annexation of uncivilized islands. For a variety of reasons which are discussed elsewhere in this book, American sentiment suddenly altered in the 1890's, and under the McKinley administration the United States made a sensational débût as an imperialist world power. As far as the Pacific is concerned, the United States in two years acquired the Philippines, Guam, Hawaii, and Samoa—including four of the best strategic harbors, and two of the most productive island groups, in the great ocean. With all Bismarck's cleverness and all the Kaiser's ambition, Germany in her imperialist career of three decades could not win so large, so populous, or so valuable a share of the spoils in the Pacific.

Two months before the Spanish-American War occurred, Commodore Dewey received from Theodore Roosevelt, then Assistant Secretary of the Navy, orders to keep his Pacific squadron ready, at Hongkong, with bunkers full of coal, for a sudden voyage to the Philippine Islands,[1] that splendid archipelago of seven thousand islands, whose total area is two and one-half times that of New York State, and whose population at that time exceeded that of New York State. The War between Spain and the United States, fought to free Cuba, afforded an opportunity to conquer the Philippines, for the latter were, like Cuba, Spanish property. Accordingly, when war broke out, Dewey's warships steamed to Manila Bay. There a German squadron and a British squadron were encountered, and it is said that the German admiral might have opposed Dewey, had not the British maneuvered their ships between the German and American lines, so as to make a German attack impossible without involving war with both England and America. Dewey, indeed, did go so far as to threaten the German admiral with war, if he interfered.[2] Secret documents

[1] Bishop, *Theodore Roosevelt*, I, p. 95.

[2] *Cf. Die Grosse Politik,* XVI, nos. 4160, 4150; Dewey, *Autobiography*, pp. 252 ff.; Diederichs' statement in *Marine Rundschau*, 1914, I, pp. 253 ff.; Jeanette Keim, *Forty Years of German-American Political Relations*, pp. 220 ff.

published since 1918 show quite clearly that the German Government had entertained some hope of securing the Spanish islands for itself. During the war Germany suggested to the American ambassador a colonial bargain whereby Germany might secure Samoa, the Caroline Islands, and naval stations in the Philippine and Sulu archipelagoes; but the United States rebuffed this overture. Later, in August 1898, a German suggestion for the neutralization of the Philippine Islands was also repulsed. Nevertheless the Kaiser refused Spain's appeal for intervention against the American demand for the Philippines and Sulus.[1] But this is getting ahead of the story. In the spring of 1898 the Germans sullenly looked on while Dewey sank the decrepit Spanish warships in Manila Bay.

The landing of troops was next in order. American forces debarked at Cavite and prepared to storm the city of Manila. But meanwhile an insurrection had begun among the Filipinos, led by Aguinaldo, a rebel who had been exiled to Hongkong, brought back on an American transport, and provided with arms and ammunition by Dewey's consent.[2] Soon Aguinaldo's insurgents had overcome the Spanish garrisons throughout the island of Luzon, and a Filipino republic had been proclaimed. Aguinaldo's republican army cooperated with the American troops in defeating the Spaniards, but the Americans alone entered Manila, when that city was captured on August 13, one day after a preliminary peace protocol had been signed between the United States and Spain.

Now arose the question, what should be done with the Philippines. President McKinley's perplexity may best be described in his own words; which touch almost every string in the familiar harmony of imperialism.

> I walked the floor of the White House night after night until midnight; and I am not ashamed to tell you, gentlemen, that I went down on my knees and prayed Almighty God for light and guidance more than one night. And one night late it came to me this way—I don't know how it was, but it came:
>
> (1) That we could not give them back to Spain—that would be cowardly and dishonorable [*national honor theme*]

[1] *Die Grosse Politik,* XIV, nos. 3801, 3806 n., XVI, esp., 4145, 4146, 4150, 4156-7, 4160, 4163, 4167-8, 4170-2, 4174-6.

[2] 55th Cong., 3rd Sess., *Sen. Doc.* 62, pt. 2, p. 343 ff.; 57th Cong., 1st Sess. *Sen. Doc.* 331, pt. 3, pp. 2926 ff.

(2) That we could not turn them over to France or Germany—our commercial rivals in the Orient—that would be bad business and discreditable; [*economic nationalism*]

(3) That we could not leave them to themselves—they were unfit for self-government—and they would soon have anarchy and misrule worse than Spain's war; [*racial superiority*]

(4) That there was nothing left for us to do but to take them all, and to educate the Filipinos, and uplift and civilize and christianize them as our fellow-men for whom Christ also died. [*Altruism, the "white man's burden" and missionary zeal. The Filipinos, by the way, were already Christians, Roman Catholics, with the exception of a small number of Mohammedan tribesmen.*]

And then I went to bed, and went to sleep, and slept soundly.[1]

The decision, truth to tell, did not come quite so suddenly, or so mysteriously, as the President's words would indicate. Mr. McKinley communed not only with his conscience, but also with his advisers. Divine light and guidance had to be confirmed by detailed reports on the economic and strategic value of the islands before the final decision was made. Dewey, among others, was asked to report, and replied that the island of Luzon was most valuable, commercially and strategically, and that the islands contained "varied and valuable mineral resources." If on first impulse he declared the Filipinos more capable of self-government than the Cubans, he later made amends by explaining that neither island was fit for independence.[2] When the peace conference met, the American commissioners were at first instructed to ask for the island of Luzon. Subsequently, the receipt of more convincing information led President McKinley to direct them to demand the entire archipelago, and he insisted that "conquest" justified such a demand, though the commissioners were more inclined to ask the islands as an "indemnity," since the conquest occurred after the peace protocol was signed.[3] Then too, there was the argument that disorders would occur in the Philippines unless American rule were continued. And there was the danger that Germany might obtain the islands. The Spanish Government was reluctant to cede its possessions, but could hardly persist in refusal. By the Peace Treaty of Dec. 10, 1898, the Philippines were ceded to

[1] C. S. Olcott, *Life of William McKinley*, II, p. 109. The comments in italics are mine.

[2] 56th Cong., 3rd Sess., *Sen. Doc.* 62, p. 383; 57th Cong., 1st Sess., *Sen. Doc.* 331, pt. 3, pp. 2982-4. *Sen. Doc.* 62 contains several very interesting reports on the value of the islands.

[3] 56th Cong., 2nd Sess., *Sen. Doc.* 148, pp. 7, 35.

the United States, and the United States promised, in the same article, to pay Spain twenty million dollars, more as a palliative than as a price.[1] In such fashion as this did "Providence" and "the fortunes of war" and "the march of events"—to use the favorite statesmanlike euphemisms for conquest—give the United States a "responsibility" for the welfare of the Filipinos.

Aguinaldo and his Filipino Republic did not interpret the designs of Providence in quite the same way. Whether Aguinaldo's troops or the Americans fired the first shot has been disputed, but at any rate hostilities broke out in the Philippines in February 1899, and an American army of 60,000 men began the second conquest of the archipelago, from the natives this time. So stubborn was the Filipino opposition that three years of guerilla warfare were required before Aguinaldo could be captured, in March 1901, and even after that small bands of insurgents had to be hunted down and dispersed. But as soon as possible, in 1902, the military government was replaced by a civil government, with Mr. Taft as first governor-general.

Educating the Filipinos

In many respects the American administration of the Philippines was extraordinarily, even uniquely liberal. As regards education, other colonial powers were put to shame. By 1924 the public school system, with 25,451 Filipino and 329 American teachers, afforded instruction for 1,128,997 Filipino children, 10% of the total population as compared with 20% in the United States, 3.5% in British India, 2.3% in the Dutch East Indies, 5% in French Indo-China. If, in the words of Governor Wood, "one of the principal objects of the schools is to teach the children to speak English," the critical student may wonder why Spanish, the language so widely prevalent before the American conquest, would not have been a more appropriate language; the answer is, of course, that Americans, like all imperialist nations, believe they are conferring a benefit by forcing their language on other peoples. In maintaining order, improving sanitation and medical service, erecting fine public buildings,

[1] Malloy, *Treaties*, p. 1690, art. 3. For the debates in Congress on the annexation of Hawaii and the Philippines, see Dennett, *op. cit.*, pp. 624 ff., and M. M. Miller, *Great Debates*, 3, chs. 5-6.

and in other respects American administrators showed themselves the peers of any colonial government.

Probably the most extraordinary feature of American rule was the rapidity and generosity with which the Filipinos were granted first partial, then increasing powers of self-government, and promises of ultimate independence. As early as 1907 a Philippine legislature was created, the lower house being elected by the wealthy classes (about 100,000 voters), the upper house being the Council of American officials. In 1913 the Wilson Administration, by appointing a Filipino majority in the Commission, made the legislature predominantly native. A still more radical step was taken in 1916, when by the Jones Law Congress substituted an elective Senate for the Philippine Commission. The preamble of the Jones Act contained the promise: "It is, as it always has been, the purpose of the people of the United States to withdraw their sovereignty from the Philippines and to recognize their independence as soon as a stable government can be established therein." Under the governorship of Mr. Harrison, who like President Wilson desired to extend self-government rapidly, with a view to preparing the islands for independence at no distant date, most of the administrative offices under the governor-general were filled by Filipinos, and as one prominent Filipino (Quezon) has said, there was "practical home rule for seven years, from 1914 to 1921." Convinced that the Filipinos during this period had demonstrated their right to self-government, President Wilson in December 1920, just before his term of office expired, advised Congress that stable government had been established in the islands, and that the pledge of independence should now be fulfilled.

A reaction came with the Republican Administration of President Harding, who appointed Major-General Wood and W. Cameron Forbes to investigate Philippine conditions. "The fortunes of war," he told the Filipinos, "revealed us to one another, and held us as your sponsors before the world"; but he reassuringly added, "Our relation to your domestic affairs is that of an unselfish devotion." The Wood-Forbes Commission, as had been expected by those familiar with General Wood's viewpoint, reported [1] that under American rule the islands had made marvellous economic, educational, and social progress; that although

[1] 67th Cong., 2nd Sess., *H. Report*, 325.

"many Filipinos have shown marked capacity for government service and . . . the young generation is full of promise," nevertheless, there had been "retrogression of the efficiency of most departments of the Government during the past few years [under a Democratic governor-general and Filipino officials] and the people were "not organized economically nor from the standpoint of national defense to maintain an independent government."

As governor-general, General Wood tightened the reins. His policy soon brought him into sharp conflict with the Philippine Legislature, whose members were strongly insistent on complete self-government. In fact, Governor Wood himself recognized the fact that the Christian Filipinos (the vast majority) desired independence, "generally under the protection of the United States," but in his opinion and in that of the Republican Party, the time for independence was not yet come.

The Philippine Assembly, however, persisted in its desire for independence. The arguments of the Filipinos were well summarized and supported by an array of facts and statistics in the Filipino Appeal for Freedom, presented to the United States by the Philippine Parliamentary Mission. This document, indeed, may be taken as a reply to the Wood-Forbes Report.[1]

In reply to the Philippine Mission, President Coolidge reminded the petitioners once more, in words that had the true McKinley ring, that American sovereignty over the islands was established not by selfish design, but by "the fortunes of war," and that this "great responsibility came unsought to the American people." The very fact that they came on this mission showed the unfitness of the Filipinos for independence. That boon they could not deserve as long as in their relations with Governor Wood they failed to recognize the truth of "the theory of the complete separation of the legislative, executive, and judicial functions."[2] If this be substituted, as the test of Philippine capacity for self-government, in place of the simpler requirement, "stable government" which was written into the Jones Act, perhaps the day of emancipation for the Filipinos can be indefinitely postponed.

[1] It is printed in 67th Cong., 4th Sess., *H. Doc.*, 511; *cf.* Senate Committee's *Hearings on Philippine Independence* (1924).

[2] 68th Cong., 2nd Sess., *H. Doc.* 485, p. 45.

The existence of economic reasons for continuing American rule can hardly be denied. In recent years the possibility of growing rubber[1] and other important raw materials in the Philippines has greatly interested official circles at Washington, as well as some business groups. American capital has been heavily invested in Philippine development and Philippine property. Moreover, various commercial and industrial interests profit largely by the advantageous tariff arrangements which have been one of the most significant features of American rule. A careful study by the United States Tariff Commission[2] shows how, in spite of the declaration of the American peace commissioners in 1898 that "the policy of the United States in the Philippines will be that of an open door to the world's commerce," the Philippine tariff was so manipulated as to favor American trade. Since 1913 there has been free trade between the United States and the islands, but on foreign goods entering the islands protective tariff duties are imposed, so as to give American goods a preference. The extent to which the United States has been able to monopolize the Philippine market is clearly revealed by figures showing the percentage of Philippine imports coming from the United States:

1893	6%
1899	7%
1908	17%
1913	15%
1925	55%

These percentages are possibly as important as the doctrine of the separation of government powers in relation to the problem of Philippine independence. And yet economic considerations will not permanently prevail over the sentimental but potent belief in self-determination which has remade the map of Europe and is now stirring the nations of the Orient.

Sugar and Destiny in Hawaii

Second to the Philippines in importance was the group of islands known as Hawaii, almost as large in area as Massachusetts, highly fertile, and so situated in the mid-Pacific as to be of first-rate importance as a naval base, commercial coaling

[1] *Cf. infra*, p. 549.
[2] *Colonial Tariff Policies*, pp. 587-600.

station, and cable landing. In the second half of the nineteenth century a number of Americans and Europeans acquired plantations in Hawaii, and soon they were exporting large quantities of sugar to the United States. Their interests were furthered by a commercial treaty of 1875, which admitted Hawaiian sugar without duty.[1] Nine years later the Queen of Hawaii granted American ships the exclusive right to use Pearl Harbor as a naval base.[2] But as American interests, especially the sugar interests, developed, such relations were not found sufficiently intimate. The sugar interests were most concerned. Americans owned sugar plantations worth about $25,000,000, seventy-four per cent of the total.[3] Favored by the treaty of 1875, which admitted their sugar free to the United States while Cuban sugar paid duty, the Hawaiian planters had increased their annual exports to $13,000,000 by 1889; but then a catastrophe occurred. By the McKinley Tariff of 1890 sugar was put on the free list, and Hawaii's preference disappeared. Prices fell and plantations lost value.

Grave was the concern which this event caused in the mind of John L. Stevens, American Minister to Hawaii, who estimated the loss to the sugar interests at not less than $12,000,000. The remedy he recommended was annexation and the payment of a bounty of $12 per ton by the United States Government to the Hawaiian sugar raisers. That a diplomat accredited to a friendly independent state such as Hawaii was, should be earnestly advocating annexation of that state, is rather surprising. The reasons given by Stevens, in his remarkable "confidential" letter of Nov. 20, 1892, are worth summarizing. Hawaii was needed as a naval base and cable station; the native monarchy was corrupt and inefficient; if America delayed, Hawaii might become another Singapore or a Hongkong, under the British flag;—and of course there was sugar. "Destiny and the vast future interests of the United States in the Pacific" —and sugar—"clearly indicate who, at no distant day, must be responsible for the government of these islands." "Annexation must be the future remedy."[4]

A few months later Stevens was able to report that events

[1] Malloy, *Treaties*, p. 915.
[2] *Ibid.*, p. 919.
[3] U. S. *Foreign Relations*, 1894, Appendix II, p. 259.
[4] *Ibid.*, pp. 181 ff.

"have moved rapidly." A committee led by two American residents held a mass-meeting of 1300 "principal citizens"—"merchants, bankers, professional men, the principal business men, and the mechanics" (Americans, British and Germans)—and organized a Committee of Public Safety, which called on the American Minister for aid. This was on Monday, January 16, 1893. Stevens at once asked the U. S. warship *Boston* to land marines. With the marines to hold off any native opposition, the Committee took possession of the government buildings and treasury, proclaimed the end of the Hawaiian monarchy, organized a Provisional Government headed by Americans, and received Stevens' blessing—immediate *de facto* recognition. Of course the Provisional Government asked for union with the United States: that was its *raison d'être.*[1] As soon as commissioners from Hawaii could reach Washington, they signed an annexation treaty, which President Harrison laid before the Senate on February 15, 1893.[2]

Had the Senate acted with the same celerity, Hawaii might have been annexed then and there. The Senate's delay, however, enabled Grover Cleveland, who was inaugurated on March 4, 1893, to withdraw the unratified treaty and thus reverse Harrison's policy. The Hawaiian Republic had to stand waiting at the door, until the Republicans returned to power at Washington, in 1897. Then President McKinley submitted the question to Congress, and by a joint resolution, July 7, 1898, passed in the midst of the Spanish-American war, Hawaii was annexed.[3]

It was later given the status of a Territory, and is therefore not a "possession," such as the Philippines, but an integral part of the United States. As such it was not separated by tariff barriers, and Hawaiian sugar planters were able to export their product[4] to the so-called "Sugar Trust" in America on terms much more favorable than would have prevailed had Hawaii remained independent. Hawaiian pineapples, too, found a ready market in the United States. To cultivate the plantations, thousands of Chinese and Japanese were brought into Hawaii as

[1] *Ibid.*, pp. 198-201, 207-218.

[2] *Ibid.*, pp. 197-205.

[3] See the Senate Committee's elaborate report, 55th Cong., 2nd Sess., *Sen. Rep.* 681; *cf.* on the whole annexation question, J. B. Moore, *Digest of Int. Law*, I, pp. 475 ff.

[4] *Cf.* 55th Cong., 2nd Sess., *Sen. Doc.* 63.

contract laborers, engaged for a certain period of years, and hired in wholesale lots through labor-agencies.[1] As a result, the native population has been swamped; Japanese laborers outnumber the native Hawaiians six to one, and there are more Chinese, more Portuguese, more Filipinos, more Americans and Europeans, than pure Hawaiians. Queen Liliuokalani, a pathetic exile after her dethronement, lived to see her country become commercially prosperous, with a fine school system, and an elected legislature, and a University, but in that country her own people were but a small minority.

In addition to the Philippines and Hawaii, the United States acquired other islands in the Pacific. Guam, a small island with an excellent harbor, was acquired from Spain in 1898, along with the Philippines; it was desirable as a coaling station and cable landing, en route from Hawaii to the Philippines. Samoa, another coaling station and naval base, was acquired in 1899, by agreement with Germany and England, as we have seen.[2] Of the various smaller islands no special mention need be made.

The Washington Conference Again [3]

Thus the United States became one of the leading imperialistic powers in the Pacific. Moreover, the digging of the Panama Canal, and the rapid economic development of the Pacific Coast states, and the growth of American business affairs in China, meant increasing American interest in what one writer has called the "Problem of the Pacific," and what another styles the "Mastery of the Pacific." There is a problem, and it is the problem of mastery.[4] At the dawn of this century six Great Powers shared in the domination of the Pacific, namely, Russia, with her naval bases at Port Arthur (until 1905) and Vladivostok; Japan with her chain of islands separating the Chinese coast from the world's highways; France, with her important colony in Indo-China and her less important island groups around New Caledonia and Tahiti, both south of the equator and pretty

[1] See interesting article, "The Labor Crisis in Hawaii," by Louis R. Sullivan, *Asia*, July, 1923, pp. 511 ff.

[2] *Cf. supra*, p. 391.

[3] *Cf. supra*, p. 355.

[4] For a trenchant though brief discussion of Pacific problems, see Bowman, *The New World*, ch. 32 and supplement, pp. 44-55.

well surrounded by British possessions; Germany, with her Kaiser Wilhelmsland and the myriad minor islands flung out between Hawaii and the Philippines; the United States, with the Philippines, situated conveniently near both the Dutch East Indies and the coast of China, and with Hawaii and Guam on the way to the Philippines, and with Samoa south of the equator on the way to Australasia, and with the Panama Canal, and a long stretch of California, Oregon and Washington exposed to the Pacific; and, most important of all, Great Britain, with her island-continent colony of Australia to preserve as a white man's land, besides New Zealand and countless strategic outposts scattered all over the southern Pacific, and with Singapore commanding the Straits of Malacca, which may not unfairly be called the Suez Canal of Asia, the Panama Canal of the West Pacific. But during the first quarter of the century, while Japan and Great Britain increased their holdings, Russia was deprived of Port Arthur and by Bolshevism rendered temporarily a zero in Pacific world-politics; Germany was driven out of the lists, and France counted for little. That left the British Empire, Japan, and the United States as the chief rivals. With their rivalry, primarily, the Washington Conference [1] of 1921-2 had to deal. The list of powers invited is not without interest. Russia and Germany were excluded; United States, Great Britain, Japan, France, and Italy were present as the five chief naval powers, and China, Holland, Portugal, and Belgium figured in the background.

The most striking feature of the Washington Conference was the adoption of the 5-5-3 ratio as a limitation on the capital ships of Great Britain, United States, and Japan, respectively, that is, acceptance on Britain's part of nominal equality with the United States, and on Japan's part, of marked inferiority. Whether the fighting strength of the three navies would be in reality exactly 5 : 5 : 3 is not of much moment in this discussion. Too much depends, in actual warfare, on chance and strategy and weather and the temperament of commanders, to make such ratios any accurate basis for predicting the outcome of a struggle at sea. However, without some marked change in methods of warfare, the ratio would mean at least that Japan would find offensive operations against California or Australia beyond her

[1] The best account is Buell, *The Washington Conference.*

strength, and, on the other hand, neither the United States nor England, single-handed, would have enough capital ships lightly to risk an attack on Japan. More significant was the termination of the Anglo-Japanese alliance, and the appearance, in its stead, of a tacit cooperation that amounted almost to an entente between Britain and America as regards the Pacific. This Anglo-American cooperation was probably of greater significance than the "Four-Power Pact" signed at Washington, providing that Great Britain, France, Japan and the United States would respect each other's insular possessions, and "communicate with one another fully and frankly in order to arrive at an understanding as to the most efficient measures to be taken" if these possessions were threatened by the aggression of any other power, and that they would hold a joint conference if any controversy should develop among themselves arising out of any Pacific question. Nominally, the Washington Conference substituted a Four-Power Pact for the Anglo-Japanese alliance; practically, it revealed an Anglo-American *entente*.

Japan's position was less weakened, however, than the foregoing paragraph might seem to imply. In the Five-Power Naval Limitation Treaty article nineteen provided that no new fortifications, and no increase of existing fortifications, should be undertaken by the United States, Japan or Great Britain, in their possessions in the Pacific, with certain exceptions. As regards the United States, the American coast, the Panama Canal, the Aleutian Islands, and Hawaii were excluded. In the case of Great Britain, the coasts of Canada, Australia and New Zealand were excluded, and posessions west of 110° E.—which would mean Singapore, where the British planned to create a great naval base. As regards Japan, the agreement applied to the Kurile Islands, the Bonin Islands, Amami-Oshima, the Loochoo Islands, Formosa and the Pescadores, and any future acquisitions. This meant that Japan would be unable to establish any formidable base of operations near the Philippines, the American coast, or British Australasia; it meant likewise that neither Great Britain nor the United States would have a fortified advanced base, of any importance, for aggressive action against Japan.

The British obviously intended, at the time, to make Singapore their chief naval station for the defense of Australasia and

India, in accordance with an investigation made by Admiral Viscount Jellicoe in 1919; but later the Macdonald Labor Cabinet announced that to promote world peace and disarm suspicion (chiefly in Japan and Holland) it would refrain from carrying out the plans for the fortification of Singapore. But the Labor Cabinet fell.

As for the United States, the interesting fact was disclosed that notwithstanding the stress which had been laid, in years past, on the importance of Samoa, Guam and the Philippines as naval bases, none of these had been adequately fortified; and the non-fortification agreement would rob them of much of their naval value. This is all the more interesting if considered in connection with the fact that the acquisition of the Philippines contributed much to create animosity and suspicion between the United States and Japan. The Philippines were in Japanese eyes a naval outpost which could be of use only against Japan, in offensive rather than defensive operations. On the other hand, American strategists and "tablecloth strategists" (if we may use that description for the amateurs who draw naval "triangles and quadrangles" on tablecloths in postprandial discussions of possible wars) learned to look on Japan as a potential menace to the Philippines. Naval bases do not always give the comfort of added security; in this case the acquisition of an admirable base simply lessened both security and comfort.

When all is said, strategic imperialism in the Pacific from 1875 to 1925 was the by-product of a certain stage of technical development in navigation and telegraphy. Warships carrying a limited quantity of fuel required coaling stations, and cables required landings. The substitution of oil for coal as fuel of warships and passenger vessels made a slight change, increasing the cruising radius and demanding the establishment of oil tanks at Hawaii and other naval bases alongside of coal depots. But further technical inventions in shipbuilding, or marked progress in aviation, or the development of radio, may easily alter the whole strategic situation in the Pacific, and deprive much-prized islands of their strategic value. Moreover, the present balance of power and the problem of mastery will be greatly altered as China comes of age, and Siberia grows populous, and Canada and Australia develop into strong white nations.

Considered merely as commercial markets and sources of raw

material, most of the islands of the Pacific are far less worth striving for than Africa and Asia. The smaller islands are negligible as markets, and produce little save coconuts, exported in the commercial form of copra for margarine and oil factories in the United States or Europe. Some of the small islands also have valuable deposits of phosphate, which is much in demand as a fertilizer. Among the larger islands, Australia, the Dutch East Indies, New Zealand, the Philippines, and Hawaii stand out, in the order named, as considerable markets for manufactured goods; it should be noted, however, that Australia and New Zealand are beginning to convert their own raw materials into manufactures. These two white colonies are important producers of wool and wheat and hides; the Dutch Indies supply a large amount of sugar and smaller quantities of rubber, coffee, petroleum; from the Philippines the entire supply of abaca or Manila hemp is derived; and Hawaii is important for sugar and fruit. Almost without exception, the larger tropical islands (this excludes New Zealand and Australia) are suited in soil and climate to plantation products such as cotton, rubber, coffee, tea, sugar, rice, tobacco, and fruits, but only the Dutch islands and the Philippines have anything like an adequate native labor supply, and the others must follow the example of Hawaii and Fiji in importing Asiatic laborers, if they are to weigh heavily in the scales of world production.

This reflection leads finally to the race problem. With the exception of the Malays in the Dutch East Indies and the Philippines, the native races of the Pacific islands have tended to wither at the touch of imperialism: they have succumbed to European diseases and to drink; they have proved ill-fitted for arduous plantation labor. The native Tasmanians are extinct; the aboriginal Australian blackfellows have been driven, largely, into the otherwise unoccupied interior; the Maoris of New Zealand have been displaced, though not exterminated, by the whites; the Fijians and Hawaiians have been swamped by Asiatic labor. The tendency thus far has been toward the replacement of natives by Asiatics in the tropical islands, and the reservation of the temperate lands of Australia and New Zealand for the white race. Perhaps the Pacific north of Capricorn will after all prove to be but a fringe of Asia and its problem but a phase of the question of the awakening Far East.

CHAPTER XVI

THE POLICY OF THE UNITED STATES TOWARD LATIN AMERICA

The Monroe Doctrine and Imperialism

In the smaller countries of Latin America,[1] writes an American publicist, "controlled by our soldiers, our bankers, and our oil kings, we are developing our Irelands, our Egypts and our Indias." The Latin-American policy of the United States—"dollar diplomacy, with its combination of bonds and battleships"—is essentially imperialist, so he believes, and "means the destruction of our nation just as surely as it meant the destruction of Egypt and Rome and Spain and Germany and all the other nations who came to measure their greatness by their material possessions rather than by their passion for justice and by the number of their friendly neighbors."[2]

Contrast this with the ringing words of Charles Evans Hughes, then Secretary of State, in his Bar Association Address in August 1923:

> We are aiming not to exploit, but to aid; not to subvert, but to help in laying the foundations for sound, stable, and independent government. Our interest does not lie in controlling foreign peoples; that would be a policy of mischief and disaster. Our interest is in having prosperous, peaceful, and law-abiding neighbors, with whom we can cooperate to mutual advantage.[3]

In other words, the United States is anything but imperialistic. Roundly Secretary Hughes condemned, in another address (at Amherst, June 18, 1924), those "writers who apparently make it their business to develop antagonism and to spread among the

[1] No attempt is made in this chapter to cover the possessions of Great Britain and other European powers in the Americas. Their development is pertinent to any study of the general effects of colonization, but as older colonies they may perhaps be omitted from this study of recent imperialist world-politics.

[2] Samuel Guy Inman in *The Atlantic Monthly*, July, 1924.

[3] Reprinted, along with many other documents on the Monroe Doctrine, in Alvarez, *The Monroe Doctrine* (Carnegie Endowment, 1924).

people of this country, who have no opportunities for judgment from personal knowledge, the notion that our policies are imperialistic, that our influence is baleful, and that mutual respect and friendship are decreasing."

Whether the United States is, or is not, pursuing a policy of imperialism in relation to Latin America, the facts set forth in this chapter should enable the reader to decide for himself if he cares to do so. Infinitely more important than selecting labels and bandying names, is the clear-sighted perception of the realities. Whether we call America "imperialist" matters not at all, but it matters much whether we understand exactly what America has done, and is doing. Such understanding is the more difficult, because no man can be wholly objective in appraising the activities of his own country; either he is blinded by the optimistic variety of patriotism, which can "see no evil, hear no evil, speak no evil"; or else with the righteous wrath of the prophet, whether through patriotism or pacifism, he finds nothing to praise, everything to blame. To be conscious of this psychological predisposition to prejudice, is perhaps easier than to free one's mind from it.

Certainly there can be no question that in the nineteenth century most of South America, all Central America, Mexico, and the Caribbean islands, were in conditions which would ordinarily constitute an invitation to imperialism. In Asia and Africa and the Pacific, countries having rich undeveloped natural resources in combination with weak governments have almost universally been subject to imperialism; one recalls Egypt, Tunis, Turkey, Morocco, Persia, Indo-China, China, Korea, not to mention more backward areas. The Latin-American states, like these, had undeveloped resources calling for European capital and for European concession-hunters, and as a general rule Latin-American governments were weak, frequently subject to revolution, lacking powerful armies or navies to repel European aggression.

Geographically, there is in some respects a marked similarity between tropical America and tropical Africa, the two great torrid continents. The northern four-fifths of South America, and also Central America, the Caribbean islands, and most of Mexico, lie within the tropics. Like Africa, tropical America has its dense jungles, its fever-stricken coastlands, its great river, the Amazon, in whose mighty basin rubber was found, as in the Congo. Like Africa, South America has a temperate southern tip, a "white man's land." Like Africa, too, the tropical portion of Latin America is predominantly not a white man's land. Mexico is about five per cent white, the rest Indian and mestizo; Bolivia, Peru, and Ecuador are likewise Indian nations, with a white and mestizo ruling class; while Colombia and Paraguay are chiefly mestizo. In Haiti, Santo Domingo, Cuba, Guatemala, Panama and Brazil, negroes descended from African slaves form a considerable part of the population, mixed in some cases with whites and Indians. The countries south of the tropics, namely, Argentina, Chile, and Uruguay, and, by way of exception, Cuba and Costa Rica within the tropics, have white majorities. These racial and geographical facts make it all the more surprising that Latin America should be politically free, for the most part, while Africa is politically subject. And it is not, as so often one hears, the expanse of the Atlantic that has protected tropical America from European imperialism. To dispel this illusion one need only look at a good globe or map, and observe that Europe has colonies in southern Africa and in the Pacific which are further distant, by water, than are Central and South America.

The political contrast between Africa and South America may be explained in part by the fact that before the age of modern imperialism there had been transplanted to Latin America, by Spanish and Portuguese colonization, a white ruling class, which to some extent had Christianized and to a less extent civilized the natives, so that it would be more difficult to plead the "civilizing mission" of Europe as a justification for European conquests in the western hemisphere, in the nineteenth century. But more important factors were the Canning Doctrine and the Monroe Doctrine.

The Canning Doctrine, formulated by British statesmen (not alone by Canning) in the 1820's, was simply that Great Britain could not permit France or Spain to reconquer the American colonies which had revolted from Spain. During the second decade, approximately, of the nineteenth century, the Spanish colonies in America, with the notable exceptions of Cuba and Porto Rico, had rebelled, and Brazil, the great Portuguese colony, had become an independent empire in 1822. Such was the situation in the 1820's, when Metternich was attempting to establish a sort of police system of the Great Powers, to repress all revolution, republicanism, and liberalism. When France was authorized by Metternich and by Prussia to use her army in restoring Bourbon autocracy in Spain, in 1823, British statesmen feared that the police system might be extended to the rebellious Spanish-American colonies, and, especially, that France might undertake to reconquer the Spanish colonies in the name of Spain but in the interest of France. If France had Spain, said George Canning, British foreign minister in 1823, "it should at least be Spain without her colonies." The British Government plainly informed France that any French intervention in the former Spanish colonies would not be tolerated.[1] The French realized that if they attempted intervention, they would have to fight Great Britain. In taking this attitude, British statesmen were actuated chiefly by fear of renewed French colonial rivalry, and by concern lest British trade with the new American republics might be disturbed, might even be seized by France.

Similar motives influenced American statesmen, but the principal motive responsible for the proclamation of the Monroe Doctrine was self-defense.[2] Secretary Hughes' cogent statement [3] that the Monroe Doctrine is "a policy of national self-defense" is historically true. This idea comes out clearly in the text of President Monroe's famous message to Congress, December 21, 1823: [4]

> . . . We should consider any attempt on their [the European Powers'] part to extend their system [Metternich's Holy Alliance or international police system] to any portion of this hemisphere as *dangerous to our peace and safety.* With the existing colonies or dependencies of any European power we have not interfered and shall not interfere. But with the governments who have declared their independence and maintained it, and whose independence we have, on great consideration and on just principles, acknowledged, [i.e. the new Latin-American republics] we could not view any interposition for the purpose of oppressing them, or controlling in any other manner their destiny by any European power, in any other light than as a manifestation of an unfriendly disposition toward the United States.

[1] *State Papers*, XI, pp. 49 ff.

[2] See especially W. R. Shepherd, "The Monroe Doctrine Reconsidered," *Pol. Sci. Quart.*, March, 1924, and address by Elihu Root reprinted in Alvarez, *op. cit.*, pp. 530 ff.

[3] Reprinted in Alvarez, *op. cit.*, pp. 413 ff.

[4] *American Foreign Policy* (Carnegie Endowment, 1920), p. 5

In another part of his message, directed against Russian expansion southward from Alaska, President Monroe strengthened the warning:

> . . . the occasion has been judged proper for asserting as a principle in which the rights and interests of the United States are involved, that the American continents, by the free and independent condition which they have assumed and maintain, are henceforth not to be considered as subjects for future colonization by any European powers.

The Monroe Doctrine, in short, contained a pledge and a warning. A pledge not to interfere with the existing European colonies in America. A warning that the United States would resent as a menace to its country any attempt to gain new colonies in America, or to reconquer the independent Latin-American states.

Needless to say, this was simply a declaration of policy, binding on neither Europe nor the United States.[1] The United States acted contrary to the letter of Monroe's declaration by wresting Cuba and Porto Rico from Spain in 1898, and what would probably be considered as European violations of the Monroe Doctrine, as now popularly interpreted, were in several cases permitted during the period between 1823 and the Civil War; for instance, the republic of Uruguay was created under British auspices, the Falkland Islands were occupied by Great Britain, Vera Cruz was bombarded by a French warship, Buenos Aires was blockaded by an Anglo-French squadron. At the time of the Civil War, Spain attempted to reoccupy the Dominican Republic, and France sent an army to install the Austrian archduke Maximilian as a puppet emperor of Mexico. These moves were pretty clearly contrary to the Monroe Doctrine, but the firm attitude of the United States, at the close of the Civil War, was at least a factor in frustrating such aggression.[2]

[1] Although Augusta E. Stetson, in an advertisement published by the *New York Times* (Dec. 2, 1923), expressed a not uncommon popular belief that the Monroe Doctrine is "as binding upon America as is our God-inspired Constitution." The advertisement was headed with a quotation from Mary Baker Eddy: "I believe strictly in the Monroe Doctrine, in our Constitution, and in the laws of God." For a sound legal view, see C. C. Hyde, *International Law* I, pp. 140-159.

[2] See especially Seward's dispatch of Sept. 26, 1863, in *U. S. Papers Relating to Foreign Affairs, accompanying the Annual Message of the President to the First Session of the Thirty-Eighth Congress*, part II, pp. 709 ff., and subsequent dispatches in the same series; *Message of the President*

That on the whole the Monroe Doctrine has been successfully maintained, is due to several factors. There was the practical certainty that any serious imperialist aggression in America would be combated by the United States—a more important consideration in recent times than in the early nineteenth century. Had all Europe been determined to override the Doctrine, the United States would not have been strong enough to forbid it. Fortunately, the Great Powers of Europe were divided; Great Britain would have viewed French aggression in America with disfavor, if not with belligerent antagonism; and probably France, Germany, or Russia would have opposed Great Britain if that power had endeavored to challenge the American policy by use of force. It need not be too naïvely assumed that Great Britain was invariably a consistently generous friend who disinterestedly lent the potential support of her fleet to underwrite the American Monroe Doctrine; as a matter of fact, some British statesmen resented the spirit of that Doctrine, and opposed its violation by Continental powers chiefly because of a very natural and very British unwillingness to permit the aggrandizement of Great Britain's European rivals.

If the attitude of the United States and Great Britain, taken in combination, shielded Latin-America from European conquest, there was no such protection against aggression by the United States. There was nothing to prevent the annexation of Texas, or the annexation of a great slice of Mexican territory in 1848, after the Mexican War, and the purchase of an additional strip a few years later. Into the earlier phases of American expansion we do not intend to enter. The Louisiana Purchase (1803), the Florida Purchase (1821), the annexation of Texas (1845), the occupation of Oregon (1846), the conquest of upper California, Nevada, Arizona, New Mexico (1848), the Gadsden Purchase (1853), and the purchase of Alaska (1867), and the attempts of expansionist statesmen to obtain Cuba and the Danish West Indies and Haiti at various times, before the last decade of the century, were due to various causes, political and economic, but they certainly were not due to the impulses characteristic of contemporary European imperialism, namely,

. . . *March 20, 1866, relating to the Condition of Affairs in Mexico.* On the other instances mentioned in the text, see convenient excerpts from Moore's *Digest* in Alvarez, *op. cit.*, pp. 40-110.

the investment of surplus capital, the seeking of markets for surplus manufactures, the quest of outlets for surplus population, the concept of the white man's civilizing mission. But in the last three decades or so, these impulses (with the exception of surplus population) have been distinctly active, and American expansion has been of a different type. There has been less of the acquisition of sparsely populated territories to be settled by the restless American pioneer; there has been instead a tendency to dominate for economic, strategic, patriotic and humanitarian purposes lands unsuited to white settlement, lands already occupied by colored populations.

In this latest period, the United States has employed methods strikingly similar to those of European imperialism. The Monroe Doctrine has been interpreted so as to resemble increasingly the "sphere of interest" doctrine so characteristic of European practice. Two illustrations may be offered. The Venezuela Boundary Affair of 1895 grew out of a frontier dispute between British Guiana and Venezuela. When Great Britain refused arbitration, Secretary of State Olney, on June 20, 1895, dispatched a note to London, explaining that any extension of the Guiana frontier would be a violation of the Monroe Doctrine, and declaring in general terms that "Today the United States is practically sovereign on this continent, and its fiat is law upon the subjects to which it confines its interposition."[1] This has been called the Olney Doctrine. As Olney also affirmed that, "distance and three thousand miles of intervening ocean make any permanent political union between a European and an American state unnatural and inexpedient," it is apparent that he went far beyond the original policy of Monroe. His truculent note was politely controverted by Lord Salisbury, whereupon President Cleveland in a special message to Congress uttered a threat of war that could hardly be described as veiled;[2] and Great Britain ultimately accepted arbitration. The other illustration is the Lodge Resolution, passed by the United States Senate (but not approved by President Taft) in 1912, declaring that the United States cannot permit the lease or concession of strategic harbors in America to foreign

[1] The whole dispatch makes interesting reading in *Foreign Relations*, 1895, pt. 1, pp. 545 ff.

[2] *Ibid.*, pp. 542 ff., *cf.* J. B. Moore, *Digest of Int. Law*, VI, pp. 540 ff.

corporations.[1] These were extreme statements, chosen because they were extreme. American popular opinion, however, and to some extent American official opinion, has increasingly taken it for granted if there is any debt-collecting to be done by force, or a punitive expedition to be dispatched, in Latin-American countries, the United States will do it. One is reminded of Theodore Roosevelt's famous declaration in 1904:—

> Chronic wrongdoing, or an impotence which results in the general loosening of the ties of civilized society, may in America, as elsewhere, ultimately require intervention by some civilized nation, and in the Western hemisphere the adherence of the United States to the Monroe Doctrine may force the United States, however reluctantly, in flagrant cases of wrongdoing or impotence, to the exercise of an international police power.[2]

Consider, in a like vein, the editorial statement of the New York *Times* (July 2, 1924) which is quoted not as a narrative of historical fact, but as an interpretation of the Monroe Doctrine:

> The duty (to intervene in Haiti) devolved upon our Government because European nations called upon the United States to bring order out of chaos and make Haiti solvent, or to waive the Monroe Doctrine and let them intervene to collect their debts and protect their nationals.

The right of exclusive intervention, a right claimed by any imperialist power in its sphere of influence, is quite generally claimed for the United States in Latin-America. Likewise the right of vetoing concessions to foreigners has been quietly exercised on several occasions since 1912, and this is the most easily recognizable earmark of a sphere of interest, whether in China or Persia or Africa or Latin America.

The United States has also pursued at times the method of territorial expansion, by lease, by purchase, or by conquest. Porto Rico was taken by conquest in 1898; the Virgin Islands (Danish West Indies) were bought by gold in 1916; the Canal Zone was

[1] *Senate Journal*, 62nd Congress, 2nd Session, p. 511. The resolution was directed against a project for the transfer of land on Magdalena Bay (Lower California) to Japanese subjects. The wording was not quite so broad as my statement. The text reads: "That when any harbor or other place in the American continents is so situated that the occupation thereof for naval or military purposes might threaten the communication or the safety of the United States, the Government of the United States could not see, without grave concern, the possession of such harbor or other place by any corporation or association which has such a relation to another government, not American, as to give that government practical power of control for naval or military purposes."

[2] *Foreign Relations*, 1905, p. xxxiv.

acquired by lease in perpetuity. The use of Guantanamo on the coast of Cuba and Fonseca Bay on the coast of Nicaragua as naval bases by the United States may perhaps be compared with the establishment of German and Japanese naval bases on the coast of China.

One must add, financial penetration. American capitalists—large and small—have invested over four billion dollars in Latin America, according to estimates given out by the Department of Commerce in 1925. Less than a fourth of this sum is represented by government bonds. The bulk of it consists of industrial and agricultural investments. Just here lies the great difference—we may pause to observe—between American loans to Europe, chiefly in the form of government bonds, and American financial interests in Latin America. In Latin America, American finance is chiefly and directly concerned in the development of productive enterprises. It is also of interest that Latin America accounts for 43% of the total American foreign investments, as compared with Canada and Newfoundland 27%; Europe, 22%, Asia and Oceania and Africa, only 8%.

American "Dollar Diplomacy" and financial control, backed up by occasional naval demonstrations or by the landing of marines, is not a unique method of controlling disorderly or insolvent countries. On the contrary, franc diplomacy and pound sterling diplomacy, as the reader will doubtless remember, were conspicuous in Morocco, Tunis, and Egypt, as was ruble diplomacy in Persia, mark diplomacy in Turkey, and yen diplomacy in China. Lending money to unstable governments, or investing money in unruly countries, has been one of the most widespread features of imperialism, and has usually led to annexations, in European practice, whereas in American practice "dollar diplomacy" leads to financial receiverships, that is to the collection of the customs duties of a Haiti or a Santo Domingo by American officials, or to other methods of financial supervision. It may be pointed out in this connection, that the American method is more subtle, achieving as it does the desired financial and economic domination, without political annexation and often, as in the case of Cuba, without much impairing political self-government. As an attempt to reconcile business interests with political principles, it has its philosophical as well as its practical attractions.

Cuba and the Spanish War

With these generalizations as food for thought, perhaps for controversy, we may proceed to consider the Latin-American countries in which American control has been particularly notable. Cuba is a good starting point. This fertile island, just about the size of Pennsylvania, with a population, in the 1890's, of about 1,600,000—two-thirds white and one-third negro or mixed—had been one of the few American colonies not lost by Spain in the early nineteenth century. During the second half of the century, with the mushroom-like development of the sugar and tobacco businesses, American capital became heavily interested in Cuban sugar and tobacco plantations, as well as in opening up iron mines and constructing railways, in supplying Cuba with manufactures, and in providing ships for Cuban-American trade. How varied and important these business interests were, and how dissatisfied with tariff and other conditions under Spanish rule, may be seen in the *Report on the Commercial and Industrial Condition of Cuba,* compiled by Robert P. Porter by President McKinley's order, at the close of the Spanish-American War, when the Washington Government was trying to make up its mind what to do with Cuba. The American capital investing in Cuban sugar and tobacco production and railways and other enterprises was not less than fifty million dollars in 1893, according to information received by the United States Senate.[1]

In 1894 there began in Cuba a rebellion, some of the leaders of which were Cubans who had been living in the United States. For several years, there was a devastating civil war between the insurgents and the Spanish forces. This civil war caused great concern in the United States, for several reasons. To begin with, it caused terrific losses to the sugar, tobacco, mining, and railway interests. The Cuban cane-sugar crop, which in 1894 and 1895, before the civil war became serious, exceeded a million tons a year, and constituted about half of the world's total production of all kinds of sugar, suddenly dropped in 1896 to 225,221 tons, the drop representing a loss of $64,000,000, and in 1897 it fell still lower. American sugar refineries, which had consumed the bulk of the Cuban crop, now stood idle.

[1] 55th Cong. 2nd Sess., *Sen. Rep.* 885, p. xxi

American concerns such as E. Atkins and Co. of Boston, owning great plantations or *colonias* in Cuba, saw their investments being wiped out by the tragic conflict in Cuba. Possibly the imposition of a duty on Cuban sugar by the Wilson Tariff of 1894 may have had something to do with the hardships of the Cuban sugar business, and, indirectly, with the disorders in Cuba.[1] American business interests were desperate with their losses in Cuba; they desired peace, order, a government and a tariff favorable to business.

In a way, one may say, these business interests provided one of the causes of the Spanish-American War. But there were other interests. American naval authorities had a strategic interest in the island which lay athwart the entrances to the Gulf of Mexico, on which border five of the United States. There was also burning popular indignation, in the United States, at the ruthlessness of Spanish procedure against the insurgents—particularly the *reconcentracion* policy, of confining civilians in concentration camps, without sufficient food or proper sanitation. American charity sent food to the *reconcentrados.* There was also a humanitarian belief that Spain ought not to be permitted to oppress and misgovern the island, and a patriotic conviction that the United States should intervene in the interest of humanity and good government, and, incidentally, of sanitation, for Cuba was becoming a contagion-spot.

Specifically asserting such grievances as the inclusion of American citizens in the concentration camps, the "wanton destruction of the legitimate investments of Americans," the stoppage of commerce, and "the uncivilized and inhuman" methods of the Spanish, and the danger of the spread of contagious diseases, the United States government assumed an attitude of protest.[2] To cap the climax, the United States battleship *Maine* was blown up in Havana harbor, on Feb. 15, 1898, whether by internal explosion, or by the Spaniards, or by the Cuban insurgents, was not known at the time.[3] American patriots assumed that the Spaniards had done the deed, and "Remember the *Maine*" soon became a popular slogan which

[1] Under the tariff of 1890 sugar had been free. 53rd Cong., 2nd Sess., *Sen. Rep.* 707, p. 42.

[2] See correspondence in 55th Congress, 2nd Session, *Senate Doc.* No. 230.

[3] It later appeared that the explosion was probably an external one. cf. 63d Cong., 2nd Sess., *House Doc.* 207.

raised the war spirit in the United States to a pitch where it could hardly be controlled.

Though the Great Powers of Europe presented to the United States an appeal for continuance of peace; [1] though Spain offered to refer the question of the *Maine* to arbitration, and stopped the *reconcentracion* policy, and liberated American citizens, and promised amnesty to the insurgents, President McKinley on April 11, 1898, without informing Congress of Spain's latest concessions, asked for authority to use force against Spain. Congress adopted a joint resolution on April 19, authorizing the President to use armed force to expel Spain from Cuba, and solemnly declaring that "The people of the island of Cuba are and of right ought to be free and independent." [2] The brief war that ensued, from April to August 1898, was long enough to evoke in the United States an outburst of a new and aggressive sentiment, a sentiment which demanded territorial booty in the West Indies and in the Philippines, forgetting that the war had been begun in the name of Cuban liberty rather than for the aggrandizement of the United States. The treaty of peace, signed on December 10, 1898, ceded the Philippine Islands and Guam in the Pacific, and Porto Rico in the Caribbean, to the United States.[3]

As for Cuba, Spain relinquished all claims, and the island was left in the possession, but not ownership, of the United States. For the ensuing three years, 1899 to 1902, Cuba was occupied by American forces and administered by an American military government, which energetically set to work to stamp out the yellow fever, and promote education, and increase the efficiency of the civil service, and construct public works. During the same period, Mr. Robert Porter as special commissioner was conducting an elaborate investigation of the commercial and industrial condition of Cuba, or rather, of the tariff changes and other reforms desired by American business interests in Cuba. The Washington government intended to grant political

[1] Sir Julian Pauncefote, British ambassador at Washington, did not think American intervention in Cuba justified. Holleben, the German ambassador, personally desired "eine öffentliche Brandmarkung dieses frivolen Angriffs." *Die Grosse Politik*, XV, no. 4140. For correspondence with Spain see U. S. *Foreign Relations*, 1898, pp. 558-768.

[2] *Cf.* U. S. *Foreign Relations*, 1898, p. 763. The resolution also disclaimed any intention of annexation or control as regards Cuba.

[3] *Foreign Relations*, 1899, p. 595.

freedom to Cuba, in accordance with its previous declarations, but American interests were to be safeguarded.

The scheme of quasi-independence which was finally applied to Cuba was an interesting improvement on European methods of imperialism. It was designed to reconcile the Cuban desire for self-government with American strategic and economic interests—to accomplish the non-political objects of imperialism, without the disagreeable political methods. A Cuban constitutional convention (1900-01) was allowed to draw up a republican constitution, with American advice. The United States Congress thereupon authorized the President to hand the government over to Cuba, on certain significant conditions, which were contained in the celebrated Platt Amendment. These conditions are worth pondering carefully: (1) Cuba could make no treaty with a foreign power that would endanger Cuban independence. (2) Cuba could incur no debts which her current revenues would not suffice to bear. (3) Cuba "consents that the United States may exercise the right to intervene for the protection of Cuban independence, the maintenance of a government adequate for the protection of life, property and individual liberty, and for discharging the obligations with respect to Cuba imposed by the Treaty of Paris on the United States, now to be assumed and undertaken by the government of Cuba." (4) The sanitary work begun by the American military administration must be continued. (5) Cuba must grant the United States "lands necessary for coaling or naval stations." To these conditions Cuba assented,[1] and in May 1902 the administration was handed over to the Cuban republic. Soon afterwards (1903), in accordance with the fifth condition, Cuba leased Guantanamo Bay and Bahia Honda, on the Cuban coast, to the United States, as naval stations, for two thousand dollars a year.[2] Cuba also agreed to a commercial treaty, Dec. 11, 1902, providing for reciprocal tariff reductions: Cuban sugar and other Cuban products were to be admitted to the United States at twenty per cent less than the duty on other foreign sugar, and American manufactures were to be imported into Cuba likewise at a reduced tariff ranging from twenty to forty per cent less than the general

[1] They are set forth in full in the treaty of May 22, 1903, ratified on July 1, 1904. Text in *Foreign Relations*, 1904, pp. 243 ff.

[2] *Ibid.*, 1903, pp. 350 ff.

tariff applicable to foreign goods.[1] In effect, the United States was assured of a virtual monopoly of Cuban trade; American interests in Cuba were assured of stable and favorable government; and the American navy had Cuban coaling stations—what more could forthright imperialism have obtained? And yet Cuba had political "independence."

The word is inclosed in quotation marks, because it was not the kind of independence enjoyed by Great Powers. If Japan had the legal right to intervene, by force of arms, in the United States, Americans would not consider the United States wholly independent. In Cuba the United States had not only special economic and naval privileges, and a veto on foreign loans and treaties, but also this right of armed intervention. The right was exercised in 1906, when the Cuban Liberal Party, hostile to American domination, instigated a revolution against the President who had been elected and installed under American auspices in 1902. For more than two years American forces occupied the island, supporting a "provisional government." Then the Americans withdrew, in 1909, leaving the Liberals in power, but again anti-foreign demonstrations and outbreaks of disorder and a negro revolt caused President Taft in 1912 to send warships to the Cuban coast. This time, occupation was unnecessary, for the Cubans elected as President a conservative engineer and business man, Menocal, who had been educated in the United States, and was friendly to American interests. When the Liberals, a few years later, again took up arms to challenge the re-election of Menocal, they received a stern warning from Washington that a government erected by force would not be recognized. Cuba, in short, was permitted to govern herself, in so far and for so long as she governed herself peaceably, without endangering American interests. Europeans might style the control exercised over Cuba by the United States a "veiled protectorate"; it has also been called a "quasi-protectorate"; perhaps it might best be described as negative supervision, although, to be sure, the financial guidance provided by General Crowder, special representative of the United States, in the post-war economic crisis, was distinctly positive.

From the economic point of view, Cuba is much more definitely dependent on the United States than many a "colony" on its

[1] *Ibid.*, pp. 375 ff.

"mother-country." An anti-imperialist writer has asserted that "practically, the economic and political life of the island is dominated from New York and Washington," and, even more explicitly, that the "ownership of Cuba lies almost completely in the hand of the National City Bank" of New York.[1] If this were literally true, there could have been no such controversy as occurred in 1923 between Cuban railway and sugar interests, and between the Cuban and Washington governments, over the Tarafa Bill for a monopolistic consolidation of the Cuban railways. The economic interests focussing in Cuba are not all concentrated in the National City Bank. Nevertheless, it is true that various American investors, including the bankers connected with the National City, have vested interests amounting to about a billion and a quarter dollars in Cuba. It is also true that the United States supplies two-thirds of Cuba's imports and buys seven-eighths of Cuba's exports. American financial and commercial interests have to a considerable extent relied upon, and in some cases have profited unduly by, American political influence. It is, of course, no secret that American diplomacy has pursued a policy of safeguarding vested interests against internal disorder or hostile legislation in Cuba.

There is, however, another side of the shield. American investments have promoted the rapid economic development of Cuba; American tariff preference for Cuban sugar has enriched Cuban planters as well as Americans owning Cuban plantations; and the conditions of life for the Cuban people under the shadow of American domination are at least in some respects better than during the chronic civil wars that preceded the Spanish war. Walter Hines Page felt that in its policy toward Cuba the United States had set an example for all nations to follow, and suggested that the policy ought to be applied to other areas. "May there not come such a chance in Mexico—to clean out the bandits, yellow fever, malaria, hookworm—all to make the country healthful, safe for life and investment, and for orderly self-government at last? What we did in Cuba might thus be made the beginning of a new epoch in history—conquest for the sole benefit of the conquered, worked out by a sanitary reformation.

[1] Scott Nearing and Joseph Freeman, *Dollar Diplomacy*, p. 193 in particular and chapter vi in general. Compare data on American investments, in R. W. Dunn, *American Foreign Investments*, pp. 119-133.

The new sanitation will reclaim all tropical lands; but the work must be first done by military power—probably from the outside. May not the existing military power of Europe conceivably be diverted, gradually, to this use? . . . And the tropics cry out for sanitation."[1]

In congratulating themselves upon their magnanimity in carrying out their pledge to emancipate Cuba, and upon the unselfish character of American policy toward Cuba, enthusiastic Americans often ignore the facts and sometimes indulge in a self-esteem that borders on hypocrisy. Nevertheless, admitting that Cuba was not set entirely free, and admitting also that there have been profits for private American interests, it may also be pointed out that instead of outright annexation the United States was content with veiled control; instead of unabashed exploitation, American interests promoted the economic development of the island. Toward Cuba the United States practised not naked imperialism but a more subtle imperialism, which left to the Cuban people a very considerable amount of self-government, and which sought its profits in the economic prosperity and political stability of Cuba. In precisely these respects the lot of Cuba has been incalculably preferable to that of Persia, Korea, or Congo.

Porto Rico

The smaller island of Porto Rico was annexed outright at the close of the Spanish War. This was pure imperialism. After a transitional period of administration by the military authorities, a civil government was established under the Foraker Act, passed by the United States Congress. Though a House of Delegates, elected by the people, was established, the controlling power was vested in a Governor-General and an Executive Council of officials appointed by the President of the United States with the advice and consent of the United States Senate. This system was liberalized by the Jones Act of 1917, which granted American citizenship to the inhabitants of Porto Rico, and created an elective Senate, but still government was far from autonomous, and Porto Ricans complained of their condition. On the other hand, there could be no question

[1] *Life and Letters*, I, pp. 271-273.

that as regards sanitation, education, and economic production (sugar, tobacco, coffee, fruit, etc.), American rule was highly beneficial. The death rate was reduced from 26 to 18.7 per thousand. Some 2500 schools were established.[1] Nor could there be any doubt that the increased commerce of Porto Rico was almost wholly with the United States. Porto Rican exports increased from 10 million dollars in 1900 to 88¼ millions in 1924; Porto Rican imports, from 10 millions to 89⅓ millions. The share of the United States in the island's exports rose from 34% in 1900 to 91% in 1924, while the percentage of the island's imports supplied by United States grew from 70% in 1900 to 90% in 1924. This was partly due to the tariff arrangement, whereby exports from the United States are admitted to Porto Rico (and *vice versa*) free of duty, whereas foreign goods are subject to the duties prescribed in the United States tariff.[2] Trade figures show that the island means many millions of dollars' worth of business to the American iron and steel industry, the cotton manufacturers, and soapmakers, as well as to American importers of sugar and tobacco.[3] If occasionally there were complaints that laborers in Porto Rico were underpaid and overworked, or that the American administration was solicitous chiefly for American interests, these were but jarring minor notes in the major cadence of prosperity.[4]

Canal Construction and Dollar Diplomacy in Central America

After the Spanish-American War, the pressure of the United States was felt in Central America. Central America consisted of five small republics (Guatemala, Salvador, Honduras, Nicaragua, and Costa Rica), besides a very small British colony of British Honduras, and the Isthmus of Panama, then part of

[1] The admirable educational system, which is equaled in few if any other colonies, owes its existence in large measure to my colleague Dr. Samuel McCune Lindsay, who laid its foundations while he was Commissioner of Education in Porto Rico.

[2] U. S. Tariff Commission, *Colonial Tariff Policies*, pp. 600 ff., for a detailed study.

[3] *Annual Report of the Governor of Porto Rico*, 1924, pp. 11 ff., 49 f. Porto Rican sugar was admitted to the U. S. free of duty, thus enjoying an advantage over the Cuban product.

[4] See Senate Committee's *Hearings on the Civil Government of Porto Rico* (1924).

the adjoining South American Republic of Colombia. In parts of Central America, American fruit interests had acquired considerable economic importance; there were also British railway interests, and German-owned plantations. Not economics, however, but strategy, was the dominating factor in the situation. For decades various plans had been discussed for the construction of a ship-canal through Nicaragua or through the Isthmus of Panama, to afford commerce a short-cut from the Atlantic to the Pacific. There was a question, however, whether such a canal ought to be American, or neutral and international. Back in the year 1850, the Clayton-Bulwer Treaty[1] between the United States and England had provided that any such canal must be unfortified, neutral, under international guarantee. Such restrictions were repugnant to the exuberant national spirit which prevailed immediately after the Spanish-American War, and from England—then preoccupied with the Boer War—permission was obtained by the Hay-Pauncefote Treaty[2] of 1901 to construct a canal under American control, to be policed by the United States, on condition that such a canal should be open to the merchant vessels and warships of all nations, in war and in peace, without discrimination or inequality of tolls.

It would have been relatively easy to obtain from Nicaragua the right to dig a canal across Nicaraguan territory, and this route was favored by a commission of investigation, but President Roosevelt and the Senate for various technical reasons preferred the route across Panama. Roosevelt obtained from Congress authority to use this route if he could make the arrangements within a reasonable time and at reasonable expense. There were two difficulties. One was the concession which a French company headed by the great canal builder Ferdinand de Lesseps had obtained from Colombia in 1878 to construct a canal across Panama, a concession which still remained valid, though the projected canal had never been built. This obstacle was overcome easily by an offer of forty million dollars to the company which held the de Lesseps concession. Philippe Bunau-Varilla, an engineer interested in this company, had exerted himself to win American approval for the Panama route, and, so Thayer

[1] *State Papers*, 38, pp. 4 ff.
[2] *Ibid.*, 94, pp. 46 ff.

claims, a New York lawyer connected with the company had contributed $60,000 to the Republican campaign fund and won the sympathetic influence of Mark Hanna.[1]

The other obstacle, Colombia, seemed to be nicely disposed of when Secretary Hay signed the Hay-Herran Treaty of January 22, 1903, with the Colombian minister, providing for a ninety-nine year lease (in imitation of the Chinese leases of 1898) of a strip of territory six miles wide, across the isthmus, for a payment of ten million dollars plus an annual rent of a quarter-million.[2] Great was the chagrin in Washington when the Colombian Senate, hoping apparently to make better financial terms, refused to ratify the treaty and adjourned on October 31, 1903. Roosevelt decided to go ahead with the canal regardless of Colombia's rights. He drafted a message to Congress, in October, 1903, recommending that the United States should build the canal through Panama even without Colombia's consent.[3] In a private letter to Dr. Albert Shaw, he wrote on October 10, 1903, "I should be delighted if Panama were an independent state; or if it made itself so at this moment; but for me to say so publicly would amount to an instigation of a revolt, and therefore I cannot say it."[4] He did not need to say it. Mr. Phillipe Bunau-Varilla and various Panamans, in the United States and in Panama, felt sufficiently confident that their action would not meet with disapproval, to launch a revolution in Panama on November 3, 1903. American marines were forthwith landed, under orders to prevent the landing of Colombian troops within fifty miles of Panama.[5] The right of secession, denied by Lincoln to the Southern States, was recognized by Roosevelt in the Colombian state of Panama.

Why the new republic of Panama was so zealously shielded and immediately recognized by the United States appeared clearly enough when a treaty was signed on November 18, 1903, whereby in consideration of ten million dollars cash and a quarter-million per annum thereafter (beginning in 1911), Panama leased to the United States in perpetuity a canal zone ten miles

[1] W. R. Thayer, Life of *John Hay*, II, p. 307. Bunau-Varilla's story is told in his books, *Panama* (1914), and *The Great Adventure of Panama* (1920).

[2] Malloy, *Treaties*, III, p. 223, and *Foreign Relations*, 1903, pp. 132 ff.

[3] Bishop, *Theodore Roosevelt*, I, p. 289.

[4] *Ibid.*, I, p. 279.

[5] *Ibid.*, p. 282.

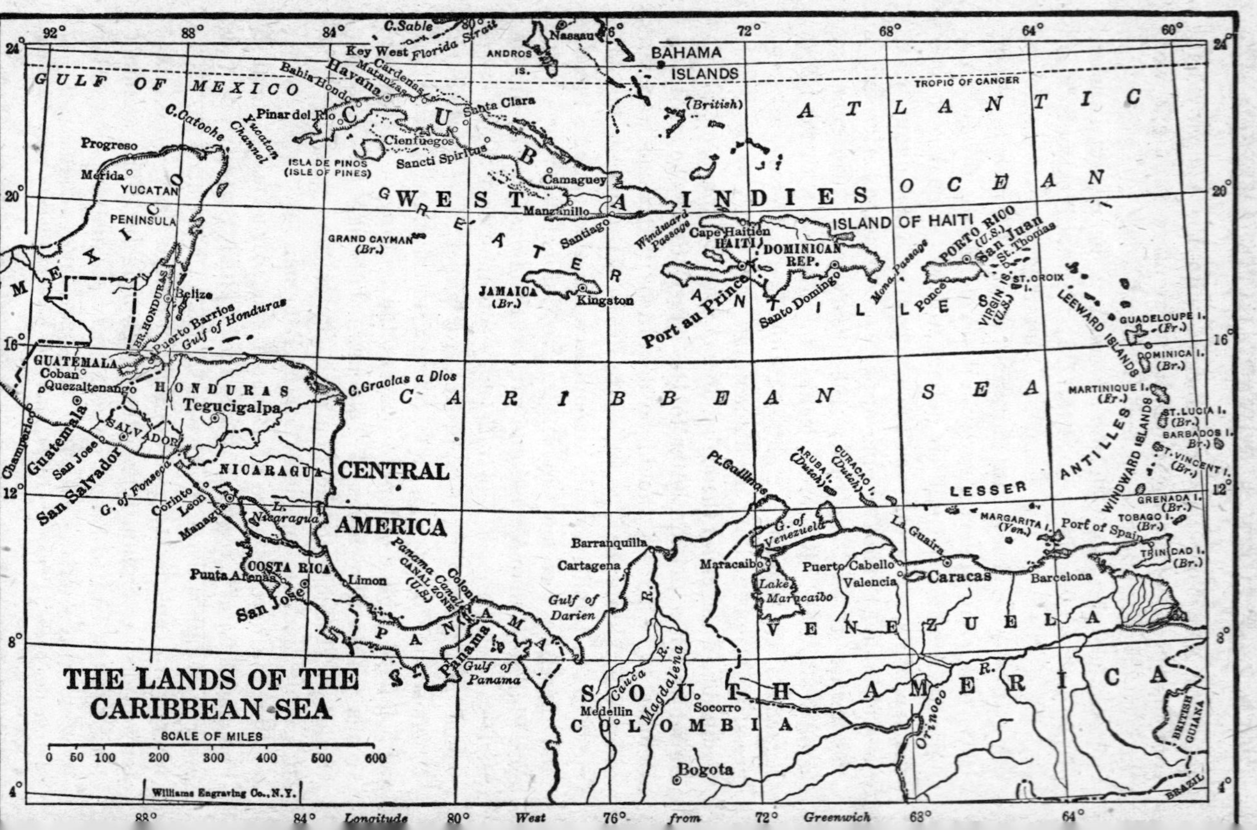

THE LANDS OF THE CARIBBEAN SEA
GULF OF MEXICO
ATLANTIC OCEAN
WEST INDIES
CARIBBEAN SEA
GREATER ANTILLES
LESSER ANTILLES
CENTRAL AMERICA
SOUTH AMERICA
BAHAMA ISLANDS (British)
TROPIC OF CANCER
ANDROS IS.
Nassau
C. Sable
Key West
Florida Strait
Havana
Matanzas
Cardenas
Santa Clara
Bahia Honda
Pinar del Rio
Cienfuegos
Sancti Spiritus
Camaguey
Manzanillo
Santiago
CUBA
ISLA DE PINOS (ISLE OF PINES)
Yucatan Channel
C. Catoche
YUCATAN PENINSULA
Progreso
Merida
MEXICO
GRAND CAYMAN (Br.)
JAMAICA (Br.)
Kingston
Windward Passage
ISLAND OF HAITI
HAITI
DOMINICAN REP.
Cape Haitien
Port au Prince
Santo Domingo
Mona Passage
PORTO RICO (U.S.)
San Juan
Ponce
VIRGIN IS. (U.S.)
St. Thomas
ST. CROIX I.
LEEWARD ISLANDS
GUADELOUPE I. (Fr.)
DOMINICA I. (Br.)
MARTINIQUE I. (Fr.)
ST. LUCIA I. (Br.)
BARBADOS I. (Br.)
ST. VINCENT I. (Br.)
GRENADA I. (Br.)
WINDWARD ISLANDS
TOBAGO I. (Br.)
TRINIDAD I. (Br.)
Port of Spain
MARGARITA I. (Ven.)
CURACAO I. (Dutch)
ARUBA I. (Dutch)
BRITISH GUIANA
BRAZIL
VENEZUELA
Caracas
La Guaira
Puerto Cabello
Valencia
Barcelona
Maracaibo
Lake Maracaibo
G. of Venezuela
Pt. Gallinas
Orinoco R.
COLOMBIA
Barranquilla
Cartagena
Bogota
Medellin
Socorro
Magdalena R.
Cauca R.
Gulf of Darien
PANAMA
Panama
Colon
Panama Canal
CANAL ZONE (U.S.)
Gulf of Panama
COSTA RICA
San Jose
Limon
Punta Arenas
NICARAGUA
L. Nicaragua
Managua
Leon
Corinto
HONDURAS
Tegucigalpa
Gulf of Honduras
Puerto Barrios
Belize
BR. HONDURAS
C. Gracias a Dios
SALVADOR
San Salvador
G. of Fonseca
GUATEMALA
Guatemala
Coban
Quezaltenango
Champerico
SCALE OF MILES
0 50 100 200 300 400 500 600
Longitude West from Greenwich
Williams Engraving Co., N.Y.

wide, over which the United States would exercise sovereign rights, including the right of fortification.[1]

Thus Roosevelt, in his own words, "took the Canal Zone." The gigantic enterprise of digging the canal was begun soon afterwards, and the canal was opened to traffic on August 15, 1914, but its completion and formal opening did not occur until July 12, 1920. Up to that date it had cost the people of the United States $366,650,000 for construction, not including the large expenditures for fortifications, or the forty millions paid for the concession, or the ten millions paid to Panama, or the twenty-five millions subsequently paid to Colombia.[2] The net cost up to 1924 was $453,266,139, of which almost three-quarters was paid out of the treasury, the remainder being provided by the sale of bonds. The net receipts, after operating expenses are deducted, have not yet risen to the point where they will pay five per cent interest on the investment. Yet the canal was unquestionably worth building. It brought San Francisco 7,873 miles nearer to New York by water; it brought Peru six thousand miles closer, Valparaiso (Chile) almost four thousand, and Japan three thousand miles closer to New York.[3] It was a factor in increasing the trade of the United States with Japan from 129 [4] to 559 million dollars a year.[5] It handled a slightly greater tonnage than the Suez Canal in 1924. It was a boon to the commerce of the world, and chiefly to American commerce. On the other hand, it must be admitted, American railways suffered because much of their former trans-continental business now went by the water route. Economic interests are rarely in national harmony.

The advantage gained by the United States in undertaking the construction of the canal singlehanded, instead of allowing it to be an international enterprise, was not commercial. By the terms of the Hay-Pauncefote treaty, foreign ships enjoy the same rights and pay the same tolls as American vessels; and when Congress in 1912 attempted to exempt American coastwise shipping from all tolls, Britain protested, with the result that

[1] *Foreign Relations*, 1904, pp. 543 ff., and correspondence, *ibid.*, 1903, pp. 230 ff. and 689 ff.

[2] *Infra*, p. 450.

[3] To Hongkong (China) and Manila (Philippine Is.) the distance from New York by water is almost as short via the Suez Canal as via Panama, although the Panama route to Shanghai is about 1500 miles shorter.

[4] The average for 1910-1914.

[5] 1925.

the tolls exemption law was repealed in June, 1914, at President Wilson's insistent and high-minded demand. The advantage, let it be repeated, was not commercial, but strategic. The United States could and did fortify the canal, so that in case of war it could be defended against attack, and so that it constituted virtually another naval base on the Caribbean Sea. This naval acquisition, however, inspired American naval experts with an earnest desire for additional naval outposts in the Caribbean, to protect the Canal. The Canal built to protect the United States now had to be protected by further acquisitions, notably Fonseca Bay, the Corn Islands, the Danish West Indies, Haiti and Santo Domingo. But of these, more will have to be said.

The digging of the Canal meant that Central America must become very definitely an American "sphere of interest," as European imperialists would say. Certainly no other Great Power could be allowed to gain a foothold near the Canal—at any rate, no foothold nearer than the existing British possessions (British Honduras, Jamaica, etc.). Increasingly the United States overshadowed the Central-American republics. Panama though "independent" was a protégé if not a protectorate of the United States; from the beginning, her existence had depended on American protection;[1] the Canal Zone, occupied by American military and naval forces was in the middle of the republic. Europeans would call Panama a "veiled protectorate."

Immediately north of Panama lies Costa Rica, better governed than its neighbors, probably because it has a larger percentage of cultured white inhabitants, and a smaller number of illiterate half-castes and negroes. In Costa Rica the mines, banks, commerce, and railways were controlled largely by foreigners, and the United Fruit Company's banana plantations were of great importance. Oil interests, however, were more decisive. In 1915 and 1916 Americans obtained extensive oil exploration rights. When in 1917 a revolutionary government headed by Federico Tinoco seized power, and seemed disposed to grant oil concessions to the Cowdray (British) interests, President Wilson refused recognition, and even though Costa Rica joined in the

[1] By article 1 of the treaty of 1903 with Panama, "the United States guarantees and will maintain the independence of the Republic of Panama." —*Foreign Relations*, 1904, p. 543.

war against Germany, still recognition was withheld, and Costa Rica was excluded from the Peace Conference. The attitude of the United States encouraged a successful rebellion against Tinoco in 1919. One needs hardly add, the new government, headed by President Acosta and less prejudiced in favor of British oil interests, was soon recognized. Presently it was reported that the British concessions were cancelled. Costa Rica is "independent," but her governments must respect the new Monroe Doctrine, the doctrine that the United States has a veto on concessions.

Nicaragua, next to the north, came more definitely under American domination. President Jose Santos Zelaya unwisely opposed American interests. When in 1909 a rebel movement "friendly to American interests"[1] was set on foot with American backing, Zelaya committed the supreme act of imprudence by executing two Americans for attempting to dynamite a troopship. Thereupon, Secretary Knox severed diplomatic relations with Zelaya's government and Zelaya was soon ousted. Now Knox's plans could be carried out. Thomas C. Dawson, who had previously been concerned in establishing the American receivership for the Dominican Republic and who had served as American Minister to Panama, was sent to Nicaragua to arrange "the reestablishment of a constitutional government," a settlement of American claims and a loan from American bankers. In consultation—on board an American warship—with the leaders who had overthrown Zelaya, Dawson made what has been called the "Dawson Pact" (1910), including provision for a loan guaranteed by customs receipts,[2] and for the election of General Juan Estrada as president. But Estrada soon found the task of governing an indignant people too much for him; and Adolfo Diaz, formerly a book-keeper in American employ, was given the presidency in 1911 and maintained in office, against the wishes of the population, by the presence of a small force of American marines at Managua and the occasional appearance of American warships off the coast. With him, Knox was able to make a convention[3] June 6, 1911, for a loan of $15,000,000 to Nicaragua, guaranteed by Nicaraguan customs receipts.

[1] *Foreign Relations*, 1909, p. 452.
[2] *Ibid.*, 1910, pp. 763-767, and 1911, pp. 652-3.
[3] *Ibid.*, 1912, pp. 1074-1075.

Though the U. S. Senate refused to ratify this treaty, other loan contracts were put through, from time to time, an American was appointed to control the collection of Nicaraguan customs revenues, and the Nicaraguan railways were pledged to American bankers. Years later, William Jennings Bryan revived the dollar diplomacy of Knox, and negotiated the Bryan-Chamorro Treaty of 1915[1] whereby in return for three million dollars, to be expended under American direction, Nicaragua submitted to American financial control, granted the United States exclusive rights to build an interoceanic canal (this, to forestall possible competition with Panama), and gave the United States a ninety-nine year lease of the Corn Islands and the right to have a naval base on the Gulf of Fonseca. Nicaragua thus became another "ward" of the United States.

Nicaragua's customs revenues were collected under American supervision. A commission of one Nicaraguan and two Americans was appointed to supervise Nicaragua's expenditures. American bankers, notably Brown Brothers and J. W. Seligman, virtually controlled the country's finances, banking and railways. And American marines prevented, or aided in suppressing, insurrections against this agreeable state of affairs.[2]

When Nicaragua's neighbors protested that the naval provisions of this treaty infringed their boundary rights, and when the Central American Court of Justice, which the United States had helped to establish in 1907, decided that this protest was just, the United States ignored the decision, and thereby delivered a mortal blow to the court.

Criticism of American policy in Nicaragua was probably responsible for the decision of the United States Government to withdraw its marines in August 1925, as a proof that the United States was not endeavoring to dominate the little republic. Moreover, a new electoral law, drafted by American experts, was adopted by Nicaragua and the American experts were invited to supervise the elections. Naval domination thus gave place to expert advice; but it requires little imagination to pre-

[1] Signed Aug. 5, 1915, and ratified June 22, 1916. *U. S. Treaty Series*, No. 624.

[2] See articles by J. K. Turner in *Appeal to Reason*, Oct., 1916, and *The Nation*, May 31, 1922; also the interesting exposé in Scott Nearing and J. Freeman, *Dollar Diplomacy*, pp. 151-171, with texts of the Bryan Chamorro treaty, pp. 321-3, and of the Brown Brothers' 1920 contract, pp. 324-32

dict that should any Nicaraguan government attempt to cancel American financial and naval privileges, the marines would again do their duty at Managua.

Honduras, a land of cattle-ranches owned by Hondurans, mines owned by American and British corporations, and banana plantations owned by Americans, has a relatively large Indian, negro and half-breed population, and a small white upper class. Such ingredients produce political instability, revolutions, dictatorships, and filibustering. Civil war between rival political factions afforded the occasion for the landing of American marines in 1924, and American intervention succeeded in restoring order.

Salvador, the smallest of the Central American republics, but densely populated, prosperous and fertile, remained independent until 1922, its commerce being conducted largely by English, Dutch and German exporters, its coffee crops increasing, its government fairly stable. In 1922, Salvador made a loan contract with Minor C. Keith, head of the United Fruit Co., for the issue of bonds amounting to a maximum of $21,500,000. Part of the issue consisted of six per cent bonds to cancel an old English loan; another part consisted of eight per cent bonds sold to New York bankers at 88% of their face value and redeemable at 105% of their face value; and a third part, seven per cent bonds. The significant feature of the contract was the provision that seventy per cent of the Republic's customs revenues were pledged to pay interest and sinking fund charges on this loan. The seventy per cent was to be paid directly to a bank named by Mr. Keith. In case of default, this bank was to transmit, through the United States Department of State, the names of two persons, one of whom would be selected by Salvador to act as Collector General of the entire customs revenue. Disputes regarding the contract were to be referred through the Washington State Department to the Chief Justice of the Supreme Court of the United States. The inference drawn by the bankers was: "It is simply not thinkable that, after a Federal Judge has decided any question or dispute between the bond holders and the Salvador Government, that the United States Government should not take the necessary steps to sustain such decision. There is a precedent in a dispute between Costa Rica and Panama, in which a warship was sent to carry out the verdict of the arbitrators."[1] Salvador, in short, becomes a financial dependency of American bankers acting with the cooperation of the United States Government.

In Guatemala, the most northerly of the six republics, the United Fruit Company grows bananas, and there are considerable American railway interests. Over Guatemala the United States did not establish control, however, perhaps because the country was farthest removed from the canal, perhaps because the administration was friendly to foreign capital and to the United States. Guatemala, for instance, offered the United States the use of its waters, ports and railways in the war against Germany, in 1917-18.

In general, it may be said that since the Panama revolution, American bankers have been rapidly acquiring control of Central American railways and other enterprises,[2] and, in cooperation with the Department of State, have been extending control over the finances of Central American governments. This is "dollar diplomacy." It has been carried on by Democrats and Republicans alike. It has been supported by marines, warships, and what we might call naval diplomacy. It has made Central America a sphere of interest of the United States, in which European intervention would be resented, in which concessions to European capitalists may not be made without danger of offending the watchful eye of the Department of State, in which American naval and economic interests hold undisputed supremacy.

The iron hand is usually covered with a velvet glove, as may best be illustrated by the Central American Conference of 1923. The Washington State Department considered it desirable to have the armies of the Central American republics reduced, and a court of arbitration established to prevent petty wars in Central America. The Court which had been established in 1908, it will be recalled, had expired in 1918, after the Fonseca Gulf case. A new court would have to be created. Moreover, there was a strong movement in Central America toward federal union, and Washington was apparently desirous of having a hand in any such federation. Accordingly, in 1922 the presi-

[1] From a confidential circular, published by *The Nation* (N. Y.) Oct. 24, 1923, p. 452. The text of the loan contract is in Dunn, *American Foreign Investments*, pp. 222 ff.

[2] For data on American holdings see Dunn, *op. cit.*, pp. 107-118.

dents of Nicaragua, Honduras, and Salvador were invited to talk matters over on board the U. S. cruiser *Tacoma,* and there a preliminary understanding was reached, with the result that the United States next invited delegates of the five republics (not including Panama) to confer in Washington, with Secretary Hughes as their host. That the affairs of Central America should be settled in distant Washington, instead of at home, seemed not to occur to Mr. Hughes. Under his tactful guidance, the conference agreed on an arbitration court; armies were limited, a free trade convention was signed, and various other unifying measures were adopted.[1] The United States presided over Central American affairs, and presided with a hand which could be gentle, though firm.

Intervention in Haiti and Santo Domingo

It is time to turn back to the Caribbean islands, as President Roosevelt turned, after he had established his foothold in Central America by taking the Canal Zone in 1903. Most of the smaller islands in the West Indies, as every American knows, are colonial possessions of England and France; Denmark had St. Thomas; and Holland owned Curaçao. The four largest islands are Cuba, Haiti, Jamaica, and Porto Rico. What happened to Cuba and Porto Rico we have seen; Jamaica was British, Haiti, however, was independent. On the island of Haiti there are two republics, the western third of the island being the Republic of Haiti, a negro state with a cultured French-speaking upper class, and the eastern two-thirds being the Dominican Republic (Santo Domingo), a Spanish-speaking mulatto state. In both republics the long arm of the United States has been felt.

Roosevelt's attention was attracted to the Dominican Republic in 1904, by the fact that the government was unstable and bankrupt. The only feasible method of protecting the European owners of Dominican bonds against loss seemed to be the seizure of Dominican customs houses, and collection of the customs revenue for the benefit of the bondholders. Germany, as the most interested European power, was reported to be on the point

[1] *Conference on Central American Affairs* (1923); *cf.* Buell, *International Relations,* p. 232, and G. Stuart, *Latin America and the United States,* chs. 12-13

of taking such action. So were France and Italy. Roosevelt, of course, would not permit this encroachment on the American sphere of interest. Moreover, the Dominican government requested American aid. Roosevelt did not desire to annex the country—"I have about the same desire to annex it," he said, "as a gorged boa constrictor might have to swallow a porcupine wrong-end to."[1] But he was willing to do police work. A plan was agreed on, whereby Americans would collect the customs and turn 55% of the revenue over to foreign creditors. This plan was put into operation quietly and immediately by executive order, though the United States Senate did not ratify a treaty sanctioning the arrangement until 1907.[2] Santo Domingo was now a financial protectorate, a bankrupt in the hands of an efficient American receivership.

The western republic, Haiti, meanwhile continued independent, until 1915. In the summer of that year the American public, or as much of it as reads the foreign news dispatches, was shocked to learn that President Villbrun Guillaume Sam of Haiti had caused two hundred political prisoners to be butchered in cold blood, and that he himself had taken refuge in the French legation, only to be dragged out and beheaded by an irate mob. That American marines should thereupon have been landed to restore order seemed natural enough. Subsequently, however, it appeared that more than a year before this bloody drama, the United States had unsuccessfully demanded the signature of a treaty giving the United States charge of the customs collection and debt service, as in Santo Domingo,[3] and that the United States Navy Department had dispatched the *Washington* to Haiti in January 1915. It also appeared that a strong reason for this forehanded action was to prevent Germany from obtaining a naval base in Haiti. It was the French, however, rather than the Germans, who landed marines in June 1915, to be followed by United States marines in July. All this seems to have occurred before the massacre of July 26 and the beheading of July 27, 1915.

After the events of July 26-27, more American marines were landed, and Rear Admiral Caperton took charge of the customs

[1] Bishop, *op. cit.*, I, p. 431.

[2] *Foreign Relations*, 1905, pp. 298 ff.; Malloy, *Treaties*, I, p. 418.

[3] *Foreign Relations*, 1914, pp. 347-350, giving Bryan's dispatch of July 2, 1914.

houses and administration against the protest of the Haitian Congress. The treaty which had been rejected by Haiti before the occupation could now be put through with ease and dispatch. A president who would accept the desired treaty was elected in August 1915, and the treaty was signed on September 16. The United States, so this interesting document stipulated, would aid Haiti in developing her agricultural, mineral and commercial resources; the United States would also name a General Receiver and a Financial Adviser to hold Haiti's purse-strings and see that the bankers owning Haitian bonds got their due; Haiti would make no new loans or changes in her tariff without obtaining consent from the White House; nor would Haiti lease or cede territory to any foreign power; and, finally, not only would the United States organize an armed constabulary to establish order in Haiti, but also American forces would intervene whenever necessary, in the future, to preserve individual liberty, life, and property. This meant a protectorate, if there ever was one.[1]

As there was inevitably some popular opposition in Haiti to this signing away of the republic's independence, it was not thought expedient to permit elections until 1922. American marines still remained in the island, and the elections went off well enough, resulting in the election of a president who promised to cooperate loyally with the United States. And still the marines remained. While the Occupation continued, American business interests were actively carrying out the treaty pledge to aid in developing Haitian resources. New York banking interests purchased control of the Banque nationale de la République d'Haiti. American capitalists bought up land, sugar mills, railways, lighting plants, and other property.

Moreover, the American naval authorities were active in promoting sanitation and road-building. The natives might not enjoy being compelled to work on the roads under the supervision of American engineers, but Americans felt that the end justified the means. Let the Haitians protest as they would, American newspapers such as the New York *Times* were joyfully certain that "the Americans are in Haiti to raise its people from a state of ignorance and savagery for which their rulers were responsible. . . ." An official American report insisted

[1] 67th Cong. 2d Sess., *Sen. Doc.* 136; *Amer. Jour. Int. Law*, supplement, X, p. 234; *Foreign Relations*, 1915, pp. 538 ff.

that the Occupation was characterized by "freedom from all suggestion of selfish aims." The United States, in short, was assuming a small share of "the white man's burden."[1]

The Haitian treaty of 1915 so pleased the State Department that an early opportunity was sought to force a similar arrangement on the Dominican Republic, since the new plan afforded so much wider scope for American control than was allowed by the Dominican treaty of 1907. The opportunity was afforded by a revolution in the spring of 1916. American marines were landed, and recognition was refused to the new Dominican president unless he signed a treaty on the Haitian model. With more patriotism than prudence, he refused, with the result that in November the American commander of the forces of occupation assumed control of the administration of the republic. Year after year the occupation continued, while American bankers increased their interests, and American marines performed the task of policing the country, and promoting sanitary and material progress much as in Haiti. In 1920, the Wilson administration announced its intention to withdraw the marines from Santo Domingo, but Wilson was followed by Harding, and Harding by Coolidge, and the marines remained. Not until the summer of 1924 were the American marines withdrawn, and then only on condition that all the acts of the American military administration establishing revenues, authorizing expenditures or creating rights in favor of third persons be ratified by the Dominican Government. Furthermore, the treaty of 1907 was replaced by a treaty signed in December 1924, which provided for the collection and control of Dominican revenues by an American receiver and his staff, until the loans of 1908, 1918, and 1922, and new loans up to a maximum (including the balance of old loans) of twenty-five million dollars, shall have been completely paid.[2] The Dominican Republic may be added to the list of Caribbean financial dependencies of the United States. The International Banking Corporation (National City Bank of New

[1] In the Senate Committee's voluminous *Hearings on the Occupation of Haiti and Santo Domingo* there is a wealth of testimony, valuable and otherwise. The Report is in 67th Cong., 2d Sess., *Sen. Rep.* 794. *Cf.* Nearing and Freeman, *Dollar Diplomacy*, pp. 133-151, 316-320; Dunn, *op. cit.*, pp. 135-6.

[2] This interpretation of the treaty was set forth in an exchange of notes in connection with the exchange of ratifications, Oct. 24, 1925.—U. S. Department of State, press bulletin, Dec. 4, 1925.

York), with seven branches in Santo Domingo, has "almost complete control over the financial life of the country," and it is estimated that a third of the Dominican sugar industry is owned by American capital.[1]

One other extension of American control in the Caribbean islands merits brief mention, namely, the purchase in 1916 of the Danish West Indies, for twenty-five million dollars.[2] These islands, now known as the Virgin Islands of the United States, were of negligible economic importance. They were acquired solely for strategic reasons, in accordance with the twentieth-century policy of the United States—the acquisition so far as possible of all important naval bases in the Caribbean region.

Oil and Turmoil in Mexico

Much more important than the diminutive republics of Central America and the Caribbean islands, with which we have thus far been concerned, is the great republic of Mexico, a fourth as large as the United States, with a population (census of 1921) of about fourteen millions. In Mexico the conditions which usually constitute an invitation to imperial conquest were present in exceptionally high degree. Mexico was, and is, a peculiarly tempting morsel for imperialists. It would have been eagerly appropriated by the United States, had imperialist sentiment there been as rampant as in France, Italy, Germany, or England. Even in spite of a stubborn anti-imperialist spirit in America, Mexico has been a sore temptation, a grave problem, one might almost say a provocation, to American imperialism.

Mexico has been a temptation because of her marvellously rich resources—her peerless silver mines and productive gold mines, her oil wells which pour out a fifth of the world's petroleum, her copper and lead. Naturally such wealth attracted foreign capitalists. The American investment in Mexican mining and smelting properties was estimated in 1902 at the figure of $80,000,000; in 1912, at $233,000,000; in 1924, at $300,000,000. The Guggenheim interests, operating through the American Smelting and Refining Company with its subsidiaries, the Ryan and Cole

[1] Dunn, *op. cit.*, pp. 133-4. For further details on the occupation of the Dominican Republic, see Nearing and Freeman, *op. cit.*, pp. 124-133, and the Senate Hearings on the Occupation of Haiti and Santo Domingo.

[2] *State Papers*, 1916, vol. 110, pp. 843 ff.

interests operating through the Cananea Consolidated Copper Company, and the Phelps-Dodge Corporation operating through the Moctezuma Copper Company, were giant figures in the Mexican mining industry, but there were scores of smaller concerns, and doubtless thousands of American small investors who depended on Mexican mines.

The oil was practically untouched until 1901 when a veteran prospector from the United States, Mr. Edward L. Doheny, began to drill wells and laid the foundations for his two great oil companies—Mexican Petroleum (Mexican "Pete") and the Pan-American Petroleum and Transport—which soon made millions annually in dividends. Standard Oil also entered the field and became heavily interested. Meanwhile a British company, the Mexican Eagle, controlled by Mr. Pearson (Lord Cowdray), became an aggressive rival from 1905 to 1913; by 1910 it controlled 58% of the Mexican output. Mexico won third, then second place among the oil-producing nations of the world, and most of her output was shipped to the United States.

Other foreign capitalists provided funds for railways. To encourage such investment, President Diaz offered attractive terms—tax remission for fifteen or twenty years, kilometric subsidies (one remembers the Bagdad Railway) ranging from six to twelve thousand dollars a kilometer; and grants of public lands. Early in the twentieth century the American capital invested in Mexican railways was estimated to be somewhere between one-third and half a billion dollars.[1] Another important foreign interest was in Mexican land, for cattle and sheep ranches or lumber. It has been estimated that from forty to sixty million acres were acquired by Americans and other foreigners, and that about $275,000,000 was invested in such land. Altogether, Consul Letcher reported in 1912, the American investment in Mexican railways, mines and smelters, and other properties, was a little over one billion dollars. More recently it has increased to about a billion and a quarter.[2] If British in-

[1] During the turmoil of Mexican civil wars it dropped to $160,000,000 or less, and is now less than the British railway investment of approximately $245,000,000. American capital, apparently, was transferred to other kinds of investment.

[2] The chief items are railroads, 160 million dollars; mining and smelting 300 millions; oil lands and refineries, 478 millions; plantations and timber, 200 millions. Dunn, *op. cit.*, p. 91. For the few facts I have given, I am indebted largely to Dunn's work and to manuscript materials placed at my

vestments amounting to about two-thirds of a billion dollars, and other foreign properties valued at a slightly lower figure, are added, the total foreign investment in Mexico is well over two and one-half billions.

Such investments were no menace to Mexico's independence as long as order reigned south of the Rio Grande. And order reigned, on the whole, during the long dictatorship of President Porfirio Diaz, a shrewd mestizo, who ruled Mexico from 1877 to 1880 and from 1884 to 1911. With one firm hand Diaz suppressed insurrections in Mexico, while with the other he welcomed foreign capital. With money borrowed from abroad some thirteen thousand miles of railways were built. Concessions were granted on generous terms to foreign capitalists who wished to exploit Mexico's mines, her oil, her land. Diaz was praised as the strong man of Mexico, an enlightened despot; he was given the G. C. B. by King Edward of England; all was well with Mexico, from the viewpoint of the foreign investor.

The whole situation changed, however, when in 1910 there began the long civil war, or series of wars, which lasted for an entire decade. The trouble arose from several causes. One difficulty was that the masses, descended mostly from the aboriginal Indian inhabitants, and converted by the Spaniards to Christianity, were illiterate, poor, and exploited. The majority consisted of peons, agricultural laborers, living in a condition not much removed from serfdom, on the great *haciendas* of aristocratic landowners, or else dwelling in backward village communities or in tribal groups which had hardly been touched by European civilization. A minority of them were miners and industrial wage-earners. Of politics these people had little knowledge; government they left to the small ruling class of creoles and mestizos. But they had sore economic grievances. The labor question affected a relatively small number, but in an acute form, for wages were incredibly low, working conditions were atrocious, and radical labor agitation was making headway, although during the Diaz régime labor outbreaks were sternly repressed.

The land question was much more serious, as it affected most of the population. Under Diaz public lands and "unclaimed"

disposal by Mrs. A. W. Marsh, who has made a detailed study of American interests in Mexico.

common lands were sold by the government to wealthy *hacendados* (estate-owners) and land speculators: probably more than a quarter of the total area was thus transferred. Ninety per cent of the villages on the central plateau were left landless, while many small owners lost their little farms and joined the ranks of discontented agricultural laborers held in bondage by debt. The census of 1910 showed that 6,000 hacendados owned 550,000 square miles; whereas only one-fourth of the land was owned by the common people in commons and small farms; and the agricultural laborers held in debt service (*peons de campo*) with their families made up over sixty per cent of the total population.[1] Here was good material for revolution. Ignorant, rebellious, shiftless workers were easily attracted to insurgent armies by the promise of pay, plunder, and the free-and-easy life of the soldier.

The situation was aggravated by other factors. The small governing class was divided against itself. Some advocated centralization; others, states' rights. Some were *cientificos,* who believed in economic progress, aided by foreign capital, and opposed demands of radicals for democracy, land reform, or labor reform. Some were "anticlericals" more or less of the French pattern, eager to legislate against the Catholic Church, while the majority devoutly upheld that Church to which the bulk of the nation gave religious adherence.

Such confusing cleavages, combined with the inability of the masses to participate in government, rendered fair elections and genuine representative government virtually impossible. Elections were usually farcical. Political leaders habitually placed more reliance on bullets than on ballots. The successful politician was the one who had a sufficient personal following, and a sufficient number of troops back of him, to seize power, and defeat or intimidate his rivals. Diaz remained in power from 1884 to 1911, and was re-elected to the presidency eight times, not because of his popularity but because he had a loyal army and an active force of armed and mounted police, the Rurales. His downfall was not caused by votes. On the contrary, when in the elections of June, 1910, he found himself

[1] For information on the land question, I am indebted to the materials placed at my disposal by Mrs. A. W. Marsh; also, H. Phipps, *Some Aspects of the Mexican Agrarian Situation;* and McBride, *Land Systems of Mexico.*

vigorously opposed, he cast the leader of the opposition, Francisco I. Madero, into jail, along with a number of his followers, and easily arranged for his own re-election. Madero, however, was no sooner released, than he inaugurated a rebellion in the north, and announced that he and his followers believed in constitutional government, extension of the suffrage, a single term for the president, free elections and free press, the right of initiative in Congress, and the restoration of lands fraudulently taken from Indian villages and small proprietors. Madero himself appears to have been sincere in these ideals, but his own family, owning a large part of the land in the state of Coahuila, were opposed to land reform, and many of his followers were doubtless interested chiefly in obtaining power.

Mr. Lane Wilson, former ambassador to Mexico, is reported to have alleged, on Jan. 7, 1913, that the Madero rebellion was paid for by the Standard Oil interests. This particular statement may or may not have been unfounded, but it is typical and significant.[1] Foreign interests, not merely oil but mining, ranching, banking, and other interests, were bound to be involved in the conflicts between rival factions in Mexico. Diaz had favored Pearson, the British oil magnate, in granting petroleum concessions; American oil interests might naturally be expected to give moral, if not financial, support to the Mexican faction opposed to Diaz. Manuel Liyo asserted that Madero promised to withdraw the Pearson concessions, and be more generous to Standard Oil. As the story unfolds itself, other instances similar to this, and perhaps better authenticated, will appear. Moreover, foreign interests were necessarily involved in another way. Any serious civil conflict in Mexico was certain to interfere with mining and ranching and possibly finance; foreign investments would be endangered, and foreign investors would demand intervention to safeguard their property. Such intervention could be by the United States alone, because there was so strong a feeling at Washington that the twentieth-century version of the Monroe doctrine would not permit European intervention.

To proceed with the story. The rebellion that began in the northern provinces in 1910 was so successful that in 1911 Diaz abdicated and fled to Europe, with well-lined pockets, while

[1] See the Senate Committee on Foreign Relations, *Hearings on Revolutions in Mexico* (1913).

Madero, of course, was "elected" president. Soon, however, Madero himself was confronted by insurrections in several provinces. One rebel "general," a former muleteer, was financed by wealthy landowners in Chihuahua, who feared land reform. Another rebellion, that of the Zapata brothers, was inspired by the opposite motives; the Zapatistas wanted more radical and more immediate land redistribution than Madero was likely to grant. The Yaqui tribe of Indians, likewise, lost patience and revolted. Moreover, a nephew of President Diaz made an unsuccessful attempt to seize power by force, was imprisoned by Madero, was liberated by rebellious military cadets. The *coup de grâce* was delivered by General Victoriano Huerta, who betrayed Madero, seized power, made himself provisional president in February 1913. Shortly afterwards Madero and Suarez, the former vice president, were put out of the way, their execution being announced with the traditional formula that they were shot "while attempting to escape."[1]

This "*cuartelazo*" or *coup d'état* put the latent imperialism of the United States to the test. Huerta was regarded in Washington (as the letters of Walter Hines Page clearly prove) as a tool of Lord Cowdray (Pearson), the British oil baron, who at this time was seeking additional concessions not only in Mexico but also in Colombia.[2] And accordingly Wilson decided not to recognize Huerta as president of Mexico. Wilson even went so far as to send an ex-governor of Minnesota, John Lind, as his personal spokesman, to invite General Huerta to get out, and to permit a free election in which he would not be a candidate. The sardonic Indian general naturally refused. In all this Wilson was acting not as an imperialist, not as a champion of American oil interests, but as an anti-imperialist, and as a democrat. Latin America, he declared in his famous Mobile Speech of October 1913, must be emancipated from foreign financial interests and concession-hunters. As Colonel House wrote confidentially to Ambassador Page on November 4, 1913,—

[1] See Priestley, *The Mexican Nation, a History* (Macmillan, 1923), for a good historical account of the events which I merely sketch.

[2] Bryan "harangued Sir William Tyrell (secretary of the British foreign minister) on the wickedness of the British Empire, particularly in Egypt and India and in Mexico." The British Foreign Office, he declared, had handed its Mexican policy over to "oil barons."

It is to be the policy of this Administration henceforth not to recognize any Central American government that is not formed along constitutional lines. Anything else would be a makeshift policy. As you know, revolutions and assassinations in order to obtain control of governments are instituted almost wholly for the purpose of loot and when it is found that these methods will not bring the desired results, they will cease. The President also feels strongly in regard to foreign financial interests seeking to control these unstable governments through concessions and otherwise. This, too, he is determined to discourage as far as it is possible to do so.

In the face of this new "Wilson Doctrine," Lord Cowdray renounced his intention of obtaining a concession in Colombia and concessions in Mexico, and the British Government permitted Wilson to handle Mexico in his own way. Page commented in a private letter, "Cowdray has, I am sure, lost (that is, failed to make) a hundred million dollars that he had within easy reach by this Wilson Doctrine, but he's game."

What would Wilson do with Huerta? The "Wilson Doctrine" meant not only opposition to financial imperialism, but also disapproval of revolutions and dictatorships in Latin America. It meant insistence on orderly, constitutional, democratic government. It meant if necessary, as Page put it, "shooting men into self-government." Now Huerta was viewed by Wilson as a despotic dictator—worse still, a dictator stained with the blood of Madero and Suarez. On the other hand, Wilson believed that Huerta's antagonists, who called themselves Constitutionalists, were genuine champions of liberty. The Constitutionalists had taken up arms against Huerta, and through their leader Venustiano Carranza they had declared their intention of restoring the constitution and granting land to the landless. With such aims, Wilson naturally sympathized,[1] and there can be little doubt that when, in December 1913, he declared his policy to be one of non-intervention or "watchful waiting," he cherished the hope that the Constitutionalists would soon be able to overthrow Huerta. But before many months had passed, Wilson found himself aiding in the elimination of the dictator. While Huerta was refused loans or arms, the Constitutionalist insurgents were permitted, beginning February 1914, to purchase munitions in the United States. In April, a boatload of

[1] American oil interests also gave sympathy and aid to Carranza, according to Mr. Doheny's testimony in 1919, 66th Cong., 2nd Sess., *Sen. Doc.* V. 9, pp. 292-3.

American marines, landing at Tampico, were arrested by Huerta's troops, and although they were speedily released with apologies, the American Admiral Mayo refused to be satisfied with less than a formal salute of twenty-one guns as reparation for what he considered an insult to the American flag. "National honor" was now involved. Wilson's hand was forced. Reluctantly but firmly he supported Admiral Mayo's demand for the salute. Huerta was willing to fire the salute if the United States would give a written promise to return the courtesy. Such a promise, Secretary Bryan felt, might appear as recognition of Huerta, and could not be made. As Huerta refused the salute without the promise, President Wilson asked Congress for authority to use force. Force was used, but in a most unexpected way; American troops were landed not in Tampico but at Vera Cruz, April 21, and after some bloodshed established themselves in that city. No salute did they obtain, but they seized a cargo of arms for which Huerta was waiting, and took charge of the customs house from which Huerta had derived revenue. Such measures definitely aided the Constitutionalists and hastened the downfall of Huerta.[1]

After Huerta's downfall in July 1914, the victorious Constitutionalist leaders, who had been expected to restore constitutional government, fell out among themselves and plunged Mexico into worse chaos of civil war. Probably the land question had much to do with the conflict. Carranza, chief of the Constitutionalists, was pledged to a program of land reform which was not radical enough to suit the Zapata faction, but too radical to please the great landowners. It is said that some of the latter bribed Pancho Villa, an ex-bandit, who had won brilliant laurels as a Constitutionalist "general," to turn against Carranza. At any rate, civil war continued among the Carranza, Villa, and Zapata factions, despite the attempts of the United States, Argentina, Brazil, Chile, Bolivia, Guatemala, and Uruguay to bring the rival leaders into peaceful agreement, and finally Carranza as the strongest of the three leaders was granted recognition by the United States and other powers, in the fall of 1915.

Carranza's recognition as president, however, did not end the civil war, nor did it settle the international difficulties. When, after many battles, Villa found defeat staring him in

[1] *Foreign Relations*, 1914, pp. 443 ff.

the face, he sought to evade disaster by the simple expedient of provoking American intervention. On March 9, 1916, he crossed the border, raided Columbus, N. M., killing seventeen Americans, and fled back into Mexico. So easy as this it was to set in motion the familiar imperialist machinery of a "punitive expedition." As France had sent punitive expeditions into Tunis and Morocco, as England had sent punitive expeditions into Afghanistan, so President Wilson now sent General Pershing into Mexico with twelve thousand soldiers to punish Villa, and eighteen thousand were stationed along the border, and presently a hundred thousand of the National Guard were brought up to the border. Invading another nation's territory is ordinarily an act of war, but if the invaded nation is a "backward" nation, it is only a "punitive expedition," and so President Wilson regarded it. Carranza, however, and many Mexicans, considered it a violation of Mexican sovereignty, and adopted so hostile an attitude that the punitive expedition against Villa threatened to become a formal war on Mexico. It would have become such, and ended in conquest, had thorough-going imperialism reigned at Washington, but Wilson accepted mediation by other American nations, and at length withdrew Pershing's expedition, in February 1917; possibly the imminence of war with Germany hastened the evacuation. The expedition had cost over $130,000,000, and Villa had not been captured or killed. The most one can say is that American national pride had been gratified.

Carranza was now free to carry out his program of constitutionalism and land reform. Just as the last American troops were leaving Mexico, he promulgated a new constitution (February 1917), which provided for a Congress elected by universal suffrage, a president elected for four years without the right of re-election, freedom of justice, and a number of radical social reforms such as the eight-hour day in industry, a free employment bureau, a minimum wage (to be fixed by each state), a public health department, and so forth. It also declared the confiscation of Church property and prohibited religious schools, thus manifesting the marked anti-clericalism of the Carranza faction. Moreover, the Carranza government proceeded vigorously with land reform. By September 1, 1919, land grants aggregating 37,434,658 acres had been annulled; a number of large estates were broken up; and thousands of acres were restored or granted to villages and Indian communities.[1]

All this may have been satisfactory enough to the White House, but not to American business interests. Against the provisions of the new constitution regarding land, labor, mines, and oil a storm of protest arose in the United States. The breaking-up of large estates, in order to give small farms to peons and common lands to villages, was a menace to Americans who owned huge ranches in Mexico. Article 27 of the Mexican Constitution, declaring subsoil products (oil and metals) to be the property of the nation, and forbidding foreigners to acquire land, mining, oil, or industrial concessions unless they waived all right of appeal to their own governments, seemed to place the oil and mining interests in jeopardy. The oil question was particularly grave. In accordance with Article 27, the Carranza government ventured to impose royalty and rental taxes on oil lands, and a ten-per-cent *ad valorem* tax on all oil produced; still worse, it announced that oil rights would be confiscated unless the companies claiming to have concessions for them at once registered their titles, and proved that they were exploiting their oil lands. To be sure, in spite of taxes and decrees, the oil companies continued to increase their output, and to pay large dividends; but they feared worse measures. With the support of the State Department at Washington, they refused to recognize the Mexican Government's right to "nationalize" oil rights which had been granted by concessions from previous governments. The Mexican question became increasingly a question of economic imperialism; whether Mexico had the right to regulate or restrict the exploitation of Mexican resources, particularly oil, by American capitalists. The leading oil companies as well as the Anaconda copper interests, and others, formed a "National Association for the Protection of American Rights in Mexico," with a press bureau on Fifth Avenue, New York City, to conduct propaganda against the attitude of the Carranza government. The Doheny oil interests offered a million-dollar retainer to President Wilson's son-in-law, Mr. McAdoo, who visited both Mexico and the White House in their behalf. And perhaps one might be warranted in the inference

[1] On the agrarian reforms see C. W. Hackett's paper in *Proceedings* of Acad. Pol. Sci., July 1926.

that there was at least some connection between the endangered oil interests and the lively agitation in the United States for active "intervention" in Mexico.

Senator Fall, later implicated in the notorious oil scandals of 1923-4, was conspicuous among the advocates of intervention. The inclusion of Senator Fall in President Harding's cabinet was sufficient indication that the new administration inaugurated at Washington in March 1921 was disposed to insist on American oil rights in Mexico. While a member of the cabinet, Mr. Fall received a hundred thousand dollars, in a satchel, as a "loan" from his old friend Mr. Doheny, head of the Mexican Petroleum Company, at least so Mr. Doheny later testified. The incident is illuminating as an instance of the methods by which imperialism sometimes operates.

The Harding Administration, as might have been expected, firmly championed American oil rights as opposed to the Mexican constitution. Without a guarantee of American rights, the Washington government would not recognize the Obregon government—which, by the way, had taken office in Mexico in 1920, after a new revolution ending in the flight and murder of Carranza. Though Obregon showed himself a capable president, and established order in the greater part of Mexico, and instituted commendable administrative reforms, and insisted that Article 27 would not be applied retroactively to the prejudice of oil concessions acquired prior to 1917, nevertheless he was denied official recognition. As the New York loan market was thereby closed to him, Obregon was willing to go far in an effort to obtain recognition. In 1922 his finance minister reached an agreement with a New York banker, Mr. Thomas Lamont of the Morgan firm, for resumption of interest payments on Mexico's debt of half a billion dollars.[1] The following year, Obregon came to a settlement with the United States Government, whereby lands obtained by Americans before 1917 were

[1] See *International Conciliation*, No. 187. By this agreement Mexico was to have made payments for the service of this debt amounting to $15,000,000 in 1923 and increasing by $2,500,000 a year until they reached $25,000,000 a year. But on the payments for 1924 and 1925 Mexico defaulted, and a new agreement was made by Finance Minister Pani and Mr. Lamont in October, 1924, for the resumption of the schedule of payments, the postponed payment of the arrears for 1924-5, and the return of the Mexican National Railways to private management. The operation of most of the railways had been taken over by the Huerta Government in December, 1914.

to be exempted from land reform laws, and mineral and oil rights conceded to Americans and exploited before May 1, 1917, were to be respected. In other words, the Mexican nationalization program would apply only to properties acquired since 1917. Further, the claims of the United States for a huge sum as damages for injuries done to Americans and their property during the tumultuous years 1910 to 1920, and the claims of Mexico for damages caused by the occupation of Vera Cruz and by the Pershing expedition, were to be settled by mixed commissions.[1] On these terms Obregon purchased recognition in 1923.

Hardly had these amicable arrangements been made when a new rebellion flared up in Mexico. Its leader, de la Huerta, a former member of Obregon's cabinet, may have been actuated solely by personal ambition; he claimed to be fighting against Obregon's attempts to interfere with freedom of election; but he was generally regarded as the candidate of the conservatives, who desired that landowners should be indemnified for confiscated estates, and that labor radicalism should be checked. It was also alleged by Obregon that de la Huerta's rebellion was backed by British oil interests, particularly by El Aguila (The Mexican Eagle Co., controlled by the Royal Dutch-Shell combine); if this be true, it is worth noting that an American oil magnate, Mr. Doheny, lent Obregon five million dollars to suppress the revolt, and that the Huasteca company, a subsidiary of Mr. Doheny's Mexican Petroleum Company, received recognition of its claims to most of the Juan Felipe Hacienda, a rich oil tract in the state of Vera Cruz.

Mexico, it may be inferred, continued to be a battleground not only for Mexican radicals and conservatives, agrarians and hacendados, clericals and anticlericals, but also for Mr. Doheny's "Mexican Pete" (American), and Standard Oil, and Mexican Eagle (Anglo-Dutch). When the Royal Dutch-Shell had bought out Lord Cowdray's interest in the Mexican Eagle in 1918, and in 1925 the Standard Oil Company of Indiana bought up a controlling interest in the Doheny companies—Mexican Petroleum and the Pan-American Petroleum and Transport—the battle lines were more clearly drawn, between the greatest American oil combine and the powerful Anglo-Dutch syndicate. The magnitude of the battle may be gauged by the capital investment

[1] *Amer. Jour. Int. Law*, 1924, Supplement, pp. 143 ff.

in the Mexican oil industry, which was estimated by the Mexican Department of Industry in 1923 at about 525 million dollars (of which 57.7% was American ownership, 33.8% British, and less than 2% Mexican). In 1924 the United States Department of Commerce issued a semi-official estimate placing the American investment in Mexican oil lands and refineries at 478 millions. And in 1925 a Wall Street firm put the figure as high as 700 millions. Mr. Doheny in 1924 gave the amount of his own interests in Mexico as $218,000,000.[1]

It must never be forgotten, however, that the Mexican and United States governments are parties in the contest. Under President Calles, who succeeded Obregon in 1924, a new crisis was precipitated by the enactment of Mexican oil and land laws. The oil law reaffirmed the inalienable national dominion over petroleum resources and required foreigners to comply with article 27 of the Constitution and seek confirmation, within one year, for concessions, leases and titles acquired prior to May 1, 1917. The land law established a "prohibited zone" of 100 kilometers from the international boundaries and 50 kilometers from the seacoasts, within which zone aliens cannot acquire lands, even as shareholders in a Mexican company. Aliens who now have such lands, however, may hold them until their death; aliens may acquire lands or mining concessions in the interior by becoming members of a Mexican company, renouncing all right to invoke the protection of their own governments, and holding their property on the same footing as Mexicans. Against this legislation there was a sharp outcry in the United States. Taking up the diplomatic cudgels for American interests, the United States Government entered protests against the new laws. What

[1] *New York Times*, March 3, 1924. The following list of ten leading companies producing oil in Mexico may be of interest. Production for 1921 is shown in millions of barrels, with percentages in parentheses.

Company	Production	Percent
Huasteca Petroleum Co. (Doheny, sold to Standard in 1925)	28.7	(15%)
Transcontinental Petroleum Co. (Stand. of N. J.)	25.5	(13%)
El Aguila or Mexican Eagle (Royal Dutch-Shell)	25.5	(13%)
Mexican Gulf Oil Co. (Mellon)	13.7	(7%)
Agwi Oil Co. (Atlantic Gulf)	12.1	(6%)
Texas Co	11.3	(6%)
International Petroleum Co. (Sinclair interests)	10.0	(5%)
Island Oil and Transport Co	8.9	(5%)
La Corona Oil Co. (Royal Dutch-Shell)	8.5	(4%)
Freeport & Mexican Fuel Oil Corp. (Sinclair)	8.1	(4%)

(The table is compiled from data supplied by Mrs. Marsh.)

the outcome will be was not clear when these pages were written.[1]

North American Interests in South America

In South America the United States has been less vitally interested than in Mexico, Central America, and the Caribbean islands, yet there has been some interest, especially in the countries bordering the Caribbean Sea, namely, Colombia and Venezuela. Colombia, after Roosevelt's maneuver with Panama, long cherished bitter resentment and showed preference to British capital in granting oil and other concessions. On one occasion, in 1913, Lord Cowdray had almost in his grasp a big concession for oil development, railways and harbor works in Colombia, when in deference to the Wilson Doctrine he dropped the negotiations. This incident revealed the importance of conciliating Colombia. Moreover, President Wilson sincerely desired to right the wrong which had been done to Colombia in 1903, and which had embittered the feelings of many South Americans toward the United States. Accordingly, on April 6, 1914, the American minister to Colombia signed a treaty expressing "sincere regret" for the Panama incident, and promising to Colombia twenty-five million dollars.[2] The Senate, however, was reluctant to ratify a treaty which seemed to reflect so censoriously on a previous administration. Roosevelt, indeed, scornfully referred to the document as a "blackmail treaty."[3] But seven years later, after Wilson had been replaced by Harding, a Republican Senate ratified the treaty, omitting the "sincere regret" clause.[4] It has been alleged, but not definitely established, that ratification was in part due to the oil interests which in other matters proved to be so influential with the Harding administration.[5] Probably the desire in Washington to conciliate Latin-American opinion in general was an important, if not the primary, reason for the payment of so large a sum to Colombia. It cannot be disputed, however, that Ameri-

[1] For the new laws, see *N. Y. Nation*, 121, No. 3137, pp. 215-216, and *Diario Official*, Dec. 31, 1925, and Jan. 21, 1926.

[2] *Foreign Relations*, 1914, pp. 163-4.

[3] *Fear God and Take Your Own Part.*

[4] *State Papers*, 1921, pp. 678-682. Ratifications were exchanged March 1, 1922.

[5] See *The New York Times*, March 14, 1921, Washington dispatch.

can capital was very active in the oilfields, platinum mines and banana plantations,[1] nor is it difficult to foresee that as the oil industry develops in Colombia a problem similar to, though simpler than, the Mexican problem will develop with it.

Venezuela has been allowed to have its dictators and revolutions without interference, as American economic interests in this country have been relatively insignificant, although quite recently prospects have opened up of important mineral and oil development.

The Lago Petroleum Company, organized in 1923, secured eight thousand square miles of oil land and soon became the largest producer in Venezuela; in 1925 it was acquired by a subsidiary of the Indiana Standard Oil, which had recently purchased control of the Doheny companies in Mexico and appeared to be launching a campaign, with the support of New York financiers, to win a dominant position in the oil lands of the Caribbean area. The chief opponent of the Standard, here as in Mexico, was the Royal Dutch-Shell combine, controlled by an Anglo-Dutch syndicate.

Being on the Caribbean Sea, moreover, Venezuela is of considerable strategic interest and may be said to fall within the American sphere of influence. Fear that Great Britain intended to extend British Guiana by encroaching on Venezuela led in 1895 to the celebrated Olney version of the Monroe Doctrine, referred to above, and to Cleveland's threat of war. Again in 1902-3 the United States stepped forward to protect Venezuela, this time against an attempt on the part of Germany, Great Britain, and Italy to collect debts by means of naval blockade. Great Britain and Italy amiably withdrew their ships, but only a threat by President Roosevelt to send the American battle fleet to the scene could convince the German Government that it would not be permitted to gain even a leased port in

[1] Dunn, *op. cit.*, pp. 74-78. Standard Oil has acquired the most important oil concessions (the De Mares concession, held by the Tropical Oil Co. of Pittsburgh). The platinum mines are worked by the South American Gold and Platinum Company, of which Mr. Adolph Lewisohn is president. The Government's finances were reorganized by Professor Kemmerer, of Princeton, in 1923. In 1926 it was announced that Colombia was negotiating with New York bankers for a loan of $45,000,000, to retire old bonds and to inaugurate a program of railway construction which will involve an expenditure of $100,000,000.

Venezuela.[1] It was on this occasion that Luis Drago, Argentine foreign minister, proposed what is known as the Drago Doctrine, namely, that European powers must not use armed force to collect debts in Latin America.[2] This Doctrine, we may as well add, was approved by a Pan-American Conference in 1906, and, in modified form, by thirty-nine nations at the Hague Conference of 1907. As modified, it condemned the use of force for the collection of public debts unless the debtor country refused arbitration or refused payment of claims established as just by an arbitration court.[3]

Pan-Americanism

In the rest of South America the interest of the United States has been less vigorous.[4] To be sure, the Monroe Doctrine applied originally and still applies to the entire southern continent, as well as to Central and North America, and the United States would undoubtedly resent European or Asiatic encroachment on the independence or integrity of any of the Latin-American republics; but the United States has evinced no concern over the settlement of large numbers of Germans in Brazil, Italians in Argentine, and of some Japanese and Chinese in several countries, nor has the United States attempted to exercise south of the equator the veto on concessions or the same strict censorship of revolutions or the police power which have been asserted in the Caribbean region. Moreover, there has been a growing tendency in the United States to regard at least the progressive "ABC Powers" (Argentina, Brazil and Chile) as associates rather than protégés; it has even been proposed that these if not other South American nations should become partners with the United States in maintaining a modified Monroe Doctrine, a mutual guarantee of independence. President Wilson, notably, in his address at the second Pan-American Scientific Congress in 1916, proposed that the states of America unite "in guaran-

[1] Thayer, *Life of John Hay*, II, pp. 284-290; Roosevelt's version in Bishop, *Theodore Roosevelt*, I, pp. 221-9; Robertson, *Hispanic-American Relations* with the United States, pp. 114-121.

[2] *U. S. Foreign Relations*, 1903, pp. 1 ff.

[3] Robertson, *op. cit.*, p. 128.

[4] That is, political interest. On the important economic interests see Dunn, *op. cit.*, pp. 61-89.

teeing to each other absolute political independence and territorial integrity."[1]

The old Monroe Doctrine was blending in with the new Pan-Americanism. The Pan-American policy proposed by Secretary Blaine in the 1880's contemplated not only friendly relations, and Pan-American conferences, but also a Pan-American customs union and a Pan-American railway, and common weights, measures and coinage.[2] His plan was never realized in its entirety, but at least a periodic conference of diplomatic representatives—the Pan-American Conference—was instituted, and later a "Union of American States," maintaining a bureau at Washington. Pan-Americanism developed mainly as an interchange of diplomatic amenities, of reciprocal assurances of good-will, rather than as the sort of economic federation Blaine had conceived. The idea prevailed that the United States and the Latin-American republics[3] should be a group of states cemented together by periodic conferences, by friendship, by a mutual regard for the peace of the Western Hemisphere.[4] In this connection, it may be noted that the United States increasingly assumed the rôle of arbitrator in disputes between Latin-American neighbors—between Costa Rica and Panama, between Chile and Peru, etc. What would happen if two South-American nations should refer a dispute to the World Court, and one of them refuse to accept the decision, and resort to force, thereby incurring the penalties prescribed under the Covenant, is an interesting and not altogether academic question; for such an incident would perhaps involve European intervention, contrary to twentieth-century versions of the Monroe Doctrine.[5]

[1] See Alvarez, *op. cit.*, for this (p. 559) and kindred declarations.

[2] Robertson, *op. cit.*, pp. 392 ff.

[3] At a meeting of the Pan-American Commercial Congress in December, 1925, Mr. Frederic Hudd, representing Canada, expressed the hope that Canada would henceforth participate in all such conferences, and the belief that no conception of Pan-America could be complete that did not include Canada. Although it was promptly pointed out that Mr. Hudd had no authority to pledge Canada's allegiance to Pan-Americanism, nevertheless the incident may serve as a suggestion that Pan-Americanism without the great Dominion is incomplete if not anomalous. Canada, it may be remarked, is the largest single field of American foreign investment and has attracted about one-fourth of all capital exported from the United States. See Dunn, *op. cit.*, pp. 57 ff., and Nearing and Freeman, *op. cit.*, pp. 19-29, on American financial interests in Canada. To my mind they demonstrate that financial and commercial interests do not necessarily imply political imperialism.

[4] Robertson, *op. cit.*, ch. 10.

[5] On the other hand, article 21 of the Covenant gives the Monroe Doctrine

Another significant phase of American policy is the principle that in Latin America orderly constitutional government must be maintained, as against revolutions and dictatorships. This was a basic principle in Wilson's Mexican policy. It was expressed by Wilson in his speech of Jan. 6, 1916, when he advocated an agreement: "That no state of either continent will permit revolutionary expeditions against another state to be fitted out on its territory, and that they will prohibit the exportation of the munitions of war for the purpose of supplying revolutionists against neighboring governments." It was reiterated by Mr. Hughes as Secretary of State. It would mean a ban on revolutions. It means that the United States insists on the practice of its own principle of constitutional government, whether the other American states are qualified for it or not. Yet, oddly enough, it has been disregarded by the United States in Haiti and Santo Domingo where American marines have on occasion exercised a purely military dictatorship; Wilson aided the Constitutionalist revolution in Mexico; and no consistent attempt has been made to censor revolutions in South America. In a word, the principle is not to be taken too literally.

As regards economic matters, the affiliations of South America prior to the Great War were chiefly with Europe, particularly with England, for British capital built the South American railways, and British, German, and French shippers handled most of South America's foreign trade. It has been estimated that before the Great War about one-fifth of British overseas investments were in Latin-America, and that the British holdings in South America amounted to about three billion dollars. But the war enabled the United States to obtain a larger share of South American commerce, and New York rivaled London as financial capital of South America.

The National City Bank, and others, established many branches in Hispanic America. North American investors bought South American bonds, and sought South American concessions. Consider, for example, the case of Peru, to whose Government an American syndicate in 1925 loaned $7,500,000 at seven and one-half per cent interest. The New Jersey Standard Oil, operating

a status in international law. It reads: "Nothing in this Covenant shall be deemed to affect the validity of international engagements, such as treaties of arbitration or regional understandings like the Monroe Doctrine, for securing the maintenance of peace."

through the International Petroleum Co., Ltd., gained control over eighty per cent of the oil production of the country. In 1925 the capital invested in Peru by the Standard Oil, the Cerro de Pasco Copper Corporation, the American Smelting and Refining Co., the Vanadium Corporation of America, and other American concerns, amounted to about $100,000,000—a fairly considerable and rapidly increasing sum, although it was only one-third of the total foreign capital invested in Peru. It was estimated that the new South American loans and investments floated in the New York money market during the year 1926 would amount to no less than $400,000,000.[1]

Toward the colossus of the north, some South American nations had long felt suspicion bordering on hostility. They resented the assumption by the United States of the rôle of protector and spokesman for the New World; they were irritated by the condescension with which North Americans so frequently dealt with South American affairs; above all they were provoked by the "imperialism" of the United States in Mexico, Central America, and the Caribbean. One eminent Latin-American publicist wrote: "To save themselves from Yankee imperialism the American democracies would almost accept a German alliance, or the aid of Japanese arms; everywhere the Americans of the North are feared."[2] This is no doubt exaggerated: it represented the attitude of extremists; yet in its way it indicates the reaction of Latin American nationalism against North American imperialism.[3]

Hoping to overcome hostile opinion in South America Wilson proposed the new version of the Monroe Doctrine which has already been mentioned, and (on Oct. 27, 1913) solemnly declared "that the United States will never again seek one additional foot of territory by conquest"; and Secretary Hughes repeatedly proclaimed that the United States had no imperialist aspirations; and indefatigable publicists have urged the substitution of a mutual guaranty for the Monroe Doctrine; and much propaganda has been directed toward the conquest of South American friendship. The substitution of Pan-American intervention for United States intervention, and of international

[1] *New York Times*, Dec. 17, 1925.
[2] F. Garcia Calderon, *Latin America*, p. 298.
[3] Consult representative opinions in Alvarez, *op. cit.*, Part II.

financial receiverships for United States financial protectorates, in the region between the equator and the United States, would perhaps keep order there more effectively, and conciliate South America, and therefore aid American trade with South America. But such a substitution will be possible only when public opinion in the United States divests itself of the spirit of domination, discards the "big stick" along with "dollar diplomacy" and learns to treat Latin American nations as associates rather than protégés. The great obstacle is not material interests, but a psychological factor, national pride, and national pride is the mother of imperialism.

CHAPTER XVII

NATIONALISM VERSUS IMPERIALISM IN EUROPE

The Survival of the Weak

Were imperialism sheer, ruthless greed—nothing more, nothing less—the smaller and weaker nations of Europe, like those of Africa and Asia, would doubtless have been swallowed up by insatiable Great Powers. That many of these impotent small nations have been permitted to remain independent is a fact of the utmost significance for any analysis of the psychology of imperialism. And that there has been a marked tendency of late toward imperialist domination of certain areas of Europe, is not less significant. These two facts require explanation.

There are really a surprising number of small nations in Europe, utterly incapable of defending themselves against any serious aggression on the part of a Great Power. In 1914 there were twenty-one such states, too small or too weak to resist a Great Power.[1] Only a few of these, namely Andorra, San Marino, the Holy See, Luxemburg, Liechtenstein, and Monaco, could be described as falling under the shadow of any Great Power; the other fifteen were independent. And some were tempting morsels. Belgium's rich coal resources could not be defended by a Belgian army which in peace boasted only 50,000 men and in war a potential 350,000—a tenth of the force France or Germany could exert. Sweden's treasure of high-grade iron

[1] Albania, Andorra, Belgium, Bulgaria, Denmark, Greece, Holy See, Liechtenstein, Luxembourg, Monaco, Montenegro, Netherlands, Norway, Portugal, Rumania, San Marino, Spain, Sweden, Switzerland, Serbia, Turkey-in-Europe. Since the Great War, Montenegro and Serbia have been merged with Yugoslav lands taken from Austria-Hungary to form the Serb, Croat and Slovene State; and the following have been added to the list of smaller states—Austria, Hungary, Czechoslovakia, Poland, Esthonia, Latvia, Lithuania, Finland. The Free City of Danzig, the internationalized Saar Basin, quasi-independent Iceland, and the new Irish Free State might possibly be included, but are not, because the first two are under the control of the League, and the second pair are under at least the suzerainty of Denmark and Great Britain, respectively.

ore, needful to the German steel industry, could not be protected by the 200,000 or so men Sweden might put into the field in case of war; nor was Spain's army of 152,000, with an estimated war strength of 200,000 any adequate guarantee of a country rich in iron, coal, zinc, lead, and other minerals; nor could 300,000 soldiers repel any powerful invader from the valuable forests, the oilfields, or the fertile grainlands of Rumania.

Such smaller nations, the German Emperor William II is reported to have said, cannot permanently remain independent units in this age of competition among gigantic economic units. Inevitably the small must gravitate into the orbits of the great. He was not alone in this conception. Pan-German fanatics dared to hope that ultimately the "Teutonic" Low Countries, and Scandinavia, and the partially Germanized Baltic provinces, and other lands, would be attached in some way as satellites or dependencies to Teutonic Central Europe embracing Austria as well as Germany. Friedrich Naumann's *Mitteleuropa* was but one of the more popular of the expositions of this general belief. The theme in a general way is analogous to that of the imperialism described in the earlier chapters of this book; the idea that great industrial nations must expand. If the German expression of the idea has been chosen for illustration, it is not because the Germans were unique in expressing it.

Why was the idea not carried out? Why were the imperialist tendencies of the Great Powers restrained, as regards the small countries of Europe? Why have small nations been allowed to continue in existence and to increase in number? Two reasons appear quite clearly.

First, the smaller European states were, almost without exception, so highly civilized and well governed that imperialists could not easily have awakened in any Great Power either the glowing indignation against "atrocities" or the humanitarian zeal for the "white man's burden" and the "civilizing mission" that are usually required for popular support of aggressive imperialism. For conquering Central Africa one could plead as justification the necessity of abolishing the slave trade; but what excuse could be offered for conquest of Sweden? No concession or protectorate or "sphere of interest" was required to enable Germany to obtain iron ore from Swedish mines, or English capitalists to develop Spanish mineral resources, because in civilized countries the ordinary processes of investment, industry and commerce suffice for such purposes. As a matter of fact, Germany did obtain iron from Sweden and oil from Rumania, and British capitalists did invest in Spain, as well as in most other countries on the Continent, and French capitalists bought the bonds of European governments, by legitimate and peaceful business transactions. The major economic factors in imperialism—making secure loans granted to an irresponsible government, exploiting hitherto undeveloped resources, opening up a market—were usually lacking.

Almost without exception, the European states were too well governed to offer the opening for imperialism; but not quite without exception. European Turkey comes to mind at once; and the European possessions of Turkey would doubtless have been taken by Great Powers had it not been for Balkan nationalism; as it was, Austria-Hungary took Bosnia-Herzegovina and Russia took Bessarabia. Another exception was Serbia, whose unstable government and unsavory record of assassinations had given Austrian public opinion some ground for the feeling that violence might justifiably be employed to punish Serbian misdeeds. Unruly Portugal, likewise, offered opportunities for foreign intervention, but was sheltered by alliance with England.

The last remark suggests a second reason. Even where some European state was turbulent enough to invite intervention, the intense rivalry of the Great Powers usually precluded such intervention. For example, an Austro-Hungarian attack on Serbia would be (and was, in 1914) opposed by Russia; a German foray into Belgium would be resisted by France and England. Rival imperialisms have occasionally neutralized each other, at least for a time, in Asia and Africa; for example before 1907 neither Russia nor England dared appropriate Persia; or again, Korea's independence was long preserved by Russo-Japanese rivalry. But in Europe this consideration was of much greater weight. In Europe the acquisition of even a small territory by a Great Power might be of immense strategic moment, might tilt the trembling Balance of Power. Strategy endowed small countries like Belgium, Switzerland, and Holland with such value that no Great Power could be permitted by the others to undertake conquest.

Consequently Europe was only to a very restricted extent a

field for imperialism. Possibly the German annexation of Alsace-Lorraine in 1871 might be called imperialistic; but it was an incident of German national unification and the German desire for its possession was certainly based less on any consideration of its economic value than on contentions that it was historically, ethnically, geographically, or strategically an integral part of the German nation. The Austro-Hungarian occupation of Bosnia-Herzegovina and Novi-bazar in 1878 and annexation of Bosnia-Herzegovina in 1908 may be set down to imperialism, or to something closely resembling the imperialism we have seen at work in Africa and Asia. There was in these actions some of the feeling of cultural superiority, some of the economic interest, much of the prestige-seeking, that are such typical elements of contemporary imperialism. Austro-Hungarian and German interests, moreover, acquired control of the Orient Railway, through the Balkans, and sought the right to construct other railways in the Balkans, and mingled economic business with political strategy in somewhat the same way that the reader has learned to recognize in China or in Asiatic Turkey. Any one eager to push the analogy may easily regard the rival aspirations and conflicting intrigues of Austria and Russia, the attempts of each to obtain political influence over the Balkan nations, as part of the story of imperialism. It is so well known that it need not be considered further here.

Economic and Military Imperialism in Europe Since 1914

The Great War of 1914 let loose latent imperialist passions. In Russia the hope of mastering the Balkans and Constantinople at last seemed realizable, as well as the design of adding German and Austrian to Russian Poland. In France ardent chauvinists dreamed of bringing Belgium and Luxemburg into the French orbit, commercially, and of establishing French domination, if not actual sovereignty, over the Saar Basin and the German Rhineland. That the French Government in some degree shared such designs is clear from the secret notes it exchanged in February and March, 1917, with the Russian Government, promising Russia a free hand in drawing the western frontier of Russia, in return for permission to annex the Saar

Basin in addition to Alsace-Lorraine, and to convert the Left Bank of the Rhine into an "autonomous" state occupied by French troops. Italy obtained from the Allies in 1915 a secret pledge to gratify the Italian desire for not only Italia Irredenta, which might be sanctioned by the principle of nationalism, but also part of Dalmatia and the Dalmatian islands and Albania—possession of which would make the Adriatic in truth an "Italian lake" and afford a foothold for Italian imperialism in the Balkan Peninsula.[1] Professor Salvemini has alleged that this program was originated by Italian shipping interests.[2] In Germany, on the other hand, a small but vociferous and influential minority clamored during the war for a thoroughly imperialistic peace: they demanded the iron area of French Lorraine, control of Belgium in one form or another, creation of a row of satellite states on the eastern border of Germany, or possibly actual annexation of Poland, Lithuania and the Baltic Provinces. Ludendorff, the masterful "Quarter Master General" who well-nigh dominated German policy in the last years of the war, seems to have lent his powerful support to such aims.[3]

German imperialist aims were balked by the fortunes of war; Russian imperialism was subverted by the Bolshevik Revolution; and Wilsonian idealism offered an obstacle at the Peace Conference to the aims of France and Italy. Yet the latter were realized in a measure. The Peace Conference planned that Italy should annex part of Albania and assume a mandate over the remainder; but revolts in Albania and a reaction against jingoism at home brought about Italy's withdrawal from Albania, and Albania became a free republic, a member of the League of Nations. France was more successful, but not wholly successful. By article 40 of the Treaty of Versailles, Germany renounced "all rights to the exploitation of the railways" of Luxemburg, and recognized that henceforth that grand duchy was no longer part of the German Zollverein; in other words, German economic control of this valuable iron-producing state was cancelled and the door was left open for French control. French plans for the Left Bank of the Rhine were modified. This populous segment of the demilitarized German nation was

[1] Cocks, *The Secret Treaties* gives these and other bargains.
[2] *Foreign Affairs*, Jan., 1926.
[3] *Ludendorff's Own Story*, I, pp. 379-380.

occupied by Allied troops, severed from the rest of Germany by a separate tariff régime. The coal mines of the Saar Basin were ceded to France, but instead of permitting France to annex the region outright, Wilson and Lloyd George succeeded in making it an internationalized territory under the political control of an international Governing Board appointed by the Council of the League of Nations, and in providing for a plebiscite in 1935. As regards both the Saar and the Rhineland, therefore, French imperialism was only partly gratified, and was partly checked by internationalism. The same tendency, it may be remarked, to impose international restraints on national imperialism, may be observed in the case of the German city of Danzig, desired by Poland for economic and strategic reasons, but established by the Peace Conference as a Free City under the administrative supervision of a commissioner appointed by the League of Nations. There was beginning to appear a significant conflict between international administration and national imperialism.

After the Peace Conference, French imperialists sought to secure by indirect means more than the Conference had granted, particularly as regards the Saar, the Left Bank, and the Ruhr. In the internationalized Saar Basin a French army of occupation was retained, French currency introduced, French schools established, French martial law declared; indeed, the measures taken by French military authorities in the Saar Territory were of such a nature that they were seriously challenged by Lord Robert Cecil and by Hjalmar Branting in the Council of the League of Nations. Ugly rumors were heard to the effect that French authorities were determined to prevent the inhabitants from voting for reincorporation into Germany in 1935. The fact that they are not heard now is an indication of the extent to which the situation has changed for the better in the last two years.

More ambitious French aims were disclosed by the "Dariac Report," a secret memorandum alleged to have been drawn up by the president of the Finance Commission of the Chamber of Deputies, and published by the *Manchester Guardian*. In this interesting document, the virtual separation of the Rhineland from Germany was urged on economic and strategic grounds. Another interesting document, cited by ex-Premier Nitti of Italy, was the alleged secret report, dated May 25, 1922, of a French military commission, which recommended not only the permanent military control of the Saar Basin, inclusion of the Left Bank in the French customs frontier, and prolonged occupation of the Rhine, but boldly pointed out the economic desirability of controlling the Ruhr Basin.[1]

These secret documents coincided to a marked degree with the tenor of French policy in post-bellum years, and with the public declarations of influential French industrialists and politicians. Poincaré as premier repeatedly announced that French troops would remain on the Rhine until Germany paid her reparations debt—which at that time seemed impossible. The Cologne bridgehead on the Rhine should normally have been evacuated in January 1925, had Germany been fulfilling the treaty terms, but French sentiment was strongly against even this partial relinquishment of the Rhine, and the decision was made by the Allies to continue the occupation until 1926. Attempts made by German "separatists" to set up a separate government in the Rhineland, independent of Prussia, were quite certainly favored, if not actually inspired, by French officials, though they may not have been instigated by the French Government itself. These maneuvers to detach the Rhineland from Prussia and to make it a buffer state dominated by France failed of fruition. They were significant as indicating a policy or desire, rather than for their results.

The boldest step toward French domination of western Germany was the seizure of the Ruhr basin by French (and Belgian) troops in January 1923. This district, on the right bank of the Rhine, was the very heart of the German iron and steel industries, and the most valuable coal-mining area possessed by Germany. Its seizure was justified by the French Government as a method of securing reparation from Germany; yet the deed could well be interpreted in line with the secret memoranda which have just been cited, and such an interpretation could find some support in the fact that French industrial magnates such as Loucheur were proposing that a portion of the stock of German industrial concerns in the Ruhr should be turned over to France. Such a plan, if it had been carried out, would have given France a permanent economic grip on the Ruhr. That would have been economic imperialism, not of the sort generally

[1] Nitti, *The Decadence of Europe*, pp. XV-XVIII.

displayed in Asia and Africa, but of a new type, better suited to Europe. But as a result of the adoption of the Dawes Plan, France evacuated the Ruhr without obtaining the desired interest in the Ruhr industries. Instead, the Allies collectively obtained a mortgage on German railways and German industries as a whole: again national imperialism was checked by internationalism. And the evacuation of the Ruhr was followed by the Locarno Conference.

French policy in Eastern Europe during the post-bellum period was also tinged with imperialism—economic and military imperialism, of a subtle form. By lending money to the members of the Little Entente (Czechoslovakia, Yugoslavia and Rumania), by providing military experts to train their armies, and by giving diplomatic support to their aspirations, and by making a formal alliance with the chief of them, Czechoslovakia, the French Government made these countries her protégés, her satellites. Such a relationship is legally quite different from a protectorate, which involves a partial transfer of sovereignty; nevertheless its practical results, in securing strategic and economic advantages, and in establishing a real though informal guidance over the policies of the protégés, were different in degree rather than in kind from the fruits of imperialist protectorates.

A more striking instance of this rarified imperialism may be found in French relations with Poland. Poland was naturally inclined toward France since the latter had been the most generous champion of extreme Polish territorial aspirations, at the Peace Conference and afterward. Moreover, as against the potential enmity of Russia or Germany, France would be Poland's most natural ally. Indeed, when a Red Army from Russia swept into Poland, menacing Warsaw, in 1920, it was France from whom the Poles obtained military supplies and military experts, and with the help of French officers Poland repelled the Bolshevists, extended her frontier to the east, and won peace with victory (by the Treaty of Riga, Oct. 12, 1920). This informal French patronage of Polish interests developed into a formal alliance. In February 1921 there was signed a Franco-Polish alliance treaty, by which the two nations agreed to "act in concert" in case either should be "attacked without provocation," and by which both agreed to cooperate in diplomatic and economic affairs. The cooperation may perhaps be described as somewhat one-sided. France made herself the resolute spokesman of the Polish claims in Upper Silesia, with the result that Poland secured a very favorable settlement in the partition of Upper Silesia, in October, 1921. It should be noted that what Poland obtained in this settlement was a rather larger share of the mining districts of Upper Silesia than strict conformity to the principle of self-determination might have allowed, and, further, that in the mines that passed under Polish sovereignty French financial interests secured a considerable measure of control. French economic imperialism, to be candid, operated through the medium of Polish nationalism—the iron hand wore a Polish glove. But the hand was there.

Moreover, France lent Poland four hundred million francs, to be used in purchasing military and other supplies in France, and in reorganizing the Polish army and railways. Thus Poland was more closely bound to her patron by finance and by military considerations. And a Franco-Polish commercial convention signed on February 6, 1922, arranged for reciprocal tariff reductions, favoring the importation of French goods into Poland and *vice versa*.

Not the old imperialism of annexation and protectorates, but a new imperialism of financial, economic and military patronage, may be seen in this Franco-Polish alliance. Less open, less brutal, less monopolistic, less secure, than conquest, the new imperialism was possible where conquest would have been quite inadmissible, and it was productive of many of the advantages obtained elsewhere by conquest. It gave France a real, though unacknowledged and insecure, influence over Polish foreign relations and Polish armaments; and it secured for French capital and French exports special favors in Poland.

Concessionaire Imperialism and Soviet Russia

By all odds the most striking instances of the newer imperialism in post-bellum Europe were those which concerned Soviet Russia. Before the war, Russia had been a field for French, Belgian, German and British investments, and the Tsar's government had borrowed heavily from France and England, but financial dependence had entailed neither political subservience nor the granting of wholesale concessions for privileged economic exploitation. War and Revolution opened the door to genuine imperialism. The war, cutting off imports of machinery and exports of grain, caused economic exhaustion, even retrogression, in Russia. This was followed by the Revolution, which in turn led to political instability and further economic exhaustion, aggravated by the Allied blockade and by Communist experimentation with the economic system. While Russia was in this condition, French support was given to counter-revolutionists, much as American support has been given on occasion to filibusters in Latin America; but the counter-revolutions were suppressed, and other tactics were needed. From 1921 on, West-European and American financial interests sought to obtain their ends in Russia through the familiar mechanism of concessions.

The scramble for concessions in Russia, beginning in 1921, may fairly enough be regarded as imperialism. In aim it was unquestionably similar to the quest of concessions in China or Turkey or Morocco; in method, however, it differed slightly, because Soviet Russia could not easily be bullied or coerced by punitive expeditions or assigned as a sphere of interest. Concession-hunters had to rely principally on Russia's crying need for foreign capital, and on such diplomatic pressure as their governments might be induced to exert, though diplomatic pressure was not very effective at Moscow. Russia did need foreign capital, however. In 1921 the Soviet Government decided upon what was called the New Economic Policy, a provisional compromise between Communism and Capitalism. One feature of the new policy was a willingness to offer industrial concessions to foreign capitalists, in order to stimulate production in Russia and thus to create conditions—so the Bolshevists argued—in which Communism might ultimately be successful. At the Hague Conference of 1922, the Russian delegates handed the allied experts a memorandum, stating that the Soviet Government was willing to offer concessions, to be exploitated by mixed stock companies in which foreign capital and the Soviet Government itself would share. There followed an elaborate list of industries in which concessions might be granted:[1]

[1] *L'Europe Nouvelle*, *fide* Culbertson, *Raw Materials*, pp. 101-2.

PETROLEUM INDUSTRY
1. Regions already exploited
    a. Baku region
    b. Grosny region
    c. Ural-Emba region
    d. Kuban region
    e. Turkestan
2. Regions prospected but not yet exploited
    Regions of Grosny
3. Unprospected regions and areas
    a. Baku region
    b. Ural-Emba region
    c. Kuban region
    d. Turkestan
    e. Province of Vologda

MINING INDUSTRY
A. Iron ore
B. Copper ore
C. Polymetallic ores
D. Coal
E. Gold and platinum

EXPLOITATION OF FORESTS
A. Thirty-three regions in European Russia
B. Caucasus
C. Siberia

PAPER MANUFACTURE

NEW ENTERPRISES
A. In the region of the Kem River
B. In the Kotlas region
C. Arkhangel region
D. Region of the Luga
E. Kuban

SUGAR INDUSTRY

MATCH INDUSTRY

MANUFACTURE OF AZOTIZED PRODUCTS

CHEMICAL INDUSTRY

ELECTROTECHNICAL INDUSTRY

AGRICULTURAL CONCESSIONS
1. Colonization concessions
2. Improvement concessions
3. Cultivation of cereals
4. Concessions for stock raising
5. Concessions for the construction of refrigerating establishments and elevators
6. Concessions for harvesting and utilizing medicinal herbs.

Such concessions usually gave the concessionaire monopolistic rights of exploitation over a specified natural resource, in a specified district, for a definite term of years, at the end of which the Government would have the right of repurchase at cost. A number of concessions were soon negotiated. Krupp of Germany and Sinclair of America, for instance, obtained concessions for agricultural development in the Don region; an English syndicate secured a concession to exploit a forest area of more than 200,000 dessiatines in the province formerly known as Vologda (now Komi); and others were reported or rumored.

But the most interesting were the oil concessions. Russia's petroleum resources, variously estimated at from eight to fifteen per cent of the world's total reserve, inspired keen desire and keener rivalry. Before the Great War foreign and Russian capitalists had built up flourishing oil industries in the Baku and Grosny districts. These, however, had been "nationalized" by the Soviet Government, and assigned to an official "trust" or governmental monopoly for exploitation, before the New Economic Policy was adopted. Such was the state of affairs when, in April 1920, France and England, represented by Premiers Millerand and Lloyd George, signed the celebrated San Remo Oil Agreement, providing for Anglo-French cooperation in seeking and exploiting oil resources in the Near East, in Rumania, in Galicia, and—what concerns us chiefly here—in Russia. After the adoption of the new policy by Russia, however, ambitious oil magnates endeavored to forget the San Remo pledge of cooperation and equal participation. Indeed, in the spring of 1922, Krassin threw a veritable bombshell into the Genoa Economic Conference by disclosing the fact that the Royal Dutch-Shell combine had been negotiating with the Moscow Government for a monopoly of the export of petroleum from Russia.

The Royal Dutch-Shell, one should explain, was the powerful Anglo-Dutch syndicate headed by Sir Henri Deterding. Wild rumors echoed through the press of further concessions to be obtained by the British. Indignantly French and Belgian oil interests vociferated against the grant to the British of oil properties they, French and Belgian capitalists, had owned in prewar Russia and lost by Bolshevist "nationalization." So strenuous were the Franco-Belgian protests, it was reported, that the Royal Dutch-Shell's negotiations fell through, and Deterding agreed to abide by the policy of cooperation with the French and Belgians in seeking the restoration of former oil properties and the acquisition of new fields in Russia. Thereupon the current of petroleum intrigue found less public subterranean channels, and only an occasional report or rumor leaked into the press regarding the progress of the bidding for Russian oilfields. A visit of Mr. Dodge, representing the Standard Oil, to Moscow was reported to have failed. A little later, the Sinclair Company was reported to have obtained a concession for large undeveloped oilfields in the Caucasus (Baku) region, on condition of floating a loan of a quarter of a billion dollars for Russia;[1] later, however, it was stated that this project, like so many others, had fallen to the ground.

An important concession was obtained in 1924 by the W. A. Harriman Company of New York, for a monopoly of the export of manganese—which is used in the manufacture of steel—from the rich deposits of Georgia, one of the states federated with Soviet Russia. Another interesting grant, for the exploitation of the Lena gold fields, was secured by a British concessionaire in 1925, but American capitalists enjoyed a half-interest in the enterprise.

American Finance and European Independence

The prominence of American concession-hunters in the Russian field was but one aspect of the startling development of the United States as the foremost contestant in the game of world finance. The Great War had transformed the United States, as has been said so many times, from a debtor into a creditor nation. The close of the war found the governments of Europe indebted to the United States government for war loans and for sundry supplies, to the amount of over ten billion dollars. Despite this huge extension of government credit to Europe, the tide of trade was flowing so strongly toward the United States, and Europe was so direly in need of funds for industrial as well as public purposes, that American bankers continued to make loans, and American investors continued to buy bonds, at a rate unparalleled in history. It was estimated that a billion dollars' worth of foreign securities, chiefly European, were being purchased in the United States each year in the post-war period.

In 1925 estimates published by the Department of Commerce, indicated that private American investors had purchased $1,665,000,000 in European government bonds or government-guaranteed securities, besides putting $450,000,000 into indus-

[1] Also an oil concession in Northern Sakhalin, later overridden by a Russo-Japanese treaty in 1925.

trial securities and direct investments. During the year 1925 American purchases of European securities amounted to about $610,000,000, and of other foreign securities about $660,000,000. J. P. Morgan and Company rescued the declining franc by lending a hundred million dollars to France; and the same firm headed a syndicate which placed in the United States half of the international loan extended to Germany in accordance with the Dawes Plan, in 1924. That Europe's need and America's affluence gave American financiers no small power in European affairs, became increasingly obvious, for American bankers could grant or withhold loans. It was this consideration that gave Mr. Thomas Lamont such decisive though unofficial authority in the London negotiations regarding the Dawes Plan, in 1924, and led some observers to believe that Wall Street held in its hand the destinies of the Old World. European observers, too, were aware of, and prone to exaggerate, America's overshadowing economic power. The fear that had once led the German Emperor to talk of the "American Peril" along with the "Yellow Peril"; the nightmare vision of Baron Sonnino, that astute Italian foreign minister who feared United States would establish a *pax Americana* in quarrelsome Europe; the apprehension expressed in his Memoirs by Count Serge Witte, the famous Russian statesman, that the United States would enthrone itself on the débris of Europe,—these and similar fears were revived and intensified in post-war Europe. Not much was said openly, except by an occasional daring historian or publicist, who might allude to the "gigantic" appetites, or the "*Ausbreitungspolitik*" of America. Rarely expressed publicly, the apprehension was not less strong, that American finance, backed by unrivalled natural resources and immense manpower, had now begun in Europe a "peaceful penetration" to be followed by imperialist domination, subtle, perhaps, and unavowed, but real.

These European fears are natural enough, but—like the nightmares they are—chimerical. Like all nightmares, they leave certain realities out of consideration. One of these realities is that though American finance in post-war years gained great influence in the world, it by no means enjoyed an irresistible power to dominate either its own government or European nations: it could make terms before extending loans, but it could not play the master as England had done in Egypt, or France in Morocco and Tunis, or Japan in Korea. Another reality is European civilization. European nations are too highly industrialized and too highly conscious of nationality to be easily or permanently dominated by a nation of kindred civilization. In a period of political instability, such as prevailed in eastern Europe after the war, or in times of extreme economic depression, imperialism of a sort is possible at the expense of European states, in proportion to their weakness and instability. But such imperialism, at least as affecting the larger nations, can hardly be more than a very subtle and rarified imperialism, nor when financial and political stability are regained, can it long endure.

Of greater significance, in the long view of events, is the striking development of internationalism as a substitute for certain functions of imperialism. The Free City of Danzig and the Saar Basin, both under the control of the League of Nations, were interesting though small-scale experiments in this direction. More important were the experiments in international financial control. First Austria, bankrupt, despairing, and impotent, was taken in hand by the League of Nations, and placed under a financial control, which stabilized the currency and somewhat revived business confidence, though it did not produce as marked an economic stimulus as might have been desired. Next Hungary, likewise bankrupt and impotent, instead of falling victim to some imperialist Great Power, accepted a financial commissioner named by the League of Nations, and rapidly climbed the hard path back to solvency. Then, in 1924, at the recommendation of the Dawes Committee of Experts, the Allies agreed with Germany for the imposition of a somewhat different form of international financial control upon Germany, for the purpose of replacing the worthless paper mark by a stable currency, and securing regular payment of reparations without destroying German economic life. The granting of a mortgage on the German railways and a mortgage on German industries to the Allies, the assignment of certain German taxes to the Commission appointed by the Allies, the provision for arbitration of disputes—these were highly interesting features, suggestive of the methods whereby recalcitrant or insolvent debtor states could be brought to book without employing such means as England used in Egypt, or the United States in Haiti and Santo Domingo. Perhaps such international politico-financial control may be called imperialism, if there be any satisfaction in using the term; but that between the British occupation of Egypt, or the American occupation of Haiti, or the French conquest of Morocco, on one hand, and the international supervision of German, Hungarian, or Austrian finances, there exists a wide gulf of difference, few unimpassioned students of world affairs are likely to deny.

CHAPTER XVIII

THE LEAGUE AND ITS MANDATES

Secret Treaties or Self-Determination

If Mr. David Lloyd George, then prime minister of England, meant what he said on January 5, 1918, he was uttering a challenge to the whole philosophy of modern imperialism as well as to the policy which his own Government had pursued up to that moment. In defining the war aims of the Allies he declared that the "principle of national self-determination" was "as applicable" to the German colonies as to European peoples, for the native chiefs and councils could be consulted as the representatives of their tribes. Applying the principle of self-determination to African and South Sea tribes was a relatively novel and certainly a revolutionary idea in itself, but Mr. Lloyd George added that the governing consideration should be 'to prevent their exploitation for the benefit of European capitalists or Governments."[1] Taken at its face value, this declaration would mean an end of imperialism for the German colonies, and once it had been applied to them, its application to other colonies could not consistently be denied. Self-determination and empire are irreconcilable foes.

Why the British premier made so amazingly radical a statement will be explained in a later paragraph, but first it is interesting to observe how diametrically opposed his utterance was to the policies hitherto pursued by the Allies. By a series of secret treaties and secret agreements the governments of the Allied Powers had arranged, in anticipation of victory, for the division of colonial spoils. France and England had exchanged notes (1916) providing for the annexation of the former German colonies in Africa. France and Great Britain promised to Italy, by the secret treaty of London (April 26, 1915), "compensation" if they enlarged their possessions in Africa, the compensation being in the form of additions to the Italian

[1] Temperley, *History of the Peace Conference*, I, p. 191.

colonies in that continent. Moreover, the British Union of South Africa expected to annex German South West Africa, which had been occupied by the Boers, and Belgium hoped to share in German East Africa, which troops from Belgian Congo had helped to conquer. As for the German colonies in the Far East, Great Britain in February 1917 had undertaken to support Japan's claims regarding the disposal of Germany's rights in Shantung and the German islands north of the equator, "it being understood that the Japanese Government . . . will . . . treat in the same spirit Great Britain's claims to the German islands south of the equator." France and Russia and Italy assented to this bargain. Thus the German colonies were to be appropriated, without reference to self-determination and without any thought of preventing exploitation.

Not only the German colonies, but also Turkey and Persia were considered legitimate spoils of imperialism. In March 1915 Great Britain and France had promised to Russia a portion of Turkey including Constantinople, and a free hand in northern Persia, it being agreed that the neutral zone in Persia should be added to the British sphere of influence, and that the claims of France and Great Britain in Turkey should be defined later. Next by the secret treaty of April 26, 1915, the Allies assured Italy that she would have Dodekanesia and her just share in the partition of Turkey, and mentioned the Adalia district of Asia Minor as being earmarked for Italy. Franco-Russian and Anglo-French agreements in the spring of 1916 assigned Turkish Armenia, in addition to Constantinople, to Russia; Syria, Cilicia, and a sphere of influence stretching eastward as far as the Persian border, to France; Mesopotamia, some ports in Palestine, and a broad sphere of influence, besides Cyprus, to Great Britain. Italy's "just share" was more precisely demarcated in 1917 so as to include not only Adalia but the whole southern coast of Anatolia and also the province of Smyrna.[1]

In sharp contrast to this official (and secret) policy of annexationist imperialism there grew up during the Great War

[1] For the secret treaties summarized above see Cocks, *The Secret Treaties;* Temperley, *op. cit.*, VI, pp. 1-22; Baker, *Woodrow Wilson and World Settlement*, I, chs. 3-4; Shane Leslie, *Mark Sykes*, pp. 250-8; Grannini, *I Documenti Diplomatici della Pace Orientale;* France, *Journal officiel*, Docs. Parlementaires, 1919, Chambre, no. 6665, p. 415.

an opposing policy, which explains Lloyd George's speech and, more important, gave birth to the existing system of colonial mandates. Opposition to imperialism was, of course, no novelty, as the early chapters of this book must have made clear. The significant features of the war-time opposition were the ideas of native self-determination and of internationalism. To trace the development of these ideas would be beyond the scope of this volume,[1] but the anti-imperialist opinions will be of interest in explaining the origin of the mandate system.

In a vivid little book that was much read in the United States, Mr. Walter Lippmann as early as 1915 reminded a forgetful public that the real "stakes of diplomacy" were being ignored by pacifists. "They will not face the fact that the diplomatic struggle, the armed peace, and the war itself revolves about the exploitation of weak territories." The task of internationalism, he concluded, was to destroy the imperialist theory that a business man must rely on his home government for support when he ventures into backward areas—"This is the central nerve of imperialism, and our business is to excise it." The method he recommended was ingenious. European conferences such as the Algeciras Conference on Morocco, should not be disbanded when they have adopted a treaty but should "continue in existence as a kind of senate, meeting from time to time" and supervising the administration of the treaty. Ultimately there would be one of these continuing conferences or international senates for each of the sore spots where world crises originate, acting as a sort of "upper house"; while a native assembly would constitute the "lower house." Colonial administration would gradually become internationalized. Men going into backward countries would look to these new institutions, rather than to their home governments, for protection; there would no longer be need of armed interventions and crises; and competitive imperialism would be deprived of its excuse and its stimulus.[2]

In England somewhat similar proposals were made. Mr. J. A. Hobson, eminent economist and anti-imperialist,[3] felt as Mr.

[1] See P. B. Potter, "Origin of the System of Mandates," *Amer. Pol. Sci. Rev.*, Nov., 1922; Walter Russell Batsell, in a book now in preparation, will cover this subject in detail.

[2] Walter Lippmann, *The Stakes of Diplomacy* (1915).

[3] His book on *Imperialism* is the classic indictment of imperialist doctrines and practices.

Lippmann did that the provisions of the Algeciras Act for international regulation of administration in Morocco indicated a direction in which a solution might be sought. He suggested that under the supervision of an international council an individual nation might be given the right of intervention and even of political control, in a backward country, under an express agreement to preserve the open door.[1] This sort of proposal had firm historic roots in the Morocco negotiations of 1906. Secretary Root, in correspondence about Morocco at that time, had referred to France and Spain as "mandatories," and Roosevelt had used the term "mandate." The name as well as the idea can be traced back at least that far, and perhaps something analogous to the idea may be found in the Berlin Act of 1885, placing the Congo basin under certain international restrictions, and prescribing, in particular, the open door. But to return to English ideas during the Great War, we find Mr. Philip Kerr, editor of the *Round Table*, speaking in 1916 of "trusteeship" and "tutelage" as the proper relationship between colonies and their possessors.[2] Kerr and other British students interested in imperial problems—a group of writers often known as the Round Table group—were probably a very important link in the chain that leads to the mandate system.

The idea of international control of colonies was given greater popular vogue through the memorandum on war aims adopted by the executive committee of the British Labour Party, in August 1917.[3] Condemning imperialism roundly, it proposed that all central Africa, from sea to sea and from the Zambesi to the Sahara—including Belgian, British and French colonies, and Liberia, as well as the conquered German protectorates—should be administered "by an impartial commission with its own trained staff," under the authority of the League of Nations that was to be established. There should be an open door for international trade, and the natives should be specially protected against expropriation and exploitation. Criticizing this program of international administration as impracticable, the Independent Labour Party published a declaration, toward the end of the same month, suggesting in place of direct interna-

[1] J. A. Hobson, *Towards International Government* (1915). *Cf.* H. N. Brailsford, *The War of Steel and Gold* (1915).

[2] Chapter V in *International Relations*, by A. J. Grant and others.

[3] London *Times*, Aug. 11, 1917, p. 4.

tional administration a plan of delegating the government of colonies to individual European states, "under the supervision of an International Commission."[1]

In somewhat modified form these conceptions found their place in the declaration of war aims adopted by the Inter-Allied Labor Conference which met in London, in February 1918. The representatives of labor organizations and Socialist parties in most of the Allied countries put themselves on record, in this declaration, as favoring the "frank abandonment of every form of Imperialism." The "colonies of all the belligerents in Tropical Africa" should be placed under "a system of control, established by international agreement under the League of Nations, and maintained by its guarantee, which, whilst respecting national sovereignty, would be alike inspired by broad conceptions of economic freedom and concerned to safeguard the rights of the natives." In particular, this system would "take account" of the wishes of the natives; it would defend their rights as regards land-ownership; and it would devote all colonial revenues to the well-being of the colonies themselves.[2]

Premier Lloyd George's speech of January 5, 1918, should be seen in this setting. It was made after the British Labour Party had been committed to its anti-imperialist platform. The clever Welsh statesman was endeavoring to dispel the idea that the Allies were fighting for the fulfilment of imperialist secret treaties (which had been published that winter). Yet he did not abrogate the treaties.

More sincere, but even less specific, was the principle laid down by President Wilson in Point Five of his Fourteen Points speech, January 8, 1918:—

> V. A free, open-minded, and absolutely impartial adjustment of all colonial claims, based upon a strict observance of the principle that in determining all such questions of sovereignty the interests of the populations concerned must have equal weight with the equitable claims of the government whose title is to be determined.

Between the lines one can easily read two conceptions characteristic of Wilsonian policy, namely, his earnest desire to prevent the peace settlement from becoming a sordid division of spoils, and his hatred—often expressed before 1918—of imperial-

[1] *Ibid.*, Aug. 29, 1917, p. 8.
[2] *Ibid.*, Feb. 25, 1918, p. 3.

ist greed and exploitation.[1] Yet the vagueness of Point Five shows how far he was from any specific plan for a mandate system. His first draft of the Covenant, made in the summer of 1918, contained no provision for such a system.

President Wilson and the Mandate System

The mandate system was in reality a compromise between the imperialist secret treaties, mentioned above, and the liberal, anti-imperialist ideas of which a few illustrations have been given. The form of the compromise was suggested to Wilson's mind by a pamphlet written, in December 1918, by General Jan Smuts of South Africa,[2] and therefore General Smuts has been regarded as the father of the mandate system. Yet the fundamental idea was not the exclusive invention of the South African statesman. He was certainly familiar with the theories of the Round Table group and the proposals of British Labor and perhaps was more a transmitter than an inventor in this matter. Curiously enough, too, Wilson might have met with the idea among his own advisers. Walter Lippmann, whose book has been mentioned, was prominent in the House Inquiry, which prepared data for the President on war aims and peace terms. George Louis Beer, who served on this Inquiry as expert on African problems, wrote a confidential memorandum on Mesopotamia, for the United States Government, in December 1918, suggesting that backward regions such as Mesopotamia might be "entrusted by international mandate to one state," and that "there should be embodied in the deed of trust most rigid safeguards to protect the native population from exploitation and also to ensure that the interests of other foreign states are not injured."[3]

General Smuts proposed that the territories formerly belonging to Russia, Austria-Hungary, and Turkey should be placed under the authority of the League of Nations, which could then "delegate its authority" over any given area to "some other State whom it may appoint as its agent or manda-

[1] *Cf. supra*, pp. 442-443.

[2] *The League of Nations—Practical Suggestions.* Dec. 16, 1918.

[3] The memorandum, finished on Jan. 1, 1918, was prepared for the House Inquiry, and is published in G. L. Beer, *African Questions at the Paris Peace Conference*, pp. 413 ff.

tary,'' subject to restrictions specified by the League in a special ''act or charter,'' and subject also to the rule that ''wherever possible, the agent or mandatory so appointed shall be nominated or approved by the autonomous people or territory.''[1] Though he here suggests the name and the mechanism, General Smuts had no intention of applying the mandate system to the former German colonies in Africa and the Pacific; nor should one expect him to, for he was one of the leading Boer imperialists, and intended that German South West Africa and German East Africa should be annexed by their Boer and British conquerors.

President Wilson, having read the Smuts plan, incorporated the provisions for mandates in his second draft of the Covenant, which was printed and distributed in January 1919. While adopting most of the Smuts provisions, even to the wording, Wilson made significant changes. He omitted Russia, and included the former German colonies, along with the former Austro-Hungarian and Turkish possessions. He strengthened the provisions for the League's authority over mandates. No weak compromise, but a genuine system of League control was to be established. Had this conception of the mandate system prevailed, many of the ambiguities and uncertainties which now embarrass the organization would have been avoided.[2]

Between the Wilson plan for mandates and the Allied secret treaties there was first a battle, then a compromise, at the Paris Peace Conference in 1919. Forgetful of his year-old pledge regarding the self-determination of the German colonies, the nimble-witted Mr. Lloyd George fired the first gun in the battle, in the Supreme Council on January 23, by proposing that the colonial spoils—in Africa, the Near East and the Pacific—should be divided up at once, even before the urgent problems of European boundaries were considered. Premier Clemenceau of France and Foreign Minister Sonnino of Italy agreed, of course, but President Wilson was opposed. Next day, Lloyd George impressively brought in the prime ministers of New Zealand, Australia, South Africa and Canada to demand with his approval the outright annexation of the German colonies which the British Dominions had seized during the war. Japan,

[1] Smuts, *op. cit.*, partly reprinted in Baker, *op. cit.*, III, pp. 94 ff.
[2] For text see Baker, *op. cit.*, pp. 108-110.

France and Italy likewise entered their claims, based on the secret treaties. President Wilson was adamant—annexations could not be permitted. "The world would say that the Great Powers first portioned out the helpless parts of the world, and then formed a League of Nations." Frankly, he thought such action "would make the League of Nations impossible, and they would have to return to the system of competitive armaments, with accumulating debts and the burden of great armies." His determination, more than his eloquence, finally brought the Allies to accept the principle that the German colonies and Turkish territories should be made mandates, instead of being annexed.[1]

President Wilson's victory in principle was in part undone by the Allies when it came to the details. The wording of the long clauses which were finally inserted into the Versailles treaty as Article XXII of the Covenant was "due in the main to General Smuts and Mr. Philip Kerr" (who had left the editorship of the *Round Table* to become Lloyd George's secretary), so a British writer informs us.[2] Under their skillful editing, President Wilson's draft became quite unrecognizable—its meaning and legal content were whittled down until they almost disappeared, and the fragment that remained was glossed over with brilliant rhetoric. The rhetoric was really charming. Where Wilson had bluntly specified the teritories belonging to Austria-Hungary and Turkey, and the German colonies, Article XXII used the orotund circumlocution:

> To those colonies and territories which as a consequence of the late war have ceased to be under the sovereignty of the States which formerly governed them and which are inhabited by peoples not yet able to stand by themselves under the strenuous conditions of the modern world, there should be applied the principle that the well-being and development of such peoples form a sacred trust of civilisation and that securities for the performance of this trust should be embodied in this Covenant.

Where Wilson had definitely given the League the sovereign right of ultimate disposal, including the right to appoint either States or an "organized agency" as mandatories, the right of supervision and "intimate control," and the right to receive appeals directly from the mandated area, the well phrased second paragraph of Article XXII left it uncertain where the

[1] For the story of these negotiations, Baker, *op. cit.*, I, ch. 15.

[2] The Right Hon. W. G. A. Ormsby-Gore, writing in Temperley's *History of the Peace Conference*, VI, p. 501.

ultimate or sovereign authority rested, by whom or how the mandatories should be selected, or how much control the League could exercise. The paragraph reads:

> The best method of giving practical effect to this principle is that the tutelage of such peoples should be entrusted to advanced nations who by reason of their resources, their experience, or their geographical position can best undertake this responsibility, and who are willing to accept it, and that this tutelage should be exercised by them as Mandatories on behalf of the League.

While "resources" and "experience" would qualify the greater Allies as mandatories, "geographical position" was inserted to give the inexperienced British Dominions the German colonies they desired. The League's rôle was left ambiguous, so that the Allies themselves might appoint themselves as mandatories and enjoy almost all the powers that could have been secured by annexations.

It may as well be explained in this connection that by article 119 of the Treaty of Versailles "Germany renounces in favour of the Principal Allied and Associated Powers all her rights and titles over her oversea possessions," and similarly article 94 of the Turkish Treaty of Sèvres (never ratified) allowed the Principal Allied Powers to draw the boundaries, select the mandatories, and formulate the terms of the mandates for Syria, Mesopotamia and Palestine. In short, the Allied Great Powers took the appointment of mandatories and drafting of mandates out of the hands of the League, where Wilson had intended to place it. The League would merely approve the mandatories chosen and terms formulated by the Allies themselves. Wilson's provision that the mandatory power should be nominated or at least approved by the people concerned was applied, in Article XXII, only to Mesopotamia, Syria, and Palestine, and in weakened form—"The wishes of these communities must be a principal consideration in the selection of the Mandatory." As a matter of fact, the wishes of the people were not consulted, and in the case of Syria at least the wishes of the natives were simply ignored. Where Wilson would have provided that the League should endeavor "to build up in as short a time as possible out of the people or territory under its guardianship a political unit which can take charge of its own affairs," and that the League could hear petitions for independence and "at any time release such a people or territory from tutelage," the final text of Article XXII did not mention the right of appeal, nor did it specify whether the League or the interested mandatory power should have the right to decide when the people of the mandated territory have become "able to stand alone."

The most striking change in the Wilson plan was the division of the mandates into three classes. The purpose of the change was to serve certain definite British interests. If Wilson's plan for the open door in all mandates had been adopted, British South Africa, Australia and New Zealand would have been in embarrassing straits. Australia and New Zealand desired mandates over the German islands south of the equator, but were determined to close the door to Japanese immigration. British South Africa coveted a mandate over German South West Africa, and desired to incorporate that territory into a tariff union with itself, rather than maintain a tariff barrier along the extensive frontier through desert country; but as British South Africa had a protective tariff giving a preferential rebate to British goods, the application of such a tariff to the mandate would violate the open door. Accordingly, Article XXII grouped South West Africa and the South Pacific Islands in a separate class (now known as Class "C"), which "can best be administered under the laws of the Mandatory as integral portions of its territory." That is, they could be administratively absorbed, and the open door which existed under German rule could now be shut, as it has been. To satisfy French and British desires, Article XXII provided that "Other peoples, especially those of Central Africa" (meaning, of course, simply the German possessions in Central Africa), need not be treated as adolescent nations preparing for independence, but may be administered virtually as ordinary colonies, under "conditions which will guarantee freedom of conscience and religion, subject only to the maintenance of public order and morals, the prohibition of abuses such as the slave trade, the arms traffic, and the liquor traffic, and the prevention of the establishment of fortifications or military and naval bases and of military training of the natives for other than police purposes and the defence of territory, and will also secure equal opportunities for the trade and commerce of other Members of the League." These are the Class "B" mandates. Only the Class "A" mandates were considered to be—as Wilson intended all the mandates to be—subject to a provisional tutelage that would end in independence; but Article XXII failed to apply to the Class "A" mandates the specific guarantees against violation of the open door or exploitation of the natives.

By such ingenious—but not ingenuous—rephrasing, General Smuts and Mr. Kerr molded President Wilson's plan of trusteeship under genuine international control into a compromise nearer heart's desire, nearer the imperialist aspirations of the Dominion premiers and of European diplomats. The denaturing of the mandate plan was carried farther, on May 7, 1919, when the "Big Three" made a provisional distribution of the "B" and "C" mandates. Great Britain was to have German East Africa (Belgium's claims[1] to a portion being ignored), British South Africa was to have German South West Africa; New Zealand would have the German Samoan Islands; the British Empire would secure the phosphate island of Nauru; the other German islands south of the equator went to Australia, and those north of the equator to Japan; and France and Great Britain would make "a joint recommendation to the League of Nations" regarding Togoland and Cameroons, for the partition of which territories they had already made a secret agreement in 1916. It was also agreed that Great Britain, France and Italy should appoint a committee to "consider the application of article 13 of the Treaty of London, dated 26th April, 1915"—by which Italy had been promised compensation if Britain and France should appropriate the German colonies in Africa.[2] It was clear that France and Great Britain intended to carry out their secret treaties so far as possible, despite having accepted the mandate system "in principle." The battle at the Peace Conference, between Wilson's conception of trusteeship and European imperialism, seemed to have ended in a compromise whereby the Allies thought they were gaining the substance of annexation under the name and form of "mandates." Probably Wilson could have purchased acceptance of his idea at no smaller price. He did not, however, obtain merely a name and

[1] *Cf. supra*, p. 97; *infra*, p. 498.

[2] Subsequently Italy received additions to Italian Somaliland and Libia at the expense of France, Great Britain and Egypt.

a hollow form of League control. The principle of trusteeship and the mechanism of League supervision were achievements whose significance and value have become increasingly clear in actual practice.

Establishment of the Mandate System

While the Allies occupied or continued to occupy and administer the territories over which they expected to receive mandates, there was much hesitation, uncertainty and delay about putting the provisions of Article XXII into effect. To be sure, a commission appointed by the Allies met in London, during the summer of 1919, and drafted terms for the "B" and "C" mandates, but France entered a reservation to these terms, as regards the recruitment of native troops,[1] and Japan likewise entered a reservation. The Council of the League, however, postponed action until August 5, 1920. Then it approved a report presented by M. Hymans of Belgium regarding the procedure to be followed. That the Principal Allied and Associated Powers (France, Great Britain, Japan, Italy and the United States) had the right to appoint the mandatories, M. Hymans was certain; but he also felt that the "legal title—a mere matter of form perhaps—but one which should be settled," must be a double title, "one conferred by the Principal Powers and the other conferred by the League of Nations." Accordingly the Principal Powers should appoint the mandatory and notify the Council, which would then approve the appointment and define the terms of the mandate. But who should draft the terms of the mandate? Article XXII left this to the Council, "if not previously agreed upon by the Members of the League." The Council decided that the Principal Powers should be allowed to draft or propose the terms of the mandates. This procedure was followed. On Dec. 17, 1920, the Council approved the "C" mandates. Then ensued a long delay before the "B" mandates were approved on July 17, 1922, and the "A" mandates for Palestine and Syria, on Sept. 29, 1923. No mandate was ever issued for Mesopotamia; instead, Great Britain set up an Arab

[1] France had been insistent on the right to recruit native troops, whereas article XXII allowed militarization of the natives only for "police purposes and the defence of territory," *cf. infra*, p. 500.

kingdom of Iraq in that area, signed a treaty of alliance (and supervision) with that kingdom on Oct. 10, 1922, and obtained the approval of the League Council on Sept. 27, 1924, for this method of fulfilling the duties of a mandate.[1]

American Interests

The delays were caused in part, but not exclusively, by the United States. It had been hoped that the United States would assume a mandate, and participate in the system. In fact, Mr. George Louis Beer, colonial expert of the American Peace Commission at Paris, was to have been head of the Mandate Division of the League of Nations Secretariat. The Senate, however, was opposed to the acceptance of any mandate, and, by withholding ratification of the Covenant made it impossible for the United States to enter the League.

The United States was soon involved in the mandate question, however, by specific material interests—oils and cables. Oil was the vital question in Mesopotamia and Palestine. On May 12, 1920, an American note was addressed to Great Britain, expressing concern at British actions which had "created the unfortunate impression in the minds of the American public that the authorities of His Majesty's Government in the occupied region have given advantages to British oil interests which were not accorded to American companies, and further that Great Britain had been preparing quietly for exclusive control of the oil resources in this region." A still more vigorous protest was made on July 28, after it had become known that on April 24, 1920, France and Great Britain had signed the San Remo Oil Agreement. The agreement provided that Britain would grant to France at current market rates twenty-five per cent of the oil secured by the British Government in Mesopotamia, or, if the oil were developed by a private company, France would be allowed to buy twenty-five per cent of the stock of the company. Such an agreement, the American note declared, would "result in a grave infringement of the mandate principle which was formulated for the purpose of removing in the future some of the principal causes of international differences." To these complaints Lord Curzon tartly replied, on August 9, that in

[1] *Cf. infra*, pp. 495-498.

view of the fact that "over eighty per cent of the petroleum production of the world is under American control," and in view of the exertion of American influence to secure cancellation of British oil concessions in Haiti and Costa Rica, "the nervousness of American opinion concerning the alleged grasping activities of British oil interests appears singularly unintelligible." As for the principles of the mandate in Mesopotamia, he referred the United States to the League Council.[1]

This controversy over oil led the United States Government to advance a claim, on November 20, to the right as one of the Allied and Associated Powers to a voice in the formulation of the mandates; in fact, Secretary Colby requested that the draft mandate forms should be submitted for the United States to consider, before being passed on by the League Council. This contention raised interesting problems. It is true that by Article 119 of the Treaty of Versailles, Germany had ceded her colonies to the "Principal Allied and Associated Powers," and as the United States was the principal "Associated" Power, these colonies could not be assigned as "B" and "C" mandates without its consent. Article 22 of the same treaty, however, stipulated that the terms of the mandates should be formulated either by "the Members of the League" or by the Council, and the United States belonged in neither of these categories. Moreover, the United States had not ratified the Treaty of Versailles, nor had it yet made any peace treaty with Germany. The whole legal situation was confused, because of non-ratification. As regards the "A" mandates—Syria, Palestine and Mesopotamia—the position was still more difficult, as the United States had neither declared war on Turkey nor signed the Turkish peace treaty at Sèvres. The Treaty of Sèvres, indeed, specifically authorized the "Principal Allied Powers" (among which the United States was not included) to select the mandatories and draft the terms of the mandates for Syria, Palestine, and Mesopotamia.

Regardless of these legal difficulties, the United States persisted in its claims, addressing itself now, by a note of February 21, 1921, to the Council of the League. Besides repeating its demands for equal opportunity in Mesopotamian oil, and for a

[1] Text of these notes and of the San Remo agreement in *International Conciliation*, No. 166; *cf.* also No. 213, by Mr. Batsell.

right to pass on the mandates, America added a new protest, against the assignment of the island of Yap to Japan under a "C" mandate, for there were important American cable interests in Yap. The negotiations that ensued are too complicated to chronicle, but the results were surprisingly favorable to the United States. The Allied Powers consented to discuss the draft "B" mandates with the United States. American oil companies secured the promise of a quarter-interest in Mesopotamian oil.[1] American interests in the Yap cables were safeguarded by a special treaty with Japan in February, 1922.[2] And by a series of other treaties with the mandatory powers [3] the United States secured in a number of the mandates the same rights as Members of the League, a pledge that vested American property rights would be respected, and a promise that copies of the annual reports on the administration of the mandates would be sent to the United States.

"A" Mandates in the Near East

The "A" mandates are the three Arab countries of Syria, Mesopotamia and Palestine. Their combined populations of about 6½ millions, largely Arabic, represent only a fraction of the Arab "race," which is scattered through the Arabian peninsula, North Africa, and other regions; in them, however, the conflict between Anglo-French imperialism and Arab self-determination is most acute.[4] The publicly professed aim of France and Great Britain in Syria and Mesopotamia was to emancipate these lands from Turkish oppression, to encourage and assist in the establishment of native governments, "freely chosen by the populations themselves," and to recognize these governments. So, at least, ran the Anglo-French Joint Declaration of Nov. 7, 1918. In the same spirit, Article 22 of the Covenant stated that these countries "have reached a stage of development where their existence as independent nations can be provisionally recognized subject to the rendering of administra-

[1] *Cf. supra*, p. 267.
[2] *Cf. supra*, p. 389.
[3] With France, concerning Cameroons and Togoland, on Feb. 13, 1923; with Belgium, concerning Ruanda and Urundi, on April 18, 1923; with France, concerning Syria, on April 4, 1924; with Great Britain, concerning Palestine, Dec. 3, 1924.
[4] On the Arabs and Arab nationalism *cf. supra*, pp. 269-272.

MANDATES IN THE NEAR EAST.

tive advice and assistance by a Mandatory until such time as they are able to stand alone."

Clearly the "A" mandates are in theory merely transitional protectorates designed to guide the Arab states into full independence. The French mandate over Syria (including Lebanon) expressly stipulates not only that an organic law or constitution shall be framed "in agreement with the native authorities," but also that France shall "enact measures to facilitate the progressive development of Syria and the Lebanon as independent States" (article 1). In Palestine, Great Britain has "full powers of legislation and administration" but must encourage local autonomy and promote the "establishment of the Jewish national home," and "the development of self-governing institutions." In Mesopotamia, Great Britain has already established an Arab kingdom and pledged herself to endeavor to secure its admission into the League of Nations.

Certain other general features of the "A" mandates are worth mentioning. The mandatory is forbidden to interfere with religious liberty, or to discriminate against any of the inhabitants on religious grounds, or to impose its own language through the schools, or to cede to another state any of the mandated territory, or to violate the economic open door, or—in the case of Syria alone— to grant monopolistic concessions for the exploitation of raw materials, or to discriminate against citizens of other Members of the League in the granting of concessions. These are liberal provisions, far in advance of the principles applied in many a colony or protectorate not subject to a mandate.

The most important and the least successful of the "A" mandates is Syria. The difficulty has been the costly failure of the French in this case to cope with Arab sentiment. Syria had been freed from the Turks, toward the close of the Great War, by British and Arab troops, and with British consent an Arab prince, Feisal, had established himself in Damascus as virtual ruler of Syria. Indeed, the French Foreign minister, M. Pichon, admitted that Feisal had the support of a majority of the population. A commission of investigation sent to Syria by President Wilson, during the Peace Conference, discovered that the prevalent desire on the part of the Syrian people was for independence and union with other Arab lands. As a mandatory they preferred United States, or, as second choice, Great Britain. Nevertheless, France insisted upon Syria as her share of the Turkish spoils, and in 1919 French troops were sent to replace the British army of occupation. The Arab leaders manifested their opposition by holding a Congress of Syrian Notables at Damascus, in March 1920, and electing Prince Feisal King of Syria and Palestine, and his brother Abdullah they nominated for the crown of Mesopotamia. As Feisal and Abdullah were sons of King Hussein of the Hejaz, the successful consummation of this plan would have meant the confederation of the leading Arab states under Hussein's dynasty. The French, however, were not to be thwarted by Arab kingdoms. General Gouraud, with 90,000 French soldiers under his command in Syria, peremptorily summoned Feisal to recognize the French mandate. King Feisal complied, but soon afterwards fighting began between his supporters and the French army. Being defeated, Feisal was expelled from Syria only to be made king of Iraq (Mesopotamia) by the British.

This unfortunate beginning handicapped the French from the outset. Having destroyed the Arab government which they found when they came, the French administrators had to build up a new government, and seek to overcome native hostility. To satisfy local desires, or possibly to offset Arab nationalism, they divided the country into five units. The mountainous area of Lebanon, in the south, with its Maronite Christian population—inclined to favor French rule—was enlarged to form "Great Lebanon" and given an independent administration, with even a national flag of its own, the French tricolor with a cedar superimposed on the white ground. Another hill country, southeast of Damascus, inhabited by a religious sect known as the Druses, was cut off to form the autonomous territory of Jebel Druse. The remainder formed three territories—Damascus, Aleppo and the Alaouite—grouped together as the Federation of Syrian States. Each of these three states, it was provided, should have a Representative Council which would send five delegates to a Federal Council, which in turn would elect the President of the Federation. This system of native authorities was paralleled and controlled by a system of French officials, headed by the French High Commissioner appointed by the French foreign minister. Later, in 1925, because the Arabs did not relish disunity, Damascus and Aleppo were combined in a State of Syria, and the Alaouite State received complete autonomy, the Federation being dissolved.

Before much progress could be made with this new form of government, the whole situation was altered by a serious Syrian rebellion. A radical French Cabinet, the Herriot Cabinet, made the mistake of appointing as High Commissioner a certain General Sarrail, whose anticlericalism antagonized the only important pro-French element in Syria, that is, the Christian minority, and whose arbitrary conduct in other matters angered other groups. Rebellion flared up among the Druses. Sairrail's efforts to restore order by having his troops burn native villages and bombard the city of Damascus only made matters worse. The rebellion spread to other parts of Syria. In dismay the authorities at Paris recalled General Sarrail, promised a reform of the constitutional laws, and sent reinforcements to the army of occupation.[1] The new governor, de Jouvenel, endeavored by conciliatory methods to persuade the rebels to lay down their arms. Syrian Arab nationalists demanded the reunification of Syria under a nationalist government, and some suggested that France should imitate the policy Britain had pursued in Mesopotamia.

The Syrian revolt was a severe test of the mandate system. Would the Mandates Commission have the courage to call France to account for maladministration? It did. France was requested to make a special report on the insurrection.[2] After considering the report, and hearing the explanations offered by the French delegate, the Mandates Commission politely announced that the French report "does not fulfil its expectations." In courteous but candid terms the Commission censured General Sarrail for allowing Captain Carbillet, French administrator of the Jebel Druse, to introduce hasty reforms regarding land tenure and public works in violation of the agreement one of Sarrail's predecessors had made with the Druse chiefs to respect their autonomy. The Commission scored Carbillet for his "abuses of authority," Sarrail for his "obstinacy" and breaches of faith with the Druses, and the French administration in general for its "oscillations" of policy and its ten-

[1] See *L'Asie Française*, Jan. 1926, pp. 9-30, on debates regarding Syria.
[2] *Rapport provisoire à la Société des Nations sur la situation de la Syrie et du Liban, Année 1925.*

dency to substitute direct rule for mandatory advice. One of the causes of revolt, the Commission frankly declared, was the subjection of the Druses to "excessive demands in the form of forced labour."[1] These were "severe criticisms," as a French imperialist journal admitted; yet the same journal praised the Commission and recommended that France should loyally carry out the mandate principle and sincerely collaborate with the Commission and the League.[2] In this spirit the French government made every effort to convince the Commission and the League Council that France intended to prepare Syria for self-government, in accordance with the mandate system, rather than practise the old policy of imperialist domination.

The conflict between Arab nationalism and French imperialism rendered the French mandate in Syria not only less successful than French rule in certain other colonies, but much more expensive than it should have been. Up to October 21, 1925, the military expenditures in Syria amounted to 2,465,000,000 francs. Syrian taxes sufficed to pay only a very small fraction of the expense. The French army of occupation, from 1919 to Nov. 5, 1925, lost 6,622 men—killed or died. The mandate in Syria was an expensive luxury for the French nation.[3]

In Palestine the British mandatory administration conflicted with Arab nationalism in a more serious and more permanent manner, but the British administrators handled the problem more skillfully than their French neighbors. Palestine, like Syria, is an Arab country. Of its total population (by the census of 1922) of 757,000, no fewer than 591,000 were Moslems, and of the 73,000 Christians many were Arabs. There were only 84,000 Jews. Yet, under the terms of the mandate, Great Britain is to aid in the "establishment in Palestine of a national home for the Jewish people," facilitating Jewish immigration, promoting the settlement of Jewish immigrants on the public and waste lands, enabling Jews to acquire Palestinian citizenship, and accepting the Zionist organization as an advisory

[1] See *Report* of Permanent Mandates Commission, 8th Session, March 6, 1926, C.144.M.58.1926 V. Also, account of 9th session, in Monthly Summary of the League of Nations, June 1926, pp. 145 ff.; Council discussion in Official Journal, April 1926, pp. 522 ff.

[2] *L'Asie Française*, May 1926, pp. 178 ff.

[3] For additional material on the French in Syria see the official annual *Rapport sur la situation de la Syrie et du Liban.*

body on "economic, social and other matters" affecting the Jewish settlement.

This remarkable project goes back to the historic Balfour Declaration of Nov. 2, 1917, pledging the British Government to aid the Zionist plan. Of the many influences which brought about that declaration, perhaps the most significant were, first, the desire of British imperialists to secure control of Palestine as a strategic protection for the Suez Canal; and, second, the belief that such a declaration would purchase for the Allies the valuable influence and financial support of Jews throughout the world.

When the Arab inhabitants of Palestine learned that Great Britain was to have a mandate for Palestine, and that the Zionist plan was to be written into the mandate, there were riots and bitter protests.[1] Great Britain, however, pursued her course. A distinguished English Jew, Sir Herbert Samuel, was sent to Palestine as British High Commissioner from 1920 to 1925. The mandate was drafted, submitted to the League Council in December, 1920, approved in 1922, and promulgated in 1923. In drafting the mandate, and in framing the new government, Great Britain endeavored to convince the Arabs that civil and religious rights as individual citizens were not to be trampled upon. The administration was to be conducted by the High Commissioner with the aid of an Executive Council of officials and a Legislative Council consisting of ten officials and twelve elected members, of whom eight were to be Moslems, two Jews, and two Christians. When the elections were held, however, the Arabs on the whole refrained from voting, and thus caused Sir Herbert Samuel to discard the whole constitution and substitute an appointed official Advisory Council for the proposed Legislative Council.

Passive resistance on the part of the Arabs, however, could not prevent the influx of Jewish immigrants, chiefly from Poland and eastern Europe, in ever-increasing numbers. By 1925 the number of Jews entering Palestine was 33,801—a startling increase over former years. To be sure, thousands of these incomers found agricultural labor in Palestine unattractive and soon deserted the country. In 1925 no fewer than 2141 Jewish immigrants forsook the "national home." The majority, how-

[1] *Parl. Papers*, 1921 (Cmd. 1540), 1922 (Cmd. 1700).

ever, remained to become citizens, establish Jewish private schools, create new Jewish-owned industries, or settle down on farms. The total number of Jews in 1925 was estimated to be 108,000, and of these three-fourths lived in towns, one-fourth on the land.

The Arabs faced the prospect, if this process should continue, of seeing the Jews become the dominant element in the business affairs, and perhaps also in the intellectual and political life of the country. Could one obliterate national sentiment, language and religious differences, this venture in Palestine might be regarded as an interesting experiment in the economic redemption of an ancient but unprogressive country, and in the creation of a "multi-national state." Certainly new roads were laid, industries founded, waste lands reclaimed, schools built by the hundred, malaria and other diseases reduced. The mandate administration even protected the scenery by forbidding the erection of ugly advertisements. Yet it is not certain that all these benefits will reconcile the Arabs, who yearn for Arab government, good or bad.[1]

In considering the first annual report of the Palestine mandate, in October 1924, the Mandates Commission of the League drew the attention of the League Council to the difficulty inherent in a mandate which sought to reconcile the fostering of a Jewish national home and the protection of Arab rights in the same small country. Even the "wisdom and impartiality" of the British administrator could not wholly surmount this difficulty. The Council refused, however, to act on this suggestion, and the British Government showed no sign of abandoning the Zionist plan.

It is worth noting that the Jewish national home project applies only to the smaller, western part of the area under the Palestine mandate. Transjordan or Kerak, east of the Jordan valley—an area sparsely populated because so much of it is desert—has been allowed autonomy under an Arab prince, the Emir Abdullah, who rules with the assistance of a British ad-

[1] See annual *Report on Palestine Administration* and also *Report of the High Commissioner on the Administration of Palestine, 1920-1925*. There is a very informing article by Leonard Stein on "The Jews in Palestine" in *Foreign Affairs*, March 1926; and a thoughtful survey of the whole problem by Quincy Wright will be published in the *Pol. Sci. Quart.* for Sept. 1926.

viser, the support of British aeroplanes and armored cars, and the aid of a small British subsidy.

The most successful of the "A" mandates is Mesopotamia, now known by its Arabic name, Iraq. Even before the war there were strong British oil, shipping, and strategic interests in lower Mesopotamia.[1] It was no surprise, therefore, when at the outbreak of war with Turkey in 1914 British troops were landed in that region, nor was it astonishing that during the war the British Government should have secured from its Allies permission to appropriate Mesopotamia and establish a sphere of influence extending about 150 miles north of Bagdad. Not content with these promised gains, however, Premier Lloyd George soon after the armistice persuaded Premier Clemenceau that the Mosul oil district, still farther north, should be allotted to Britain rather than to France, although by the Sykes-Picot agreement of 1916 it had been earmarked for the latter. The new arrangement hinged on Anglo-French negotiations regarding the share France was to have in Mesopotamian oil, as well as upon British consent to French plans regarding Syria, but at length these negotiations were concluded, and the mandate for Mesopotamia was assigned to Great Britain in the spring of 1920. The terms of the mandate, however, were not submitted to the League of Nations for approval until December, 1920, and not until 1924 was the status of Mesopotamia definitely settled. In part the delay was due to the long oil negotiations with the United States which have already been reviewed.[2] But it was due also to difficulties in Mesopotamia.

In Mesopotamia, as in Syria and in Palestine, there were Arab Nationalist leaders who desired union or confederation of the Arab states, and bitterly resented both the breaking-up of the Arab area into several mandates and the subjection of their country to British administration. During the years 1919-1920 this resentment took the form of a fairly serious Arab rebellion in Mesopotamia. Convinced that the maintenance of an unpopular British administration by crude military methods would be impossible, because of the protests of the overburdened British taxpayer if for no other reason, the British Government sent Sir Percy Cox to Mesopotamia with orders to conciliate the natives. He promptly appointed an Arab Cabinet, with British

[1] *Cf. supra*, pp. 254-255.

[2] *Cf. supra*, pp. 260, 263 ff., 485 ff.

advisers attached to each ministry, but for a permanent native government a monarch seemed necessary. The choice was none other than Prince Feisal, ex-king of Syria, who had been overthrown by the French. He came to visit, but remained to reign. With a certain amount of proper guidance an election was held in which 96 per cent of the votes were cast for Feisal as King. Having been duly crowned on August 23, 1921, and installed in office, King Feisal proved a statesmanlike ruler, evincing "tact and wisdom" not only in his relations with his subjects, but also in his "steady reliance on the help and friendship of His (British) Majesty's Government."[1]

With King Feisal the British drew up a "Treaty of Alliance," signed on Oct. 10, 1922, which contained the provisions that would otherwise have been incorporated into a mandate. Religious freedom, the use of native languages in schools, the rights of minorities, the open door,[2] are guaranteed as in an ordinary mandate. Great Britain undertakes to provide the Kingdom of Iraq with advice and assistance, including military and financial aid, while on the other hand Iraq agrees "to be guided by the advice" of the British High Commissioner on "all important matters affecting the international and financial obligations and interests of His Britannic Majesty." By a supplementary agreement the number of British officials and their salaries were fixed. This relationship is pretty clearly what the provisions of Article 22 of the Covenant intended for "A" mandates. No less in harmony with the Covenant was the provision in the Iraq treaty that Great Britain will use her "good offices" to secure admission of Iraq into the League of Nations "as soon as possible," thereby terminating the treaty and the mandatory tutelage. If Iraq should not be admitted to the League, the treaty would remain in force twenty years. By a subsequent agreement, in 1923, the twenty-year term was reduced to four (dating from the ratification of peace with Turkey, and therefore expiring in 1928). In 1925, however, in order to secure Mosul under the terms of the League Council's decision, Great

[1] *Report on 'Iraq Administration, October, 1920-March, 1922*, p. 17.

[2] As regards taxation, commerce, navigations, exercise of industries or professions, treatment of shipping and aircraft, for all members of the League and other powers with which Great Britain may make treaties promising privileges equal to those of League Members. The circumlocution refers to the United States. It is significant that there is no clause on monopolistic concessions.

Britain agreed to renew for twenty-five years her treaty obligations toward Iraq, or in other words, to prolong the mandatory relationship for twenty-five years, subject to the possibility that it might be ended earlier by the admission of Iraq to the League.

This method of fulfilling the principle of mandatory trusteeship was approved by the League, although no mandate charter has been issued as in other cases. On September 27, 1924, the Council of the League accepted the Iraq treaty, with supplementary British pledges, as giving effect to Article 22 of the Covenant, it being understood that an annual report would be made on this as on other mandates, that the terms should not be altered save with the Council's consent, and that British obligations should terminate when Iraq enters the League.[1]

To reassure British critics who were fearful lest the prolongation of the British mandate to the year 1950 might commit Great Britain to an expensive obligation, Premier Baldwin predicted that the mandate would probably expire (by the method indicated) before the maximum of twenty-five years had elapsed, and, he explained, Great Britain was not required to spend money or keep troops in Iraq, but merely to lend cooperation and advice. As a matter of fact, it was estimated in 1925 that Great Britain had spent 150 million pounds sterling on the occupation and administration of Mesopotamia, and was still expending more than four millions sterling per annum, although the British army of occupation had been reduced to some air squadrons and one battalion of infantry. The return on the investment must depend on the future development of the country. Probably British political influence aided the British-controlled Turkish Petroleum Company to secure its concession, in 1925, for exclusive prospecting rights, but the company's profits will depend on the settlement of the Mosul boundary dispute with Turkey,[2] and upon the success of the prospecting, and upon the drilling of oil wells and the construction of a pipe line to the Syrian coast. Cotton and grain likewise are potential assets, and are being cultivated on an ever increasing irrigated area, yet these also depend on the extension of irrigation, as well as upon general conditions in Iraq. On the other hand, British tax-

[1] League of Nations, *Official Journal*, V, pp. 1346-7; for text of treaty, *Treaty Series*, XXXIV.

[2] *Cf. supra*, p. 266. It now seems settled in Britain's favor.

payers may possibly derive some satisfaction from the knowledge that on the whole the British administration has been remarkably successful, under difficult circumstances, in establishing a friendly and apparently stable native government, in extending the railway system, in encouraging agriculture, in laying foundations for a modern educational system, in providing hospital facilities and combatting epidemics, despite the fact that such humane reforms and economic enterprises have been sadly handicapped by the paucity of the funds left after defraying the heavy military expenses.[1]

"B" Mandates in Central Africa

Six "B" mandates were carved out of three former German colonies, as follows:—

		Area (sq. mi.)	*Population*
Togoland	British Togoland	12,600	185,000
	French Togoland	22,000	747,000
Kamerun	British Cameroons	31,000	550,000
	French Cameroun *	166,489	2,771,000
German East Africa...	Tanganyika Territory (British)	365,000	4,125,000
	Ruanda-Urundi (Belgian)	21,235	3,000,000

* Not including 107,000 sq. mi. which had been ceded from French Equatorial Africa to German Kamerun in 1911 and were simply reincorporated into French Equatorial Africa.

It will be noticed that France secured most of Togoland and Kamerun, the western colonies, whereas Great Britain took German East Africa. Belgium, indignant at being ignored in the first distribution of mandates, persuaded the British to relinquish the northwestern corner of East Africa, which Belgian Congolese troops had occupied; this district, by the way, is much more important in population and productivity than its small area would indicate, for it includes some of the finest African highlands, where cattle are plentiful.

Between the Arab "A" mandates and these "B" mandates there is a world of difference. The latter are without exception

[1] Details in *Review of the Civil Administration of Mesopotamia*, 1920 (Cmd. 1061); *Report on 'Iraq Administration, Oct., 1920-March, 1922; Report on 'Iraq Administration* (annual since 1922); *Report of the British Financial Mission*, 1925.

tropical lands, much of their surface is covered by the dense equatorial jungle and drenched by tropical rains. Their inhabitants are uncivilized negroes, ranging in culture, or lack of it, from cattle-growing tribesmen to forest savages. Obviously there can be no national self-determination here, as in the case of the Arabs. Mandates, in this case, must not mean transitional tutelage over adolescent nations, but must give the mandatory power "full powers of administration and legislation," to govern the country "as an integral part" of the mandatory's territory.

As a matter of fact, the policy has been generally pursued of governing through the native tribal chieftains, wherever possible. As the British report on Togoland for 1923 declares, "The general policy adopted since the British occupation has been to support native rule and rulers." The Belgian report for 1924 contains the interesting statement: "The chiefs are the pivot of native policy. . . . The importance of their rôle is of the first order, and a wise organization of chieftainships is the most potent means of action one can have. Where the chief is won over to European influence, just and respected, progress is rapid, order assured; where the chief is hostile, tyrannical or without authority, our influence on the population is, on the contrary, very ineffective." In some cases the chiefs are allowed to collect the taxes, turning over a certain percentage to the central administration, or are used as agents to recruit native labor, and quite generally they are entrusted with the local administration, subject of course to the laws of the colony and the advice or orders of the white officials. So strongly do the British prefer this method, that where no prominent native chiefs exist, they "discover" them, and deliberately build up their authority. This, indeed, is done in other British West African colonies, as well as in the mandates; but it is fairly characteristic of the problem of government in the mandates. Otherwise one must install white officials—and it is not easy to provide a sufficient number in torrid colonies. In regions where the native villages have no tribal organization, direct administration is necessary, but even so, the lower administrative ranks are filled by natives.

The prime difference between a "B" mandate and an ordinary colony is that in the former the administration is more definitely responsible before the world for a just and beneficent policy toward the natives.[1] The very terms of the mandates prescribe explicitly that the mandatory must abolish slavery as soon as possible, suppress the slave trade, exercise a strict control over the arms and liquor traffic, prohibit compulsory labor except for essential public works, supervise labor contracts so as to protect the natives from exploitation. Accordingly, the mandatories have prohibited the slave traffic and abolished slavery in law, although in some cases the institution of domestic slavery among the natives is too firmly rooted to be at once eradicated. Fairly elaborate laws regulating the terms of native labor contracts have been promulgated. The importation of arms and distilled liquor is usually restricted rigorously. It is interesting—for Americans—to note that the French policy is to promote the consumption of "hygienic beverages" such as wines and beer, instead of the deadly whiskey, gin and rum.[2] The mandates also forbid the raising of native troops except for "local police purposes and for the defence of the territory." On this point, however, the French were so insistently dissatisfied that in the French mandates a clause is added allowing these native troops to be used elsewhere (in Europe, for example) in the event of a general war, to repel an attack or for defense of territory. Despite the importance which France attached to this permission, the reports show only 1017 native soldiers in French Cameroun and 455 in French Togo for 1923-1924.

The most important issues affecting the welfare of the natives are hygiene, education and missionary work, land and labor. In the first of these the mandatories seem eager to make as good a showing as the expense of sending doctors to Africa will allow. For instance, the French in 1922 boasted of having administered 200,000 vaccinations in Cameroun. Missions enjoy a guaranteed religious freedom, and are conducting most of what educational work there is—and it is little enough. In French Cameroun, for example, there were in 1924 some 4700 natives attending mission schools and 3300 attending government schools, or less than three students per thousand of population—about the same ratio that prevails in the neighboring French colony of Equatorial Africa. It is a difficult problem, made more difficult by the im-

[1] Even before the adoption of the mandate system, Central Africa was subject to various international economic and humane restrictions—see Beer, *African Questions*, part iii.

[2] *Rapport annuel . . . du Cameroun*, 1924, p. 11.

possibility of securing or paying adequate numbers of teachers, native or white. As for the land problem, to guard against the expropriation of the natives that has been so grave an evil in colonies like Kenya and Congo, the mandates bind the mandatories to "respect the rights and safeguard the interests of the native population." Since the natives have no conception of individual real property, it is not a simple matter. In the French mandates an attempt seems to have been made to establish European ideas of land-ownership immediately by the drastic measures of declaring the private domain of the state to include all vacant lands and even the lands around native villages utilized but not owned by the villagers (and, by the way, all lands formerly owned by Germany). These lands the government could sell or lease to individuals or companies. Obviously much will depend upon the spirit in which the administration deals with the question, whether too large a portion of these lands are assigned to concessionaires. On the other hand, to protect individual native properties, the French are endeavoring to have the natives register or "matriculate" their lands. In Tanganyika, the British have declared all lands to be public lands, which may be granted to planters for ninety-nine years' use, but not sold outright. How such measures will work out in practice is not yet clear, except in so far as the desire of the mandatories to make unimpeachable reports may afford a reason for predicting a policy of safeguarding native interests.

The mandate provision against compulsory labor is most significant, as in many African colonies the natives have been forced to work for government or private interests, sometimes in lieu of other taxation, sometimes for wages that scarcely concealed the resemblance of forced labor to slavery. The mandatories may employ forced labor only on essential public works and with "adequate remuneration." In some cases a labor on public words (e.g. railways and roads) is required as a form of taxation or *corvée*—in French Togo, four days a year; in French Cameroun, ten days; in Tanganyika, long enough to earn the amount of the hut tax in money.[1] Forced labor for private plantations or other private enterprises, however, is not allowed according to the letter of the law. Yet in some regions where native chiefs

[1] The British Report on *Labour in the Tanganyika Territory* (1926) is particularly detailed and illuminating.

or village headmen "recruit" young negroes to become contract laborers—that is, to work under contract for a certain number of weeks or months—it is practically inevitable that an element of compulsion will enter into the process. The aim is that labor should be free. But it is not always easy to "inspire the native with a taste for work," in the words of a French report on Cameroun.

Any description of the "B" mandates would be incomplete without mention of one more typical feature, the detailed guarantee of the open door. For all Members of the League there must be "complete economic, commercial and industrial equality"; concessions for the exploitation of natural resources must be granted without distinction of nationality; and monopolistic concessions are prohibited. For commerce, the open door is so genuine that until 1924 England had a larger share than France of the market in French Cameroun. Concessions, on the other hand, quite naturally tend to be sought by and granted to subjects of the mandatory power, more than by foreigners. Nevertheless, it may be fairly said that the open door is a reality. The fact is the more interesting in view of the cost of the mandates to the mandatories. In Tanganyika and British Cameroons there have been regular deficits, to be defrayed by the British taxpayer; Belgium has granted a subsidy of 1,200,000 francs a year to balance the budget of her mandate; only France has been able to make the taxes collected in the mandates provide a surplus over expenditures, in order to accumulate funds for ambitious programs of railway construction and other public works.[1]

"C" Mandates in the South Seas and South Africa

There remain a few other ex-German colonies to be considered, namely, South West Africa and the Pacific Islands. These were put into a separate class of mandates, as we have seen, for quite specific reasons—because the Australasians wished to exclude the Japanese from the islands in the South Pacific, and because

[1] For further details on the "B" mandates see the annual reports published for each mandate and submitted to the League of Nations. For comparison between German and mandate administration see statistical tables in Foreign Policy Association, *Information Service*, II, no. 2, and read *German Colonization Past and Future* (1926) by Dr. Heinrich Schnee, a former German colonial governor.

British South Africa wished to incorporate German South West Africa into its own administrative and preferential tariff system. In both cases, the "open door" provision could not be applied. The absence of this provision is one of the principal characteristics of the "C" mandates. Another striking characteristic is their relatively small population, less than three-quarters of a million all told, as appears from the following table:

	Area (sq. mi.)	*Population*
South Sea Islands (Japan)..................	800	42,000
New Guinea (Australia)	89,000	400,000
Western Samoa (New Zealand).............	1,250	38,000
Nauru Island (British Empire).............	10	2,000
South West Africa (Union of South Africa)..	322,000	228,000

The islands assigned to Japan are hundreds in number and small in importance, except as cable or radio stations, or as coaling stations and potential naval bases. Yap, which occasioned such controversy between Japan and the United States[1] and caused so many newspaper readers in 1921 to consult their atlases, is one of these diminutive islands.

The insular possessions of Germany south of the equator were appropriated by Great Britain and her Dominions, New Zealand taking the strategic but small Samoan islands, Australia assuming the mandate over "New Guinea" (former Kaiser Wilhelmsland, Bismarck Archipelago, and German Solomon Islands), and the British Empire in its collective capacity reserving for itself the microscopic but valuable atoll of Nauru, which produces two hundred thousand tons of phosphate a year. Of all the islands except Nauru the chief product is borne by the picturesque coconut palm, the kernels of whose fruit are dried and exported under the trade name copra.

South West Africa[2] achieved singular prominence among the "C" mandates through the Bondelzwarts rebellion, the culmination of long-standing difficulties between whites and blacks. Under German rule before the Great War the colony had attracted some twelve thousand German settlers, many of whom secured large cattle ranches while others devoted themselves to business or to operating the profitable diamond mines. German colonization had created two acute native grievances, for the Hottentots and Bantus resented the occupation of most of their

[1] *Cf. supra*, p. 389. [2] *Cf. supra*, pp. 102 f., 117 ff.

lands by the whites, and they were unwilling to be forced into the position of ill-paid laborers on ranches or in mines. "An exhortation to labour is not popular anywhere, least of all in South West Africa, where from time immemorial the Hereros and Hottentots have been the proud possessors of vast herds of stock and the land they roamed over. Constant wars with the European invader caused the loss of everything, except what the generosity or political acumen of the European left them. One can quite understand their feelings against the farmers who now occupy the land. . . ."[1] Against the Germans there had been a long series of native insurrections, sternly repressed, leaving bitter racial antagonism in their wake. When British South Africa took the country, some eight thousand Germans remained, and thousands of British settlers joined them (11,000 British by 1921). These white farmers owned almost half a million head of cattle and over a million head of sheep and goats, whereas the natives had only some 66,000 cattle and 650,000 sheep and goats.

The British endeavored to pursue a more humane policy than their predecessors, in certain respects. They prohibited, for example, the flogging of native servants and laborers by the white farmers. In certain other matters, however, the new masters of the land were severe. Because the whites complained that there were too many hunting-dogs killing game, the British administration in 1921 levied a dog tax of one pound sterling for the first dog, ten pounds for five dogs. Many of the natives, of course, were too poor to pay any such tax, and consequently in four months over one hundred members of the Bondelzwarts tribe alone were condemned, for non-payment of the tax, to pay a fine of two pounds or spend two weeks in jail. To obtain the money for tax and fines, the natives would have to work for white ranchers and mine-owners. While the dog tax exasperated the natives, there were other grievances, too, such as the practice of condemning native "vagrants"[2] to work, and the fact that natives were not allowed to have branding-irons, although they were required to pay thirty shillings for them. As a result,

[1] Memorandum by Major Herbst, secretary to the Native Affairs Department of the Union of South Africa, Permanent Mandates Commission, *Annexes to the Minutes of the Third Session*, p. 333.

[2] Natives found wandering abroad who could not prove legal ownership of at least ten head of cattle or fifty head of small stock.

"there was much ill-feeling and enmity" and there were constant reports "that the Hottentots were about to rise against the whites."

One small tribe of Hottentots, the Bondelzwarts, did rise, in 1922. Somewhat less than six hundred warriors, with their women and children, went on the warpath. Against them the Government sent a force of 390 men, with machine guns and airplanes, and the planes bombed the rebel camp. About a hundred warriors and two children were killed; how many were wounded could not be told, because the Hottentots carry their wounded with them in retreat. Thus rebellion was crushed. And the cattle owned by the tribe were captured or stampeded.

When the Assembly of the League met in 1922 a colored delegate from Haiti ventured to criticize the conduct of South Africa, and the Assembly adopted a resolution expressing its "confident hope" that the Permanent Mandates Commission would consider the matter and "be able to report that satisfactory conditions have been established." Obeying this strong, though courteously worded injunction, the Commission devoted much of its third session, in July and August, 1923, to a discussion of reports which had been received from an investigating commission appointed by South Africa, and to a virtual cross-examination of Major Herbst and Sir Edgar Walton, who appeared in behalf of South Africa. The Commission's report [1] was in effect a rebuke to South Africa, and so unwelcome a rebuke that the delegate of that country issued a statement that, "The Commission, I am afraid, has failed altogether to realise the situation in South-West Africa when the Union of South Africa assumed the responsibility of government." If the Commission had ever been in South Africa, he declared, it would have been impossible to write such a report, "a Report which will, I fear, be read in South Africa with bitter feeling." [2] Nevertheless the League Assembly, in September 1923, expressed its regret that satisfactory conditions had not yet been reported in the Bondelzwarts district.

Under the lash of such international reproof, South Africa took pains, in its next annual report on the mandate, to announce

[1] Permanent Mandates Commission, *Annexes to the Minutes of the Third Session*, pp. 290 ff.

[2] League of Nations document, A.48.1923.VI. (C.550.1923.VI).

that the objectionable laws had been modified, that most of their cattle had been returned to the Bondels, that rations were being given to the indigent and free medical service to the sick. Moreover, the Administrator whose policy had been criticized came in person to the next meeting of the Mandates Commission with a very elaborate and conciliatory report, and with tactful words of praise for the Commission's work. The root of the trouble in South West Africa, he explained, was the too sudden change from the "iron discipline" of the Germans to the "more lenient policy" of the British toward the natives, especially the abolition of flogging. The natives construed British humanitarianism as weakness, and were encouraged in their hope of recovering their ancestral lands. He took pains, however, to show that South Africa had really improved conditions by more humane laws, by setting aside additional lands as native reserves, by promoting education. The negroes were not being forced to work, but it was hoped that as their wants increased economic pressure would induce them to seek employment.[1]

Some Defects

The Bondelzwarts affair undoubtedly demonstrated the effectiveness of the weapon of public criticism as wielded by the League of Nations, but it also illustrated one of the fundamental defects in the mandate system. Dissatisfied as it was with the reports transmitted to it by South Africa concerning the rebellion, the League's Permanent Mandates Commission considered itself incompetent to send an investigating commission of its own to South West Africa. Nor could it summon witnesses from the territory. It could only bring moral pressure to bear, by means of courteous criticism, to induce South Africa to supply further information. Again, when the rebellion of 1925 occurred in Syria, the Commission did not dispatch field agents to investigate conditions in Syria, but rather requested France to make a special report on the situation. To supplement the reports of the interested powers, which are, after all, *ex parte* evidence, the Mandates Section of the League prepares *dossiers* of information culled from the press, parliamentary debates, and other sources. Moreover, the experienced colonial experts who sit on

[1] P.M.C., *Minutes of the Fourth Session*, pp. 42, 46, 59, 78, 112, 119.

the Mandates Commission are not easily hoodwinked. Yet the inability of the League to send out inspectors or investigators, whose reports could be set off against those of the interested governments, remains a regrettable weakness in the mandatory system.

Charged with the responsibility of ensuring administration of the mandates in harmony with the humane principles of the Covenant, the League is nevertheless inadequately equipped with specific powers for the fulfilment of its task. It cannot, or does not, issue orders for the improvement of conditions, or injunctions to check objectionable practices. The Mandates Commission feels that it cannot consider petitions—from the Arabs of Palestine for instance—which question the terms of a mandate, for the terms can be modified only by the Council. If only the Council, on which all the mandatory powers are at present represented, can alter the mandates, and if the Council's decisions must be unanimous under the Covenant, a mandate can hardly be modified without the consent of the mandatory (unless the matter becomes an international "dispute likely to lead to rupture," in which case the interested parties would have no vote). It is even less probable that a mandatory power could be deprived of its mandate on account of misgovernment, since the mandatories were selected by the Allied Powers rather than by the League. A test case would probably lead to ingenious legal complications. The probability of such a case is, however, very small. Even the Mandates Commission considers the transfer of a mandate a "very remote contingency."[1]

Still more fundamental is the problem of sovereignty, or of ultimate authority, which Article 22 discreetly evaded. In the Hymans report (1920) on the fulfilment of the article, the question of the legal title over mandates was lightly regarded as "a mere matter of form perhaps," and it was assumed that in the "B" and "C" mandates the mandatory would enjoy "a full exercise of sovereignty," subject to the obligations prescribed in the Covenant. The "mere matter of form," however, soon appeared to have remarkably practical and material angles. What nationality could be claimed by inhabitants of a mandated territory, when applying for passports? If the mandatory power conferred or imposed its own nationality on the inhabitants, the

[1] *Report on the Work of the Third Session*, p. 5.

mandate system would be very similar to annexation. On this point, the conclusion was that the inhabitants of a mandate should enjoy a separate nationality, although individuals so desiring could be granted the nationality of the mandatory.

The ownership of public lands presented another angle of the problem. Could France treat the public lands in the Cameroun and Togo mandates as French public property? The answer, in this case, was that such public lands, and budget surpluses, must be considered the property of the mandated territory and used for the benefit of that territory. Again trusteeship was differentiated from annexation.

Even more urgent was the practical question whether a mandatory power could guarantee the protection of loans, investments of public and private capital in mandated territories, as it could in its own possessions. The possibility of the revocation, transfer, or termination of a mandate, "remote" as it might be, was sufficient to act as a deterrent to such investments, and yet investments were urgently needed for the economic development of the mandates. Accordingly the Council at the request of the Commission declared, in September 1925, that financial obligations and vested rights would have the same validity as if the mandatory were sovereign, and that a mandate could not be terminated or transferred unless the Council had been assured in advance that financial obligations would be fulfilled and vested rights respected.

The problem of sovereignty again took concrete form in 1925, when the Mandates Commission learned that there was a considerable agitation in South Africa for the eventual incorporation of South West Africa into the Union. The High Commissioner for the Union seemed to believe that South West Africa might in time be given independence, and then a treaty could be arranged whereby the white ruling class would agree to incorporation of the territory as one of the states of the Union. On this problem views differed, but an authoritative member of the Commission expressed the opinion that the spirit of the mandate system would be violated if "upon the demand of some ten thousand white settlers," a small minority of the population, the mandated territory were to be annexed.

From these instances it is apparent that the League is not disposed to concede sovereignty to the mandatories. It is even more obvious that the League, with its very limited powers, does not enjoy sovereignty itself. It is still more patent that only in a highly metaphysical sense could one regard sovereignty as being vested in the mandated territories themselves. Perhaps the legal arguments may be left to jurists; the practical difficulties, however, which arise from the vagueness of Article 22 are apparent to any layman, and must be considered as constituting one of the inherent defects of the present mandate system.

The Value of International Criticism

The mandate system may be toothless, but it is not bootless. Although under the terms of Article 22 the Mandates Commission has specific authority only to "receive and examine the annual reports of the Mandatories and to advise the Council on all matters relating to the observance of the mandates," nevertheless the work of the Commission has been surprisingly effective and significant. This happy result is due in part to the wisdom which has been displayed in appointing members of the Commission. Five members are citizens of non-mandatory states, and have shown no backwardness in criticizing the mandatories. Four are citizens of mandatory states, chosen not as national representatives but as experts on colonial questions. For instance, Sir Frederick Lugard, former British governor of Nigeria and author of books on Africa, was chosen as an experienced and enlightened colonial administrator, and has evinced admirable detachment in the criticism of British, as of other, mandates.

Unless one has carefully compared the reports and minutes of the Permanent Mandates Commission with the successive reports of the mandatories, it would seem incredible that the power to "receive and examine" the annual reports on the mandates could have been made to mean so much as it does. By means of questionnaires the Commission has elicited information on topics which the mandatories might have wished to leave untouched. By detailed comments on the annual reports it has suggested new policies, or better methods of achieving desirable ends. It has administered reproof—courteous but unmistakable—to Belgium, France, Britain, or Japan, with no apparent discrimination between Great Powers and small. And often it gives praise, or expresses its appreciation of commendable changes undertaken at its suggestion, no less courteously.

The range and spirit of the Commission's work cannot possibly be appreciated without sampling its reports. In commenting on the British report on Cameroons, it draws attention to the "unsatisfactory condition of public health," and suggests that if it is difficult to secure British doctors, Great Britain should employ doctors of other nationalities. It "notes with satisfaction," in 1925, that France is "paying special attention" in Togoland "to the development of vocational and agricultural training—a policy which coincides with the views expressed by the Commission last year." It "hopes" that South Africa will spend more money on native education of a practical kind. It "asks to be informed" whether slavery has been abolished in the Transjordan area of the Palestine mandate, and hopes that more money will be provided for village schools in Palestine. It inquires why there is an increase in the quantity of gin imported into British Cameroons in 1924, and asks that the next report on this area may "contain a clear explanation of any definite plan which the mandatory power may have for improving native agricultural methods, for guiding the moral and social evolution of native life, and for suppressing such customs as cannibalism, which are repulsive to humanity." It congratulates New Zealand on the constant decrease in the death rate in Samoa, but "is concerned to note the very high mortality" among prisoners in Belgian Urundi. Belgium is asked to explain whether the labor levy of 42 days' work per year required by native chiefs in the Belgian mandate, and the further requirements of forced labor for road work, are not inconsistent with the mandate. When it appears that some 6000 natives are employed in building the Midland Railway in French Cameroun, working a ten-hour day, with only one white doctor to care for the sick, and that the death rate is 80 per thousand, the Commission expresses the desire that France should improve the medical service. South Africa is called upon to give detailed explanations regarding land legislation in South West Africa, to show that the interests of the natives are not being overridden.

The Commission has also the function of considering petitions or complaints regarding the administration of mandates, but up to the present time this function has not been fruitful. In 1925, however, it suggested that its right of receiving petitions be interpreted with sufficient latitude to include memoranda and memorials of all kinds relating to the administration of the mandated territories. It is easy to see how this interpretation might lead to the development of a very important extension of the Commission's activity.

Another potential function—it is not much more than that now—is the formulation and recommendation of general colonial policies. At present, of course, it is not difficult to discover behind the queries and comments of the Commission on the annual reports which come before it a set of principles or policies such as the encouragement of native education, improvement of public health, protection of the natives against forced labor and abusive exploitation. A bolder step, however, was proposed in 1925 by M. Orts, the Belgian member, when he suggested that the time had come for the Commission to call to the attention of all the mandatories the danger of making excessive demands upon native labor. "The vast programmes of public works," he said, "the railways planned to cover enormous distances, the large industries which were being set up, the mining and agricultural exploitation of the country, the new concessions which had to be worked at a profit—all these operations implied at every turn a new and pressing appeal for native labour." The results might be tragic. Natives taken far from their homes to labor on railways, plantations or mines, developed tuberculosis or other diseases. The mortality was alarming. Another member of the Commission pointed out that recent reports showed a decrease of the native population. The Portuguese member thought that alcohol and syphilis, rather than work, caused the high mortality. M. Rappard observed that reliable statistics would tell the story: if they indicated excessive death-rates, it would be incumbent upon the administrators to explain the reason. Finally it was agreed that a question to bring out this information should be inserted in a questionnaire.

Whether the Mandates Commission issues some general pronouncement on this topic or not, the fact that it can be discussed as it was is significant of the spirit which the mandate system has tended to develop. Whether the Commission issues orders and general rules of policy or not, its criticism of mandate administration is not futile. Whether the jurisdiction of the commission is legally extended to other colonial possessions, or all colonial possessions, or is restricted to the fourteen existing mandates, the influence of the system cannot be confined by artificial boundaries.

A keen British critic of imperialism, advocating the extension of the mandate system to all subject peoples, wrote the pregnant sentence, "In fact, it is hardly conceivable that the mandate system, if honestly applied, and the old imperialism can exist side by side."[1] That the "old imperialism" will surrender, or that the ten nations owning colonies will hasten to place their possessions in the hands of the League, in the near future, only the most sanguine internationalist will dare hope. Yet it is true that the "old imperialism" and the new "trusteeship" cannot live together in so small a world as ours. The idea of trusteeship, the public criticism of administration in the mandates, and the careful study by the Mandates Commission of specific policies which benefit or injure the natives, must inevitably, though perhaps insensibly, influence the administration of colonies legally outside the mandate sphere, and thus bring imperialism more under the control of humane principles and international public opinion. As the French minister of colonies, M. Albert Sarraut, declared in 1923, "Reforms accomplished in one place will inevitably penetrate elsewhere. Whether we like it or not, colonial questions have ceased to be purely national; they have become international, placed under the eyes of the world."[2]

[1] Leonard Woolf, *Mandates and Empire* (1920, pamphlet), p. 18.

[2] *Afrique française*, 1923, p. 254, quoted in Buell, *International Relations*, p. 352 note. Buell's discussion of the mandate system and its desirable extension, pp. 339-352, is valuable in this connection.

CHAPTER XIX

CONCLUSIONS

THE MEASURE OF IMPERIALISM

To view modern imperialism in proper perspective, one must in some way sum up the aggregate results of such varied events as the partition of Persia, the conquest of Tunis, the Hawaiian revolution, the Agadir crisis, the Riffian revolt, intervention in Haiti, the Boer War, the Twenty-One Demands, and the thousand and one other episodes that have gone into the making of this chapter in contemporary world history. What these things have meant in terms of human hopes and fears, of cultural enrichment, of spiritual stimulus and strife, no statistics can ever reveal, nor can the historian do much more than guess. One can measure, however, some aspects of imperialism. One can gauge the size of empires, at any rate.

Ten imperialist nations of to-day possess colonies and protectorates which, taken together, are seven times the size of Europe and half the earth's total land surface. Six hundred million human beings, a third of the human race, are directly subject to imperialist domination. Even these figures, astonishingly large as they may appear, are admittedly incomplete. Yet it is problematical whether one should add Norway's recent acquisition of Spitsbergen, or Denmark's colony of Greenland, or Iceland. On the other hand, we have omitted countries such as China, Persia, Turkey, Abyssinia, Afghanistan, and several Latin-American states which have been very definitely affected by imperialism, though at the moment they may be considered independent. If they were included in our totals, we would have about two-thirds of the world, with more than a billion inhabitants, in colonies, protectorates, and "backward countries" which have been subject to European, American, or Japanese imperialism.

The relative importance of modern imperialist conquests may

be suggested by comparing them with achievements which bulk large in conventional histories. Republican France has outdone the warlike Charlemagne. The "New World" discovered by Columbus was less extensive than the realm conquered by modern imperialism. The empire of Julius Cæsar was much smaller than that of George V. More extensive than Napoleon's conquests were the territories won for Britain by Cecil Rhodes.

A survey of existing empires (see Tables I and II) discloses the fact that while in general modern imperialism has accompanied industrialism, the results have not been proportionate to the economic importance, or to the size and power, of the empire-building nations. The present distribution of colonies can be explained by no simple principle, but only by that complex interweaving of forces which—for want of a better name—we sometimes call chance.

While Spain has lost all but a poor remnant of her vast dominions, Portugal, her less powerful neighbor, retains two very large African colonies, besides several smaller possessions. Though she ranks fourth on the list of empires, Portugal is unable to develop her colonies or even to give them good government, for the mother-country is lacking in the industrial and financial resources and the political capacity for large-scale imperialism. Indeed, the Portuguese colonies are being invaded by British and other foreign capital and are so insecurely held that before 1914, as we have seen in another connection, Great Britain and Germany planned their partition.[1]

Holland, too, possesses in the East Indies an empire quite out of proportion to her own magnitude in area, population, or industry. In population the Dutch empire ranks third, in commerce fourth, in area seventh. It is doubtful whether the Netherlands could have secured so generous a portion in the nineteenth-century rivalry of world-powers, had the East Indies not been inherited as a legacy from the period, centuries ago, when Holland had one of the foremost navies.

Belgium has in Congo an empire even larger, though much less valuable, carved out of virgin territory by a foresighted king, before the appetites of the Great Powers had been thoroughly whetted. Belgium was able to purchase the Congo from her king in 1908, because rivalry among the Great Powers permitted

[1] *Cf. supra*, p. 119.

none to interfere, but had there been interference Belgium would have been too weak to defend her claims. In such fashion Belgium fell heir to a colonial empire larger than either Japan, or Italy, or the United States possesses, and almost as large as the one Germany held before the Great War.

TABLE I

PRESENT-DAY COLONIAL EMPIRES—AREAS [1]

Areas of colonial possessions and protectorates [2]
(in thousands of square miles)

	Africa	*Asia*	*Pacific* §§	*Americas*	*Total*
British *	4,203	2,126	3,279	4,008	13,616
Russian **		6,400			6,400
French †	3,773	317	10	36	4,136
Portuguese	927	7	1.6		936
Belgian	931				931
United States ††	37		122	752	911
Dutch			734	55	789
Italian	780				780
Spanish	132				129
Japanese §		86	28		114
				Total	28,742

[1] Perhaps one should include also the Norwegian possessions of Spitsbergen archipelago and Bear Island; the Danish possession of Greenland as well as the "independent" kingdom of Iceland, which is bound to Denmark by a personal union; and other minor quasi-colonial possessions. These, however, seem hardly to belong in a class with the empires given above.

[2] These terms are used in a broad sense, regardless of technicalities.

* Comprising the Dominions and all parts of the Empire as listed in the *Statesman's Year-Book*, excepting Great Britain and Ireland. Egypt is included though nominally independent. Mandates also are added.

** Asiatic Russia, estimated, not including portions of Mongolia occupied by Soviet forces.

† Including mandates and Algeria, although the latter is in certain matters considered an integral part of France. Including also the French zone of the Moroccan protectorate.

†† Including areas listed in Table IV.

§ Including Chosen and Port Arthur on the mainland; and Formosa, southern Sakhalin, the Pescadores, and the mandated islands in the Pacific. Perhaps one should add the Manchurian sphere of interest.

§§ Including Malay Archipelago, Australasia, and all islands of the Pacific.

While Portugal, Holland, and Belgium have disproportionately large shares, three Great Powers—Germany, Japan, and Italy—were peculiarly unsuccessful in attempting to occupy their proper places in the sun. In the period from 1871 to 1914

TABLE II

Present-Day Colonial Empires—Populations

Populations (in millions) of colonial possessions and protectorates[1]

	Africa	*Asia*	*Pacific*	*Americas*	*Total*
British	65	333	8	11	417
French	35	23	x	x	59
Dutch			50	x	50
Russian		35			35
Japanese		19	4		23
United States *	1,5		11.4	9	22
Belgian	11.5				11.5
Portuguese	8		x	x	9
Italian	1.9				2
Spanish	1				1
				Total	630.

x indicates population of less than one million.
[1] For explanation of interpretation of these terms, see notes to Table I.
* *Cf.* Table IV.

Germany was clearly superior to France in power, population, and industrial development, and yet this puissant Germany could obtain hardly more than a fourth of the colonial area that a weakened and humiliated French Republic was able to appropriate. In population, in commerce, in potential value, the German colonies were not to be compared with those of France or those of Britain. In part this anomaly was due to Bismarck's caution; in part, to clumsy diplomacy which enabled France, Russia, Britain, and Italy to combine against Germany on colonial questions. The hope of rectifying the situation was one of the will-o'-the-wisps that German statesmen pursued during the Great War, but the will-o'-the-wisp vanished "somewhere in France." After 1919, having lost even her former colonies, Germany stood alone among the industrial giants of Europe, the only Great Power without an empire.

Japan's phenomenal rise to power and dramatic entry into the area of world politics might easily give rise to the false impression that the vigorous island empire of the East has made large conquests. As a matter of fact, despite the three wars she fought at ten-year intervals, Japan still stands at the foot of the list as regards the area, and in fifth place as regards the population and commercial value, of her colonies, whereas her population of sixty millions and her rank among the Great Powers might entitle her—if there were any principles in the matter—to as large an empire as the French, or at least as valuable an empire as the Dutch. To be sure, if we include the Japanese sphere of interest in Southern Manchuria and Eastern Inner Mongolia, Japan's share appears less niggardly, and if Japanese imperialists had succeeded in their design of bringing China under Japanese tutelage, as the Twenty-One Demands of 1915 stipulated, their empire would have been second only to that of Great Britain.

The most striking case is that of Italy, a Great Power second to none in national pride or imperial ambition, boasting an African empire—Libia, Eritrea and Somaliland—which impressively covers 780,000 square miles, as seen on the map, but which includes so much desert land that its total population is less than two million souls. Commercially, it is the least valuable of all the ten empires. If the Fascisti have set apart April 21 as a "National Colonial Day," and if in 1926 no less a personage than *il Duce*, Mussolini himself, visited Tripoli with pomp and circumstance, urging Italian emigrants and Italian capital to develop the empire, it is because Italian imperialism is founded less on accomplished facts than on a faith which sees populous provinces and prosperous plantations in a parched and unpopulated wilderness.

By way of contrast, we turn to the more successful empires of France, Britain, Russia, and America. Considering the handicaps under which it labored, the French Republic has achieved miracles. The dawn of the imperialist age found France weak, isolated, overshadowed by victorious Germany. In shipping she was inferior to Germany and Britain, and likewise in the "heavy industries" such as cotton and iron, which have been such dynamic factors in imperialism. But France had francs for investment, and gallant soldiers and explorers, and astute diplomats. Francs paved the way for soldiers in Tunis and Morocco. Soldier-explorers penetrated jungle, desert and prairie, rounding out French Equatorial and French West Africa, and connecting them with French North Africa in one unbroken realm. Other soldiers subdued the large island of Madagascar, and admirals conquered province after province in Indo-China.

This work was carried on in the 1880's with the consent of Bismarck, who was willing that France should find in Africa compensation for Alsace-Lorraine. After Bismarck's fall, skilful French diplomacy secured Russian, Italian, and English support for French aggrandizement. French imperialism was more successful in its military and diplomatic phases, than as regards commerce or colonial settlement. There are only about half a million French settlers in French North Africa, although it would be difficult to find a region better suited for French colonization: the distance from the homeland is short, the climate is pleasant, the resources are rich, the native population is not too dense. France has no "surplus population" to pour into these colonies. As regards commerce, too, the French achievement has been less impressive than one might expect after consulting the map. French North Africa, West Africa, Equatorial Africa, Madagascar, Indo-China, the lesser possessions in the Pacific and the Caribbean, and the Syria mandate, make up an empire a third as large as Britain's, two-thirds as large as Asiatic Russia, and four times as large as any other, yet the total commerce of this vast domain is barely one billion dollars,[1] as compared with the eleven billions of the British possessions. Equatorial Africa and Madagascar are of relatively small value. The important colonies, commercially, are Algeria, Indo-China, Morocco, West Africa, Tunis, and Syria, in the order named, but the commerce of Indo-China and Syria is not with France. India, Canada, or Australia alone is more important in trade than the entire French colonial empire. The colonial empire of the United States has fifty per cent more commerce than the empire of France.

How far Great Britain has outstripped all competitors appears clearly enough from the tables given in these pages. Whether one takes area, or population, or commerce, as the measure of achievement, the British Empire is greater than the eight others combined, unless one throws Siberia into the scales, and even then the statement is still true except for area. Much of the empire, to be sure, is a heritage from an earlier age of colonial expansion, but almost half of it has been added by modern imperialism since 1874. In size and commerce these recent acquisitions outrank those of France or of any other rival.

[1] In 1924, as compared with 906 millions in 1922.

TABLE III

COMMERCIAL VALUE OF THE CHIEF COLONIAL EMPIRES [1]

	Total Commerce (in millions of dollars)	Commerce with Mother-Country (in millions of dollars)	Mother-Country's Share in Total Commerce of Colonies (in percentages)
British (1923-24)	11,079	3,778	34
American (1923-24) *	1,542	1,194	77
French (1922)	906	441	49
Dutch (1924)	898	100 **	11
Japanese (1923)	607	430	71
Portuguese (1924)	59	? †	? †
Belgian (1924)	44	22	50
Italian (1922-23)	21	7 ††	33 ††
Russian		no comparable data	
Spanish		" " "	

[1] See notes to Table I.

* *Cf.* Table IV.

** Including a generous estimate for Dutch share of Dutch West Indies trade. For the East Indies the 1924 commerce was 860 million dollars, of which Netherlands enjoyed 8½%, or 73 millions.

† Data not available.

†† *Annuario Statistico* (Rome 1925) gives total commerce for 1921 as 351 million lire, of which Italy enjoyed 115 millions or 32.5%. Assuming this percentage for 1922-23 gives the figures above.

For Britain's preeminent acquisitiveness, several reasons may be suggested, without pretending to offer any complete, scientific explanation. To begin with, England felt earlier and more keenly than any other Great Power the economic pressure which imperialism seeks to relieve—the pressure of surplus goods and surplus capital on a temporarily saturated market. Partly as a result of this pressure, and partly because of insularity, British policy was effectively concentrated upon empire, while France and Germany quarreled over the old Alsace-Lorraine grievance, while Russia and Austria intrigued in the Balkans, while the United States was absorbed in domestic affairs. Moreover, it should be recognized that Great Britain had a more ample supply of capable empire-builders, missionaries, overseas traders, and capital to lend or invest than did her rivals. Her navy, too, was unrivalled. Furthermore, British settlers in South Africa and Australasia have been zealous in urging expansion.

The overshadowing significance of the British economic empire in southern Asia does not appear from the ordinary map, which shows British territories colored in a uniform pink or red, apparently well distributed in three equivalent groups—Canada and

Newfoundland; Africa; and Australasia and India. Such a map gives factitious importance to unpeopled wastes in Australia and northern Canada and the Sudan, while it conceals the magnitude of India. If a map could show population, it would reveal India as three-fourths of the British Empire. India is by far the greatest market ever acquired as a colony by any industrial empire. In this respect, Britain's Asiatic possessions bulk larger than all British Africa and British America combined. The rounding out of the Indian Empire, and the policy of surrounding India with buffer states, naval bases, and spheres of influence, as well as the policy of vetoing railways which might approach India through Mesopotamia and Persia through Afghanistan, may be regarded as fairly logical corollaries of the progress of British trade and investment in India. To India should be added the recently magnified importance of rubber plantations and tin in the Malay States and the Straits Settlements, and the British oil interests in southern Persia and Mesopotamia, and British railway-building and commerce in the Yangtse Valley, if we would appreciate the importance of southern Asia in Britain's empire.

In the partition of Africa Great Britain secured a peculiarly desirable share. In South Africa and Rhodesia the British have the diamond and gold mines, and a large area fit for white colonization. In Egypt they secured what all modern industrial empires have sought, an important supply of raw cotton, while in East Africa and the Sudan they possess the most promising area in Africa for the future development of cotton plantations. Tanganyika, Nyasaland, Kenya and Uganda are of minor economic importance, but they serve as middle links in the territorial chain connecting South Africa with the Sudan and Egypt, and thus they complete the realization of Rhodes's project of a Cape-to-Cairo empire. Nigeria, Gold Coast, and the other British colonies in West Africa are commercially important, thanks to cocoa and the oil palm. Great Britain's share of Africa may be only a little larger than that of France, but it is almost twice as populous and of much greater commercial value.

In Africa and in southern Asia British imperialism since 1874 has been principally concerned, as the imperialism of other nations in the same period has been concerned, with the economic

ARCTIC OCEAN
GREENLAND
Parry Is.
Hayes Peninsula
North Devon
Baffin Bay
Melville Sound
Banks Land
Victoria Land
Baffin Land
Davis Strait
Pt. Barrow
ALASKA
Yukon R.
Arctic Circle
Dawson
Mackenzie R.
DOMINION OF CANADA
Hudson Bay
Iceland
Bering Sea
C. Farewell
Sitka
York
Nain
Labrador
Prince Rupert
NORTH AMERICA
Aleutian Islands
Queen Charlotte Islands
Vancouver I.
Vancouver
Victoria
Winnipeg
L. Superior
Quebec
Montreal
Ottawa
Quebec to Glasgow 2553 m.
NEWFOUNDLAND
St. Johns
Miquelon
BRITISH ISLES
N.Y. to Glasgow 3000 m.
to Liverpool 3062
N.Y. to Southampton
Vladivostok to Victoria 4320 m.
Yokohama to Victoria 4200 m.
Chicago
Toronto
Halifax
San Francisco
UNITED STATES
New York
Washington
St. Louis
Yokohama to San Francisco 4750 m.
Honolulu to Victoria 2340 m.
Honolulu to San Francisco 2098 m.
Los Angeles
Bermudas
Charleston
New Orleans to Liverpool 4561 m.
To Southampton 4669 m.
NORTH ATLANTIC OCEAN
Azores
Madeira
Canary Is.
NORTH PACIFIC OCEAN
To Yokohama 3380 m.
Tropic of Cancer
Honolulu
Sandwich Islands
New Orleans
MEXICO
G. of Mexico
Havana
Bahamas
WEST INDIES
Cuba
Haiti
Guadeloupe
Dominica
Martinique
Barbados
C. S. Lucas
Mexico
Acapulco
Belize
Jamaica
Caribbean Sea
Grenada
Trinidad
Honolulu to Panama 4711 m.
Guatemala
CENTRAL AMERICA
Colon
Panama
Caracas
VENEZUELA
Georgetown
Cayenne
Cape Verde Is.
Bathurst
Freetown
Palmyra
Fanning I.
Christmas I.
Gilbert Is.
Baker I.
Suva to Honolulu 2738 m.
EQUATOR
COLOMBIA
Quito
ECUADOR
Galapagos Is.
Guayaquil
Phoenix Is.
Jarvis I.
Malden I.
Starbuck I.
Ellice Is.
Union Is.
Tongarewa
Manihiki Is.
Marquesas Is.
Amazon R.
Para
BRAZIL
Pernambuco
Rotumah
Samoa Is.
Suwarow I.
6593 m.
Lima
Callao
PERU
SOUTH AMERICA
Bahia
Fiji Is.
Suva
Tonga or Friendly Is.
Society Is.
Cook Is.
Paumotu or Low Archipelago
BOLIVIA
Iquique
Sucre
St. Helena
Tropic of Capricorn
Auckland to Panama
Pitcairn I.
Ducie
Asuncion
PARAGUAY
Rio de Janeiro
Kermadec Is.
Auckland to Honolulu
SOUTH PACIFIC OCEAN
Valparaiso
Santiago
CHILE
ARGENTINA
Montevideo
Rio de la Plata
Buenos Aires
SOUTH ATLANTIC OCEAN
Auckland
Wellington
NEW ZEALAND
Chatham Is.
Valdivia
Tristan da Cunha
Dunedin
Bounty Is.
Antipodes Is.
Wellington to London 11,970 m.
Patagonia
Wellington to Rio 6688 m.
Falkland Is.
Stanley Harbor
South Georgia
Strait of Magellan
C. Horn
Drake Strait
South Shetlands
South Orkneys
Graham Land
Antarctic Circle
Longitude West from Greenwich

THE BR

ARCTIC OCEAN
C. Chelyuskin
New Siberia
Nova Zembla
North Cape
Narvik
NORWAY
SWEDEN
Stockholm
Archangel
Obdorsk
SIBERIA
Yakutsk
ARCTIC CIRCLE
Yenisei R.
Lena R.
Obi R.
Petrograd
Copenhagen
RUSSIAN REPUBLIC
Moscow
Tobolsk
Tomsk
Omsk
TRANS-SIBERIAN
Irkutsk
Amur R.
Okhotsk
Sea of Okhotsk
Saghalien
Kamchatka
Bering Sea
Aleutian Islands
Kurile Is.
GERMANY
Berlin
Vienna
RUSSIA
Orenburg
Volga R.
Odessa
Sea of Aral
Caspian Sea
Black Sea
Brindisi
Constantinople
OTTOMAN EMPIRE
Rome
ITALY
Mediterranean Sea
Malta
Cyprus
Port Said
Cairo
Suez
TRIPOLI
EGYPT
Tashkent
Andijan
Merv
Teheran
PERSIA
Kabul
AFGHANISTAN
BALUCHISTAN
Delhi
INDIA
Calcutta
Bombay
Karachi
Bahrein Is.
Mecca
HEDJAZ
Red Sea
Wady Halfa
ANGLO-EGYPTIAN
SUDAN
Khartum
Kuria Muria Is.
Kamaran I.
Aden
Perim I.
Socotra
Arabian Sea
Laccadive Is.
Goa
ABYSSINIA
SOMALI LD.
Aden to Zanz. 1720 m.
Lond. to Cal.
7933 m.
Madras
Ceylon
Colombo
B. of Bengal
Andaman Is.
BURMA
Rangoon
SIAM
FRENCH INDO-CHINA
Penang
Malacca
Singapore
Sumatra
MONGOLIA
MANCHURIA
Kharbin
Vladivostok
Sea of Japan
Hakodate
Pekin
Port Arthur
Wei-hai-wei
Kiao-chau
Kobe
JAPAN
Tokio
Yokohama
Nagasaki
Shanghai
CHINA
TIBET
Lhasa
Yangtse-kiang
Hankow
Canton
Hong-Kong
Manila
Philippine Islands
China Sea
Labuan
Borneo
East Indian Archipelago
Celebes
Vladivostok to Victoria 4320 m.
Yokohama to Victoria 4260 m.
Yokohama to San Francisco 4750 m.
To Honolulu 3380 m.
Bonin Is.
NORTH PACIFIC OCEAN
TROPIC OF CANCER
Ladrone Is.
Caroline Is.
Marshall Is.
Gilbert Is.
Baker I.
EQUATOR
Phœnix Is.
Solomon Is.
Ellice Is.
Santa Cruz
Rotumah
New Guinea
Thursday I.
Port Darwin
New Hebrides
Fiji Is.
New Caledonia
Suva
TROPIC OF CAPRICORN
Port Denison
Brisbane
Norfolk I.
Kermadec Is.
Lord Howe I.
Sydney to Suva
Sydney
Canberra
Auckland
NEW ZEALAND
Wellington
Chatham Is.
Dunedin
Bounty Is.
Antipodes Is.
Auckland I.
Campbell I.
Macquarie I.
NORTHERN TERR.
WESTERN AUSTRALIA
AUSTRALIA
SOUTH AUSTRALIA
QUEENSLAND
NEW S. WALES
VICTORIA
Coolgardie
Adelaide
Melbourne
Tasmania
Hobart
Perth
Fremantle
Albany
Java
Batavia
Christmas I.
Cocos Is.
Colombo to Albany
London to Melbourne 11,055 m.
INDIAN OCEAN
Maldive Is.
Seychelles
Chagos Archipelago
Amirante Is.
Mombasa
Pemba I.
Zanzibar
Madagascar
Rodriguez I.
Mauritius
Réunion
C. Town to Colombo
Kamerun
Congo R.
BELGIAN AFRICA
Leopoldville
CONGO
Boma
ANGOLA
RHODESIA
PORTUGUESE EAST AFRICA
BRITISH EAST AFRICA
SOUTH-WEST AFRICA
Bulawayo
TRANS.
O.F.S.
Durban
CAPE OF GOOD HOPE
Cape Town
Port Elizabeth
St. Paul I.
Amsterdam I.
Cape Town to Adelaide 5603 m.
Cape Town to Hobart
Pr. Edward Is.
Crozet Is.
Kerguelen
Kaiser Wilhelm II Land
Enderby Land
ANTARCTIC CIRCLE
Wilkes Land
King George V Land
Longitude East from Greenwich
WILLIAMS ENGRAVING CO., N.Y.
15° 30° 45° 60° 75° 90° 105° 120° 135° 150° 165° 180°

EMPIRE.

exploitation of colored peoples, rather than with white settlement. But at the same time, another sort of British imperialism has been displayed in relation to what are now known as the Dominions—Canada, Newfoundland, Australia, New Zealand, the Union of South Africa. It is significant that with the exception of Natal and the Transvaal, these territories were acquired before the beginning of the period to which this book has been devoted. They were the products of an earlier age of colonization. No other contemporary empire has anything to compare with them. And the policies applied to them by Great Britain are not applied by other nations, nor are they extended even by Great Britain to her other possessions. Indeed, one of the vital factors in British policy toward these Dominions is the cultivation of an imperial patriotism somewhat akin to nationalism rather than to imperialist domination.

Nevertheless there is an important connection between the Dominions and imperialism. The desire to prevent Gladstonian liberalism from bringing about a final rupture between the English-speaking colonies and the mother-country was probably uppermost in the minds of many British patriots of the Victorian age, whose efforts to preserve the Empire soon blended in with the more aggressive imperialism which they helped to create. To many Englishmen imperialism still means strengthening the ties between Fngland and the Dominions rather than the exploitation of Asiatic or African possessions.

The two varieties of imperialism doubtless strengthened each other. But their methods were, from the very nature of things, quite different. Canada could not be ruled like Egypt, through a Khedive with British advisers; Australian settlers could not be mowed down like dervishes before British machine-guns. White colonists[1] insisted on self-government, which is the antithesis of imperialism, for in the strict sense imperialism means the exercise of power, domination. For domination it was necessary to substitute federation or some other form of association. This problem of "imperial federation" and the whole subject of Britain's relations with the Dominions have been so amply described, discussed, and disputed by publicists and

[1] It should be remembered, however, that South Africa is not a white colony, but black, with a dominant white minority, although as a self-governing Dominion it is ordinarily thought of as belonging to the group of white colonies.

scholars that it would be an impertinence to attempt even a summary in this place. What needs to be emphasized here is the fact that the Dominions are not the British Empire. It is now the fashion to substitute the new term, "British Commonwealth of Nations" for the old name, "British Empire," but only if one ignores all except the self-governing colonies is the new name more accurate than the old. In addition to the Dominions there is still the Empire. Most of the Empire—as regards population rather than area—is colored, and not self-governing. Moreover, the Dominions as they mature are being entrusted with a share in the task of governing the subject empire. South Africa and New Zealand and Australia have their mandates and dependencies. In short, there is both a British Commonwealth and a British Empire, and the Commonwealth rules the Empire.

The imperialist expansion of Russia is not easily compared with that of France or England, because it is difficult to say whether Siberia should be regarded as an integral part of Russia. Had it been separated from Russia by the ocean, perhaps it would have been a Russian Australia. Being contiguous to Russia, it was settled by Russians, chiefly in the late nineteenth century, and to-day it is both administratively and racially part of Russia. If we exclude Siberia, and consider only the quite unmistakably imperialist acquisitions made in the period from 1850 to 1914, Russia ranks third, being only less successful than England and France in imperialistic aggrandizement. The following tabular summary is a convenient means of recapitulating Russia's gains:

Russian Acquisitions, 1850-1914	*Area* (square miles)	*Population*
Far East	350,000	750,000
Amur region, part of Maritime Province, and northern Sakhalin.		
Central Asia	750,000	9,000,000
Turkestan, Bokhara, Khiva and Trans-Caspian Province.		
Acquisitions in Kuban and Caucasus region	50,000	4,000,000
Total annexations	1,150,000	13,750,000
Spheres of interest in northern Persia, northern Manchuria, and Outer Mongolia	2,100,000	14,500,000
Grand total	3,250,000	28,250,000

The figures, it must be admitted, are only rough estimates in some cases where no definite statistics exist, but even approximations serve to show the relative importance of the acquisitions.

The Bolshevist Revolution, of course, has somewhat altered the situation. Northern Persia is no longer a Russian sphere of interest. Outer Mongolia, formerly a sphere of influence, has been occupied by Russian troops and partly sovietized, although Russia has promised to evacuate it. In northern Manchuria, the Bolshevists have renounced some of the privileges obtained by the Tsar, yet they have attempted to control the Chinese Eastern Railway. The Russian dependencies in Central Asia have been given new governments patterned on the soviet style, and "allied" with rather than subject to Muscovite Russia. In a word, while denouncing "capitalistic imperialism," the Bolshevists have practised their own sort of Red imperialism and have retained most of the tsarist empire in Asia. It is an empire so large that its economic development is beyond their industrial and financial capacity. Yet as her economic revival proceeds, Russia may measure up to the task.

As Russia colonized and absorbed Siberia, so the United States during the nineteenth century acquired and colonized vast territories on the North American continent—territories which cannot possibly be considered as colonies, since they are now States in the federal Union. The settlement of the West is a most important phase of the nineteenth-century expansion of the dominion of the white race. It has been left out of the picture in this study of imperialism, and it cannot be compared with the overseas imperialism of Europe, yet it should not be quite forgotten in this comparative review. The figures given for the American empire in the accompanying table (Table IV), it must be borne in mind, include only outlying dependencies and therefore fail to give the true measure of American expansion.

Even so, the figures may astonish those who have paid more attention to the anti-imperialist utterances of contemporary American statesmen than to the statistical record of their acquisitions. If one considers merely the outlying territories and possessions which have been won since the Civil War, the American colonial empire is over 700,000 square miles in area, with a population of almost 13,000,000 and a commerce of almost

$700,000,000. It ranks ninth in area and seventh in population, but fifth in commerce.

TABLE IV

THE COLONIAL EMPIRE OF THE UNITED STATES

	Area (square miles)	Population	Commerce † (dollars)
OUTLYING TERRITORIES			
Alaska	590,884	60,000	88,905,000
Hawaii	6,449	307,000	188,541,000
DEPENDENCIES			
Philippine Islands	115,026	11,076,000	243,356,000
Porto Rico	3,435	1,347,000	172,478,000
Virgin Islands *	132	26,000	2,559,000*
Samoa *	58	8,000	294,000*
Guam	210	13,000	967,000
Wake and Midway Is.	29	x	x
LEASED TERRITORY			
Panama Canal Zone, Guantanamo, Fonseca Bay, Corn Island	527	27,000	
Total Possessions	716,750	12,864,000	697,100,000
NOMINALLY INDEPENDENT DEPENDENCIES ‡			
Cuba	44,164	3,369,000	724,595,000
Haiti	11,072	2,045,000	28,872,000
Dominican Republic	19,325	897,000	51,843,000
Panama	33,667	443,000	16,250,000
Nicaragua	49,200	638,000	21,797,000
Liberia	36,834	1,500,000	2,528,000*
Total nominally independent dependencies	194,262	8,892,000	845,885,000
Grand Total	911,012	21,756,000	1,542,985,000

* 1923.
† 1924, *Commerce Year Book.*
‡ Whether these should be included, and whether other Latin-American countries might also be added, must necessarily be a matter of opinion. I have selected the countries which are definitely under a form of control which Europeans might be tempted to describe as a protectorate, quasi-protectorate, or veiled protectorate. Technical classification is difficult if not impossible, but the fact of control is indubitable. *Cf. infra* and ch. xvi.

But if Canada is part of the British Empire, and if Egypt and Iraq are under British control, then by the same standards Cuba, Haiti, the Dominican Republic, Panama, and Nicaragua are to be reckoned as falling in some degree under the control of the United States, for they are subject to military intervention, which Canada is not; their foreign affairs are to some extent submitted to American guidance, or at least to an American veto; their economic life is in considerable measure under American supervision; and they are protected against non-American encroachment quite as genuinely as any French or British protectorate. Liberia may perhaps be added to the list, without serious dispute. Some readers would wish to add other Central American republics, or Mexico, or Colombia and Venezuela; but these are excluded for the reason that American intervention in their affairs is less formal, less continuous, less analogous to the "protectorates" of European imperialism. Taking then, this fairly conservative list of quasi-dependencies—Cuba, Haiti, Santo Domingo, Panama, Nicaragua, and Liberia—and adding it to the list of territories and possessions, we obtain a grand total that will put the United States colonial empire in sixth place for area, and for population, and in second place for commercial value. For a non-aggressive nation, the United States has done remarkably well, as compared with rivals candidly intent on imperial expansion. Only Great Britain has done better.

Such a review as the foregoing ought to bring out clearly at least the fact that present-day empires are not accurately proportionate to the rank, power, prestige, wealth, or industrial needs of their possessors. Several small countries have more than their share; Italy and Japan have less; Germany has nothing; Britain has a fourth of the world. Nor can one defend this situation on the ground that colonial empires are the reward of enterprise, foresight, and civilizing capacity. If the preceding chapters have shown anything, they must have demonstrated that the present distribution of colonies depends, in the case of Portugal for instance, on explorations that are now almost ancient history; or, as in the case of Belgium, on the enterprise of an individual rather than of a nation; or, as in the case of France, partly on fortunate diplomatic combinations; or, as in the case of Czechoslovakia's lack of colonies, on a nation's being unable to take a hand at the right moment. The very suggestion that empires are a measure of the civilizing capacity of the governing powers needs only to be uttered to be recognized as absurd.

Does Imperialism Pay?—The Problem of Marketing Surplus Goods

How keen and how hazardous the rivalry of imperialist nations will continue to be in the future must depend primarily on what answer the public gives to the question: Does imperialism pay? Now that imperialism has almost literally gained the whole world, one may appropriately ask: what shall it profit? What have been its dividends, material and moral?

The question is too complex, despite its brevity, to be disposed of neatly in a final formula or a facile phrase. The answer can be obtained only by summing up the profit-and-loss account in each of half a dozen departments of activity, and combining the net results. An exhaustive study of each item would require more than one volume and more than a single lifetime. In the end, some of the benefits and evils of imperialism would still be imponderable, and the final judgment would be subjective rather than scientific, for no scientific balance can be devised to weigh ships against schools, raw materials against wars, profits against patriotism, civilization against cannibalism.

Nevertheless several of the crucial items can be objectively considered. Indeed, they call for consideration, because the facts are so astonishingly at variance with Mid-Victorian opinions that still pass as honest currency. The purpose of this and the following sections is to survey what seem to be the most significant of these opinions and facts, in relation to the value of imperialism as a solution for the problems of marketing surplus goods, investing surplus capital, relieving surplus population, providing raw materials, and promoting the welfare of the colored races.

First and foremost among the economic arguments advanced by imperialists of the late nineteenth century and still widely accepted to-day, is the vital need of an industrial nation for colonial markets in which to dispose of surplus manufactured goods. If the reader will turn back to Chapter III he will find that this was the plea of men like Chamberlain and Jules Ferry, of Lugard and Leopold. "What our great industries lack," said Ferry, "is markets"; and for markets he annexed colonies. "Trade follows the flag," so the slogan ran, and the conclusion followed that one should raise the flag in Africa, Asia, and Malaysia. Nor is the idea dead, though now it is practised less by flag-raising than by the maintenance of discriminating tariffs to monopolize for the mother-country the markets of her empire. Statistics are hardly needed to prove that the problem of marketing surplus manufactures is growing more acute as mass-production makes headway.

To what extent can imperialism solve the problem? The amount of colonial trade is impressive. The total, for the ten empires listed in Table III, is over fifteen billion dollars—at least a fourth and perhaps almost a third of the international trade of the world. The trade of the Dominions and colonies of Great Britain, including India, is eleven billion dollars, 74% of the total trade of the world's colonies; the possessions and protectorates of the United States account for 10%, or a billion and a half; the French colonies, 6%, or about one billion; the Dutch, 6%; the Japanese, 4%; the Belgian, one-third of one per cent; the Portuguese, two-fifths of one per cent; and the Italian, one-seventh of one per cent.

Each of these imperialist nations is striving, to some degree, to monopolize the trade of its possessions. Though the doctrine of the "Open Door" may seem to receive much lip-service, in reality the open door has been swinging shut, in one colony after another, during the last half-century. In the most valuable colonies of France the door is closed by what is euphemistically styled tariff "assimilation." An "assimilated" colony has, with minor modifications, the same tariff as the mother country. In other words exports to and imports from France are in general free, whereas against imports from other countries the high French protective tariff applies. This is tariff discrimination in its purest form, designed to monopolize the colonial market. Algeria was assimilated in 1884, Indo-China in 1887, Madagascar in 1897, Tunis in 1898; and so also were minor French colonies in the western hemisphere. As the trade of these colonies is seventy per cent of the total commerce of the whole French colonial empire, it is obvious that "assimilation" is the prevailing French policy. To a few less important colonies, such as Senegal, French Guinea, and French Oceania, preferential tariffs are applied, admitting French goods at rates of duty less than the rates charged on foreign goods.

Japan, like France, pursues the policy of assimilation, and has assimilated her chief possessions, namely, Formosa, Sakhalin, and Korea. Italy has established the preferential rather than assimilated form of tariff discrimination in her African colonies. The United States has assimilated Porto Rico and Hawaii, and established preferential tariffs in the Philippines, Guam, and the Virgin Islands. In the British Empire differential duties were adopted by the self-governing Dominions, under the name of "imperial preference"; and preferential rates have also been established in Rhodesia, the British West Indies, Cyprus, and Fiji. Portugal practises tariff discrimination except in certain minor colonies.[1]

Clearly the prevalent tendency has been toward discrimination and monopolistic policies. There are, however, some exceptions to the rule. The United States maintains the open door in Samoa, which has little commerce. So does Spain in Spanish Morocco and the Canary Islands. The Netherlands have a tariff for revenue, without discrimination, in the East Indies. Great Britain has refrained from imposing differential tariffs, in general, in the all-important Indian Empire as well as in the Malay States, many of the minor African and Pacific colonies, and Egypt, which is nominally independent. In several of these cases Great Britain is pledged by treaty to maintain the open door. France is bound by the Algeciras Act of 1906 to preserve the open door in Morocco; by the Berlin Act of 1885 she is required to afford commercial equality in Equatorial Africa; and she applies equal duties also in Somali, Dahomey, and Ivory Coast. Germany, before she lost her colonies, pursued an open door policy, which has been modified under the mandate system; it should be noted specially that the open door provision was deliberately omitted from the "C" Mandates.[2] It is not an exaggeration to conclude that the prevailing policy is one of discrimination and monopoly, and that the open door is maintained by way of exception to the rule, usually because of treaty obligations, or in minor colonies, or for some special reason.

Monopolistic imperialism seems to have been fairly effective in some instances as a means of securing colonial markets. The

[1] See the valuable study, *Colonial Tariff Policies*, published by the Tariff Commission, 1922.

[2] *Cf. supra*, pp. 482, 503.

Philippines in 1900 purchased only 8% of their imports from the United States, but after discriminating tariffs had been applied, the figure rose to 45% in 1913 and 57.5% in 1923. Of Porto Rico's purchases about 40% came from the United States in 1899, but 90% in 1924. For Hawaii the proportion was 89% in 1925. France supplies 63% of Algeria's needs, 65% of the imports of Tunis, and 78% of those of Madagascar. Such percentages are the more impressive when one remembers that colonial trade is increasing more rapidly than world trade. The colonial market expanded by 51% in the decade 1913-1923, while the world market was expanding by 22%.

On closer examination, however, these facts are less convincing. Discriminating tariffs do not always achieve their purpose. The exceptions are so important that one wonders if there is a rule. To cite only three conspicuous instances, Canada purchases only 17% of her imports from Great Britain, and 67% from the United States, despite "imperial preference"; French Indo-China, though "assimilated" to France, buys only 40% from the mother country; and Korea, while under an open door régime, received 63% of her imports from Japan, whereas after "assimilation" to Japan (1920) the percentage was precisely the same in 1922.[1] On the other hand, fairly monopolistic conditions are found in a number of "open door" colonies. British exports enjoy 80% of the open Nigerian market, and 54% of India's import trade; while France has a more monopolistic grip on the open door markets of Morocco (64%) and Equatorial Africa (52%) than on the severely protected market of Indo-China. A fair conclusion is that colonial tariff policies reserve for the mother country a larger share of the colonial market than she would otherwise have, but they are only one of the factors in the situation, and they are by no means so universally effective as one might expect them to be.

The broader question, whether imports follow the flag into colonies, may be attacked in the same manner. As we have seen, numerous colonies buy more than half their imports from their mother-countries. But the political fact that they are colonies is not in all cases the reason for the economic preference they show the mother-country. If you examine the export statistics of the United States, for example, you will find that we enjoy on

[1] In 1924 it rose to 68%.

the average about twenty per cent of the markets of foreign countries, but that we control more than half of the market in our possessions. However, we also control more than half the market in Canada, and in various countries bordering on the Caribbean Sea which are not our dependencies. We monopolize the markets of Canada, Mexico, and Colombia more effectively than the market of the Philippines. In short, geographic situation and trade facilities are more important than the flag in directing commerce. Andrew Carnegie once shrewdly observed, "One of the purest fallacies is that trade follows the flag. Trade follows the lowest price current. If a dealer in any colony wished to buy Union Jacks, he would order them from Britain's worst foe if he could save a sixpence. Trade knows no flag."[1]

Before accepting the steel magnate's view, it is wise to look at the facts still more closely. Belgium supplies 56% of the imports of her own colony, the Congo, and England provides only 11%, but in the British West African colony of Nigeria Belgium's trade is negligible whereas the British share is 80%. France supplies only one per cent of the imports of India and of the Philippines, and three or four of Siam's; but she provides 40% of the imports of her own colony, Indo-China. Political ownership alone can explain such a discrepancy. Similarly, Great Britain supplies only two or three per cent of the imports for Indo-China and five for the Philippines, but 15% for the open Dutch East Indies, 17% for independent Siam, and 53% for British-controlled India. The United States has 55% of the Philippine market, but only 6% of the Indian, 3% of the Indo-Chinese, 6% of the Dutch East Indian, and 3% of the Siamese. Netherlands has only one per cent or less of these Far Eastern markets except in the Dutch East Indies, where the Dutch before the war supplied over 30%, and since the war a somewhat smaller but still substantial portion (17% in 1923 and 8% in 1924).

The conclusion must already be clear, though it could be buttressed with any quantity of statistics if necessary, that ownership of a colony does not invariably enable the mother-country to monopolize the market for her own surplus goods, but does enable the mother-country as a rule to enjoy a somewhat larger share of the colonial market than would otherwise be hers. That

[1] *Imperial Federation*, p. 23.

is to say, by imperialism one gains not the whole trade of a colony, but only a percentage over and above what trade one would have obtained without political possession. Imperialism affords an additional margin of marketing facilities for an industrial nation's goods.

How important the margin is, can be gauged only by making unscientific assumptions as to how large the market would be if political ownership were in other hands. Instead of attempting so delicate a speculative task, we may more profitably deal with the relative importance of the total colonial market, remembering always that the relative importance of the market is considerably greater than that of the margin. The clearest case, naturally, is that of the British Empire. India, the Dominions, and the British colonies provide markets for two-fifths (42% in 1924 and 43% in 1925) of Great Britain's exports. But the vast French colonial empire absorbs only 13% of the exports of France,[1] and the outlying territories, dependencies and protégés [2] of the United States take only one-ninth of the exports of the United States. Belgium alone, or Great Britain alone, is a larger consumer of French goods, and therefore more important as a market for France, than the whole French colonial empire. The British Dominion of Canada is more valuable as a market, to the United States, than all the American colonial possessions and protégés; Great Britain is twice, Europe five times as valuable. Holland sells (1924) about eight times as much to Germany as to the Dutch East Indies. Belgium in 1923 sold three times as much to Argentine, ten times as much to Holland, and almost twenty times as much to France, as to the Belgian colony in which King Albert believes Belgium's future lies. Japan in 1924-25 sold 15% of her exports to Korea and Formosa; but the goodwill of her chief customer, the United States, is three times as valuable to her as the possession of these colonies. For the other empires, colonial trade is of still less relative importance. Germany before the war sold to her own colonies about half of one per cent of her exports.

To get a truer perspective, one should remember that we have been considering, thus far, only *external* trade. If *internal* trade

[1] For 1921, the last year for which, at the time of writing, official data are conveniently available in the *Annuaire Statistique.*
[2] As listed in Table IV for 1924-1925.

within the nation were taken into account, the colonial markets would shrink still further in relative importance. It has been estimated that in the United States internal traffic is ten times the volume of the nation's foreign trade. Census figures show that in 1921 for every dollar's worth of domestic manufactures exported across the frontier, twenty-one dollars' worth was consumed at home. For every dollar's worth of goods sold in the United States, about four or five cents' worth was sold to foreign countries, and only a fraction of a cent's worth to the American colonial empire. In the general economy of the nation, then, colonial trade is a small factor. Except in the case of a few outstanding possessions such as Canada, India, Australia, and the Dutch East Indies, imperialism means merely securing an additional fraction of a market that is relatively small, if not insignificant, as compared with the volume of internal and external trade in general. In no case except that of Britain can the colonial market be considered as a major factor in the export problem, and even Great Britain, if she lost her empire, would be losing not 43% of her external markets, but only the marginal fraction of that 43% which accrues as a result of political ownership.

Against the gain set the cost. Many colonies are operated at a deficit, so far as the government's finances are concerned, and the deficit is paid by the taxpayer of the mother-country. Most colonies are acquired at a considerable cost, whether in the form of a purchase price or in the form of military and naval expenditures. As one of the chief purposes of armaments, especially of naval armaments, has been to defend colonies against seizure, and to maintain the diplomatic prestige and influence which make colonial acquisitions possible, part of the armaments expenditures of the last half-century must be entered in the debit column of imperialism. Add to that the cost of occasional wars, such as the Russo-Japanese War, and of countless native insurrections, and the charges become so heavy as to cast some doubt on the net value of imperialism, measured in dollars and cents, to the taxpaying public in general. In the case of Italy and of pre-war Germany, the net result of colonial ventures in Africa cannot be calculated as anything other than a loss.

We can push the analysis farther if we recognize that the cost of imperialism falls on the government treasury, hence on the taxpaying public in general, whereas the direct gain from colonial markets is enjoyed by the corporations, firms, and individuals who do business with the colonies. To be sure, the general public may possibly derive an indirect profit through the raising of the level of business prosperity, but, since it has been shown that colonial markets are a relatively small item as compared with the volume of internal and general foreign trade, it is at least uncertain in most cases whether the indirect profit outweighs the direct cost to the whole body of taxpayers.

To certain branches of industry, however, the colonial market is very important. These are, above all, cotton and iron. The making of cotton cloth is one of the greatest world industries, and it is an industry in which the problem of surplus production is acute. It has been estimated that the cotton-goods manufacturers of the United States should export twenty per cent of their output in order to keep their mills running at capacity.[1] In practice, however, the exports do not attain this figure, because world competition in this trade is little short of frenzied. Now it so happens that cotton goods are one of the commodities that can be sold in considerable quantities to colonial populations. For the owners of American cotton mills, colonies are valuable. The conquest of the Philippines, for example, enabled these owners to supplant their British rivals in an important market. Almost one-fifth of the cotton-goods surplus exported from the United States is disposed of in the Philippines, Porto Rico, and Hawaii.[2] These possessions are twice as valuable to the cotton industry as to American industry in general. Similarly, French cotton mills market 37% of their exportable surplus in the French colonies, and find in Algeria their largest external market. The colonies, by the way, consume the cheaper grades of cloth, whereas more expensive grades are sold to the United States, Belgium, England, and Germany. Still more dependent on colonial markets is the British cotton industry, which once dominated world markets, but, losing its grip on Europe and America, found compensation in Asia and Latin America, and above all in India. In 1913 India was taking three billion yards of British cotton cloth a year.[3]

[1] L. Bader, *World Developments in the Cotton Industry*, p. 179.
[2] *Statistical Abstract*, 1923.
[3] Bader, *op. cit.*, p. 47 and ch. 5.

Iron vies with cotton as king in world politics, and like cotton seeks colonial markets from which competition can be barred to some extent. The British iron industry, as was indicated in an earlier chapter,[1] found it impossible to keep pace with its American and German competitors in the world market, and fell back more and more on safe colonial consumption. The figures for the decade 1900-1910 show what happened. During that period the exports of British iron and steel, hardware, cutlery, railway rolling stock, tools, ships, and other iron and steel products, increased by about £23,500,000; but of this increase £14,000,000 represented new colonial business. The British colonies, which took 33% of the exports in 1900, took 40% in 1910. Turning to the American iron and steel business, we find that what in the 1880's was still an "infant industry," unable to supply domestic demands, swiftly gained in power until it was producing a large surplus that had to be sold, or dumped, on foreign markets. After the Great War the amount of the surplus was from one-fourth to one-third of the total output. In normal times only a small fraction of this goes to Europe; most of it is sold to Canada, Latin America, and the Far East; fully one-sixth of it goes to American territories, dependencies and protégés.

The general conclusions to be drawn from these facts seem to be: (1) Colonial trade is much more advantageous to a few industries, notably the cotton and iron industries, than to industry in general. (2) It is impossible to calculate the precise indirect gain, if there is any, which accrues to the public through increased general business prosperity, or to balance that gain against the direct costs, which are material. But the relative importance of colonial trade as compared with the total volume of internal and external trade is so slight, except in a few cases, as to afford little basis for imperialist oratory of the type made popular by Jules Ferry and Joseph Chamberlain, and to offer little compensation for the risks of war encountered by aggressively imperialist nations. Imperialist propaganda, however, exaggerates the supposed rewards and supports a policy of differential and monopolistic colonial tariffs. The result of such exaggeration is that for the sake of gaining relatively trifling increments of colonial trade great nations cheerfully incur heavy

[1] *Cf. supra*, p. 26.

colonial and military expenses and too often deliberately jeopardize their largest markets and the peace of the world.

Investing Surplus Capital

Surplus goods and surplus capital are twin problems born of eminently respectable parents—thrift and profit. Thrift dictates that wage-earner and capitalist alike save part of their income. Profit suggests the investment of savings in interest-bearing bonds or profit-bearing stocks, either directly or through savings banks and insurance companies. Thus the amount of invested capital on which industry must earn an income in normal times is being continually and rapidly increased. This means simply that more goods, and then still more goods, must be produced and sold. If, however, the investment of savings and the increase of production outstrip the growth of population and the rise of the standard of living, you have the problem of surplus goods, which leads to the struggle for colonial and other markets; or, if markets are not found, to price-cutting, losses, and bankruptcies. There is, however, an escape—temporary if not permanent. Accumulating surplus savings of capital may be invested abroad, rather than in over-productive home industries. The export of surplus capital can be a substitute for the export of surplus goods. As a matter of fact, the two are in a sense identical, for the "export of capital" often means merely exporting goods on credit, where one could not get cash.

This is the remedy the leading industrial nations have chosen. It is hardly necessary here to repeat the statistics of foreign investments given on an earlier page.[1] Nor is it necessary to remind the reader of the aggressive rôle of investment interests in Egypt, Morocco, China, the Near East, and Latin America. It will be more interesting to discuss four controversial aspects of the problem: first, the relation between the flag and the financier; second, the effect on the colonies and backward countries; third, the effect on labor at home; fourth, the effect on the capitalist régime.

(1) The association between finance and diplomacy has become intimate for fairly obvious reasons. No government can easily turn a deaf ear to the grievances or the desires of banking,

[1] *Cf. supra*, pp. 31 f., 415, 469 and Index.

oil, and mining syndicates or of other well-organized investing interests which can bring to bear upon officialdom all the power of gigantic concentrations of capital as well as the influence of intelligence and sophistication in international affairs. On the other hand, the diplomat occasionally finds the banker a most useful ally when it is necessary to cement an alliance with loans, or to consolidate a sphere of influence against foreign concession-hunters, or to discipline a foreign government by withholding credits. Against this very natural association—which is so well expressed in the now classic phrase "dollar diplomacy" —it is equally natural that protests should be uttered, protests based on the economic democrat's instinctive distrust of "capitalism"; or on the political democrat's fear that his government is being corruptly controlled by Wall Street, or the Bourse, or the City; or on the pacifist's well grounded belief that dollar, franc, sterling, mark, lira and yen diplomacy has often led to international conflict; or simply on the feeling that as against the combination of "bonds and battleships" the small nations do not get fair play. There is force in these protests, mixed as they may be with passion or prejudice. Yet two observations may be made. First, if dollar and diplomacy could be divorced, and if foreign investments were given no political protection, there would still be foreign investments, but—if one may judge by the past—there would be more filibustering, more "strong men" of the Diaz type, more subsidized revolutions and counter-revolutions in backward countries—in a word, more anarchy. The other observation is that finance is becoming international to a very significant extent. Witness the Chinese Consortium, the reconstruction of Austria and Hungary, the Turkish Petroleum Company, the Katanga copper mines, the African diamond industry.[1] In proportion as the most influential investment interests learn to pursue the international consortium and international syndicate method, the danger to peace will disappear.

(2) There may still remain the problem of fair play for the natives of the colony or for a weak and backward nation. That brings us to the second topic. On one hand it ought to be reasonably clear that, by and large, the investment of surplus capital in a colony or backward country does promote the material

[1] *Cf. supra*, pp. 370 ff., 471, 267, 92.

development of that country. When capital waves its magic wand over jungle and wilderness, railways, mines, oil-wells, cities, plantations, wharves, factories, power-plants, telegraphs, and warehouses appear. Of the profits, the native population may at first receive a niggardly share. On the other hand, with material progress are linked the vices, diseases and problems of modern industrialism. Backward countries such as India go through the Industrial Revolution, with its low wages, child labor, excessive working hours, overcrowded slums; colonies suffer from high mortality rates due to labor conditions unsuited to native physique. The medal has its two faces. Perhaps it is not unduly optimistic to hope that the evils of uncontrolled exploitation and the problems of economic transformation are passing phases which will in time be corrected, as they have been, at least partly, in progressive countries, while the benefits of industrial progress will be more enduring. Let those who will lament the invasion of the Orient by hustling business and noisy machine, or the passing away of tribalism in Africa. Ruskin uttered noble protests against modern industrialism, but he gave lectures in Manchester and Edinburgh, and he received royalties from books printed by modern industrial methods of mass-production.

(3) A typical labor attitude toward investment imperialism is expressed in a little red-covered textbook, *An Outline of Modern Imperialism*, issued by the Plebs League and distributed by the Independent Labor party, for the use of labor colleges in Britain. The writer points out that British capitalism has built in Germany, in Japan, in India, factories which compete with British factories. "Thus capitalism is forever changing customers into competitors." Colonies and backward countries offer to capitalists new "spheres of exploitation" where labor is cheap, unorganized, and unprotected. The products of such native labor, being cheap, compete with those of the mother-country, "and cause more lasting and more widespread unemployment and misery there." Thus, the conclusion follows, "the workers of the advanced country who provided the means for the creation of a new competitor suffer a second time, and possibly more terribly than they did from their original and direct exploitation."

Plausible though this argument may sound, it is based on the same false assumption as neo-mercantilism, namely, that the growth of industry in one country necessarily competes with and injures the industry of other countries. There is no need to argue the principle in abstract economics. On this point we have facts. The rise of "competing" industries in Germany did not impoverish Britain, but made Germany the largest buyer of British goods in pre-war Europe. The development of factory industry in India has not prevented, but rather has helped to cause, the phenomenal increase of India's imports of manufactures ("articles wholly or mainly manufactured") from £9,500,000 in 1904, to £15,000,000 in 1910, and to £174,700,000 in 1923-24. India's imports of cotton manufactures increased by 66% in the decade 1913 to 1923. Her imports of cotton piece goods from Great Britain are larger since the war than in 1913. The total sale of British cotton manufactures to India rose from £25,000,000 in 1910, to £38,000,000 in 1913, and to an average of almost £50,000,000 in the years 1920-24. Likewise India's imports of other manufactures from Britain, especially iron, steel and machinery, increased during the same period. Industrialization in India means increased production, and therefore increased buying power, and therefore increased imports. India's per capita imports almost doubled between 1913 and 1925. The building of cotton mills in India does mean competition for British mills making the same type of goods, but for British industry in general it means a larger Indian market. The part may suffer, but the whole gains. Hence the investment of surplus capital in colonies and backward countries does not necessarily mean increasing unemployment and poverty for labor in the investing countries; the facts so far indicate the reverse, for labor as a whole.

(4) But—coming to the fourth point—the export of capital does affect the future of capitalism. It has been pointed out that under present conditions the normal tendency of prosperous industrial nations is to produce surplus goods which are not consumed at home and surplus capital which cannot be invested at home without reducing the rate of profits or glutting the market with unsaleable goods. Therefore foreign markets and foreign investments are sought.

Marketing surplus goods and investing surplus capital in backward countries and colonies is all very well, so long as those countries and colonies remain backward. There is still much room for surpluses in the building of railways, roads, mills, dams, irrigation canals, and a thousand and one other enterprises in Asia and Africa and Latin America. But each such enterprise established by foreign capital will in time produce profits, if it prospers, and of the profits a portion will be available for reinvestment. Infant industries created by foreign capital help to relieve the need for foreign capital. We have seen the process illustrated most strikingly in the United States, once a favorite field for British investments, but now producing its own surpluses and seeking foreign investment fields. India will undoubtedly undergo the same transformation from debtor to creditor, and other borrowing nations, one after another, in proportion as they progress, will cease to be fields for foreign investment and become rivals in exploiting what fields are left. Unless some other solution is found, the gradual transformation of backward countries into surplus-producing countries will cause fiercer competition for markets and for the fewer remaining investment opportunities in backward countries. In other words, economic imperialism will become more intense and more bitterly competitive. Well-informed observers of world affairs have predicted this process. Some Socialists add that the outcome will be "the formation of a world consortium, consciously organising the whole material and labour resources of the world for the benefit of a small oligarchy."[1]

The one fact that is not duly appreciated in such arguments is that there are two safety valves—the birth-rate and the standard of living. Backward countries and colonies are not necessities but luxuries for expanding capitalism. Increasing consumption caused by increasing population or by rising standards of living would, without colonies, afford some room for profits and expansion. It is only when consumption lags too far behind production that additional outlets for surpluses are required in backward countries. Fundamentally, economic imperialism is a symptom of overgrown production and excessive profits—"overgrown" and "excessive," be it explained, only in relation

[1] *An Outline of Modern Imperialism* (Plebs League), p. 126. For discussion of these ideas see Nikolai Lenin, *Der Imperialismus als jüngste Etappe des Kapitalismus* (Hamburg, 1921); M. Pavlovitch, *Foundations of Imperialist Policy* (London, 1922); Rosa Luxemburg, *Die Akkumulation des Kapitals* (Berlin, 1913).

to the domestic requirements of goods for consumption. But the lag between consumption and production may be reduced either by diminishing production or, more comfortably, by increasing consumption, until the annual surplus (represented by savings from wages and profits) is normally not much more than sufficient to provide the additional factories, mines or other productive enterprises needed to satisfy a rising standard of living or an increasing population. More simply stated, this means more wages and more spending, and less profits and less investing. "Less," of course, is only used in a relative sense; the total absolute amount of profits and investment may increase; but the ratio between that amount reinvested and the amount spent must be smaller. One can already discern a tendency in this direction. A continuation of this tendency might quite conceivably reduce the surpluses of capitalism in measure as economic imperialism becomes impossible. As it becomes more difficult to export surplus capital, the remedy is to spend the surplus.[1]

"Surplus" Population

The value of imperialism as an outlet for "surplus" population is not difficult to estimate. Germany in the 1880's and in more recent years Italy and Japan have been pointed to as countries suffering from the supposed malady of overpopulation. As an excuse or justification for their efforts to gain colonial empires the "surplus population" argument has been frequently employed. The conventional view of the situation is that such countries, having more people than can be fed on their restricted areas, must have colonies into which the surplus of hungering human beings may overflow. Imperialism is prescribed as the remedy for overpopulation. "Italy's surplus man power must emigrate," declares Mussolini.[2]

It is a poor remedy. The colonies Germany obtained during the period from 1884 to 1914 were extensive enough, and in them were many great open spaces, but as outlets for German emigration they were of no importance whatsoever. Germans did not care to go to German colonies. According to official

[1] Compare Foster and Catchings, *Profits*, and J. A. Hobson, *Imperialism*, in this connection.
[2] *N. Y. Times*, July 24, 1926.

German statistics there were only 23,952 Germans in all the German colonies, just before the Great War. That was the imposing result of thirty years of imperialism. More than that number of Germans immigrated to the United States in two years, 1912 and 1913. Italy has acquired an African Empire, which now has somewhat less than 30,000 Italian inhabitants—less than the number of Italian immigrants to the United States in the year 1923-24. New York City contains more Italians, twenty-five or twenty-six times more Italians, than the whole Italian colonial empire. Japan annexed Korea in 1910, and ten years later the total number of Japanese in the country was 347,850, most of them being in commerce, public service, and industry, rather than in agriculture. In Formosa there were about 178,000 Japanese in 1922. Imperialism has been a conspicuous failure in providing homes for the surplus inhabitants of Germany, Italy, and Japan.

One reason for the failure is that these nations failed to obtain the most desirable territories for colonization. In large part, the best territories had already been appropriated—North America and South America, Australia, New Zealand, South Africa, Algeria. Japan had to content herself with Sakhalin, which is too cold, and Korea and Formosa, which are more densely peopled than France. Italy obtained regions as arid as they were extensive. Germany secured few regions fit for white settlers, but much jungle and some desert.

The more important reason for the failure, however, was economic and social, rather than geographical. Germany did not make full use of the colonizable areas she had. Mussolini finds it necessary to urge Italians to go to Libia. Japanese immigrants prefer the United States to Korea as a destination. Immigrants rarely have the capital required to set up plantations in undeveloped territory. Immigrant laborers seek lands where they can make a good living, not wildernesses to conquer. To be sure, there are always a few adventurous souls who like to be pioneers, but the masses want high wages, economic opportunity and comfort.

One wonders, after all, just what "surplus" population is. As compared with Canada's 2.3 inhabitants per square mile, Germany's 328, and Italy's 329, Japan's 392 may seem excessive. The situation of Japan seems still more grave if one leaves out of consideration the island of Hokkaido, which is too cold to be attractive to Japanese settlers; perhaps one could obtain a figure of 485 for the density of population in the chief Japanese islands. The population of any country can be made to appear denser by eliminating the barren or uninhabited regions. But even 485 or 500 per square mile appears not very excessive when compared with 479 for Massachusetts, 566 for Rhode Island, 573 for Netherlands, 648 for Belgium, and 701 for England. Netherlands and Belgium are not overpopulated; and though they have colonies they have few emigrants. To be sure, the soil of either of these countries, and of many others, does not suffice to provide food for the population. But it is mere twaddle to talk of "overpopulation" simply because the domestic production of food has to be supplemented with imports. Every city imports food. New York City has a population density of almost 21,000 per square mile, yet its people do not starve, as a rule. What matters is not the density of the population per square mile, or the acreage of grainfields, but the ability of the population to buy food from regions where there is ample room for grainfields. And the ability to buy food depends on industrial, commercial, and financial development. Overpopulation is merely economic underdevelopment. Ten million Indians supporting themselves by hunting would probably mean overpopulation in the United States. Yet a hundred millions can support themselves in the same area by combining industry, finance, and agriculture.

Economic underdevelopment may be due to lack of capital and of modern industrial methods, as in India and China. It may be due to lack of coal and iron or other raw materials. Italy, we know, suffers the handicap of having practically no coal and iron. Japan has coal and iron, but not in large quantity. If the root of the trouble is found in these deficiencies, then the question of surplus population is transformed into the problem of raw materials to which the next section is devoted.

Raw Materials and Imperialism

"The fight for raw materials plays the most important part in world politics, an even greater rôle than before the war." These are the words of Dr. Schacht, president of the German

Reichsbank, as reported in *The New York Times* of March 26, 1926. And his conclusion was that "Germany's only solution is her acquisition of colonies." Dr. Heinrich Schnee, former governor of German East Africa, conspicuous since the Great War in the agitation for the restoration of some colonial territory to Germany, has made similar pleas, based on the assumption that great industrial nations need colonies to supply them with raw materials.[1] Fascist Italy "must expand or suffocate," Mussolini asserts.[2] France owes her greatness to her colonies, which provide her with raw materials and markets, so we read in a recent book issued under the auspices of the General Staff of the French navy.[3] Nationalistic monopolies of raw materials, Secretary Hoover warns the world, "can set up great malignant currents of international ill-will."[4]

Some of the reasons which lie behind such statements as these are worth stating and criticizing in this discussion, brief as it must be. All important industrial nations have become more and more dependent on imported raw materials. In some cases it is cheaper to import than to produce the raw materials: that is why England imports Australian wool. In other cases the domestic supply is inadequate; that is why Italy has to import iron. Often industries are established where they can obtain coal or power, labor, and capital, but not the raw materials they require: such is the situation of the British cotton industry. Or again, an industry may have local supplies of its principal raw materials, and still need to import minor but essential ingredients; as the United States steel industry imports chromite from Rhodesia and Cuba. Taken in the aggregate, such imports have reached immense proportions. The value of imported raw materials consumed by the industries of the United States is shown in the following table:

Year	*Imports of Raw Materials*
1850	$ 407,141
1875	50,387,008
1900	210,391,745
1925	1,430,012,763

[1] H. Schnee, *German Colonization Past and Future* (London, 1926), and address in *Proceedings of the Academy of Political Science*, XI, no. 4, pp. 172-173.

[2] *N. Y. Times*, July 24, 1926.

[3] J. Tramond et A. Reussner, *Éléments d'histoire maritime et coloniale contemporaine* (Paris, 1924), pp. 410-411.

[4] Speech before Chamber of Commerce, Erie, Pa., Oct. 31, 1925.

Great Britain's needs are even greater. In 1900 she used foreign raw materials worth 172 million pounds sterling; in 1924, 400 millions (two billion dollars). France in 1925 imported twenty-nine million francs' worth; Germany, six and a quarter billion gold marks' worth. In short, billions of dollars, francs, marks, lira, yen, and hundreds of millions of pounds sterling are reaching out into the most remote quarters of the earth to secure the ores, the fibres, the gums, which are fed into the hoppers of their factories.

The quest for raw materials becomes imperialism when it deals with backward and tropical countries. Sir Frederick Lugard, British empire-builder, writes: "The tropics produce in abundance a class of raw materials and foodstuffs which cannot be grown in the temperate zone and are so vital to the needs of civilized man that they have in very truth become essential to civilisation. It was the realisation of this fact (as I have said) which led the nations of Europe to compete for control of the African tropics."[1] And not only the African tropics! The process of extending control over tropical sources of raw materials is quite as active in the American, Asiatic, and Pacific tropics. One thinks of Cuban sugar and tobacco, Mexican oil, Manila hemp, Indian cotton, Malayan rubber. In tropical countries the large-scale production of plantation products requires fairly stable and favorable government. Planters want protection for their crops and their persons; oil men must obtain concessions; their bankers insist on security. How closely this situation is bound up with imperialism must be clear, especially if the reader has scanned the preceding chapters, in which the details were set forth. One should add, that the same motive is operative also in non-tropical countries which have raw materials without strong and stable governments. Japanese efforts to obtain control of Chinese iron mines and coalfields may perhaps serve as an illustration.

The tendency of business men actively engaged in obtaining raw materials to ask protection and aid from their own government, and even to demand annexations, meets with a favorable response from the statesmen and the public in so far as the idea of national wealth is popular. Many a Frenchman, for example, looks on the phosphate mines of French North Africa

[1] *The Dual Mandate in British Tropical Africa* (1922), p. 43.

as an addition to the wealth of his nation. Such material treasures are something the public can visualize, something the statesman can understand. Who can doubt that a colony with rich mines, or a mandate permeated with petroleum, is a prize worth winning, worth quarreling for, worth fighting for? It requires either sophistication or high-mindedness to entertain such doubts. The altruist denies that war for material gain is ethical. The student of economic imperialism denies that the average Frenchman gains any substantial share in the Tunisian phosphate mines, or the average Englishman in the Kimberley diamond fields. If an Englishman wants an engagement ring, he pays for the diamond, as if he were not a fellow-countryman of the late Cecil Rhodes; if a Frenchman wants phosphate to fertilize his farm, he buys it at a price, and at approximately the same price that a Spaniard or an Italian would pay.

The desire for colonial supplies of raw materials has been stimulated since the Peace Conference by the inter-Allied debt situation and the depression of European exchanges. It has been argued that France can more easily maintain the franc and meet her obligations if she obtains raw materials from her own colonies than if she has to buy them from foreign countries. Prominent British statesmen have applied the same principle to their own debt problems. Premier Baldwin himself has asserted that the more Britain turns to her own Dominions for raw materials, rather than to America, the better it is for British exchange and for the payment of the British debt to the United States. At a recent conference on international relations,[1] a distinguished Swiss journalist, Dr. William Martin, expressed the opinion that the European countries needed to depend on their colonial resources in order to pay their debts to America. At the impressive British Empire Exhibition at Wembley the idea is put in the form of the slogan, "Keep your money in your Empire." Into the intricacies of exchange, we cannot enter here. But we may observe that this point of view is exaggerated, to say the least. Except for Great Britain no European country can expect in the near future to depend on its colonies for the major portion of its raw materials. Italy, England, and

[1] National Conference on International Relations and Problems, Briarcliff Lodge, May, 1926. See the discussions, in *Proceedings of the Academy of Political Science*, July, 1926.

France are paying deficits on colonial budgets and investing large sums of capital in colonial debts, railways, and other enterprises. Colonial raw materials have to be paid for, even though in most cases the payment is not made through international exchanges.

While Europe is growing more interested in raw material imperialism because of debts to the United States, the latter is being aroused by its Department of Commerce for very different reasons. Secretary Hoover discovered the fact that "there are at present governmentally controlled combinations in nine[1] raw materials," our imports of which, if prices remain at their present level, "will cost us about $1,200,000,000 for 1926." And there are "some twenty or thirty other commodities in the world which could likewise be controlled by action of one government or by agreement between two governments." The attempt of governments to control prices of such monopolistic supplies "raises a host of new dangers." Mr. Hoover believes that it "not only threatens the sane progress of the world but involves great dangers to international good will." And he informs us that the Department has "endeavoured to stimulate our industries to provide for themselves independent sources of supply."

Above all, the rubber situation aroused Mr. Hoover's ire. Rubber is one of the newcomers in the front rank of raw materials. Although it was used by the Aztecs before Columbus discovered America, it was not consumed in large quantities until the latter part of the nineteenth century. Charles Goodyear's invention of the vulcanizing process stimulated the industry. Gradually the use of rubber grew—for cables, insulations, rubber shoes, rubber coats, hot water bottles, rubber boots, bicycle and carriage tires. Wild rubber trees and vines in the jungles of the Amazon valley, of Central America and Mexico, and of Central Africa, supplied such demands. But toward the year 1900 the automobile began to come into use, slowly at first, then with amazing rapidity. In the United States, for

[1] Egyptian long-staple cotton, camphor, coffee, iodine, nitrates, potash, mercury, rubber, and sisal. See Secretary Hoover's statement in *Trade Information Bulletin No. 385*, issued by the Department of Commerce. Also, *Crude Rubber, Coffee, etc., Hearings before the Committee on Interstate and Foreign Commerce*, House of Representatives, 69th Cong., 1st Sess., on House Resolution 59 (1926).

example, 3700 automobiles were manufactured in 1899, and 131,000 in 1909, and almost 2,000,000 in 1919. Wild rubber no longer sufficed to provide the tires for the swiftly multiplying number of motor cars. Fortunately for the automobile industry, Sir Henry Wickham had carried rubber seeds from Brazil to London, long before the big demand for rubber arose, and the seeds had been planted in Ceylon, British Malaya, India, and the Dutch East Indies. In these colonies the rubber plantations soon covered millions of acres, and their output soon overshadowed the wild rubber of Brazil and Congo. The following table shows what happened:

Year	*American and African Wild Rubber (tons)*	*Total Plantation Rubber (tons)*	*Plantation Rubber from British Cols. (tons)*	*Plantation Rubber from Dutch E. I. (tons)*	*Percentage of Plantation Rubber Produced by British*	*Average Price per lb. (cents)*
1905	59,320	174	174		100	
1906	62,004	577	577		100	
1907	66,013	1,157	1,157		100	
1908	64,770	1,796	1,796		100	
1909	70,370	3,386	3,386		100	
1910	73,477	7,269	7,269		100	
1911	68,446	14,383	14,383		100	
1912	73,834	30,113	28,088	2,025	93	
1913	63,280	51,721	46,186	5,535	89	
1914	48,052	73,153	63,992	8,970	87	65
1915	54,740	114,277	96,095	17,811	84	66
1916	51,086	158,993	128,010	30,443	81	72½
1917	56,751	221,187	175,382	44,889	79	72
1918	36,711	180,800	136,926	43,345	76	60
1919	50,424	348,574	257,484	88,189	74	49
1920	36,464	304,671	226,081	75,522	74	36
1921	23,903	276,746	200,959	72,227	73	16
1922	27,878	378,232	271,589	102,171	72	17½
1923	26,685	379,738	237,434	137,158	63	29
1924	28,000	386,703	205,027	175,298	53	26

In the early years of the twentieth century, before the plantations were producing, the price of "fine Para" rubber varied between 70c and $1.50 a pound, and in 1910, when the American automobile output was suddenly expanding, the price rose as high as $3.00 a pound. The plantations were then producing less than a tenth of the world supply. As the plantation output increased, however, the average price was brought down to 65c in 1914; it rose only slightly during the war; and after the war it fell to 16c in 1921. That was the year in which automobile production in the United States took its big slump from 2,205,197 cars to 1,592,041.

The automobile slump caused a crisis in the rubber plantations. Before 1921 the plantation profits had averaged about twenty per cent. But with rubber at sixteen cents in 1921 the situation was serious. Sixteen cents was less than cost. The United States Department of Commerce estimated the cost of production at from twelve to eighteen cents a pound, allowing nothing for profit; including a profit of fifteen per cent, the price would have to be from 24c to 32c a pound. Large stocks of unsold rubber were accumulating. The planting of new trees for future production stopped, and the weaker plantations began to go to the wall. Such was the situation when the British Colonial Secretary in 1921 appointed a commission, headed by Sir James Stevenson, to investigate possible remedies. The plan recommended by the Stevenson committee was adopted, in the form of ordinances, by Ceylon, Straits Settlements, the Federated Malay States, and other British Malayan colonies. In essence, it aimed to restrict the production and export of crude rubber in such a way as to keep the price in the neighborhood of thirty to forty cents a pound—a reasonable enough figure. The method, however, was clumsy. The amount produced by each plantation in the year 1919-1920 was taken as "standard production," with some allowance for new trees. No one could export rubber without a licence, or export more than his quota without paying a heavy export tax. The export quota for each plantation or company was fixed at 60% of "standard production" for the first quarter-year; then, if the average price for the first quarter had been less than 25 cents (1*s*), the quota would be reduced; if the price were above 30 cents (1*s*. 3*d.*) the quota would be increased.

At first the Stevenson scheme failed to produce a very marked change. The average price for 1923, the first year, was only 29.45 cents, and for 1924 it was still less, 26.40 cents. But the automobile industry in the United States was recovering. The number of automobiles produced by American manufacturers rose from about 1,600,000 in 1921 to 3,900,000 in 1923, and 3,600,000 in 1924. Moreover, balloon tires were coming into general use. As a result, the demand for crude rubber increased, and prices rose, and speculators, foreseeing a shortage with higher prices, bought wildly, driving the price up suddenly in 1925 until it reached the high point of $1.21 a pound. It was the increased use of rubber, rather than the Stevenson restrictions, that caused the rise; and it was speculation rather than sound economics that produced the absurdity of $1.21. The Stevenson scheme, however, bore the blame.

The situation was particularly difficult because the producers were mainly British whereas the consumers were largely American. The United States normally purchased more than three-fourths of the world's output of crude rubber. To be sure, the British had offered in 1922 to supply the American industry with rubber at 35 cents a pound for five years; that was an approximately fair price, but rubber in 1922 was selling at just half that price, and the American manufacturers rejected the bargain. In 1925, however, they paid, on the average, 73 cents. The Department of Commerce figured it out that the United States paid out $430,000,000 for crude rubber in 1925, and that this was $200,000,000 more than it would have been at 1924 prices. Secretary Hoover uttered his philippics against the British rubber monopoly. There was a Congressional investigation.[1] New interest was taken in the possibility of producing in the Philippines a supply of rubber under the American flag. But in the Philippines there was a difficulty: there was a law restricting to twenty-five hundred acres the land any corporation could acquire or lease. Yet men like the vice-president of the American Chamber of Commerce in the Philippines insisted in public speeches that Congress would remove this restriction, and that America should have its rubber plantations under the Stars and Stripes. Meanwhile, Harvey Firestone, the great tire-maker, was inserting two-page advertisements in the ubiquitous *Saturday Evening Post*, carrying the slogan, "Americans should produce their own rubber." To set the example, he announced that he intended to create huge plantations in Liberia.[2] On the other hand, the United States Rubber Company, apparently willing to waive the flag, pursued the policy of establishing plantations, under American ownership but under foreign flags, in the East Indies—94,000 acres in the Dutch East Indies, and 30,000 acres in British Malaya,

[1] *Hearings on Crude Rubber, Coffee, etc.*, cited above.
[2] *Cf. supra*, p. 110.

with seven million trees producing twenty million pounds of rubber a year, and representing an investment of something like $25,000,000.

What relieved the situation, however, was not the planting of new trees—for it requires six or seven years for a new plantation to come to productive maturity—and not Secretary Hoover's campaign which according to one shrewd critic tended to "nourish the panic," but rather certain economic reactions.[1] High prices of themselves checked buying, and thus lessened the competition in the buyers' market. High prices of themselves resulted in the automatic increase of the Stevenson quotas. High prices and Secretary Hoover's advice alike stimulated tire-manufacturers to utilize "reclaimed" or old rubber, thus lessening the demand for new crude. And, finally, while the British were restricting their exports, the Dutch East Indies increased theirs, naturally enough, from 102,000 tons in 1922, to 137,000 in 1923, to 175,000 in 1924. Doubtless some of this increase was due to the maturing of trees already planted, and some to "rubber bootlegging." The net result of these combined factors was to bring the price of rubber down to 90 cents in January 1926, and to about 41 cents in the summer of 1926.

The rubber episode was significant in showing not only the possibilities, but also the limitations of such experiments. It helped to raise prices little when prices were too low, and too much when prices were too high. It occasioned a panic in the United States and called forth exchanges of recriminations across the Atlantic. It handed over to the Dutch a large share of the business which the British producers had hitherto enjoyed, and it stimulated American rubber companies to seek rival sources of crude rubber outside British Malaya. It was certainly no unmixed success.

Another kind of nationalistic interference with colonial raw materials has been exhibited here and there in the imposition of differential export taxes. The purpose of these is to give manufacturers in the mother-country an advantage over other manufacturers in purchasing raw materials. For instance, when the United States acquired the Philippine Islands the export tax on Philippine manila was increased from 37½ cents to 75 cents per 100 kilos and in 1902, while this heavy tax continued

[1] Jacob Viner, in *Foreign Affairs*, IV, p. 593.

to be levied on exports of manila to foreign countries, manila shipped to the United States was freed of duty. Thus foreign cordage manufacturers had to pay 75 cents per hundred kilos more for their manila hemp than was paid by Americans.[1] Similarly the British imposed differential export duties on tin ore mined in the Malay Peninsula, in order to give the tin smelters of Cornwall an advantage over their rivals in Perth Amboy and Brooklyn. Again, in 1920, in order to wrest from Germany the industry of crushing oil from the palm kernels produced by British West Africa, the British imposed a differential export tax of £2 a ton on palm kernels shipped outside Britain. Incidentally they injured an American palm oil industry which had sprung up rapidly since the beginning of the war (that is, since the blockade had stifled the German industry). On the whole, however, such differential export taxes have been relatively rare, and comparatively unimportant in international life. Yet to some extent they have contributed to the development of the imperialist attitude toward raw materials.

Perhaps the most important factor in popular psychology regarding this problem is the feeling that it is perilous to be without supplies of necessary war materials in time of war. In a world where peace is insecure, so this train of thought runs, a nation should endeavor to provide itself with adequate materials, under its own flag, where no foreign nation can cut them off. Those who consciously or unconsciously allow this idea to influence them usually forget that obtaining a safe supply of this or that material is quite a different thing from having assured supplies of *all* the essential war materials. The United States is unusually generously endowed by nature, yet it is stated on good authority [2] that there are at least thirty materials essential to war, which are produced either not at all or in quite insufficient quantities in the United States.[3] Some of these—chromium and shellac, for instance—are items that are little in the public eye, yet vital in war industry. To obtain adequate

[1] U. S. Tariff Commission, *Colonial Tariff Policies*, pp. 590-600.

[2] See Wm. Redfield, *Dependent America*, p. 209.

[3] Antimony, camphor, chromium, coffee, cork, graphite, hemp, hides, iodine, jute, flaxseed, manganese, manila, mica, nickel, nux vomica, opium, platinum, potassium salts, quicksilver, quinine, rubber, shellac, silk, sodium nitrate, sugar, tin, tungsten, vanadium, wool.

supplies of them all would be a sheer impossibility for the United States, and even more fantastic for other countries. Real self-sufficiency in war-time materials is a delusion.

The intensification of imperialist interest in raw materials, especially since the war, has meant keen international rivalry and has done much to embitter international relations. If the economic results had been wholly satisfactory, perhaps one could pay the political price with less regret. But too often the economic results have justified neither the price paid nor the optimism with which many imperialist ventures have been launched.

Take as an illustration the question of cotton. By temporarily interfering with the supply of raw cotton from the United States, the Civil War aroused the mill-owners of Lancashire to look about them for other sources of supply, so that they might be less dependent on America. Indian cotton production was increased, gradually. Egyptian production was greatly stimulated, and Egypt passed into Britain's hands. Attempts, more or less successful, were made to grow cotton in British West Africa, East Africa, Sudan, and other possessions. France and Germany, too, endeavored to foster cotton-growing in their African protectorates. Italian imperialists dreamed of bountiful cotton crops in the Italian colonies. Yet by 1914 all Africa, with the exception of Egypt, produced only 35,000 bales; and in 1925 only 250,000 bales, as compared with some 16,000,000 produced by the United States and 900,000 by the independent countries of South America. The growing of cotton in various parts of Africa and the Orient is, of course, advantageous in giving colonies an additional source of livelihood, and in supplementing the rather uncertain and often inadequate American supply. But neither Great Britain, nor France, nor Italy, nor any other European nation-empire has come within reach of the desired goal of self-sufficiency in raw cotton. Moreover, India may be expected increasingly to consume a larger share of her own raw cotton in her own mills. Most of the cotton grown in the French empire goes to Japan and China, rather than to France, for manufacture, because Indo-China, the chief producing colony, is nearer to Japan and China than to France.

The foregoing instances may serve to suggest a thought that

is devastating to the conventional imperialist view of the raw materials problem. The popular notion is that a nation naturally obtains the raw materials which its colonies produce. The actual facts, however, do not conform to this rule. France owns New Caledonia, and on that island are found certain rare minerals, notably cobalt and nickel; but the cobalt of New Caledonia goes to Belgium, and two-thirds of the nickel goes to Belgium. The British own the Malayan colonies which produce more than half the world's crude rubber, but the crude rubber goes mainly to the United States. The graphite of Madagascar goes to England, not to France. French imperialists are eloquent on the topic of Tunisian phosphate, but French official statistics show that France receives less than half of the phosphate and other mineral produce of Tunis.

The point is that raw materials, in general, are color-blind. They recognize no national flag. They follow the laws of supply and demand, and of distance and transportation costs. They obey economic rather than political control. The producers have the familiar human tendency to sell to the highest bidder, regardless of nationality. Only by embargoes or by the imposition of differential export taxes can this tendency ordinarily be overruled, and such methods are rarely employed. They cannot be employed generally. If France should forbid Tunisian mines to sell phosphate to foreign countries, it would probably injure the prosperity of Tunis and of influential French capitalists, who would register effective protests. If Great Britain, instead of merely introducing a scheme to stabilize prices for the benefit of British Malayan rubber plantations, should ruin those plantations by prohibiting all export of rubber to the United States, the British Malayan colonies would become a grave problem, and the plantation owners would move heaven and earth, including Downing Street, to repeal the prohibition. This point need not be overstated as an inviolable law; on the contrary, we know that economic "laws" can be overruled to some extent by political interference. Nevertheless, the economic self-interest of colonial producers is strong enough to act as a formidable obstacle to any attempt on the part of an imperialist nation to monopolize an important raw material produced in its colonies but needed by foreign consumers able to pay a better price than their competitors in the mother-country.

Admitting that normally raw materials will go to the highest bidder, and that Belgians will have to pay for Congolese products, and Frenchmen for Tunisian phosphate, and Englishmen for Australian wool, just as if they were not Belgians, Frenchmen, or Britons, still the question may be raised whether it is not better for a country's foreign exchange and general prosperity, or at any rate if it is not more satisfactory, to pay the purchase price to one's colonial fellow-countrymen rather than to foreigners. Leaving the reader free to answer this delicate question in accordance with his own sentimental predilections or theories of international exchange, we may simply take note of the fact that in a number of rather important instances the premise of this principle is false. The colonial producer is not necessarily a fellow-countryman. Some of the rubber plantations in British Malaya, for example, are owned by the United States Rubber Company, and large plantations in the Dutch East Indies are really British and American. Similarly, in the British mandate of Iraq the oil wells of the Turkish Petroleum Company will pay somewhat less than half their dividends to British investors, the larger share being divided among French, American, and Dutch interests. British capital has an important share in the Katanga mines of Belgian Congo. American capital is interested in African diamonds. British and Belgian capital own productive enterprises in the Portuguese colonies. If the present process of vertical trust-building, by which great industries seek to extend their ownership over their raw materials, continues, we may expect to see the political map more and more hopelessly blurred by the world-wide network of investments.

There is one more point to be considered here, and it is the pivot of the whole matter. The question is whether through imperialism it is possible and desirable to achieve national self-sufficiency in raw materials. Such self-sufficiency seems to be the goal toward which imperialist efforts tend, and—to change the metaphor—the rock on which imperialist arguments are builded. The answer must be factual rather than theoretical. Let France, with her very large empire, be taken as an illustration and test. Two-thirds of the imports of France are raw materials. But merely one-tenth of those raw materials comes from French colonies. The other nine-tenths France must import from Great Britain, the United States, Germany, Belgium, South America. After fifty years of active imperialism, France has achieved ten per cent of self-sufficiency—and ten per cent, of course, is not self-sufficiency at all. If a French imperialist heard the statement that the most important colonies of France, from the economic point of view, were the United States, Germany and Great Britain, he would doubtless gasp. But it is true. The chief providers of raw materials for French industry—colonies in that economic sense—are these three Great Powers. France does get over fifty per cent of her cattle, rice, manioc, fish, and ground nuts from her colonies; she gets between ten and fifty per cent of her imported wines, hides, tobacco, rubber, meat, fruits, olive oils; and she gets a small percentage (one to ten per cent) of her wool, wood, cotton, coffee, grain, cacao, lead, sugar. It has been estimated that if colonial supplies were fully developed, and if the price factor were not considered, France could depend on her colonies entirely for her supplies of hides, rubber, vegetable oils, wool, cotton, and some of the metals. But she would still remain dependent on foreign countries for the coal to smelt her iron ore, for zinc and tin, lead, manganese, oil (unless new fields are tapped), nitrate (unless it is made from the air), mercury, platinum, and sulphur, and other rather necessary materials. To annex supplies of all of these would require more than the imperialist genius of a Delcassé.[1]

Other countries would serve equally well to illustrate the point. From its dependencies the United States obtains much sugar, fruits, hemp, and tobacco, and some fish, gold, copper, coconut oil and minor products; but thus far political expansion has not materially helped to make the United States independent of Malayan rubber, Indian jute, Japanese silk, British tin, Canadian nickel, Canadian asbestos, Australian and South American wool, Indian and Russian manganese, Rhodesian chromite, and other important items on the list of imports. Japan needs raw cotton, iron, rubber, hides, wool, flax and hemp, wood pulp, and oil; but from her colonies she gets little of these, although some day Korea's undeveloped mines may somewhat

[1] On these French needs and resources, I have used the *Annuaire statistique* for 1923 and A. Sarraut, *La Mise en valeur des colonies françaises* (Paris, 1923).

relieve the demand for copper, iron, and coal. At present Formosa supplies camphor, and some tea, sugar and coal; Korea exports rice, beans, cattle, and gold; Sakhalin is supposed to contain valuable oil and mineral resources. Holland has to import from foreign countries iron, coal, cotton, and various metals; whereas her colonies supply sugar, coffee, tea, cinchona, tobacco, rubber, copra, tin, and oil, enabling the Dutch to act as middlemen, rather than rendering Holland self-sufficient. Italy needs cotton, coal, iron; but colonial supplies are largely in the stage of fervent hopes. Belgian Congo produces, above all, copper, and also palm nuts, gold, ivory, palm oil, diamonds; but Belgium needs coal, various minerals, phosphates, cotton, and other items not supplied in quantity by Congo. Portugal needs coal, cotton, and fertilizers, but her colonies provide coffee, rubber, sugar, coconuts, and cacao.

But what of Britain? If her empire is not self-sufficient, surely none can aspire to be so. A few years ago a British scholar compiled statistics showing that the empire produces more than half the world's supplies of a dozen or more minerals, including asbestos, chromite, cobalt, feldspar, gold, manganese, mica, nickel, tin, tungsten, molybdenum, monazite; and a substantial percentage of a dozen or so more.[1] In many items it is or could easily become self-sufficient. Yet there remain certain deficiencies, notably cotton, copper, and fertilizers, besides quicksilver, platinum, and sulphur, with which at present even this greatest of all empires does not seem to be able to supply itself. Even if enough cotton were produced, by strenuous efforts, there remain the minerals, which must be discovered if they are to be produced. The British people can not yet practise the motto, "Keep your money in your own Empire."

Even for Great Britain, but infinitely more so for other empires, self-sufficiency in raw materials seems unattainable, certainly in the near future. And except in the case of Britain and the United States, colonial possessions supply only a relatively small fraction of raw material requirements. If these are the economic facts, it is sheer folly for nations dependent on other Great Powers for the bulk of their supplies to let illusory hopes of imperial self-sufficiency interfere with the international

[1] P. Evans Lewin, *The Resources of the Empire and their Development* (British Empire Series), 1924.

reciprocity and good will which are necessary to their own prosperity.

The whole problem can be viewed from a different angle. The feudal state and city state of the Middle Ages proved too small for the economic facts of early modern times, and were united into national states. The national state of yesterday found itself too small to include the raw materials and markets its industries craved, and so nations expanded into nation-empires. All the Great Powers of to-day are nation-empires rather than simple nations, with the sole exception of Germany, and Germany is a nation against her will. Now the nation-empire finds itself inadequate. Even its expanded frontiers do not include all the needed materials and markets of industry. It is too small. The next step seems to be world-wide international cooperation, reciprocity, and regulation. Nations hesitate to take the step, inevitable as it may be, because public opinion and public sentiment cling to doctrines which were formulated to fit the economic facts of a generation or two generations ago. It takes so long to convert the public to a new doctrine that often the doctrine is out of date before it wins general acceptance. Men were slow to accept the gospel of imperialism which a few professors, business men, and journalists began to preach in the seventies and eighties of the last century, as a solution of the economic problems of their day; but in the end imperialism spread. Now it is being applied, a mid-Victorian policy in a very un-Victorian age.

It is this survival of mid-Victorianism that makes it so difficult to perceive the plain facts of the present situation. We see not the facts but a mid-Victorian mirage. If the mirage could be cleared away, and sentiment laid aside for the moment, two things would become reasonably clear. First, that in increasing the variety and quantity of raw materials that may be used for the comfort of mankind imperialism has performed a very genuine service. Second, that in so far as imperialism attempts to attain monopoly or self-sufficiency it is running counter both to economic facts and to the international good will on which peace ultimately rests. If these facts may be taken for granted, it is not difficult to argue, though it is beyond the scope of this book to propose in detail, that in place of short-sighted antagonisms and rivalry among empires what is needed to-day is the gradual development, through international conferences, of international agreements against unfair practices in the control of raw materials.[1]

The Civilizing Mission

In all this reckoning of business profits and economic balances we have left out of account the high humanitarian purposes which have played so conspicuous a part in imperialist eloquence and in public sentiment. After all, if Frenchmen sacrificed blood and treasure to build their empire in Africa, they believed it was to fulfill their "*mission civilisatrice,*" as well as to gain raw materials and markets. Englishmen do not always weigh the "White Man's Burden" in pounds sterling. President McKinley spoke of civilizing the Filipinos, not of exploiting them. In discussions of what is often now called "economic imperialism" one should not forget that imperialism is also non-economic. One may even doubt whether it would have much potency if it had no idealism. Imperialism, to many, means going into unhappy, backward lands, and bringing education, Christianity, civilization, sanitation, and progress to the benighted heathen races.

If this be imperialism, the student has the right to ask: what has been accomplished, to date, in civilizing the backward races? One acid test that is easily applied is the extent to which imperialist nations have promoted education in their colonies. Something like a million negroes are now receiving some sort of schooling in the African colonies, largely thanks to the devoted efforts of Catholic and Protestant missionaries, while in Asia and the East Indies many millions are being educated. This is an achievement and a benefit which should not be minimized nor forgotten. But it is less than the reader of imperialist speeches and writings might have been led to expect. It is less

[1] On this problem of raw materials see further Acad. Pol. Sci., *Proceedings*, July, 1926; Moon, *Syllabus on International Relations* (N. Y., 1925), pp. 169 ff.; W. S. Culbertson, *International Economic Policies* (N. Y., (1925), ch. ix; W. S. Culbertson and others, *Raw Materials and Food Stuffs*, in *Annals* of Amer. Acad. Pol. and Soc. Sci. (Phil., 1924); Lewin, *op. cit.;* Sarraut, *La Mise en valeur des colonies françaises* (Paris, 1923); P. d'Agostino Orsini di Camerota, *Espansionismo italiano odierno* (Salerno, 1923); W. C. Redfield, *Dependent America* (Boston, 1926); U. S. Tariff Commission, *Colonial Tariff Policies;* Commerce Committee Hearings on *Crude Rubber, Coffee, etc.*, cited above; Gini, *Report on the Problem of Raw Materials* (League of Nations, 1922); International Labor Office, *Enquête sur la Production.*

because establishing schools in colonies is no easy task. It costs money, and as a rule colonial budgets are strained by other burdens, if they do not actually show deficits. It calls for teachers, but for a teacher to leave home and family, and journey to some distant and semi-civilized colony, and learn the native language, requires a rare degree of courage and adventure.

Giving due weight to these factors, we still must observe that most imperialist governments give much less support to education than to raw materials, tariffs, and railways. The Belgian Government, in its *Annuaire statistique* for Belgium and Congo, while giving full details of commerce and administrative matters, does not even consider school statistics for Congo interesting enough to include; from the budget figures there given, however, one learns that a little over two million francs (not much more than a hundred thousand dollars and only one per cent of the Congo budget), was appropriated for education in 1923. For education in the great colony of French West Africa last year only 7,400,000 francs, less than half a million dollars, could be spared out of a budget of twelve times that figure.

And small appropriations bring small results. They would be still smaller, were it not for the fact that in many African colonies the work of education is carried on by missionaries, either with or without financial aid from the administration. In Algeria out of every thousand inhabitants there are only 46 children attending school. If elementary education were as widespread, say, as in the United States, there would be about 200 instead of 46. For Madagascar the ratio is 40.5; for Tunis, somewhere between 22 and 28 according to different statistics; but for French West Africa—as soon as we get into tropical Africa—the ratio drops to 3! In the French Cameroun mandate it is also 3. In Belgian Congo, according to the report of an American educational investigation,[1] the ratio is 26. In the British African colonies the ratio varies widely; Uganda has 50,

[1] On education in Africa there is much very interesting material in the report entitled *Education in Africa* prepared by Thomas Jesse Jones as chairman of a commission sent to investigate African education by the Phelps-Stokes Fund. This first report was published by the Fund in 1922. Another field investigation led to a second report, *Education in East Africa*, likewise prepared by Dr. Jones, in 1925. For some of the material in this chapter I am indebted to these reports, as well as to official year-books published by Belgium, France, etc., and to the always handy *Statesman's Year-Book*.

South Africa 40,[1] Gold Coast 17, Nigeria only 7 according to the American investigators, but over 30 according to the *Statesman's Year-Book,* which includes a large number of Mohammedan schools. For Portuguese Angola it is 1 by one report, 11 by another. In quasi-independent Liberia it is between 3 and 4.

It is hardly necessary to characterize these ratios by saying that they represent heroic endeavors on the part of missionaries and a pitifully inadequate effort on the part of governments. Standards vary so widely from one colony to another that the ratios cannot be fairly used as a basis for contrasting the policy of one country with that of another; but the ratios are accurate enough to show clearly that the powers which partitioned Africa have considered economic development more important than schools for the natives.

If the quantity of education given to the African natives is small, the quality is a matter of dispute. In some cases the "education" consists of the rudiments of the "three r's"' with a smattering of the language of the European government. Now the tendency is to question the value of such teaching, and in some colonies the attempt to force a European language on children in the elementary grades is being abandoned. Portugal, however, still insists that printing textbooks in the native languages, or teaching in the native languages, is not to be allowed, except as a makeshift while the pupils are learning Portuguese.[2] On the other hand, the investigating commissions sent out by the Phelps-Stokes Fund recommended that in the elementary classes the tribal language should be used, and the European tongue introduced only in the upper grades. It is also interesting to note that the commissions urged that not merely the "three r's", but also agriculture, hygiene, industrial skill, and morals ought to have a prominent place in the curriculum.

For Asiatic colonies the problem is different, but the quantity of education is small, as in Africa. In British India the ratio is only 37.7—the masses are remaining illiterate. In Cochin-China, the French provide schooling for only 22.5 children per thousand inhabitants. In the Dutch East Indies the figure is 38.

[1] This figure applies to the Bantu population, in the Union of South Africa, excluding the whites. *Official Year Book of the Union of South Africa,* no. 7.

[2] *Education in Africa,* p. 232.

These ratios may be compared with 59 for independent Siam, 16 for China, 150 for Japan, 20 for the Japanese colony of Korea. The value of Western educational ideals and methods in Asia is too deep and intricate a question even to broach here, where we are considering principally the degree of sincerity with which the "civilizing mission" has been carried out.

Americans may perhaps derive some satisfaction from the knowledge that the United States has taken the task of education much more seriously than European powers have done. In Hawaii there is practically universal elementary education. In Porto Rico the ratio per thousand inhabitants is 175 (compare this with 125 for British Jamaica, 117 for the Dominican Republic, and 37 for Haiti). In the Philippines it is 120, as compared with 38 for the Dutch East Indies and 22½ for Cochin-China. An educational survey made by a commission headed by Professor Paul Munroe of Columbia University found that there is still room for improvement in the Philippines. The average Filipino child goes to school less than three years, and gets only the merest smattering of English and the "three r's." Despite the large sums that have been spent to teach them English, the Filipinos adopt the language slowly, and English is spoken habitually in not more than one or two per cent of Filipino homes. Moreover, it has been said that the rapid development of a sort of education imperfectly suited to Philippine needs has led to an alarming increase of "*ilustrados*"—"white collar men" seeking clerical and political positions. That, however, is a criticism which strikes at the root of American and European, as well as of colonial education.

Into the question of the success and achievements, or failures, of missionary efforts in colonial territory we cannot enter seriously here; nor would the writer, after having visited the international missionary exhibit at the Vatican in 1925, with its bewildering wealth of impressive material, consider himself qualified to make any summary of missionary work. That would call for a more intimate knowledge of many countries than any one person is likely to acquire. There is one point, however, that may confidently be asserted. The extension of European political and economic control over pagan lands has not had the effect of Christianizing the natives. The statistics of conversions difficult to compile and more difficult to interpret, show that while in some of the Pacific islands and a few parts of Africa very considerable percentages of the native populations have become at least nominally Christian, most of Africa and Asia have remained pagan and Moslem. It may properly be suggested, furthermore, that although in many colonies the missions obtain small contributions for their schools from the public treasury, this financial gain is offset by the psychological effect of imperialism. While the missionary has been bringing the Gospel to the natives, the traders too often have brought rum and guns, and traders and soldiers and officials have brought violence, fraud, and venereal disease.

No estimate of the benefits of imperialism to the natives can ignore the interrelated problems of land, labor, and taxation. The land problem is particularly acute in the more backward parts of Africa. How wholesale expropriation was carried out in Congo, and with what tragic results, we have already described in some detail.[1] In East Africa vast plantations have been granted to white planters, who rarely cultivate more than a small fraction of the princely estates assigned to them. In some of the African colonies the natives have been crowded into "reservations," where there is not enough pasturage for their herds, and not enough fertile land for their food crops, which are moved about from field to field to prevent exhaustion of the soil. Sometimes, as in Kenya, the motive has been to convert a black man's homeland into a "white man's country." Sometimes it has been to compel the natives to seek employment as laborers on white men's plantations; for the native who has plenty of land for his crops, and forests for hunting, or pastures for cattle, is not enthusiastic about becoming a wage-earner. The vital problem for humanitarian imperialists is to protect the native against the loss of his land; and it is no easy problem when the tribal-minded native does not understand, as he does not usually understand, European ideas of land-ownership. In recent years Britain, France, and Belgium have framed fairly elaborate laws to protect native rights to the soil, in some of their colonies. The League of Nations Mandates Commission has given particular emphasis to this problem.[2]

[1] *Cf. supra, pp.* 85 ff., 113 ff. [2] *Cf. supra,* p. 501.

Labor is another difficult problem. In the Pacific islands, where natives are disinclined or physically ill-suited to plantation labor, the problem has been solved by importing coolies—Japanese laborers in Hawaii, Indians in Fiji. In Asia, there is surplus labor, cheap and willing, and the problem there is not wholly unlike the European labor problem of a few generations ago; it is a problem of long hours, low wages, child labor, and the beginnings of the struggle between capitalism and incipient trade-unionism. In tropical Africa, however, the problem is how to make the natives work at all, for Europeans. Actual slavery is everywhere condemned, and vanishing; it lingers longest in the form of domestic slavery among the natives themselves. Compulsory labor, once the fashion in Central Africa, is falling more and more under censure, though it is still utilized by governments when they need natives for railroad or road construction, or other public works, and it is still exacted in some colonies in lieu of taxes. But increasingly compulsory labor is being disguised or transformed into other devices. One ingenious substitute is "contract labor": natives are "recruited" by an agent or by native chiefs, to serve as laborers for a definite term of two or three months, and are transported in gangs to the place of labor, where, being under obligation of contract, they are compelled to serve out their term. Where the native understands the contract, and accepts it freely, the system may be relatively innocuous; but it is an open secret that in many cases the native is ignorant or is coerced by authority.

Taxation is a favorite method of stimulating native industry. In many African colonies hut and poll taxes are imposed, ranging from fifty cents to several dollars per capita. The amount seems small enough, by our standards, but to a negro without money it is a large sum. He can earn it by working on a plantation or in a mine, for white employers, at wages that vary from five cents a day, or less, in Congo, Northern Rhodesia, and other regions, to six or seven cents in Kenya, perhaps twenty cents in the interior of Nigeria, and fifty cents or more in South Africa. At such wages it takes a native months to save enough to pay the tax for his family.

Small wages, it should be pointed out incidentally, mean small purchasing power. Here there is a real conflict of interest between the European manufacturers and merchants who hope to sell their goods to the colonies, and the colonial planters and mine-owners who want cheap labor. The conflict is broader than Africa. In the *Statistical Abstract of the United States* there is a table showing the per capita imports of various countries—a significant table. A few of the figures may be quoted for purpose of illustrating the point: British India, $2.21; Dutch East Indies, $5.64; French Indo-China, $3.63; Belgian Congo, $1.21;[1] Portuguese colonies, $3.64; and we may add Kenya and Uganda, $5.35; French West Africa, $3.25; Nigeria, $3.49. If the imports of Europeans in the colonies were deducted, the figures would of course be still lower. The purchasing power of the natives in most colonies is extremely small, simply because the natives are poor. In Gold Coast, however, where the natives as independent farmers have been "enriched" by cacao production, the per capita imports are two or three times as high—$11.12 in 1924. In the Philippine Islands they are $12.45. In North Africa they are still higher, ranging up to $33.54 for Tunis. Porto Rico, thanks to the sugar industry, has the amazingly large figure of $62.71. And perhaps it will not seem strange that the white Dominions of Canada, Australia, and New Zealand, with well paid labor, import even larger quantities of foreign goods. The conclusion to be drawn is apparently that humanitarianism may have its economic advantage; that protecting the natives in colonies from unbridled exploitation by planters may be beneficial to the export interests, as well as gratifying to the humanitarian.

In this, as in so many other matters, European imperialism stands at the crossroads, with conflicting interests and ideals tugging at either sleeve. On one hand, the development of plantation production is just making its lusty beginning, and as it grows it may be expected to call more and more loudly for cheap native or coolie labor. On the other hand, the idea that the natives should be protected against expropriation and exploitation; that they should be educated to industriousness rather than coerced into industry, seems to be making rapid headway among publicists and administrators. The issue is just as sharp, though not so often perceived, between the doctrine

[1] According to the Belgian *Annuaire statistique* the figure for 1924 would be about $2.65.

of exclusive and monopolistic imperialism, which is being more fervently preached in Europe to-day than ever before, and the doctrine of international reciprocity, which is being hardly less zealously proclaimed both in Europe and America. The same issue appears as between the increasingly prevalent practice of tariff discrimination and raw material controls, on one hand, and the growing financial internationalism that is manifested in consortiums, syndicates, and loans. The difference of opinion as to whether colonies should be assimiliated in culture and language to the mother-country, or should be provided with education adapted to their needs and traditions, is also becoming more sharply defined. Gravest of all, from a political viewpoint, is the conflict between the rising tide of colonial nationalism or self-determination, as exemplified in Egypt, India, and the Philippines, and the determination of imperialists to preserve imperial dominion.

These conflicts may best be summed up in one transcendent issue. Compulsory labor, exclusive colonial tariffs, attempts to achieve imperial economic self-sufficiency, the policy of forcing the mother-country's language and culture on the colonies, and insistence on domination, are the ingredients of one form of imperialism that is by no means decrepit or defunct. Protection of native land rights, abolition of compulsory labor, readjusted education policies, the open door, and gradually increasing self-government for colonies capable of it, are policies that belong with a type of imperialism now associated with the word "trusteeship."

"Trusteeship" is not confined to the mandate system under the League of Nations, although the implications of the principle are being more fruitfully studied by the Permanent Mandates Commission than by any other organization. In Great Britain and at Geneva one hears Englishmen express the belief that, not only in the mandates, but in the other British colonies too, Britain is the trustee if not the mandatory of civilization, charged with the double guardianship of the welfare of the natives and of the interests of the civilized world. The idea is not unfamiliar in America, and on the Continent. It is an idea toward which the internationalization of finance, the world extension of industrial ramifications, the uneasy stirrings and questionings of native populations, and above all the development of publicity and public opinion are driving.

If international opinion—or, to use Dr. Nicholas Murray Butler's happier phrase, "the international mind"—continues to develop as it has developed in recent years, it can hardly fail to assail the strong citadels of self-seeking imperialism. Yet about those citadels there hangs a mist, obscuring unsightly facts and lending glamor to illusions. It is no more than a fog of Mid-Victorian misinformation, accumulated in the form of prejudice and venerable sentiment. Once the fog is dissipated, perhaps those citadels of narrow vision will vanish, and in their place mankind may establish an edifice in which enlightened national interest and humane internationalism may be at one, and at peace.

INDEX

INDEX